REVISED AND UPDATED

THE GREAT RECKONING

PROTECT YOURSELF IN THE COMING DEPRESSION

JAMES DALE DAVIDSON

AND

LORD WILLIAM REES-MOGG

SIMON & SCHUSTER

NEW YORK   LONDON   TORONTO   SYDNEY   TOKYO   SINGAPORE

SIMON & SCHUSTER
Simon & Schuster Building
Rockefeller Center
1230 Avenue of the Americas
New York, New York 10020

Designed by Irving Perkins Associates
Manufactured in the United States of America

10   9   8   7   6   5   4

Library of Congress Cataloging in Publication Data

Davidson, James Dale.
    The great reckoning : protect yourself in the coming depression /
James Dale Davidson and Lord William Rees-Mogg.
        p.   cm.
    Includes bibliographical references and index.
    1. Economic forecasting.   2. Business forecasting.
3. Depressions.   4. Financial security.   I. Rees-Mogg, William, date.
II. Title.
HC59.15.D38   1993
338.5'42—dc20   92-46435
                                                                        CIP

ISBN: 0-671-86994-9

ACKNOWLEDGMENTS

We thank those whose thoughts we have appropriated and misappropriated. Their names are cited in the text and their quoted remarks in the endnotes. It is easier and more polite to take people's ideas on loan and use them as they intended. We admit to a greater pleasure in straight-out misappropriation. That, after all, is what authorship is about. An author is like a tyrant over the page, a government that can tax the thoughts of the living and the dead. Sometimes, if the ideas are particularly rich and the author is lucky, the taxation is confiscatory. In our case, the wealth of information we found in the writings of others has been turned very inefficiently into a mini–public works project. The typescript arrived some years late. We only wish our advance had been calculated on a cost-plus basis.

We learned a great deal in the process of researching our topics. It was particularly fun to rediscover an essentially lost work—William Playfair's *An Enquiry into the Permanent Causes of the Decline and Fall of Powerful and Wealthy Nations*. He spoke to us across the centuries as an author whose concerns were essentially too far ahead of his time to be appreciated in 1805. We appreciate him today, and can't help but think that others will when his work again becomes accessible in a modern edition. We had other help and more tangible encouragement from our friends and colleagues; our agent, Theron Raines; and the good people at Simon & Schuster: Dominick Anfuso, Cassie Jones, Carolyn Reidy and Jack McKeown.

While acknowledging our debts we should say that we owe much to the great thinkers of Western civilization. They did most of the heavy lifting that went into this book. We would be proud to have enlarged their ideas in any way. Once upon a time, such a statement would have been outrageous because presumptuous. Now it is considered outrageous for far sillier reasons. It is now deemed to be retrograde in some circles to uphold the contributions of great thinkers who happened to be European or white males. The current narrow-mindedness is unfortunate and counterproductive—but it unhappily arises from profound causes.

Less controversially, we have called upon large numbers of friends and associates for advice, help, and research assistance. In some cases, the assistance took the form of lively discussions over dinner or late-night chat over the telephone. As Robert Louis Stevenson said of talk, it not only "cheers the flight of time among our intimates," it is also an essential preparation for almost any endeavor. He also commented, "No measure comes before Parliament but it has been long ago prepared by the grand jury of the talkers; no book is written that has not been largely composed by their assistances. Literature in many of its branches is no other than the shadow of good talk." We thank Mrs. Thatcher for denationalizing British Telecom and making transatlantic talk easier.

Here are some of our friends to whom we offer special thanks; they helped us advertently or inadvertently: Michael Aronstein, Lee Auspitz, Greg Barnhill, Amy Bayer, Carter Beese, Josh Bigger, Natalie Bocock, Kingsmill Bond, Bill Bonner, Clementina Brown, Jim Buchanan, Tom Crema, Robert Czeschin, Dennis Davidson, Kent Davis, Adrian Day, John Deuss, Pauline Downs, Presley Edwards, Lee Euler, Marc Faber, Mark Frazier, Arthur Goodhart, David Hale, Rita Hamilton, George Hecksher, Paul Hewitt, Neil Howe, Mark Hulbert, Kathleen Juhl, David Keating, Dick Lamm, Nancy Lazar, Becky Manges, Steve Newby, Mancur Olson, John Rickmeier, Frank Riess, Nick Roditi, Bea Romack, Fiona Shields, David Shulman, Lenny Smith, Rita Smith, Tom Stanton, Nils Taube, Gordon Tullock, Gary Vernier, David Weil, Jack Wheeler, and Chris Wood. If you are one of the many others who helped, and we have failed to thank you here, please don't take us off the Christmas card list. We appreciate every bit of help we get.

Dedicated with thanks to our friends:
Carter Beese, Bill Bonner, John Deuss, Marc Faber, Kathleen Juhl, Frank Jungers, Steve Newby, Jim Rogers, Nils Taube, and Gary Vernier

The harvest is past, the summer is ended, and we are not saved.

—Jeremiah 8:20

CONTENTS

BEYOND THE POSTWAR WORLD

The general conclusion is that wealth and power have never been long permanent in any place. . . . and that they travel over the face of the earth, something like a caravan of merchants. On their arrival everything is found green and fresh; while they remain, all is bustle and abundance, and, when gone, all is left trampled down, barren and bare.

—WILLIAM PLAYFAIR,
*An Enquiry into the Permanent Causes
of the Decline and Fall of Powerful and
Wealthy Nations,* 1805

NOVEMBER 1992: *The Great Reckoning* first appeared in print a few weeks before the failed coup against Gorbachev in August 1991. It spelled out a comprehensive forecast of "how the world will change in the depression of the 1990s." To a surprising extent, the world did change, and in much the way we forecast:

- The Soviet Union is gone.
- The Cold War is over.
- The Japanese stock market did follow Wall Street's path after 1929.
- Property investors in Tokyo did lose trillions.
- In America, layoffs by large corporations averaged almost 2,000 per business day as the much-forecast economic recovery failed to materialize, in spite of 24 interest rate cuts by the Federal Reserve.

- Nominal personal income growth in the United States was the lowest for 35 years.
- Business failures as a percentage of GNP reached a record high.
- After 31 consecutive monthly increases in the unemployment rate, Great Britain seemed poised for an even deeper and longer slump than it suffered in the Great Depression.
- The world's largest real estate developer, Olympia & York, filed for bankruptcy.
- A national referendum on the constitutional future of Canada was resoundingly defeated.
- Practically every bank in Scandinavia became insolvent.
- In Sweden, the model welfare state tottered at the brink, as overnight interest rates were raised to 500% and unemployment benefits were slashed in an unsuccessful attempt to fend off a run on the currency.
- The worst rioting in decades swept Los Angeles, Toronto, and other cities.
- America's bellwether state, California, flirted with financial ruin, falling billions behind in payments to employees and suppliers. Banks refused to cash its IOUs.
- U.S. President George Bush suffered the greatest 18-month drop in popularity of any president in history, culminating in an election defeat in which he polled a lower percentage of the popular vote than Herbert Hoover received in 1932.
- While the former Soviet republics were stalked by hyperinflation, deflation gathered momentum in the West. The CRB index of commodity prices dipped below 200, a multi-year low beneath its closing price from December 30, 1977.
- A brutal civil war rages where Yugoslavia used to be. News reports that seem to be recycled from the 1930s tell of concentration camps and mass murder under the banner of "ethnic cleansing."

Such are the developments likely to figure in future economic histories of the 1990s. All were forecast or anticipated and explained in *The Great Reckoning*. Many of these forecasts were not simple extrapolations or extensions of trend, but major departures from what has been considered normal since World War II. We warned that the 1990s would be dramatically different from the previous five decades. Reading the news of 1991 and 1992, it appeared that themes of *The Great Reckoning* were borne out almost daily.

We see these developments not as examples of isolated difficulties, trouble here, trouble there, but as shocks and tremors that run along the same fault line. The old order is being toppled by a megapolitical earthquake that will revolutionize institutions and alter the way thinking people see the world.

The effects of this great change are especially jarring because they coincide with the collapse of a great credit cycle, the sixth since the 17th century. Dying governments and dying industries must tumble into bankruptcy before the cycle is complete.

A DECADE OF DEPRESSION

We said that the 1990s would be a decade of depression. To a greater extent than conventional wisdom would allow, this forecast, too, has come true. Britain is clearly in depression. *The Financial Times* said on October 16, 1992, "The British economy is like a battered car on a steepening descent." The same can be said of Scandinavia. New Zealand and Australia entered slumps years ago and have not recovered. Unemployment in Canada has reached 11.8% as we write, 30% higher than it stood at the end of 1930.

In many respects, the state of the U.S. economy in 1991 and 1992 was much like it was at the onset of the last depression, and perhaps worse. Some telling evidence to this effect is available at your local library in the business pages of the *Wall Street Journal* from 1930. They record details of the first stage of the deepest depression in history. So far. If you had time to read them you could find that almost every story about the economy of the early 1990s was already reported more than 60 years ago in better prose.

- Experts were predicting gains in homebuilding because of lower interest rates.
- The stock market was coming off a record-setting April.
- Lots of individual companies were showing signs of distress.
- The Federal Reserve was cutting the discount rate.
- Much of the world was already in depression, but no one seemed to care.
- Congress was drafting legislation for bank reform.
- Commodity prices were sinking.
- Loans were shrinking in spite of easy money.

Then as now most economists in the United States were expecting a rapid recovery. The Harvard Economic Society wrote on May 17, 1930, "Business will turn for the better this month or next, recovering vigorously in the third quarter and end the year at a level substantially above normal."

The first phase of the Great Depression lasted more than a year in the United States and other non-debtor countries. It was marked by an orderly drop-off in income, just as in the early 1990s. In Britain, which was in debt to the United States, consumer spending even continued to rise. The early misery of the last depression in Britain was felt mainly by the sectors of industry that had already been suffering during the 1920s due to structural adjustment and overvaluation of the pound.

In France and the Scandinavian countries, the first stage of depression was also fairly benign after 1929. Industrial production in France, for example, was flat in 1930, and only began to fall in 1931 as exports shrank.

Then as now there was a steady pressure on employment that led to the erosion of income and radiating stresses in the major economies. But the deeper falloff into the second stage of depression did not occur until later in 1931, as financial strains grew and debt liquidation accelerated.

The crucial difference between the depression of the 1990s and that of the 1930s is that the first phase of depression has been dragged out. Governments are playing a much larger role in economies today. By borrowing against the future to preserve the past, politicians have so far been able to prevent the collapse in income and the debt liquidation associated with the second and deeper stage of depression in the 1930s. Special circumstances in two leading economies have also helped defer a deeper downturn. The shopping boom generated in Germany by reunification and the massive borrowing required to finance it have kept German money supply growth high, exaggerating the strength of the real economy. In Japan, the tradition of "lifetime employment" has also *postponed* job losses, thus forestalling the collapse in income in the leading creditor country.

Notwithstanding these special considerations and the role of automatic stabilizers, such as unemployment insurance and banking bailouts, in delaying the progress of depression, its underlying dynamic remains much the same. As Yogi Berra might have said, the early 1990s were a case of *"déjà vu* all over again,"* with many parallels to developments in the early 1930s:

- Economic growth has been the weakest since the 1930s. All the leading economies, including the United States, are either contracting or stagnant. GDP data in the U.S. suggest otherwise, but are distorted, as we outline later. The much less closely monitored "Coincident Indicators" show that the U.S. economy is weaker as we write in November 1992, than in the spring of 1991 when the recovery allegedly began.
- Debt levels have reached the saturation point in all the leading countries, which has put the credit cycle into reverse, arresting the tendency for spending growth to be financed through debt growth. Because spending can no longer be accelerated by rapid debt growth, income

has started to fall, and credit problems are growing in all the leading economies.

- Real asset prices have been under sharp deflationary pressures. The fall in property prices is most acute in countries which had the greatest access to world capital markets in the 1980s: Japan, Britain, the United States and other English-speaking industrialized countries.

- As the Japanese boom has faltered, Japan has reduced its imports just as the United States did after 1929. The huge and mounting Japanese trade surplus requires that other industrial countries balance their trade deficit with Japan either through capital imports, which are shriveling, or through surpluses in trade with the primary product producers.

- The financial crisis of 1931 and the demise of the gold standard has an obvious parallel with 1992's financial crises in Europe and the meltdown of the European Exchange Rate Mechanism. The crises even happened in the same month. Britain "temporarily" left the gold standard in September 1931, devalued its currency, and transmitted deflation to the countries that remained on gold. In 1992, Britain "temporarily" left the European currency grid in September and devalued the pound.

The downturn of the early 1990s has been a depression, but not yet a Depression with a capital D. It is unlike the familiar recessions that have come and gone since World War II. Yet only Britain among the advanced countries has experienced a fall in output as severe as that of the 1930s, and nowhere in the West has unemployment reached the extreme levels seen in the deepest stage of the last depression. Furthermore, the condition of the United States, Germany and Japan remains ambiguous enough as of this writing to sustain debate about whether they are contracting at all. If this is depression, as we believe, then the worst of it is still to come.

What Comes Next?

Part of the argument in the second edition of this book is that the containment of depression which appeared to have been successful through the end of 1992 cannot ultimately work. It is a policy of postponement, not of prevention. The multi-trillion-dollar losses suffered due to malinvestments in the 1980s are real. They can only be disguised until the good credit of governments is exhausted.

Running huge debts to postpone a further decline in living standards has been naively considered a policy success by the few observers who acknowledge that the current environment is a depression. But this may be the misunderstanding of the century. By running down its own balance sheet, government is insuring that it will lack the capacity to alleviate the worst suffering when the depression finally gets out of hand.

Programs to prevent debt liquidation, such as the Federal Deposit Insurance Corporation, Fannie Mae, The Pension Guarantee Board, The Resolution Trust Corporation, and a whole host of other subsidy programs, do not alter the basic contractionary forces in the system. On the contrary, they make them worse. They add to the total debt burden, and do so in a way that exhausts the good credit of the government even before the contraction has reached its deepest stage. Far from being a policy to prevent or contain depression, this is a policy that guarantees absolute ruin if it is wrong. History shows that once nominal growth slows in a heavily indebted economy, there can be no recovery until the excess debt is eliminated. Political efforts to expand debt, enthusiastically supported by all quarters today, do nothing to lift the burden of debt service, which is the cause of slow growth and faltering incomes in the first place.

Altogether too many people have become complacent about deflation. Markets have treated bad new as good news, rising on falling earnings and signs of weakness because the first effect of deflation has been to cut interest rates, and thus push liquidity into stocks. Nobody from Toledo to Tokyo believes that the inevitable consequences of deflation are inevitable. But watch out. Debt has grown too large to be sustained out of cash flow. As soon as the balance sheet is depleted, a deeper crisis of asset liquidation will catch the world by surprise.

This may be closer than you think. Only a handful of rich countries retain the latitude to maintain, let alone increase government spending. Even if politicians stand ready to bail out insolvent banks, and subsidize their constituents with falling incomes, the losses will show up somewhere in the system, in the form of currency devaluation, punitive interest rates, higher taxes, inflation, or some other measure of economic distress. If recoveries do not emerge soon, bond and currency markets will force cuts in real public expenditure, shocking millions who have staked their lives on the promise that politicians would protect them from economic difficulty.

Witness the example of Sweden. As you have heard many times, Sweden was the model welfare state. It is today a less than model welfare state with an insolvent banking system and a yawning budget gap to close. In the September currency crisis, the government in Stockholm was obliged to slash spending by more than 20 billion krona, in spite of the weakest economic environment since the Great Depression. The markets forced the Swedish authorities to act in order to fend off devaluation. Even that was not enough.

On November 19, 1992, the market devalued Sweden's currency by almost 10 percent.

The difference between the national finances of Sweden and those of the United States is considerable. But it is only one of degree. Sooner or later, unless a vigorous recovery rescues impaired asset values, and allows the United States to close its growing structural deficit, the United States will face a financial crisis of the sort that has already struck Sweden, Italy, and other nations in Europe, and which is threatening Canada and Australia as we write.

While the election of President Clinton appears to have given a boost to confidence in the United States, we expect that the resulting bounce in the economy will prove temporary. The strain on the federal government's balance sheet will continue to grow until the authorities no longer have the capacity to stand in the way of debt liquidation. Then the second, deeper stage of depression will begin. We explain this in *The Great Reckoning*, and tell you how you can protect yourself from some of the worst consequences.

Budget deficits, lax monetary policy, credit guarantees, and palliatives such as make-work employment will continue to offer short-term gains to politicians, but at the expense of threatening broad economic collapse when the cycle plays itself out. *The Great Reckoning*, as the title implies, may be postponed, but we do not believe it can be avoided. In due course, politicians will be obliged to retrench in order to preserve constitutional stability. This will surprise the same people who were dumbfounded when the Berlin Wall came down. We expected and forecast the fall of Communism. Just as we believed it was impossible to sustain an economic system which attempted to prevent anyone from profiting, so we believe it will prove impossible to sustain a political economy which attempts to prevent anyone from losing. In the long run, the market is more powerful than governments.

Of course, we don't pretend that every thinking person must necessarily agree with our interpretation of events. We are groping to understand changes that have only begun to unfold. Subsequent developments may not continue to move in the direction that we have foreseen. Perhaps the high valuations of the U.S. stock market are justified and a recovery really is just around the corner. Perhaps the depression can be contained, and not lead to the deeper stage of downturn and debt liquidation that we anticipate. Time will tell.

It is certainly true that our view of the world is shared by few economists or other experts. As we write, most observers remain confident that recovery is at hand. We doubt it. In past credit cycle unwindings, depression did not bottom until excess debt was liquidated. Very little has been liquidated to date. This is one of a number of factors that tell us that the world economy still faces a second and deeper stage of depression to come.

This view may seem extreme and unwarranted. But exactly the same thing would have been said in 1930. The leading economists of that day saw no hints then that the economy was about to take a deep dive. It would be easy to assume that this failure to forecast was due to a lack of knowledge that economists now have well in hand today. Not so. In fact, even contemporary mainstream economists, using current forecasting techniques, were unable to predict the 1931 downdraft retrospectively. This was reported in an article published in 1988 in *The American Economic Review.* As an exercise to find out why forecasts from the early thirties were so poor, three economic historians reformatted the data from that period in ways compatible with modern forecasting techniques. They even added reconstructed time series unavailable in the thirties.

All the data were then examined for the statistical picture they painted of the economy, and forecasts were generated using the same techniques now employed by most business and government economists today. The results: they saw nothing indicative of deflation. They failed to forecast the initial downturn in 1929. And their forecasts based on 1930 data indicated "a speedy recovery."

They saw no hint of deep depression then. They see none now. The reason, we believe, is that the data that are most reliable in measuring the health of the economy during the normal inventory cycle do not probe the part of reality where the credit cycle contractions take hold. More on that later.

Needless to say, the mere fact that most economists are complacent about the dangers of a global meltdown today is no argument that one is likely. The reasons we see a second stage of depression looming is that events are confirming the arguments spelled out in this book. They are following a pattern in the 1990s similar to that of the 1930s and other modern depressions dating back to the early 18th century. Maybe the results will be different this time. We could be wrong. Any economic forecaster has to be constantly aware of the possibility of being wrong. We therefore look all the time for the signs that our expectations in *The Great Reckoning* will prove to be too pessimistic.

Unfortunately, at the moment the signs are confirming that the world depression is not responding to the measures that are being taken. The United States may be in the best shape of the three major industrial areas of North America, Japan, and the European Community.

The United States has established two significant advantages. The first is that the dollar is now undervalued in terms of purchasing power, and therefore American exports are very competitive. They certainly need to be competitive against Japan, but the overvaluation of the European currencies is an opportunity for American exporters and a very important one. The United States has also followed the logic of low short-term interest rates during a recession, and at least the American economy is not being dragged down as the European economies are by interest rates more appropriate to a boom.

That does not mean that the American economy is in good shape. Recovery, where it exists, has remained local, and the broad recovery which everyone hopes for has not happened, certainly not yet. Even after bouncing on the election of President Clinton, confidence remains low and the low values of commercial real estate undermine the banking system.

In Japan something much more frightening is happening. There have been no transactions of significance in Tokyo real estate for about twelve months. The market is supposed to be only about 30 percent below its peak, but a true market with normal activity could well be down by 60 percent like the Tokyo stock market. The Japanese banks face losses that dwarf those of the U.S. savings and loan debacle. And corporate earnings are plunging. It is only a matter of time until hard-pressed Japanese corporations begin to lay off large numbers of employees who imagined that they had the security of jobs for life. This will probably cause a political crisis and a further sharp fall in share prices. The unwinding of the Tokyo bull market in shares and property is certainly far from complete.

Europe is in an extraordinary position. A high cost, high currency-value island in a sea of lower costs, not competitive with Japan in exports, with labor costs that probably average 50 times those of China and India and almost as many times those of Eastern Europe—the European Community is looking increasingly like a sand castle with the sea coming in. Because it has the most unrealistic cost structures, it faces the most potentially severe deflation of any of the three major trading areas.

The only thing to be said for the European economy is that it did not participate fully in the inflation of asset values. The costs that are already out of line are imposed by the currency system which has been jacked up by German interest rates. Both the interest rates and the currency values of Europe seem likely to fall but not until there is a more severe downturn in Germany itself.

In Britain we have further evidence of history repeating itself, a nation that made the mistake of deflating in a depression. It is a policy which destroyed half the democratic governments of the world in the early 1930s and severely undermined the popularity of John Major's government. He managed to convert an April 1992 election victory into record low ratings in opinion polls just six months later. Through no choice of his own, the pound was forced out of the European Exchange Rate Mechanism in the currency crisis of September 1992. This obliged Major to reverse course and adopt a policy of attempting to reliquify the economy by lowering interest rates. Whether this will work is yet to be seen. As we write, the number of business insolvencies in England and Wales has reached a new high. One in 38 English companies operating in the past year has failed. *The Financial Times* reports "no evidence that the reduction (in interest rates) has improved consumer or business confidence."

The world scene does, therefore, remain a very dark one. We are still looking for the factors which would lead us to qualify the forecasts made in *The Great Reckoning*. Day after day, more of them appear to be coming true:

- We said that credit demand would fall as interest rates declined. It has.
- We forecast that long-term interest rates in the U.S. would remain stubbornly high as the slump unfolded, in spite of dramatic ease on the short side. The spread between T-bills and 30-year T-bonds reached a record in 1992.
- We argued that the propensity of consumers to spend would decline as middle class living standards eroded. As 1992 unfolded, politicians, economists, and business leaders complained that consumers had not returned to the spending patterns of the 1980s.
- We forecast that there would be a surge in downgrades of municipal bonds in the United States. There was. In July and August of 1992, the spread between Treasury bonds and municipal bonds widened to a record amount.
- We said taxes would skyrocket. Tax increases at the state and local level raised the effective tax record in the U.S. to the highest in history.
- We claimed that the terms of income redistribution would shift as depression set, in order to mobilize the underclass to join the work force. Since *The Great Reckoning* was first published, 15 U.S. states have proposed reforms designed to alter the behavior of welfare recipients in the direction forecast.
- We explained why a clamor for national health insurance would sweep America as it follows Britain's path into bankruptcy.
- We argued that decaying infrastructure would create crises in American cities, a fitting preamble to headlines that announced the collapse of a neglected tunnel system which flooded downtown Chicago at a cost of more than a billion dollars.
- We said that there would be a movement toward for-profit secondary and elementary schools in the United States. This got a dramatic launch

in 1992 when Benno Schmidt, the President of Yale University, resigned to become CEO of Project Edison.
- We argued that industrial output would plunge in the former Communist countries. It did, dropping 40 percent or more in some regions.
- We forecast that Russia would slash its foreign aid budget, leaving the Third World even more bankrupt than during the Cold War. In fact, Russian aid vanished completely.
- We further argued that the end of the Cold War also would lead Western donors to curtail aid to bankrupt Third World nations. It did. Nations like Kenya, formerly large aid recipients, were cut off as their geopolitical significance faded. Sweden, formerly the most generous donor country, slashed its foreign aid budget across the board.
- We said that those Third World dictators who were supported by Communist praetorian guards, such as Mengistu in Ethiopia, would be rapidly overthrown. It happened.
- We forecast that the breakdown of order in the world's bad neighborhoods would lead to such unbridled chaos that the governments of some backward countries would effectively be placed into receivership under United Nations supervision. This happened much as we imagined. In December 1992, United States troops were deployed to Somalia as part of a UN peacekeeping effort intended to protect emergency relief shipments against attack by warlords and roving teenagers with machine guns. Central authority had completely disappeared.
- We forecast that the movement toward disarmament would accelerate, with devastating consequences for California real estate. It did, as whole categories of strategic weapon were scheduled for elimination, and military spending in both the former Soviet Union and the United States fell—along with California property values.
- We theorized that Germany and Japan would move to develop independent foreign policies, as the importance of Washington's nuclear shield faded. They did. A *Journal of Commerce* story on Japanese aid to Vietnam reported it as "the clearest sign yet that Japan is setting an independent foreign policy."
- We explained why Italy might default on state debt. In August 1992, it became the first G-7 country to default on state debt since World War II.
- We forecast that weapons from disintegrating Soviet nuclear arsenals would find their way into dangerous hands. News reports in the spring of 1992 told of the sale of three former Soviet nuclear weapons to Iran.
- We said that religious fundamentalism would gather strength around the world, with Islamic fundamentalists making particular strides. This

became headline news when the Islamic Salvation Front appeared poised to win a landslide victory in the aborted parliamentary elections in Algeria. Fundamentalists also gained ground in the former Soviet Republics, the Sudan, and elsewhere.

• We argued that protectionism would intensify. It did. The GATT world trade talks broke down over agricultural subsidies. *The Washington Post* headline from November 6, 1992, could have been written on November 6, 1929: "U.S. to Hit Europe With Stiff Tariffs." The Smoot-Hawley Tariff bill that amplified trade war and deepened the last depression was originally conceived to protect agriculture. As the postwar world collapses, history has a way of repeating itself.

I'm not a shmuck. Even if the world goes to hell in a hand basket, I won't lose a penny."

—DONALD TRUMP, 1989

Those who read the first edition of *The Great Reckoning* will not be surprised by apparently random news stories about change and turmoil in all parts of the globe. Many are linked by the hidden logic spelled out in *The Great Reckoning*. We warned that a "return to tribalization and tribal thinking" would sweep the world. It has. Pick up any newspaper. The same theme of devolution and breakdown of large systems runs beneath the surface of many of the decade's top stories:

Serbs kill their Bosnian neighbors.
Separatists in Quebec seek to splinter Canada.
Eskimoes assume direct control of tracts of land larger than France.
Zulus battle Xhosas in South African townships.
Slovaks and Czechs break up Czechoslovakia.
Rap singers urge blacks to kill whites in the United States.

Like vandals chipping away loose bricks from an old house, small groups and fractions of groups reassert their own special interests against the cosmopolitan interests that all people share. Sikh separatists kill Hindus in India. IRA bombers blow up innocents on a London street. In the derelict remains of the czar's empire, tribes not heard for centuries fight to break fractions of breakaway regions into smaller fractions. The Ingush people battle the Ossetians while the Azeris battle the Armenians. Every day an old tribe makes new demands against the whole.

The 1990s sure aren't like the 1980s.

—DONALD TRUMP, 1991

It is no coincidence that the news of the early 1990s recalls dark themes of delusional politics and ethnic animosity of the 1930s. After half a century of economic boom, economies have begun to shrink and political horizons have begun to shrink as well. As forecast, the competition for scarce jobs and the shock of economic losses has brought extreme nationalist movements back to life in the heart of Europe, most notably in Germany, where refugee camps have been trashed and burned and neo-Nazis riot almost nightly. We spell out in *The Great Reckoning* why the delusional response to economic stress is entirely predictable. Even the content of the delusions is remarkably similar from one episode to another. It is no surprise that many resentful Japanese unhappily rushed to embrace conspiracy theories blaming "Rothschild" and "the Jews" for the falling markets in Tokyo. In a world with growing legions of unhappy losers, it may be important for you to anticipate coming episodes of delusional thinking.

In this updated edition, we explain in more detail why "politics will likely move backward, as in the 1930s." Sour moods have already proven almost as contagious as high German interest rates within the European Community, confounding expectations of rapid economic and monetary union. We forecast that "resurgent nationalist pressures on European governments" would frustrate hopes for European integration, just as they dashed plans for a "United States of Europe" in the last depression. Our fears were confirmed when Danish voters rejected the Maastricht Treaty, and the ratification process, once taken for granted, began to stall in other countries. Here you will find our argument revised in the light of two years of events and further research into the dynamics of depression.

Compared to many books that attempt to analyze the future, *The Great Reckoning* has yielded many non-trivial predictions that actually came true. If we had pretended to conjure our forecasts from tea leaves, or base them on astrology, we would be on the cover of the *The National Enquirer*. But we are not clairvoyants or modern-day imitations of Nostradamus. We are not even interested in making detached forecasts. Unless predictions about the future are connected to an explanation that makes sense, they are little better than fortune cookies. False or true, they leave you every bit as much in the dark about why things happen. We don't mean to hand you a big bag of fortune cookies without the crumbs. Our purpose here is as much to explain as to predict. If we can reveal even some of the hidden seams and connections between events, then you may be able to use that understanding to form your own judgments in ways that would never occur to us. That is our hope.

We recognize, of course, that because our analysis is unconventional, its credibility is closely related to its usefulness in forecasting the course that events actually take. But there is a sense in which the mere attempt to summarize or catalog a list of accurate predictions actually trivializes the deeper argument of the book. If you are a serious reader, we hope that you will look beyond the sometimes incidental forecasts to think about the deeper meaning of our argument. It explains such issues as:

- Why matter will be controlled at the atomic level, and the implications for medicine, political theory, and even family life. Designer children will become a reality.
- Why microtechnology will make central government control over all functions more difficult.
- Why technology is forcing the downsizing of corporations, destroying smokestack industries, and undermining the power of labor unions.
- Why mental work is becoming more important than physical labor.
- Why the end of the Cold War raises the probability that weapons of mass destruction such as nuclear weapons will actually be used.
- Why information-based technologies not only promise to reduce the drain on natural resources, but can also displace natural resources.

What we see unfolding is far more important than any specific forecast about the economy.

A New Phase in World History

All the stunning changes that have occurred since the fall of the Berlin Wall in 1989, however unthinkable a decade ago, are merely first installments of a broader upheaval in human affairs. The 1990s could mark the climax of a major phase of history that began in the decade when Columbus sailed for America. Hints from a variety of sources suggest that the technological change and economic exhaustion that brought the Cold War to an end will also bring about a new world disorder, as well as a new organization of work. The industrial economy based primarily upon the manipulation of raw materials at a large scale is giving way to the information economy based upon the manipulation of data at a small scale.

Such dramatic change necessarily involves "crises" in the original sense of the word. These are never wholly random events. They occur under circumstances in which societies have rendered themselves increasingly crisis-prone.

The world economy, especially the Japanese and American parts of it, were in just such a state as the 1990s began. Vast sums of debts owing within and across borders made continued prosperity almost everywhere dependent upon many of the weakest debtors continuing to meet their obligations.

Unhappily, some of the weakest debtors were also among the largest. In the United States, core financial institutions, like money center banks, savings and loans, insurance companies, and even the government itself, were skirting the edge of insolvency. A generation of budget deficits without tears had spread complacency about the ability of Americans to consume without paying. But the unpaid bills, though out of sight and out of mind, continued to compound. By 1992, gross interest on the national debt claimed 62 cents of every dollar of federal income tax. Meanwhile, a reasonable guess at the foreign indebtedness of the United States was about $850 billion—a sum approximately double the total of U.S. exports, which were running at less than $425 billion. Debt-to-export ratios of 200 percent or more are high by the standards of Third World countries. If the same arithmetic that pushed Argentina, Brazil, and Mexico over the brink into debt crisis in the 1980s continues to do its work, the world's key economy—the United States—will suffer a debt crisis in the 1990s.

FINANCIAL ARMAGEDDON

Debt cannot go on compounding faster than output forever. At the rate it expanded in the United States in the 1980s, interest payments would consume 100 percent of GNP by the year 2015. No such thing will happen. Long before debt reaches that extreme, it will be wiped away. Either an economic deflation will cause the financial system to implode, or a political inflation of an extreme kind will obliterate much of the value of debts denominated in dollars.

One way or the other, we expect a great reckoning. A settling of accounts. We expect the long economic boom and credit expansion that began with World War II to come to an end. The end, when it comes, will not only reveal the insolvency of many individuals and corporations, it may also bring bankruptcy to the welfare state and widespread breakdown of authority within political economies. Such far-reaching transitions cannot occur without touching your life and the lives of those you love. More than you may now imagine, you are vulnerable to financial, economic, and political collapse. You may even be vulnerable to physical violence. The better you can foresee the revolution of the 1990s, the better it will be for you, and not merely in financial terms, but in other ways as well. Your family relationships, your livelihood, the community in which you live will all be altered for better or worse in the Great Reckoning. To prepare for these changes requires thinking anew. It means looking beneath the surface of events to identify the deeper causes of economic and social change. This book is an attempt to do that.

The Great Reckoning is an analysis of an event just beginning to unfold— the final depression of the twentieth century. In an earlier book, *Blood in the Streets,* we explained why such a depression was a likely consequence of the decline of American predominance in the world. It was merely one of a number of converging reasons to expect a crisis of transition in the 1990s. Other reasons include:

1. The compounding debt crisis. Interest rates exceeded the growth of economies during the 1980s—pushing debt to historically unprecedented heights at a time when a normal business cycle downturn was due.

2. The insolvency of financial institutions in many parts of the globe. From New York to London to Tokyo, many commercial banks, insurance companies, and other financial institutions were poised to follow the U.S. savings and loan industry down the chute.

3. The collapse of state-dominated economies. The lands of the former Soviet Union, Eastern Europe, along with much of Africa and parts of Latin America were in a deeper slump by 1992 than any Western country experienced in the Great Depression.

4. The crash of Asian stock markets. Normally, crashes prefigure downturns.

5. The end of the Cold War. It will lead to sweeping reductions of military spending. Historically, falling military budgets have been associated with economic retrenchment.

6. The saturation of markets for most of the products that comprised the postwar economic boom. This implies growing profit pressures and significant job losses in established industries.*

---

* Dr. Cesare Marchetti, a physicist working in Austria, has developed an unorthodox theory of market saturation. Marchetti's approach has almost nothing in common with the work of any market-sensitive economist. Instead of arguing that price movements explain everything, Marchetti ignores prices and money altogether. Marchetti measures only physical quanitites in his work—BTUs of energy consumed, or passenger miles driven, cars per capita, etc. He treats the development and penetration of innovations and products in the economy as if they were populations of living species. He argues that the growth and spread of automobiles into the markets of the Western world, for example, can be described by the same logistic equation that describes the penetration of rabbits into Australia, or any other form of ecological competition.

7. The appearance of a destabilizing technology. The microchip is a subversive invention. The Information Revolution made possible by the microchip helped overturn Communism and will contribute to the death of the welfare state.

8. It is time for a downturn in the long-wave economic cycle. A rhythm of boom and bust in which depressions have recurred every fifty to sixty years is evident for as long as records have been kept. The late-twentieth-century credit cycle that began in the 1930s is the sixth major credit cycle since the beginning of the eighteenth century. Each of the other five ended about a decade after commodity prices peaked in the leading economy. Commodity prices peaked in 1980 in both the United States and Japan.

A Longer Phase of History

The end of the postwar world is more than the eclipse of a single economic power, America, or the collapse of state-dominated economies. These developments, far-reaching in themselves, appear to be coinciding with the twilight of another, much longer phase of world history. The Atlantic centuries, five hundred years of unprecedented progress during which the world has been dominated by European powers and their successors, may also be nearing their climax. Not only may financial and manufacturing predominance be taken up by a non-Atlantic power—Japan—but the underlying conditions that precipitated the great explosion of modern progress may themselves be coming to an end. A millennium that has witnessed ever-accelerating technical change seems destined to end in dramatic fashion. A shift in the technology of power brought about by the microchip may profoundly alter the organization of life.

The Economic Fallout of the Atomic Age

Even the consequences of nuclear weaponry have been underestimated and misunderstood. Such weapons have been with us for almost half a century. Their frightening potential for destruction has been well canvassed. What has been widely ignored, however, is the impact of fusion on the value of money. The absence of deflation since World War II has given steadily rising prices the appearance of being driven by an inexorable natural force. Yet the whole story has not been told. Only now are we coming to the climax of the long and unique economic cycle that began with World War II. For reasons we explore later, this economic cycle was fundamentally altered by nuclear weap-

Nikkei Average (1981–92) vs. Dow-Jones Industrials (1921–35)

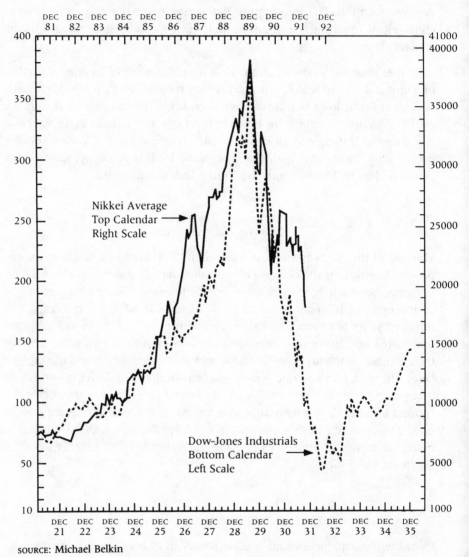

| DEC 81 | DEC 82 | DEC 83 | DEC 84 | DEC 85 | DEC 86 | DEC 87 | DEC 88 | DEC 89 | DEC 90 | DEC 91 | DEC 92 |

Nikkei Average
Top Calendar
Right Scale →

Dow-Jones Industrials
Bottom Calendar ←
Left Scale

| DEC 21 | DEC 22 | DEC 23 | DEC 24 | DEC 25 | DEC 26 | DEC 27 | DEC 28 | DEC 29 | DEC 30 | DEC 31 | DEC 32 | DEC 33 | DEC 34 | DEC 35 |

SOURCE: Michael Belkin

onry. Sweeping disarmament, long delayed since the war's end, could lead to lower prices and deflationary debt implosion.

We hope that microtechnology and nuclear weapons will not prove destructive on a mass scale. But it would be surprising if the fallout from these profound inventions did not spread over many aspects of modern life, even if—as we hope—the nuclear warheads themselves remain confined to the test sites and silos. Major transitions in the technology of power have always had sweeping effects. As Robert O'Connell noted optimistically, there has been a "coincidence between historical clusters of weapons developments and periods noted for generalized creativity. The Hellenistic period following the conquest of Alexander the Great constituted such a time frame. The Italian Renaissance marked another. These were times of energy and optimism, brief spans when tradition loosened its grip on men's minds and freed them to explore possibility." Unhappily, not all the revolutions touched off by weapons transitions tip the contests of life towards freedom and openness.

A CYCLE OF CENTURIES?

There is also another hint that the 1990s may be a decade of sweeping change. It is one we only half believe ourselves, like a note that one can scarcely hear. Yet you should consider it for reasons we explore more fully later. There may be a cycle of centuries that culminates at the millennium, a largely overlooked and unexplored pattern in the ups and downs of human progress. As the year 2000 approaches, you should be alert to the strange fact that the end of each century divisible by five has witnessed a major transition in Western civilization. Precisely five centuries ago, in this decade at the end of the fifteenth century, the Gunpowder Revolution exploded in Europe and Columbus sailed for America. It was in the 1490s that Western Europe finally emerged from the demographic depression that began with the Black Death in 1348. Indeed, it was then that the world first began to think of itself as a world. Five centuries earlier, at the turn of the tenth century, the Middle Ages began, as the European economy recovered from the long coma known as the Dark Ages. Five hundred years before that, at the end of the fifth century, Rome fell, as the last legions in Gaul disintegrated. And twenty centuries ago, in this decade, Christ was born.

It may seem absurd to expect another major turn in a cycle of centuries when we cannot prove that there is such a cycle and have no idea what mechanism could drive it. Nonetheless, there is reason to suspect that the patterns of history are more complex and bizarre than educated opinion has commonly thought. Growing evidence suggests that many phenomena that appear random are actually biased by some hidden order.

Empires Fall and So Do Economies

The theme of our previous book, *Blood in the Streets*, was that the decline of American predominance in the world would prove economically destabilizing in far-reaching ways. The collapse of empires has always been a cause of economic upheaval. In the past five hundred years, the Spanish, Dutch, and British empires all fell. In their wakes the world suffered through debt default, financial turbulence, trade disruptions, and worse. The twilight of the British predominance earlier in this century was a period of war, revolution, monetary convulsion, and worldwide depression. In 1945, America emerged as a new economic and military superpower. Monetary stability was restored. Trade expanded and the world became prosperous again. But it was a Cold War prosperity, which placed a heavy financial burden on the United States. Within a few decades, U.S. gold reserves were overtaxed. The international monetary system collapsed, leading to currency fluctuations and disorder in the world pricing system. This was followed in short order by the OPEC shock—the most widely noted part of a 3,400 percent increase in international grand larceny. Third World governments, emboldened by the defeat of the United States in Vietnam, stole overseas American investments almost at will. Economic growth in the years after 1973 fell worldwide by 50 percent. Now, less than half a century after it began, the era of American predominance has all but drawn to a close. As it does, the world is once again in jeopardy of economic reversal. With America lumbered with debts, and sagging beneath the financial and military burdens of policing the globe, pressure is building for further upheavals in trade and finance of the kind that followed the collapse of British supremacy in World War I. Nothing short of a revolution in weaponry or the most muscular surge of productivity that America has ever seen is likely to change it.

So we argued in *Blood in the Streets,* which was first published in May 1987. That book contained a number of predictions that were considered improbable or even ridiculous:

- We forecast another 1929-style stock market crash. Investment professionals were almost unanimous in denying that any such thing could happen again. Less than six months later, in October 1987, the markets of the world were convulsed by the most violent sell-off of the century.
- We predicted the impending collapse of Communism. Again, experts scoffed. Yet 1989 brought the proof that "no one could have predicted." Revolutions swept away the old regimes in Eastern Europe, while hastening the death of Communism in the Soviet Union itself.
- We also stated that the multi-ethnic empire the Soviets inherited from the czar "will inevitably crack apart." This forecast was considered silly until a few weeks after the first edition of this book was published, when the whole world watched the Soviet Union crack apart on television.

- At the height of the Reagan arms buildup, we said that the world stood at the threshold of sweeping disarmament. This, too, was considered unlikely. Yet the following five years brought the most rapid movement toward disarmament since the 1920s.
- Our forecast that Third World debt would never be repaid was ridiculed by reviewers. While top bankers and government officials argued that the problems of the debtor countries would prove temporary, we suggested that they faced economic collapse. By July 1989, the World Bank was reporting that financial institutions in backward countries were "insolvent on an unprecedented scale." Even the U.S. treasury secretary was urging banks to accept partial debt forgiveness as an alternative to total default or repudiation.
- At a time when most middle-class families in America, Britain, and other countries were acting on the assumption that residential real estate could only go up in price, we warned of an impending real estate bust. By 1992, Olympia & York, the world's largest property developer, had filed for bankruptcy, with prices still falling from London to Tokyo, as well as in most parts of the United States.
- When many economists and politicians in the United States and Western Europe were pointing to Japan for evidence that governments can successfully rig markets, we said that the Japanese financial assets boom would end in a bust. The 49 percent decline of the Nikkei Dow index during 1990, from 38,915 on the last trading day of 1989 to 19,782 on October 1, was a deeper drop than Wall Street suffered in 1929.

We also forecast the widespread bankruptcies of U.S. savings and loan institutions. They happened. We said that the income share of blue-collar workers would continue to decline. It has. We predicted the increase in protectionism, intensified terrorism, and more.

Much of what we predicted has come true, some of it dramatically so. When the first edition of The Great Reckoning was published, we listed two that stood out as not having been borne out by events. Tokyo property prices had not yet registered dramatic falls. And the leading industrial democracies had not yet clearly succumbed to the slump that was already then spreading through much of the rest of the world. Now they have. Estimates of total losses in the Japanese property market range as high as 50 percent or $10 trillion, a loss of wealth equivalent to every stock market on earth plunging to zero.

Even more modest estimates, in the range of $3 trillion, amount to a loss of wealth roughly equivalent to that if all of China had disappeared. Losses of this magnitude cannot help but be felt in the real economy, not just in

Japan, but around the globe. As we write, Japan shows every sign of dipping into depression, with bankruptcies surging to record levels, and industrial production having fallen for eleven straight months. Europe is also suffering an economic downturn unlike any experienced since World War II.

Megapolitics: A Shortcut to Understanding

We do not claim any particular expertise in most of the areas on which our predictions touched. We are not authorities on Japanese or Soviet history, the international arms race, mortgage banking, or the current balances in the treasuries of Third World countries. To the contrary, our forecasts in *Blood in the Streets* were not based on a lifetime of study of these issues themselves. Rather, they were logical implications of a broader theory about the way the world works. We call this the theory of "megapolitics."

According to this theory, historic changes in the ways that societies organize are largely determined by the physical limits on the exercise of power. In essence, we imagine how the world would change if there were no laws or constitutions, and human affairs fluctuated solely according to the changing dictates of physical force. We do not mean by this, of course, that we imagine every outcome everywhere to be determined by violent struggle. Far from it. But raw power has a more sweeping impact than people in generally peaceful Western societies tend to suppose. As technology and other factors change the limits within which force can be exercised, they change society. Part of this book is a history of violence, which illustrates these points. In our view, what philosophers used to call "the state of nature" is always with us. Its workings may be disguised, or buffered. Yet even the most polite and prosperous nations ultimately have no choice but to evolve according to the changing costs and rewards of projecting and resisting power.

Strange though this way of thinking may seem at first, it offers valuable hints about the way the world is tending, hints that can help you see beyond today's headlines. As we showed in *Blood in the Streets,* there are significant and profitable insights to be gained by understanding the logic of violence. That lesson was driven home again by Saddam Hussein's short-lived conquest of Kuwait and the ensuing Mideast war that disrupted markets, bankrupted businesses, and made new fortunes. Learning to think megapolitically can be of vital importance to you if you have wealth to protect . . . or if you seek to build wealth in the face of difficult circumstances.

You can depend upon the fact that normal channels of information will seldom give you advance warning of major political and economic events. The world just doesn't work that way. The dictates of mass communications and the limits of conventional thinking make it rare for the media to convey any message that involves a chain of reasoning of more than two or three steps. The media skim the surface, like birds skimming bugs from the surface of water, shying too far away from the deeper currents and undertows to notice which way they are tending.

Put simply, the media will tell you little of value about the deeper causes and consequences of events. Where complex patterns of cause and effect point to conclusions that have not already been demonstrated by immediate experience, they will simply be ignored by most people. This is why there is little public analysis of any phenomenon that involves a change from current trends. And there is almost no megapolitical analysis in mainstream information sources. It is taboo. Those who enjoy the inherited luxury of peace tend to focus on proximate causes and ignore the ultimate determinants of the way the world works—in large measure because those determinants are out of sight.

In Western democracies, social change is in most respects channeled through the political process. It has become second nature to assume that elections and debates are what matter most in the everyday ordering of life. They are not. Behind politics, as important as it is, are the megapolitical factors that ultimately determine how societies function. Unhappily, in this world of sin and sorrow, weapons are the ultimate instruments of change. And it is with the impact of weapons that human consciousness and the human spirit must contend.

As we are seeing throughout most of Eastern Europe and the Soviet Union, it is not enough to merely proclaim that a free and prosperous commonwealth will henceforth exist where one has not existed before. The rules that make for productive living—the constitution and laws—do not inaugurate themselves. Nor are they held in place by good intentions. Before violence in society can be controlled, the costs of policing violence must be low. It must be relatively easy to overpower those who act in violent and predatory ways. Whether this is possible depends upon many factors beyond the reach of political authorities. The ultimate constitution of society is determined not by what people say nor by resolutions passed in a solemn assembly. As Winston Churchill once said, "The cheers of weak, well-meaning legislatures soon cease to echo and their votes soon cease to count."

The ultimate constitution is determined by factors that alter the costs and rewards of resorting to violence. Historically, there have been four prime factors that have established the boundaries where power is exercised: technology, climate, topography, and the work of busy little microbes. At different times and places, each has exerted a determinant influence on affairs, though not necessarily in isolation from the others. Of these, technology's importance has grown as civilization has evolved. It is now the most important megapolitical influence. It helps determine how governments form, how long they endure, and who has a voice in controlling them.

In *Blood in the Streets* we focused largely on the technological foundations of power. Changes in scale economies in the production process and the shifting balance between the offense and defense in weaponry help explain the meanderings of history. They determine the size at which groups organize their livelihoods and defend themselves most effectively. They explain why imperialism blossomed in the last half of the nineteenth century—when the great powers enjoyed extraordinary, and decidedly temporary, advantages in offensive weaponry—and receded in the twentieth century, when the advantage swung toward the defense. These same factors also help explain the rising level of instability in the Third World, the dynamics of revolution, and the increasing menace of terrorism. As we will explore, when upheaval costs less you get more of it.

THE REVOLUTION OF THE 1990s

The reason we focus on these deep determinants of historic change is that we believe that a major transition in history is already underway. The collapse of Communism and the liquidation of the Soviet Union marks the end of the bipolar organization of the world that has predominated since 1945.

The crucial date in this turnabout was November 9, 1989. This was the day the Berlin Wall fell. Whatever political leaders may have thought or said, November 9, 1989, changed more than the traffic flow in Berlin. It changed the flow of power around the globe. It marked the end of the Cold War period in which real power was controlled in Moscow and Washington. This has far-reaching implications, not just for Europe, but for Africa, Asia, the Middle East, and Latin America. The fall of the Berlin Wall will add to the rubble in the Third World. The mostly backward countries over which Moscow and Washington maneuvered for forty-five years have suddenly become just substitute players in a game that is finished. The 1990s will be a cold decade for the weak who must battle the strong for the savings of the thrifty.

We will move towards a world without a leader, to a multi-polar world, marked by economic competition rather than military confrontation between superpowers. North America, dominated by the United States, will compete with the Pacific rim, dominated by Japan, and with the European Community, dominated by Germany. Some have hailed this new competition as "the end of history," a new era in which the great ideological division that rent the Western world will disappear along with Communism, and leave no further questions to be decided. A sillier notion is hard to imagine. The new threats to peace that seem likely to emerge in the nineties could make even the most hard-nosed Cold Warrior nostalgic for days when ponderous Communist bureaucracies were the principal enemies of progress. Witness the murderous ethnic wars that have erupted in Eastern Europe and the former Soviet Union. Consider how they could be compounded by the breakdown of central authority that once held control over tens of thousands of nuclear weapons and paid the scientists who built them.

The new world of economic competition will be one in which North America begins with an advantage that is also a liability—its near monopoly on twenty-first-century military power. The lopsided U.S. victory in the Gulf War increased perception of U.S. military strength. This carries undoubted advantages. It will slow the collapse of the dollar. The currencies of dominant military powers tend to stand at a premium relative to the interest rates and trading position that would otherwise determine their value. The United States will, in practice, be able to do better deals in trade negotiations because of its superior military power.

In some respects, however, America's near monopoly on twenty-first-century military power may prove a disadvantage. This hardly sounds logical. But think carefully. In purely commercial terms, dominance in military technology is far less advantageous than dominance in a consumer sector like electronics or automobiles. Unless the United States is actually prepared to employ military force against Germany and Japan, its superpower capacities will avail little in economic competition. And to the extent that the United States does serve as the world's policeman, dampening conflict and aggression in the Third World, it is providing a public good that all the leading trading nations can enjoy. Furthermore, the very act of policing property rights, as police in big cities frequently find, is more likely to incite animosities than reap dividends. Even the U.S. military campaign to secure Gulf oil supplies against Saddam Hussein may prove economically more useful to Germany and Japan, both noncombatants, than to the United States and the United Kingdom, who bore the burden of the fighting.

We have argued for some years that the problem of world disorder has been growing steadily harder and more expensive to handle—in part because of the increasing costs of projecting power. In the wake of the Gulf War, the international security of property appears to have changed for the better. Like world stock markets, world order depends partly on expectation. Since the Vietnam War the expectations about the use of American defense power had become negative, both in the United States itself and in the rest of the world. The devastating defeat of Iraqi forces in the Persian Gulf War changed that impression. The new expectation is that the justified use of American military power will be successful.

This expectation is likely to last for some years, possibly until the end of the century. It may appear therefore that United States military supremacy can assure stability. Unfortunately, this is unlikely. While the prospects for world order have definitely been improved in the wake of the Gulf War because expectations have been changed for the better, the trend in purely technological terms has not changed. As we explain in detail, the ultimate logic of the Information Revolution is to undercut the effectiveness of offensive weaponry and undermine all organizations operating at a large scale.

Remember that essentially defensive military technologies can temporarily swing the advantage to offensive use *when they are monopolized*. When Western powers were the only ones in possession of machine guns during the nineteenth century, they used them to devastate Asian and African forces in battle. It was only later, when machine guns faced each other in World War I, that their true implications for defeating the projection of power were revealed. The ratio of American and Allied casualties to Iraqi dead from the Gulf War may never be precisely known. But it is not unlikely that the Iraqis lost five hundred or more per each casualty they inflicted. It was a lopsided defeat, equivalent to the massacre of the Dervish Army by the British Camel Corps in the Battle of Omdurman on September 2, 1898. For the time being, America is the only superpower. But this may not have as many salutary effects as one would wish.

The very success of high-tech military measures against Saddam is likely to discourage future Third World tyrants from fielding targets against which such superweapons can be effective. The apparent invincibility of American forces against massed land armies will be all too apparent. It will be understood in the Third World even better than it is understood in the United States. No doubt most Americans will feel a sense of pride and power over the effectiveness of American weaponry. But it will be like the pride of machine gunners who decimated cavalry charges in World War I. Not a very useful guide to future conflict because there won't be many more cavalry charges to decimate.

Saddam Hussein assembled the largest and mightiest of Third World armies. Laser bombs and cruise missiles proved it was an anachronism—a force better suited to World War I trench warfare than the automated battlefields of the twenty-first century. With one exception, Saddam's tactics, including use of poison gas, could have come from General Falkenhayn's field manual at Ypres in 1915. That one exception was terrorism. General Falkenhayn did not employ terror against civilian targets. It was Saddam's only successful weapon.

In the future, Third World tyrants will emulate Saddam's successful use of terror, and not bother assembling massive field armies in trenches—just as they no longer field cavalry divisions. The lesson of the Iraq War is that an army massed for a war of maneuver is no longer a viable force against a high-tech air force. Third World dictators can still be ruthless tyrants, but they can no longer be tyrants on the march. Their armies will continue to be instruments of terror against their own populations. But they will not be found massing on borders for frontal assaults against neighboring countries. Future aggression will be undertaken by guerrilla war, subversion, and terror, tactics that cannot be countered by cruise missiles and bombardments targeted from space. Henceforth, Third World dictators will rely less on armies and more on terrorists. When they gain nuclear weapons, they will deliver them by overnight express, not by missiles that can be shot down.

Much of the military capital accumulated by the United States during the Cold War will be of little effect against terrorists and guerrilla bands. It will be all but useless in economic competition. And as unhappiness over burden-sharing in the Gulf showed, it will no longer command the fiscal and monetary allegiance of Japan and Germany. Therefore, the United States will be under increasing threat in the decade now opening. Before it ends, the dollar will cease to be the world's reserve currency. America's allies will no longer be obliged to support the dollar or fund U.S. deficits in order to forestall major cuts in U.S. military spending. Such spending will henceforth be of much less importance in fending off the crippled successors to the Soviet Union. And Saddam Hussein's luckily ill-timed Iraqi invasion of Kuwait notwithstanding, American military power will come to be seen as insufficient to control disorder at the periphery. American military power could defeat any Third World military force in a head-on confrontation. But America cannot occupy and control the Third World.

The military equipment and structure the United States has purchased with trillions in Cold War spending is largely unsuited to combating the threats of the 1990s. The new and ancient enemies of Western civilization that will emerge to disrupt the peace will not be continental powers like the former Soviet Union, or even anachronistic 1930s-style dictators like Saddam, but small countries and fragments of countries, bands of terrorists, religious fanatics, drug lords, and criminal gangs. They will not be deterred by Patriot missiles, much less intercontinental ballistic missiles and nuclear attack submarines.

The macro-terror of the Cold War will be replaced with micro-terror of growing technological sophistication. The crack-up of the Soviet Union left behind alienated and impoverished populations who possess the world's largest collection of unregistered guns. The KGB notwithstanding, millions of sophisticated weapons disappeared from Soviet arsenals on the black market in exchange for hard currency. It must be considered likely that many of the 35,000 nuclear weapons spread around the former Soviet empire have fallen into the hands of those who would pay hard money to have them. Reports placed at least three tactical nuclear weapons in Iran by spring, 1992. Officials in Belarus told James Davidson in April 1992 that tactical nuclear weapons formerly stationed there had been removed, adding, "But we can't be sure where they went. For all we know, Saddam Hussein has them." If this was a joke, it is only half funny. The collapse of central authority has placed weapons of frightful power up for grabs by Islamic fundamentalists, fanatical ethnic separatists, like General Dzhokar Dudayev, who has threatened to bomb Russian nuclear plants, renegade military units, or just plain criminals. Any of these may pose threats to peace that would far overshadow the dying threat of Communism.

> *The colors on the map are dripping.*
>
> —ROD STEWART

For forty-five years, the map of Europe was frozen by Cold War. This was the longest period of stable borders in Europe since the fall of Rome. The 1990s will be a boom time for map-makers. It will be a period of devolution, not just in Europe, but throughout the globe. Multi-ethnic empires will come apart. We will see the breakup not just of the Soviet Union . . . but of India, Canada, China, Yugoslavia, Ethiopia, and other countries.

The Neighborhood Power Equation

The increasing futility of policing the globe is not merely a matter of concern to generals and strategic planners. It affects you. The fall of empires is just the most obvious consequence of the declining capacity of governments everywhere to maintain control on a large scale. As technological change makes it ever more costly to project power, and ever cheaper to resist, the capacity of governments to maintain order inside their own borders is likely to shrivel to a level more typical of the Third World. Changes in the power equation imply not merely the fall of empires, but the fall of neighborhoods. There are already areas in urban centers in the United States, and to a lesser extent Britain, where police have effectively lost control. These are precisely the neighborhoods where puzzling social pathologies are mushrooming. Violence, crime, drugs, broken families, abused and neglected children, the failure of education, are all symptoms of the collapse of civilized authority. When disorder at any level effectively prohibits individuals from participating in the larger economy, it gives rise to perverse and even self-destructive behavior. Part of this book is an analysis of the functional logic of such "irrationality."

The Retribalization of the West

As the Information Revolution proceeds in the 1990s, the scale of power in the world will continue to devolve. Smaller and smaller groups will gain military effectiveness. Violence will tend to reassert itself as the common condition of life.

How quickly this tendency is realized depends in part on the appeal of liberal, Western values to violence-prone groups at the margins of the modern economy. As we shall see, the evidence is not encouraging. The more disaffected the violence-prone become, the more likely it is that modern states, especially those with multi-ethnic populations, will mimic in some degree the kind of social collapse that has overtaken Lebanon. There, almost every neighborhood or valley is under the armed sway of a separate gang or militia. The members of the pro-Iranian terrorist group Hezbollah are scarcely more brutal than the gangs of Los Angeles or the followers of the drug lords in New York or Washington—they are merely better armed. The rioting that swept Los Angeles in 1992 showed how vulnerable large cities are to disruption. As violence-prone groups become more militarily threatening, we will see a reversion to conflict along tribal and ethnic lines, as well as a further breakdown of the infrastructure that supports urban living. This is not as farfetched as it may seem. A consequence of the depression of the 1990s could be a full-scale migration away from major cities in the United States.

The continued trend toward predominance of defensive weaponry has a potential to break up trading areas and weaken or destroy many organizations operating at a large scale. Unless some new accident of technology intervenes to raise the scale of weaponry, and to restore the megapolitical advantage to larger political units, the world will be increasingly vulnerable to economic devolution and decline.

Fluctuations in the exercise of raw power are important to the evolution of economies at all levels. Changes in technology, especially military technology, have set the stage for an increase in the perverse effects of violence everywhere. We showed in *Blood in the Streets* that many apparently random events—the rise of OPEC, the U.S. defeat in Vietnam, Third World debt troubles, and even the falling income share of blue-collar workers—are not so random as they seem. They are intimately connected consequences of changes in the physical limits on the exercise of power.

The Subversive Microchip

Not only is the postwar world coming to an end. But the technological transformation that undermined Communism—and thus effectively ended the
Cold War—will alter the way we organize our work. The microchip has set
in motion what promises to be the third great revolution of human life,
comparable in its sweep to the Agricultural Revolution that set history in
motion and the Gunpowder Revolution that initiated the great surge of human
progress at the end of the fifteenth century. As the fall of Communism has
already demonstrated, this new transition will involve major shocks to over-
grown bureaucratic systems now ripe for ruin. We expect something more
than mild business-cycle downturns in the 1990s. If we are right, you will
see a crisis in the original sense of the word. In the days before TV newsmen
started describing every story as a "crisis," the word was not merely a term
of suspense. It had a specific meaning now largely lost. A "crisis" was "a
turning point, a critical time, or a decisive turn." It was "a state of affairs in
which a decisive change for better or worse is imminent."

The revolution of the 1990s will involve not only crises of economics and
politics. It will involve crises of culture. It will remake the modern mind,
altering values and changing beliefs. The postwar obsession with consumption, self-indulgence, and debt, now so conspicuous in America, but a feature
of all advanced consumer societies, will be tested and found wanting. As the
religion of secular consumerism is left behind like a rusting tail fin, sterner
religions that involve real moral principles and angry gods will make a comeback. For the first time in centuries, the revelations of science will seem to
enhance rather than undermine the spiritual dimension in life.

While it is difficult to speak of a "frame of mind" of a whole society, we
are all nonetheless aware that there are moods in the lives of nations as well
as in the lives of individuals. Special ways of seeing things survive for a time,
then pass away. Some of these have a very short season. They drift in and
out of consciousness and are gone. Others, like the ideas of the Cold War,
last for decades. Still others, like the perceptions and attitudes that form the
culture of Western progress, have endured for centuries.

As the year 2000 approaches, the ideas that define the struggles of human
consciousness will be split in more directions than ever before. Society will
be more diverse and more violent. The occult notions of race and tribe will
confront the mainstream of Western civilization with a new struggle, as menacing as the fading conflict between capitalism and socialism. Crime will be
politicized. The bankruptcy and growing weakness of the nation-state will
draw into sharper resolution the conflict between those who struggle to earn
their way and those who live upon the redistributed wealth of others. The

division between the skilled and the unskilled, between the culture of earnings and the culture of entitlement, will widen as society is stretched to pay its overdue bills.

THE REVOLUTION OF THE 1490s

> The thing that hath been, it is that which shall be; and that which is done is that which shall be done: and there is no new thing under the sun.
>
> —ECCLESIASTES 1:9

History's nearest analogy to the current revolution in the technology of weaponry was the transition from mechanical to chemically powered weapons five centuries ago. It set in motion some of the more profound changes in human history. The rise of the West, the "Renaissance," and the "Reformation" are just a few of the names given to aspects of the revolution in human life that accompanied the spread of gunpowder. In a roundabout way, the Newtonian world view that has informed the modern intuition was itself a product of gunpowder. Improvements in metallurgy, driven by the search for better guns, allowed improvements in optics, which led ultimately to the telescope, which Newton used to spy gravitation and calculus. As we shall explore, the mathematical inventions Newton devised to complement seventeenth-century technology still dominate what remains of "modern" common sense. Such was the sweep of the Gunpowder Revolution. Few events have ever loomed so large in subsequent history, and at the same time been so little understood.

We say this not as historians of politics or science but as lovers of books, who read widely and speculate on what we read. Some of our speculations are no doubt adventuresome. For this we make no apology. We are trying to formulate an overview of complicated issues. To take full account of all the complexities would be like setting out to draw a map at a scale of 1:1. If it could be done, it would be a waste of time. For our work to be of use to you, we must simplify reality. We must draw conclusions.

The subject of this book is much broader than just the economy or markets. It is an exploration of the hidden logic of power, and how a change in the boundary forces that govern the use of power affects everything else. The end of the postwar world is not an accident, but a necessity. It is driven not only by the normal feedback of hideous cost, which brings every human extravaganza to an end. It is also an early casualty of the microchip. This triumph of miniaturization is a development we will analyze from several perspectives. It will alter the balance of power between peoples, shift the incentives for predatory violence, rearrange the way that people think and even the content of their prayers.

Understanding and the Profit Motive

Although Marxism is dead, the market has not triumphed as a matter of ideas, but as a matter of megapolitical reality. A "Marxist mist," to use Jean-François Revel's phrase, still hangs over our intellectual culture and clouds the vision of many. Thus any attempt to escape from general unhappiness, or profit at all, is suspect. This is one reason that investment books as a genre are held in low esteem by much of the intelligentsia. They see every work that aims to provide practical advice as yet another version of *How I Turned Two Cruddy Outhouses into a Million Dollars of Real Estate.*

No doubt some investment books are written for simpletons. Yet the indictment is overdone. An analysis may benefit as well as suffer for being harnessed to the profit motive. Investors often tolerate more complexity than casual readers precisely because they have a keener incentive to learn. This incentive is straightforward. The better you understand the world, the more likely you are to profit. In a sense, therefore, the profit motive is a profound tool of learning. It encourages individuals to broaden their perspectives and understand cause-and-effect relationships that may have an impact on markets. This is why a periodical aimed toward investors, like the *Economist,* offers more comprehensive coverage of world affairs than one aimed at a more general audience, like *Newsweek.*

Far more than is generally realized, the range of human understanding has been widened by the profit motive. A feature of this book will be to explore some of the surprising consequences of this tendency. The political values, ideas, and metaphors we live by are informed by a complex web of incentives that have only rarely or recently been understood. There is powerful evidence suggesting that reason and science are the traveling companions of social mobility. A society that has no use for information about getting ahead is likely to have little use for reason either. Its day-to-day life is likely to be ridden with demons and delusions. Even more surprising is the close connection between social mobility and the study of history.

As heretical as it may seem to institution-bound historians, the study of history has essentially been a self-help project. That it no longer holds such value for the current generation of students, who shun history for more practical disciplines, is evidence of a failure among historians. They have abandoned the old-fashioned notion that history has lessons, and thus emptied their classrooms. The most compelling of all reasons to study the past has always been to foretell the future.

For fundamental reasons, such information has been in strongest demand among societies that afforded individuals a scope for upward mobility. When and where upward mobility has been forbidden, history has been forgotten as well. Caste-bound societies, like India or the Roman Empire in its dotage, have produced little or no history, only myths and fabricated genealogies that offered few insights into the future because they offered few reliable details of the past. Exact sequences, records, and dating of events have been the building blocks of forecasting.

The distant grandfather of today's historian competed with soothsayers and astrologers in foretelling the future. In fact, if one looks far enough into the past, the historian and astrologer have a common ancestor. The scribes who first recorded "omen texts" and chronologies in Babylon and China were engaged in a form of augury. Historian Donald E. Brown notes that they "collected information on conjoined occurrences so that these could be used to predict human events." By recording practically any event that happened on given days, they were not only linking together by date many events that could have been associated only by coincidence, they were also establishing a record of historic knowledge that pointed the way toward objective accounts of what really happened. Since timekeeping in the ancient world was reckoned almost entirely from the heavens, it was a short step from recording the dates at which events occurred to correlating them with influences from the heavens. At a time when causation was not well understood, it was just as plausible, and certainly easier, to look to the heavens as a source of regularity in human affairs than to sort out the governing influences from a closer study of human affairs themselves.

In ways that casual observation would be unlikely to reveal, the social mobility of the marketplace was and remains a prerequisite for the rational view of life that makes science possible. The accounting requirements of mercantile society gave rise to many innovations of mathematics. The algorithms of arithmetic were first learned by traders and spread through society as the rise of capitalism spread the need for skills of reckoning. Roy Harris, professor of linguistics at Oxford, argues that the great invention of written language itself arose primarily from the necessity of maintaining a record of inventories in ancient agricultural societies. The written word was a bastard child of accountants before it was adopted by poets.

We do not apologize for the fact that we write books oriented toward helping you to survive and profit. In a sense, we are employing history in its original use, as a guide to practical affairs. The twelfth-century Chinese historian Fei Kun said, "History records good fortune and disaster responding to events, and should display the intention of encouraging and warning." This is no less true today than it was for the Sung emperors. The best hints that life affords about the future are found in the past.

Our excursions into theory are attempts to understand the unfolding revolution of the 1990s and beyond. We do not pretend to have all the answers. But we do believe that we have uncovered ideas with implications that could be important to you. They may help you in your investments. They may also help you order your life during what could prove to be the most important decade of the century.

The message of *Blood in the Streets* was that power matters. That is a message of this volume as well. We do not pretend that it is a simplistic single cause of everything that happens. Power's reach, however, goes further than is commonly believed. In our view, neither the worldwide boom in financial assets during the 1980s nor its subsequent end should be understood as events out of the blue. Both are consequences of profound disruptions of the equations of power. Just as the decline of British power early in this century led first to World War I and then to financial booms that ended with 1929 and the Great Depression, so the decline in American power evident since the late sixties also precipitated financial fluctuations of an extreme kind. The worldwide depression that you are now living through is its direct aftermath.

A Challenge to Prevailing Perceptions of Reality

Most people do not wish to hear even a constructive warning about an event as frightening as depression, let alone one that could be associated with a revolution in the organization of social life. Warnings about major economic changes or social upheavals are never heeded nor taken seriously by the great majority. In the past, when anyone has warned of depression, he has been laughed at or ignored. Even if we had not understood this from our readings of history, we were well instructed by the reception accorded to *Blood in the Streets*. A reviewer in *Newsweek* who dismissed our analysis as "an unthinking attack on reason" spoke not just for himself, but the times.

We assumed as we wrote *The Great Reckoning* that it would be no better received by reviewers and the news media. Of course, we would have been pleased to be proven wrong. We were not. Although the North American first edition is now in its 11th printing as we write, a disproportionate share of the sales came in Canada, where *The Great Reckoning* became a widely discussed, number one nonfiction best seller. In the United States, sales have come almost entirely by word of mouth. The book received little national notice. As the U.S. economy weakened, and more of our forecasts came true, the American media stopped discussing them altogether.

In a society with few qualms left, where the daily fare of television is talk of incest, child abuse, and photos of Madonna in bondage, there is one topic the American media remain reluctant to touch. The ideas in this book. Television producers who would jump at the chance to book a discussion of kinky sex, or a recipe for cheesecake that won't make you fat, feel that they must protect the public from the taboo idea that depression is even a possibility. On more than one occasion when some forecast in *The Great Reckoning* had been spectacularly confirmed by an event such as the death of the Soviet Union or the Los Angeles riots, the stalwart people whose job it was to get some commercial attention for the book in the United States were told to forget it. Ours were just not ideas that America's television networks felt they could talk about.

One editor who did write a favorable mention of *The Great Reckoning* received a reprimand from the owner of the magazine stating that "the only issue of your publication that should report the forecasts of Davidson and Rees-Mogg is the last issue. Even if we thought they were true, why would we tell anybody?" Others who did not get that message directly got it indirectly.

You might expect that as the economy weakens, some of the gatekeepers of ideas who previously dismissed our analysis would soften their critical attitudes, and perhaps even acknowledge that *The Great Reckoning* anticipated important developments that others missed. This has not yet happened yet, and remains unlikely. In fact, we expect to be subjected to even more vitriolic attack as events vindicate our views. If the past is a guide, we will be denounced as unqualified, our characters will be called into question, and we will even be blamed for causing or contributing to the depression that we have merely seen coming.

There is a reason for such a perverse reception to a considered warning. We are struggling to develop a new paradigm of understanding. This new paradigm challenges received views of reality on a range of sensitive issues. When people's sense of reality is threatened, they feel angry. When people feel angry, they feel justified in saying nasty things. The reason that our argument is taboo while Madonna in bondage isn't is that our arguments threaten the shared sense of reality upon which many people have built their lives, while her antics do not. The views we set out in *Blood in the Streets* and amplify here clash at a number of points with received opinions about the way the world works and how it is tending.

- Among American readers, especially, there has been an inclination to reject any argument that supposes the hegemony of the United States is nearing an end. As that student of history, J. Danforth Quayle, frequently said to great applause in the lecture hall, "The declinists are wrong." Many Americans refuse to acknowledge the obvious signs that the era of American predominance is drawing to a close.

- Both the political left, who sympathized with Communism, and the anti-Communist right, who dedicated themselves to struggle against it, were roundly offended by our prediction that Marxist systems were destined to collapse. Reality has largely overtaken those objections. But as we enter the final decade of the twentieth century, political debate remains trapped within mental constructs informed by the technology and ideology of the nineteenth century.

- Our views are offensive to both parties that contend for power in the modern welfare state. We deny their central premise—that any political faction can guarantee prosperity. Indeed, we go further. We doubt that the secular utopia of the welfare state can survive the revolutionary impact of the microchip. The hope that government can provide everyone with a high standard of living, good health, and security against misfortune, quite apart from his abilities and values, has been an article of faith in all Western democracies for most of this century. It is now an anachronism, bound to be disappointed, no matter how reckless the monetary or fiscal policy any set of leaders chooses to adopt.

- The idea that volatility and crashes are integral to the functioning of markets as complex systems is another concept that has few visible adherents. Yet much evidence points in just that direction, some of it newly buttressed by discoveries in the emerging science of chaos. To treat market crashes as accidents is to miss their fundamental similarity to other complex systems in nature. When pressure builds along fault lines in the earth's crust, the quake that eventually results is not an accident, but a consequence. The same is true of market crashes. They are not truly random events, but reflections of stresses that have built up in the world system.

- Among modern peoples in general there is an almost instinctive rejection of any notion that recognizes the inherent nonlinearity of life. Much of the contemporary perception of reality is based more on seventeenth-century physics than on the discoveries of our own science. The educated public who think about the economy keep wanting it to have laws of motion like the planets, hence the largely artificial notion of "equilibrium," around which economics is taught. In fact, the economy, with its turbulence and complexity, bears more resemblance to the behavior of clouds in a weather system than to the routine movements of the heavenly bodies.

- There is a deep prejudice against any theory that highlights the inter-connectedness of life in a nonmagical way. Many minds balk at any long chain of reasoning, whatever the character of the conclusions it supports. This prejudice is all the more emphatic when the logic suggests that certain political or social developments are broadly deterministic, or that each stage of human history does not afford the same possi-bilities. In part, this disregard for causes and consequences is a form of intellectual evasion. What is truly random cannot be predicted or explained. By pretending that practically everything is random, we paradoxically allow ourselves to shirk responsibility for those circum-stances where our own actions could have an effect in altering outcomes for the better. To those who do not wish to understand, all news is a surprise.
- There is a widespread assumption that economic progress since World War II has become permanent. Practically everyone in modern indus-trial countries accepts the unargued conviction that another depression is no more likely than an invasion from Mars. This illusion is part of a general overestimation of the powers of governments. Only the res-idents of rich countries where governments still function with a sem-blance of competence could believe it. In the rest of the world, where they don't, depression, and even destitution, have been quite contem-porary phenomena throughout the postwar period. As a matter of simple logic, it is unclear why political measures that failed to stop economic collapse in Argentina should be expected to work so much better in the Northern Hemisphere. We argue that they don't.

THE GREAT RECKONING

Taking a longer view, the crucial mistake that runs through contemporary perceptions of reality is the deep reluctance to face the all-embracing action and reaction of nature. Life is not static. It is turbulent to its very essence. Human societies, like all complex systems, are constantly fluctuating. This fundamental ebb and flow is the source of cycles in human affairs, including economic cycles. As Emerson says, there is a "deep remedial force that un-derlies all facts." At every point where something goes up, nature is constantly compensating by finding a way to bring it down. "Superinduce magnetism at one end of a needle; the opposite magnetism takes place at the other end. If the south attracts, the north repels. To empty here, you must condense there." Nature always keeps its accounts in balance.

This is the fundamental truth that underlies the Great Reckoning. It is another way of saying that everything has its price, that there is no such thing as something for nothing; that all bills must be paid. Every attempt in history to avoid paying by enlarging debts has ended in tears. "Always pay; for first or last, you must pay your entire debt. Persons and events may stand for a time between you and justice, but it is only a postponement. You must pay at last your own debt. If you are wise, you will dread a prosperity which only loads you with more." So Emerson said. It is still true today.

The failure to perceive that nature is a better accountant than politicians probably explains our common hubris and indifference to history. It is quite usual for peoples to imagine on a fair day that it will never storm again.

"A severe depression like that of 1920–21 is outside the range of possibility," the Harvard Economic Society proclaimed in 1929. Perhaps those who say the same today are right. We hope so. But we worry about signs that more of our forecasts have begun to come true.

The decline in the relative power of the United States and the death of the Soviet Union are bound to be fundamentally destabilizing, economically as well as politically. With one of the two world empires weakening at home and the other gone, many of the variables that for long periods have been treated as constants will begin to fluctuate, changing every equation of value in the world economy. Even developments that seem clearly positive, like the decline of military spending, will have far-reaching and surprising consequences. Falling military effort is deflationary. We forecast that the end of the Cold War would bring an end to the real estate boom in California and deflate other prices across the globe. That forecast has only just begun to come true.

As much as we sympathize with the longing for freedom throughout the defunct Soviet empire, the rise of nationalism in formerly captive lands is not a wholly positive phenomenon. The news of 1992 makes it only too clear that the reassertion of nationalist and tribal identities is not a matter about which to cheer. In the past, it has been associated with breakdown, ethnic antagonisms, trade protectionism, and economic collapse. Normally, when economies collapse, freedom is lost as well.

We expect the nineties to be a decade of escalating economic and political disorder unparalleled since the 1930s. We are prepared to offer you evidence and logic in support of some rather unorthodox views. In this respect, this book, like *Blood in the Streets* before it, is a thought exercise, an attempt to judge the rough shape of the future by extrapolating from the past. Our aim is to help you anticipate and respond to events that will bewilder most of our fellow citizens. If you are an investor, we believe that reading this book will help you find many ways to profit, as well as avoid losses. Yet even if you do not self-consciously think of yourself as an investor, take heart. We hope you will find much here to interest and stimulate you.

This book, like its predecessor, is as intellectually honest as we know how to make it. In his review of *Blood in the Streets*, Sir Martin Jacomb described it as having been written with a "frighteningly unsentimental objectivity." Too much writing about the world today is geared more to being politically "correct" or avoiding offense to inflamed sensibilities. We have tried not to blink at facts and let political or ideological blinders mask our perception of reality.

That said, however, we are not disaffected from Western culture, and feel no inclination to pretend otherwise. We do not believe that material wealth is a fraud or an encroachment upon the human spirit. It is written in Ecclesiastes: "A feast is made for laughter, and wine maketh merry: but money answereth all things." Sane people would like a laugh or two. They would also like a few dollars or some other convertible currency in their pockets.

As is always the case with a book of nonfiction, our most original thoughts are the thoughts of others. In spite of our interest in nonlinear change, our method of analysis shares much in common with that of Adam Smith, Adam Ferguson, Thomas Malthus, David Ricardo, and other political economists of the eighteenth and nineteenth centuries. We are simply applying their insights about price theory in a larger context. They argued that incentives matter, that humans respond to costs and rewards. We agree. We owe much of our further inspiration to contemporary thinkers like James Buchanan, Mancur Olson, and Gordon Tullock, who have extended the methods of economic analysis to political and constitutional questions. We are applying their techniques to analyze the most encompassing constraints of all, the costs and rewards of exercising physical force. Like amateur painters who have stolen the brushes of professionals, we have the tools even if we lack the art to use them properly.

Recognizing that ideas are often informed by incentives, we also indicate a prejudice. We are the purveyors of investment products, including a newsletter, *Strategic Investment*, and some private investment partnerships. We are also private consultants. In a sense, therefore, this book is an advertisement for our view of investment.

This does not mean, however, that we hope that our projections of hard times comes true. Quite the contrary. We are not wishing for a depression to demonstrate how clever we are. We intend our warnings to be constructive and helpful. Those who heeded our argument in *Blood in the Streets* that real estate prices were building on a cloud of false expectation know that the value of forewarning can be substantial. One couple wrote to credit us with saving them tens of thousands of dollars. In spite of such gratifying comments, we would rather be wrong than right. Our warnings are like admonitions to buy insurance—more likely to be appreciated when calamity has struck. We would much rather that it did not strike, for all the obvious reasons. We fear the economic, social, and political consequences of depression. We have businesses and interests established long ago that cannot easily be made depression-proof or unwound. Like everyone else, we have a vested interest in prosperity.

And while we are confessing our sins, we may as well repeat again that we do not pretend that our forward vision is 20/20. Indeed, from what we understand of economic history, it would be startling if we were able to accurately gauge details of time and place in advance of the actual events. Our claims are more modest. We simply believe that it is possible to anticipate events rather than merely react to them. Lessons to this effect have been driven home since the earliest days of human interaction.

The Book of Genesis tells the story of Joseph. By listening to Joseph's hint, the Pharaoh rightly anticipated the seven lean years that followed seven years of plenty. From that date to this, it has always been true that the future belonged to those who prepared for it.

CHAPTER ONE

THE MEGAPOLITICS OF PROGRESS AND DECLINE

VIOLENCE AS A CATALYST AND CONSEQUENCE

OF CHANGE

One of the lamentable principles of human productivity is that it is easier to destroy than to create. A house that takes several man-years to build can be destroyed in an hour by any young delinquent who has the price of a box of matches. . . .

The power to hurt—to destroy things that somebody treasures, to inflict pain and grief—is a kind of bargaining power, not easy to use but used often. In the underworld it is the basis for blackmail, extortion, and kidnapping, in the commercial world, for boycotts, strikes, and lockouts . . . it underlies the humane as well as the corporal punishments that society uses to deter crime and delinquency . . . It is often the basis for discipline, civilian and military: and gods use it to exact obedience.

—THOMAS SCHELLING,
Arms and Influence

ON JANUARY 26, 1990, a strange event occurred in the Best Food Market in Houston, Texas. A thief armed with two pistols held up the store. This may not seem so strange. You no doubt know how an armed robbery works. The strange part was that the thief didn't. The store manager, in a rare feat of salesmanship, persuaded the thief to sell his guns. The thief actually obliged. He handed over loaded firearms in exchange for two hundred dollars cash. This was such an astonishing twist on the normal logic of violence that tabloids in the United States trumpeted the story: "Holdup Victim Tricks Bandit into

Selling His Guns: . . . Then Forces Thief to Flee Empty-Handed." The accounts made much of the apparent stupidity of the robber, describing him as a "flea-brained felon." He had confused the rules of the game he was playing, and failed to grasp something crucial—that the almighty dollar is not almighty. It is always hostage to the power of the gun.

This is so fundamental, so ultimate a fact of life, that it is almost never mistaken on the battlelines of society, at those points where the rule of law is contested by violence. In such a showdown, violence can be bettered only by superior force, not by good intentions, much less by mere pieces of paper with ink on them. Gary Cooper could not have won the showdown in *High Noon* if he had reached into his wallet instead of his holster. The attempted robbery of the Best Food Market was clearly the exception to the more common experience where violence holds economic behavior hostage. Yet the mistake the "flea-brained felon" made—failing to appreciate the ultimate importance of power—is actually quite common. People who live in delightful, well-mannered suburbs, who never have to physically contest for their lives and property, often fail to grasp the subtle logic of violence. It is a mistake seldom made by hardened criminals. Criminals are normally connoisseurs of power's subtleties. They understand, as law-abiding people sometimes do not, that laws are merely wishes on a piece of paper unless there is sufficient power to enforce them. The ultimate law is the law of the jungle. The law of the desert. The law of the dark alley in the inner city. It is the law that says that what is yours by right and justice is yours only so long as you—or someone—can protect it.

The Paradox of Violence

At the banquet table of Nature, there are no reserved seats. You get what you can take. You keep what you can hold.

—A. PHILIP RANDOLPH

Humans always have incentives to employ violence to obtain what they want. Yet this is a fact that most peaceful cultures discourage individuals from bringing clearly into focus. You have often heard it said that "crime is a sickness" or "war never solves anything." Such views are profoundly misleading. They reflect a combination of wishful thinking and the workings of a taboo against violence that is an important cultural contribution to civic peace. Encouraging people to believe that violence never achieves anything can be a useful way of discouraging free-lance violence. But it would be a mistake for you to stop thinking at the boundary of this taboo. Imagine that violence has no role to play and you are like someone holding a map upside down and noticing only that greasy fingerprints smudge the colors. Some criminals are sick. Some wars are indeed economic disasters, launched by madmen. But to focus on the deranged or unwholesome character of those who resort to violence is to miss its deeper logic. It is crucial to understanding many of the historic and economic changes of the 1990s—such as the explosion of terrorism and crime, the collapse of Communism, the coming world depression, the bankruptcy of the welfare state, the impoverishment of the Third World, the growth of tribalism and racism, the menacing challenge of Islam, and the revival of morality and religion in Western societies. All these apparently random phenomena are actually connected and driven by the logic of violence.

The reason that people resort to violence is that it often pays. In some ways, the simplest thing a man can do if he wants money is to take it. That is no less true for an army of men seizing an oil field than it is for a single thug taking a wallet. Power, as William Playfair wrote, "has always sought the readiest road to wealth, by attacking those who were in possession of it."

The challenge to prosperity is precisely that predatory violence does pay well in many circumstances. War does change things. It changes the rules. It changes the distribution of assets and income. It even determines who lives and who dies. It is precisely the fact that violence does pay that makes it hard to control.

Even more troublesome and confusing to many people is the fact that the chief deterrent to predatory violence is the threat of still greater force, sufficient force to insure that violence, for all its simplicity, will not pay. This is the paradox of violence. Part of this paradox is the fact that upper- and middle-class values have for centuries been sensitizing individuals to violence. In other words, the more people conform to the values that have made for modern prosperity, the more repelled they are likely to be by the steps that are sometimes needed to suppress free-lance criminal behavior.

A moment's reflection shows that this is indeed a difficult problem to unravel. The ultimate cure for violence is superior force. It sounds like a simple contradiction, but it isn't. To achieve peace, a society must find ways to muster enough force to suppress predatory violence and curtail the incentives to use it. Seldom can force be deterred by persuasion, as in the foiled robbery of the Best Food Market. Power means more than talk. To police predation effectively, some group must control the physical means to overpower *anyone*. This is why the nature and character of weapons is so important. Weapons are the primary tools that determine the capacity of individuals and groups to employ violence. Obviously, if criminals were armed with AK47s and police had nothing but water pistols, thieves would rampage with impunity. Indeed, the thieves would soon become the government. You would have to apply to them for low-interest loans or permission to park your car.

The logic of violence implies that more than one game of human interaction is going on in any social setting. The first game, as Jack Hirshleifer has observed, is the economic game. It accounts for most constructive human activity. It is the game in which individuals attempt to profit by working within the rules. When people build and work, buy and sell, they are participating in the economic game. But this game supposes that people are willing to abide by the rules. The second game comes into play when they are not. This is the political game—in which individuals seek to profit by changing the rules to their own benefit. This second game of constitutional politics is constrained by the existing constitution and other conceptions of legitimate behavior. The third game is subject to no such constraints. It is the most basic game of all, the game in which there are no rules, and outcomes are constrained only by raw power. This is the game of megapolitics, what Hirshleifer calls the "politics of raw power and conflict." He writes,

> The highest and biggest game of all is *nonconstitutional* . . . politics. This biggest game of social interaction is subject only to the laws of nature. There are no property rights, and the ultimate arbiter is the physical force of individuals or the coalitions they can form.

It is the game that ultimately determines how the world changes, yet it is a game that few understand.

The logic of power is more often disguised than transparent. Subtle differences in incentives and relative capacities to employ violence can create tremendous differences in outcomes. The poet George Herbert wrote:

> *For the want of a nail, the shoe was lost;*
> *For the want of a shoe, the horse was lost;*
> *For the want of a horse, the rider was lost;*
> *For the want of a rider, the battle was lost;*
> *For the want of a battle, the kingdom was lost!*

It is unlikely that the economic future will turn on "want of a nail." But it may turn on something equally as subtle, perhaps the want of a computer chip. The malfunction of a single circuit in a complex weapons system, like a Patriot missile, could tilt the outcome of a battle, and thus send history ricocheting along a different course. Indeed, the inputting of a single wrong coordinate, or a mistaken keystroke by the programmer, could produce dramatically different results. Precisely because many of the catalysts for far-reaching change may be apparently insignificant, you must think closely and carefully about how changes in the current power equation would ripple through society. The best way to do that may be to revisit some crucial transitions in the past. The "raw politics of power and conflict" in the past holds lessons for today.

A Megapolitical Light on History

Very deep is the well of the past. . . . No matter to what hazardous lengths we let our line they still withdraw, again and further into the depths.

—THOMAS MANN,
Joseph and His Brothers

Much of our analysis in the rest of this chapter is centered on events in the past. This detour is a way of illustrating how various megapolitical factors have altered the form of government, the way it is controlled, how economies function, and even the way people think. Megapolitics—or the logic of violence—largely explains when and where democracies evolve, and why they fail. Megapolitics determines when there is slavery and when freedom prevails. Megapolitics explains why women got the vote. It explains why prosperity exploded after the Gunpowder Revolution five hundred years ago. It offers a strong hint about why most societies in antiquity banned borrowing. And why the effective use of gunpowder led almost immediately to a theological declaration on the part of Protestant religious leaders in support of the morality of lending at interest. Megapolitics explains why imperialism was successful in the nineteenth century, and receded in the twentieth. Megapolitics even suggests why Jews and Moslems don't eat pork, while pig feasts are sacred to the rites of primitive peoples in the rain forest. In short, megapolitics helps explain what people think as well as the way they act. It explains why socialism grew as an ideology of the nineteenth century, while the scale of enterprise was rising, and collapsed in the twentieth century, when the scale of enterprise fell.

Like a hammer pounding a precious metal, power changes the shape of society. A realistic forecast of how these changes will unfold in the future depends upon an understanding of the way the world has worked in the past. This is especially true when you are thinking about the dynamics of change. Major economic revolutions are so few in number that one must literally look back to the Stone Age to gain a full perspective on the patterns involved.

Yet as important as this raid on history is, there can never be merely historical answers to questions about the future. Much of what we need to learn from the past depends upon contemporary understandings. When we journey into history we are all "Connecticut Yankees in King Arthur's Court." What we can see depends in part on what type of flashlight we take in our pocket. If we could be magically transported back five, ten, or fifteen centuries ago, much less to the Anatolia of 10,000 B.C., we could learn something about the political economies of those periods. But most of what we could learn would not depend upon what people living then could tell us. In many cases, they would have understood little of what was happening themselves. The most interesting insights from the past are not discoverable in the past but in the present. The record of the past is like Pharaoh's dream in the Book of Genesis, a jumble of largely unintelligible details—seven lean cattle—that mean little without interpretation. Our purpose is to interpret.

THE MEGAPOLITICS OF PRIMEVAL LIFE

For tens of thousands of generations, there was no civilization. There was no written language. There was no government, nor larger organization of society at all. There appear to have been few settled communities, none larger than a village. Wandering bands of fifty or fewer lived by hunting, fishing, and gathering foods in the wild. Population density was extremely low. For example, estimates of the Stone Age population of France go as low as sixteen hundred.

Our primeval ancestors traveled frequently, but usually without a settled home to return to. Their migratory habits helped them resolve disputes. When members of the band argued with one another, it was a relatively simple matter for one faction or the other to walk away if the argument could not be settled. Frequent movement also kept people healthy. Because they did not live in close contact with their own waste and barnyard animals, they were free of the infectious diseases of civilization. Nonetheless, they faced the risk of early death due to hazards of wounds, and infections such as gangrene.

Little Work, No Savings

Anthropologists believe that our ancestors in the primeval economy "neither collected nor maintained" food surpluses. It seems certain that they did not work very hard, probably no more than two hours per day. Anthropologists observing remaining hunter-gatherer societies, such as Eskimos, Australian Aborigines, and Bushmen in the Kalahari Desert, find that they spend little time collecting food, even in their harsh habitats. When circumstances oblige them to work longer one day, they usually take off the next few days to talk and relax. They save nothing.

No Theft, No Government

Humans in the primeval phase of existence had little or nothing to steal. Other than a few personal ornaments and weapons for hunting, they had no private property. Ownership of other resources was held in common, or to be more precise, factors that we today consider resources—like land—were not resources, and therefore were not owned by anyone. Primeval society had no occupational specialization, no structure of leadership, nor any formal hierarchy for settling disputes. Decision-making was democratic for fundamental megapolitical reasons. All men were trained as hunters to kill big animals, and those in good health were of practically equal military power. Violence seems to have been rare, in part because the groups could dissolve and look for food somewhere else in a vast countryside almost empty of other humans. When crimes did occur, they were punished by ostracism, shunning, and blood feuds. When there was plenty of room to roam and essentially nothing to steal, neither crime nor government could have been paying propositions.

CLIMATE AND POWER IN THE AGRICULTURAL REVOLUTION

Simultaneously, climatic changes altered the balance of nature, both in northern regions along the fringes of the retreating glaciers, and in the subtropics where a northward shift of the trade winds spread desiccation across what had earlier been good hunting territory in the African Sahara and adjacent parts of western Asia.

—WILLIAM H. McNEILL

The first major change in the boundary conditions that govern the use of violence was climatic in origin. About thirteen thousand years ago, a global warming began that put an end to the last Ice Age. This change in climate appears to have had dramatic effects on the primeval economy. Over a period of about five thousand years, the warming of the earth made it impossible for humans in many parts of the Northern Hemisphere to support themselves by hunting large animals. As the warming proceeded, forests of evergreens and beech trees began to take over the grassy plains that had once supported the vast herds upon which humans had depended for food. With grazing lands vanishing, animals like the woolly mammoth and the giant elk vanished with them, hunted to extinction by hungry humans. Our ancestors seem to have turned to gathering wild grasses, like barley and wheat, because it was the only way they could survive.

About four hundred generations ago (or about 6000 B.C.), they began planting seeds and became farmers. Farming was the most sweeping innovation in human existence. Farming spawned government, civilization, history, war, writing, and organized religion on a large scale, among other things. Farming required planning ahead. It made calendars and time-telling important. It was a revolution that spread through the whole of life.

The Megapolitics of Grain Farming

Grain farming made possible the accumulation of enough surplus food to support centralized authority in cities. The word "civilization," like "civility" and "citizen," is derived from the Latin *civitas,* for city. Before grain farming there were no cities or civilizations. Farming allowed for a staggering increase in the size of human populations by making it possible to support many more people in the same area. Rice farming in China, for example, was able to feed fifty thousand times more mouths than a hunter-gatherer economy in the same area. As farming grew in importance, and farm populations expanded, they inevitably pushed hunter-gatherer groups aside. The commotion stirred up by farmers as they moved into new regions depleted resources and scared away game.

Heightened Incentives for Violence

Farming altered the incentives to use violence, in part because it increased population dramatically. Higher population densities antiquated mobility as a solution to disputes. If two farmers quarreled, it would be unlikely for one to simply abandon his field and wander somewhere else, as foragers in conflict could. After the ready supply of good land had been occupied in any region, the land itself became an economic resource as it never had been to foragers. Farmers had to work much harder than foragers ever did—up to thirty-five hours a week to prepare the fields and harvest crops in the Northern Hemisphere. This required the development of private property in land. No one would work all year to raise a crop if someone else could wander by and freely harvest it. In order to grow food surpluses, someone had to have the right to exclude others from the produce of the field.

The Seeds of Taxation and Theft

The difficulty of securing property claims played a major role in raising the scale of human communities. Farming produced a food surplus upon which nonfarmers could survive. It therefore gave a tremendous added incentive to employ and organize the use of force. Farming made government possible, and, indeed, necessary as the scale of human society rose. It was no longer sufficient for human communities to divide into bands of fifty or fewer as had foragers in the primeval economy. An agreement among a handful of families to reserve the produce of a field for those who planted it was likely to mean nothing to outsiders who came around to plunder after the harvest. For a stable farming community to survive, it had to be big enough to fend off attack by the largest expedition of bandits that could operate in the local area. This logic turned the descendants of foragers into the citizens of empires.

Settled agricultural society made both taxes and crime paying propositions. Where there was accumulated wealth to take, there was always someone willing to take it. A good way to understand how government originated is literally to imagine how a group of bandits would have behaved under the megapolitical circumstances created by the Agricultural Revolution. The temptation to settle down among the conquered people and extract a regular tribute rather than returning sporadically to loot and pillage must have been obvious. It saved a lot of meandering. It avoided the possibility that another band of looters would pass through the vicinity and take a first swipe at the harvest. The logic of pillage required that warrior bands who preyed on farming communities settle among their victims. Greed and fear drove them to expand the number of farmers subject to their plunder as well as suppress competition from other looters operating nearby. As the ancient maxim had it, "The Treasury is the root of kings."

Farming made slavery and its gray equivalent, serfdom, profitable for the first time. There was hard labor to be done in the fields. The output of that labor could be stored and consumed by someone other than the person who did the work. Farming created other forms of occupational specialization. Small numbers of artists, architects, builders, and craftsmen, like jewelers and potters, found markets for their wares.

The Microbes of Power

Farming necessitated sedentary living. As animals were domesticated, and large numbers of people came to live in close contact with them, the result was another profound consequence of the Agricultural Revolution, one that still affects you today—the diseases of civilization. These diseases, "a sort of soldiers who for their smallness are not visible," became a potent factor in the exercise of power. On more than one occasion, peoples weakened by the onslaught of new microbes, for which they lacked immune response, have fallen prey to invaders or internal collapse. This was a major factor in the spread of agricultural communities as well as in the conquest of North and South America by European invaders during the early modern period. The tendency for cosmopolitan peoples to carry diseases that become "potent biological weapons" has played an important role in history.

The Agricultural Revolution greatly increased the environmental impact of humans. As hunters and gatherers for tens of thousands of generations, humans did little more to change the world than bears. But farming so increased the human population and led to such a dramatic increase in the use and depletion of resources that local ecologies were affected. The human presence was stamped upon the environment for the first time. This was true even in antiquity. Mycenae, from which King Agamemnon sailed to launch the siege of Troy, seems literally to have been destroyed by erosion due to disruption of the ground cover by farming and the harvesting of trees. According to Eberhard Zangger of Cambridge University, the Mycenaean bay was closed by a current carrying soil from the eroded Mediterranean coastline. Once closed, the harbor became a lake, then silted over. Soon, what had been the seat of a fabled civilization became a malarial swamp.

Armies Spread the Word of the Gods

Farming also gave birth to religions of broader than tribal appeal. Purely local deities were superseded as the first empires formed in the ancient Near East and began to exercise power at a larger scale. Armies were the incubators of new religions. When they marched abroad they carried gods with them. The seams, or border regions between empires, gave birth to more profound religions of adjustment to agriculture. In the words of historian William McNeill, "In certain regions, where rival cultural traditions mingled, reflective minds were stimulated to grapple anew with great questions of human destiny. One such region was eastern Persia, where Mesopotamian and Indian influences met, and Zoroastrianism arose. A second was Israel, where Mesopotamian and Egyptian civilizations confronted each other, and Judaism took shape." The Hebrew war god, Yahweh, was enlarged with the widening of human horizons. A 360-degree view was required for a poor people facing the armies of empires on either side. As McNeill put it, "Logic indeed required monotheism. Neither Yahweh nor any other deity or deities could retain a merely local sovereignty in an age when the face of nations and peoples depended upon actions in distant Assyria and Egypt."

Accounting for Language

Agriculture was also the seed from which written language germinated. To collect taxes on a broad scale, you must be able to keep records. Written language, which is a feature of only about 10 percent of all human tongues, appears to have originated as a way to solve problems of inventory-keeping in ancient agricultural societies. Hunting and gathering cultures never developed writing because they never developed taxation at a large scale, and never needed to keep track of four thousand sheep, or a thousand bushels of grain. For similar reasons, arithmetic became necessary to calculate inventories and compute calendars that helped guide farmers in planting.

Governments Dissolved by Drizzle

The new possibilities introduced by farming dramatically altered life-styles, principally by raising the scale of human communities. But many of the advantages we associate with the emergence of civilization, like written languages, profound religions, and thriving cities, did not universally accompany agriculture. Not all farming groups could sustain larger forms of organization. The equations by which the logic of violence raised groups from fifty or fewer to empires of millions were very delicate. Until relatively recently they did not depend so much upon weaponry as on other megapolitical factors such as climate and topography. The lay of the land, the flow of a river, a small shift in wind patterns could dramatically alter the incentives that drove groups together.*

A shift in patterns of rainfall, for example, could destroy civilizations, as seems to have been the case with the Pueblo Indians of North America. The shift from summer thunderstorms to winter drizzle was a megapolitical development of great importance. When summer rainfall declined, irrigation systems created to utilize thunderstorm precipitation became less important. Less water fell in the cisterns, so farmers were less dependent upon the political organization that controlled the water. When winter drizzle replaced summer downpours, farming conditions favorable to detached individuals improved. As a result, political systems began to disintegrate when climate changed. Iben Browning wrote of the death of Pueblo Indian civilizations:

*To many minds, the idea of minor changes having profound effects is counterintuitive. We discuss the character of such nonlinear changes in greater detail in chapters 8 and 9.

About 1180, the weather got cooler and precipitation shifted to winter snow and drizzle. Irrigation systems—lacking thunderstorm water—ceased to function. Yet aggradation began again; hunting/gathering/farming on an individual basis improved. The forms of civilization became a liability rather than an asset.

The people walked away.

Difficulties of a similar character inhibited the growth of large communities in the interior of Africa prior to the advent of modern military technology. While occasional empires waxed and waned in sub-Saharan Africa, there were few places in that vast region where climate and topography conveyed permanent advantages to communities forming at a large scale. For thousands of years after agriculture was introduced, the interior of Africa was almost without cities. One of the few was Timbuktu, an oasis town near the Niger. It prospered during the Middle Ages as a trading center, "the meeting point of the camel and the canoe." But Timbuktu's fortunes faltered as the desert spread and the waters that occasionally inundated the fields surrounding the city dried up. By the time that European travelers began to visit the interior of Africa, Timbuktu was a dusty ruin, barely more viable than the abandoned Pueblo settlements.

Even where climate and topography combined to make for fertile growing conditions, which was the case in many parts of interior Africa, they did not convey advantages that enabled communities to stabilize and protect themselves on a large scale. This was so pronounced a feature of life in the interior of Africa that historians of Africa have treated it defensively. Basil Davidson wrote in *Africa in History*, "The notion that some special virtue lies in the politically 'small' becoming the politically 'large,' whether by absorption or conquest of neighbors, may fit the conventional traditions of Europe and America: it has seldom fitted those of Africa." The point, of course, is not that "politically large" is virtuous in the sense that honesty and kindness are virtues. Quite the contrary. If the prevailing megapolitical conditions allow societies to become "politically large," it is mostly or entirely an accident. But it is an accident with consequences. When societies are not favored by megapolitical conditions that enable them to form and stabilize on a large scale, many of the advantages of civilization cannot emerge.

In a country divided into a thousand petty states, mostly independent and jealous of each other, it is natural that wars frequently originate for very frivolous provocations. The wars of Africa are of two kinds, one called *killi*, that which is openly avowed; and the other, *tegria*, plundering or stealing. These latter are very common, particularly about the beginning of the dry season, when the labours of harvest are over, and provisions are plentiful. . . .

The insecurity of property arising from this constant exposure to plunder, must necessarily have a most baneful effect on industry. The deserted state of all the frontier provinces sufficiently proves to what degree it operates.

—Thomas Malthus,
Principle of Population, 1802

The lack of economic progress in the interior of Africa for thousands of years was largely due to the lay of the land and quirks of climate. In most regions, they offered few advantages to any party seeking to organize on a large scale. Each of thousands of petty states could temporarily hold its own poor plot of ground, but none could suppress the constant wars and plundering, nor even halt the marauders who beset the "no-man's-lands." When Europeans first penetrated to these regions, according to Malthus, they found "many extensive and beautiful districts entirely destitute of inhabitants." No one could build much of value where his property or his life might be forfeit at any moment. The effect of the incessant wars and violence was to keep most of Africa and most Africans in destitution. In the period before Europeans arrived, as many as three out of four black African males were slaves.

Hydraulic Civilizations

By contrast, civilization developed rapidly in another part of Africa—Egypt. There, as in the river valleys of Mesopotamia, climatic conditions required the organization of hydraulic systems for irrigating crops. So long as the Nile overflowed its banks, the Egyptian political structure was almost guaranteed to operate at a large scale. It was certainly not as vulnerable to upheavals arising from fluctuations in climate. Under such megapolitical conditions, individual farmers faced a very high cost for failing to cooperate in maintaining the political structure. Without irrigation, which could only be provided at a large scale, crops would not grow. No crops meant starvation. Given the choice, farmers stayed around to be oppressed by the despotic governments that formed along the Nile. When the water didn't flow, moods turned nasty. Even in Egypt, where the Nile drained the rainfall from much of Africa, droughts did happen. Dynasties often fell when the Nile did not flood. The Pharaoh of Joseph's tale in the Book of Genesis was an exception in improving his position during seven years of dearth. Normally, droughts meant depression for the court as well as the subjects.

Inequality of Power and the Form of Government

When farming multiplied the incentives to employ violence, it not only created government, it created a new dilemma about how to control government.

The occupational specialization necessitated by farming created for the first time significant gaps in the megapolitical power of individuals. Unlike the primeval hunting society, in which all men were armed with weapons for felling large animals, and were well trained to use them, the majority in most agricultural societies lived behind the plow. The plow is not an effective weapon. Neither is the artist's brush or the potter's wheel. The development of metal weapons gave a soldier a major military advantage over an unarmed farmer. As a consequence, power in an ancient grain-farming state like Egypt became highly centralized. Whoever had a preponderance of expensive weaponry could control the irrigation system and thus hold a life and death control over the peasants. Indeed, there was a strong tendency for the system to become more closed and stratified as time passed.

Middle-Class Topography

Why were the Greek city-states not as despotic as ancient Egypt? We believe that the answer lies with differences in megapolitical conditions. It was not so much because the idea of democracy was more compelling to Greek ears than elsewhere. Nor was it because they were the first to think of democracy and equality. As we have seen, democracy and equality really were primitive ideas—because equality of power was a feature of primitive life. The uniqueness of Greece was that local conditions of climate and topography made it easier for Greek citizens to arm themselves and retain real military power. Because of this, more people were able to retain a voice in the political process in a more economically advanced society.

The key was that Greece is open to the sea. If you tried to measure the shoreline of the Greek isles and the Greek basin, you would find that it is extremely long. It was possible to develop a lot of land for farming, and yet be no more than twenty miles from the sea in most cases for the Greek city-states. This was crucial. It allowed the Greeks to market their products easily at a time when it was cheaper to ship goods from Syria to Spain than to cart them seventy-five miles overland. This gave the Greeks tremendous advantages in trade over inland areas that might also have been climatically suited to farming olives and grapes, two of the more profitable crops of the ancient world.

Unlike grain farming, which prospered on flood plains with centrally controlled irrigation, olive and grape farming could prosper as small-scale operations. Even a small plot of land—ten acres, fifteen acres—could support an independent freeholder, who could then trade his wine and oil for grain to feed his family, and retain a significant profit. This meant that, compared to people elsewhere, there were many Greeks who were relatively well off in ancient terms. They were rich enough to buy metal weapons and armor.

The ultimate basis of aristocratic primacy was, of course, removed when the farmer-hoplite became the decisive factor on the battlefield.

—WILLIAM MCNEILL,
The Rise of the West

In the Classic Age of Greek city-states, the typical soldier was a hoplite, a farmer or the owner of rural property who was armed for heavy infantry duty at his own expense. Because he was heavily armed, he could not be ignored. And his military effectiveness depended upon close cooperation with other highly motivated hoplites who fought shoulder-to-shoulder in a phalanx. The logic of the phalanx made equality between the hoplites an essential ingredient of classic Greek culture. But this logic did not extend to those who could not afford arms. By and large, they were ignored. The Greek notion of liberty and a democratic vote were not ideas for everybody. Greek liberty was for the people who had the military means to express it—those who could afford weapons. Athens at its height may have had a population of about 250,000 persons. Of that number, perhaps 80,000 were slaves. They had no voice in politics. Neither did women, because they, too, lacked weapons. There may have been 30,000 to 40,000 citizens in all (adult males were citizens). Most citizens had some property. Three-quarters of them had at least some rural property. Much of that property was worked by slaves who were not rich enough to buy the weapons to assert their voice and liberty. The Greek notion of freedom closely followed megapolitical boundaries. It was only for those sufficiently well armed to enforce their claim for it.

Likewise, the stability of the Roman republic, while it lasted, depended on the preservation of real military power by yeoman freeholders. In Italy, as in Greece, the original foundation of military might was a citizen soldiery out-fitted at private expense. However, the very success of the Roman military undermined the economic position of the small freeholders. The advancing legions captured large numbers of foreign troops who were pressed into service as slaves in the domestic economy. The addition of large numbers of slaves into Italy significantly raised the scale of agriculture in the countryside. It became common for wealthy landholders to own numerous estates farmed by gangs of slaves.

SLAVERY IN ROME

By the last days of the Roman republic, in the middle of the first century B.C,
approximately three out of seven persons in Italy were slaves. In that slaves
were overwhelmingly men rather than women and children, it is possible
that the majority of men in ancient Rome were not just poor, they were slaves.
Something important can be deduced from this. Prevailing weaponry obviously created a wide gap between the real power of those who could afford
weapons and those who could not. Otherwise, a majority or near majority
of the male population of ancient Italy could not have been enslaved. Slave
revolts were few and far between. They were also notably unsuccessful.
Clearly this would not have been the case if it had been easy for propertyless
males to compete militarily without access to weaponry.

While the propertyless artisans and workers in the cities were not restricted
as severely as slaves, it is equally obvious that they could have posed no real
threat of taking up arms against the state. This is clear from the fact that the
city of Rome itself did not even have a professional police force to monitor
urban unrest during the republican period. It was only when the city became
overcrowded and the proportions of the poor grew significantly that they
could pose any incipient military threat.

The First Welfare Program

The tribune Publius Clodius launched one of history's first welfare programs
by arming some of Rome's poor in the fifties B.C. This significantly increased
the threat of urban violence. It therefore obliged the government to buy off
the potentially more violent mob by offering free food—the first installment
of the infamous "bread and circuses." The urban mob became increasingly
menacing from that point forward because its military power had been decisively enhanced. Even so, the power of the poor was that of an incendiary
device.

Once the dole was introduced, the size of the bribe it entailed naturally
tended to escalate over time. The availability of free food made the opportunities in the workplace seem even less attractive to large numbers of the
Roman poor. So they stopped working. As the size of the mob rose, it became
more important. And greater efforts were extended by factions of the leadership to manipulate it. There also appears to have been a coarsening of the
mob itself, which became less self-sufficient and more prone to violence as
time passed. Remember the grim logic of the bread and circuses. It could be
replayed in the 1990s.

In any event, the great majority of the poor never had a voice in the Roman system, except in later times as a mob. The poor could be ignored while they were militarily insignificant. Although weaponry was primitive by today's standards, its relative costs were high. Effective arms were hard to come by, all the more so because manufacture was monopolized in state factories. Later, when the uproar in the streets became a major factor in the power equation, Rome had ceased to be a republic.

The Change in Power Changes Institutions

The small holders who had been the foundation of Rome's republican tradition had long since been impoverished. Most had lost their land, squeezed by the economic burdens of taxes and war. Conscripted freeholders were often taken from their fields to fight. They thus paid disproportionate costs for the ceaseless wars. The spoils, however, were hogged by the senatorial elite. For a long time, entrance into this elite was highly restricted. Even the wealthy landowners from other areas of Italy were not incorporated into the power structure. The small holders who traditionally had exercised some influence in government were declining in megapolitical power, while the new wealthy outside of Rome were gaining in raw power. The extreme conservatism of the Roman senatorial class was a costly mistake. The wealthy in other portions of Italy were quite capable of mobilizing military resources. When their claims for a share of power were rebuked, they were in a position to back their ambitions with raw force. Debilitating civil wars broke out, which further aggravated the tenuous position of the small holders.

The refusal of the Roman Senate to adequately distribute the rewards of victory in proportion to the costs that were borne in the fighting seriously undermined the stability of the republic. It became common for military commanders to pay pensions or bonuses to their troops from their private fortunes. Not surprisingly, this produced a circumstance where the troops owed a greater loyalty to their commanders than to the government. In due course, the distribution of raw power was no longer dependent, even in part, on the votes of well-armed yeoman freeholders. It was dependent upon the shifting allegiances of economically dependent legions and an impoverished mob. Under those megapolitical circumstances, it was hardly surprising that the republic was superseded by an empire with autocratic rule from the top.

The Roman approximation of popular government could not long outlast its eroded megapolitical foundations. When real power devolved to a few wealthy landholders, who commanded the allegiance of the legions from their private means, the constitution changed. The change was from one in which a large number of small property holders at least had to be consulted about policy—because they had military power—to one in which only their pay masters had to be consulted.

The Death of Barbarian Democracy

The stability of democratic systems has always rested upon an underlying military equality of the electors. This was verified by the many transitions between tribal and settled societies—including the examples of barbarian tribes that conquered Rome. White and Asiatic pastoralists and nomads abandoned elective rule and democratic councils in response to the substantial differentiation in actual military power that arose in settled societies.

Practically all barbarian tribes began as migratory clans, with little settled property. They were governed by crude democratic counsels. Economically, these tribes were mainly pastoral. They tended to shun crop farming. In general, the pasturing of herds was done on communal land. Herds were privately owned. The typical tribesman had at least some sheep, cattle, and horses. Overall wealth was frequently held in quite unequal portions, but this inequality was immaterial in the military sense. A horseman with one mount and three sheep was not necessarily inferior at arms to one with three horses and one hundred sheep. While local variations colored the practice of these tribes, they all followed a similar pattern. The Suevi, the Vandals, the Alans, the Burgundians, the Visigoths, the Astrogoths, the Slavs, the Bulgars, the Magyars, and the Norse Vikings, who became known as Normans, all tended to shuck off their democratic structures when they conquered other peoples and came into possession of settled territories. The new territorial arrangements involved a change in megapolitical conditions that soon ended the de facto military equality of tribal life.

TECHNOLOGY AND THE DEVOLUTION INTO THE DARK AGES

> The stirrup, by giving lateral support in addition to the front and back support offered by pommel and cantle, effectively welded horse and rider into a single fighting unit capable of a violence without precedent. The fighter's hand no longer delivered the blow: it merely guided it. . . . Immediately, without preparatory steps, it made possible mounted shock combat, a revolutionary new way of doing battle.
>
> —LYNN WHITE, JR.,
> *Medieval Technology and Social Change*

The stirrup was a simple invention—an attachment to a saddle that allowed a rider to steady himself with his feet. No one would mistake this apparently innocuous development for a political act. Yet many people would make the mistake of assuming that it was innocuous. Far from it. The stirrup was a megapolitical invention of surpassing importance. It changed history, probably doing more to alter political institutions than any politician who ever lived.

How?

The stirrup made feudalism not only possible, but probably inevitable.* Developed at the turn of the fifth–sixth centuries A.D., or just about fifteen hundred years ago, the stirrup was a minor addition to the outfitting of a horse. Yet it decisively tilted the power equation. Stirrups enabled heavily armed knights to keep their balance while fighting at full gallop. The result was a tremendous increase in the effectiveness of armored cavalry—whose charges could no longer be resisted by infantry.

Power in the Hands of a Few

This might not have had far-reaching consequences if all infantry had simply been able to mount up and fight from horseback. But this was impossible. Society was too poor to support a broadly based cavalry. For one thing, hungry horses needed to be fed. In many areas, there simply was not enough fodder to field more than a small number of horses. Armor was also expensive. Furthermore, fighting on horseback was a skilled art. To carry a heavy lance at full gallop, or wield a battle axe from atop a horse while covered in heavy armor, required years of practice. Along with the other costs of equipping and training cavalry, these limitations assured that only a small fraction of the adult male population could go mounted into battle.

This had far-reaching consequences. Because a relatively small number of knights was suddenly able to carry the day against much larger numbers of infantry, commanders sought to field knights. In A.D. 740, Charles Martel made a now-famous shift toward heavy cavalry. By 864, Charles the Bald "issued the Edict of Pitres, ordering all free Franks who owned a horse or could afford to keep one to serve mounted." A perfectly logical thing to do under the circumstances. But this, too, had its effects. It meant that the proportion of the community with true megapolitical power declined. It de-

---

*Some historians have objected to "technical determinism" as an explanation for the social change that culminated in feudalism. See, for example, R. H. Hilton and P. H. Sawyer, "Technical Determinism: The Stirrup and the Plough," *Past and Present*, April 1963, pp. 90–100. Their argument is weakened dramatically by a failure to grasp the significance of the fact that English military methods could remain anachronistic prior to the Battle of Hastings because Britain was an island.

clined so low, in fact, that our word "imbecile," which today describes the weak of mind, appears to be derived from the Gothic Latin word *imbelle*. It originally was applied to the "scorned" mass of peasantry who were weak because they were unarmed.

With real megapolitical power falling into the hands of a necessarily tiny minority, it was inevitable that the minority should begin to expropriate wealth for itself. That is exactly what happened. Not only did battle tactics change, so did political institutions. As historian William H. McNeill wrote: "Whenever superior force came to rest in the hands of a few elaborately equipped and trained individuals, it became difficult for central authorities to prevent such persons from intercepting most of the agricultural surplus and consuming it locally. 'Feudalism' was the result."

Once the breakdown of central authority began, the tendency for power to decentralize fed on itself. With local powers seizing a greater share of available revenues, the more encompassing entities of government ran short of cash. Those whose job it was to administer justice, for example, were no longer paid. Or if they were paid, they found themselves isolated, without sufficient support to perform their task. A judge who decided a case against a powerful local figure, for example, might be lucky if he were ignored altogether. Otherwise, he would be killed. Local powers became laws unto themselves. They could get away with being arbitrary and corrupt, so they were. The result was a dramatic decline in the security of person and property. Under such conditions, economies collapsed and populations dwindled.

As the process continued, it became ever more costly and futile for central authorities to attempt to subordinate local officials. And the more local officials stole, the less commerce could take place, and the weaker the economy became. Historian Carroll Quigley summarized what happened:

> In this way, as the economic system wound down, with decreasing commerce and money flows, transportation became more difficult and more expensive; as roads washed away and bridges collapsed, the capturing of strongholds at any distance became less and less likely, the royal power became dispersed, localized, and privatized, until by 950, there was no state, no public authority, and no royal power at all. All power had become local, private and dispersed in what we now know as feudalism. The European Dark Ages had arrived.

The story of the stirrup illustrates how a minor change in military technology could remake political institutions. An innovation as simple as a piece of leather fitted to the saddle of the horse helped change history. It tilted the power equation, allowing the petty local lord to become a law unto himself. A law without appeal, except to heaven—the authority to which people increasingly turned. There was no help for them on earth. The result was a sharp narrowing of horizons. A partitioning of life. The economy shriveled within the walls built by rude and violent men.

THE GREAT POWER OF THE DARK AGES

The Dark Ages were a period when European civilization was at its weakest. Perhaps the most expansive activities of these centuries of darkness were the far-ranging expeditions of the Vikings. They came from the Scandinavian fringe of Europe to plunder. In the eighth century, Vikings burnt Paris, Cologne, and London. They also set off on the northern route across the Atlantic along much the same path followed today by a transatlantic passenger jet. They went northwest to Iceland, to Greenland, and on to North America. Their exploits provide fascinating evidence of the complexity of the economy of violence.

The fate of the Viking expeditions to North America exemplifies the interdependencies between the various megapolitical factors that govern the use of power. Properly understood, climate, topography, microbes, and technology are not separate and distinct, but dynamically intertwined. As ecologists frequently tell us, technology changes climate. Climate also changes technology. Both affect the evolution of microbes, which can have effects that counteract or offset the impact of technology in establishing the boundaries where power can be exercised. This interrelation is particularly illustrated by the first European attempts to settle North America, which began almost exactly one thousand years ago and five hundred years prior to Columbus.

When the Vikings first came to Greenland, they were not hallucinating, it was green. But as the weather got colder in the centuries after A.D. 1000, settlers found it more and more difficult to farm. In time, areas that had once been hospitable were covered in ice. Greenland's population, never much above thirty-five hundred, spiraled downward, with significant consequences for the future of North America.

The adverse climatic changes in Greenland assured that North America would not become a Norse colony. The dwindling population of Vikings was too small to sustain the usual endemic diseases that are the consequence of settled agricultural society in which humans live in close contact with domesticated animals. As Greenland became colder, it became less hospitable to the diseases of civilization as well as to people. The Vikings quite rationally went prospecting for a more hospitable climate. They found one in "Vineland" somewhere on the North American coast. But they could not keep it. Because the would-be Viking settlers came not from Europe, but from a sparsely populated mid-ocean stopping place, they did not carry with them European childhood diseases. Without the microbes, the Vikings were unable to decimate the Indian populations as later white settlers did. The Norse had better weapons than the Indians, but not enough of them to overpower the native populations in the absence of an effective tool of biological warfare. If they had come with measles, this book would probably be written in some form of mongrel Danish.

The Purchased Power of the Medieval Merchants

European commerce recovered significantly after a semblance of order was restored around the millennium, the year 1000. Money, which had almost completely disappeared during the Dark Ages, came back into circulation. The sudden upsurge of economic activity after the stagnation of the previous centuries enabled economic pioneers, like the Jews, "to become Europe's first *nouveaux riches.*" By the standards of later times, European commerce in the Middle Ages was meager, and certainly inferior to the prosperity of China or the Islamic world. As Playfair wrote of Europe, "Wealth was confined to a few insulated spots." Among them were the trading republics in Italy and the Hanseatic League to the north, "which owed their prosperity . . . partly to the contempt with which sovereigns, in the days of chivalry, viewed commerce."

These medieval republics were founded upon the equality of military power that could be purchased and commanded by the upper stratum of merchants. Poor city dwellers never enjoyed the franchise because they had no effective weapons and no way to get them. Their opinions were generally of little military consequence. Although this sweeping judgment was occasionally challenged by revolts, these were seldom successful. As in Roman times, revolts of the propertyless urban poor were usually acts of desperation during periods of depression or famine. These uprisings were always short-lived. They seldom produced any lasting gains for their participants.

The Topography of Freedom

The few medieval regions that maintained or reasserted an elective voice for the peasants were precisely those where yeoman farming and infantry had special megapolitical advantages. The mountainous country of Switzerland was far more hospitable to small-scale farming than to the large feudal estate. Even so, it wasn't very hospitable. Farming in the Alps conferred a military rather than an economic advantage to the small holders. The steep mountains and almost impenetrable passages effectively neutralized the advantage that the heavily armed knight enjoyed over the foot soldier on flat terrain. After rugged Swiss fighters decimated an Austrian army in a mountain ambush in the thirteenth century, isolated Swiss communities were effectively freed from the political domination of the landed aristocracy who had held sway over much of the rest of Europe. The basis of the later Swiss prosperity was laid in the late medieval period in which Swiss pikemen became the premier mercenaries of Europe. They rented their services for cash, then retired to unassailable redoubts in the mountains. The foundation of Swiss economic prosperity was the topographical advantage that enabled Swiss archers and pikemen to preserve their independence over the heavy cavalry that predominated elsewhere.

The advantages the Swiss enjoyed were shared to some extent by other regions with similar topography. For example, small farmers in the mountains of Italy were much more successful than their lowland cousins in maintaining their freedom. A photograph of the Republic of San Marino leaves little doubt as to how it has maintained its independence since the year A.D. 885. It towers atop Mount Titano, rising 2763 feet above the flat plain of Romagna below. San Marino was a natural citadel commanding a hundred-mile view in every direction. The topography of heavily wooded Sweden, with its many lakes and rivers, also limited the military value of heavy cavalry. As a result, Swedish peasants still owned a majority of land at the end of the Middle Ages.

Paradoxically, among the few other areas of Europe where the yeoman presence was preserved was on the lowland flood plains of what is now the Netherlands. In this absolutely flat terrain, medieval peasants retained more freedom than was common for their contemporaries elsewhere in Western Europe. Why? They were distinguished, in part, by the higher skill levels required by the reclamation and preservation of land from the sea. But skill alone did not have a determinant megapolitical importance. Skilled Flemish peasants who were lured east to help reclaim Polish marshlands received promises of freedom that were honored at the outset and later revoked. This revocation of the liberties of the transplanted peasants from the Netherlands was evidence that their freedoms were sustained, in part, by the topography of their homeland. Skilled artisans of eastern cities were frequently enslaved and carried away by Mongol and other nomadic raiders. The only skills of importance in preserving freedom have been military skills.

If Flemish and Dutch peasants were more free than their contemporaries in the lowlands of Europe during the Middle Ages, it was because the unique terrain of those regions, like the topography of mountainous Switzerland, conveyed a military capacity to the peasants that they lacked elsewhere. Peasants who farmed reclaimed lands could not easily be dispossessed from their properties, or subjected to the same level of infeudation as peasants

elsewhere, precisely because the lowland peasants, far more than their contemporaries, had a capacity to destroy the economic value of their land if it
was taken from them.

With portions of the recovered lands lying at or below sea level, these lands
could be inundated by sabotage of the dikes. The result was that otherwise militarily powerful lords were discouraged from seizing peasant lands in
lowland regions. The lords had the military capacity to take the lands,
but not to protect them against sabotage. The predominant powers were
better off settling for smaller rents and taxes from a prosperous and relatively free peasantry than they would have been at trying to subjugate the
peasants at the risk of a devastating sabotage of the principal asset base of
the economy.

It took a thousand years for society to absorb the devolution of the Dark
Ages and rebuild a prosperity that rivaled that of the ancient world. This
period of consolidation and recovery culminated in the second great
revolution in the organization of violence—the Gunpowder Revolution.
It became history's most explosive transition in the organization of human
affairs.

THE GUNPOWDER REVOLUTION

Gunpowder destroyed the existing political ecologies of late medieval Europe.
It shattered an equilibrium in which the defense had long been predominant
over the offense, an equilibrium that had built up over centuries in keeping
with the logic of mechanical weaponry. Along with other inventions of the
same era, like the printing press and the magnetic compass, gunpowder rev-
olutionized life. While gunpowder had been known in Europe for some time,
its impact was decisively demonstrated in 1494. In that year, a French army
led by King Charles VIII carried along new siege guns on an invasion of Italy.
The new cannon reduced the walls of a fortress of an Italian ministate to
"rubble" in only eight hours. It is no exaggeration to say that modern history
began at that time. A few years earlier—before the new technology—"this
same fortress had made itself famous by withstanding a siege of seven years."

The importance of this development was deeply impressed upon contemporaries. Francesco Guicciardini, writing around 1528, saw the impact of
gunpowder weapons with remarkable clarity.

> Before the year 1494, wars were protracted, battles bloodless, the methods fol-
> lowed in besieging towns slow and uncertain; and although artillery was already
> in use, it was managed with such lack of skill that it caused little hurt. Hence it

came about that the ruler of a state could hardly be dispossessed. But the French, in their invasion of Italy, infused so much liveliness into our wars that, up to the [present], . . . whenever open country was lost, the state was lost with it."

Gunpowder gave powerful new advantages to the offense, while raising the scale of warfare. The cannon, for example, shifted the balance toward the offense. It made it easier to knock down walls. Fortresses and local strongholds that were almost impervious to attack before cannon were made more vulnerable to power projected from afar. And they became ever more vulnerable as the quality of cannon improved. Small arms also shifted the scale of battle in favor of larger political entities. Because a soldier using a blunderbuss required less training than an armored soldier fighting hand-to-hand, the number of troops that could be deployed rose tenfold.

Larger Scale in Governance

This jump in the scale of fighting had a sweeping impact on the scale of political organization. Put simply, because of gunpowder weapons, political entities got bigger. In the year 1500 there were approximately five hundred independent political bodies in Europe. That number fell to about twenty-five on the eve of World War I. Ninety-five percent of the petty states of late medieval Europe were blasted away by gunpowder. So great was the centralizing impact of the Gunpowder Revolution that the European powers who were the first to undergo this revolution ended up controlling most of the rest of the globe. Europe went from being a backward area with few resources to become the home of empires. In 1914, European powers commanded 84 percent of the world's land surface. Great Britain alone controlled one-quarter of the globe.

As borders and barriers fell under the centralizing thrust of new weapons, the potential for economic growth rose. The result was a feedback mechanism that nourished itself. Expensive cannon and muskets conveyed an advantage in battle. To enjoy that advantage, however, groups had to be wealthy, and thus usually large. As political units became more encompassing, they also grew richer. The additional wealth supported armies of a still larger size, which were then even more difficult for the remaining local powers to resist. Gunpowder further reinforced the advantages of wealth by taking away the physical edge that poor societies previously had enjoyed over rich ones. William Playfair explains:

While human force was the power by which men were annoyed, in cases of hostility, bodily strength laid the foundation for the greatness of individual men, as well as of whole nations. So long as this was the case, it was impossible for any nation to cultivate the arts of peace, (as at the present time,) without becoming much inferior in physical force to nations that preferred exercising the body, as rude nations do, to gratifying the appetites, as practised in wealthy ones. To be wealthy and powerful long together was then impossible.

Changes in the logic of violence introduced by gunpowder compounded advantages for those states that emerged victorious from the centuries of almost constant warfare that reshaped the map of Europe. Greater wealth made possible technological and managerial innovations that gave rise to the Industrial Revolution, which raised still further the scale of warfare. The Industrial Revolution so dramatically improved the firepower of weapons as to make it impossible for small groups or non-Western societies to resist the military power of the nation-state.

This fundamental change in the equation of power took the better part of five centuries to play itself out. Along the way, it had many far-reaching but not always obvious consequences. Among them were the expansion of trade, the growth of capital markets, the rediscovery of representative government, the renaissance in art, and major changes in ethical and religious precepts. The processes by which these developments unfolded were far from simple. We do not pretend to give a satisfactory account of them here. But we will give a few illustrative examples to suggest how an invention that opened society precipitated cultural changes to reflect that new openness.

Gunpowder Opens the Door for Money and Merit

Gunpowder helped break down the relatively closed, hierarchial societies in which wealth primarily consisted of titles to land. In the closed feudal world, what mattered most was not what you were capable of doing, but who you were. A person's prospects were defined by his lineage much more than by his individual identity. In general, it was the local, hereditary powers with castles on the hill at whose expense central authority was expanded. These central authorities tended to ally themselves with the emerging capitalists. Money had become an essential ingredient in meeting the high costs of contesting for power. "The discovery of gunpowder," as Playfair observed, was "wonderfully adapted for doing away the illusions of knight-errantry, that had such a powerful effect in making war be preferred to commerce."

As the importance of money grew relative to rank, culture changed to reflect this fact. There was a rebirth of realism, portraiture, and individualism in art, characteristics that, prior to the invention of photography, were always associated with open societies. Symbolic and nonrepresentational art were almost exclusively the product of closed societies in which individuals did not enjoy plentiful opportunities to advance on their own merit.

Theological Consequences of Gunpowder

When the Gunpowder Revolution opened such opportunities to a much broader spectrum of society, it also helped precipitate a major change in religious doctrine. The Protestant Reformation, which began early in the sixteenth century, can be crudely and simply understood as a theological justification of savings. In fact, the Protestant denominations became among the more effective vehicles for the promotion of savings ever devised. They contributed to this end through a variety of means. In the first place, they provided an immediate theological justification for saving and lending money at interest. As we explore further in another chapter, gunpowder broke the taboo on usury. Protestant leaders like Luther, Calvin, and Zwingli defended the payment of interest on money lent, and thus significantly increased the return on money.

They also greatly discounted the costs of operating and supporting churches. One of the chief charges of Luther and the other reformers against the Catholic Church was that it had grown too opulent. Protestant denominations, at least in the beginning, built simple, even austere churches. And they garbed their ministers in the same spirit. Plain black frocks replaced the often opulent robes of the priests and bishops of the Catholic Church.

A Major Curtailment of Income Redistribution

This spirit of pruning costs carried over to the religious calendar in ways that altered the relationship between rich and poor. Gunpowder significantly improved the relative strength of the industrious over the indolent. Gunpowder not only opened the door for ambitious people to advance on their own merit, it also diminished the importance of physical strength in protecting one's property. It therefore helped to neutralize the need for constant redistribution that plagued medieval peasant communities. Protestant denominations reflected this change by scrapping forty feast days of saints and other holidays. Rogation Day, Shrove Tuesday, and many others were no longer celebrated. These holy days or "holidays" had provided the occasion for almost weekly revels in medieval Europe.

Reform of the religious calendar was an integral part of the theological revolution that reduced the costs of living a pious life. The shift in emphasis from good deeds to faith as the key to salvation helped lift the burden of redistribution that had made it all but impossible for the more industrious peasants and burghers to accumulate capital. It was normally they who had to outfit the table at the incessant village feasts that dotted the old calendar. So much was consumed in these frequent revels that in and of themselves they almost provided a minimum for survival by the poor or the unindustrious. The Puritan rejection of both the feasts and the doctrine that provision of alms and good deeds were keys to salvation effectively cut the tax rate for industrious Protestants. It helped launch a new middle class of prosperous farmers, tradesmen, and freeholders. It also obliged those among the population who consumed more than they produced to work harder. The poor could no longer depend as before upon alms and feasts at the expense of their neighbors.

Moderation in Food and Drink

Puritanism lent still another hand to savings by discouraging consumption. From the earliest Protestant sect, the Moravians, private as well as public opulence was generally frowned upon as sinful. Protestant sects barred the faithful from holding private parties, even on such traditional occasions as baptisms, weddings, and wakes. The throwing of grain at weddings was banned, along with dancing, dressing in fine clothes, and overindulgence in drink. Frequently, alcoholic beverages were banned altogether and other dietary austerities were encouraged. The attempt to discourage alcohol marked a crucial distinction between the emerging middle-class culture, which emphasized self-control and discipline, and that of the lower classes, who consumed prodigious quantities of beer. Per capita consumption figures for seventeenth-century England were "higher than anything known in modern times."

A penny saved is a penny earned. The compound effect of many pennies saved was to greatly facilitate the accumulation of capital by individuals and families who had never had any before. As money capital in liquid form was required to pay the mounting costs of waging war, central authorities, whatever their private inclinations, were more or less obliged to tolerate the evolution of capitalism. In this respect, there was an inherent connection between the Gunpowder Revolution and the revolution in the religious and moral life of Western society.

The Poor Gain Arms

The Gunpowder Revolution decisively tilted the internal power equation in society to the advantage of the industrious, and thus helped lift living standards to an unprecedented extent. Part of the lift-off advantage that gunpowder provided in societies that later became rich derived from the fact that the poor could not afford guns. Therefore they could not use the new technology to maintain or increase their claims on the wealth of others.

Needless to say, they attempted to stake such claims anyway. Among the many doctrines put forward when gunpowder blasted the lid off feudal society were demands for redistribution of wealth. Anabaptists, such as Thomas Münzter, proclaimed doctrines of radical communism at the same time that the merchant Protestant leaders were promulgating new religious doctrines that helped undergird the emergence of capitalism. Münzter asked, "Why groan we in poverty while others have delicacies? Have we not a right to the equality of goods, which, by nature, are made to be parted without distinction among us?" His call for the redistribution of all wealth was keenly received among destitute populations in Germany and elsewhere in the early sixteenth century. But luckily for later generations, the sixteenth-century poor lacked the military capacity to halt the accumulation of capital by redistributing wealth. Münzter was defeated in Frankenhausen and swiftly beheaded. His followers later created "disturbances at Amsterdam, and an insurrection in Westphalia. . . . But the constituted authorities of the times put an end to these delusions, by . . . killing and executing the ringleaders of the sect."

But as society became more wealthy, the balance of power began to shift toward the poor. By the second half of the nineteenth century, the technical quality of small arms improved dramatically. They no longer misfired half the time. And their relative price fell. The broad dispersal of effective weapons among the poor gave them added megapolitical power. This contributed to the abolition of slavery, as well as to the broader extension of the franchise. When more of the poor came to vote, government soon began redistributing income on a much larger scale.

Until the nineteenth century, representative or democratic decision-making was almost always stabilized by the exclusion of a large percentage of the population from the vote.* Typically, all women, children, and propertyless males were excluded from the tribal councils, the ancient republics and democracies, and the medieval merchant republics, like Venice. They were also forbidden to vote in the early years of the American republic.

Our argument is that these exclusions were not puzzling, but predictable.

---

*Where the poor were a majority, the temptation for them to rob the rich through the ballot box was too obvious to be ignored. Consequently, they were barred from the ballot box wherever the rich had the megapolitical power to exclude them, which was almost everywhere.

They were based upon the megapolitical reality that individuals could be excluded from decision-making in any setting where they lacked the command of resources or raw power to influence the outcome by force.

Gunpowder, Slavery, and the Franchise

Although the exercise of raw power is measured across many dimensions that have fluctuated over time, there is one obvious indicator that individuals can be excluded from the decision-making processes with impunity—the existence of chattel slavery. No one who is a slave is in any position to express himself militarily. Since slavery is a denial of full individual autonomy, it is clear that it can exist only when and where megapolitical conditions leave at least some stratum of the population almost totally powerless.

As we have seen, this was frequently the case in ancient times. That was certainly true in the Dark Ages, during the medieval centuries, and well into the modern period. Yet slavery rapidly faded away in modern countries during the middle decades of the nineteenth century—precisely the time when the most radical extensions of the voting franchise began. Why? Part of the reason may have been the sudden success of moral arguments against slavery. These arguments, hardly novel in the nineteenth century, had lain ignored through all the Christian centuries up until that time. If there was any novelty in them, it was the sudden perception that they had to be taken seriously. In ancient times, the Christian church, later derided by Friedrich Nietzsche as providing "a religion for slaves," was itself an extensive slaveholder. In late Roman times, the church became a predominant landholder. Slaves worked the land.

The religious mediation of slavery was primarily limited to injunctions to treat slaves kindly. When slavery waned on church lands, it was due less to religious scruples about recognizing the rights of slaves than to the decline of the slave market arising from a conjunction of (a) low reproductive rates among the slave population who were almost entirely male, (b) plagues that resulted in rural depopulation, especially in the Christian West, and (c) a decline in the slave market due to drying up of the supply of military captives. Yet even though slavery was a marginal phenomenon after the fall of Rome, it continued uninterrupted until the early modern period. Even during the medieval centuries when serfdom largely took the place of chattel slavery, domestic slavery and the slave trade never were entirely eclipsed. Indeed, our word for "slave" is derived from the ethnic identity of the medieval slave, who was ordinarily a "slav." Even in the English legal tradition, the most liberal of the early modern legal systems, slavery and indentured labor were retained, at least in the colonies, through the early part of the nineteenth century.

Why the change? Our answer is that megapolitical conditions changed. In this case, the change was attributable to the evolution of weaponry. The proliferation of small arms, especially pistols, sharply raised the price of holding slaves. As small arms became more dependable and their costs fell, the dangers of the slave rebellion rose. These dangers were evidenced as early as 1791, when a slave revolt broke out in Haiti. Napoleon sent twenty-five thousand French troops in 1801 to restore slavery, but with little success. The cost of controlling slaves had taken a significant jump. As small-arms technology rapidly improved, slavery receded into the margins of the world economy.

As a parallel development, in the areas where representative institutions existed and were retained, the right to vote was rapidly widened.

The Pistol Gives Women the Vote

The movement towards the enfranchisement of women, which was a late-nineteenth-century phenomenon, coincided with further refinement of small-arms technology. Small, dependable pistols allowed disgruntled females practically as much military potential as males. It is probably no coincidence that the first place where women got the vote was on the American frontier, in Wyoming, where women were well armed with pistols and knew how to use them. The standard academic argument is that women in Wyoming got the franchise because the state was thinly populated and wanted to qualify for statehood by raising the number of voters. This really explains nothing. Other thinly populated frontier states had sought and been denied statehood earlier without enfranchising women. It was only when cheap effective pistols became widely available after the Civil War that women got the vote.

It is important to note, however, that the modern expedient of holding elections to decide the control of government was not the predominant solution in Eastern Europe, western Asia, and other areas, where average income levels did not reach the point where the ordinary individual could afford a rifle or pistol during the time when such weapons were at a technological match to the weapons of a well-armed military. Where income growth lagged, there was no fundamental necessity for constitutional arrangements to accord an equal voice to the opinions of every man. The spread of cheap weaponry may have made slavery an anachronism and necessitated an extension of the franchise where it existed. But where militaries came to control rapid-firing machine guns, automatic cannon, and other specialized weapons, an electoral decision process itself was no longer a megapolitical necessity. Given that a state was to preserve sufficient freedom to allow an open electoral process, the system could no longer be stabilized by restricting the franchise.

In the modern period, therefore, it is no longer possible to resolve the fundamental instability of popular government with the kinds of solutions that maintained the classic civilization of the Greek city-states. It was no longer possible to achieve a representative or democratic system in which a small group of property holders could determine the resolution of political conflicts without respect to the opinions of a large cross-section of militarily irrelevant, propertyless freeholders and slaves. Aristotle's belief that the ideal republic should disenfranchise the workers was antiquated by gunpowder weapons.

CHAPTER TWO

THE INFORMATION REVOLUTION

THE MEGAPOLITICS OF THE FUTURE AND THE
CONSTITUTIONS OF THE PAST

It is an extraordinary era in which we live. It is altogether new. The world has seen nothing like it before. I will not pretend, nobody can pretend, to discern the end. But everyone knows that the age is remarkable for scientific research. . . . The ancients saw nothing like it. The moderns have seen nothing like it till the present generation.

—DANIEL WEBSTER, 1847

DANIEL WEBSTER'S words from 145 years ago remain true for the present generation. Because they remain true, the acceleration of technological change should warn us that seemingly settled parameters of megapolitical power may be subject to dramatic change in the decades to come.

THE THIRD REVOLUTION

The Information Revolution, much rumored but little understood, is the third great revolution of human life. Its effects have already begun to unfold. It is a revolution in which the new growth area of the economy is the manipulation of information at a very small scale rather than the mass processing of raw materials.

Like all true revolutions, the Information Revolution is also a revolution

83

of power. Miniaturized technologies miniaturize institutions. In time, the microchip will destroy the nation-state. It will give small groups and even individuals the capacity to employ violence in ways that could overturn governments and destroy large organizations.

On the simplest level, the progress of the Information Revolution has been easy to recognize. Thousands of computer companies have been founded in the past twenty years as computational capacities have skyrocketed. More recently, biotech firms have created a stir in the market. Practically every office now has a fax machine, a remote copier that allows documents to be transmitted instantaneously from afar rather than taking the old-fashioned tour of the post office.

Yet, as easy as it is to acknowledge these new product developments, it is much harder to see that they entail an entirely new principle of human control over nature. It is harder still to credit how quickly this transformation could occur by extrapolating from past product cycles. Microtechnology, unlike any past breakthrough, is the first to significantly increase the speed at which mental work can be accomplished. So far, most of these improvements have been limited to lower-order calculations, like adding or sorting files of information. But relatively minor advances in Artificial Intelligence could have an incredible compounding effect on the speed of the Information Revolution. Once computers a million times faster than an unaided mind can be harnessed for higher-order thinking, the equivalent of a million years' worth of design work could be accomplished in a single year. It won't work quite that smoothly, but that is the direction towards which technology is tending. As computational capacities compound by orders of magnitude, they promise to destroy the old economy just as surely as farming displaced foraging.

Consider as a paradigm example of the old industrial economy the manufacture of a lawn mower. Vast amounts of raw materials are required at every stage of the process, to extract iron ore from the ground, to transport the ore to a smelter, to melt it in a blast furnace, shape it into ingots or mill it, and then transport it to yet another factory. There, it is transformed once again, stamped or pressed or milled into parts, which are then welded, bolted, or otherwise fastened together to become a lawn mower.

Each stage of the process of creating a lawn mower involves the transformation of raw materials at a large scale. This requires energy, most of it stored in the form of other raw materials: coal, coke, or petroleum. To make lawn mowers operate requires still more energy, in either an internal combustion or electric engine.

The production of manufactured goods involves raw materials in large quantities at every stage of the process. It also tends to require large numbers of people working together in a coordinated way, and large sums of capital to fund the construction of the factories and assembly lines.

By contrast, the manipulation of information through computers requires very little in the way of raw materials. The paradigm example is that of the computer programmer, whose energy source to produce a multi-million-dollar software product could be as little as a peanut butter sandwich. Programmers do not employ blast furnaces to do their work. They are footloose and detached. They do not have to work in any particular sequence or only on certain shifts. Unlike miners or workers on an assembly line, computer programmers can work when and where they please. They require only small sums of capital. Some highly successful software companies have been launched with investments of only a few dollars.

Not only do new information-based enterprises use little in the way of natural resources themselves, they also displace natural resources in innumerable ways. The lawn mower of the Information Age will come in an envelope. It will not be pushed but planted. Genetic engineering of grass seed will produce new types of turf that automatically grow to an optimum height—and then stop. The new bioengineered grass will require neither fertilizer nor insecticides. It will make lawn mowers obsolete.

The benign example of new seed displacing the lawn mower suggests how the Information Revolution will displace demand for fantastic quantities of raw materials. Computer-assisted design will make it possible in a few years to effectively transport products as digital impulses over telephone lines. A computer-aided design program or blueprint will be transmitted from the other end of the earth in seconds, much as letters are now transmitted by fax machine. Revolutionary new techniques of stereo lithography, pioneered to rapidly produce design prototypes, will ultimately displace much of the old manufacturing process itself. They will allow individuals to make their own highly specialized products. Robots will execute three-dimensional blueprints by depositing small drops of high-tech plastics at every point along the designs. The resulting products will be fabricated to a higher precision than was possible with industrial molds. And they will be produced almost instantly.

The potential savings of raw materials will ramify as the transmission of information displaces large quantities of product now laboriously wrapped and shipped individually. A great many products that are now transported from here to there will be fabricated by computer-driven systems at the point where they are needed. High-tech materials and composites will be pre-shipped, just as fax paper is today.

These examples suggest how microtechnology will transform the economy in the years to come. They only hint at the kind of change that can be expected in megapolitics.

The Megapolitics of the Information Revolution

The exponential consequences of the impact of semiconductors on all institutions have only been hinted at by the fall of Communism. The increasing costs of projecting power, driven far higher by the impact of computers on weapons systems, helped bankrupt and break apart Europe's last multi-national empire. The Soviet Union collapsed, in part, because its economy could not adapt to the decentralizing impact of the new technology. As we explore in more detail later, the microchip made the command economy obsolete.

It also made possible new types of gunpowder weapons, more accurate, self-contained, and deadly than any known in the past. Stinger missiles knocked multi-million-dollar airplanes from the sky. "Smart bombs," cruise missiles, and stealth technologies have increased the impact of conventional explosions by applying the detonations to targets with surgical precision. It is estimated that it would have required nine thousand bombs of the kind carried on a B-17 in World War II to take out the Iraqi Defense Ministry—a job accomplished by two intelligent bombs carried on a single stealth fighter in the 1991 Gulf War.

A first consequence of some of these sophisticated and expensive weapons appears to have been a shift in the balance of power to the advantage of the United States. As encouraging as such a development must be to those who long for a "New World Order" in the 1990s, any stabilization is unlikely to be more than temporary. Over the longer term, the megapolitical impact of microtechnologies will be devolutionary in the extreme.

The fact that the world has not instantly shattered into thousands of mini-states does not make the megapolitical logic of the computer any less subversive. Perhaps today's early stages of the Information Revolution could be compared to the early stages of the Gunpowder Revolution five hundred years ago. The new high-speed computers of the 1990s are the equivalents to Charles VIII's new high-compression cannon of the 1490s. Their potential for reorganizing life reaches far beyond what has as yet been demonstrated.

Just as farming antiquated the primeval economy based upon forage, and later gunpowder weapons antiquated the ancient political economy whose boundaries were set by mechanical weapons and human force, so the Information Revolution will overturn the modern economy whose borders are policed by the gun. The speed with which this revolution unfolds may be in doubt. But its logic should not be.

This can be seen most clearly by thinking about some of the future developments that microtechnology could make possible. They will include some extraordinary conventional weapons, perhaps even some that could be programmed to recognize and target specific individuals. But quite apart from the wonders that may prove possible along those lines, microtechnology will also create and enlarge new types of unorthodox weapons.

Advances in miniaturization and computer technology not only imply the replacement of raw material with information, they also promise in time to give humans control of nature at the molecular level. The human genome project has already begun a mapping of the specific functions of genes. Early stages of genetic engineering will make possible the elimination of many of the approximately thirty-five hundred genetic-based diseases that now plague humanity. As the specific genes that control human development are identified, it will be possible for parents to determine at conception the race, sex, height, hair color, eye color, complexion, intelligence, and athletic abilities of their offspring. Designer children will be a reality after the millennium.

The same developments that promise to make possible the taming of diseases and a Brave New World of control over the species open up many other possibilities with which we are ill prepared to cope. It will be possible, for example, to muddle the characteristics of the species. Only one part in one hundred separates humans from the nearest neighbors on the genetic map. Only one part in one thousand separates individuals from one another. These very narrow boundaries could be smudged by the transplantation into humans of genes from practically any living creature.

Genetic engineering on this scale also allows the development of new and more deadly biological weapons that could be unleashed by small groups, criminal bands, or terrorists. Large cities and concentrated populations will be increasingly vulnerable to disruption and attack.

Yet even these possibilities are tame compared to what may well lie ahead. It may be possible in the future to adopt the techniques now used in genetic coding to build molecular computers, and then to set them to work in molecular engineering.

As unlikely as it may seem, a supercomputer could be possible in a form so tiny that it would fit comfortably in a single human cell. Such molecular computers would make possible the construction of numerically controlled assemblers for manipulating matter at the atomic level—what is known as *nanotechnology*. As long ago as 1959, Nobel laureate Richard Feynman spoke of "the possibility of maneuvering things atom by atom." He declared then that it would prove to be "a development which I think cannot be avoided."

This perhaps unavoidable science would have unavoidable megapolitical consequences. Human control over nature at the molecular level implies a new, post–industrial strength magic. Scientists who study nanotechnology believe that within decades self-replicating molecular "machines" will be able to construct practically any product the heart desires—almost without assistance from human labor. Inanimate objects—from an automobile to a baked

Alaska—could be programmed for assembly in much the same way that living organisms are programmed by genetic encoding, built cell by cell, or molecule by molecule, from a soup of raw ingredients.

Think what that might mean.

Not only would nanotechnology open a new horizon of material abundance, it would also create an entirely new dimension of control over human behavior.

Those who design nanotechnology will be able to totally control or even physically alter other human beings. Invisible machines, programmed through Artificial Intelligence, could literally force anyone to behave in any way the ultimate programmer wished. It would no longer be necessary to put a gun to someone's head to force obedience. You could program the desire to obey directly by altering the genetic programming of the brain on a molecular level. This could go far beyond what is now imagined in terms of genetic engineering. It would not be a matter of correcting a gene or two that might predispose someone to diabetes or cancer. It could be possible to manipulate humans at the molecular level so thoroughly as to turn them to pillars of salt like Lot's wife.

When molecular assemblers are unleashed, the distinction between living organisms and other forms of matter would be thoroughly muddled. You could have robots with human characteristics collecting the garbage. Or humans with robot characteristics. They could be programmed to love garbage, and derive great happiness from dusting antique window sills.

The Slavery of the Future

Slavery could return. But it would not be the slavery of field workers bending under the lash. No one would need most forms of human labor because nanotechnologies could be programmed to do almost everything now required of human labor. As Jeffrey MacGillvray of the MIT Nanotechnology Study Group asks, "What forms of human labor will still be of value after self-replicating molecular machines provide material goods in virtually unlimited quantity at almost zero cost?" The answer is practically nothing that was ever done by slaves, except the provision of entertainment. Let your imagination work. Slaves will be anyone without control of the nanotechnology and they will do anything that might have been asked by Aladdin when he rubbed his lamp.

A common misunderstanding would be to suppose that governments could control or police nanotechnology to prevent any such thing happening. They could not.

In the first instance, it is altogether unlikely that any government among the leading nations would stifle its own computer industry to prevent research into Artificial Intelligence, molecular computing, or the other precursors of nanotechnology. If the United States were to attempt to do so, for example, that would only assure that future development in these strategically critical areas was the property of Japanese, European, or Indian scientists.

Nor is it in keeping with the nature of nanotechnological power—if such power should ever come to pass—that guards could monitor programmers to somehow prevent them from putting such profound breakthroughs to any use they choose. This would be about as futile as sending someone with a pistol to stand guard against a virus. No one with a pistol could enforce any control over a nanotechnological programmer—any more than he could stop a microparasite from entering a room on the next gust of wind. The pistol packer could be peacefully lobotomized by unleashed molecular assemblers before he learned or comprehended the meaning of the keystrokes the programmer had entered.

For all the capacity of governments to employ force at a large scale, they have scant capacity to manipulate the world molecule by molecule. When science places such control within the reach of human ingenuity, it is all but certain that the far-reaching powers it unleashes will be controlled by individuals rather than governments. Most likely, they will be controlled by a single individual.

Perhaps the best way to understand how nanotechnology would work is to think in terms of magic. As with Aladdin's Lamp, nanotechnology will ultimately change the world according to the whim of the person who finds it. That is its logic. Much of the charm of Aladdin's tale lies with the essential fact that the almost unlimited powers the genie granted were not shared by everyone, and could not be. If they had been, no one could have enjoyed the magic, even the peasants who never rubbed the lamp. An essential element of magic is that it cannot be egalitarian. Everyone cannot use it. In fables, access is always controlled by "secret words" like "Open Sesame." These are the equivalents to passwords employed to control access to computers. The reason that power bordering on magic must be controlled is that it is deadly. As scientist Eric Drexler wrote of molecular technology, it could be used "to cheaply tranquilize, lobotomize, or otherwise modify entire populations." The nanotechnological equivalent of a genie would be the deadliest weapon that the world has yet known—far more deadly than atomic weapons because it could be used invisibly, anonymously, and without danger to anything or anyone other than the targets. If everyone had Aladdin's lamp, everyone would be dead. The arrangement would last only so long as it took for one person to wish that he alone had the genie. That would take only a few seconds.

The megapolitics of nanotechnology points clearly to total rule, not just by the few, but by one person, who would have godlike powers. The person who controlled the replicators could expect to outlive Methuselah and the patriarchs. Nanotechnology could repair human cells and counter the aging process. This figure could program others to do whatever he wished, or more benignly, he might prevent them from doing things he did not wish. He could stop them being violent. Or playing loud music. Or dropping candy wrappers on side streets. He could stabilize his own power by making everyone else too stupid to comprehend the nanotechnological secrets. In effect, a new god would cast humans out of the Garden of Eden.

It is one of the divine mysteries of human existence that the ancient religions have taught humans how to interact impotently with a god. In the future, to borrow German philosopher Immanuel Kant's phrase, there could be a new "perfect freedom," in the sense most of us would not recognize. The human will would be made to coincide with the will of those programming the replicators.

The revolution in the economic predicament and the changing frontiers of power that will accompany molecular technology assure that the human population will either be much changed or much diminished in numbers. Material abundance at negligible cost will shift the boundaries of scarcity. It will increase the premium on leisure and privacy. In such an environment, anyone who survives will face a power gap in relation to those who control the replicators as wide as that separating men from gods. Ordinary people, if they exist, will have no more control over the exercise of power than a box of noodles. The triumph of information technology will shift the boundary decisions about power to a miniaturized dimension in which those without the secret passwords and knowledge of the program will be unable to operate.

Therefore it should hardly be imagined that the ideas of democracy and equal voice in government have in any sense triumphed for all time. They have not. As in the time of Aristotle, the triumph of ideas remains contingent upon the megapolitical facts of the moment. The institutions of political economy that we take for granted today are artifacts of technological conditions that are changing. Contrary to absurd proclamations of the "end of history," one can see that a tremendous revolution in the exercise of power is already underway. Even if miniaturization is never carried to the ultimate extremes of nanotechnology, it threatens a radical devolution of power.

THE RELATIVITY OF POWER AND THE CONSTITUTIONS OF THE PAST

Understanding the dynamics of power and the incentives to use it are the keys to understanding how societies evolve. Power relations are constantly subject to revision as megapolitical factors change. Power is never absolute. It is always relative. As William Playfair, one of the early pioneers of megapolitical analysis, wrote in 1805, "Power is altogether comparative." It depends entirely upon the capacity that one group has in confrontation with another. This is illustrated by some compelling historic comparisons:

> The Romans, for example, may very justly be called the most powerful nation that ever existed, yet a single battalion of our present troops, well supported with artillery, would have probably destroyed the finest army they ever sent into the field. A single ship of the line would certainly have sunk, taken, or put to flight, all the fleets that Rome and Carthage ever sent to sea. The feeblest and least powerful of civilized nations, with the present means of fighting, and the knowledge of the present day, would defeat an ancient army of the most powerful description. Power is entirely relative; and what is feebleness now, would, at a certain time, have been force or power.

As Playfair suggests, what is power today may not be power tomorrow. The troops that seemed invincible at the turn of the nineteenth century would have been a laughing stock on a battlefield a hundred years later.

Artifacts of Power

This is a matter of importance far beyond the battlefield. All of the political institutions of the world are artifacts of megapolitical conditions as they existed sometime in the past. One of the clearer examples of this is the House of Lords, in which Lord Rees-Mogg sits. In the past, no important decisions could be enacted in England without the approval of the lords, who commanded private armies and great wealth. The House of Lords is an anachronism in today's world. But so are the Diet in Tokyo and the United States Congress. Any established institution of power reflects megapolitical conditions as they used to be.

This is even true of nations. It is important to remember that the boundaries drawn on maps are artificial. They, too, are artifacts of megapolitical conditions that existed sometime in the past. There is no inherent size at which human ecologies naturally form borders. They can be tiny, like primitive bands made up of fewer than one hundred persons. Or gargantuan, like the British Empire, upon which "the sun never set." They can be any size in between.

Historically, it has been rare for human societies to organize at a large scale because the technology of weaponry has seldom conveyed overwhelming advantages to any group. Empires and large political systems have existed for less than one percent of the time that human beings have been on earth. Most human societies have been the political equivalents of mom-and-pop grocery stores, small groups that last for a generation or two and disappear. There has never yet been a single government commanding enough power to become the custodian of violence for the entire world.

Thus, there is always some anarchy at the heart of the world system. When there are hundreds of governments or even thousands of governments, it is less likely that any one of them will have the capacity to police predatory violence on a global scale. Like a blanket pinned loosely together from many bolts of cloth, the world order is always a bit frayed and weak at the seams, even in the most stable of times.

The more governments there are, the worse. When many groups exercise power at a small scale, and every little hill is under the control of a different group, as in Somalia, economies tend to falter. Indeed, much of the advantage of avoiding anarchy is lost if power can be established only on a tenuous, fleeting basis. It is far better when the technology of power makes those who control the government reasonably secure from physical attack.

Why Thieves Should Be Monopolists

Society is produced by our wants, and government by our wickedness.

—WILLIAM GODWIN

When there are no commanding heights of power, only small hills, over which contending groups wrestle or maneuver in uneasy balance, the incentives to use predatory violence proliferate. It becomes more difficult to prosper economically. Plunder becomes more attractive. And because power is less stable, it becomes more difficult to control those who seek to monopolize it. The "king of the mountain" may stand on such a slippery slope that he could not expect to survive long enough to realize a share of the substantial gains that any society realizes from containing violence. Under such conditions, there is little to prevent those who command what passes for government from employing their power to terrorize and pillage society.

The logic of force, therefore, is such that the more armed groups there are, and the more nearly equal they are in power (which is really another way of saying the same thing), the more anarchy and predatory violence there will be. Without an overwhelming power to suppress violence, it proliferates, and many of the gains of economic and social cooperation go up in smoke.

When the Law Is Outgunned

The horrors that occur when violence is given full reign are well demonstrated by history. Consider the example of China in the 1920s. After the collapse of the monarchy in 1911, China descended into anarchy. Although there was notionally a government, it was essentially a government of water pistols. It exercised little real power over most of the country, which consequently fell under the yoke of marauding armies, bandits, and war lords. No authority was strong enough to establish a monopoly of force by suppressing the various bullies who took turns shaking down society. By 1928, there were eighty-four separate armies roaming around China, plus eighteen independent divisions and twenty-one brigades.

Untold millions died as warlords fought back and forth across the countryside, pillaging and looting with abandon. In a single five-month period in the 1929–30 winter, the once-wealthy city of Iyang in West Honan changed hands among various bandit armies seventy-two times. A new band of thugs seized control on an average of once every two days. Anyone who was suspected of possessing even a vestige of wealth was fair play for kidnapping and torture. As an official report put it, "When they capture a person for ransom they first pierce his legs with iron wire and bind them together as fish are hung on a string. When they return to their bandit dens the captives are interrogated and cut with sickles to make them disclose hidden property. Any who hesitate are immediately cut in two at the waist, as a warning to the others." Merchants from Chengtu, capital of Szechuan Province, protested, "We have nothing left but the grease between our bones."

> When Providence divided the earth among a few lordly masters, it neither forgot nor abandoned those who seem to have been left out in the partition.
>
> —ADAM SMITH

Even if one believes that governments are little better than large bands of thieves—as they sometimes appear to be—it is in most cases incomparably better to live with one settled group of thieves than to run for one's life from even more violent and predatory bandits who clash and loot under anarchy. At least when governments become the main custodians of violence at a large scale, they have some incentive to let citizens prosper, if only so they can collect more taxes. The roving bandits and looters who compete under anarchy lack even these weak incentives to moderation.

One of the best ways those in power can increase the bounty they have to consume or distribute is to encourage those whom they tax to be more productive. This alone is enough to account for at least some enforcement of property rights. Even the Mafia and other criminal gangs honor this principle in practice by "protecting" those whom they shake down from the violence of others.

When predatory violence can be contained, economies can become quite prosperous in spite of all the obstacles that politicians and criminals put in the way of free and efficient use of private property. Free markets make societies richer. Richer societies not only afford better lives for those who inhabit them, they can also better bear the costs of military power.

Incentives and the Power Equation

Thus the capacity to control violence is fundamental in yet another sense to the functioning of societies. When megapolitical conditions make the attainment of sufficient military power dependent upon greater national wealth, as has generally been the case in recent centuries, leaders have stronger incentives to tolerate the emergence of private property rights, sound money, and economic freedom. This accounts for part of the reason that Soviet authorities did not fall into the last ditch to save Communism in Eastern Europe. As an imperial power, the Soviet Union faced rising costs as the trend in weaponry turned in favor of small groups. An ever more productive economy would have been required to maintain the same relative burden of military cost.

Changing military costs cut into the incentives for those in power to tolerate free economies in other ways, as well. For nonimperial powers and splinter groups claiming authority over small areas, it may be less essential to observe property rights when the costs of effective defensive weapons fall. Attracting fanatical followers may be more important militarily than supporting a larger military establishment. Incentives to promote commerce may also be less pronounced in very violent times, when the possession of wealth may inhibit military effectiveness by tending to make people "soft" or less willing to fight. The "invisible hand" that sometimes steers and constrains those who have power to observe property rights may go limp when megapolitical conditions change.

This is why the power equation is of such crucial importance to you. The continued survival of civilization, much less prosperity, depends upon there being only a limited number of entities that can employ destructive force effectively.

Unfortunately, the trend of technology is increasing the number of groups that can employ predatory and destructive violence. This trend has a number of dimensions:

1. *The military balance between offense and defense is shifting in favor of the defense.* The military balance between offense and defense does not necessarily indicate which side in a battle is the aggressor. It refers to another concept— whether it is cheaper or more costly to consolidate jurisdictions than to break them into smaller units. The easier it is to project power from the center to the periphery, the more the offense is at the advantage. The more difficult and costly it becomes to suppress local violence, the more the defense is at the advantage. As one or the other gains the upper hand, political ecologies expand or contract. Sometimes, the balance changes because of innovations in weapons themselves. Sometimes the changes involve nonmilitary technologies or other megapolitical factors that raise or lower the costs of projecting power. As the 1990s began, power in the world appeared to be devolving. The trend in weapons was making it more costly to project authority and cheaper to resist. Notwithstanding U.S. success in the Gulf War, borders and barriers were proliferating. The number of political units in the world was growing as separatist movements and ethnic clashes increased. Even within large societies, violence was skyrocketing. And so was misgovernment.

2. *The scale of predominant technologies is rapidly falling.* The trend toward miniaturization evidenced in microcircuitry and computer chips has a parallel in the falling scale at which human livelihoods are most efficiently organized. As we explained in *Blood in the Streets*, this is an important reason for the collapse of Communism, the most centralized of all economic systems. Falling scale dictated by technology is also breaking up smokestack industries and undermining labor union power in Western countries. As the economy switches from processing raw materials to processing information, the size of the operations required to handle the tasks is tumbling. The most productive steel mills no longer employ tens of thousands as they did in 1950. They employ one hundred people. Information processing involves few raw materials. It involves primarily mental work, rather than physical labor. In 1950, seven of ten workers employed in Western Europe and North America worked with their hands. Now the ratio is rapidly reversing.

The shift in the skills required of the work force has troubling implications for violence during the transition period. It means that educated people who

cultivate mental skills will receive ever greater income in comparison to those
who don't. This is exactly as it must be if the compensating changes in behavior
among the unskilled are to occur. In the long run, higher returns to people
who educate themselves should heighten interest in learning. But the achievement of significant gains in education will not come overnight. It will only
materialize after a cultural confrontation and a revolution in educational
methods, which are the subjects of other chapters. Until this cultural confrontation is faced and resolved, however, matters are likely to get worse.
The rapid falloff of jobs for the unskilled has led to a decline in self-discipline
and a surge in violence and crime. A historian of violence, Ted Robert Gurr,
put it this way:

> The well-documented decline in violent crime during the nineteenth century
> coincided with the inculcation of habits of discipline among urban industrial
> workers by schools, churches, and factories . . . a discipline that was enforced by
> increasingly professional police forces. The bottom of the U-shaped crime curve,
> from the 1920s to the 1950s, coincided with the maturation of industrial society.
> The rising rate of violent crimes that began in Britain and the United States in
> the 1960s is a consequence of the transition to post-industrial society, which
> provides ever fewer job opportunities for poorly trained people at the bottom of
> the social ladder. The black underclass in our urban ghettos has its counterparts
> among the growing numbers of alienated, unemployable youths in Europe's old
> industrial cities.

Paradoxically, the shift to higher returns from education has led not to a
renovation in the culture and habits of those at the bottom of society, but to
an attack upon the mainstream culture of achievement. Why the strange
reversal of blame? It is actually quite in keeping with the logic of violence.
An increase in the repertoire of skills required to earn income in the
market automatically increases the relative attractiveness of seeking what
one wants by violence. Crime is easier than calculus. And when large numbers
are attracted to crime, they inevitably rationalize by blaming someone
else.

The upsurge of crime and transfer payments can be understood as part of
the same phenomenon. For the unskilled, the resort to violence is a shakedown operation. And transfer payments, make-work jobs, and the like can
be understood as attempts to buy off violence-prone, poorly skilled people.

This coincides with a growing tribalization of society, which also reflects
the increasing military power of small groups. The meanderings of technology
that are reducing the scale at which livelihoods are organized is also reducing
the minimum size that groups must achieve to defy central authority effec-

tively. The cost and magnitude of the operation required to suppress local violence is rising, while the scale and cost of the effective resistance is falling. This is why the Soviet empire fell apart. It is why Yugoslavia dissolved into bloodshed. And why the better-mannered Czechs and Slovaks splintered Czechoslovakia into bits. It is why Canada, India, South Africa, Israel, and other multi-ethnic states will have difficulty surviving the decade. Even a nation as stable as the United States has been since the Civil War will be severely strained by growing tribalism and ethnic division. Wherever you look on the globe, you see that almost every multi-ethnic society has a Balkan heart. Germans riot against immigrants. Albanians in Macedonia fear a blood-bath. Indian tribes in North America resort to violence to reassert aboriginal claims to much of the continent. This return to tribalization and tribal thinking reflects the falling scale of weaponry.

During the high tide of Western civilization, which lasted through the early part of this century, it was very difficult for small groups to resort to violence without exposing themselves to ruinous costs, especially in the advanced societies themselves. Military weaponry at a scale necessary to inflict significant damage on society was exceedingly expensive and required large numbers to deploy successfully in battle. Even weapons that could be operated by three or four persons, like tanks, have heretofore been too expensive for a small group to afford. The high costs of effective weapons kept them from wide use.

Today many conventional weapons that were once essential to wage warfare are still prohibitively expensive. But they are no longer essential to resisting central authority. Terrorists will not take over your neighborhood by driving in with tank battalions. But they may cut off the water supply. Or blow up a power station. Or poison people with chemical or biological weapons. And the authorities will be hard pressed to stop them. Some weapons that make it extremely difficult to suppress local violence are falling sharply in price due to the advent of the microchip. The hand-held missile is such a weapon. As the Afghan rebels showed, it can be ruinously expensive to attempt to suppress even a handful of determined people armed with Stinger missiles. And on the horizon are many new weapons that could be effectively unleashed by only a handful of people, which large-scale command systems have practically no means of countering. Biological weapons, for example, now require sophisticated installations to produce, but even that may change in time. They certainly do not require large forces to unleash. Even one terrorist with biological weapons could cause horrifying casualties in big cities. As the cost of such weapons continues to fall, groups at a smaller and smaller scale will obtain the effective capacity to thwart central authority and disrupt the peace.

3. *The threat of retaliation is of declining value in deterring the use of weapons of mass destruction as they proliferate.* Paradoxically, the collapse of the Soviet empire, which appears to remove the threat of great-power nuclear war, is driven by the same causes that are now making the use of nuclear weapons by small nations and terrorists more likely. The doctrine of mutually assured destruction, or MAD, succeeded in deterring the use of nuclear weapons during the Cold War. But it could have little deterrent effect when the potential enemy is not a large nation-state. The threat of large-scale annihilation cannot be effectively used to deter aggressive behavior of small groups.

This can be understood in terms of the distinction between weapons of duress and weapons of destruction. Until recently, this distinction was mainly of interest to police science. Experts in that field have long distinguished between weapons of destruction that kill, and weapons of duress—like tear gas or truncheons—that can be used to alter behavior. Weapons of duress also might be called weapons of persuasion. They force people to submit rather than endure further physical punishment. Where groups are concerned, weapons of destruction have traditionally been weapons of duress as well. By killing some members of a group with a weapon like a gun, it has often been possible to oblige surviving members of the group to submit. The more formidably destructive offensive weapons, however, such as nuclear, chemical, or biological weapons, are useful as weapons of duress only when they are targeted against large groups. You cannot drop an atomic bomb on a terrorist. For the terrorist, it is true, as Dylan Thomas said, that "after the first death, there is no other."

This has frightening implications. A terrorist is unlikely to be deterred from employing weapons of mass destruction by the threat of massive retaliation. A mad bomber who would risk death to blow up an airplane is willing to risk death. Period. He is unlikely to be further deterred because his target is bigger. Indeed, the logic of terrorism makes it more attractive for terrorists to blow up or poison a whole city than to kill a few innocent tourists on an intercontinental flight.

For fundamental reasons, weapons of mass destruction are more likely to be used, the greater the number and smaller the scale of the groups who can obtain them. The vulnerability of large governments and centralized targets is therefore likely to continue growing during the 1990s. Large cities rather than military targets will be at growing risk as effective weapons of destruction are dispersed ever more widely throughout the world.

The Power Equation Is Destabilizing

The current power equation is therefore highly destabilizing. Technological trends are making it possible for ever-smaller groups to attain military effectiveness. Power is devolving. At worst, this will mean a dramatic upsurge in violence, and even the unleashing of weapons of mass destruction by small nations and terrorist groups. At the least, it means a continuation of the trend toward more governments in the world. The total has more than tripled since World War II. Beyond a minimum point, the greater the number of sovereign governments exercising power, the more of a snarl they will make of everything.

It is like what might happen if you tried to stage a football game, but instead of playing on a normal stretch of field, with one set of rules applying throughout its length, you passed into a new jurisdiction every ten yards. The new referee would whistle the play dead. A legal kick at mid-field might be a misdemeanor somewhere else. The confusion of multiple rules, as you passed from one jurisdiction to another, would defeat the game completely.

In this respect, life is no less serious than a game. Multiplying borders and barriers is like erecting fencing, or stringing nets across important dimensions of existence. The more and smaller the units that exercise sovereign power, the greater the number of transactions that will be hung up.

Encompassing Systems and Big Government

The breakdown of large political systems and the proliferation of borders and barriers are likely to be inimical to economic growth and human freedom. This is a point that is likely to be misunderstood, so it requires some elaboration. Much political debate in the modern period had rightly focused on the evils of centralized control and the dangers of totalitarianism in which practically every aspect of life is dictated from afar by a powerful central government. We agree with those concerns. Wherever government at a large scale exists, it is crucially important that it be controlled in ways that maximize human liberty. However, it would be a mistake to suppose that megapolitical changes that could destroy the capacity to maintain order at a large scale are likely to encourage the realization of freedom or progress. Quite the contrary. Historically, freedom has tended to be submerged when order at a large scale was destroyed. The alternative to encompassing trading areas and multinational empires is not likely to be the proliferation of prosperous, peaceable communities developing according to their own dreams, but something far worse: spreading violence, depredation, and economic decline.

Generally speaking, the larger the scale over which order is exercised, the more conducive it is to progress. Of course, we are not saying that small systems cannot outperform large ones. They can. But their prosperity is usually dependent upon exploiting a larger world system of free trade and exchange, arrangements that small political entities are usually incapable of providing for themselves. A small polity like Monaco or Hong Kong, for example, could hardly prosper, or even survive, in a world in which goods could not flow readily across borders.

The question is really whether the world is likely to be a more prosperous place if the number of groups who can employ violence increases. You need only think of an extreme case to see the answer. What would happen if every person had the capacity to set off a nuclear attack? Obviously, the world would already have been blown to cinders. The continued survival of civilization, much less prosperity, depends upon there being only a small number of entities that can employ destructive force effectively. Unfortunately, as we have seen, the thrust of technology is moving in the direction of devolution. And that means you can expect a rising tide of violence and misgovernment to spread more widely in the coming decades. In less than two years since the first edition of this book was published, evidence of devolution has accumulated almost daily. The Soviet Union, Yugoslavia, and Czechoslovakia are gone. Three nations have become 23, with new fissures and fragments on the way. These changes reflect the early stages of a revolution in the organization of life. The hand-held missile and even new categories of weapons made possible by the microchip promise to revolutionize the whole of life.

Counterexamples

The wonder is that the devolution implied by the present power equation has not been more fully felt. The logic of our argument suggests that terrorists and tribal groups could be making life unbearable in even advanced countries. Yet the news includes some that is positive. The proposed unification of the European Community, if it is ultimately consummated, is an example of a move against the megapolitical tide. The same can be said of the North American Free Trade Agreement, encompassing the United States, Canada and Mexico. While the attempt to reduce borders and barriers and achieve greater regional economic integration may partly reflect the emergence of trade blocs, it is certainly a more open response than wholesale protectionism and trade war.

Time Lags

It would be a mistake, however, to suppose that these examples of economic integration are decisive evidence that the logic of megapolitics will not apply in the future as it has in the past. There have typically been long lags between the introduction of new technologies and the consequent changes in political organization and economic life that they implied. Gunpowder, for example, was known in Europe as early as 1242, and there is evidence of guns in use in Florence as early as 1325. These early weapons, however, could not be used effectively. One of the first hints that chemically propelled weapons would play a major role in future warfare was the use of cannon by the Turks in taking Constantinople in 1453. Nonetheless, it was another forty years before the Gunpowder Revolution exploded in the heart of Europe.

Likewise, the history of almost every far-reaching innovation in weaponry shows a long lag, of a generation or more, before the tactical possibilities that were always implied in the weapons were realized. It is quite possible that we are enjoying the last rose of summer where civic peace is concerned.

The megapolitics of devolution have already resulted in breakdown in much of the world. The backward nations in Africa and Latin America, as well as the post-Communist countries in Eastern Europe, are prisoners of violence. Even if their rulers do wish to establish property rights and a rule of law, the current power equation makes their job formidably difficult. Economies that have long been perverted by expropriation, arbitrary edict, price controls, and distorted forms of ownership cannot be transformed into sound systems with the wave of a wand. Such a transformation involves lots of pain and time. It takes many years to produce the benefits of a predictable legal system, impartial protection of private property rights, and regular taxation rather than arbitrary pillage. As G. W. F. Hegel put it, a suitable constitution cannot be "a mere contrivance." It must be "the work of generations." The benefits of such an evolution, if it were to occur, would not necessarily fall to the persons who are currently making decisions. Nor can they be instituted over the objections of those who have the power of the veto by violent force. Recognition of these facts goes a long way toward explaining many of the puzzles and frustrations of modern history.

The Conditions for Prosperity

Prosperity can occur only where the perverse effects of violence are minimized. This requires relatively stable rules. As Nathan Rosenberg and L. E. Birdzell point out in *How the West Grew Rich,* an important element in the growth of prosperity in the Western world since the fifteenth century was the evolution of institutions that reduced the risks of trade. "Among them were a legal system designed to give predictable, rather than discretionary, decisions, the introduction of bills of exchange, which facilitated the transfer of money and provided the credit needed for commercial transactions; the rise of an insurance market; and the change of governmental revenue systems from discretionary expropriation to systematic taxation—a change closely linked to the development of the institution of private property." Although the authors may not see it as we do, the characteristics they cite as essential to prosperity are all fundamentally connected to the distribution of raw power in the world.

As Mancur Olson has shrewdly observed, the principal reason that poor countries are poor is that they lack a crucial element required for economic development—"a stable government that reliably provides law and order, impartially protects private property, and enforces contracts." This is not to say that such countries lack laws against theft, or that they have failed to draft commercial codes, although some of the post-Communist countries are deficient even in these measures. The problem is greater. Laws alone are merely words. They do not always describe the realities that people live by. In a backward country, like Zaire or Peru, laws may mean little. The law may say that you can import or export a product without paying bribes to numerous petty functionaries, but the reality is that you can't. The constitution of Lebanon states that laws are enacted by the parliament. Among them are provisions that ban kidnapping. Yet the Lebanese parliament building was largely abandoned for years because many of its members refused to enter the Beirut district where it is located for fear of being kidnapped or murdered.

Contrary to common impressions, the impoverishment of the backward regions has little to do with the history of Western colonialism. Nor is it due to a lack of capital and skilled workers. These are as much the consequences as the causes of poverty. If the principal problem were a simple lack of capital, the income it would earn in poor areas would be higher than in more advanced regions. Capital would flow in like water running downhill. Similarly, if there were really a shortage of skilled personnel in Third World countries, the wages they earn would be higher than in rich countries. There would be a net migration of skilled persons into poor countries. This, of course, is not the case. Most poor countries are losing skilled workers. And the few wealthy persons who continue to live in such places go to great lengths to ship most of their savings abroad, a reflection of the fact that property rights are likely to change with the next strong wind.

With megapolitical trends making it ever more difficult to suppress violence, the result to be expected in backward countries is not a sudden surge of progress, but a relapse into destitution. Overall consumption in Latin America dropped by 13 percent over the decade of the 1980s, and it could plunge even further in the 1990s as world depression lowers prices.

Why Violence Has Not Yet Swamped the West

The logic of devolution is the same in advanced Western countries as it is in the former Yugoslavia or Somalia. But the results to this point have been far less destabilizing. A principal reason is that the prosperity of Western societies has given individuals keener incentives to expand commerce and uphold the laws. This strength of the West is partly cultural and partly economic. The two intertwine in complicated ways. Western culture has sensitized people to violence as part of the process that made them fit for commerce. And the grand success of centuries of commerce has tended to reinforce this taboo on violence. The repression of violence increases the economic incentive to uphold the laws and observe property rights. This can almost be measured by the composition of the national balance sheets.

Roughly speaking, the more peaceful and stable a society, the greater will be its financial assets relative to tangible assets. As John Stuart Mill emphasized, a "long exemption . . . from military violence or arbitrary spoliation" is essential to "a long-standing and hereditary confidence in the safety of funds when trusted outside of the owner's hands." For financial assets to become a very substantial fraction of the whole, people must be confident that contracts will be enforced and money entrusted to others repaid. But this is precisely what one cannot be sure of in unstable Third World countries. Yale economist Raymond W. Goldsmith has extensively studied the balance sheets of leading countries over recent centuries. His data show that there was a steady increase in the percentage of financial assets from very small fractions—just 11 percent of total assets in Great Britain in 1688—to more than 60 percent of the total in this century. The richest countries have tended to have the highest percentage of financial assets—with Switzerland having the highest sustained ratio of any country. Not surprisingly, Switzerland is also perhaps the most stable and law-abiding of all the nations in the world.

The Economic Value of a Sound Constitution

As capital builds up, it is like padding that protects social institutions from megapolitical shocks. Consequently, institutions and laws in prosperous societies can outlast the megapolitical conditions that brought them into existence. Poorer societies, however, have smaller capital buffers to shield themselves from megapolitical reality. In a way we seldom think about, the rules of a society have value in themselves. It is a matter of incentives. The increment to lifetime income for living under the laws of Switzerland rather than Swaziland or Bolivia is enormous. People respond to this fact in the normal way. This is why Switzerland is not only more prosperous, it is more stable. Political and constitutional stability tend to rise as wealth accumulates.

This does not mean that every law will always be followed by every person in a rich country. But a constitution will be honored in broad measure so long as the rules continue to pay off for those who have the power to change them. This is why economic decline is destabilizing. As incomes fall, the incentive to adhere to the rules of society falls as well. This is true whether or not the rules would be productive of higher incomes over the long run.

Although physical force is the ultimate determinant of the rules by which a society operates, power cannot be adequately understood in isolation from the incentives to use it. People do not do everything that is within their power to accomplish. A man may have the capacity to burn down his own house. Yet barring strange circumstances, he has no incentive to do so. Most people who set their homes afire do so by accident.

The incentives facing large groups, much less whole societies, are more complex than those facing individuals. While at any given time the rules of a society may not reflect the actual balance of physical force among individuals and the groups they form, distributions of wealth and physical power cannot long diverge. Eventually, societies change to reflect the changing power equation.

Electronic Feudalism?

Unless the growing capacity of small groups to employ violence is countered by new technologies and vigorous action, we can expect a dramatic shift in political institutions, with far-reaching economic effects. The result could be economic decline in the advanced countries and even electronic feudalism.

Feudalism, after all, was the response of agricultural society to the breakdown of public order. The privatization of public services is not necessarily equivalent to feudalism. Far from it. But the privatization of protection and the substitution of private alternatives to public infrastructure could be the parallels during the twenty-first century to the building of castles on the hill.

It is already clear in the United States, at least, that those who are relatively secure in their lives and properties owe that security more to having isolated themselves successfully from criminals than to the effectiveness of public law enforcement. People who live in upper- and middle-class neighborhoods are not prone to rob and murder one another. In neighborhoods where criminals live or to which criminals have greater access, violence and crime are sky-rocketing.

According to privatization expert Mark Frazier, homeowner associations have grown from six hundred to forty-five thousand in the United States since 1964. Homeowner associations are organized to deliver services, particularly neighborhood watches and crime patrols, on a private basis. They repay their costs by deterring violence. Each 1 percent reduction in crime victimization rates translates into about a three-hundred-dollar rise in the value of a private home. The police and public justice system have shown little capacity to thwart crime in those areas that are readily accessible to criminals.

A further breakdown of public order would expose people in even good neighborhoods in urban areas to heightened dangers of predatory violence. If that happens, two consequences are likely: (a) a surge of vigilantism as private citizens attempt to protect their lives and property on their own, and (b) the further retreat of the wealthy from central cities into the countryside to escape the growing costs of urban breakdown and misgovernment. In a sense, the test of the coming decade will be whether vigilantism (the private attempt to secure the peace in public spaces) will prevail over high-tech feudalism (the private protection of property rights in private spaces).

Power Always Matters

Wealth neither appears nor disappears randomly. The prosperity of peoples and nations is intimately connected to the power equation. The past five centuries have been an extraordinary period of progress in human affairs, in large measure because megapolitical conditions made it possible to suppress the perverse use of violence, and thus create a more encompassing, open economy.

Technological change can have a far more sweeping impact than casual observers looking at close range would suppose. The Gunpowder Revolution altered the political ecology of Europe and then the world in ways that greatly increased the potential for economic growth, opening many previously closed societies. Now the thrust of technology that set in motion a five-hundred-year opening of the world system is being overtaken by new technological developments, from the atomic bomb to the microchip, which threaten to destabilize the megapolitical foundations of progress.

Whether you prosper or merely struggle to survive is determined in large measure by the interaction of the basic factors that govern the use of violence in the world. To a far greater extent than most people believe, prosperity is always a hostage to the meanderings of power. Megapolitical changes, especially improvements in the tools of violence we know as weapons, can dramatically alter the power equation. They play a crucial role in determining whether it is militarily feasible to suppress the use of force that some humans are always tempted to use against others. In the 1990s, you will have to hope for miracles—that criminals and terrorists will not recognize the deterioration of the power equation and, like the thief who was bluffed out of the Best Food Market, will kindly hand over their weapons.

CHAPTER THREE

AMERICA FOLLOWS IN BRITAIN'S FOOTSTEPS

If all other methods of adjustment fail, we shall, in the extremity, suffer such a fall in the exchange value of sterling and in the levels of employment and expenditure in this country as to force our consumption of imports within the straitjacket of our financial capacity to pay for them.

—Secret British Treasury Memo,
March 1942

HALF A CENTURY ago, the British Empire was in trouble. Worse trouble than most people knew. Hitler. The Blitz. Skimpy rations and bad hamburgers. These were only part of the trouble. Britain was broke, a nation living on foreign borrowing at an immense scale. The end of World War II meant the end of the financial lifeline from abroad. President Truman canceled Lend-Lease* on August 17, 1945. When the foreign money ceased to pour in, Britain's economy went into a stall that ended only with the advent of Prime Minister Margaret Thatcher.

There are troubling similarities between the British economic situation then and America's today. Indeed, America is suffering the classic symptoms of a nation in decline. Since the eighteenth century, those who have thought

---

*Lend-Lease was a program enacted by Congress on March 11, 1941, allowing the president of the United States to transfer resources to any country whose defense was vital to America. It was basically a program for subsidizing Great Britain.

systematically about the rise and fall of nations have noted similar symptoms of decline: high taxes, high prices, widening gaps between the rich and poor, strong special-interest groups, failures of motivation, a decline in education and everyday competence, a high tendency to import, high budget deficits, and more. It was common opinion in the Enlightenment that faltering empires suffer moral breakdown, lose their civic spirit, and divert ever more of their energies to nonproductive pursuits. Writing "Of the Decline of Nations," Adam Ferguson said, "Whole bodies of men are sometimes infected with an epidemical weakness of the head, or corruption of heart, by which they become unfit for the stations they occupy, and threaten the states they compose, however flourishing, with a prospect of decay, and of ruin." In 1766, when Ferguson wrote, there was no Congress of the United States. Long before *The Bonfire of the Vanities*, Ferguson described the moral atmosphere of a society heading for a fall:

> The individual considers his community so far only as it can be rendered subservient to his personal advancement or profit: he states himself in competition with his fellow-creatures; and, urged by the passions of emulation, of fear and jealousy, of envy and malice, he follows the maxims of an animal destined to preserve his separate existence, and to indulge his caprice or his appetite, at the expense of his species.

Sometimes fact follows fiction and life imitates art. Those who have read Tom Wolfe's sinister fantasy of life in New York in the 1980s can see in newspapers ample evidence that it is a fantasy coming true. Episodes that could have been cut from the book as overdrawn are detailed regularly in the headlines. For many Americans who live outside New York, Wolfe's novel must at first have seemed unreal. It is the story, as almost everyone knows by now, of a wealthy young New Yorker, of old family, who is involved in a hit-and-run accident in the Bronx. The protagonist, Sherman McCoy, is rapidly destroyed by unscrupulous media, craven colleagues, a politicized system of law, and one helping too many of "Veal Boogie Woogie." He is also the victim of deepening ethnic divisions and animosities, particularly between New York Jews and blacks.

The Bonfire of the Vanities is the story of the end of an era, of the wasting of an educated man who lacks the street smarts to make it in a world where the rules have changed. Before he knows it, Sherman McCoy is no longer an investment banker, just as New York City is no longer the capital of international finance.

Tom Wolfe's novel is one in which the rich can see themselves as decadent and threatened. In New York, it is easy to feel that one is moving through a little corridor of safety, to and from Wall Street, or the pricey neighborhoods that rim Central Park. They are zones of sanctuary in what Pete Hamill has called a "barbarized city." It is the same in many other major cities in America.

Intellectual Retreat

On the eve of the last depression, William Butler Yeats described a vision of impending chaos in "The Second Coming." He was making a poem, not an economic forecast, when he wrote, "Things fall apart; the centre cannot hold." Yet that was soon true. The world trading system, centered on London, did fall apart. The center could not hold. Some of Yeats's images are surprisingly close fits with what the years brought.

The poet tells us that even before the collapse of the world economy had been registered in the cash markets, it was prefigured in the psyches of men. He could see in the twenties, "The best lack all conviction, while the worst are full of passionate intensity." Even before depression and war stretched the bounds of civilization to the limit, there was much evidence that the spirit of the leading figures in Europe had "become enfeebled in conduct."

The erosion of the real power of the leading nation, Great Britain, was followed by an epidemic of renunciation of the principles of which the British Empire had long been the foremost champion. As Winston Churchill put it in a speech on March 18, 1931, "Many itching fingers were stretching and scratching at the vast pillage of a derelict empire." Demagogues like Hitler and Mussolini stirred crowds with emotional harangues denouncing free markets, liberal democracy, and free trade. Even in Britain itself, a fickle intelligentsia lost confidence in some aspects of British traditions. The Oxford Union resolved never again to fight for King and Country.

> But in the prevailing climate, Thomas Jefferson and all the Founding Fathers are in disrepute. (The Constitution, according to the 1989 New York State report, is "the embodiment of the White Male with Property Model.") . . . And since most of Western culture, according to this view, has been a testament to "male power and transcendence," it is similarly evil and must be discarded. This includes not only patriarchal books like the Bible and sexist subjects like traditional history, with its emphasis on great men and great deeds, but also the natural sciences and even the very process of analytical thinking itself.
>
> —JOHN TAYLOR,
> "Are You Politically Correct?"

The erosion of the real power of America has led to a parallel renunciation of what America stood for, a renunciation that appears to be more harsh within the intellectual community in America itself than in the world at large. The peoples left behind by Communism in Eastern Europe and the former Soviet Union have become, in many cases, vigorous proponents of the American way of life. But the affirmations of free markets and liberal democracy that swept Leipzig and Beijing surprised America's elite campuses. Faculties and students alike have turned against the culture that produced them far more than Oxford or Cambridge ever turned against the British culture, even during the dark days of fiscal crisis and retreat in the 1930s.

The intellectual atmosphere at many universities in the United States has turned hostile, not just to many aspects of American society, but to the larger inheritance of Western civilization itself. The devolution of megapolitical power, which has given small groups growing capacities to disrupt society, has fostered a parallel assertion of new ideologies of separateness. In campuses across America, from Berkeley to New Haven, the magic word is "oppression." Say it out loud and you may get to ride for free on a city bus. Any group that claims to be "oppressed" is suddenly possessed of an asset, an entitlement upon which to leverage claims for redistributed wealth.

The advocates of the new "oppression" ideologies share a common premise. They presume that culture has no role to play in preparing either an individual or society for success or failure. They seem to think that culture's sole purpose is to disguise and perpetuate claims for privilege among the dominant groups. This extreme relativism has led to an active and hostile rejection of the culture of Western achievement.

As more groups maneuver to claim privileged status among those officially designated as "oppressed," any statement that offends their sensibilities is shouted down. One of the favorite terms of abuse is "racist," a once-useful word that has been emptied of meaning. Or worse. In many cases, the meaning of "racist" has been reversed. According to the militant critics of Western culture, a "racist" is now someone who believes that everyone should be judged as an individual, rather than according to ethnic identity, sexual orientation, or some other defining characteristic of separateness.

An undergraduate at the University of Pennsylvania who found herself on the "diversity education committee" wrote a memo to fellow committee members eagerly declaring a "deep regard for the individual and my desire to protect the freedoms of all members of society." A college administrator returned her memo with the word "individual" underlined as if it had been misspelled. This comment was attached: "This is a 'RED FLAG' phrase today, which many consider RACIST." Other terms of abuse, in addition to "Eurocentric," are mostly *neologisms*, newly coined words that reflect new definitions of "oppression." They include "sexist," "classist," "phallocentric," "ageist," "ableist," and even "lookist."

The hypersensitivity to any hint of offense that these terms suggest reflects society's growing vulnerability to disruption. By seeking to expunge and suppress any thoughts or concepts that might conceivably give offense to anyone, the new ideologists of oppression say they are making it easier "to learn to live with everyone." Bowing to divisiveness may be a tribute to the growing megapolitical power of small groups. But teaching people that they are oppressed is more likely to encourage confrontations than to appease them. It embitters the groups to which it caters. It also ill prepares them to compete in the world. The noisiest opponents of Western culture are not content just to attack American institutions, they also attack the sciences, intellectual rigor, and logic itself as tools of oppression. To be "logocentric" is now supposed to be a matter of shame. Faculty and students in many American educational institutions are being instructed not to pay too much heed to the meanings of words or the logic they imply. The dean of the Graduate School at Rutgers, Catherine Stimpson, denounces "objectivity and intellectual rigor" as "a lot of mishmash" used by people "trying to preserve the cultural and political supremacy of white heterosexual males."

Individuals are valued not according to their character or achievements, but according to their ethnic identities. A woman who applied for an opening for a professorship of Latin American literature at Hampshire College was turned down because she had Italian and Jewish ancestors. Although she was an Argentine, "her Third World ethnicity was considered insufficiently pure," as John Taylor reported. "Her heritage made her, in the words of one faculty member, 'Eurocentric.' "

The tendency to assign rewards according to status rather than through competition is a common characteristic of closed societies. To the shrewd investor, it is a leading indicator that should not be ignored. When there is a common perception that prospects for economic growth in a society have diminished, the focus of energies tends to shift away from acquiring competence and productive skills. More attention is devoted to struggles for redistributing wealth. These inevitably become worse than a zero-sum game. They undermine future prosperity, doing more to suppress the creation of wealth than they can achieve in redistributing it. The deemphasis of science and intellectual rigor, for example, undermines the very knowledge and skills that, according to Rosenberg and Birdzell, enabled the West to become "conspicuously richer and more powerful than the rest of the world."

The new ideologies of oppression also undermine productivity in other ways. They complicate hiring, promotion, and management in American firms, and dramatically expand legal costs and contingent liabilities from litigation. The next generation of America's elite lawyers, inculcated in "oppression studies" at Yale and Harvard, are concocting theories to justify lawsuits that would have been beyond the imagination of British courts, even during the high tide of Labour Party rule.

In almost every respect, members of the American intelligentsia have turned against the culture that produced them far more viciously than was ever the case in England during its decades of decline. Even theologians in America have adopted views that amount to little less than the renunciation of American society and Western civilization itself. Professor Stanley Hauerwas, of Duke Divinity School, denounces the great books of Western learning with this sendoff: "The canon of great literature was created by high-Anglican ass——s to underwrite their social class." The silliness of so many American intellectuals, and the growing renunciation of culture among institutions of learning, are clear symptoms of a nation in decline. As in interwar Britain, but even more so, we see in America's universities what Paul Johnson calls "an ostensible concern for humanity forming a thin crust over a morass of funk." It is one example among many of the United States taking longer strides as it follows in Britain's footsteps on the well-traveled road to ruin.

I have watched this famous island descending incontinently, fecklessly, the stairway which leads to a dark gulf. It is a fine broad stairway at the beginning, but after a bit the carpet ends. A little farther on there are only flagstones, and little farther on still these break beneath your feet.

—WINSTON CHURCHILL

The British are expert witnesses to the twilight of empire. They lived through it. When leaders of Lord Rees-Mogg's generation were children, the British Empire encompassed one-quarter of the world, a far-flung patchwork of pink on the maps. On a visit to New York in 1989, Lord Rees-Mogg remarked how similar America's predicament seems to that of England some years ago. He was trying to order tea in the Waldorf Hotel, a task that called for patience. After waiting a long while for service, he observed that the condition of the famous New York hotels was a metaphor for the decline of empire. A magnificent physical plant was understaffed and inefficiently run. The television did not work. The sink was stopped up. Room service might come or it might not. It reminded him of being in an English hotel when England faltered. The sense of encroaching ruin was so palpable that he said that one would not have been surprised to learn that there were "barbarians in the basement."

These comments came to mind a number of times since, as we studied the decline of empires. There can be no doubt that there is a disturbing similarity between conditions in Britain half a century ago and those in America today. America is following the same path to decline that Britain followed, and its predecessors before it.

Financial Parallels

England lost her position as the dominant political and financial power in the world. . . . [A] highly unstable and destructive political situation developed and with it a series of weak or minority governments. Voter support was purchased by large social expenditures unmatched by increased production. The result was a flight of capital, a massive increase in the national debt, a loss of monetary reserves, a loss of exports, a rise in imports, huge international borrowings, a disastrous inflation, and an unprecedented rise in interest rates.

—SIDNEY HOMER,
A History of Interest Rates

America in 1990, like Britain half a century earlier, is a nation living on foreign borrowing at an immense scale. The dollar now, like the pound then, is a currency under pressure. Its value has been sustained in the late eighties by the Japanese version of Lend-Lease, a massive influx of funding for America's current account deficit. This lifeline of foreign credit had already begun to fray by 1991, as the plunge of the Japanese stock and property markets took its toll. It is bound to snap altogether now that the Cold War has ended, just as Lend-Lease was canceled at the end of World War II. Like Britain then, America today has insufficient savings to finance a hugh structural deficit and have enough left over for needed investment. In 1992, government borrowing absorbed approximately 70 percent of new credit.

This is a symptom of deeper problems. A characteristic of empires in their twilight is that they are burdened with high costs and inflexible leadership. In each case where a predominant country has faltered since the sixteenth century, it did so after its leaders stiffly resisted efforts to cut costs to competitive levels, opting instead for higher taxes and more spending. In each case, resources were fatally overextended. Economic supremacy was forfeited to another country enjoying lower taxes and lower costs.

States have endeavored, in some instances, by pawning their credit, instead of deploying their capital, to disguise the hazards they ran. . . . The growing burden too, is thus gradually laid; and if a nation is to sink in some future age, every minister hopes it may keep afloat in his own.

—ADAM FERGUSON

This pattern should be of telling interest to a modern American. The unprecedented growth of federal spending and huge deficits over the past two decades provide a clear warning signal that the United States is stumbling over the same challenge that ruined its predecessors. By the mid-1980s, the U.S. federal deficit for one year exceeded the gross national product of 158 of 167 countries. Interest payments alone swallowed all the individual income tax collected from everyone living west of the Mississippi River.

Another bleak sign is the record number of incumbents winning reelection to Congress. In the eighties, almost 99 percent of members of the House of Representatives seeking reelection were returned to office. Even the 1992 election, which brought more turnover than any in decades, saw mostly voluntary retirement. More than 90 percent of incumbents who sought another term won. There was more involuntary turnover in the Politburo of the USSR before *perestroika*. Indeed, U.S. congressmen in the 1980s had more job security than the Politburo in North Korea. Only in benighted Albania before its collapse was there less turnover in leadership. Strangely, American leaders became more entrenched the more they failed to face up to the tough choices. The huge overhang of officeholders seemed to confirm the political advantage of selling favors and wishful thinking as two principal policy planks of America's leadership.

A Pattern of Overextending Resources

Throughout the whole of the earth, we see the same causes producing nearly the same effects; why do we remain in doubt respecting their connection?

—WILLIAM PLAYFAIR, 1805

There is no better example of a nation that underwent an imperial crisis of costs and spent itself into oblivion than Spain, the great power of the early modern period. Leadership of the Spanish government was totally dominated by tax-consuming interests: the military, the bureaucracy, the church, and the nobility. Long after it became obvious that the Spanish economy was in trouble, Spain's leaders resisted every effort to cut costs. Like American politicians today, they could not believe that the money would ever run out. Each new setback to the economy was treated as an occasion to launch a grand new program. Taxes were tripled between 1556 and 1577. Spending went up even faster. The deficit rose, even as Philip II's "six-hundred-ship navy," the Armada, sank. By 1600, interest on the national debt took 40 percent of the budget. Spain descended into bankruptcy and never recovered.

A similar pattern of high costs and rigid leadership marked the decline of late-seventeenth-century Holland. The Dutch had escaped from Spanish rule to succeed Spain as the world's leading economy. But Holland's heyday did not last long. It was cut short by high costs and high taxes that fatally overextended resources and undercut the economy. Historian Jan de Vries put it succinctly:

> Increased costs, particularly in the last third of the seventeenth century, robbed Dutch trade of its dynamism. As the costs of defense forced taxes up, the high costs of urban living forced up wages. . . . And as so often happens in societies when new conditions threaten their leadership, an inflexibility permeated Dutch institutions.

THE BRITISH CATCH THE BRITISH DISEASE

A similar crisis of costs overtook Holland's successor, Great Britain, in its twilight as a world empire in the 1920s. After two centuries at the pinnacle of the world economy, Britain began to overtax its resources before World War I. The high costs of the fighting left Britain practically broke. Taxes and inflation skyrocketed after 1914. In just four years, British private investors lost the greater part of a century's accumulation of foreign investments.

British leaders, like the Spanish and Dutch before them, responded to the crisis not by cutting costs but by proposing expensive new spending ideas. The British military was the most expensive anywhere, yet important factions of the army and the cabinet wanted to garrison Armenia, send troops to Afghanistan and Iraq, and even invade Russia. Meanwhile, domestic spending was rising wildly. Lloyd George had inflamed grandiose schemes for social reconstruction with his promise to "build a nation fit for heroes to live in." Political competition rapidly upped the ante. For every spending idea the Liberals dreamed up, the Labour Party proposed even more expansive programs.

Yet the problem was not that spending was too low, but too high. For Britain to have restored its competitive position, it needed to reduce the strains on its overextended resources and lower costs. Parliament seemed paralyzed. The only significant pressure for cost-cutting came not from within the political leadership but from the outside. A popular reform movement known as the Anti-Waste League, led by a group of the more vigorous industrialists, spurred British opinion to fight "the prevailing concomitant evils of excessive government spending and high levels of taxation."

Under pressure from the Anti-Waste League, the prime minister appointed a Committee on National Economy from outside the Parliament to slash costs. This committee, headed by Sir Eric Geddes, made sweeping recommendations, especially for cuts in the military. Some of these cuts were actually implemented. But not many. Like automatic cuts threatened under the now defunct

Gramm-Rudman-Hollings law, the cuts of the "Geddes Axe" mostly failed to materialize. The few cuts that were made were not nearly deep enough to lower costs to levels enjoyed by major competitors. Then as now, resistance of spending constituencies to meaningful cost reduction predominated over efforts at reform.

Britain sank lower and lower. Its productivity growth, once the highest in the world, collapsed. As British industry fell behind, it gave up its markets to foreign competitors, forgoing growth of living standards as a result. Seventy-five years ago the only people on earth richer than the English were Americans. Today, more than twenty countries have higher living standards.

The revenues of the state were wasted on the soldiers.

—WILLIAM PLAYFAIR

It is significant that in each case the leaders of the faltering empires responded to the crisis of costs in more or less the same way. Proposals for reform were ignored. Costs were not reduced to competitive levels; instead, spending, especially for the military, was maintained or increased, fatally overextending resources. Predominant economies seem suddenly to lose their flexibility when a shift in conditions (such as technological innovation) makes high costs within the government (rather than high costs within industry) the main obstacle to continued economic vitality. In the past, this has always been associated with a heavy burden of military spending. In effect, when leaders are required to decide between restoring the competitiveness of the domestic economy and maintaining their international military authority, they opt to preserve the empire.

For most of the postwar period, American military spending far outstripped that of the other advanced democracies. It was approximately seven times that of Japan and more than twice that of western Germany. A total of ten trillion dollars was invested, much of it on the most lavish military compensation the world had ever seen. The average career soldier retired at the age of thirty-nine. He could expect to receive $228,000 in pension benefits, plus free medical care for life.

In no case where a leading economy has faltered have members of the public failed to see that trouble was at hand. Many reformers advanced plans to cut costs, but those who favored reform lacked the power to take decisive measures. An observer in Spain over three hundred years ago, noting the frustration of every effort at cost-cutting reform, wrote that "those who can will not and those who will cannot." This was true in Hapsburg Spain, but it was no less true of the efforts of the Anti-Waste League in parliamentary Britain in the twenties.

Part of the explanation for the decision to maintain the empire at all costs, while sacrificing the long-term strength of the home economy, seems to be institutional. Tax-consuming interests in the military and bureaucracy, along with financiers with major interests abroad, have more intense incentives to cultivate the leadership, whatever the form of government. Not infrequently, they are the leadership. Persons with the nearest access to the levers of power, who tend to benefit most from the status quo, are usually reluctant to undertake reforms whose first effects would be to whack their own pocketbooks.

The few cases where costs were cut were precisely those where the leadership of the faltering countries themselves stood to gain. For example, the one cost-cutting proposal that the Spanish leadership could readily accept was the abolition of the ruff collar—a dress requirement at court that had saddled the nobility with ruinous laundry bills. The greater the personal incentive the leadership enjoys for lowering costs, the more successful their efforts are likely to be.

Parallels Compound

Outsiders find the sight of this great country struggling to eliminate a fiscal deficit, so modest in itself but so large when set against net savings, astounding and disturbing in equal degrees.

—*FINANCIAL TIMES*

The United States is today struggling through a similar crisis to those faced by its three immediate predecessors as the world's supreme economy. The U.S. costs for attempting to police the world were gigantic. The U.S. fiscal deficit was far worse than Britain's or Holland's ever was. To find a comparable example of fiscal decay for a leading nation you have to return to the Hapsburg Empire in the declining years of the sixteenth century. Efforts at reform that would lower costs have been hampered by the same sort of institutional rigidity that defeated reform efforts at the court of Philip II.

Faltering Competitiveness

The signs of America's relative decline are converging and unquestionable. Japanese productivity is increasing at three times the U.S. rate while European productivity increases at twice the U.S. rate.

—JACQUES ATTALI, PRESIDENT,
European Bank for Reconstruction
and Development, 1990

Britain in decline demonstrated a "lamentable want of energy and enterprise" in exploring open markets, as Correlli Barnett put it. The same is so of Americans. America's competitiveness, however, tumbled far faster than that of Britain. In 1948, at the beginning of the postwar era, the United States produced 44 percent of the world's industrial output. The U.S. economy was *eight* times larger than that of Japan. The recovery from war naturally reduced the U.S. share of the total world economy. But the falloff was far greater than can be accounted for simply by the progress of other countries. The fact that other countries grew rapidly does not explain why U.S. productivity growth collapsed. In almost two decades following the 1973 oil shock, which was itself a follow-on effect to the decline of American power, U.S. productivity growth was the lowest in the industrialized world.

By the mid-eighties, the United States was still enjoying one of the highest living standards of any country, but it was also running the highest trade deficit in history. This was sustained by massive foreign borrowing, which turned America from a creditor to the world's largest debtor in a few short years. Put simply, the United States had ceased to be internationally competitive. More industrial plant was obsolete in America than anywhere else in the advanced world. And that trend seemed likely to continue because the United States had the lowest rate of capital investment—about one-third that of Japan.

U.S. exports had taken on the composition of those of an underdeveloped country. The top ten products by value included only one manufactured item—aircraft. The others were mainly raw materials and farm products.

The top six U.S. exports to Japan were:

1. Corn seed
2. Soybeans
3. Coal
4. Wood
5. Cotton
6. Wheat

The top U.S. imports from Japan were:

1. Automobiles
2. Tape recorders
3. Trucks
4. Office machines
5. Parts for office machines
6. Computer chips

In effect, the United States had become "a natural resource colony" of Japan. When American trade negotiators pressed the Japanese to open their markets to U.S. goods, talks centered on possibilities for more export of U.S. beef and rice.

Failing to compete effectively in the markets for mature products, Americans pin hopes, as Britain once did, on new industries arising from scientific inventiveness. Yet, like the British of several generations ago, Americans seem unable to capture the commercial advantage of new ideas. British science invented antibiotics, radar, and the jet plane, yet it fell largely to American companies to profit from them. More recently, American science invented such blockbuster products as VCRs and semiconductors. But Japanese competitors increasingly have captured their commercial potential.

Imperial Lassitude

The slow reflexes of response in exploiting new technology are not merely coincidental. In Shakespeare's words, "The hungry lion feeds best." A people who have experienced world supremacy are inevitably tempted to slacken their efforts and enjoy the superior life-style that great power implies. At the same time, the requirement to maintain a far-flung military establishment drains skill and capital away from commercial enterprise. This explains a portion of the imperial lassitude. But more is involved.

Education to Rule

The educational system of a hegemonic power is likely to be geared toward training mandarins. It is a cliché that an Oxbridge education earlier in this century trained students for the civil service, rather than civil engineering. America's elite education today is also more adept at training persons to redistribute income than to produce it. Ten lawyers graduate in America for every engineer, as compared to ten engineers for each lawyer in Japan.

The Most Inefficient Legal System in History

The high deadweight costs of America's incomparably inefficient and expensive legal system weigh on competitiveness as they never did upon the previous modern powers. In 1990, there were more lawyers in the United States than all the rest of the world combined. America had four times as many lawyers per capita as Great Britain, five times as many as Germany, ten times as many as France, and fully twenty times more lawyers than Japan. There were fifty thousand lawyers in the city of Washington alone, more than all of Japan. The consequences have been staggering to American justice and society. America has been infested with lawsuits. The costs of settling them is 400 percent higher than in the average of the other advanced economies. An editorial in the *Wall Street Journal* suggested why:

> Drunks and tort lawyers are surely toasting this week's award of $9 million to a visibly plastered Mexican dishwasher who stumbled in front of a New York subway train and woke up missing one arm. In awarding this jackpot, a Bronx jury heaved all blame on the Transit Authority for failing to "take charge" of the man.
>
> Other recent awards against the TA include $4.3 million for a thug who was shot in the back by policemen and crippled after mugging a 71-year-old man; $1.2 million for an unsuccessful suicide who jumped in front of a train and lost his legs; and $8.2 million for a homeless man who stumbled over garbage left by other homeless people, fell onto the subway tracks and was badly burned by the third rail, plus $5 million for a brother chasing him trying to take him home. If the cases are typical, a third of the loot stands to go to brazen and imaginative tort lawyers.

Simple legal procedures have been complicated and delayed to a degree that is almost without precedent. A comparison in the 1970s showed that it was one hundred times more costly to probate an estate in America than it is in England. To make matters worse, it took seventeen times as long in America to see probate to completion.

It is hard to describe how much harm the legal system of the United States does and how little good. The combination of vast law firms, litigation for profit, tight government regulation, and grotesque costs is regarded by many economists as one of the reasons why American industry has ceased to be competitive with Japan. At the same time that the legal system frustrates productive activity, it encourages crime. So many innovations have been pioneered to keep criminals out of jail in America that criminal justice has become a farce. Criminals have rational contempt for the law. As the mother of one young tough told the press after her son failed to show up for arraignment three weeks after being placed on probation, "I'm more afraid of the system than he is. . . . He has absolutely no fear of the court." And for good reason.

As Thomas Plate showed in his book *Crime Pays!,* the rewards of crime are greater than its costs. Thanks to America's legal system, the odds of committing a felony and escaping without serving prison time are as great as 100:1. An extensive investigation of the overloaded justice system published in December 1990 by the *Los Angeles Times* reported the following conclusions:

—Police take hours to respond to burglaries and other property crimes, if they respond at all, and most of the cases are never investigated.

—Prosecutors trade guilty pleas for lesser sentences for nearly every crime, including homicide, rape and robbery.

—Many felons are routinely released from overcrowded jails after serving only small fractions of the statutory punishments for their crimes. Only 0.3% of detected felonies result in long prison terms.

—Probation officers rarely, if ever, see tens of thousands of the convicted criminals who are supposed to be actively supervised.

—When a convicted criminal violates his probation and a Superior Court judge issues a bench warrant, the odds are less than 1 in 12 that the person will be arrested on the warrant.

Los Angeles detective Robert E. Readhimer specialized in investigating scrap metal thefts. He told the *Los Angeles Times* that even metal thieves who steal hundreds of thousands of dollars' worth of property are routinely jailed on misdemeanor counts and quickly released. One suspect named Calvin W. Edwards was said to face no more than ninety days in jail for his seventeenth conviction.

Not surprising, given these facts, the crime rate in America far outstrips that in any other industrial country. Robbery was 1700 percent higher in America than in Japan. To protect against crime that the legal system was unable to deter, Americans hired more than one million new security guards from 1975 to 1988. As Judge Richard Neely has pointed out, the major reason that Americans have turned increasingly toward private guards to prevent crime is that money spent on private guards is far more efficient. It costs as much as $150,000 to put a police officer on the street in a major urban area. "But the average uniformed state or local police officer spends only about 2 percent of the time actively patrolling. The rest is spent responding to calls, doing paperwork, supervising accident scenes, lecturing schoolchildren and testifying. It takes little imagination to understand that for every $100 worth of police hours our tax dollars purchase, only about $2 or $3 will be spent to prevent crimes."

Untold billions were also spent on locks and security systems. In the Northeast, many auto owners even paid dealers and repairmen to remove their own radios, to forestall junkies from smashing their windows to gain entry to their cars. This spending did not contribute anything productive. It merely fended off still greater losses because the U.S. government was incapable of effectively protecting citizens from the piracy of criminals.

A century ago, one could walk almost anywhere in a large American city without fear of physical attack. Newspaper readers were shocked by a report in 1892 that a man walking in the North Bronx, New York, had been mugged by an armed gunman. The news was so sensational that it became a headline story as far away as Philadelphia. As Roger Lane reports, the New York police were so thrown for a loop by the case that they eventually concluded "that the gunman must have worked for Buffalo Bill." In the 1990s, muggings are no longer news. They have become almost an expected toll that one pays for trying to live in or do business in an American city. Life, limb, and property are safe almost nowhere in a major urban area. In Los Angeles, gangs have taken to using the freeways in lightning raids on heretofore safe suburbs. In Jacksonville, Florida, the American Automobile Association warned its members not to travel on Interstate 295 because of a recurring danger of sniper fire. Local gangs have taken to shooting at passersby.

Perhaps the most frightening consequence of the breakdown of law and order has been the upsurge of violent carjackings. Widespread use of anti-theft devices has made it more difficult for criminals to steal parked cars. At the same time, the breakdown of the judicial system has made punishment for auto theft so rare that more than 300 cars are stolen for each auto theft that results in a prison sentence. As Morgan O. Reynolds reports, "Someone considering an auto theft can expect to spend only 4.2 days in prison." Criminals have taken by the thousands to stealing cars at gunpoint with the drivers inside. Victims are assaulted while stopped at traffic lights, run off the road, or even followed home and attacked when they leave their cars. In one widely reported case, a young mother driving her baby to daycare was intercepted by armed bandits in broad daylight, thrown out the passenger door, and dragged two miles to her death. Her child was thrown out the window.

> "What a vast difference there is between the barbarism that precedes culture and the barbarism that follows it."
>
> —FRIEDRICH HEBBEL

When barbarians sacked Rome in the fifth century they came from without. America's barbarians are home grown. It is difficult to imagine a system of accounting that would accurately gauge the damage they do. Billions must be lost just because growing numbers of people are frightened to leave their homes. Stand on a street corner in downtown Detroit at eight o'clock in the evening—if you dare. You will find it all but deserted. Crime and fear of crime are choking the life from once great cities, jeopardizing much that is vital to commerce and culture.

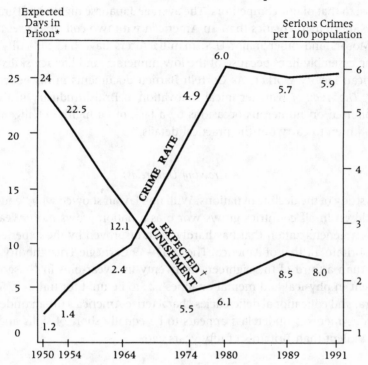

Punishment Down; Crime Up

* Median prison sentence for all serious crimes, weighted by probabilities of arrest, prosecution, conviction and imprisonment.
† Figures for expected punishment for 1991 not available.

Source: Updated from Morgan O. Reynolds, "Crime Pays, But So Does Imprisonment," National Center for Policy Analysis, NCPA Policy Report No. 149, March 1990, Appendix A, Table A-1.

Technically Deficient Workers

Throughout recorded human history, the ebb and flow of the love of achievement—and the resentment against its success—have been major forces behind the rise and fall of civilizations. While a civilization is in ascendance (which is to say, when the morality of achievement has the upper hand), people tend to derive their cultural and social ideals from the class above them. . . . But if and when resentment morality gains the upper hand, civilization enters a slow decline. . . . lower class values begin to spread upward.

—ROBERT SHEAFFER,
Resentment Against Achievement

Like Britain's half a century ago, America's technical education is deficient relative to that of our competitors. The average Japanese high school graduate knows more mathematics than an American with two college degrees. General Motors and other major U.S. manufacturers have had difficulty automating assembly lines because of the low numeracy and literacy skills of the American factory worker. As Correlli Barnett documents in his penetrating study, *The Audit of War*, technical innovation in British industry in the past was aborted on numerous occasions by a lack of "a highly intelligent class of workmen to carry out the practical details."

A Growing Underclass

In his study of the decline of nations, William Playfair showed why "education of children in all countries grows worse as a nation grows more wealthy." This is a generalization that has hardly been disproven by the experience of Great Britain, or that of America. The 1937–39 Carnegie Trust inquiry found more than a third of the eighteen- to twenty-five-year-olds in Glasgow "so deficient in physical and mental qualities" as to be unfit for training. Similar cultural and educational deficiencies characterize America's urban underclass. Indeed, America's underclass appears to be equally short of skills and even more violent than Britain's of fifty years ago.

An Engineering Gap

In the past, American engineering was preeminent in the world. Americans invented standardized parts and mass production. Now American engineering shows some of the same debilities that characterized British engineering during the twilight of the empire. According to a McKinsey study, America is now suffering from a widening "engineering gap." In relative terms, America has 15 percent fewer engineers than Japan. And unlike the ingenious Yankees of the past, who organized designs to fit production, current American engineers sometimes seem to be oblivious to the commercial consequences of their designs. They often redesign new parts when standardized parts would do, and they tend to be extravagant with materials. The McKinsey comparison showed that car doors produced by an American automaker cost twice as much to make as those in Japan. Most of the difference was attributed to engineering weaknesses. As reported in the *Economist*, "the doors were stamped out in such a way that half the sheet metal was wasted."

Comparisons on the broader measures of practical expertise are more doleful. On a per capita basis, western Germany has more than twice as many scientists and engineers as the United States. France and Italy have 50 percent more. Canada has almost five times as many. And the United States has barely a sixth as many scientists and engineers as Japan.

Procurement Failures

We are frequently led into error by mistaking money for riches; we think that a people cannot be impoverished by a waste of Money that is spent among themselves.

—ADAM FERGUSON,
Of the Decline of Nations, 1767

A key measure of engineering competence is the big-product development program of which military procurement provides a prime example. During World War II, at a time when American military procurement was operating with extraordinary efficiency, British procurement was having its problems. Consider the Convenanter tank, of which nineteen hundred were built. The design flaws and defects were, according to Correlli Barnett, "so numerous and so fundamental" that it had to be "redesigned and remade in most of its parts." Even so, the tank was so deficient that it never saw action in a battle.

Today, American military procurement has caught the British disease of old. Many major weapons systems developed in the United States within the past two decades—such as the C-5 transport plane, the B-1 bomber, and the Navy's attempt at producing a new minesweeper—have been plagued by design flaws, production delays, and exorbitant cost overruns. Total cost estimates for procurement of twenty-five major weapons systems launched between 1971 and 1978 had increased by 223 percent by 1981.

The quality of many American products has tended to suffer as work has grown more sloppy. A study at the Harvard Business School reported that products from American assembly lines turned up with seventy defects, on average, for every one in Japan.

Disregard for Cold Financial Facts

The median net financial assets of Americans earning from $40,000–$50,000 a year, including cash, savings accounts, stocks and bonds are $1,200.

—HON. ROGER PORTER,
White House Advisor on Domestic
Policy, 1989

Of course, if one were to ask American political leaders whether the nation is declining economically, the suggestion would be indignantly dismissed.

Their complacency would be buttressed by some establishment historians and economists. Joseph S. Nye, Jr., for example, argues that the U.S. percentage of the global economy in the late eighties was actually higher than it was in 1938. That is reassuring, to be sure, but it does not address the main facts of the case. Neither does Nye's observation that the U.S. productivity advantage in 1945 was greater than Britain's was at its height. Nye makes much of the fact that U.S. defense spending had declined from about 10 percent of GNP in the 1950s to about 6 percent. He contrasts the United States to seventeenth-century France and Spain, which devoted three-quarters of total government spending to the military. The United States, therefore, was not engaged in imperial overreach, because it spent just 27 percent of its federal budget on defense. By this logic, France and Spain would have been in better financial condition in the seventeenth century if, in addition to their military budgets, they had increased social spending and created sweeping entitlement programs.

Professor Charles Hulten argues that the appearance of a decline in the real pace of growth is in some respects a statistical artifact. Massage the trend line and the drop in growth after 1973 does not look so alarming. Hulten writes, "What one thinks about lagging growth, therefore, is a matter of which figure one finds most persuasive." Hulten suggests that the decline in productivity could be due to "the difficulty of measuring service-sector output accurately in the nonfarm-nonmanufacturing industries." The appearance of decline could be caused by "a measurement bias." It is always true, of course, that statistics are disputable. But the surest evidence that something is amiss in American growth rates is the meager improvement in living standards. By 1990, real weekly earnings in nonagricultural industries had fallen back to 1961 levels. And median real family income of American families had retreated back to 1973 levels. And those figures are calculated on a pretax basis. The *Economist* concludes: "Had the economy and living standards grown after 1973 at the same pace as before, real incomes would today be 50 percent higher than they are."

Those who deny that the American economy is following the path to decline that Britain and other rich nations followed generally ignore the cultural and political evidence. And they take a complacent view of the issue of relative decline. They point out that America is rich, and therefore continued economic progress doesn't matter so much anyway. As one academic advocate of higher taxes put it, "For a country as rich as America is, getting richer faster is not a very important goal."

There is hardly any national sense of urgency to tackle the tough questions that must be faced in order for America to renew itself. The popular press is full of arguments that deficits do not matter—as if debt could indefinitely continue to compound faster than income. It is the economics of euphoria. In America today, as in Britain half a century ago, there is an almost giddy sense of liberation from the straitjacket of financial solvency.

Health Care as a Right

Americans now believe that the ability to pay should not bar people from having whatever they need. Britain took its major leap into welfare socialism when the treasury was empty. So now in America, as forecast in the first edition of this book, popular opinion has moved unmistakably to the view that health care at public expense is a right.

This was an easy forecast to make. The multiplication of health care costs is both cause and consequence of America growing poorer. As fewer Americans have been able to earn their livelihoods by producing tradeable goods, which are subject to sharp competition in more or less saturated markets, the economy has had a hard time moving forward. The major area of growth has been the service sector, particularly health care, where costs cannot be contained by direct foreign competition and where markets cannot be saturated because death is the ultimate sentence of our maker. Unhappily, this implies that there is always a demand for more health care, especially where those who receive the added treatments do not have to pay for them with their own money.

Rapid cost escalation in uncompetitive health services has helped disguise the weakness of the economy while making it poorer. For example, from March 1991 through October 1992 health care jobs in the United States rose by 430,000, while total payroll employment of all kinds was up by just 65,000. In other words, if health care costs had not been expanding rapidly, net employment in the U.S. economy would have fallen by 365,000 jobs over that period.

This shows up in the GDP accounts as "growth," but it is actually a measure of mounting inefficiency. It has never been plausible that Americans, as a whole, could become more wealthy simply by getting sick and paying one another ever more inflated sums for care. Yet in the early 1990s, the burden of medical cost appeared in the backwards mirror of statistics as a measure of wealth. Americans appeared to be richer because they paid more for health care that others bought for less. Dr. Henry Heimlich, of Heimlich Maneuver fame, reports that his experimental cancer therapy costs $300,000 a week to administer in the United States, $15,000 a week in Mexico, and just $2,000 a week in China. Same therapy. Same technology. It just costs from 20 to

150 times more in the United States. By embedding and multiplying costs without competition, the health sector has continued to "grow" in an accounting sense. But it is like the abnormal growth of a cancerous cell, consuming more resources without contributing a commensurate improvement in well-being. Indeed, the explosion in costs has not even significantly bettered statistical measures of health. Greek men have longer life expectancies than Americans, with about one tenth the outlay for medical care.

At the absurd rate American health care costs compounded in recent years, they were on course to absorb the entire U.S. economy in the next century. This will never happen, of course. Bankruptcy will interrupt long before unproductive health care costs turn the whole U.S. economy into a coast-to-coast sanitarium. By 1992, consumption of health care already accounted for 14.6 percent of nominal disposable income—up from 9 percent in 1980. Americans spend more than three times as much as Britain, per capita, on doctors, hospitals, and other medical services.

With health care bankrupting many individuals, while making small and even large businesses less competitive with foreign companies that operate without such hideous costs, it was all but inevitable that a cry would rise up for adoption of a latter-day version of the National Health Service. People going broke always wish for someone else to pay the bills. It is a marker on the road to bankruptcy. As in so many other respects, history repeats itself.

"History as Bunk"

Of the many possible views of history, the most common in America today is that it has nothing useful to tell us. The inventor of the assembly line, Henry Ford, said that "History is bunk." That was an outrageous statement seventy years ago. Today, almost everyone seems to agree. This is particularly evident among young people. Surveys of students suggest that they have little or no grasp of the past. They cannot say in what half century the Civil War was fought, much less recognize more subtle patterns in history. What Madonna said about her latest boyfriend or girlfriend is much better known than what Winston Churchill said during World War II. Madonna has had far more press than Churchill, who is a largely unknown figure for those who came of age in the past two decades.

When world historic figures are forgotten a generation after their death, it is a clear hint that popular culture has discounted history almost to the vanishing point. It is also a warning that even emphatic evidence that history is repeating itself will not be heeded because it will pass unnoticed. This has been the case in America during the early 1990s. News on the economy has been a full color replay of black-and-white newsreels from 1930. But few recognized Herbert Hoover's words in the mouth of George Bush, because few knew or remembered what Hoover said.

The detachment from the past is so complete in the United States that even encouraging comparisons with the last depression pass unnoticed. To be sure, there have been a few hopes expressed that President Clinton will engineer a legislative whirlwind equivalent to the first "100 days" of the New Deal. But this talk remains only half coherent because it implies the need for a remedy to depression without first accepting that there is a depression, or analyzing how its progress today compares to the depression of the 1930s.

Is Rome the Last Place to Be Sacked?

Because America has clearly been following in Britain's footsteps, a case could be made that America is due to have a milder depression in the 1990s than many other leading countries. A characteristic that America clearly shares with the Britain of the 1930s is that America has also ceased to act like a creditor. It now acts like a debtor. The United States of the 1990s, like Britain after 1931, has shown little interest in preserving the value of its currency. Indeed, during the Bush Administration, Treasury Secretary Nicholas Brady took every opportunity to express his hope that the dollar would fall in value against the currencies of other leading countries. The administration backed that ambition with an eagerness to slash interest rates—precisely the policy that a debtor would prefer.

If history were to repeat itself literally, the depth of America's depression in the 1990s would be comparatively shallow. As of the autumn of 1992, a strong case could have been made to support this. Just as Britain suffered a very mild depression in the 1930s, when it was the fading power, the depression in North America so far has been far less traumatic than it might have been, in both cases because of aggressive and early interest rate cuts.

We continue to expect that a deeper downturn lies ahead. But it is at least possible that the duration of America's slump in the 1990s will match that of Britain in the 1930s, which was just two and a half years. British growth resumed by the last half of 1932, and output for the entire year was actually up, although by an almost invisible 0.2 percent. It then rose by 4.2 percent in 1933, and averaged over 5 percent a year through 1936.

In spite of its many structural problems, the British economy significantly outperformed the U.S. economy during the 1930s. In fact, British growth was so much stronger that taking the 1920s and the 1930s together, British growth matched U.S. growth of 40 percent. In other words, while the fading power lagged behind during the disinflationary financial boom decade of the 1920s, it recovered all of the lag during the decade of outright deflation in the 1930s.

If the same pattern were to repeat itself today, and industrial production in Japan were taken as the measure of comparison, then the drop in U.S. output would be almost at an end, and we could expect cumulative growth of about 20 percent over the rest of the decade—a far better performance than the 0 percent growth experienced in America during the 1930s.

There are other reasons to suggest that the depression in the United States will be less severe than that in Japan:

1. There has been less speculative excess in the United States today as compared to Japan, just as there was less of a boom in Britain during the twenties than in the United States.

2. There is a high likelihood that the United States will soon abandon its effort to be the policeman of the globe, just as Britain did in the 1930s. As a result, the world will go unpoliced—as it did then. Wars, revolutions, and chaos will overtake other places, leaving extensive Japanese overseas investments and trade arrangements unprotected. Because of language and cost barriers, Japan is unlikely to become as broad a haven for fleeing capital as stable nations in Europe, particularly Switzerland. As the dust settles, the U.S. economy will gain from budget savings that would otherwise have gone to provide protection for others.

3. An upsurge in protectionism by the United States will mean that America, like Britain before it, will no longer be the buyer of last resort in the world economy. As trade barriers go up, they will have a less negative impact upon the United States with its huge domestic market than upon Japan and the smaller European and Asian export economies (not to mention Third World primary product producers).

The 1930s were the only decade in this century when the British economy strikingly outperformed the American economy. By some measures, Great Britain grew more rapidly during the 1930s than in any other decade since the 1850s. As depression was settling over America, John Maynard Keynes, who was the economic philosopher of Britain's withdrawal as the world leader, boasted: "England is really richer than she has ever been before; . . . succeeding in bearing a burden of taxation, debts and standard of living which is at least twice as great as that of any other country."

Change the name, and Keynes's pronouncement may well seem to apply to America in the 1990s. As the fading empire turning in upon itself, there is at least a possibility that the United States may enjoy a decade of relatively stronger performance than Japan. The final collapse of the postwar system may have a less adverse impact upon some American assets, and perhaps even lead to a short-term revival of the dollar. The pound revived in the 1930s. The dollar might revive temporarily during a short squeeze on dollar debtors. Nonetheless, by the end of the 1990s, we expect the dollar to be significantly lower against the yen. The eventual collapse of the dollar to the fifty-yen level, which we predicted in *Blood in the Streets*, will probably await the emergence of full-blown Japanese leadership. The pound took its steepest dive after the United States had emerged as a hegemonic power at the end of World War II. But the relative financial status of the United States in 1990 was far worse than that of Great Britain in 1930—a factor that may accelerate the dollar's fall.

Another factor that is far worse in the United States today than in Britain sixty years ago is the potential for social unrest. As we explore in later chapters, the United States is far more ethnically divided and violence-prone than Britain ever was.

These factors did not stand in the way of a stronger performance on Wall Street than on Japanese exchanges during the first stage of depression in 1991 and 1992. As we write, the S&P 500 has reached a new closing high. This is what you would expect by extrapolating from the 1930s. By contrast, the Japanese markets are well off their highs, and may take decades to recover to their predepression peaks. In the 1930s, share prices in the London market

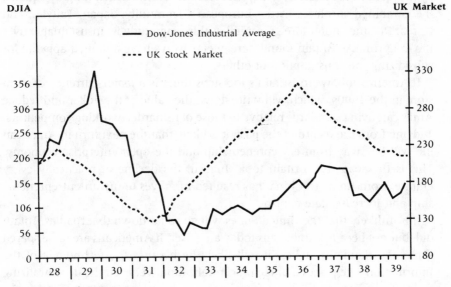

The British Stock Market vs. the Dow-Jones Industrial Average

SOURCE: Strategic Investment

recovered considerably above their 1929 highs, whereas American stock prices did not match their 1929 highs until 1954. A repetition of the pattern along the same magnitudes would yield an apparently preposterous high of about 4750 on the Dow. But this requires only a 50 percent increase in Dow stock earnings over 1990 levels if price/earnings ratios are held constant.

We doubt that will happen. But it could. It may be that as a fading power, America is due for a milder depression than we expect. If the United States is following in the United Kingdom's footsteps, as it seems to be, then not every step is necessarily a treacherous one. The question is really whether history is going to repeat itself almost literally, or whether, as we suspect, many of the changes in relative position between America of the 1990s and Britain of the 1930s are not changes for the worse.

What Comes Next?

The history of three thousand years, and of nations that have risen to wealth and power, in a great variety of situations, all terminating with a considerable degree of similarity, discovers the great outline of causes that . . . ruin states and empires.

—WILLIAM PLAYFAIR

It would be wrong to overdraw the parallels, but it would be equally wrong to ignore them. The widely accepted view that the decline of America's economic fortunes has been reversed during the Reagan years is not supported by the facts. In the late 1980s, the U.S. current account deficit roughly equaled the combined surpluses of the European Community, Japan, Taiwan, and Korea. Reliance upon foreign capital at this magnitude is unsustainable over the long run. As Britain found, foreigners always have a limited appetite for subsidizing the consumption of others.

If America follows in Britain's footsteps there is a major currency crisis in store in the 1990s, which will write down the value of the dollar and reduce American living standards relative to those of its harder-working competitors. Judging from the record of the past, it is likely that the next turn in American life will be away from entrepreneurship and the open enterprise economy. This is the road that Britain took. Indeed, the decline of practically every empire, from Rome to China, has resulted in moves to thwart entrepreneurship and increase state control.

It is unlikely that the United States will go so far down that road as Britain did, but not because Americans today are wiser. If Americans are to be spared some of Britain's mistakes, it will likely be because the technology of the Information Age places a brake on centralization. yet even the decentralizing technology that may save us from some of the worst features of industrial socialism is not an unmixed blessing. As we pointed out in *Blood in the Streets*, the same technology that is decentralizing enterprise is also decentralizing the control of violence. This puts real power in the hands of criminals, terrorists, and drug lords. Nowhere is this trend more apparent than in Washington, D.C., where the murder rate in 1990 of eighty per one hundred thousand was almost twice as high as the murder rate in Dodge City in 1871, when there was essentially no police or justice system at all. At that rate, the odds of being murdered over a lifetime in Washington are about one in sixteen. Among children under twelve, murder is now the leading cause of death. The ghettos of Glasgow were never that wicked.

> As in a hall, in which there has been a sumptuous banquet, we perceive the fragments of a feast now become a prey to beggars and banditti; if, in some instances, the spectacle is less wretched and disgusting; it is, because the banquet is not entirely over, and the guests have not yet all risen from the table.
>
> —WILLIAM PLAYFAIR

The question of whether America is in decline has been widely debated. Many have formed the understandable impression that the collapse of Communism and victory in the Cold War mean a triumphant future for America. According to Samuel Huntington and others, America's economy has already been renewed. We hope for all the obvious reasons that this cheery view is correct. But we doubt it. We see too many parallels between the United States of 1990 and Great Britain of fifty years earlier to believe that America has painlessly crossed the threshold from decline to renewal in a few short years. Victory in the Cold War may expose America to the same debilities from economic competition that Great Britain faced after victory in World War II.

In the new world of economic competition and Third World conflicts, it will be less necessary for America's allies in Europe and Japan to continue supporting the dollar or financing the deficits. The result to be expected is a crisis sometime early in the 1990s, a crisis of transition.

Imperial overreach and economic decline are not superficial problems that can be whisked away by a change in marginal tax rates. They involve incentives and relationships deeply imbedded in the political and economic system. Their cure will be measured in terms of generations.

CHAPTER FOUR

JAPAN FOLLOWS IN AMERICA'S FOOTSTEPS

I am inclined to think that our Relations with Japan are going through the usual and unavoidable stages of the Intercourse of strong and Civilised nations with weaker and less civilised ones.

—LORD PALMERSTON,
justifying the destruction of the port
of Kagoshima by the Royal Navy,
1864

The U.S. 7th fleet is chasing a renegade Japanese nuclear submarine through the Straits of Moluccas in the Western Pacific when suddenly the high-tech sub decides to show the Americans that bigger is not always better. In maneuvers of unsurpassed skill, it singlehandedly cripples the six U.S. submarines. Captain Umieda, its commander, declares as his goal "a war for independence from U.S. domination."

"Japan hasn't changed a bit since Pearl Harbor," snarls the commander of the defeated American fleet.

Sound far-fetched? It's the plot of a comic book called "Silent Fleet" read today by a quarter million young Japanese.

—ALAN MURRAY and
URBAN C. LEHNER, 1990

THE DECLINE of one empire is often the rise of another. As American economic supremacy has given way to relentless international competition, especially Japanese competition, the stage has been set for another perilous transition of world power. Such transitions are rare in modern history. There has been only one in the last two centuries. Not surprisingly, therefore, the lessons of the decline of empire have been easy to neglect or misunderstand. In particular, it would be easy to assume that the transition period is one of growing advantage for the rising power. Historically and logically, this is untrue. In the first instance, the declining power itself is likely to be the beneficiary of its own weakness, while other nations, poor or rich, suffer more in the chaos and depression that accompany a breakdown of the world system. It may be only when the new empire finally emerges to predominance, after a trauma of transition that may be decades long, that the old empire settles into its debility.

JAPAN—THE NEXT HEGEMONIC POWER?

If there is to be a new supreme power in the world, it is likely to be Japan. To some, and perhaps to some Japanese, this conclusion might have seemed surprising even a few years ago. Now it no longer does. During the Cold War, Japan was the only industrial nation pledged to pacificism by its constitution. It was only potentially any kind of military power at all. Yet immediately the Cold War ended, the Japanese parliament authorized the dispatch of Japanese troops abroad on peace-keeping missions. Though the debate was rancorous, a major part of the internal opposition was motivated by fear that Japan would indeed resume wielding the military power it had abandoned after World War II.

As 1992 ended, there was a growing awareness in Japan that economic prowess alone would not afford Japan the weight in world affairs that would be exercised by a nation with military might. Prof. Fuji Kamiya spoke for many Japanese when he interpreted the cancellation of Russian President Boris Yeltsin's scheduled visit to Tokyo in September 1992 as a gesture of "contempt." According to Kamiya, "the Russians have little regard for a country like Japan, economic superpower or not. Russians respect military muscle, and they know very well that Japan is puny."

Before the end of the decade, and perhaps sooner, Japan will once again be a military power. And it is likely to be a nuclear power. Hints to that effect accumulate. Foremost on the list is a major new Japanese program to import plutonium from France and Britain. The schedule of imports now planned would be enough to give Japan the world's largest stockpile of plutonium— up to 100 tonnes. Eight kilograms of high-grade plutonium are sufficient to make a nuclear bomb. The developments of an independent Japanese nuclear force would confirm Japan's emergence from American predominance, and further increase frictions between the two countries.

The Twilight of the Postwar World

Only ten or fifteen years ago, if you had asked anyone which nation was likely to replace the United States at the top of the world order, he probably would have answered the Soviet Union. Yet events of the early 1990s suggest that, if the world is again to be organized under the predominance of any nation, it is more likely to be Japan, possibly Germany, and certainly not the remnants of Soviet Russia that will next be supreme in world affairs. Not only did Japan surpass the United States in total wealth in 1987, it has also eclipsed the faltering Soviet economy in every measure except the output of weapons and the marshaling of men under arms. While the United States and Russia have exhausted one another, consuming talent and resources in a costly arms race, Japan has emerged as the world's foremost industrial and trading power. It is Japanese rather than German competition that roils the constituents who write to American congressmen.

America today is like a man wearing a coat cut to his figure as it was decades ago. The fit is uncomfortable and growing more so. The consensus of American politics and the alliance of the industrial democracies are vulnerable to rapid change. They have rested upon arrangements forged in the late forties, when America was protecting the world from Russia. Now Communism has collapsed. Russia is bankrupt. And America is no longer rich enough to play its established role as world policeman. A major subtext in the story of the American move into the Persian Gulf to counter Saddam Hussein's invasion of Kuwait was the question of who would pay the bill. The hat was passed from country to country, amid complaints that Japan was shirking its fair share of the costs.

This was foreshadowed in the spring of 1987 by President Ronald Reagan. In the twilight of his term and under fire from Congress on other scores, Reagan was firmly supported in his decision to make European nuclear peace with the Soviet Union, and to start a trade war with Japan. Historians could look back someday at these events as a turning point in world relations.

These are, after all, two of the most explosive problems that statesmen have had to deal with in modern times. The balance between Russia and Germany has unsettled Europe throughout this century, and was a contributing cause to both world wars. The need of Japan for open markets, both to import and export, was the motivation of the Japanese imperialism that led to Pearl Harbor in 1941.

Yet events of the early 1990s confirmed President Reagan's sense that Japanese industrial competition was indeed more of a threat than Russian military competition. This was highlighted in December 1991, when the Soviet Union ceased to exist, and President George Bush chose that historic moment for a pathetic trade expedition to Tokyo, in which he pleaded with the Japanese authorities to require Japanese consumers to buy more American automobiles and other products. There could scarcely have been a stronger symbolic confirmation that the world had indeed changed. In a way the change had been foreshadowed five years earlier. President Reagan's intellect was often ridiculed, but his intution never should be: he came from a profession of imagination rather than reason. In 1987, he seemed to sense that the timing was right for a great switch of roles. He determined to make peace with the Soviet empire, and enter into combat with his too successful Asian allies.

History Points to Japan

The emergence of Japan as the nation most likely to succeed America as the guardian of the world economy is also plausible for historical reasons. Japan is America's ally. Every modern transition of world supremacy has involved an ally or former colony of the previous hegemonic power. Holland was a breakaway possession of Spain. England was an ally of the Netherlands, and from 1689 through 1702 both states shared the same sovereign, the Dutch-born William III. The United States was a former colony and intimate ally of Britain. Never has a principal challenger to power such as France, Germany, or Russia ultimately succeeded. Not only were the challengers hobbled by the formidable opposition of the predominant power, they were also subject to the same economic stress and burdens of high cost that exhausted the Spanish, Dutch, and British empires, and are now bankrupting America.

Japan Inherits a Daunting Task

As America sheds its role as the world's policeman, much of the danger and vulnerability will lie not within America's borders but elsewhere. Nowhere will the consequences be felt more strongly than in Japan. With Germany preoccupied by reunification and the integration of Europe, Japan is the heir apparent. Japan is the nation that will face the unhappy choice between bearing the lion's share of the costs of maintaining the world economy or bearing the lion's share of the losses when the world economy falters. As trying as a breakdown of the world trading system will be for the United States, history suggests that the challenge will be even more trying for the world's rising power, Japan.

The trend of microtechnology makes it increasingly difficult for any nation to police a disordered world. The declining scale of effective weaponry and the shift in advantage from the offense to the defense are trends that point to the disintegration of empires and nations. For Japan to overcome these trends in the wake of American withdrawal will be a far more difficult and costly challenge than that which faced America after the effective end of the British Empire.

As we argued in *Blood in the Streets*, the transition between British and American predominance from 1914 to 1945 shook the world no less than a violent earthquake. The political, monetary, and military foundations upon which markets operated were severely tested. In more than one instance, they gave way, and as they did, prosperity—like a weakened building— tumbled into the chasm. The result was disorder: a world unpoliced, in which property rights and free trade were abridged or abolished in many places, and millions perished in brutal wars.

Can the World Be Organized Cooperatively?

In 1945, the emergence of a new international order, under American lead- ership, was allegedly a cooperative effort. And in some nontrivial ways, true cooperation between the leading Western powers was involved. It would be understandable for many in Japan and elsewhere to nourish the hope that cooperation can yet emerge as the alternative to either a costly breakdown in the world system or an even more costly effort of Japanese reconstruction. We share that hope, but doubt that it will be realized. Cooperation has always been a suboptimal solution for the very reason that government exists in the first place. Groups and nations are prey to similar relational incentives. Just as individuals are unlikely to voluntarily supply mechanisms to secure prop- erty rights, or maintain order in the absence of government, so groups of governments will do too little to secure property rights internationally, main- tain access to markets, and achieve the common good of world monetary stability.

The united world condemnation of Saddam Hussein after the invasion of Kuwait gave rise to new optimism about the effectiveness of the United Nations. Experts rushed to suggest that the promise of the UN as an effective peace-keeping agency might finally be realized half a century after it was conceived. This is possible but unlikely. The success of cooperative institu- tions, like NATO or the United Nations, is inevitably limited by the logic of group incentives. These point to an irresistible tendency for "the 'exploita- tion' of the great by the small." Except under the press of a life-and-death emergency, weaker and poorer countries with less to lose will persistently tend to undercontribute to the provision of any common good sought by the alliance.

The experience since World War II, during which cooperative arrangements have been given their fullest test ever, strongly supports this conclusion. American contributions to NATO, the United Nations, the International Monetary Fund, and especially the defense of the Pacific rim have been disproportionately large in every case. Even as America has visibly staggered under a growing military burden, other nations, including Japan, have been slow to shoulder a larger share.

It may be that the press of greater difficulties in the years to come will sharpen the incentives to cooperate. It is possible that some future plan organized under Japanese leadership will prove to be something other than a disguised Japanese hegemony, organized largely at Japanese cost. But we doubt it. If the argument of this book is right, there is a secular trend toward disorder that will cause economic hardship in many countries. Typically, economic downturns sharpen the demands of selfish, local interests and reduce international cooperation. Indeed, this is one of the chief reasons that slow growth periods are times of protectionism and trade war. Cooperation, by itself, is unlikely to answer the need for international order between governments when it is the very lack of cooperation between individuals that accounts for the existence of governments in the first place.

Cooperation and the "Jacquerie"

The message of history is that cooperation declines along with economies. As world growth prospects diminish, ethnic solidarity and nationalism increase. Horizons narrow. Groups tend to hoard political advantages and seek regulations that reserve for themselves as much as possible of the smaller pie. As growth is less robust or nonexistent, the competition for scarce jobs and diminished markets grows nastier. Those who are not economically secure fear change that entails any adjustment or sacrifice for them, quite apart from whether that change might make the world better off. Even leaders who personally understand the importance of cooperation are often afraid to compromise selfish local interests.

Witness the reluctance of French authorities to expose inefficient and highly subsidized soybean farmers to international competition, an issue that threatened to torpedo world trade talks throughout the early 1990s. While it appeared as we wrote in late November 1992 that the French would ultimately be overriden by their European partners, a solution, if it proved to be a solution, emerged only after headline threats of a 1930s-style trade war precipitated a crisis. The episode was hardly the clear vindication of international cooperation that one might wish.

Indeed, the contentious nature of world trade talks in the early nineties points to a future of increasing difficulty. Rather than demonstrating the ease

with which cooperative solutions to common problems can be found, it con-
firms the difficulty of sacrificing the special interests of local constituencies
for the broader good. Even where agreements were reached, they were settled
on terms far removed from the ideal of free trade. What was emerging from
the 1980s onward was a regime of managed trade, where market access was
negotiated on a basis that accommodated the vested interests of powerful
local producers. The points of breakdown came where the claims of the more
stubborn of the vested interests clashed. Japanese rice farmers, for example,
heavily subsidized and inefficient, were bitterly opposed to competition from
other Asian and American producers. American rice farmers welcomed free
trade. So did American soybean farmers. But American sugar farmers, themselves inefficient and heavily subsidized, took the same attitude toward outside
competition as Japanese rice farmers, or French oilseed producers. The ins
and outs of this obstinacy were determined mainly by the comparative productivity and political muscle of the various local groups.

Megapolitics of Tradewar

Rural interests in France, like their Japanese counterparts, enjoy power be-
yond their proportions because of unequal representation in the National
Assembly. Yet the reason that French leaders blocked an agreement was not
merely fear of political punishment. Their thinking was more megapolitical.
They feared social unrest, perhaps even bodily harm. At the height of the
French farmers' violent protest against revision of the European Community's
Common Agricultural Policy in 1991, government ministers were prohibited
from leaving Paris "because they faced personal danger from rampaging farmers." Likewise, European Community President Jacques Delors justified his
reluctance to compromise the farm subsidy question as follows: "We can't
let prices fall so brutally or let one-third of our farmland become desert. There
are already threats to public order from the farmers in two or three European
countries."

The agreement that appeared to have defused the trade war commits the
European Community to sharply reducing the acreage farmers in Europe may
employ for planting oilseed crops. Ten percent of European farm land is to
be set aside permanently, according to the accord. Another provision prohibits
EC farmers from exporting subsidized beef to Asia.

Even if unrest does not result in 1993, the hope for maintaining social
peace is a delicate one, not only in Western Europe but elsewhere as well.
M. Delors will not be the only leader to fear a "Jacquerie," or peasants'

rampage, in which economic losers revolt against falling prices by burning down the chateaux, as French peasants, or *les jacques*, did in the fourteenth century. The dangers will be especially pronounced in Eastern Europe, because the Eastern Europeans lack the leverage that Washington exerted in GATT world trade talks. In large measure, this is because they lack the purchasing power to buy appreciable quantities of foreign goods. They therefore lack a significant lobby in the form of exporters in the capitals of other countries who can counter growing pressures for protectionist restriction of low-cost imports.

In spite of pious talk welcoming Eastern European nations into the capitalist system, high-cost producers in Western Europe have slammed the door on competition from Eastern Europe. Although the EC is the logical outlet for trade for the nations just emerging from Communism, the few products produced in Eastern Europe that might be competitive in Western markets, such as steel and farm produce, have been stopped at the border. In fact, just as the United States and Western Europe appeared to pull back from the brink of trade war, steel companies in the EC were celebrating victory in an eighteen-month campaign to bar imports of seamless steel tubing from former Communist countries on grounds they were being "dumped."

Deflation Closes Borders

It is difficult to keep borders open in times of deflation. Existing trade agreements permit imposition of punitive tariffs and antidumping duties to protect domestic industries from competition by goods that foreign producers sell for less than the cost of production. During a boom or an inflationary period, antidumping provisions are relatively benign. But in a deep recession or depression, where demand is falling and goods can only be sold at liquidation prices, as was the case for Eastern European steelmakers, treaty provisions made to prohibit dumping can be invoked to close borders and cramp trade.

The world came to the brink of open trade war in the autumn of 1992, when the degree of economic distress in the three leading trading areas— Western Europe, North America, and the Asian rim—was minimal compared to what might be expected if depression once again reached the depths experienced in the 1930s. In such an environment, it would take almost superhuman negotiating ability, probably lubricated with lots of cash, to keep borders open. This is a particularly worrisome note for the Japanese. As a nation with a huge trade surplus, Japan will suffer more than others if cooperative efforts fail to maintain open world markets. Trade war would merely add another dimension to an already deteriorating situation in Tokyo.

Japan and the United Nations

The likelihood of cooperation working to resolve world economic challenges is not as great as many hope. It is further diminished by the anachronistic organization of the United Nations. Neither Germany nor Japan, the two leading creditor powers of the 1990s, has a permanent seat on the United Nations Security Council. The UN is an organization that reflects the Allied victory in World War II. Germany and Japan are the losers of World War II. Even more ominously, the fact that the leading creditor is distanced from the councils of power in the major international organ of cooperation has a precedent in the last depression. At that time, the United States was the leading creditor, and was not a member of the League of Nations, a factor that may have contributed to the breakdown of international cooperation in dealing with the depression.

THE SECULAR TREND TOWARD DISORDER

The higher absolute levels of prosperity achieved during the decades of Pax Americana, especially in the stable industrial democracies, mask the long-term megapolitical trend toward disorder. For all America's might and wealth at the close of World War II, it was never strong enough to restore a world system as liberal and open as that which existed before 1914. Even during the peak years of American hegemony, a significant fraction of the world's peoples lived in closed Marxist systems, where international property rights were recognized minimally or not at all. In other areas of every continent, the treatment of property rights was far from the ideal of universal protection for private investment that was the mainstay of international law before 1914. Even at the height of its power in the wake of war, America was too weak to enforce such a standard. The generally reduced growth of financial assets relative to tangible assets measures like a seismograph the growing instability in the world.

Prior to this century, economic growth was reflected in a higher ratio of financial to tangible assets. Financial assets essentially reflect trust, the trust that promises to pay will be honored. This trust must decay when property becomes less secure and contracts more violable. During this century, it has improved only in those countries that were backward when the twentieth century opened. They have tended to see a growth in financial assets from very low levels because of modernization. This was true in India, South Africa, Mexico, Yugoslavia, and even Italy. But it has not generally been true of countries that were in the first tier of advanced economies before World

War I. Belgium, Denmark, France, Norway, Sweden, the United States, and especially Great Britain have seen their financial interrelations ratios tumble since World War II. Only in Switzerland, which remains a model of middle-class rectitude in a disordered world, has the financial interrelations ratio continued to grow. It was appreciably higher in the last quarter of the twentieth century than it had been early in the century.

At the turn of the twentieth century, the West Shore Railroad 4 percent bond traded to a high of 114¾, to yield 3.48 percent. The bond was not due for redemption until the year 2361. Today, no one could sell a bond set for redemption three or four centuries hence. It would be easier to peddle insurance against nuclear war. The trust that obligations will be met is shakier than it was at the turn of the century. And the trust in governments to sustain the value of money is even shakier. This is reflected in an increase in long-term interest rates during the twentieth century, which may either be a temporary blip or a reversal of the trend to lower long rates that had continued since the end of the Middle Ages. If you consider the value of financial assets in 1990 compared to what they would have been if trends in place at the beginning of this century had held intact, it is apparent that the breakdown of order in the twentieth century has cost the world tens of trillions in missing financial assets.

Reflagging and Flagging Power

Consider that in 1912, before the stability of the British Empire was ruptured, anyone who could plausibly have passed for British had protection almost anywhere on the globe. American traders took advantage of it running caravans of tea and silk from Kalgan to Urga over the plains of Outer Mongolia. They were able to protect their property at practically no cost to themselves. They merely flew the Union Jack from the lead and trailing camels. Mongolian bandits, hardened fighters as they were, had learned that violence against British merchants invited deadly punishment. A small detachment of British troops, armed with Maxim guns, could wipe out almost any number of Mongolian horsemen. Consequently, commerce and property rights were secure in 1912, even in Outer Mongolia, a region as remote then as it is today. The entire British military budget at that time was just seventy-five million pounds.

In 1990, America's military budget was about three hundred billion dollars, a huge multiple in real terms of what Britain spent seventy-five years earlier. Yet the costs of projecting power have risen so far that to show the American flag in remote areas of the globe today is to invite attack as often as to forestall it. The famous contemporary incident of American reflagging in the Persian

Gulf was possible only under the cover of a huge armada, ships that cost more to build than the entire gross national product of Iran. Even then, the Kuwaiti tankers that ran up the Stars and Stripes were attacked and several were severely damaged. And Kuwait's apparent alliance with the United States clearly counted for little in the mind of Saddam Hussein when he invaded and seized the whole country in an attempt to force up oil prices.

Costs Rising on a Geometric Curve

The technological trends that have led to the devolution of power throughout the twentieth century appear to be accelerating. As they do, the cost of policing the globe is rising on a geometric curve. The logical expectation, therefore, must be that Japan, or another country, will face far more difficult obstacles as the emerging empire of the twenty-first century than America or Britain ever did. The transition between American and Japanese hegemony may drag out longer than the thirty years it took to reorganize the world economy under American leadership. The results could be unhappy for Japan.

The period when the old power is no longer effective, yet no new power has emerged, is a time of rising borders and obstacles to trade. It is a time of economic reversal and instability, when the contradiction between the integration of world markets and the separateness of selfish political entities is most acute. Functions crucial to growth simply go undone. The old power is no longer willing or able to serve as the guardian of commerce. It is no longer rich enough to be the guarantor of money and debts or the buyer of last resort. Until some new power steps into the void, the world economy will struggle in disorder. In the words of Sir Martin Jacomb, "An unpoliced community is hell for those who inhabit it."

The Japanese Assets Collapse

The first edition of this book forecast "a collapse of the value of Japanese stocks and real estate more drastic than any that has yet occurred." It was a simple forecast based upon the assumption that the classic pattern of the credit cycle would repeat itself. We saw it unfolding in Japan even before the initial 1990 crash, which took the Nikkei Dow down by 49 percent—a greater drop than Wall Street suffered in 1929. We warned that the greatest asset boom in history would be followed by history's greatest asset bust. So far, at least, events have not altered that expectation.

Every nation that has yet emerged as a leading financial power in the modern world has ridden a roller coaster of boom and bust during the transition period. It is a wild ride that lasts for decades. First comes a property-rights shock, like the OPEC Shock of 1973, touched off by the military weakness or vulnerability of the fading power. For the better part of a decade, inflation ensues. During this period, the emerging power starts to outperform the fading power decisively. This happened for Japan in the late 1970s, when its auto and electronics industries began to accumulate massive profits in world trade.

During the early stages of the transition, asset prices in the emerging economy are capitalized at modest or even trivial levels. In the early seventies, the market value of IBM exceeded that of the whole Japanese stock market. It takes years for the buildup of liquidity to drive up investment assets to prices that are lofty by international comparison. Through the late 1970s and early 1980s, real estate and stock prices in Japan compounded rapidly. But it was only after 1985 that they began to reach levels that seemed expensive. They later become extreme.

The manic phase of the boom lasts for several years. By 1988, it was said that a single prefecture of Tokyo was worth more than all of Canada. Yet this was not the peak. Even after assets reach extreme valuations, they go on to still greater extremes. At the peak of its value, when NTT, the one-time Japanese telephone monopoly, was privatized, it was worth more than the entire German stock market. In the classic assets mania, markets outrun any rational valuation based on yield or cash return. Stocks and properties come to sell at absurd prices on the expectation that they will appreciate to still more absurd prices. And they do. They defy gravity, moving from one lofty new high to another, month after month, year after year, long enough to lure otherwise prudent people into mortgaging their gains to reinvest in the inflated assets on margin. Before the market can top, everyone who could conceivably be drawn in must have already become a buyer. And debt levels supporting the asset prices must be many times higher than any that could conceivably be serviced out of the cash flow yielded by the investments themselves.

Then comes the bust. Just as everyone has come to count on the idea that the lofty asset valuations are permanent, there is a crash. This tends to happen nine to ten years after the peak in commodity prices, and fifteen to twenty years after the initial property-rights shock that set in motion the decade of inflation. Tokyo's 1990 crash fits that pattern exactly. It is one of the strongest hints that the troubles in Japan, as well as those in the rest of the world, are not the result of a superficial inventory cycle, or recession, but those of a major world depression that is still to reach its deepest stage.

Examples

- Commodity prices peaked in London in 1711. The South Sea Bubble burst in 1720. Depression followed.
- Producer prices peaked in London in 1763. The London stock market crashed again in 1772. Depression followed.
- Commodity prices peaked in London in 1816. The London stock market crashed in 1825. Depression followed.
- Wholesale prices peaked in New York in 1864. A worldwide assets crash began in May 1873. Depression followed.
- Wholesale prices peaked in the United States in 1919. Wall Street crashed in 1929. Depression followed.
- Commodity prices peaked in Tokyo in 1980. The Tokyo stock market peaked in 1989 and crashed in 1990.

The crash is then followed by a long wind-down period, interrupted by numerous suckers' rallies, which absorb cash from optimists expecting an early recovery. Ultimately, assets are deflated by about 90 percent. As we write, the process is only about 60 percent complete. The Nikkei Dow is rotating between 16,000 and 17,000, with a prospect of a sharper bear market rally before it resumes its plunge back to late-1970s levels.

Of course, the authorities in Japan, along with many informed observers in the West, express confidence that the markets have already bottomed out and begun to recover. They share the conviction, apparently supported by several recent decades of experience prior to 1990, that Japanese markets do not function as those in the West do. Many smart people really believe that. We don't. Notwithstanding the fact that the Japanese are culturally more amenable to rigging markets, with their traditional respect for *gaman*, the virtue of bearing losses and pain without complaint, the Nikkei Dow has followed much the same course as the Dow Jones average on Wall Street followed after 1929. Indeed, the Japanese market has tumbled 10,000 points beneath where it stood when the first edition of this book was typeset.

We continue to believe that the deepest stage of depression is to come, and that Japanese markets will provide the key to determining how severe the depression will be and how quickly it will run its course.

Stock Markets and the Rise and Fall of Empires

For all that has been written about investment booms and busts over the centuries, seldom has the connection between the asset booms and the rise and fall of empires been clearly drawn. Undoubtedly, a major reason for the obscurity of the connection is that its major regularity is counterintuitive. It would be easy to guess that major busts occur in the markets of fading powers. It is certainly true that the relative performance of such markets suffers as the old power is eclipsed. But the conditions of economic decline are not suited to engender collapses of historic proportions, precisely because the symptoms of decline are ordinarily widely recognized. Imperial decline (or even the perception of imperial decline) is likely to create extraordinary buying opportunities when pessimism is overdone—provided the system survives. When the evidence of growing difficulty is on the minds of investors, it is difficult to sustain the kind of optimism that drives up prices to preposterous levels. You cannot fall off the floor.

On the other hand, the ingredient of optimism is available in abundance precisely when a new power is emerging. It is probably for this reason that many of history's epic busts have occurred in the markets of rising powers during the transition after the defeat or retreat of the old empire.

TULIPOMANIA AND THE RISE OF THE NETHERLANDS

In the seventeenth century, Holland first achieved independence of Spain, then emerged as the world's principal power a few decades later. As Amsterdam became the unchallenged financial capital of Europe, a speculative boom overflowed from the primitive Dutch stock markets around 1634 into flower marts. The focus of interest: a Turkish perennial only recently introduced into Europe—the tulip. The result was the tulipomania, a buying euphoria for tulips that has become a textbook example of a popular delusion. In fairness to the Dutch, their passion for rare flowers was merely part of a general appetite for rarities of foreign origin, such as Chinese porcelain, Turkish carpets, and Italian paintings. The latter have retained their fascination for the rich of all cultures, perhaps because they are more durable and less easily reproduced than tulips. But in the conditions of the seventeenth century, tulips were a preferred rarity for speculative trade. For one thing, the bulbs were smaller and more easily transported than porcelain or paintings. For another, they could be traded almost like coins or tokens in a futures market. In their dormant state, the bulbs presented little by way of appearance that could feed disagreements of taste. They all looked more or less like exotic onions.

During the height of tulipomania, in November 1636, single bulbs sold for prices equal to ten years' wages of the average worker. Such extreme valuations could not last long. In a pattern that continues to characterize overbought markets, the collapse was swift and terrifying. Prices fell by more than

90 percent, leaving behind a massive crazy quilt of defaulted futures contracts. Although discontented sellers appealed to courts and to the Provincial Council at the Hague, it was beyond the power of the government to reinflate a bubble that had so decisively burst.

Notice that the tulipomania was largely confined to Holland. There was no mad rush to buy bulbs in other countries. Stock jobbers in both London and Paris put tulips on sale in the stock markets in 1636, but with minor success. The boom and bust were confined to the markets of the emerging financial power.

ANOTHER ROUND OF BOOM AND BUST IN THE EIGHTEENTH CENTURY

England's Dutch king, William, died after a riding accident early in the eighteenth century. His death marked the effective end of the era of Dutch predominance. The first decades of the eighteenth century were disrupted by a costly world war of the kind that frequently erupts when new military challengers seek to rearrange the world order. In 1714, soon after the fighting ended, interest rates on high-quality debt reached almost 9 percent—their highest level since the 1570s—and a level that would not be matched or exceeded again until the 1970s. Rates then declined sharply. The result was a surge of postwar prosperity, leading to financial asset booms of historic proportions in both Britain and France, the two nations challenging to succeed Holland as the world's dominant economy.

As there were few cross-border capital flows between the two countries, the Mississippi Scheme in France and the South Sea Bubble in Britain were treated at the time as quite separate events. Yet both booms ended in spectacular crashes within months of one another in the fall of 1720. Little has been made since of the fact that they occurred simultaneously, except that they are frequently grouped together under the category of stock manias. If our argument is correct, however, it is no coincidence that the two most extreme financial booms and busts in British and French history occurred precisely as both nations competed for dominance after a major upheaval of world power.

The Mississippi Scheme

Limitations of space prevent us from considering both the Mississippi Scheme and the South Sea Bubble in the detail that they deserve. Both stories unfolded in remarkably similar fashion, with the exception that the French government went to extreme lengths in the futile attempt to prop up the faltering Mississippi issues. Even a paper money inflation of Latin American dimensions failed to halt the collapse for more than a few months. The British government, on the other hand, did little to interfere directly with the progress of the South Sea Bubble as it occurred. A reason that the British were more willing than the French to allow the market to work may have been that the British economy was a good deal stronger than the French. Although the competition for world dominance continued for almost another century, Britain's financial power ultimately allowed its armies to prevail.

Though the French people were carried to extremes of optimism about their prospects during the Mississippi Scheme, the regent who ruled France was inclined to desperate measures, partly because of his intimate knowledge of the condition of state finances. Burdened with debts incurred during the long spendthrift reign of Louis XIV, the treasury was so bare upon his death in 1715 that the Duke de St. Simon advised the regent to convene the Estates-General and "declare a national bankruptcy." Wars had been underway for fifty-one of Louis XIV's seventy-two years in power. Not only was France at the edge of fiscal bankruptcy, but French military capacity had been physically beaten during the almost constant warfare in the quarter century before 1713. France's improved standing in the world pecking order was attributable more to a rapid falloff in Dutch power than increased French vigor.

In any event, we shall examine the British boom and bust in greater detail because Britain ultimately succeeded the Netherlands as the leader of the world economy.

The South Sea Bubble

The unaccountable Frenzy in Stocks and Projects of this Year 1720 may by some be thought to have taken up too much Room in this Work: But we are persuaded that others, better judging, will approve of the perpetuating . . . the Remembrance thereof, as a Warning to After-ages.

—ADAM ANDERSON,
The Origin of Commerce, 1764

The South Sea Bubble took its name from a company ironically founded without a name by the Earl of Oxford in 1711. The company's original plan was to fund a portion of the British debt as a speculation in tax-farming. The merchants who originally clubbed together to form the company were to be paid by a direct interest in government duties on a variety of goods. They also were granted a monopoly on trade to the South Seas. Hence, the name.

The boom, however, was hardly confined to the shares of one company. It was a broadly based rally across the whole English market, which had grown rapidly since 1688. Near the top, of course, the number of new issues peaked, with some so frothy that their like has scarcely been seen since. One company was floated to carry on trade with Greenland. Another was "a company for carrying on an undertaking of great advantage, but nobody to know what it is." Deposits of two pounds each actually were subscribed for one thousand shares of this unspeakable enterprise in just five hours of one day. The promoter of the company decided not to press his luck and left the country that evening, money in hand.

The peak prices of the boom were reached on August 1, 1720. Fifty-four days later, on September 23, 1720, shares of the South Sea Company, and with them the whole London stock market, collapsed. Although the Bank of England stepped in on the morning of the crash to back the bonds of the South Sea Company, the attempt was futile and the authorities bowed to the judgment of the market.

THE PAST IS PROLOGUE

The South Sea Bubble established a trading pattern that was repeated almost identically in 1929, as we shall see. It also advanced the practice, which also has persisted in busts to this day, of parliamentary inquiries, ex post facto laws, and other recriminations against anyone who appeared to make money from the boom or the ensuing collapse. Some of the directors and officers of the South Sea Company were hounded into prison, and most were obliged to forfeit 90 percent or more of their entire property, even those who had violated no law that had existed in the time of the boom. Not only the directors and officers, but stockbrokers too were obliged to face government inquiries in the search to uncover any peculations that might have gone unremedied. It was not a time when the public agreed with Dr. Johnson's sentiment, "There are few ways in which a man can be more innocently employed than in getting money."

This is not to say that there were no charges to answer for in the South Sea Bubble. Some of the minor issues certainly involved gross fraud. Or so we would say today. But this judgment from the vantage of more than two and a half centuries is colored by different standards than those that prevailed then. Fraudulent conversion—or converting another's property to your own use—was not illegal in early-eighteenth-century law. But bribery was. Evidence was brought forward that shares of the South Sea Company had been issued as bribes to secure favorable legislation from Parliament. It is probably an inevitable feature of a financial assets boom that it throws up people to positions of prominence who are willing to play fast and loose with the rules of prudence, if not the existing laws of the country. At the peak of the boom, it is they who make the scandals that are merely incidental, but are later misjudged to have played a crucial role in having brought the country from a fabulous boom into depression.

Contrary to what is often thought, it is a sign of efficient adaptation to the requirements of the time that those who are most adept at manipulating money come to manage great sums of it during a financial assets boom. It is no more surprising than the fact that large sums flow into the hands of mining engineers during a gold boom.

The details of the individual cases are not as important as the general conclusion they support about human nature and the likely behavior of governments in the wake of a big bust. There is an enduring human need for scapegoats, arising from at least two directions: (1) the refusal of most people to accept responsibility for their own mistakes; and (2) the misconception that any significant event must be the consequence of someone's volition. Together, the two provide a powerful impetus to revenge-seeking. The wider the pain, the more intense the scapegoating effort is likely to be, even if it carries over to individuals who did nothing wrong except make or preserve their capital by withdrawing from the overvalued market before it fell.

Scapegoating will almost certainly become a major factor in the life of Japanese society in the mid-1990s. There was a strong hint to that effect in the summer of 1992, when a number of Japanese publications began to offer explanations for the collapse of the Japanese stock market to a new postcrash low. In spite of the fact that Japan has few Jews, and foreign involvement in Japanese markets has been minimal, a widely heard explanation for the assets crash was that it was engineered by Jews and Jewish-dominated U.S. investment houses. As we analyze in more detail later, this is a classic delusional response. It has much in common with the hallucinations of the prairie populists in the United States during the deflation of the late nineteenth century. They said, "Rothschild did it," attributing the fall in their asset values to the machinations of a faraway cabal. The next step in this search for scapegoats will be to seek out those Japanese imagined to have entered into the conspiracy and facilitated its success. Recriminations will abound.

There are few societies in the world today where the rule of law and the sense of fair play are strong enough to allow investors who escape with conspicuous profits from a big bust to retain their earnings without paying some penalty. The prudent businessman or investor will be guided in his behavior by the standards that seem likely to apply after the day of reckoning.

In any event, the great stock market busts of 1720 did not spill over to Amsterdam. The Dutch had already suffered their great crash eight decades earlier. The year 1720 was bust time for London and Paris. Within eighteen months, a depression began that lasted, by some accounts, through the middle of the century.

Forgotten Crashes

It would be a mistake to skip over the crashes and convulsions of the next two centuries as we zero in on 1929. All long-term credit cycles end with asset crashes in the markets of the leading economy. Measuring from crash to crash, the dates of the modern credit cycles are as follows:

Span of the credit cycles	Duration
From 1720 to 1772	52 years
From 1772 to 1825	53 years
From 1825 to 1873	48 years
From 1873 to 1929	56 years
From 1929 to 1990	61 years

The crashes and resulting depressions appear to be less intense and traumatic when the end of the cycle does not coincide with a shift in world economic predominance. The Dutch tulipomania, and the South Sea Bubble and Mississippi Scheme did. The next three credit cycles unfolded during the long period of British hegemony. While they involved severe trauma for those who were caught unprepared by them, they do not stand out in economic history in the same vivid outline as the South Sea Bubble or Wall Street's crash of 1929.

As we explored in *Blood in the Streets*, the London market sold off to extremely low valuations around the time of the Battle of Waterloo in 1815. Many traders feared a British defeat. They were mistaken, however, and when this mistake became known the market rallied in a buying frenzy. It continued to gain ground for another decade, and indeed, with interruptions, for the rest of the nineteenth century. There was, however, a postwar crash marking the end of the credit cycle in December 1825.

The primitive U.S. stock market collapsed along with the prices of cotton land in the Panic of 1837. This, however, was mostly a real estate collapse. The majority of listed shares were banks that expired with the underlying value of their collateral.

Germany, which never became a predominant power, and never even developed a substantial stock market, nonetheless had its greatest collapse in 1873 after Prussian victory in the war with France and the subsequent founding of the German Empire in 1871. The greatest losses in Germany came with the collapse of land values after a period of raging optimism.

There was also a collapse on Wall Street in 1873, which foretold the end of the Civil War–Crimean War credit cycle and the beginning of the same world depression that brought on the German collapse.

1929 AND AFTER

By far the greatest financial trauma in modern history, however, was the Wall Street crash of 1929. It was the crash that marked America's emergence as the world's predominant economic power. It is etched in modern memory as the harbinger of the Great Depression of the 1930s. We discuss many aspects of the crash and preceding events in other chapters. Here we will focus on features that may help illuminate what is in store in the future, especially for Japan.

3800 on the Nikkei Dow?

The Japanese stock market has followed Wall Street's pattern before and after 1929 with remarkable affinity. Its initial decline brought it down by slightly more than Wall Street fell in 1929. Its subsequent suckers' rally was somewhat extended in duration, but not in price. If patterns of the past continue to be replayed, the rally in the fall of 1992 will place itself out, and Japanese stocks will again slip down an erosive curve that will take it to an ultimate low by sometime in 1994. The ultimate low after 1929 in the United States came almost three years after the market peak—in July 1932. Markets in Japan, like those throughout the world, appear to be moving more slowly in this cycle, reflecting the fact that the first phase of depression has been extended.

While the speed of the unraveling may be in doubt, the conditions that would push Tokyo to extreme lows are all in place, as we analyze below. We continue to expect the Japanese market to follow the trail blazed by the Dutch, French, English, and American markets in great-credit-cycle unwindings. This would make for an ultimate low in Tokyo of roughtly 3800 on the Nikkei Dow—about a 90 percent drop.

Although many countries had sunk into depression before the market crashed in 1929, the deepest stage of the world slump came only after the collapse of the American market squelched world liquidity, halting foreign lending. This hint suggests that a trigger of the second and deeper stage of depression this time will be the withdrawal of Japanese investment as a consequence of the collapse of asset markets. As we write, gathering evidence points to exactly this outcome. The liquidation phase appears to be drawing closer.

Investment Winds Down

We suggested in the first edition of this book that this liquidation would probably not occur during "a brief interlude of continued Japanese investment overseas while the market recovers from its initial decline to the October 1, 1990 lows." In fact, Japanese investment abroad did not come to a halt in 1991. Japanese companies made $31 billion in direct foreign investments that year. This was almost a 40 percent drop from 1990 levels, a substantial reduction but by no means the total withdrawal of Japanese capital that could help trigger an implosion of the world financial system.

There were several reasons why the Japanese continued to recycle capital into the world system in the early stages of this depression:

1. Like Americans after 1929, many Japanese executives did not recognize the decisive change that was heralded by the stock market crash. Some Americans continued to invest abroad in 1930. The Japanese followed in their footsteps in 1991.
2. Far more than American business in 1930, which had matured during the heyday of free trade sponsored by the British Empire, Japanese executives were taught to be sensitive to the dangers of protectionism by their experiences in America and Asia in the 1980s. Recognizing that protectionism could close lucrative foreign markets to their goods, the Japanese undertook the systematic building of assembly plants offshore. This policy continued in 1991, and to a lesser extent in 1992.
3. Japan, unlike America after 1929, is an aging society with a relatively tight labor market. Many Japanese companies therefore adopted the moving of low-skill manufacturing jobs offshore to free highly skilled Japanese workers for more valuable activites.
4. The Japanese were forced to recycle part of their 1991 trade surplus to the United States as a contribution to pay a share of the costs of Operation Desert Storm. This political tribute, in combination with voluntary Japanese investment in 1991 and early 1992, helped forestall the collapse in world liquidity that we still expect to help trigger the second and deeper stage of depression.

The Coming Collapse of Japanese Investment

As we write, evidence has begun to mount that the well of Japanese liquidity is running dry. Gurgling sounds fill the air. This is true in spite of the fact that some economic news from Japan seems bullish by American or European standards. For example, unemployment remains a low 3 percent. And Japanese exports rose to a twenty-sixth consecutive monthly record in 1992, contributing to an all-time-high $9.2 billion monthly trade surplus.

Superficially, it sounds as though Japan is in great shape. American politicians would jump for joy to have such results. But analysis of other dimensions of the Japanese economy shows that underlying conditions are much less robust than they seem.

Reported Japanese corporate profits have fallen by more than 30 percent, and are likely to be down by 50 percent or more by the end of the fiscal year. Although GDP is still barely positive as we write, it will turn negative in 1993, following industrial production downhill.

The rapid wind-down of Japanese corporate profits is resulting in a distinct slowdown in investment. After a $3 trillion spending binge between 1986 and 1991, Japanese corporations are stuck with lots of unused capacity and idle plants. Capital outlays were down by 11.9 percent in 1992, while inventories of unsold goods were rising at a 20 percent annual rate.

Credit Slowdown

As profits have fallen, the top Japanese companies have begun to be conscious of the need to avoid taking on new debt. Consumers are also shunning credit. Department store sales have been down for eight months in a row as we write. Year-over-year credit growth in Japan continues to decline steadily from month to month. The money supply is declining. For the first time ever, Japanese M2 has turned negative on a year-over-year basis.

The faltering credit pulse of the Japanese economy cannot be easily ramped up because total bank loans remain far too high a proportion of the economy. Total debt stood at an astonishing 262 percent of GDP. The Japanese economy is overborrowed. Weak credit growth, in turn, places downward pressure on asset prices, which further undermines the banks' position.

The unraveling of the credit spree and the fall in the stock market are adding to already significant downward pressures on Japanese real estate. Stock and real estate markets are closely intertwined in Japan because many property owners mortgaged their land at inflated prices to buy stocks on margin at precrash prices. At the time, the exaggerated values of many Japanese companies were justified on the basis of their hidden assets in the form of massively appreciated properties. During the late 1980s, vast amounts of surplus cash were diverted into real estate and stock speculation. Prices jumped to unprecedented levels. Real estate in Tokyo rose in value by almost 80 percent from 1986 to 1987 alone. This assets boom inflated the capital of Japanese banks, alowing them to finance a worldwide credit binge. Japanese banks counted in their capital unrealized gains from property and stock holdings, a marvelous alchemy when asset prices were rising.

The most obvious vulnerability in Japan's financial system has long been the ground on which it sits. Before the crash, real estate prices in Japan were preposterous. They are still preposterous. A single prefecture of downtown Tokyo was once valued higher than the whole of Canada. In Taiwan, only two hours away by plane, prices were one-twentieth of Tokyo levels. At the peak of the boom, office space in the center of Tokyo rented for 88,000 yen per *tsubo* per month. A *tsubo* is 35.6 square feet. Even compared with overpriced London and New York, Tokyo remains at a huge premium. In the summer of 1990, the payback period on a new Tokyo office building was as long as 150 years. And still the building continued. Rapid growth in office demand would be needed to prevent vacancy rates from rising simply because so much new space is coming available.

Clearly, Japanese real estate values had reached an unsustainable extreme. According to Gregory Clark, a longtime resident of Japan who teaches economics at Sophia University, the value of all property in Japan at the end of 1987 was "twice that of the value of all land and resources in the entire United States." As Japan is less than 4 percent the land area of the United States, that would put the unit value of Japanese property at approximately fifty times that in the United States.

Postwar Overhang

This is an overhang of the postwar era. After World War II, a conscious decision was made to overrepresent rural interests in the Diet. This was partly America's doing. At the time, no one worried about industrial competition from a war-ruined Japan. Americans in the occupation government were more concerned about controlling the future direction of Japanese politics. One of their solutions was to give rice farmers a disproportionate say in politics. Times have changed, but farmers who represent just 5 percent of the population control 18 percent of the potential votes and approximately 25 percent of the normal turnout.

One thing led to another. To preserve the rice farmers meant not only heavy subsidies that cost Japanese taxpayers forty billion dollars a year, but other distortions that produce far higher indirect costs. These include fifty billion dollars in higher food costs, plus hundreds of billions in higher housing costs due to subsidies of farming in urban areas. Property taxes have charged farmers as little as 1 percent of the rate they would pay on the same land in residential use. This has enabled farmers to sit under the shade of persimmon trees in urban areas, dreaming of capital gains on artificially scarce land, while the average young couple pays twice the percentage of income for housing as a couple in overpriced New York.

Inefficient Building

Even the meager portion of land available for housing is utilized inefficiently. The predominance of low-rise residential structures keeps housing density lower than it should be, given world-record real estate prices. The traditional preference for low-rise building in Japan is entirely understandable given the frequency of earthquakes. But improved architectural techniques have greatly enhanced the survivability of taller buildings. Even if that were not the case, however, the Tokyo skyline is dotted with high-rise commercial buildings. It makes little sense to work in high-rise structures but insist upon sleeping in a two-story building. As Marc Faber points out, an earthquake is just as likely to strike during the day as at night. An adjustment of the Japanese residential housing stock to reflect these probabilities is long overdue.

The press of higher prices in the Tokyo metropolitan area can only accelerate the inevitable. It is amazing that social discontent over the housing predicament in Japan has not already forced the government, in spite of the farmers' lobby, to abandon policies that keep real estate in artificial scarcity. Housing costs are so ridiculous that the purchase price of a decent house cannot be paid in the lifetime of an average urban worker. Banks are now writing "two-generation" mortgages in which the eldest son or another heir is expected to continue payments after the original purchaser retires. New entrants into the job market, for whom housing is priced out of reach, waste many hours commuting in and out of the remote suburbs, or live in tiny rooms that hardly befit the image of the Japanese as the richest people on earth.

Tax Policy Immobilizes the Property Market

The artificial scarcity of housing has been compounded by a tax policy that imposes a punitive 80 percent capital gains levy on real estate profits—except on proceeds that are immediately reinvested in a property of equal or greater value within the year. This policy, slightly modified in 1987, has helped to immobilize the property market, reducing the effective supply and driving up prices. Further, by discouraging owners from taking profit directly by selling their land, the tax provides an inducement to extract gains indirectly through borrowing. As a consequence, it has become commonplace to borrow 90 percent or more of the value of appreciated property.

Kiting profits is fun and easy while prices are rising. But real estate in Japan cannot continue rising in real terms. Even after a major market decline, a great part of its value is patently artificial. Any adjustment that releases supply could send prices plunging further. They could fall by 90 percent and still be high by world standards. Much more modest reductions have already created major problems for the Japanese banking system and the whole world economy.

JAPANESE BANKS FACING TROUBLE

But the real reason why Japan faces a looming credit crisis is the exposure of its biggest banks to the property market. A December 1987 study by the Washington Econometrics Forecasting Services points out that if real estate in Japan were suddenly revalued back to the levels which prevailed in 1984, it would result in the loss of wealth in Japan exceeding $3 trillion. That is a decline in collateral which even Japan's big banks would have trouble stomaching, and they are the world's biggest. Of the world's ten largest companies, eight are Japanese and six of these are Japanese banks. The very size of the Japanese banks means that a credit crisis in Japan caused by a crash in property values there would have deflationary consequences throughout the world.

—CHRISTOPHER WOOD,
Boom & Bust

The Japanese banking sector is exposed to a real estate debacle that could be many times more costly than the S & L collapse in the United States. The unwinding of prices has put the leverage that worked to inflate the financial sector into reverse. Real estate debtors, many of whom borrowed to invest in shares at much higher prices, must be sitting on huge losses, not all of which have yet been called by the banks. The point of no return appears to be somewhere below 14,000 on the Nikkei Dow. If prices move decisively below that level, forced selling could accelerate the deflationary implosion. Shareholders could be obliged to liquidate their holdings in order to stop their losses and make good on highly geared real estate debt. Not only would the market be hit by sellers looking to raise cash, but its asset base would be simultaneously unwound, since falling real estate values would wipe away corporate assets. The value of land under offices and factories, now incorporated into share prices, would shrivel as land values fell. A drop in corporate assets typically is reflected in lower share prices. With profits already plunging, a further unwinding of the market would feed on itself.

In spite of the damage done in Tokyo to date, we believe that we are still in the preliminary stages of the unraveling. There has not yet been panic selling to bring the market down below its previous equilibrium valuations. In past credit-cycle unwindings, asset markets in the leading economies have contracted by about 90 percent, falling to subnormal levels.

Before the big bubble during the 1980s, the Japanese stock market was capitalized in a range between 20 and 34 percent of nominal GNP—with the single exception of 1972, when a rapid monetary expansion temporarily brought stock prices above 50 percent of nominal GNP. If you assume that rapid monetary expansion will not occur under current conditions, and take an average ratio of stock valuations to the nominal GNP that prevailed before the bubble, the Nikkei should be valued at about 8000. Even this depressed level, however, represents just an 80 percent decline. We think it will go lower. The losses in the property market will have feedback effects on the real economy that almost guarantee a 1930s-style debt implosion.

Trillions Lost

At the top of the bubble, Japanese property prices were worth somewhere between $16 trillion and $20 trillion. Realistic estimates suggest that during 1991 and 1992, Japanese property prices may have fallen by 50 percent— although the magnitude of the drop has been disguised by the drying up of sales. There have been few transactions of any significance among the bubble properties. Alexander Kinmonti and Keiko Ohtsuki of Morgan Stanley calculate that falling rental values and growing vacancies imply that "site values in the center of Tokyo rationally ought to settle at 30 percent of their peak theoretical values. They go on to suggest that this may overestimate the decline that is likely to take place. They say, "The fall necessary to restore a balanced market should be around 45 percent."

They may be optimistic. Most estimates of office demand by experts extrapolate from boom conditions. They also tend to overlook the significant impact of new technology in displacing demand for expensive center-city real estate. New communications technologies will soon make telecommuting more practical, and thus undercut the property values in the center of Tokyo, just as in other cities. Nonetheless, if the Japanese property market has already shriveled by 50 percent, or if it suffers such losses in the future, the total loss of wealth implied is from $8 to $10 trillion—equivalent to having all the world's stock markets crash to zero.

A Mountain of Bad Debt

Not all those massive losses will necessarily show up on the books of banks. But many of them will. The plunge in Japanese stock and property markets has directly undermined the banks' collateral and capital. They are even more short of capital now than meets the eye, because far more of their loans are nonperforming than they have acknowledged. Our best guess, based on soundings from Tokyo, is that Japanese banks had between $400 and $500 billion in nonperforming assets at the end of 1992. This is only a guess. The accounting for nonperforming assets in Japan is flexible, and reporting requirements are skimpy, so the true total may be lower, or it may be higher. If real estate prices plunge further, the banks losses be higher.

After having kept a brave face for two years after the Japanese stock market crash, the banks are now facing a more ominous situation. There is a rumor as we write that a bank in Osaka is on the verge of failing. The bank in question is not large enough to bring the house down. But the story is significant because it reflects the breakdown of cooperation between the government and the banking sector.

In the past, the bigger banks have been persuaded to swallow loss-making institutions or lift a portion of their bad loans. Now all the big banks are worried about their own situation and are unwilling to take on further burdens. Fuji Bank has even announced its first-ever branch closing.

The Japanese banks are losing deposits at a rapid clip, for two reasons that they cannot control: corporations are drawing down cash balances, and consumers are transferring funds to the government-owned postal savings system, which is far more isolated from the bad-loan problems.

Faced with falling deposits and shrinking capital, the Japanese banks have had no choice but to curtail lending. The problem here is not merely that many of the Japanese banks will be outside the Bank for International Settlements capital standards. The damage would be every bit as great, even if the standards had never been agreed upon. As it is, they could be waived or fudged. But what can't be "waived away" are the real losses. A banking system with impaired capital cannot lend on the scale to which its customers have become accustomed.

A credit crunch is the inevitable result. Bank lending in Japan grew by just 0.7 percent in the six months ending September 1992. Loans to small and medium-sized Japanese companies have been sharply curtailed. They formerly accounted for 56 percent of all commercial credit. Smaller accounts are historically more dependent on banks than large companies are, and have accounted for most of the record surge of business failures. What was already a serious problem for small business in Japan as 1992 came to end will soon be a big problem worldwide.

Global Consequences

The liquidation in Japan has only begun. It is a tremendous deflationary event, bound to have far-reaching consequences. When the world's largest creditor suffers losses of the magnitude now being endured, they are inevitably felt right around the globe. Japanese banks were a major engine of credit creation, accounting for 25 percent of total world credit growth in recent years. Now that the assets crash has wiped away their loan loss reserves and much of their capital, they will be unable to lend at accustomed levels. Not only will the Japanese real economy continue to contract, Japanese companies will curtail their foreign investment. Japanese banks will cease to recycle the trade surplus. This will act as a drag on activity in other regions.

As the Japanese boom has faltered, Japan has reduced its imports, just as the United States did after 1929. The huge Japanese trade surplus requires that other industrial countries balance their trade deficit with Japan, either through capital imports, which are shriveling, or through surpluses in trade with the primary product producers in the underdeveloped countries.

Lending by Japanese banks to the rest of the world has followed the same pattern as direct investment. It peaked with the Japanese stock market in 1989 and has since fallen in half, to $100 billion annually. We expect it to plunge by 1993 to $20 billion annually or less, a 90 percent drop from the peak.

The constriction of Japanese lending, including concessionary lending to the former Soviet Union and the Third World will both reduce the purchases by these economies of goods in the world market; and increase selling of commodities that they produce. After 1929, one of the major causes of plunging commodity prices was the withdrawal of capital from the periphery. Furthermore, Japan itself is the largest importer of natural resources. As the Japanese economy slows, Japanese imports will slow, and commodity prices should fall. This chain of events will accentuate the trade deficits that Europe and North America are running with Japan, increasing protectionist pressure. It will have particularly negative effects in Canada, which is heavily dependent on sales of raw materials to Japan, its largest trading partner after the United States.

The Pacific rim and the United States are also likely to be hurt. They have been the main centers of Japanese investment. The Pacific rim, including the dynamic growth regions of southern China, has been one of the few bright spots in the world economy. But it is still largely a region that lives by manufacturing and transshipment of goods to outside markets. If the rest of the world, particularly Japan, goes into a slump, deflationary pressures will be felt throughout the Pacific.

Not only will the contraction in Japan help slow the Asian economies, it will also be another blow to the economy and property values worldwide. Japanese speculators were active in real estate internationally. The Japanese banks were also major lenders to non-Japanese property investors, including Olympia & York.

A particularly ominous sign that Japanese capital will no longer be available internationally passed almost unnoticed in November 1992. A high-level German investment mission to Tokyo was entirely rebuffed. The Germans, leading creditors during the 1980s boom, have found their resources increasingly strained by the high costs of reunification. They came to Japan hoping to interest Japanese investors in purchasing distressed properties in eastern Germany. They came away without a penny.

A Big Sell Order

Rather than helping other economies to meet growing capital needs by stepping up foreign investment, the unraveling in Tokyo has reached the stage where more aggressive liquidation of foreign holdings is likely. A significant portion of more than $75 billion the Japanese have invested in U.S. real estate is likely to be on the block in 1993 and 1994.

More Bad News for California

This is particularly bad news for California, where a lot of the investment is concentrated. As we write, the California economy is still reeling, and in spite of the protracted budget stalemates in 1991 and 1992, it appears that the state will face still another deficit of $7 billion to $9 billion in 1993. More retrenchment lies ahead.

A move by the Japanese to dump their U.S. real estate would also be bad news for U.S. banks. If Japanese holders unload showplace properties at distressed prices, it would further undermine the collateral on U.S. property loans. And more than that, it would end any fleeting hope that Japanese institutions could conceivably come to the rescue of insolvent money-center banks in New York and elsewhere. At the moment, it would be difficult to be very optimistic about some of them surviving on their own. Among the possible insolvent banks are Chase Manhattan, Chemical, and Citibank. Sometime in the 1990s, it is not unlikely that some of these large U.S. banks will have trouble surviving on their own. The difficulties of the Japanese banks make it unlikely that they will be in either the position or the mood to take on insolvent banks from New York to California.

Can the Japanese Turn Back the Deflationary Tide?

The crucial question is whether the Japanese authorities are correct in assuming that they can halt the slide of their financial system toward debt implosion and depression. They believe they can. Japanese authorities remain confident that they can avoid the "mistakes" of the U.S. authorities after 1930, when the money supply imploded by 30 percent. Therefore, while they think that further drops of as much as 20 to 30 percent in the Nikkei Dow are possible, they do not expect a drop down to 3800—which would be equivalent to the fall of the U.S. market after 1929.

Herbert Hoover organized the equivalent of an eighty-billion-dollar stimulus package in today's terms during the first two years of the depression.

—THE GREAT RECKONING,
first edition, page 407

It is far from obvious, however, that the Japanese authorities are in any sense more nimble or competent than their counterparts in the United States were after 1929. In fact, their behavior in the two years following the crash makes an unfavorable comparison with the dramatic action undertaken by Herbert Hoover in a fruitless attempt to stabilize the American economy. Hoover was a genuine student of the business cycle, and probably better informed about the intricacies of the economy than any other world leader of this century. Contrary to song and fable, Hoover did not sit on his hands as the economy imploded. He sought vainly to reverse the collapse, using every method available to the Japanese today, including pouring concrete.

As we reported in the first edition of this book, "Hoover organized the equivalent of an eighty-billion-dollar stimulus package in today's terms." He started putting it together within a month of the stock market crash in 1929. Ironically, news in August 1992 that Japan will pour more than Y10 trillion into infrastructure spending provided another haunting example of history repeating itself. Ten trillion yen is roughly equivalent to $80 billion. The attempt by the Japanese authorities to suppress the earthquake of depression has led them to follow, almost pace for pace, in Herbert Hoover's footsteps. But note that they are about two years slower off the mark than Hoover was. As Christopher Wood, Japan Finance Editor of The Economist, put it, "The Japanese make Herbert Hoover look like a 100 metre sprinter."

Consensus Crumbles

Far from proving to be supermen, the aging Japanese leadership find themselves on the defensive. Facing an unprecedented collapse in wealth, the Japanese authorities will no doubt ease further, and rig up a stimulative package of domestic infrastructure spending similar to Hoover's road- and dam-building binge. But they will not be able to reinflate the bubble by pouring concrete. The losses are real and they will eventually have to be faced.

The Japanese leadership seems to have a difficult time responding to a crisis when they are not being pressured from the outside, as they have been through much of the 1970s and 1980s by the United States. As economic stresses have mounted, there has been an uncharacteristic breakdown in the Japanese political consensus. There is no effective coalition of support to bail out the banks, as there is in the United States. Bad loans are growing rapidly, and could soon swell beyond the capacity of the banks themselves to deal with them.

Not surprisingly, the banks are asking the government for help in managing these huge losses. They want a Japanese version of the US Resolution Trust Corporation to refund the bad debts with someone else's money. They are also seeking reform of the postal savings system to limit the competition for deposits that they face from the government.

Industrialists facing unaccustomed losses are insisting that if the banks receive help, then they should as well. Many ordinary citizens also appear to be more than normally agitated by the prospect of seeing their tax money tidy up balance sheets for the bankers.

LDP to Break Up?

Various ministries and factions of the ruling Liberal Democratic Party remain in dispute over what to do. Before the depression bottoms, we expect the LDP to break into separate parties. Its legitimacy will be severely tested when the tradition of lifetime employment is scrapped—which is bound to happen. As we write, news has come that Shintom, an electronic company of medium size, has been forced by the slump in world demand for video equipment to halt production at its factory at Kofu, with the outright elimination of ninety-four jobs. By early 1993, one or more big corporations will shock the system by beginning to lay off staff in large numbers. Japanese corporate profits are plunging. It is only a matter of time until unemployment rises to shocking levels by Japanese standards. In the polite words of Takeshi Noda, economic planning minister, "We are one step before entering into the phase of employment adjustment."

Time will tell whether it is as easy to stop deflation as the Japanese and others now expect. The crucial question is still the same one that economic historians have argued about ever since the 1930s. It is whether the deflation of the 1930s was really a policy mistake that could have been easily corrected by a more determined policy of monetary ease—or a more highly determined follow-on effect of the inflationary boom.

Our guess, which is not orthodox opinion, is that deflation was not a mistake but a consequence. It could well be a consequence in the 1990s. When all is said and done, the Japanese authorities will be no better able to roll back the tide than Herbert Hoover, who in spite of his bad press was one of the more able men of this century.

WEAK FOUNDATIONS

In many ways, the whole structure of postwar Japanese investment has rested upon arrangements forged in the late forties, when American predominance was at its height. General Douglas MacArthur, the United States viceroy in Japan, helped reorganize the Japanese economy and government. Japan was forbidden from becoming a military power. And the internal balance of votes in the Japanese parliament was tilted in favor of rural interests who were expected to be less enchanted by the blandishments of Communism.

Rather than use America's great power to force open Japanese markets to U.S. goods, successive American administrations allowed the Japanese free access to American markets. This helped shore up conservative political dominance in Japan. The United States cooperated in the protection of two Japanese voting blocs of conservative bent that otherwise would have been decimated by international competition: farmers and small retailers. Japanese farmers are only one-quarter as efficient as American farmers. They could not have stayed in business if the United States had insisted upon free access to Japanese markets for American food exports thirty or forty years ago. Japanese retailing is not quite as inefficient as Japanese farming, but almost. Merchandising in Japan is dominated by hundreds of thousands of inefficient mom-and-pop shops, most of which stay in business only because they have been protected from competition of American-style discount and department stores. U.S. administrations allowed free access to American markets without demanding reciprocity because it was a way of strengthening Japan and thus indirectly assuring that Japan would not stray from the anti-Communist coalition during the Cold War. Now American economic power has shrunk to the danger point. The old arrangements can no longer be sustained. And new arrangements cannot be forged without exposing the whole rickety structure to the dangers of collapse.

The Coming Test of Japan

Every great nation that has approached world predominance has suffered a great crash just as its fortunes were rising on a cycle of optimism. To all outward appearances, Japan is a great nation. A Japanese population half that of the United States has created half again more wealth than Americans. The Japanese have done it by being better educated, harder working, more efficient, less violent, cleaner, and more polite than the inhabitants of other industrial countries. Japanese also know far more about other peoples than other peoples know about them.

Japan was the first society in Asia to industrialize successfully, a transformation attributable to the extraordinary vigor of the Emperor Mutsuhito's reforms, especially as contrasted with the failed efforts of the T'ung-chih Restoration in China. Japan grew while China stagnated because, at a crucial time, modernizing reforms carried the day over bitter opposition.

Now another test faces Japan. Atlantic powers have dominated the world for five centuries, since the Portuguese first sailed around Africa and into Asian waters. Japan may be the next world leader, and therefore the first non-Atlantic power to predominate in the modern world. But there is another possiblity—that there will be no new supreme power in the world. The end of the American century may not usher in a Japanese century, just a century of confusion. The test is still to come.

Great financial crises tend to give rise to political crises. In other countries where elections are held, major crashes have often led to changes of government. Whatever party is in power when the music stops faces the recrimination of voters. Japan has not yet experienced such a peaceful revolution since the establishment of the postwar system. The leaders of oppostion parties have no experience of anything but opposition.

The Next America or the Next Argentina?

Early in this century, Argentina was one of the world's most vital and richest economies. It had grown rich under the sponsorship of Great Britain, relying on British capital, selling into British markets, and living under rules inspired by the distant British, rules that were backed up on more than one occasion by the British Atlantic Fleet. Then British power receded, and the framework in which the Argentine economy had grown broke apart. The Argentines could never recover stability. The weakened liberal faction of wealthy exporters that had dominated Argentine affairs during the heyday of growth could no longer win elections. And the dictators of the left and right would not adopt liberal policies. In effect, the Argentine society was one of the worst causalties of the decline of the British Empire.

An extension of the franchise brought the Radical Party to power in 1916. The doleful effects of its redistributionist policies initially were masked by the export boom associated with World War I. The end of the boom revealed the fragility of the prosperity that Argentines had come to take for granted. The new leaders of government were acutely aware of the ineequalities of wealth that had become pronounced in Argentina's headlong rush for wealth. They also had a long experience of proposing reform. Suddenly, they were in the position to act upon their speeches. The onslaught of legislation they unleashed sent Argentina on the road to ruin. When cadets at the military academy overthrew the government during the Great Depression, in September 1930, the once-soaring national self-confidence had been shattered.

Nothing of the sort is likely to happen to Japan. But as an exporting nation in close symbiosis with a fading power of another culture, Japan has some of the vulnerabilities of Argentina sixty years ago. Economies operate upon an artificial political scaffolding. That scaffolding cannot simply be knocked down without dramatic consequences. Urban wage earners in Japan are correct to complain that it is unfair that they must pay the world's highest prices for the lowest-quality housing among industrial countries. They are correct, as well, to claim that it is unfair to deny them access to cheap American food. It is unfair. But it is an unfairness that American itself helped to author years ago under very different economic circumstances. Unfairness is now deeply embedded in the Japanese political economy. Its consequences are reflected in artificially high asset values in Japan and around the world. It is a system that can no longer be sustained, and will not be changed without tears.

The ongoing assets crash and its aftermath will challenge Japan as nothing has since defeat in 1945. A nation that has grown as rich as it can within the rules of the postwar world will have to find its way to new rules and the solution of old problems. Japan will have to reinvent a military. It will have to spend hundreds of billions to rehouse much of its population to the standards of middle-class life—without destroying the vitality of industry.

If history is a guide, the coming world depression will be more severe in Japan than in many other countries. For reasons we explore later, the sudden drop in wealth and income gains in Japan is likely to encourage the militancy of unions, a slackening of work effort and investment in education, and more extensive income redistribution. Whether Japan emerges at the dawn of a new century as the nation capable of leading the world and not just the champion of urban congestion is yet to be decided.

CHAPTER FIVE

THE NEW GERMANY AND EUROPE IN THE 1990s

Whatever the faults and ambitions the Germans had were amply shared by the other major nations of the modern era. But unlike Britian, Russia or the United States, the Germans lacked the space to work out their abundant vitality. Moreover, because of geography, Germany's vitality was an immediate threat to the rest of Europe.

—DAVID CALLEO,
on Imperial Germany (pre-1914),
The German Problem Reconsidered

EASTERN AND WESTERN EUROPE NEED EACH OTHER

The next century could look back at 1989 as a turning point in the balance of the world. It was the year when the Soviet Union withdrew from Afghanistan and attempted to return to Europe. The Berlin Wall fell, as we predicted, ending the division of Germany.

The withdrawal of Communist power from Eastern Europe, followed by the disintegration of the Soviet Union, seemed to mark victory for the West in the Cold War, and it certainly raised the confidence of Western Europe. However, the disintegration of the Communist system of authority let loose forces that Communism had ruthlessly contained, particularly the forces of nationalism. Local conflicts between different tribes occurred in many parts of the Soviet Union itself, and the seventy-year-old state of Czechoslovakia was peaceably divided between the Czechs and the Slovaks.

By far the most tragic event was the outbreak of civil war in what had been Yugoslavia. This had a much greater impact on the public imagination in Germany than it had in most other West European countries, let alone the United States. The process of breakup was started by increasingly aggressive assertions of Serbian nationalism, but a decisive step was the recognition of the Croat and Slovene declarations of independence, followed by war between Serbs and Croats in Croatia, and then between Serbs, Croats, and Bosnians in Bosnia.

The Croats, like the Serbs, are a Slav people and speak the same language. But in terms of history and religion they are linked to the German people. Croatia and Slovenia belonged to the Austro-Hungarian Empire until 1918, and an independent Croatia was an extremely brutal ally of Hitler in the Second World War. The Croats are Roman Catholics, whereas the Serbs belong to the Greek Orthodox Church and the Bosnians are Muslims. These religious differences mark off different tribes that are not otherwise divided by physical or language characteristics. In this context religion is not important as a spiritual belief but as a tribal label. The same is true in Northern Ireland, where "Catholic" and "Protestant" are labels for hostile tribes rather than true indicators of strong religious conviction. The conditions in Yugoslavia are like those of Nigeria or on the streets of Los Angeles. In the absence of strong central authority, tribes or gangs fight each other. The breakdown of Communist authority was welcome from many aspects, but it allowed the revival of tribal war in Europe.

When the twentieth century opened, European empires controlled 84 percent of the earth's surface. Europeans were "the lords of human kind," wrote V. G. Kiernan, and had been since the end of the fifteenth century. From the Gunpowder Revolution until World War II, it was mainly Europe's feuds that prevented it from dominating the rest of the world completely. The parts of the other continents that came within Europe's reach had fallen into the European orbit. European settlers from Portugal, Spain, Holland, France, and England took over North and South America, Australia, and New Zealand from their aboriginal inhabitants. These vast terrains were not only peopled with Europeans, they were also restocked with European flora and fauna. Other continents, especially in their temperate zones, came to resemble little Europes. And where Europeans did not total dominate the lands they found— as in India, China, Indonesia, and Africa—they forced backward societies to do what they probably would not have done otherwise: modernize.

But in 1990, Western Europe was no longer the seat of empires. It was home to mountains of subsidized surplus cheese and hardened arteries. Its people were still rich but hardly in the mood for imperial expansion. Unlike the overlords Oliver Goldsmith satirized, Europeans no longer had "pride in their port, defiance in their eye." Such swagger no longer paid. The European military advantage over the periphery had been dissipated by the world wars. And irresistible technological trends had reduced it ever since. What was rebuilt from the rubble of World War II was not the European empires but European industry. Europeans, especially West Germans, had learned to prosper as the staging grounds of the Cold War. While America paid trillions to hold Russia out of the heartland of Europe, Europeans put much more of their capital into productive investment.

THE "DEMOGRAPHIC TIME BOMB"

Europe was weakening in demographic terms during the late twentieth century even as its living standards rose. In the words of French expert Jean-Claude Chesnais, Europe was facing a "demographic time bomb"—a growing " 'Africanization' and 'Islamization' " caused by immigration from the south shore of the Mediterranean. The wealthy, aging populations of Western Europe were abandoning jobs that could not be filled by their sons and daughters. This time bomb of Africanization and Islamization may be partly diffused by another migration—the rush of Eastern European refugees fleeing toward the West to escape economic collapse and even civil war in the East. The relaxation of totalitarian controls, now inevitable because of the breakdown of authority in the former Soviet Union, will free millions of people, and not merely Soviet Jews, to emigrate. Already hundreds of thousands of them have found refuge in the European Community.

The pressure from the outside has been matched by a decline in the birth rate of all the countries of the European Community. People are so concerned with world overpopulation that they often regard any sign of reduced population growth as desirable. That is a common attitude in the United States and also in Europe. Yet a combination of rising external population pressure with a declining internal birth rate presents exactly the same features as the closing decades of the Roman Empire, which was destroyed by population movements.

The European demographic trends are negative. Of the twelve countries of the European Community, only Ireland—where abortion has been subject to a constitutional prohibition—is reproducing at a stable rate. To maintain a population each woman needs on average to produce 2.1 children. In Italy and Spain, Catholic countries with a strong tradition of large families, the birth rate has now fallen to 1.3 percent, well below the replacement level. Italy and Spain are two of the main receiving countries for African immigration, and Africa has a much higher rate of population growth than Eastern Europe or Russia.

Apart from immigration, this pattern of an aging population will put increasing pressure on Western European economies. The balance between young and old is shifting in favor of the old. This will mean slow economic growth and rapidly increasing welfare costs. As the European Community countries are already high-cost, high-welfare economies, the burden may become insupportable. For instance, West Germany, before reunification, had the lowest proportion of children under fifteen of any country in the United Nations.

If one treated the European Community as a single nation, one would be forecasting a stable population over the next twenty years followed by a rapid decline. Even during the period of stability, the average age would be rising quite rapidly, as the baby boom generation gets older. If present welfare standards for the elderly are to be maintained, large-scale immigration of young workers will be needed. But these run into the obstacles of tribal feeling. Immigration is already an acute political issue in most EC countries, and has created growing anti-immigrant parties of a fascist type.

THE EAST-WEST DIVIDE

> It cannot be maintained that these peoples too belong to the unity of our nation; their customs and constitution have ever separated them from it. In that epoch they exercised no independent influence, but merely appear subordinate or antagonistic: now and then lapped so to speak, by the receding waves of the general movements of history.
>
> —LEOPOLD VON RANKE, 1824

Few today remember that the separation papers between Eastern and Western Europe were not drawn up by Stalin. His Iron Curtain merely traced in barbed wire a line drawn by German philosophers early in the nineteenth century. Leopold von Ranke and his contemporary G. W. F. Hegel were themselves noticing an ancient division in the fates of Western Europe, the western part of the Eurasian land mass with the longest borders on the open sea, and the broad, stolid interior of Eastern Europe. It was a region with a different social history. The Gunpowder Revolution came late to Eastern Europe. And feudalism lingered late. In Eastern Europe, peasants were less successful in escaping to more or less autonomous cities than they were in the West. The traditional German folk wisdom, *Stadtluft macht frei*, or "Town air makes a man free," was not as true in the East, where population densities were thinner and nobles maintained more control over the towns. After the decline of the Hans towns in the Black Death, Eastern European serfs were increasingly tied to the land. They certainly were not free to run away to Antwerp or Cologne and go to work in crafts and manufactures. The result was that Eastern Europe became less commercially important as time passed, lingering behind the West in the development of modern institutions, including the nation-state.

William Playfair, writing about the same time as Hegel in 1805, saw clearly that the collapse of Poland in the late eighteenth century was caused by the late arrival of the Gunpowder Revolution in Eastern Europe, which had led to the preservation of feudalism:

> When the feudal system was established all over Europe, nations under its influence were so far on an equality; and as they all emerged from that situation nearly about the same time, Poland excepted, they still preserved their relative situations. The Poles during this change in other states, comparatively lost power. Amongst the alterations produced, was that of placing in the hands of the sovereign all the disposable revenue and force of a country, with which standing armies were maintained. Those irregular militias, till then composed of the barons and their retainers; a species of force, at best far inferior to regular armies, became useless; but particularly so, after the modes of fighting had been changed by the invention of gunpowder, and the adoption of large trains of artillery, which could never have been employed in the feudal armies.

People whose megapolitical power is weak never lack for contempt, even among philosophers in more advantageously situated lands. Hegel dismissed the East of Europe. He acknowledged that "the Slavs have to some extent been drawn within the sphere of Occidental Reason," because "sometimes, as an advanced guard—an intermediate nationality—they took part in the struggle between Christian European and unchristian Asia." Yet he believed that they were not part of the same history. He said, "This entire body of peoples remains excluded from our consideration, because hitherto it has not appeared as an independent element in the series of phases that Reason has assumed in the world."

Ironically, it was a Hegelian in a bad mood, Kark Marx, whose philosophy of Communism contributed so much in the long run to bringing the two ends of Europe together. Communism did not make Eastern Europe into Western Europe. And it certainly did not make Eastern Europe rich. Indeed, the trillions in losses that Communism imposed on Eastern Europe in the past half century helped lay a perverse groundwork for the current accommodation. A capitalist Russia threatened German domination of Central and Eastern Europe prior to 1914. But Communism destroyed Russia economically, and thus mitigated a major source of conflict.

Today, a united Germany could for the moment be the natural economic master of the whole of Europe—without the sabers rattling in any quarter. First Napoleon, then the Kaiser, then Hitler invaded Russia in fatal attempts to consolidate control over Central Europe. Now a desperately bankrupt Russia is inviting Germany to take a larger role. The Russians need foreign investment on a massive scale, and Germany has been one of two principal savings nations, along with Japan. If the Russians were to obtain even a fraction of the trillions of dollars they need, much of it would have to come from Germany. That helps explain why East Germany was allowed to reunite with the Federal Republic. It was the largest "red tag sale" of all time. Whether it was a development of "Reason" of the sort that Hegel would have approved, we cannot say.

Unfortunately, at the very point where a powerful Germany could have been the fulcrum for a wider European development, the great German economic engine started to splutter and stall. First of all, Chancellor Helmut Kohl mishandled the reunification by promising a one-for-one exchange between the West and the East German mark. Much more important, the West Germans all underestimated the financial cost of redeveloping East Germany, and the social difference created by forty years of separate development— one free-market, the other Communist.

Early in 1991, the cost of restoring East Germany was being estimated in Bonn at about DM60 billion, or $2,400 per head of the population of East Germany. By the end of 1992, actual expenditure committed was DM350 billion, nearly six times as much. The eventual cost may well be DM1 trillion, or $40,000 per head of the East German population. This expenditure has exhausted the West German surplus, with little left over for investment in the rest of East Europe and the former Soviet Union.

At the same time, the German economy is weakening in terms of international competition, as is the European economy generally. High interest rates have held the D Mark at unnaturally high levels relative to the dollar and, even more dangerously, the yen. German investment in new productive equipment in West Germany is much lower than Japanese investment in Japan. Germany's industrial strengths are in relatively old-fashioned technologies, including heavy engineering, automobiles, and heavy chemicals. The growth mix of the German economy is not as strong as that of Japan or even the United States.

At the same time German industry is heavily regulated by the Länder, the federal government, and the European Community, and has high redundancy costs when labor has to be reduced. Most German businesses are run in a very bureaucratic manner. In all, German industry is beginning to look like General Motors, a superb organization of the 1960s, with some very high-quality middle technology, but overmanned, overregulated, and overbureaucratized.

This is a potential crisis for Germany, but also a potential crisis for the European Community. Germany is the industrial engine of Western Europe, and for that reason is also the predominant political power. The whole plan of the European Community, and particularly the Maastricht Treaty proposals for a further stage of European unity, presuppose that the German economy will be able to carry the broader European burden. A middle-tech, bureaucratized, high-unit-cost economy, based on a rapidly aging population, cannot be expected to carry East Germany, Eastern Europe, Russia, and the European Community. Germany is likely to suffer from everyone's overexpectations, including those of the Germans themselves.

These anxieties about the future of the German economy are widely held in Germany itself. There are substantial layoffs in German industry, particularly in the car industry. Germany has been moving into recession in 1992, and few Germans expect that the recession will clear away before 1994. Some recent studies of the German car industry suggest that it may be in a permanent decline in the face of Japanese competition, forced back into market niches. Yet the other European economies are not strong enough to make good any deterioration in Germany.

Probably the strongest of the other economies of the European Community is that of France, which shares with Germany a central geographical position in the market. French unemployment has been high throughout the 1980s and has now risen to over 10 percent. In world terms, the franc is an overvalued currency, certainly comparing French costs to American or Japanese, let alone those of the developing Asian economies. French attitudes are strongly protectionist, and France has become the most protectionist of all the European countries.

Italy is corruptly governed and has too much debt. Most of the Italian debt is expressed in terms of lire and much of it is internally held, which makes what would otherwise be an intolerable debt level perhaps less serious. A significant part of the Italian economy falls outside the knowledge of government; this black economy is a handicap when it comes to government debt service but may be an advantage in that it frees a sector of the Italian economy from the burden of overregulation, which is such a handicap to Europe as a whole. The countries immediately around Germany—Luxembourg, Belgium, and the Netherlands—really form part of the German economy. They are dependent upon it for demand, and German prosperity has maintained a very high level of prosperity among its neighbors. Their economies should no longer be regarded as independent economies. They may not be part of a single Europe, but they certainly are part of a single greater German economy.

Unfortunately, they also share the problems of the German economy in terms of their own domestic industry. The Netherlands, which has a very long financial and industrial tradition, has the same problems of bureaucratization of industry and overregulation as Germany does. One of the great Dutch companies, Phillips, the most important European company in consumer electrical and electronic goods, has been going through a crisis very similar to that of General Motors, trying to deal with the enormous burden of bureaucracy and overmanning left over from the industrial structures adopted in the 1950s and 1960s. All Dutch companies have the same problem—the low growth rate of the economy and overmanning—and most have too large an overhead.

The British economy was one of the weakest in Europe until the reforms of the 1980s. Britain has experienced a more prolonged depression in the 1990s than almost any other country, seeming to share the difficulties of the American and the European economies. The British housing debt is a long-term depressant on consumer demand, and significant sectors of British industry have disappeared because they were unable to compete with the Japanese. In terms of bureaucratiziation and enforced overmanning through trade union restrictions, Britain is somewhat better off than the other major European economies, having faced the issue under Margaret Thatcher at a time when other European countries felt that they did not need to do so. Britain's percentage of government expenditure to GDP is significantly lower than that of the other major European countries.

Greece, Portugal, and Ireland are poor countries that Europe can well afford to help during boom periods, but they are an added burden rather than an added resource, and the convergence under the Maastricht Treaty means trying to bring up their living standards to those of the rest of the European Community. The Danish economy is a high-cost Scandinavian economy relating strongly to that of Germany. The Danes are reluctant to become more dependent on Germany, and that was a major reason for their rejecting the Maastricht Treaty in the referendum. Spain is essentially a weak economy midway between that of Greece and Portugal on the one hand and Italy on the other. Like Italy, Spain faces the problem of severe government corruption.

The individual outlook for the European countries is therefore rather discouraging. The optimism of the late 1980s has given way to an increasing feeling of what might be called Euro-pessimism. Yet the attempted political and economic development of Europe is still in the hands of the politicians of the 1980s, particularly Chancellor Kohl and President Mitterrand, and seems to be based on 1980s assumptions.

There is a great contrast between the ambition to create a single European market, in which considerable but not complete progress has been made in 1992 and in the earlier years, and the ambition to create a single European Community as envisaged in the 1991 Treaty of Maastricht. The danger is that the single-market concept will be damaged by the attempt to move beyond it to some sort of federal European government.

At present the Maastricht Treaty of 1991 has been ratified by a number of European parliaments, has been passed by a large majority in a referendum in Ireland, has been passed by a very narrow majority in a referendum in France, and has been rejected by a narrow majority in a referendum in Denmark. The British Parliament has not yet ratified the treaty. Ratification is much more difficult in Britain than it has been in Germany, though it is generally agreed that the treaty would not be ratified by a referendum in either country.

In Britain Maastricht is regarded as too federalist, giving away too much power that belongs at present to the sovereignty of the House of Commons. In Germany it is regarded as giving away too much of the power of the Bundesbank to a European central bank; that is resented because it would mark the end of the D Mark, which the Germans trust, and replacement by a single European currency controlled by a central bank, some of whose members would come from countries with a much worse record of inflation than Germany's.

Among expert opinion in Europe there is a widespread disillusionment about the Maastricht scheme. Indeed, it satisfies hardly anybody. The scheme started out with a clear federal intention, but the European nations were not ready for federation. The Maastricht Treaty therefore has varying degrees of federal application, and leaves the balance of power tilted toward federation, but in a rather disorderly and illogical way. It does not actually succeed in creating a European federation but it does impose certain objectives in the economic area that only a fully federal system could be expected to achieve. From either a federal or an antifederal point of view, the Maastricht Treaty is a muddle.

For this reason the most frequent comment that one hears in Europe about Maastricht is that it does no harm for the parliaments to ratify it because it can never come into effect. The essential objective is a single European currency. The treaty recognizes that it is not possible to have a single currency if every European government is pursuing quite separate economic policies.

The obvious question is whether one could have, either in theory or in practice, a single currency and a single economic policy while retaining twelve independent governments that range from the strong and well-organized to the incompetent and corrupt. Again the danger seems to be that Germany, with the strongest economy, could be loaded with the responsibility for the whole.

German doubts about Maastricht arise because it would allow the weaker governments of Europe to lay their burdens on the stronger economies while at the same time giving the stronger economies less control of their own economic policies. Germany would not be able to run her own currency, would not even be free to run her own fiscal policy, but would have burdens like that of the Italian debt dumped on her. If, as was the case immediately before the reunification of Germany, the Germans felt that they could bear any burdens, then perhaps they could bear the weight of the rest of the European Community while they were sorting out the policies that had led to the particular economic difficulties of the other European countries. Now that Germany has found that the 17 million people of East Germany are actually more than the German economy can handle satisfactorily, it seems less and less possible to support the problems that could arise in the more than 200 million non-Germanic people of the rest of the European Community.

At an earlier stage we felt able to take an optimistic view of the development of the European single market, and we are still convinced that the single market in itself is good for Europe and is potentially good for the world. But we do not believe that the convergence of the European economies, which is envisaged in the Maastricht Treaty, can be achieved in the time scale that Maastricht set. We therefore do not believe that a single European currency is either desirable or possible in the next ten years. We do not believe that the individual European countries are ready for a stage of federation that goes beyond the stage of the single market. We are concerned that the European Community will be able to contribute far less to the world economy than seemed likely a few years ago.

Our forecast now would run as follows:

1. Trade inside Europe will continue to grow as a result of the reduction of border restrictions on trade. There will be more mergers and joint ventures between major European companies and the pattern of business organization in Europe will follow the single market, with a few large European companies emerging instead of a few large companies in each sector of each nation. This will improve the international competitive capacity of Europe and give Europe some of the advantages of the United States. It is likely, however, that the reorganization will be done by joint venture rather than full merger because

of the remaining nationalist aspirations of the individual European countries. The pattern will be the joint ventures entered into by Britain's G.E.C. with Alsthom and with Siemens rather than the full-scale mergers that have taken place inside individual countries.

2. Because of the high costs in Europe and the lack of competitiveness of European labor against labor in the Far East, Europe will continue for the time being to have very high rates of unemployment. That will be politically and socially damaging. These high rates of unemployment will tend to be reduced as the population ages and the new entrants to the labor market become much fewer. During the 1990s, European unemployment will probably be in the zone of 15 to 20 million.

3. The present European welfare systems, with their heavy emphasis on guaranteed pensions and benefits in old age, will become an increasing burden. They can barely be sustained during the 1990s but may well not be sustainable in the next century. Governments will be increasingly concerned to raise birth rates and to reduce the cost of taking care of the aged. Whatever the progressive reformers are urging, the politicians may become keener on euthanasia—a new social issue—and less keen on abortion as an instrument of social policy. Indeed it is notable that Ireland is the only European country with a strict no-abortion rule and a stable population base. In most European countries, abortions plus live births are still running at a full replacement level. It is abortion that has changed European demographic projections.

4. Europe cannot afford to be a high-cost, middle-tech island in a low-cost, high-tech world. The ability of the Bundesbank to resist inflation by keeping the German currency at an artificially high level will be reduced by the declining competitive advantages of the German economy. Relative to other currencies, European currencies are likely to fall in value and European interest rates to come nearer to the world average. These pressures will be accentuated by the pressures of unemployment on governments and by the changes of European government that are likely to be caused by the European depression.

5. The Bundesbank will remain the de facto central bank of Europe and will win its battle against the single currency with a federal government. Chancellor Kohl will be replaced as Chancellor either before or after the next German election but probably by mid-1994. The Bundesbank will continue to exercise a relatively austere influence despite the need to keep European currencies at a competitive level, but its power will be nothing like as great as it was in the 1980s. Britain will not rejoin the Exchange

Rate Mechanism. The convergence criteria of the Maastricht Treaty will not be met by the other European countries. There will not be a single European currency in the 1990s and probably not in the first decade of the next century either.

6. Because the European economy is losing its competitive edge, Europe will be relatively protectionist, particularly against Japan. There will also continue to be conflict with the United States. This will have the effect of reducing the competitive efficiency of the European economy still further and making many European businesses excessively inward-looking. The United States will have considerable reason to complain against Europe's reluctance to be a good partner in GATT. The difficulties that have arisen over the Uruguay round will persist. European protectionism may become intense.

7. It is likely that the most compatible countries—Austria, possibly Norway, Finland, and Sweden—will become members of the European Community inside the decade, but even they will find it a slower and more difficult process because of the more protectionist attitude. The European Community will not expand into Eastern Europe. There will not be a surplus sufficient to create major convergence through investment in the Eastern European countries, let alone the countries of the former Soviet Union. The progress toward a Europe stretching from the Atlantic to the Urals will be slow and disappointing. France in particular will continue to exercise a crucially protectionist role. French governments are likely to prefer a small Fortress Europe trying to defend high living standards against the competitive force of the outside world. Britain is likely to be a consistent but unsuccessful protagonist of Europe as a free-trade influence.

8. The pressures of emigration into Europe combined with the pressures of crime, which is now strongly entrenched in Italy because of the drug trade, will make European countries reluctant to have greater freedom of movement for people. Indeed, the commitments to have open borders inside the European Community are already being watered down and may eventually be withdrawn altogether. At present there are very great differences between the number of East European refugees that have been taken by different European countries, with Germany much more open than France or Britain. Germany will become more restrictive as the pressure of immigration intensifies, and Britain will certainly not become less restrictive. The only point at which restrictions will be eased will come when the European economies cannot be sustained without substantial increases in immigrant labor. Then the people who will be allowed in will, in the main, be young people with skills, from European countries outside the EC.

9. The prospect of free capital movement will create a severe problem in financing the Italian national debt. This will probably lead to a major Italian inflation, because their burden of debt compounding at high rates is unsustainable. An Italian default seems extremely likely given the size of the debt, the weakness of the Italian government, and the widespread manipulation of the Italian system by criminal forces.

10. None of the European currencies will be completely satisfactory as a store of value or as a reserve currency. The German mark would have become the reserve currency of Europe to a much greater degree if Germany had not undertaken the burden of East Germany and were not plainly faced by other economic burdens of an excessive kind. In Russia, the dollar has continued to be acceptable because it is plainly so much better a currency than the ruble. The dollar may not be the hardest currency in the world, but it is hard enough for the Russians. There will be greater tolerance of the dollar for a longer time than might otherwise have been expected in Europe. Probably the yen is the world's best prospect as a reserve currency for the first quarter of the next century, but Europeans are not accustomed to think in yen terms.

11. European countries that stay outside the European Community but have free trade relationships with it, which is the position of the Scandinavian countries for the time being, may suffer in their pride but will not suffer significantly in economic terms. The regulatory cost of the Brussels system— as with the regulatory cost of the Washington system—is a considerable burden on European industry. The Maastricht Treaty alone provides for at least thirty additional cost burdens on European industry.

12. The Europe that is being created is unfortunately highly bureaucratic. The current dominant forces in Brussels do not think in terms of industrial costs, although costs are the critical problem for European industry. At present industrialists see the net advantage from having a broader area of relatively free trade and are prepared to accept the regulatory costs. However, the single European market is now becoming established, and much stronger industrial protests against the regulatory and other industrial cost burdens seem likely to follow. The need to meet external competition alone will make that inevitable. The industrialists are likely also to be in favor of free trade with the rest of the world. But we cannot be confident that this will overcome the protectionist pressures.

Historic precedents suggest that free trade is contrary to the natural political order. The resolution to reduce trading barriers is a characteristic of the top of a long secular boom. It may not survive the political pressures that will emerge in a slump.

We strongly support the move to dispense with borders and barriers in the European Economic Community. If it could be implemented, all the countries of the European Community would benefit from the improved efficiencies of a broader free market. The stimulus would be especially vigorous in the Iberian peninsula. But the impact would not be limited to Europe itself. The United States, East Asia, and even the Third World would benefit, as they did from the spurt of growth associated with the advent of the Common Market in the 1960s.

The benefit of freer trade is not in doubt. What is in doubt is the capacity of political decision makers to complete all the complex negotiations needed to realize that benefit. History provides many examples of political decisions that betrayed the long-term best interests of everyone. Generally speaking, free trade has been an anomaly. Progress in eliminating trade barriers has been hard to come by, especially in times when trade was not generally growing. Most of the success that has been realized occurred in two periods: the third quarters of the nineteenth and twentieth centuries. Not coincidentally, these were the times when first Great Britain, then the United States, peaked in terms of economic hegemony. As we spelled out in *Blood in the Streets*, American economic power is now waning, increasing the prospect of a continued depression in the West and a closure of the world economic system.

There is a parallel between today's proposals for reducing trade barriers in Europe and proposals made in the twilight of British predominance during the late 1920s. It is little remembered today that the World Economic Conference sponsored by the League of Nations adjourned on May 23, 1927, with a resolution "in favour of abolishing or reducing to a minimum the system of import and export prohibitions." A schedule was set up for the gradual elimination of "all trade restrictions and prohibitions." Proposals were even put forward to abolish "invisible barriers to trade." The British ambassador, Sir Arthur Salter, argued for creation of a "United States of Europe." The record of discussion and negotiation over this proposal is spelled out in his book *The United States of Europe and Other Papers* (1933). The French diplomat Aristide Briand, later prime minister, was also a vigorous advocate of uniting Europe in a single free-trade area. Briand is best remembered as the coauthor of the Kellogg-Briand Pact outlawing war. Unhappily, his proposal for an economically integrated Europe turned out to be as unrealistic as his hopes to eliminate the use of force in international disputes.

In the period after World War II, Europe faced great challenges, which were successfully overcome. There was the challenge of the threat of Communism and the economic challenges of recovery and of a single market. With this record of success it would be wrong to write off Europe or the ability of the European nations to respond to new challenges. Nevertheless, the challenges of the 1990s, which are different, are very serious.

Despite the European Community, Europe is still divided by national economic self-interest. France, which professes to be one of the most European of European nations, pursues national self-interest with particular ruthlessness, but all the European nations do so to a considerable extent. This economic selfishness is a permanent force in favor of protectionism, which could damage Europe's position in world trade.

The European population is aging and will decline, and this will raise still further what already are the highest welfare costs in the world. European industry also suffers from its relatively low technological base—technology of the 1970s rather than the technology likely to be most profitable for the next century—and it suffers from the bureaucratic system that has been reinforced by the Brussels Commission.

The real challenge for the European Community, as for the United States, is competition with Asia. That is not only or even primarily competition with Japan but competition with the lower-cost developing countries, with all their potential. If the countries of the European Community are not able to overcome the problems of the 1990s, then what Spengler forecast in *The Decline of the West* is likely to go a stage further. In the next century Europe will have far less power in the world than in the second half of the twentieth century, which itself was period in which Europe had far less power than in the first half of the century, let alone in the heyday of European power before the outbreak of the First World War. From that tragedy, which began in Sarajevo, Europe has never completely recovered.

CHAPTER SIX

LATIN AMERICA TAKES OVER COMMUNISM AND OTHER IRONIES OF THE END OF THE COLD WAR

The spirit of mutiny swept the land. . . . Having freed itself from inherited fears and imaginary obstacles, the mass did not want to, and could not, see the real obstacles in its path. Therein lay its weakness, and also its strength. It rushed forward like an ocean of tide whipped by a storm. . . . It was as though someone were stirring the social cauldron, right to its very bottom, with a gigantic spoon. . . . Workers' strikes, incessant processions, wreckings of country estates, strikes of policemen and janitors, and finally unrest and mutiny among the soldiers and sailors. Everything disintegrated, everything turned to chaos.

—LEON TROTSKY

THE BRIGHT people in the American State Department used to fret that Marxism had history on its side. They feared that once a country fell under the spell of Communism, it could never again break free. The Alliance for Progress was launched because of this vision. Billions in foreign aid were pumped into Central and South America. Big banks were encouraged to lend more billions, never to be repaid, on the understanding that it was in America's interests to increase the flow of funds to unstable Latin regimes. Further sums of treasure went to support anti-Communist armies in El Salvador and the Contra rebels fighting in Nicaragua. All this was to prevent Communism from taking over Latin America. Now we see that it turned out rather differently. Communism has not taken over Latin America. The truth is more nearly the other way around. Latin America is taking over Communism.

The breakdown of Communist systems everywhere is both political and economic. Its financial implications will spill over through the entire world. As Marxist systems have lost their political grip, following many decades of economic failure, they have come to resemble more nearly the unstable Third World countries than the prosperous democracies of the West. In 1992, more boundaries shifted than in the previous forty-five years combined. New nations, or nations not heard of for centuries, have risen up to take their place on the map. It is possible that continental Russia and the remains of the former Soviet Union will be convulsed by revolution and even civil war for many years to come. Having enjoyed, at least briefly, the rule of an elected president, Russia will probably end the decade neither prosperous nor democratic, but with a nationalistic, fascist regime led by a Slavic version of Juan Perón.

What was once East Germany will no doubt have a better fate. It will gradually develop into a Western European–style democracy as the Siamese twin of West Germany in a reunified Reich. But as the turmoil and almost nightly rioting against foreigners showed in 1992, the residues left behind by Communism are highly combustible. It will take the wealthy German state many hundred of billions of D marks to scrub them clean. And it is by no means clear that the task can be completed in this century.

In Czechoslovakia, the challenges of reconstruction have already split the country in two. Without the resources to peg wage rates at Western European levels, the government in Prague had no choice but to price its reform program on market terms. By most economic measures, this program, designed by Vaclav Klaus, has been a success. Inflation was slashed from 55 percent to 10 percent in a year. The budget deficit was virtually eliminated. Even the balance-of-payments deficit for 1991 was held to just $200 million, less than the U.S. deficit for a single day. Yet even Eastern Europe's most successful reform program did not prevent rising tribal tensions between the Czechs and Slovaks from shattering the republic. The market reforms produced bids for investment in the more advanced Czech Republic, fewer in the Slovak regions. In an era of rising tensions, the forces of devolution turned this development difference into a border. Time will no doubt prove this divorce much to the disadvantage of the Slovaks. If the Czechs continue their market reforms, they may recover the relative prosperity that made theirs one of the more advanced economies in Europe before World War II. The Slovaks, like most of Eastern Europe and the remains of the Soviet Union, have a future much like the past of Latin America.

Before World War II, Eastern Europe and China followed the same patterns of instability as Latin America. As the ideological dictatorships that have held sway in the Marxist systems lose their grip, an anarchic situation could develop that could become more or less permanent. The Argentine economy was for years in a state of inflationary collapse, despite spasms of democratic government. It may be again. A cycle of weak dictatorship and weak democracies, the army stepping in and stepping out, and ever-higher inflation is familiar in the history of Latin America in the late nineteenth and twentieth centuries. Poland's economy in 1992 was in even worse shape than Argentina's before democracy returned. The same was true in Hungary, Rumania, what was once Yugoslavia, Bulgaria, and Cuba. Such crippled systems need reform that weak and ineffective governments find hard to achieve. Realistic pricing causes unrest among impoverished urban populations. Closing uneconomic enterprises and dismantling bureaucracy means unemployment. This, too, leads to unrest. The path of least resistance is to subsidize everybody with printed money. Triple-digit inflation is already common in Eastern Europe and the former Soviet states. Indeed, hyperinflation is so severe in Russia, and economic collapse is so complete, that at ruble exchange rates prevailing in late 1992, Russian GDP stood at $30 billion, or about one-half of one percent of U.S. GDP.

Such is the legacy of Communism. First in Poland, then throughout Eastern Europe, and now in the former Soviet republics themselves, decades of lies and oppression draw to an end with the collapse of Stalin's empire. As we forecast in *Blood in the Streets*, the Communist system was brought down by a crucial megapolitical development—the microchip. It would have died anyway of its many deficiencies and functional contradictions. But it died sooner and more suddenly because there was no way for the lumbering command economy to accommodate the decentralizing impact of microtechnology— the new growth sector of the world economy. Neither could the impact of microtechnology be ignored.

It could not be ignored because the transistor helped spread information and undermine totalitarian control. As radio and television became more common throughout the Eastern bloc, it became ever more difficult for Communist authorities to dam the flow of information reaching their people. And no item of information was as crucial to the revolutions of 1989 as news from Afghanistan that the Soviet military had been defeated. Illiterate Afghan peasants had harnessed the microchip, in the form of deadly new Stinger missiles, to effectively immobilize Soviet air power. In the process, the mujaheddin demonstrated for all to see that offensive Soviet military might could be neutralized. Moscow could no longer impose its will by military edict, even on its own borders. Not a year passed between the Soviet withdrawal and the collapse of Stalin's Eastern European empire.

Just as American defeat in Vietnam almost twenty years earlier had precipitated an upsurge in confiscation of American investments abroad, including the oil concessions swallowed by OPEC, so Russian defeat triggered a sudden rush of rebellion. Hammer-and-sickle emblems came crashing to the ground from Warsaw to Bucharest. Military defeat in Afghanistan meant not just the end of the Soviet empire, but the public disgrace of the command economy in Russia as well.

It meant the end of a century of enchantment with the doctrines of Marx. His ideas will still be in books. And many of them will still be believed. But they will be believed mainly in American universities and backwater, Third World mining towns. Marxism at long last has ceased to be a contemporary ideology. It is now of the past. Just as Plato and Aristotle, and even Thomas Aquinas, are figures of the past, whose thoughts were informed in conditions other than our own, so Marx speaks to us now across the divide of history.

THE FAILURES OF MARXISM

Of course, dedicated Marxists may not yet be ready to accept that judgment. They would claim that there are still deep truths to be learned from the study of Marxism. We would agree but for different reasons. Little though Marxism did for workers in practice, its rise and fall tells us something about the fortunes of the industrial worker. This is something that could be important to understand.

The building of factories for mass employment, along with the spread of firearms, gave unskilled workers a rare opportunity to seize wealth. Every such shift of megapolitical power engenders a new ideology to justify the new outcome. When a new power comes along to pay the piper, the result is a new tune. Marx met that demand for a new ideology by concocting a wide-ranging justification for workers seizing the property of the owners. Ironically, his ideas proved most useful to workers in situations where conditions of offsetting power prevented them from being entirely carried out.

It was in Western countries, where workers did not seize all the property of the owners, that they got the highest gains. Fifty percent of something is more than 100 percent of nothing. The "class struggle" was most successful from the workers' standpoint where the capitalists continued to control the state and the Marxists failed.

On a more profound level, however, we believe that class conflict explains little. Rich and poor alike have always squabbled over the good things of life. And they are likely to squabble even more in the decades to come, as opportunities for the unskilled and uneducated to earn income by manual labor shrivel. Yet rarely do these squabbles become historic transformations. If you try to specify the conditions under which class struggle determines the direction of history, you are left with a puzzle. Most of the explanation must be smuggled in from elsewhere.

Wrong though Marx was in many ways, part of his theory of historical development is valid. He was right in thinking that historic change is sometimes caused by changes in the underlying means of production. This is one of the truffles of truth to be dug for in the enchanted forest of Marxism. History is a process, and, according to Marx and Engels, "circumstances make men just as men make circumstances." It does seem to be true, as Marx argued, that "social revolution" results when "the material forces of production in society come into conflict with the existing relations of production." That is what we are seeing in Marxist societies today.

Yet Marx offered little guidance in predicting when such "revolutions" will arise. Even if you accept the Marxist definition of "exploitation," which we do not, it is certain from history that exploitation *per se* is not the determining factor. Marx himself recognized that "exploitation" was not necessarily destabilizing. In fact, exploitative systems could be highly stable, as was the case in what Marx called the "Asiatic Mode of Production"—the Oriental despotism that endured for centuries on end.

Ironically, a deficiency of the Marxist system of dialectical materialism as a theory of history is that it is not determinist enough. It offers an abundance of political rhetoric and jargon, but little basis for predicting how anything will turn out. Many potentially far-reaching changes are external to the dynamic of the system. For example, suppose a new disease, a latter-day version of the Black Death, or a more easily communicable version of AIDS, were to strike humanity, killing or debilitating everyone except a small minority who happened to possess an exotic blood protein that provided protection from the infection. Such a development would lead to a historic change of dramatic dimensions. Yet it would have utterly nothing to do with "surplus value" or the other preoccupations of Marxist ideology. While such a prospect is hypothetical, it is not far different from what actually happened to Native American populations on their first encounter with white men carrying European diseases. A theory of historic change should make sense of such developments.

Furthermore, Marx's deification of workers has proven to be misleading. It not only led to an underestimation of the importance of entrepreneurial decisions by capitalists and managers in the production process—a mistake that proved disastrous for Marxist systems in practice—it also erected barriers to understanding the actual "law of motion of modern society." In effect, Marx and his followers set up a giant billboard emblazoned with a political slogan, "The workers are the vanguard of history." This was not only misleading in itself, it blocked the view of the social landscape. It made it more difficult to predict how technological change would actually shift political power and redistribute income.

For example, our prediction in *Blood in the Streets* of the impending collapse of Communism was a deduction derived from the role of microtechnology in reducing optimum firm size. We explained why Communism is an artifact from a rare period of history when staple mass production industries operated most efficiently at a gigantic scale. We also showed why the decline in the optimum scale of enterprise has far-reaching implications for Marxist systems that effectively operated as economy-wide holding companies under the control of the Communist Party. Such systems were antiquated by the computer. Marxist analysis offers no such insights. For all the talk about "material forces of production in society," Marxism is mainly a romantic vision rather than objective analysis of how change in crucial technological variables alters economic and political arrangements. The failure of the Marxist systems, which Marxists failed to predict, is only one example of this shortcoming.

Another is the impact of the declining scale of production enterprises in Western countries on the income share of factory labor. Marxists, of course, would claim to have predicted this as part of their permanent prediction of increasing "exploitation" of the workers, leading to the long-expected collapse of the bourgeois system. But such ancient forecasts, dating back more than a century, do not touch on the primary facts of the situation, which are precisely the opposite of those that Marx claimed could be predicted "with the precision of natural science." This bears explanation. What is happening is not that capitalists are suddenly succeeding in exploiting the workers, but rather that technological change is making it more difficult for workers to exploit the capitalists.

Contrary to the popular misconception, employers do not generally and routinely "exploit" employees. They may ask them to do stupid things. They may be petty and aggravating. They may drive down morale. But employers like that tend to go out of business. They do not "exploit" workers by somehow forcing them to toil for less than their market-clearing wages. The practice in democratic countries is precisely the reverse. The advent of large-scale enterprises in the late nineteenth and twentieth centuries enabled labor unions to extract higher wages for their members—higher than would be justified by their true economic contributions. They did this by threatening to strike or, in many cases, sabotage the operations of the enterprises in which they were employed. Since companies operating on a large scale tend to have high capital costs, which make even temporary losses of output costly, management in most cases found it prudent to pay workers more than would have been required by the strict economic costs of replacing them. In essence, industrial workers received a political payoff in addition to their economic wage—a legalized shakedown payment for not sabotaging the operations of the firms where they worked.

Such shakedown payments were most readily achieved in industries most vulnerable to sabotage. Railroads, for example, can easily be derailed. Consequently, they were among the first industries worldwide to be unionized. The same is true for most mining operations, especially deep shaft mines. The possible damage from blockading or flooding a mine was great. In most cases, mine management found it prudent to accept union demands for higher wages rather than risk costly damage to the operation. As a consequence, the share of income earned by uneducated or poorly educated workers rose sharply as the scale of enterprise grew during the first half of the twentieth century. Some of this gain was due to productivity advances arising from a larger scale of enterprise. Another part was due to blackmail or, to put it more politely, the exploitation of the capitalists by the workers.

The economic change of recent decades has been from the primacy of manufactures to that of communications, from machine power to electronic power, from factory to office, from mass production to small teams. As the scale of enterprise falls, so does the potential for sabotage and blackmail in the workplace. Smaller-scale operations are much more difficult to organize by unions. Partly, this is because they tend to be smaller, more footloose targets. Many deal in services or products with negligible natural resource content. In principle, these businesses could be conducted almost anywhere. They are not trapped at a specific location, like a mine or a port. If operations become uncomfortable because of union demands, a firm operating on a small scale can move. Such firms also have an added inducement to escape union demands for monopoly wages. Smaller firms tend to have more competitors. If you have dozens or even hundreds of competitors tempting your customers, you cannot afford to pay your employees more than they are actually worth. If you alone tried to do so, your costs would be higher than your competitors' and you would go broke.

The decay of union power as economies move into the Information Age is hardly a random development. It is a predictable consequence of the declining scale of enterprise and therefore the increasing costs of redistributing income through disguised blackmail. Both the economic base and the class ideology of socialism are in rapid decline. The industrial worker, having had his summer of class power, must now give way to new interests and ideas, based on emerging rather than declining technology. Because unions can no longer extract political blackmail from employers as readily as they used to, it is hardly surprising that the share of income claimed by essentially unskilled workers is falling while the percentage earned by the well-educated and the capitalists is rising. Contrary to the animated assertions of union officials and their supporters, the decline of unions, and the resulting shift in the distribution of income, are not evidence of increasing "exploitation." In democratic countries, at least, it was the workers who exploited the capitalists during the phase of technological development that was characterized by large-scale output. The unique legal immunities that exempted unions from laws against intimidation and violence during strikes became a feature of law in practically every stable representative system.

These laws reflected a megapolitical fact. Unions had the raw force to close down and sabotage not only individual firms but whole economies during times when economic activity was disproportionately focused in a few gigantic firms. They also had votes to sanction their actions through the political process. Technological change has now eclipsed the raw megapolitical power of unions. The smokestacks have become the Rust Belt, the factory worker is a dwindling minority, and his ideology is a dwindling minority ideology. The new class is the electronic class, whose work is individualistic, often incentive-rewarded, personal rather than impersonal, and related to communications that span the world. It is a far, far better way of life.

This new class does not want to live in a factory state of imposed uniformity, which is entirely alien to its work experience and social needs. This is a quasi-capitalist class, with a strong desire for home ownership, freedom of movement, and personal independence. To the electronic class, the ideologies of market capitalism—John Locke, Adam Smith, John Stuart Mill—are more relevant than the ideologies of nineteenth-century state socialism, whether in the totalitarian form of Marx or the milder, democratic form of the Fabians and the union movement. Many of the factories that were built for mass employment from about 1770 through 1960 have already been closed down. This has happened first in Great Britain and the United States, the first two leading manufacturing powers. As other nations follow through the stages of economic development, more than factories will be closed. We will also board up or demolish the factory consciousness, Stalinism, dark inner cities with their tower block public housing—"machines for living" in Corbusier's infamous phrase—public schooling based on the factory method: in short, the whole smokestack society.

The withdrawal of unions' extraordinary legal status will be part of this process. As mass-production factory jobs fall away and the growing number of entrepreneurs and would-be entrepreneurs find greater political expression, unions will lose their legal power to intimidate and employ violence in strikes. This is already evident in Great Britain and the United States. The sudden addition of millions of unemployed East Germans, the disruptions inherent in reunification, and the mass closure of Stalinist industries are also likely to undermine union power in the new Germany. As other nations emerge from the era of large-scale mass production, unions will lose their extraordinary legal footing there as well. To steal a comment from Engels, the cause of this development is not "to be sought in the minds of men, in their increasing insight into eternal truth and justice, but in changes in the mode of production."

This change in the "mode of production" is ironically hidden from the Marxist who misperceives the character of exploitation as an economic problem. But exploitation or no, the industrial worker whom Marx imagined as his hero is on the way out. The megapolitical logic of technology is the same in socialist economies as in the West. This is a truth now being verified by the restructuring of Marxist economies. This has meant a loss of industrial jobs and a plunge in wages for factory workers even in the former Soviet Union. As we write, workers in Russia are commanding an average wage of less than $15 a month.

The fantasy that the workers are the vanguard of history has defeated the systematic analysis to which Marx aspired. Not only has it tended to obscure the changing relationships between technology and political outcomes, thus cloaking rather than illuminating important developments, such as the twilight of Communism, it has also discouraged understanding of developments in the past. The romantic identification with peasants, workers, and the poor in general, so common among intellectuals, has naturally tended to block appreciation of features of economic development that run counter to this prejudice. As a consequence, some of the more important generalizations about the impact of economic change on societies are hidden from view. In the first instance, this disguises the past. But even more important from our perspective, it also disguises the future. A more realistic grasp of what actually happens when societies move up and down the scale of economic development forms a more reliable basis for forecasting events such as the collapse of Communism, and the consequences that follow from it.

Gorbachev Did Not Kill Communism

When the full story of the Communist collapse is detailed in history books, it will no doubt become more clear than it is at this writing that Gorbachev did not give away his empire. Many in the West, seeing the changes for which they were unprepared, credited Gorbachev for engineering freedom for the nations occupied by Stalin after World War II. But Gorbachev was not the author of these events. He was merely carried along by the flood of revolution. He appeared to be the master of his own policy, but in fact, he was like a man shooting the rapids: It is the water that steers the boat, and the helmsman is carried by the flood. Gorbachev tolerated the revolutions of 1989 that freed Eastern Europe because he had little choice. Attempts by Erich Honecker and other hardline Communists in East Germany to crush demonstrators militarily were vetoed by the Soviets, not because Gorbachev wished to give away Eastern Europe, but because he did not wish to embroil Soviet troops in civil war. A crackdown could have resulted in a bloody revolution.

It was too late to save East Germany, the rest of Eastern Europe, or even the Soviet Union, as the failed coup of August 1991 proved. The Communist economies had simply collapsed. They could not go on. The shortages were too acute. There was too much pollution. The goods were too low in quality. Distribution had failed. Food production had failed. After decades of peace, the former Communist economies looked as though they had just emerged from the devastation of a world war. It was only the devastation of socialism.

The theory that human societies ought to be organized from a single command center to ensure equal distribution of benefits has been disproven. This theory made the bureaucratic masters of the state the true sovereign power. They represented the industrial workers, the proletariat, but in name only. In fact, the Soviet Union after 1917 became a slave society in that the power of the state was subject to no control by the citizen. Similar systems were imposed on the satellite nations of Eastern Europe. But even in Western Europe, compromised versions of socialism with a democratic face had failed. Attempts to retain the sovereignty of the individual in terms of political elections, but create the sovereignty of the state over what was termed "the commanding heights of the economy," brought economic stagnation to Great Britain in the 1970s and Sweden in the 1980s. Centralizing economic power for the state through nationalization acts, punitive taxation, and controls over trade and finance brought long-term problems.

The theory of socialism proved to be a lethal blunder. There are reasons in politics, psychology, sociology, philosophy, and information theory why economic socialism is a failure. As we argue elsewhere in this book, new developments in the understanding of complex systems discredit in yet another way the idea of benign economic planning. There are now many proofs that socialism cannot succeed over the long run. Much of the important work that establishes the counterarguments to Marx has been done by those trained in the Viennese academic tradition, including Karl Popper, Friedrich von Hayek, and Ludwig von Mises. People prefer to live in an open society. But it is also far more efficient.

The primary arguments are those of motivation. John Locke, the seventeenth-century philosopher, argued that people need economic liberty because they want different things. That is where the phrase "the pursuit of happiness" comes from. Adam Smith argued that people would supply goods and services for profit that they would not supply for charity. Ludwig von Mises argued that it is not a question of plan or no plan, but of whether the individual should plan for himself or someone else should plan for him.

One can reinforce these arguments by studies of information theory developed in the computer age. These show that a successful communications system requires a strong flow of information, a capacity for rapid response, and feedback of action taken. A tennis champion will have an accurate perception of what is happening on the court, a rapid ability to play the ball, and rapid recognition of the impact of his shot—information, action, and feedback.

The market system has all these qualities. The information flow and the feedback are maximized because all the potential buyers and sellers operate through the market. The market knows what the bureaucracy cannot possibly know, and eliminates those traders or producers who are not able to respond quickly. Competitive pressures mean that the best-qualified survive.

The socialist command system is not like this at all. It knows little and responds bureaucratically. It does not know what demand is, except through the length of lines and the volume of complaints. It has no automatic feedback. It is like a blind, one-legged centenarian on the center court at Wimbledon.

The political collapse became inevitable because people were fed up with Communism. The system had exhausted its resources, and exhausted the patience of the people.

After the August 1991 coup, Mikhail Gorbachev found himself in the position of a polar bear on an ice floe. The ice was breaking up and bits were floating away. It was a process he could not prevent. In the end there was no place for him to stand, nothing but icy water. The age of Communism in the modern world is over.

HYPERINFLATION AND DEFLATION

When the first edition of this book was published, we predicted that the formerly Communist countries would follow the Latin American model, with weak social order and inadequate economic development. This is no longer a conjecture. It is a fact. The consequences have indeed been inflationary for those countries emerging from Communism and deflationary for the world. Locally bankrupt systems always tend to deflate demand internationally. This looks likely to be true of the former Communist economies for some time to come.

1. The more bankrupt the former Communist systems become, the wider the circle of debt default they will spread. The Russians have already slashed foreign aid to the former client states like Cuba, Nicaragua, Ethiopia, and Angola. This has aggravated the bankruptcy of these nations, leaving them with fewer resources with which to meet their debt obligations. Debt defaults undermine the collateral of the whole international banking system, slowing lending worldwide.

2. The death of Communism also means the death of the Third World. It foreshadows a significant drop in the level of Western aid and assistance to the poor countries of the South, because these countries will no longer be able to play off the East-West rivalry. It will appear to Western political leaders to be far more crucial to provide available aid to stablilize Russia and the other former Soviet republics, still heavily armed with nuclear weapons, than to pour more money into Kenya or Zaire. The Russians and their former allies in Eastern Europe will command a major share of international development aid. They will also consume the attention, though not necessarily the funds, of private investors.

3. There will be less effective demand from the bankrupt economics, which will tend to slow international trade and reduce commodity prices. Even defaults on official debt that do not directly undermine the banking system tend to deflate demand. As we write, Russia is in default on many billions in debts contracted by the former Soviet Union, including U.S. grain credits that were paid with religious punctuality before the Soviet collapse. Until the default is perfected, subsidized grain sales to Russia will be halted, putting deflationary pressure on the prices of food commodities.

4. Pressed to accumulate hard currencies, the post-Communist countries will be obliged to sell anything they can in world markets. Closed systems with runaway inflation tend to reduce imports more than exports. Latin America has run a trade surplus in recent years while inflation ran amuck and living standards tumbled. The countries left behind by Communism will also be obliged to dump any products they can sell to get hard currency, while importing less from abroad.

5. Industrial output in the former Communist countries has plunged. This has reduced raw-material demand to a far greater extent than could be offset by the meager increase in demand for manufactured products from the West.

6. The liquidation of the Soviet Union and the drop in military spending among the successor states is putting significant downward pressure on West-

ern military spending. As we explore later in detail, lower military spending is deflationary.

7. As we explained in *Blood in the Streets,* one of the easiest elements of reform to achieve in Eastern Europe and the former Soviet Union is reform of agriculture. At the time of the czar, Russia was a major food exporter, notwithstanding the muddled incentives inherent in the closed village system of community property that still lingered from the Middle Ages. Under this system, peasants were discouraged from improving productivity because all land was owned by the village. The most productive plots were periodically expropriated by the village elders and redistributed, usually for their own benefit and that of their families. When this backward arrangement was finally scrapped after the Revolution of 1905, Russian agriculture experienced an explosive growth of productivity. This reform was possible even for the weak czarist regime. It is reasonable to expect a similar result from the dismantling of collective farms today. As of 1992, little progress had yet been made in dismantling collective farms in most of the former Soviet Union. When reform accelerates, the productivity of Russian agriculture should explode. There have already been some modest improvements in the distribution system arising from a greater private role in the economy. If crops grown in the former Soviet Union but now allowed to rot in the fields were brought to market, there would be little need for the republics to import food. Any halfway coherent reform of farming implies a major drop in grain imports, and thus lower prices for most staple foods worldwide.

8. While some reforms are bound to bear fruit, especially in the farming sector, it is unlikely that they will succeed in making the former Soviet Union an attractive home to a large influx of foreign capital. Therefore, the potential for an investment boom centered on the reconstruction of those countries may remain merely a tantalizing prospect, like Lord Baden-Powell's speculation at the end of the last century that the woolen industry would get an immense boost if only every African could be convinced to wear a suit. The foreclosure of the opportunity to invest up to one trillion dollars in the reconstruction of Russia implies that there will not be a capital spending boom to mask the transitional effects of lower defense spending.

9. The collapse of income in Eastern Europe and the former Soviet Union places severe stresses on the high-wage economies of Western Europe. One of the reasons that the reunification of Germany has proven so expensive is that the authorities have felt compelled to manage the integration in a way that did not undercut the prevailing high wages of western Germany. The costs of insulating the high-wage economy have proven to be very large,

including penal German interest rates that have depressed growth throughout the European Community. If East German labor had been priced at wages that realistically reflected its productivity, the cash costs of reunification would have been far lower, but with the consequence of deflating the bloated costs of Germany industry and the generous welfare benefits that underpin those costs. One way or the other, however, the collapse of Communism will reduce wages in Western Europe. The proximity of many tens of millions of workers in Eastern Europe whose wages are on a par with those of India or China cannot help but place growing downward pressure on high-wage economies in Germany and the rest of the European Community.

10. The death of Communism marks a shift from a bipolar world, with two military camps allied with Washington or Moscow, to a multipolar world of economic competition. This shift will fracture the Western alliance. In the future, there will be at least three major blocs. North America, dominated by the United States, will compete with the Pacific rim, dominated by Japan, and the European Community, dominated by Germany. In the past, the move to a multipolar environment in world politics has destabilized the international economic system, contributing to deflationary collapse.

This last point is particularly important, and perhaps likely to be misunderstood. As Charles Kindelberger emphasized in his explanation for the Great Depression of 1929, one of the chief reasons for the collapse was that there was no longer a single country willing or able to discharge the following functions:

1. maintaining a relatively open market for distress goods;
2. providing countercyclical, or at least stable, long-term lending;
3. policing a relatively stable system of exchange rates;
4. ensuring the coordination of macroeconomic policies;
5. acting as a lender of last resort by discounting or otherwise providing liquidity in financial crisis.

The breakup of the postwar world means that there will no longer be a single country willing and able to perform these functions.

As we explained in *Blood in the Streets*, the fall of Communism will reduce the relative prosperity of the United States and undermine the U.S. dollar. Germany and Japan, the world's principal creditors, will no longer be obliged to subsidize America's budget deficits and support the U.S. dollar. They will no longer need to fear that the exposure of economic weakness in America would lead to significant cuts in American military spending, because American military might will be less important to their security. If the past is a guide, Japan and Germany will go their own way, developing their own foreign policies, rather than subsidizing America to enable it to continue serving as the world's leader.

In the spring of 1992, German Chancellor Helmut Kohl and Japanese Prime Minister Miyazawa seemed to fulfill our prediction. They decided to increase their bilateral cooperation and coordination without involving the United States. They agreed that the two countries should "play roles commensurate with their increased international importance." Sources close to Kohl said at the time that a more independent policy would be needed because the U.S. appeared adrift and inwardly focused.

Given the volcanic situation in the former Soviet Union, it is likely that Germany will shift from subvening America's deficits to subsidizing Russia. The German government will have a strong interest in helping to provide Russia with food and other essentials in order to stave off a flood of refugees fleeing economic collapse.

Japan has other priorities. It, too, will go its own way, concentrating new investment in China and the nearby Pacific regions, areas that attracted the lion's share of Japanese interest before World War II. To be sure, Japanese manufacturers have a great stake in plant and equipment in the United States, which they will use as an export platform. It will be more difficult for the European Community to exclude cars made in America by Japanese companies than to exclude Japanese cars made in Japan. But the trade tensions between Europe and Japan are likely to grow in any case, with the United States seen increasingly as playing a weak hand.

From the perspective of late 1992, it seems unlikely that the United States will be able to exert effective pressure to maintain an open world trading system. Indeed, it is doubtful that many American political leaders would even want to. Part of the suspense surrounding troubled world talks to draft a new treaty for the General Agreement on Tariff and Trade (GATT) was the common perception that the U.S. Congress was becoming far more protectionistic. It seemed to many observers that any agreement signed and submitted for ratification could be torn to shreds in the Congress.

During most of the postwar period, the United States helped Japan, Taiwan, South Korea, and other countries of the Pacific rim develop their economies by allowing them to maintain relatively closed investment and trade policies in exchange for their diplomatic support in the Cold War. The security arrangements worked principally to the advantage of the Pacific rim countries. The United States did not use its power when it might have to insist that these major trading partners open their markets to American goods at a time when American products were overwhelmingly superior. Now the eclipse of the United States as a manufacturing power has taken away much of the American incentive to seek free trade. It has certainly shifted the political balance within the Congress. Protectionist sentiment has grown, and policy has changed accordingly. Except in farm products, American policy during the 1980s was to erect trade barriers rather than pull them down. That policy is likely to continue in the 1990s.

The United States no longer has the financial capability to provide countercyclical lending, nor serve as the lender of last resort. Like Great Britain in the late 1920s, the United States can no longer bail out other countries in trouble. Unlike Britain then, however, the United States has already become a debtor nation; it must effectively borrow from abroad in order to bail out another country. A banker whose till is bare cannot be a dependable source of new money.

Nor can the United States by any stretch of the imagination police a system of stable exchange rates. That capability was exhausted in 1971 when Richard Nixon repudiated the international monetary system of fixed exchange rates. To put it simply, the United States no longer has the financial power to stabilize the world economy. And neither Germany nor Japan is in a position to immediately assume that function. Therefore, the world economy will be increasingly exposed to much the same danger of deflationary collapse that transpired in 1929.

Good-bye to the Subsidized Dollar

There are other important implications of the end of the Cold War for Americans. It means the end of the subsidized dollar. Because the collapse of Communism goes a long way toward lifting the military threat to Germany and Japan, it weakens the incentives those nations previously had to support the U.S. dollar through thick and thin. This was demonstrated in the grudging support forthcoming from Japan and Germany for the U.S. military campaign to liberate Kuwait. American opinion deeply resented the impression that both Japan and Germany were acting as freeloaders on America's military. The attitude in Tokyo and Bonn was that they were being dragooned into subsidizing America's military industries.

Henceforth it will be less important for America's former allies to provide roundabout subsidies to American military spending by supporting the dollar in moments of crisis, or investing large sums to finance U.S. budget deficits. More of the German and Japanese surpluses will go into the rebuilding of

East Germany, and into other regions of investment opportunity. Relatively less of the world's capital will be available to invest in the United States.

This will probably require the United States to run a more restrictive fiscal policy during the 1990s than during the last twenty years of the Cold War. Nothwithstanding huge potential savings on the order of $150 billion annually from the reduced military threat, there will be a major political struggle within the United States over how to bring the federal budget under control.

Fiscal and monetary pressures may even lead the United States to follow in Britain's footsteps and introduce domestic capital controls. We touch on this possibility elsewhere.

A Post-Communist Boom?

Any transitional difficulties arising from the end of the Cold War would have minor economic consequences in the 1990s if Russia and the other post-Communist economies could successfully follow the path of reform. The best case would have the Commonwealth of Independent States transformed into a pluralist society, based on a market economy, with loose federal arrangements between the different nations, and with friendly relations with Eastern Europe and the West generally. This is what Mr. Yeltsin was aiming for in some of his reforms.

This best case would be extremely favorable for the whole world economy. East Europe and the CIS post-Communist economies could absorb and justify heavy investment, which Western Europe, Japan, and to a lesser extent the United States would have the financial and political incentive to provide—if the structure were in place to receive it.

There could be a massive market for environmental cleanup if the people of the CIS and Eastern Europe can improvise some way of paying to close the open wounds left behind by Communism. The former Soviet Union, in particular, is a poisoned land. Chernobyl became an international symbol of environmental damage. But it is merely the most famous part of a widespread catastrophe that seems likely to worsen as the system collapses.

The seventy years of Communism, or forty years in East Europe, have caused an astonishing amount of damage, waste, and loss of social and industrial investment. The need for investment is great—far more than these crippled systems can provide on their own.

How can we gain an understanding of the magnitude of capital that would be required to bring the former Soviet Union and its one-time satellites up to a par with the capitalist countries? One measure we can use is the value of equities listed on the stock markets of the eleven major non-Communist countries. These countries have a population of seven hundred million, and a market of equities worth approximately ten trillion dollars. That works out to an equity of about fourteen thousand dollars per head of population.

The post-Communist world has half this population, and is perhaps at one-third of this level of industrial development. There is therefore a missing industrial and commercial equity caused by socialist waste and inefficiency on the order of three trillion dollars. To give some idea of the scale of three trillion dollars: Annual current capital spending by the whole of West German industry was running at about two hundred billion dollars in the late 1980s. The missing equity in the post-Communist world, required to bring these countries into industrial balance with their neighbors, is the equivalent of fifteen years of West Germany's total investment. This is far beyond the capacity of these countries to provide for themselves in the next decade. Even dramatic cuts in military budgets and significant gains from reform would still leave the CIS and other post-Communist economies dependent upon a massive influx of foreign capital.

If such an investment opportunity were forthcoming, it would make a deep depression unlikely. Economies seldom falter while massive investment projects are underway. The post-Communist boom would be like a postwar boom in the replenishment of missing industrial capacity, and the raising of standards of production efficiency. It could help tide the world over what otherwise stands to be a major transition crisis. Practically everything in the former Soviet Union and Eastern Europe needs replacement or upgrading.

Unfortunately, the current weakness of the post-Communist economies, which makes the need for capital investment so tantalizingly obvious, also makes it unlikely that the opportunities can be realized. With a handful of exceptions, most of the existing factories in the post-Communist countries are throwbacks—smokestack industries of the 1920s. They produce low-quality, even shoddy goods. They are so shoddy, in fact, that the much-discussed problem of valuing state assets in nations emerging from Communism may be more academic exercise than economic necessity. For all practical purposes, the Communist plants are worthless.

This is clearly demonstrated in what was East Germany, which has been so closely studied by the West Germans. Within days after the currency union between the two Germanies, most East German goods had disappeared from the shelves in East Germany. They had been removed by store managers who knew them best because, compared to Western goods, they had simply become unsaleable. A conspicuous example is the Trabant automobile, the smelly, grimy, and expensive little vehicle that was commonly seen on the streets of Eastern Europe in the dark days of the Cold War. As the *Wall Street Journal* reported, none of these vehicles could be sold "now that East Germans can buy, for less money, bigger and infinitely better Western-made Fords,

Volkswagens, Opels or Fiats.'' Even the processed raw materials and chemical stocks produced in East German factories were with few exceptions uncompetitive in cost, and too low in quality to compete in world markets. Most of the antiquated factories that produced these goods threw off pollution so foul that they threatened to turn much of Eastern Europe into a gigantic waste dump.

Because the Stalinist economy was not designed to operate efficiently or turn a profit, the productivity of the enterprises it created is strikingly low. The few plants that do produce goods of competitive quality are dramatically overstaffed. Peter Drucker explains:

Central Europe's most efficient steel mill, Witkowice in Czechoslovakia, produces about the same tonnage of steel as it did in 1938, but with a substantially larger work force. In the West, even an inefficient steel mill turns out 2½ times the tonnage per worker that it did 50 years ago, or about three times what Witkowice does.

Even the plants in Central Europe that have kept abreast of technology are overstaffed. The Tungstram works outside of Budapest, of which General Electric recently acquired control, make a first-rate light bulb. But they employ almost 50% more people, proportionately, than do GE, Siemens and Philips in their light-bulb plants in the West.

Wherever you look in what was East Germany, the economy was crippled by a grotesque growth of overheads of every kind. When the old regime fell, East German radio had a staff four times as numerous as in West German radio systems. The most telling statistic of life in the East German police state, however, was provided by revelations of the size of the Stasi, the secret police. In 1939, Hitler employed 40,000 Gestapo officers to control a population of 80 million Germans: one secret policeman to two thousand citizens. Herr Honecker required 104,000 Stasi to control 17 million East Germans: one secret policeman to 165 citizens. Even the secret police were 90 percent less productive than prewar.

What is to be done with the legions of secret police? And the superfluous army? And the thousands of surplus teachers of Marxism-Leninism? Not to mention the many Communist Party cadres and the vast central bureaucracy that long held a first claim on resources? The people who filled these posts have no function to serve in a market economy. They will have to find new work, as will millions of industrial employees of antiquated, overstaffed East German factories. The transition will require unprecedented unemployment, with as many as four million persons, about 45 percent of the work force, losing their jobs. This is a greater loss of employment than has ever occurred over a short time in a market economy, even in a severe depression. The Germans have attempted to find answers to these questions, having spent hundreds of billions of marks without as yet succeeding. As we write, Kohl is attempting to negotiate an all-party "Solidarity Pact" that would form the basis for more heroic measures to stop the collapse of the eastern German economy. Yet the terrifying fact is that East Germany was the most efficient of the Communist economies, more productive than any other Warsaw Pact country and far more productive than the now dissolved Soviet Union itself.

This shows why the prospects of a post-Communist boom are not bright. Their knowledge of East Germany has given many West Germans a very pessimistic view of the outlook for the former Soviet Union. After all, what was East Germany has all the advantages of the reunification process, and even so, it will be a very great strain on the powerful German economy. Russia and other former Soviet republics start from a point much lower than East Germany, have a population sixteen times as large, and are far less Westernized in culture, while enjoying none of the benefits of Germany's stable system of law.

The West Germans measure the task of rebuilding the eastern landers, and they see how much harder it is going to be than they at first thought. They go on to measure the task of redeveloping the former Soviet Union, and many are coming to believe that it is actually impossible. Unlike the countries of Western Europe, the former Soviet republics lack a structure of law, property rights, courts, well-developed insurance markets, or even double-entry book-keeping, an innovation that was well established in the West five hundred years ago.

The vast majority of large enterprises and almost all the banks in the former Soviet Union were insolvent when the hammer-and-sickle banner was pulled down from the Kremlin for the last time. The Soviet Union had had no provisions in its banking law to account for bad debt. Banks were simply instruments of state policy that advanced funds to state-run enterprises at the direction of central authorities. Their assets included little cash, and mostly worthless loans.

This legacy made it almost impossible for Mr. Yeltsin's reformers or their counterparts in the other former Soviet republics to control the emission of currency or discourage additional lending to the bankrupt sector. The introduction of sound accounting, or any rough test of solvency with a stable ruble, would have required a massive liquidation of banks and state enterprises, up to 80 percent of which were thought to be insolvent.

When the central plan disappeared, the gigantic enterprises that were the hallmark of Stalinism did not adjust their output to the markets. They certainly did not fire excess staff and curtail expenses as if their survival depended upon becoming profitable. Most continued to produce and stockpile goods more or less as they had previously done, billing one another for the shipments, and when money was not forthcoming from ultimate customers in the market, demanding additional "credit" from the banks.

In effect, the former Soviet "enterprises" behaved as the U.S. Department of Agriculture might behave if suddenly told that funds would no longer be available from the treasury to pay salaries and that henceforth it would have to survive on its own. The USDA would hoard its cash and lobby like fury to reverse the decision. Its determination would be reinforced by the fact that no one in high authority in the Department of Agriculture has even a remote hint of how that sprawling bureaucracy could be made self-supporting in the market. Perhaps a divine genius could devise a way to keep 5 or 10 percent of the operation going as a self-sustaining enterprise. That would still leave 90 percent of the operation to be liquidated.

The former Soviet "enterprises" are not all that hopeless. But many are. Much of what they produce has no value in the market. As a measure of their malfunction, consider that Russia's annual output of natural resources— such as oil, natural gas, gold, copper, platinum, and coal—would be worth somewhat more than $100 billion if it were all sold in cash markets. But at prevailing exchange rates in November 1992, Russian statistics indicate that the whole of Russia's GDP is worth just $30 billion, less than a third of the value of its raw-material inputs. By implication, the output of Russia's economy would more than triple in value if the domestic manufacturing and service economy were shut down completely. Instead of contributing value, they subtract it. They are best understood not as enterprises in the Western sense, but as bureaucracies or lobbies. They survive through their influence over government policy—an influence exercised because they employ vast numbers of people.

The former Soviet republics have gone in an instant from one system allegedly run by the workers to several systems linked in a daisy chain of bankruptcy, now totally dominated by executives of the old state enterprises. There has proven to be little difference. Rhetorically, the sorry results are no longer justified under the rhetoric of Marxism. In principle, the former Soviet republics are now market economies. But other than a sprinkling of recently launched businesses, and some small shops that have been privatized, the free market continues to operate mainly in the crevices of the system. Young people and others who have already adopted a commercial spirit line up by the thousands in open markets in parking lots in all the big cities to sell pathetically small inventories of goods. Attractive young couples take turns holding up a single new dress or shirt for sale. They stand patiently for hours waiting for a customer. An old man comes to the farmers' market with a single new pair of army boots, which he eventually hawks for the equivalent of two dollars.

That is the reality of the market in the former Soviet Union. For too many people there, it is a matter for after-hours and weekends, not the substance of their workaday lives. As we write, the system is still stuck at the same impasse that was highlighted at the Kremlin's penultimate May Day parade in 1990. Placards carried by the official marchers announced: "Market Economy—Yes. Unemployment—No." Unfortunately, that is like calling for everyone to move house, but without permitting any of the furniture to be touched.

The essential virtue of the market is precisely that it discourages the waste of resources, including human talent. And that is precisely what many in the former Soviet Union are resisting.

Yet even if the leaders were willing to recognize that transitional unemployment was a necessary price for shedding the command economy, the system appears to be too unstable to absorb the shock. In spite of its appearance of menacing power from the outside, and the totalitarian controls its exercised for more than seventy years, the Soviet state collapsed. Only a popular and widely supported government could undertake the task of creating a market economy almost from scratch. The present power equation—which threatens to undermine central authority everywhere—makes it difficult to establish a sound system of law and order under which a market economy can emerge. The bankrupt Third World countries and the bankrupt Communist systems share this common difficulty. They lack the only factor of production that cannot be imported: a stable government to keep the peace and enforce a productive set of property rights.

The post-Communist countries have the advantage of relatively well-educated populations who share the broad features of Western culture. Indeed, seventy years of deep freeze in the former Soviet Union has preserved attractive aspects of nineteenth-century life that have melted away under the hot wind of commercialism in the West. There is scarcely a provincial city in the former Soviet Union that is not home to a ballet and an opera company. They draw big crowds. The few restaurants and night spots seem to be on their last call by about 9:30. There is a quite conservative air about the people, little evidence of aliented youth. No purple hair. The lack of any commercial attractions has probably helped preserve family life. Legions of parents are busy on Saturdays entertaining their children in the parks. The people of the former Soviet Union are decent, good people, although they conspicuously lack a sound work ethic and a general understanding of markets.

These few debilities could be set aside rather quickly if incentives could be reformed. Unfortunately, the odds seem be against it. Much of the difficulty

lies in the fact that many members of the population—including large numbers of pensioners, along with millions of former Communist Party functionaries, officials of collective farms, superfluous military officers, and
bureaucrats—believe that they have far more to lose by the reform of the
economy than they stand to gain by economic growth. Some of them are
probably right. For more than seventy years, economic benefits in the Soviet
Union were obtained not by work but by political influence or by bribing
officials. Normal profit motives were perverted. In its turn, the government
had to bribe its people with subsidies on basic foodstuffs and rent. Food was
of very low quality. But prices were unrealistically low, so low that they
distorted much of what remained of ordinary economic management. Prior
to reform, bread in the Soviet Union was cheaper than grain. As a consequence, it was frequently fed to animals.

Undoubtedly, most citizens of the former Soviet Union would agree that
Communist pricing policies made no sense. Western pollsters who have sam-
pled opinion confirm this judgment. But people left behind by Communism
have few resources to sustain themselves during a transition to a free system.
Unlike Western societies that enjoyed the advantage of having significant
numbers of financially independent burghers, wealthy farmers, and an aristocracy who had cash to invest during their transition to capitalism, the
orphans of Communism are too equal in their poverty. Many people were
well stocked with rubles when the Soviet Union collapsed. But the rubles
soon became worthless. Only a bare statistical trace of the population has
any wealth in hard currency. The fact that a transition to a free market would
open investment prospects and markedly improve living standards in the long
run is less compelling to persons who might starve in the meantime. Policies
that require a transition period longer than a few months risk triggering
explosive social unrest.

Why an End to Inflation Is Unlikely

Much of the problem might be corrected if value could be restored to the
ruble. Chronic inflation is another feature that the former Communist governments share with governments in Latin America, Africa, and elsewhere
that are too weak and ineffective to extract resources needed for public purposes by taxation. These governments, like the former Soviet governments,
are also too weak to resist costly demands for subsidies from inefficient enterprises and other spending constituencies. Given their circumstances, they
extract resources from society in a harmful and inefficient way, but in the
only way they can—by depreciating the currency. This option is always open
to them because the currency is under their control. They control the printing

presses. Their control elsewhere is more problematic. In underdeveloped
countries, the low per capita income, the small scale of most private enterprises, and the backward nature of transportation and communications systems make it very difficult for governments to operate over a wide geographic
area. This, of course, is exactly what governments must do if they are to be
effective—operate over the whole vast terrain of the country.

Notwithstanding its nuclear weapons, Russia has most of the features of
governmental incompetence that plague underdeveloped countries. Even
more than Latin governments, the Russians monopolized all large industry,
most of which consequently operated with great inefficiency. Under the press
of necessity, the Russians have made an attempt at reform. But it has been
Latin America–style reform—grand promises and comprehensive programs
promised, but only small and marginal changes delivered. As in Latin America,
the principal reform in the former Soviet Union has merely been to talk of
reform. But talk, especially freer speech, has its consequences. As police-state
controls weakened, most of the stick that formerly obliged managers and
workers conform to discipline from the center has been whittled away. But
the carrot—an effective price mechanism, private ownership, and sound
money—is only a seedling that has barely taken root. Of course, there are
few or no profits to be taxed from the gigantic Stalinist enterprises that require
massive infusions of inflated currency to stay alive. This has led to punishing
taxation on the small fraction of the economy that could be geniunely described as private enterprise. In the countryside, agriculture has still not been
reformed in most of the former Soviet republics, because privatization means
the end of the line for the powerful managers of the giant collective farms.
Consequently, farming continues to suffer chronic, almost unbelievable waste,
with as much as a quarter of the crops allegedly rotting in the fields.

We say "allegedly" because the fact that so many people find ways to
survive the cold Russian winters testifies to their ingenuity in obtaining and
consuming food that statistically should not be there. Much of what is said
to rot or be lost in the harvest actually does rot or is lost. But some of it is
stolen or diverted into other distribution channels, acts of improvisation that
put food on many tables that might otherwise be bare.

Economic activity in the former Soviet Union has been rendered more
incoherent by the multiplication of jurisdictions, a problem with little modern
precedent even in Latin America. Output in the former Soviet Union was
consciously subdivided among the republics. Often, there was only one supplier of any civilian good in the whole of the Soviet Union. Now the various
republics have become independent nations. And separatist movements
within the republics are busily drawing new borders from Tiraspol to Ru-
thenia. This devolution creates new dilemmas for an already staggering econ-

omy. Factories sometimes find that their main component suppliers and customers are now in other countries. The entire rationale of some enterprises has been rendered ludicrous in light of international pricing—importing corn to fatten pigs for export to another part of the former Soviet Union where the pork will sell for less than the price of the corn.

The incoherence of borders involves another problem common to the Third World, the inability of the state to enforce laws that it promulgates. Large areas of the former Soviet Union are under de facto control of local military units, warlords, and clashing ethnic factions. Whatever the doubtful maps suggest, there are areas of gray, where no authority protects commerce or enforces property rights.

Upon consideration, therefore, the leftovers of the former Soviet Union do share many of the debilities of underdeveloped countries. The Soviet Union left behind few financial assets other than worthless currency. It therefore had no social groups with significant financial wealth who have a stake in prohibiting inflation. The former Soviet Union had the balance sheet of a Third World economy—which is what it was. A Third World economy with nuclear weapons. The Soviets attempted to operate on the largest possible scale, and failed. Their bureaucracy was notoriously corrupt and inefficient. The transportation system they left behind is in many respects primitive. Communications are far worse than those of Latin America. By stifling the pursuit of profit in commerce, the defunct Soviet government foreclosed the collection of significant tax revenue. It also assured that the cultural attitudes and values that accompany the operation of efficient private enterprises would not develop. As Mancur Olson writes:

> Characteristically, in the underdeveloped societies of today as well as in the preindustrial West, leaders of large organizations have been unable to prevent corruption by their underlings. As the great Indian sage, Kautalya, put it more than 2,000 years ago: "Just as the fish moving under water cannot possibly be found out either as drinking or not drinking water, so government servants employed in government work cannot be found out while taking money for themselves."

The obstacles to the end of inflation in the former Soviet republics are quite similar to those that stand in the way of an easy solution to the inflation problem that has plagued Latin America for most of this century.

By contrast, the West grew rich at a time when wealth was very unequally distributed, so savings for investment were much easier to come by than would have been the case with greater equality. Traders and investors who operated in conditions of turmoil could largely protect themselves from inflation by holding the profits of their investments in gold or silver coins. Residents of the former Soviet republics must make do with dollars.

Citizens of the former Soviet republics may include many who are potentially entrepreneurs of great talent. But most are only potential entrepreneurs, except for the few who grew rich fiddling the defunct system, and an even smaller number with access to Western investment capital.

The most likely course is for the former Soviet states to continue in the footsteps of Latin America. There reform, and talk of reform, have spread out for generations, with weak, ineffectual governments coming and going without ever taking decisive action that actually addresses the underlying difficulties. In such a scenario, the former Soviet Union would remain backward and poor. Yeltsin and the reforms would become even more discredited, with authoritarian methods coming in and out of favor, as they do in Latin America.

"Turning a Fish Soup Back into an Aquarium"

We believe that we are coldly realistic about the obstacles facing the former Soviet republics. Nonetheless, we must indicate a prejudice. In April 1992, James Davidson was appointed an adviser on economic reform to the former Soviet Republic of Belarus. In the years that we have offered our judgments and advice in *Strategic Investment* and books, we have operated on a paradigm apart from most of the investment world. We have tried to be objective, and not merely say what would sell. We have forecast wars, revolutions, recessions, and even depression. Sometimes we have regretted having to forecast these unpleasant developments. We would have preferred not to have to tell you about a world falling apart. But given that it was falling apart, we wished to find ways to help put it back together. Thinking about how the post-Communist economic reform might be made to work is a step in that direction. But the task is formidable.

That is not to say that reform is actually impossible. Intelligent and well-meaning people in all the former Soviet republics are seeking inventive solutions to the dilemmas of reform. We have offered them ideas in the spirit of friendship, and with full recognition of the obstacles. We will continue to do so. Societies that slide to the edge of the economic abyss often keep sliding the full way in. But sometimes they discover a freedom of action that more stable societies lack. When there is nothing left to lose, and no more to be wrung out of a bankrupt system, what Mancur Olson calls "redistributive coalitions" sometimes loosen their grip. After many decades of runaway deficit spending and hyperinflation, Argentina has balanced its budget while America cannot.

When this chapter was first written, we anticipated that the post-Communists economies would follow in Argentina's footsteps. Now we wish they would. At the time, the example Argentina was setting was altogether different. In the summer of 1989, the Argentine annual inflation rate briefly reached 1,000,000 percent. Productivity collapsed because employees had to flee from their jobs several times a day to spend unwieldy wads of devalued paper money before it became even more worthless. Sound money would have done wonders. Everyone agreed. Even Carlos Menem, the new President of Argentina. He did something about it. The exchange value of the Argentine peso used to devalue by the hour. As we write, it has been stabilized at one-to-one against the U.S. dollar for 19 months. Because the peso is backed by 100 percent dollar reserves, it will certainly remain stable for several more months, vindicating at least a while longer "the Menem Miracle."

It is a miracle that raises our hopes not just for Argentina, but also for Russia, Belarus, and all the countries now suffering with hyperinflation and economic collapse. We say this, unconvinced that Argentina's reforms can be made to stick in the turmoil of world depression. Nonetheless, they stand as a brave example that escape from overdetermined economic failure may be possible.

A Chance Worth Taking

We are investing small sums in Belarus and the other former Soviet republics, and urging others to do so as well. The difficulties stated throughout this chapter will keep cautious investors on the sidelines for obvious reasons. It is not improbable that any investment made now in any of the former Soviet republics could be totally lost. But while the odds are stacked against success, that is only part of the story. For an investment that does work, the profit payoff would not be 10 percent or even 10:1. It could be 100:1 or even 1,000:1. These are odds that support targeted investment on a small scale. They will not justify massive investment of the sort required to absorb the slack in Western economies. The world depression will not be ended by a recovery in the former Soviet economies—even if those economies begin to grow as vigorously as Argentina has since President Menem stabilized the currency. Nonetheless, if a foundation for improved economic performance can be laid in spite of deteriorating megapolitical conditions, it would raise our hopes, not just for the former Soviet Union but for the whole world in the century to come.

Much is at stake. Social peace and prosperity for all the peoples emerging from the rubble of Communism hang in the balance, as does Mr. Yeltsin's survival and that of the other reformers. For the West, our future is at stake as well. The resolution of the question of post-Communist reform could come to a crisis point very quickly. It could be another trigger of the larger revolution of the 1990s. Or it could vindicate the Argentine example that economic miracles can happen, even if for a short time.

The most likely fate for the former Soviet Union is to experience further stages of upheaval, probably including reactionary crackdowns and drawn-out secession struggles. Before long, it is probable that Mr. Yeltsin will be ousted and his place taken by a Slav nationalist figure with strong ties to the military. It is a possibility of great political and economic danger.

Real incomes have plunged to the vanishing point, and public discontent is rising. There is a prospect of economic collapse, revolution, or even civil war of the kind seen in the former Yugoslavia. Clashes between the authorities in Moscow and ethnic separatists at the periphery could escalate into full-scale warfare. There are many points of contention that indicate a growing danger of conflict between Russia and Ukraine. The frightening possibility exists that such conflicts could involve the capture of nuclear or chemical weapons by dissidents, nationalist revolutionaries, armed fundamentalists, bandits, or even hardliners seeking to provoke a crackdown. The logic of Cold War deterrence was based on the assumption that the central command structure of the superpowers would retain internal control over the many thousands of warheads dispersed on both sides. With the disintegration of the Soviet Union, that assumption is clearly antiquated.

Indeed there are many questions to which the decade of the 1990s seems likely to provide answers:

- What happens if a local authority seizes control of nuclear warheads or chemical weapons stockpiled on its territory?
- What happen if nuclear power facilities are threatened with attack, or appear on the verge of an accident because unrest cuts off the flow of crucial supplies, or blocks essential personnel from reporting to work?
- What happens if there is a breakdown of the food and supplies distribution network in remote areas, leading troops assigned to guard and maintain weapons to abandon their posts in search of food? Or sell their weapons on the black market?
- What happens if militants attack nuclear weapons facilities or seize stockpiled weapons?
- What happens if terrorist nations or terrorist groups hire scientists and technicians from the former Soviet nuclear program who can no longer earn a living wage?

These are hypothetical questions, but hardly questions that are remote from the facts. We have been informed that at least one shipment of enriched uranium smuggled from Russia by Polish black marketeers has been seized by police in Munich, Germany. According to our sources, this led the German government to protest formally to the Russian government over the need to step up control over radioactive material in that country. Unhappily, the Russians have little or no control over much of the nuclear material going to or from nuclear plants. Estimates vary on how much has been stolen so far, but sources indicate the primary recipients of the contraband are Israel, Pakistan, China, and possibly even Iraq. Early in 1992, Iran reportedly obtained three tactical nuclear weapons from former Soviet arsenals in Kazakhstan. It would hardly be surprising if one or more of the estimated 31,000 warheads accumulated in the former Soviet Union had fallen into other unauthorized hands.

ANOTHER CHERNOBYL?

With energy needs in Russia outstripping the capacity of the crumbing economy, and the nuclear industry falling apart, German experts worry that it could only be a matter of time until another aging Russian reactor suffers a Chernobyl-style meltdown. Such a meltdown could be a body blow to European economies already reeling from the world slump.

The growing prospect of such disaster is more than a caution against taking large short positions in grains. It is a reminder that not all needs are necessarily occasions for investment. If the West were not in a slump, and capital were plentiful, Germany, Sweden, Switzerland, and other countries in Western Europe that might be threatened by fallout from another nuclear accident would find it in their own interests to invest the billions it will take to stabilize the Russian nuclear industry. But the problem is so unwelcome, and the costs so enormous if funded at a Western scale, that it is unlikely either the capital or the will can be found to make the remedial investments that would be needed.

It is probable that the benign interlude that followed the disintegration of the Soviet Union is drawing to a close. While we continue to hope for the best, a turn for the worse should not be a surprise. The loss of empire and the breakdown of internal order in the former USSR has already led to a mass revival of Russian nationalism. A military coup is not unlikely, perhaps leading to a fascist organization of industry of the Latin American type. It is well to remember that Hitler's Nazi movement proclaimed itself to be "National Socialist" and Mussolini's roots were also in socialism. The step to a fascist dictatorship in the Soviet Union, or what remains of it, will be a short one later in the 1990s.

This could lead to a serious revival of international tensions and confrontations within Central and Eastern Europe. However, it is unlikely that Russia or other successor states to the Soviet Union would seek a confrontation with Western Europe or the United States in the 1990s. Nations undergoing deep traumas normally turn inward, as the United States did after Vietnam. It is more likely that relatively isolationist sentiments will prevail in Russia for the rest of this decade, and that military spending around the globe will continue to fall in real terms.

When crises do emerge, the Russian leadership may find it in its interests to make common cause with Western nations in seeking to restrain the explosion of Islamic power on its southern borders. The military danger may come in confrontations between splintering pieces of the former Soviet Union, particularly between Russia and Ukraine, among the republics of the Transcaucasus, or between Russians and Islamic republics with close ethnic ties to Iran.

Islam is certainly a movement of faith, and could be a movement of shifting boundaries. The former Soviet Union had about a quarter of its population in states that are predominantly Islamic. Those states were occupied in the czarist era of primitive imperialism, when Islam was at its weakest. They were retained in the period of Marxist revolution. But Marxism is now dead and Islam is reviving.

The good news of the death of Communism is only the bright side of a two-sided coin. The dark side is that destabilization of the Eastern bloc, and the fall of the false prophet Marx, could throw up new and ancient enemies to threaten the peace and prosperity of the West.

CHAPTER SEVEN

MUHAMMAD REPLACES MARX

THE NEW NORTH-SOUTH DIVISION

OF WORLD POLITICS

Oh, Arabs, Oh Moslems and faithful everywhere, this is your day to rise and defend Mecca, which is captured by the spears of the Americans and the Zionists. Burn the soil under the feet of the aggressors and invaders.

—SADDAM HUSSEIN,
August 10, 1990

FIVE CENTURIES ago, in 1483, the first news report ever printed in English was John Kay's translation of an account of the defense of the island of Rhodes against an Islamic assault. The fact that it appeared at all reflected the degree of anxiety about the challenge of Islam, even in a country as remote as England was then from the Mediterranean.

We expect Western anxiety about the challenge of Islam to dominate the news once again in the coming decade. The followers of Muhammad have passed the followers of Marx in the night. Marxism is dead. Marx was not only a false prophet, but, like all secular prophets, a short-lived one. With Islam, history has to be measured in centuries. Now Islam is on the move again. It could prove as frightening to the West, and perhaps as economically disruptive, as the stolid Soviet empire ever was. This was driven home by the trillion-dollar losses in world capital markets following Saddam Hussein's invasion of Kuwait—and the war that resulted to set it right.

The collapse of socialism does not end the division of world opinion, nor does it settle the clashes of interest that have sparked conflict through the ages. What you should expect in the years to come is a shift in the battle-ground. The new division of world politics will be much less an East-West division than a North-South division. It will be a division between the rich world of material progress and market economies in the Northern states, and the more backward, heavily populated lands to the South. Governments that still retain a tolerable competence will come under assault from peoples in regions where governments have proven almost uniformly corrupt and inept. Modern, secular ideas about living will be confronted by older, even ancient religious strategies for organizing human affairs. To an extent few would have expected a few years ago, Russia and the post-Communist nations of Eastern Europe will find themselves increasingly allied with the leading capitalist powers in opposition to the rise of Islam and the militance of the South.

Of all the religions of premodern, traditional societies, Islam is the most vital. It is a crusading faith, whose energy appears to be renewed and militant. And the location of Islamic societies on the southern borders of Europe and in the globe's leading oil exporting regions assures that they will play an important geopolitical role so long as the world economy is powered by fossil fuels.

In a sense, the shift back to a religious rather than a materialist enemy of capitalism reflects the reversion to conditions that prevailed before the Gun-powder Revolution launched the great explosion of modern progress. It is the logical cultural consequence of the faltering of governments.

In most parts of the South, it never proved possible to establish modern governments that were capable of organizing law and order on a large scale. Even during the centuries of cheap imperialism when megapolitical conditions favored the export of government, colonial administrations were mainly gov-ernments for Europeans, grafted over traditional systems. They disturbed but did not displace older ways of life. When technological change made it too costly for the metropolitan powers to retain control over the periphery earlier in this century, they withdrew. They left behind the equivalent of a heavy saddle hitched to a chicken. Immature and incomplete governments, armed with modern weapons, were grafted upon societies with primitive markets, low income, a minimal division of labor, poor infrastructure, and the cultural characteristics appropriate to those conditions.

As the closing decades of the postwar period have well demonstrated, governments in backward countries in Africa, Asia, and Latin America are incapable of providing conditions necessary for the full development of mar-kets. Their laws are arbitrary and corruptly enforced. They expropriate in-vestments. Debauch the currency. And steal practically anything that can be broken up and hauled away. Under such conditions, markets have not been allowed to develop as fully as they have in Northern Europe, Japan, or North

America. The bulk of society in the South cannot depend upon governments and markets vulnerable to misgovernment to provide security for retirement and substitute for the other practical functions that religions served in the organization of traditional life. As the twentieth century draws to an end. religions will offer an increasingly attractive alternative to incompetent governments, especially in societies too unstable to develop large-scale markets.

How Religions Undergird Markets and Governments

The hypothesis we are considering is that the social function of a religion is independent of its truth or falsity, that religions which we think to be erroneous or even absurd and repulsive, such as those of some savage tribes, may be important and effective parts of the social machinery, and that without these "false" religions social revolution and the development of modern civilization would have been impossible.

—A. R. Radcliffe-Brown,
"Religion and Society"

One of the mysteries in the ordering of human life is the way that otherwise inadequate or even dysfunctional social systems can be made functional by religion. Religions enable sometimes petty and dishonest human beings to work with one another by depending upon a power greater than themselves. This is no mean achievement. If people followed only in the footsteps of economists, and did anything or everything they could get away with to raise their own profit and shirk costs, the world would indeed be an unpleasant place, full of violence, savagery, and deceit. One person would murder the next to steal a pair of shoes—provided that shoes were worth more than a bullet. Progress would be tripped up at every turn by nearsighted, selfish behavior. Many of the gains of social life would disappear, swallowed whole by incentive traps.

Incentive Traps and Religions

There are more incentive traps in life than you might suspect. Sometimes they are called "public goods" problems. Sometimes they are called "prisoner's dilemmas." But most of the time they are called nothing at all because they are simply ignored. Unless you have closely studied problems of the environment or political economy, chances are high that you never have been introduced to the discussion of such incentive traps. They are complex. And almost as invisible as a gambler's marks on a deck of cards. Unless you set out patiently intending to find them, you probably would know them only by their results. They abound where life's troubles abound. Depletion of resources. Pollution. Budget deficits. Waste. War. Crime. Wherever you find people behaving in sorry ways, it is a fair bet that an incentive trap lies at the heart of the matter.

An incentive trap is a situation where what seems narrowly profitable for the individual is bad for the group and possibly even bad in the long run for the individual himself. Consider a fanciful example, of a credit card. With an ordinary credit card, say an American Express card, the only things you really need to worry about are keeping it from being stolen and avoiding the temptation to buy too much on credit. The more you charge, the more you personally will have to pay.

But suppose you shared an American Express account with five hundred other people. Each of these five hundred people would have a card with the same account number as you. At the end of each month, you would each pay 1/500 of the bill, regardless of how much you personally had charged.

What would happen?

You would be caught in an incentive trap. You would get the full benefit of any purchase you made, but you would have to contribute only 1/500 of the cost of paying for it. Your incentive to spend would be five hundred times greater than if you had to pay the full cost on your own credit card. And, of course, the same would be true for everyone else. Each of the cardholders would get the full benefit of anything he could consume or carry away at 1/500 of its ordinary price. Under such an incentive trap, everyone would spend like a congressman and the whole group would soon be bankrupt.

Even so, that would not stop a cardholder who was rational from spending all the faster. Anyone who tried to avoid the looming bankruptcy by passing up spending opportunities would achieve little. He would bear 100 percent of the costs of his good deed himself while realizing only 1/500 of the benefit. He would still have to pay for all the wild spending of 499 other people. He would end up no less bankrupt than the others. He would merely enjoy fewer of the benefits along the way.

This is an extreme example of an incentive trap, a situation involving many individuals or groups in which there is a significant disproportion between the benefits and costs of some action. It clearly shows how relational incentives can lead people into outcomes that no one would favor.

Of course, the example we concocted above is unusual because it could easily be avoided. Everyone would be far better off simply by paying his own bills. And that is in fact the way that credit cards work. By contrast, the incentive traps of ordinary life are not so easy to escape. They are not usually voluntary arrangements. They are circumstances into which people are thrust, invisible pits and valleys through which we stumble in navigating the local environment.

Religious Solutions to Incentive Traps

Even though incentive traps have been around forever, they have been explicitly identified and studied only in recent times. In the past, societies attempted to overcome these problems primarily through the invention of taboos and religious practices rather than by directly analytical means.

Some primitive tribes developed quite elaborate patterns of ritual to overcome incentive traps. The Maring people of New Guinea, for example, like many others, constantly threaten to overgraze and deplete the local environment. Theirs is an incentive problem that Garrett Hardin has described as "the tragedy of the commons." Nobody owns the forest upon which all the local people depend for their livelihood. Consequently, everyone has an incentive to consume as many resources as possible, which they do particularly by raising herds of hungry pigs that devour the vegetation and overrun the forest floor. The Maring have found a religious answer to this public goods dilemma. They throw elaborate pig feasts for their ancestors, in which they dramatically cut back the pig population. These are followed by wars between rival clans, which have the effect of balancing claims on the resources of the forest. The ritual wars create a no-man's-land, a sanctuary that prevents overharvesting the forest. Vegetation grows back. In time, new pig herds are raised, resources are pushed once more near their limit, and the whole cycle repeats itself.

Strange as it may seem, the social functions of the religious pig orgies in the rain forest are similar to those of taboos against eating pork that are common to the desert religions. Both help overcome public goods dilemmas unique to the setting in which they emerged. The taboo against eating pork is shared by Muslims and Jews. We often hear it rationalized as a health measure. It is said that wise old prophets made eating pork taboo to avoid trichinosis. This is unlikely. In the desert conditions in which both the Muslims and Jews lived, trichinosis is a nonproblem. The more probable reason that desert cultures forbade the eating of pork is because the pig is basically an animal of a wet climate. It cannot sweat. It therefore requires a lot of the desert's most precious resource, water. To keep pigs in a desert is to crowd out people in favor of animals that have a diet very much like people, require large amounts of water, and are of much less practical value in a primitive economy than cattle, goats, or sheep. Pigs cannot be milked. They cannot be shorn. They cannot be hitched to a plow.

Nonetheless, pork is a delicious and highly prized luxury food around the world. As Marvin Harris reports, there is anthropological evidence that Middle Eastern peoples raised pigs in early settlements that were very sparsely populated. But as population grew sixty-fold and deforestation spread between 7000 and 2000 B.C., it became ever more costly, and even dangerous, for desert tribes to raise pigs. The huge leap in population, combined with environmental degradation, created a "tragedy of the commons" over the use of water. It meant an upsurge in conflict, made all the more dangerous because keeping pigs in a desert environment was an invitation to military weakness. A few pigs wallowing at the oasis could consume water and food that would support a number of people. In times of invasion or conflict, the pigs could expose their owners and neighbors to great danger. Pigs, unlike people, could not take up arms to defend the community.

That is the proximate reason why pork is taboo in religions of the desert. Moslems and Jews banned pigs for essentially the same reason that the peoples of the rain forest placed pigs at the center of their religious rituals. Both groups attempted to overcome an incentive trap—a "tragedy of the commons"— that threatened vital resources.

Nonreligious Solutions Require Developed Markets and Competent Government

In a wealthier society many "tragedies of the commons" could be resolved by creating private property in the threatened resources. But such a solution can be effective only where government or some other institution can wield enough physical power to protect and enforce property rights. This can happen only when megapolitical conditions permit. The power equation in primeval rain forests or in the deserts of the Middle East at the dawn of history did not permit effective privatization of many vital resources. People were too poor. Raw power was too equally distributed. There was no government that could effectively bar persons of similar physical strength from letting their pigs run free in the forest. And the only defense of the desert water hole from the next marauding tribe was the walled fort, which could not be garrisoned by pigs to fend off attack.

The mysterious solutions that ancient people found to their incentive traps were often religious ones. Rituals, taboos, and rules of conduct made it "unclean" to behave in ways that could threaten the social life of the community. Religions helped resolve incentive traps when markets were too undeveloped, and governments too weak to provide other solutions.

"Rigorously Fixed" Behavior

Religious answers to incentive traps are indeed very good solutions in the conditions under which they emerged. This is demonstrated by the fact that some devout Jews and Moslems today, living in London or New York, still honor the taboos of their fathers. But their voluntary adherence to these survival strategies of long ago is by no means sufficient to suppress the demand for pork. The world at large consumes pork in quantity. If overcoming some incentive trap today really did depend upon avoiding pork, we would be in deep trouble. The religious solution to public goods dilemmas depends upon everyone, or almost everyone, behaving in the same way. It requires, as the great pioneer of anthropology of religion Robertson Smith put it, that behavior be "rigorously fixed."

In the typical impoverished society, religion is not a matter of choice. It could not be. The more crucial the role that religion plays in overcoming the incentive traps a community faces, the more mandatory it must be. It cannot merely be an argument that you accept or reject as you see fit:

- "Honor your ancestors—throw a pig feast."
- "Don't eat pork, if you do you will be 'unclean.' "

These are not logical propositions to be debated, nor beliefs that appeal to the intellect in the modern Western sense. They are divine writ, injunctions that help a group escape from an incentive trap arising from local megapolitical conditions. They work, so long as they are followed almost unanimously. What Basil Davidson wrote about African life was true of every society where religion played a crucial role in organizing social life: "Their systems of behaviour—their systems of religion, if you will—had to be . . . mandatory." There cannot be freedom of religion in societies that depend upon religious solutions to incentive traps.

" 'All,' " He Says, " 'Think This; but I Do Not Think So.' "

It is not a coincidence that freedom of religion is prized in the Western tradition but not prized in poorer societies where markets are underdeveloped and governments have only a marginal ability to enforce property rights and maintain order. Prior to the Gunpowder Revolution, and the Reformation it set in motion, freedom of religion and even the freedom to form individual judgments on matters of faith scarcely existed in Christian Europe. Consider the story of Peter Abelard, a leading scholar of the twelfth century. He was a bright and learned man, much honored in later centuries, who brought down upon himself the wrath of the whole medieval church. Abelard argued what would today be obscure and trivial points about the power of the devil and the theological reasons that Jesus was born. Yet the very fact that he questioned even a part of received religious doctrine unleashed a firestorm of outrage. Saint Bernard, speaking for the church elders, responded in much the same spirit as the Ayatollah Khomeini reacted to Salman Rushdie. Saint Bernard said:

> Which shall I call the more intolerable in these words—the blasphemy or the arrogance? . . . Does he not deservedly provoke every man's hand against him, whose hand is raised against every man?

Too free a thinker for his time, Abelard was eventually castrated.

The Megapolitics of Religious Freedom

Freedom of religion is possible only where governments function competently on a large scale. It was the advent of new megapolitical conditions—the Gunpowder Revolution—that made religion, in Radcliffe-Brown's words, "primarily a matter of belief." The new technology of power facilitated the development of markets and the growth of the nation-state, developments that altered religion's previously crucial role in organizing social life. The fact that freedom of religion became possible in the most advanced economies over the past few centuries is itself evidence of religion's declining importance. Religion could only become a matter of choice when it no longer mattered so much what religion one chose.

This is confirmed by the brief development of religious freedom in the ancient world. At the high-water period of Roman power and prosperity, for example, there was broad tolerance in religious matters, and even a competition in religious practice. Upper-class pagans, and humanists like Cicero, remained half-heartedly faithful to the gods of Rome, while materialist atheism of an almost modern kind spread widely. There were also dozens of other religions competing locally and throughout the empire for adherents. Egyptian cults were prominent in Greece. The cult of Osiris spread into Italy, especially among farmers. The emperor was worshipped. Mithras was a popular god among the legionnaires. The cult of Dionysus was present throughout the empire, "and was closely linked to men's hopes of immortality." And, of course, Judaism and Christianity, the enduring religions of Western civilization, were also widespread.

But the period of tolerance and religious freedom was short-lived. As the Roman Empire collapsed, "abandoned to inroad, to pillage, and at last to conquest, on her frontier," freedom of religion disappeared. It was a casualty of economic ruin and the collapse of social order.

Now that megapolitical conditions have changed in a way that undermines social order and weakens economies, an upsurge of religious fundamentalism is the natural consequence, especially in less wealthy societies. This is already evident in the Islamic world. It is likely to be even a more prominent feature of social relations in the coming decade. You can expect less religious tolerance as economies decline, and the practical importance of religion rises in meeting common concerns.

Islamic Societies Destabilized by Oil Wealth

By a strange coincidence, most oil-exporting countries are either Islamic societies, such as Saudi Arabia, Iraq, Libya, and Iran, or societies with a large Islamic influence, such as Indonesia, Nigeria, and the former Soviet republic of Kazakhstan, tapped by informed sources in the oil industry to be the most exciting production prospect since the opening of the Middle East fields earlier in this century. In the more traditional Islamic societies, the oil money that poured in during the OPEC price hikes of the 1970s hit with an effect like a water cannon blasting a mud hut. It dissolved many traditional patterns of behavior, without creating new developed market economies or truly modern states to take their place. The result was Islamic revolution in Iran, and an upsurge of militant fundamentalism in Egypt, the Gulf states, Saudi Arabia, and beyond.

By transplanting Western products, habits, and desires into societies only a generation or so removed from the Middle Ages, oil wealth was destabilizing. This has also been true to an extent wherever traditional societies have come under pressure from modernization and people have come to feel that the promises of development would not be fulfilled for them. They have seen that the impact of oil wealth made it less likely that traditional, religious solutions would continue to function. The fundamentalist reaction, therefore, was most acute among those who were exposed to oil wealth without actually pocketing the royalties themselves. The Palestinians in Kuwait, for example, were more drawn to fundamentalism than wealthy Kuwaitis with flats in London. Likewise, Pakistani and Egyptian guest workers, unlike the Saudi princes, came home empty-handed and embittered from the 1986 oil bust.

It is not a coincidence that the country in the Middle East that became the bastion of fundamentalism, Iran, was too heavily populated to allow its oil revenues to make everyone rich, as almost happened in the Gulf emirates and Saudi Arabia. As the world economy slows, and rapid population growth in young Islamic societies stalls the increase in per capita income, the result to be expected is an upsurge of Islamic fundamentalism.

Algeria, a Hint of Things to Come

A taste of things to come was provided by events in Algeria in 1992. Algeria, like Iran, is a nation that has enjoyed an influx of oil revenue under a regime of authoritarian modernizers. As in Iran, the oil revenue trickled into even the most remote village, but not enough of it to provide financial security or even a good job to legions of young people. When disappointing economic results stimulated demands for free elections, Algeria's longtime military rulers bowed to popular requests and did allow one round of a multiparty voting to take place. The Islamic Salvation Front—or FIS, as it is known by its French initials—looked to be a landslide winner. The results showed the popular appeal of Islamic fundamentalism in North Africa, especially among the young, who voted overwhelmingly for the Islamic Salvation Front.

The second and final stage of the election was aborted in mid-January 1992, when a military-backed council seized power to block the fundamentalists. The leaders who inspired the coup are thoroughly secular in outlook, no less so than the Shah. They are part of the generation who brought Algeria to independence from France. Most are European-educated. They believe the ideas that were taught in French universities and discussed in French cafés in the 1950s.

Because they were once Marxists or Marxist-influenced, the Algerian military leaders have not been shy about employing authoritarian methods to suppress the Islamic Salvation Front and its supporters. Clashes between Algerian security forces and Muslim fundamentalists in the months after the elections were aborted left 150 dead and 700 wounded. A number of militants from the Islamic Salvation Front were condemned to death. At least 30,000 others were arrested and placed in detention camps in the Sahara. They included about 200 local mayors and over 100 Front candidates for the canceled parliamentary elections. A thoroughgoing attempt has been made to eradicate all local organizations that support fundamentalism, including religious institutions. As we write, news reports indicate that Algeria's ruling council has decided to ban labor unions thought to have supported the FIS in the first round of elections.

We doubt that the attempt to eradicate Islamic fundamentalism in Algeria will succeed. Megapolitical conditions are against it. And the FIS has a useful ally in Iran, which has reportedly funneled vast sums to Islamic fundamentalist organizations in other countries. French and Moroccan intelligence agencies report that Iran gave more than $100 million, perhaps as much as $200 million, to the FIS.

From Cold War to Holy War

You can look to Iran to become a major platform for exporting revolutionary Islamic fundamentalism in the 1990s, just as the former Soviet Union was once an active agent of support for Marxist revolution. This is a development that has not yet struck public consciousness. The mood in the West is one of relaxation and thankfulness at the end of the Cold War. It is in a way similar to the attitude that prevailed at the end of World War II when the foundation of the Cold War was being laid but few noticed the work in progress. Several years passed before George Kennan's article on containment and Winston Churchill's "Iron Curtain" speech crystalized public understanding of the hostile character of Soviet Communism. Now, many of the early manifestations of Islamic fundamentalism as an imperial ideology have passed unremarked. We followed many of its developments in 1992 in *Strategic Investment*.

Qods Force to Spread Islamic Revolution

Our sources indicate that Tehran has set up an agency of subversion known as "Qods Force" ("Qods" means "Jerusalem" in Farsi), which has been assigned the task of underwriting fundamentalist revolution in Islamic societies. The founding commander of the Qods Force is said to be Brig. General Ahmed Vahidi, who reports directly to Iranian President Hashemi Rafsanjani. Its intelligence director, Mohammed Jafari, is reported to have an extensive background in Euro-terrorism. Qods Force director of operations, Commander Mosleh, led Revolutionary Guards forces in Lebanon from 1982 to 1984 and is believed to have masterminded the 1983 bombing of the U.S. Marines baracks in Beirut.

Iran is clearly an imperial power on the march. And it is most likely now a nuclear power. There is considerable evidence that Tehran has purchased at least three tactical nuclear missiles from Russian-controlled missile sites in Kazakhstan. Iran has also contracted with Cuba to teach its pilots how to fly low-level nuclear bomb runs with its newly acquired and nuclear-capable MiG 29s.

One of Tehran's ambitions has been to expand its borders eastward to encompass Farsi-speaking western and northern Afghanistan. It would also like to turn the remainder of Afghanistan into a fundamentalist republic. The champion of Iran's Afghan ambitions is Gulbuddin Hekmatyar, a fundamen-

talist leader who passionately hates the West and reveres the Iranian aya-
tollahs. Gulbuddin is seeking to seize control over Afghanistan from the
coalition of fighters who overthrew the old Soviet-installed government. Gulbuddin is a member of the majority Pushtun tribe. His principal opponent,
Ahmad Shah Massoud, is from the Tajik regions of northern Afghanistan.
Given the tribal nature of their support, there is a real possibility that the
struggle between the two guerrilla leaders will turn into a Pushtun-Tajik ethnic
war, which may partition Afghanistan. Massoud, "The Lion of Panshir,"
would break much of northern Afghanistan away and merge it with Tajikistan,
leaving Gulbuddin in charge of a pro-Iranian fundamentalist regime in the
south.

Iran Targets Egypt and Saudi Arabia

Iran is willing to project military power in support of Islamic fundamentalism.
It dispatched 10,000 troops to Sudan in 1992, to back the fundamentalist
military junta in Khartoum against the rebel Sudan People's Liberation Army
(SPLA) fighting for independence in the south. Among the Iranian detach-
ment were reportedly 2,000 Qods Forces, whose mission was not to fight the
SPLA rebels but to export the Islamic Revolution to Egypt and Saudi Arabia.
Soon thereafter, Egyptian authorities imposed a state of emergency in Upper
Egypt to stem a tide of fundamentalist violence. Communication routes with
the Governate of Aryut were closed for a time, and 4,000 Egyptian riot troops
were dispatched to the area, in addition to 2,000 regular soldiers. Dozens of
Islamic fundamentalists were arrested after violent clashes with local Coptic
Christians resulted in death, injury, and the destruction of local stores. A large
number of automatic weapons were confiscated, and many Egyptians fear
the unrest could spread.

The Iranians hope so. A training center for spreading revolutionary Islam,
equivalent to the old Patrice Lumumba University in Moscow, has been
opened in the Imam Ali Garrison, a former palace of the Shah outside Tehran.
Agents are being trained from Egypt, Algeria, Saudi Arabia, and the Central
Asian republics, particularly Tadjikistan. The Fourth Division of Qods Force,
known as the Ansar Corps and led by Commander Qa'ani, reportedly has
been assigned the specific mission of subverting the newly independent republics of former Soviet Central Asia: Azerbaijan, Kazakhstan, Turkmenistan,
Kirghizia, Uzbekistan, and Tajikistan.

Religion and the Disappearance of Natural Resources

In most of these places, Islam is an increasingly attractive alternative to failed development strategies, rising population pressures, and the breakdown of civil order. Another powerful inducement to the renewed religious visions of discontent is the adverse shift in the terms of trade between North and South. Natural materials and physical labor, the two major endowments of the overpopulated regions of the South, are being rapidly eclipsed. Raw commodities, almost without exception, were selling at lower prices in real terms in 1990 than they had a decade earlier. The eclipse of natural resources in the Information Age has been accompanied by an increase in the importance of mental work and a fall in the importance of physical labor. These fundamental trends undermine prospects for economic development in the regions of the globe that have not already achieved high levels of per capita income.

For reasons already touched upon, the economic prospects for the underdeveloped world are further diminished by the collapse of Communism. It removes a major incentive for the transfer of resources to the South. Weak states at the periphery will no longer be the focus of geopolitical struggle. Henceforth, the post-Communist countries of the East will be more attractive targets for investment, partly because their collapse would be more threatening to the West, and partly because they already share more cultural affinities with the West. The wealthy donor countries of the North, with few exceptions, will have much stronger reasons to look east across the heartland of Europe than to Western Asia, Africa, or Latin America.

The Retribalization of the World

These practical reasons point to a coming upsurge in religious fundamentalism, particularly Islamic fundamentalism. Traditional values and patterns of behavior that atrophied during recent generations are destined to make a comeback as the capacity of the governments wanes. This revival will not be confined merely to Islamic societies, nor even to the Third World. Religious and tribal revival will be spread everywhere by the rise in power of small groups and the logic of economic decline. Hindu militants will be more militant. And so will the Sikhs. Survivors of aboriginal tribes will rediscover the lost rites of their ancestors. In New Guinea, the armed cargo cults will insist that the world's largest copper mine be returned to the jungle. It will be more difficult still to build a golf course in North America, as Indian tribes claim that the third tee is the sacred precinct of a holy hunting ground. Millions of small animals will perish in blood sacrifices to the gods of Santeria, the Caribbean voodoo cult that has taken root in Florida, California, and New

York City. And of course, there will be a renewal of Christian conviction and a further spread of fundamentalism in almost every Christian community. Lapsed Jews will also tend to return to the traditions of their forefathers.

Why Islam Will Define the North-South Struggle

The revival of religion will not merely be a revival of Islam, but Islam will come to define the terms of conflict between North and South. Islam is the religion of Europe's southern border. It is the world religion that historically has posed the gravest threat to the Judeo-Christian tradition. It is also the religion of the frontline states that confront Israel and oppose the aspiration of the Jewish people for a Mideast homeland. Even more important, however, Islam is the faith of those who control the world's oil wealth. Islamic states, alone among those that are less economically developed, are likely to control sufficient wealth and resources to challenge the advanced capitalist world in macro as well as micro terms. As the events of 1973 and the Islamic revolution in Iran later in 1979 showed without doubt, oil is a weapon that can be used with broadside economic effects. Whoever controls oil has a grip on the prosperity of the industrialized West.

Notwithstanding the fact that oil is declining in importance along with other raw materials as a factor in economic growth, it remains the lifeblood of modern economies. Transportation, petrochemicals, and power generation are crucially dependent upon the ready availability of oil supplies. Islamic states alone have the capacity to halt the flow of oil that lubricates world commerce. Some of the regimes with their hands on the spigot are militarily weak and unstable, as Iraq demonstrated by its lightning conquest of Kuwait in the summer of 1990. This increases the scope for contention over who controls the oil.

Taken together, these facts suggest that the North-South conflict will come to be seen in terms of the religious differences between Islam and the largely Christian North. It is one of the strange cycles of human affairs that the conflict of the 1990s and beyond will repeat some of the terms and anxieties of John Kay's first English news report five centuries earlier.

ISLAM BETTER FITS 1990 THAN 1890

For reasons that are worth exploring, Islam is better suited to the economic world of the 1990s than it was to the world of the 1890s. Its doctrines, at least in some readings, fit the megapolitical conditions of devolution and the breakdown of order.

Terrorism and the Megapolitics of the 1990s

Some Islamic sects have approved terrorism as a legitimate tactic. That well suits them to current circumstances, as terrorism is likely to be of growing military importance as the year 2000 approaches. In the wealthy countries of Europe, North America, and the Pacific, most people demonstrate by their behavior that they are more interested in profits than the promise of heaven. But Islamic militants, reared in poor economies and a different culture, are more willing to fight and die for their faith.

> Overall, the mighty US military isn't designed for fighting in this Middle Eastern desert or in many of the other Third World hot spots where war is most likely to erupt.
>
> —WALL STREET JOURNAL,
> August 28, 1990, "U.S. Military Lacks Some Tools It Needs in the Middle East Crisis"

Terrorists will be able to slip between the seams of superpower military establishments. The United States alone spent ten trillion dollars during the Cold War in developing a formidable military force. But the money was largely invested in anticipation of conflict on a large scale with another superpower. The United States has far less capacity to project power against irregular forces at the periphery, in spite of the success against Saddam Hussein.

Shifts in the power equation have made it increasingly difficult for remote powers to control events effectively anywhere over anyone's intense objections. Although the United States easily succeeded in ousting Saddam Hussein from Kuwait, the fact that a resort to war was necessary is itself testimony to the decline in the perception of Western military power. Iraq, after all, is a small nation, with a population roughly equivalent to that of Belgium. Imagine the likelihood that Belgium would have attempted blatant aggression, and then defied the world, inviting war with Great Britain, France, the United States, and more than twenty-five other countries. It could not have happened at any time in the past several centuries. Yet Saddam Hussein tried it because he was convinced that the United States was incapable of winning a war at a distance even with his small country.

> We are living on a bluff.
>
> —GENERAL SIR AYLMER HALDANE,
> Commander, British forces in Mesopotamia, August 1920

The difficulty of Western military forces maintaining control over the Middle East was great in 1920. But it has increased over this century. Almost exactly seventy years before Saddam Hussein seized Kuwait, British troops were fighting a widespread rebellion in Mesopotamia, as Iraq was then known. Even at that time, military experts were privately concerned that the costs of projecting power into a hostile Middle East would prove too high.

Then, as now, a main concern was securing the supply of oil. In one of the first effective uses of air power, the British were able to squash the rebellion and install a pro-British monarchy, which Saddam Hussein later opposed as a youthful assassin. Twenty-one years after the first rebellion in Mesopotamia, in 1941, the Iraqi Army, under Rashid Ali, staged a pro-Nazi revolt. Once again, British forces "disposed of" the Iraqis with "relative ease." So overwhelming was British power at the time that the Iraqi Army was placed on a near-starvation diet to keep it from causing more trouble. "Rations were cut down by 1,000 calories a day below what was considered necessary by medical authorities. . . ."

Again in the early 1960s, with the monarchy gone, an Iraqi dictator announced his intention to invade Kuwait. Once again, the British Army moved to oppose the Iraqis, and the crisis passed. By 1990, there was no British Army in the Middle East to protect Kuwait, nor any other credible force that could take up the slack. Because of low confidence in United States power and resolve, Gulf states had hitherto declined to allow American land forces to be based on the Arabian peninsula. The primary United States military contingent was "over-the-horizon," a naval flotilla in the Indian Ocean. Defense experts put the costs of this force at fifty billion dollars a year. It was a fifty-billion-dollar force better suited to mid-ocean combat with the Soviet Union than close operations in a narrow waterway like the Persian Gulf. For example, the U.S. Navy was almost totally lacking in minesweepers, a potentially fatal weakness. The United States had to borrow minesweepers from Britain and Italy. American logistics capacity to move troops to shore was strained. President Bush had to commandeer commercial airliners, rent cargo ships, and call up the reserves. Once on shore, the United States possessed little equipment designed for desert warfare. The sharp run-up in the price of Mine Safety Appliance and Survival Technology stock reflected the lack of gas masks to counter Iraqi chemical weapons.

Most United States troops were lumbered with extremely heavy tanks that could be brought to the Persian Gulf only with great difficulty. They were too heavy to travel on bridges even on well-engineered European roadways. They got a mere four thousand feet to the gallon. The United States also had too few cargo ships to deliver the tanks. And those that were available were too slow. Once in combat, U.S. troops would be dependent to a large extent upon helicopters that "are noted for performing poorly in harsh Third World weather conditions," reported the *Wall Street Journal*. None of these drawbacks prevented the success of the U.S. mission against Saddam Hussein. But it required almost a united front, including the now deceased Soviet Union and all of the Western industrial countries, to bring one Third World dictator to heel.

The strained U.S. position reflected changing megapolitical conditions, which have narrowed the cost advantage of the Western powers over the traditionally backward societies at the periphery. The price of policing the Persian Gulf had skyrocketed, up from twenty-five million pounds in 1920 (about a billion pounds in today's money), a sum that Churchill thought was ridiculously expensive. That was the annual cost for operating the British military garrison during combat. Experts suggested that the outbreak of hostilities in 1991 added up to one billion dollars per day to U.S. costs. Implied annual costs for U.S. forces in Middle East combat were more than three hundred times higher in real terms. And Britain subdued a restless Mesopotamia on its own, with a handful of troops. U.S. forces were joined by Arab armies, and the forces of many other nations whose costs amounted to billions more.

It appeared that almost complete cooperation among the major and minor powers was required to force Iraq's Saddam Hussein to back down. U.S. forces on the ground were supplemented by contingents from Egypt, Syria, Morocco, Pakistan, Bangladesh, and other countries.

A False Dawn of Power?

For all the obstacles and costs that stood in the way of successful military action, the United States had one significant advantage in confronting Saddam that it lacked in Vietnam. Saddam presented a huge target to hit. The million-man Iraqi Army was a World War I–style massed force, not a guerrilla group hiding in the jungle. The early days of air war showed that the World War III air power America had purchased at such great expense was capable of striking military targets with astonishing precision. The capacity to destroy command and control centers, bridges, and other key facilities from the air without obliterating civilian targets convinced world markets that the war was over, even before the ground fighting had begun. The markets were proven correct.

Saddam Hussein set up a situation where American power could be used effectively. That appearance of renewed capacity to police violence in the Middle East could provide a last hurrah of American predominance. Just as the Falklands War revived the perception of British power in the world, though it might have ended otherwise had Argentina possessed a few more Exocet missiles, so the successful routing of Saddam Hussein might produce a false dawn of American power. The impression that American military muscle will be used effectively could last for a surprising time.

But American military operations against Iraq, however successful, could only obscure the fundamental megapolitical logic, not change it. The next crises of the postwar world will find the power equation even more unfavorable to the suppression of violence.

The difficulties faced by the superpowers in confronting a conventional force operating at a distance, like the Iraqi Army, are compounded one hundred times over in confronting irregular terrorist bands and small groups. Such groups can inflict severe damage on the operation of vulnerable large-scale systems. And the military capabilities of the Northern powers are not yet focused enough on the post–Cold War threat to provide effective countermeasures. You cannot kill a fly in your home, even one that carries a deadly contagion, with a smart bomb. Even less would you wish to employ a hydrogen bomb. The terrorist, like the fly, will make life miserable for the superpowers in the 1990s. The huge increase in the cost of suppressing piracy and terrorism is the major reason you should expect more of them in the future.

Law and Domestic Order

The hard-nosed Koranic law is well matched to the rigors of justice at a time when social order is generally breaking down. Islamic penalties for theft and murder are swift and sure. They work. A survey of crime around the globe compiled for *Business Traveler* magazine in 1988 found that Dubai, in the United Arab Emirates, a traditional Islamic society, had per capita rates of violent crime that were only a bare chemical trace of those in big American cities. For example, there were 5,387 assaults per 500,000 persons in Los Angeles. There was none at all reported in Dubai. Zero. The same went for kidnapping. There were no kidnappings in Dubai in 1986. The number of muggings, relative to population, was 778 times higher in New York. Auto theft per capita was 425 times higher in Los Angeles than Dubai. And you were 31 times more likely to be murdered. Early in this century, an authority wrote, "The Prophet hoped by the mere terror of his name to make complete security reign throughout Arabia. . . . "As the capacity of governments to police society recedes, the record of stricter Islamic justice in preserving order and protecting property will attract adherents.

Part of what makes Islamic law effective in discouraging crime is that it is "old-time religion," unamended by modern sociology and sophisticated apologies for crime. All religions discourage theft and murder. But where Islamic law is in force, this discouragement does not speak in a soft voice. Muhammad, the Prophet of Islam, promulgated a specific, detailed law. He sat as a judge in the community of Medina, where he handed down decisions that serve along with the Koran as the foundation of Islamic law. In orthodox Islam, there has been no new law since the Prophet died on June 7, 632. If punishments for crime in North America or Western Europe were meted out according to standards of justice in Christian countries in the seventh century, infractions like mugging, murder, kidnapping, and grand larceny would not be undertaken so lightly.

Islamic Law and the Economy: The Taboo on Usury

The relative inflexibility of Islamic law has poorly equipped Islamic societies for prosperity in the age of smokestack industries. Part of the reason is that Islam retains the ancient taboo against lending money at interest. "Allah hath blighted usury" says the Holy Koran. This injunction echoes similar condemnations of usury in the Bible. The Old Testament placed limits upon lending:

> Thou shalt not lend upon usury to thy brother; usury of money, usury of victuals, usury of anything that is lent upon usury. Unto a stranger thou mayest lend upon usury; but unto thy brother thou shalt not lend upon usury, that the Lord thy God may bless thee.

This passage from Deuteronomy did not ban lending at interest altogether. But medieval church fathers read it in that light. They quoted a passage from Luke 8:35, " . . . lend freely, hoping nothing thereby."

The ban on lending was too widespread in ancient societies to have reflected merely a local misunderstanding of capital markets, or a failure to anticipate John Locke's argument that "the price of the hire of money" should always be free. The taboo on usury served a function. It helped stabilize backward societies at the edge of subsistence. The reason is hinted at in another Biblical passage, Nehemiah 5:4–5:

> We have borrowed money for the king's tribute, and that upon our lands and vineyards . . . and, lo, we bring into bondage our sons and daughters to be servants . . . neither is it in our power to redeem them, for other men have our lands and vineyards.

Borrowing when there were few or no income-producing capital assets, other than land and human labor, tended to be destabilizing and militarily dangerous. Military success in antiquity often turned on whether a society retained a significant number of freeholders. A person with a stake in the society he fought for tended to make a better account of himself than a peasant soldier or an indentured servant. The trouble, however, was that while yeomen may have been successes at war, war did not tend to make successes of yeomen. Wars tended to impoverish the very freeholders who were the most able and dependable fighters. It sometimes called them from their fields, so they could not tend to their crops. It also drove up taxes. These twin evils were compounded by the occasional drought, which reduced the yield from farming below the break-even point. Given the high interest rates that are common even today in backward economies, running into debt was rarely a way for a small holder to rescue his livelihood. Generally, when small holders went into debt they lost their property and their freedom. Sometimes they legally pledged their persons as collateral for a loan. At other times, their bondage was debt bondage. In either case, the result was social unrest that destabilized the system.

Muhammad had seen in the Mecca of his own time how a disproportionately large population of the poor, fraught with discontent, could militarily weaken a system. This was not because the poor themselves were able to overthrow the local elite. It was rather that they had no reason to defend the system when it did come under attack. Muhammad exploited such a weakness in taking Mecca. It was common in antiquity for states to be weakened by dispossessed freeholders and insolvent debtors. This happened in almost every Greek city-state. It was the reason for Solon's reforms in ancient Athens. He found a city simmering no less than Mecca. Solon stabilized the situation by prohibiting lending on the security of a person's body, and decreed a general cancellation of debt similar to the Biblical Jubilee.

Indirect Tax Limitation

The injunction against usury was an artificial means of ensuring a wider distribution of property. It was also a roundabout, religious limitation on taxes. By narrowing the availability of credit to finance tax payments, usury bans discouraged high taxes. They made it relatively easier for the small owners to avoid being squeezed off their lands by the oligarchies that both started wars and tended to hog the primary spoils of war.

In late republican Rome, where there were no prohibitions against usury, the senatorial class effectively dispossessed the small holders. They frequently plunged the country into war, reserving the bounties for themselves, while shifting the costs to the yeomen. A clear example is Sulla's war tax laid in 84 B.C. It was financed by the senatorial elite, at interest rates above 50 percent.

In due course, most of those who went into debt lost their lands. In effect, the oligarchy got away with more than if they had stolen the lands directly. They laid the tax, pushed the small holders into insolvency, and earned exorbitant returns for financing those who attempted to escape from the snare. To short-circuit this unhappy process, religions, including Islam, made the payment of interest taboo.

In the Christian world, the ban on usury lingered through the Middle Ages, but was blasted away by the Gunpowder Revolution. Almost immediately after gunpowder weapons came into wide use, Protestant reformers discarded the old taboo. Huldreich Zwingli, the Protestant reformer who set Zurich on the path to becoming a world banking center, emphatically denied that lending was sinful or contrary to the Bible. In Sidney Homer's words, Zwingli argued that "the obligation to pay interest flows directly from the commandment to 'render to all their due.' " Luther and Calvin also disputed that it was sinful for a Christian to lend money. While the Catholic Church did not fully lift its injunctions against money lending until 1836, capital markets and banks began to function in Western Europe almost as soon as the change in megapolitical conditions made investment on a larger scale possible.

Islam and the Scale of Enterprise

As the scale of enterprise rose over the past five centuries, and banking developed in its modern forms, it became ever more difficult for a nation operating under Islamic law to compete. A strict prohibition on lending for interest prohibits a passbook savings account, as well as a fixed-interest government bond. It hobbles credit markets to preserve a taboo that has been militarily anachronistic since gunpowder replaced the sword. Without credit markets, large-scale industry is hampered. Its high capital costs require that money from many hands be pooled together for investment. But where money cannot be borrowed, much of it must either come from abroad, which is to say, from people who are not confined by the same ban on usury, from the state, or from roundabout, inefficient forms of banking of a kind that prevailed in the Italian city-states in the late Middle Ages.

As it happens, Islamic societies have indulged in all three. But without producing any notable successes in industrial competition. During the whole modern period of large-scale, smokestack industries, Islamic manufacturers never competed on a world level. It was simply impossible for countries operating under Islamic law, hampered by inflexible restrictions on usury, to invest large sums of capital as well as nations with efficient banking systems and bond markets.

By a stroke of luck, or perhaps Allah's blessing, much of the wealth of the

Western industrial countries has been transferred back into Islamic hands in payment for oil. The more thinly populated and traditional societies on the Arabian peninsula where the Prophet Muhammad lived are awash in oil. The governments that control this oil are among the few creditor countries in an indebted world. It is wealth that makes them attractive to aggressors. It also gives them the opportunity to develop new intellectual capital.

In the Information Age, the traditional Islamic prohibition against usury will be less damaging to economic efficiency. Even if it is not set aside by an Islamic Luther, the falling scale of enterprise implies lower capital costs, and thus marginally less damage done by limiting debt markets.

Lower Oil in Slump

Of course, another fall in the oil price could have a rapidly destabilizing impact on the Islamic world. If the slump does develop as we forecast, the oil price could go much lower than most people now think—in spite of its crucial importance and dwindling supply.

In the depression of the 1930s, oil was one of the few growth sectors. Although prices were depressed, demand rose sharply, and oil companies were among the leaders in profit performance. If the world suffers a deeper depression in the 1990s, as we expect, the oil market and oil industry this time are unlikely to fare as well.

Of course, we don't pretend that it is easy to form a clear statistical snapshot of future oil prices. Forecasting is always difficult, and there are special problems in this case:

1. The elasticity of oil demand is subject to considerable time lags. It is unclear how rapidly a depression would cut into consumption.

2. The impact of economic growth in raising oil demand during the 1980s has been obscured because it was entirely canceled by conservation and substitution effects.

3. A straightforward link between economic growth and oil consumption is complicated by currency effects. In the event that the dollar tumbled in the early stages of a depression, lower oil costs in local currencies outside the United States could help sustain demand. (Alternatively, a higher dollar could accelerate declines in demand outside the United States.)

It is possible, though unlikely, that oil demand would rise enough relative to economic output to hold consumption up in the early stages of a depression. The following factors, however, suggest that demand would fall significantly:

1. Oil consumption in the last recession in 1982 fell by 13.8 percent in the second tier of industrial countries (excluding the United States, Western Europe, and Japan). These countries suffered the brunt of recession more than the larger economies. A deeper slump would presumably reduce oil demand everywhere.

2. A Salomon Brothers study attributes 17.6 million barrels per day of oil consumption to economic growth since 1980. A 1930s-style depression would wipe away much of that growth.

At the depth of the last depression in the United States in 1933, GNP fell to the level of 1922. In Germany, the economy bottomed in 1932 at 1908 levels. In Great Britain, Gross Domestic Product (GDP) bottomed in 1932 at roughly 1926 levels. Italy bottomed in 1931 at 1926 levels. Japanese GDP figures are unavailable, but industrial production bottomed in 1931 at 1928 levels.

On average, if you exclude the German case as an outlier, the leading industrial countries lost about six years of growth. An equally severe depression bottoming in the mid-nineties would, by implication, reduce oil consumption outside the old Communist bloc by about eight million barrels per day.

The 1986 Collapse

A 12 percent reduction in oil consumption, combined with a modest increase in non-OPEC output, sent prices reeling below ten dollars per barrel in early 1986. The reduction in demand was quite gradual because it was largely attributable to capital investment. As much as 80 percent of the drop between 1979 and 1986 was due to substitution of coal, nuclear power, and natural gas for oil in electricity generation and industrial boilers.*

The important point here is that a drop in demand of six to seven million barrels per day over seven years ultimately resulted in a price collapse during a boom. A depression could result in a similar drop in a much shorter time. It is unlikely that OPEC and other producers would be able to manage production declines of the magnitude needed to keep prices from tumbling.

---

*This may slightly overstate the importance of fuel substitution, because demand for energy in all forms fell per unit of GNP, thanks to substantial increases in the energy efficiency.

Oil Output in a Depression

Historically, commodity producers have reduced output only minimally during past depression periods. In the early stages, output of some commodities actually tends to rise as prices fall. Most output shutdowns are either forced politically, through domestic cartels, like agricultural production boards (or, in the case of oil, the Texas Railroad Commission), or are necessitated by bankruptcy.

There is little likelihood that the core Gulf states could agree prospectively to divide output reductions among themselves to the degree necessary to hold prices, unless they were forced to do so by military intervention, either on the part of Iraq, Iran, or some other power. As Iraq's attack on Kuwait emphasized, the Gulf states have been unable to agree on production cutbacks with less than a third of capacity idle. Indeed, this is why Saddam invaded Kuwait in the first place. With the oil price slipping, rich producers like Kuwait and the United Arab Emirates would not agree to limit production as Saddam demanded. Absent a large army, able to deploy around the entire oil-producing world, it would be almost impossible to find a way of portioning more painful cuts. Credible attempts in that direction would probably await severe price falls.

It is hard to make dependable estimates of excess capacity among the non-OPEC producers. But potential additions to supply of one hundred thousand to two hundred thousand barrels per day certainly seem reasonable in Mexico, Malaysia, and Norway. It is quite likely, judging from both recent behavior and the record of the 1930s, that poor nations will produce as much as possible to maximize income at lower prices.

It is also difficult to make sound estimates of potential output increases in China and the Soviet Union. They would not appear to be great. China may have a large potential, but it is unlikely to be a factor in export anytime soon. Indeed, rapidly growing Chinese demand will counteract some of the decline in demand in the industrialized West.

The former Soviet republics are another story. Output fell significantly in the turmoil following the collapse of the Soviet Union. It may fall further, or at least not increase significantly in 1993. But there is now little doubt that gross mismanagement and backward technology held oil output in the late Soviet Union to a fraction of what it could have been. Now that Western companies are entering Russia, Kazakhstan, and other former Soviet republics, you can expect an astonishing surge in oil output in the next few years, as fields are developed and facilities such as pipelines are put in place to handle the new production.

Another potentially large contribution to supplies for export from the former

Soviet Union could arise from conservation and more efficient use of oil that has traditionally been wasted. When the Soviet Union died, oil was priced for domestic use at $5 per barrel. Consequently, little effort was expended to conserve it. Apartment buildings, for example, lacked individual thermostats. Residents regulated temperatures in the winter by opening the window. With more realistic pricing, and the introduction of energy-saving technologies that would pay for themselves in short order, the former Soviet states should free large amounts of oil for export.

In the early stages of the downturn, output into the world market from some countries would probably increase as prices fell. Eventually, high-cost output would be shut in, but not before prices tumbled, and stayed down for a considerable period.

United States Is High-Cost Production Area

The highest-cost production is in Alaska, an area where the producers have made huge investments that could be jeopardized if they attempted to shut in their wells. They are unlikely to abandon production quickly. Other high-cost areas tend to have high amortization costs, but lower marginal costs. At the time of the last oil drop, *Petroleum Intelligence Weekly* estimated that the marginal cost of operating much of the North Sea oil was as low as two to three dollars per barrel. Even if these estimates are too low, the oil price could drop dramatically without much curtailing of output.

As consumption fell, you could get a huge glut of oil. Prices could tumble toward the marginal costs of production in the low-cost area—the Mideast. In 1986, a number of oil experts were quoted as expecting oil prices to drop to six to eight dollars a barrel if OPEC did not trim output. As it turned out, output was curtailed—for a variety of reasons. U.S. Mideast policy was a contributing factor.

The Political Response to Falling Prices

The United States has shown through the shipment of arms to Iran, the reflagging of the Kuwaiti tankers, and the response to Iraq's 1990 invasion of Kuwait that some efforts will be made to safeguard oil flows and the domestic oil industry in the United States. But these policies also demonstrate the limitations of roundabout mechanisms for controlling oil and the oil price.

In 1986, some factions of the U.S. government, led by then–Vice President Bush, wanted to raise the oil price and said so publicly. A Detroit newspaper responded with a headline that encapsulates the political problem with overt actions to shore up the oil industry, "Bush to Michigan: Drop Dead." President

Reagan was unwilling to support direct moves to raise oil prices. But oil became entangled in the great foreign policy fandango of the Reagan years, the Iran-Contra affair.

Perhaps coincidentally, the United States began sending arms to Iran at a time when Iran was pressuring Saudi Arabia to curtail production. The military progress made by Iran was quickly followed by a reversal in Saudi policy. The price of oil stabilized.

With a high portion of world oil production concentrated in a small, thinly populated Gulf region, it is likely that that area would be the main stage of international political intrigue during a depression period—without necessarily producing a major lift to oil prices in North America.

Only a sustained shutdown of the oil fields due to direct military intervention would be likely to offset a fall in demand of six to eight million barrels per day. The most likely political response to falling prices would involve drastic oil import controls and domestic output cartelization in the United States. The import controls would probably come first, perhaps in conjunction with exchange controls in a dollar crisis. Historically, major shifts in policy regimes are unlikely for the first two to three years of a depression.

Unlikely though it may seem in the wake of the high prices in the fall of 1990, in a depression you could see oil trade below five dollars per barrel. Political responses might cushion the fall, and prevent world prices from dropping as low as Gulf production costs, but you could not count on political maneuvering to keep prices from reaching severely depressed levels.

Evidence from other downturns suggests that the more prices are held up artificially, the longer they take to bottom out. This has been a general characteristic of asset declines across countries in past depressions. There may be a tradeoff, therefore, between a sharper, briefer price decline and a more gradual but longer-lasting drop.

Consequences

Here are some implications of this scenario for the oil industry:

1. Profitability in all segments of the oil industry would tumble.
2. Domestic American production earnings would be hurt more than foreign earnings because of higher costs.
3. The more highly leveraged firms and sectors would be hit especially hard.
4. Exploration and drilling activity would come to a standstill.
5. The portion of world oil output in high-cost regions, especially North America, would decline.

6. The heavily indebted oil industry in the Third World would be starved for capital, perhaps opening opportunities for foreign investment.

7. After the ultimate recovery of demand, the industry should return to higher profitability, barring major technological breakthroughs in exotics, such as fusion, solar power, or superconductivity.

The integrated international oil companies would be hurt by depressed prices, but perhaps less than other oil firms. As a group, they suffered less in the 1985–86 oil price drop than other segments of the oil industry. But a number of the second-rank firms were weakened and stand to be more vulnerable. Texaco was hurt by the courts. Phillips and Unocal ran up huge debts to fight takeovers. Occidental took on debts for acquisitions.

The U.S. exploration and energy service segments should be severely hurt. In 1985 and 1986, domestic oil exploration almost collapsed. The number of operating onshore oil rigs plunged 40 percent on a year-over-year basis. A steeper drop would leave little room for profitable operations. In the past, industry-specific assets of failing companies in areas with excess capacity went for salvage value. The FDIC will probably end up owning many energy assets.

The oil industry in the Third World is eighty billion dollars in debt. A real downturn would shrivel cash flow and make it very difficult for these mostly nationalized entities to raise investment capital. Portions of some of them might actually be thrown back into the market as a means of relieving bankrupt governments from their debts.

The international financial system would be undermined, with a high likelihood of political chaos in many regions, especially in Saudi Arabia and the conservative Persian Gulf sheikdoms.

"THE AFRICANIZATION OF EUROPE"

Europe faces an Islamization or Africanization as the demographic and economic gap between the two banks of the Mediterranean Sea widens and people move from south to north.

—JEAN-CLAUDE CHESNAIS

As the 1990s began, Third World countries were experiencing a rate of population growth double that in Europe a century ago—the period when Europe's expansion reached its peak relative to the rest of the world. Africa and the Near East, which already have young populations compared to the average age of Europeans, are poised for a further population explosion in the 1990s.

What amounts to a demographic time bomb is ticking away on the southern shores of the Mediterranean. In Europe to the north, which has been richer longer than any other area of the world, the normal trend to lower fertility among the rich has dropped fertility rates below replacement levels. For the European Community as a whole, there are about 1.2 million fewer births per year than would be needed to maintain population.

This means that in the future, the European populations will be disproportionately made up of old people, whose retirement costs will weigh upon economies with too few young workers. By contrast, on the African shore of the Mediterranean, fertility is at its historical maximum. Each woman has, on average, from four to six children. The annual African surplus of births over the replacement rate is fifteen million. In Africa, there will be many young people crowding in search of jobs in immature and unstable economic systems.

The combination of depopulation in regions of wealth with overpopulation in nearby regions of poverty creates almost irresistible pressures for migration. As Albert Sauvy, the French demographer, succinctly put it, "If wealth does not go where people are, people naturally go where wealth is." This dynamic, which explains the dramatic influx of Latin Americans into the United States, will be even more powerful in Europe because the gap in purchasing power between the European Community and Africa is almost twice that between Latin America and the United States.

The migration into Europe seems likely to proceed no matter what happens to the oil price. But it will certainly be amplified if a collapse in oil prices deflates the economies of the Middle East. Projections suggest that the Middle East alone (including Iran) could reach a population of three hundred to four hundred million by 2030, considerably higher than the expected number of descendants and survivors of what is now the European Community.

If large numbers of Middle Eastern and African migrants compete with Eastern European refugees to swarm into Europe in the 1990s and beyond, as now seems likely, the result will not only be a migration of individuals, it will also be a migration of cultures and value systems. It will be a migration of Islamic power. Demographers now estimate that "the great majority" of new immigrants "would be made up of Moslems originating in the Mediterranean crescent running from Marrakesh to Istanbul." An influx of fifty million Moslems over the next few decades would bring into Europe many of the tensions and difficulties that the United States and Great Britain have faced in attempting to balance the clash of cultures in multi-ethnic societies. A growing population of disgruntled Moslems will be the shock troops of change in Europe as the year 2000 approaches.

"The Gospel Cannot Be Introduced Without Tumult"

During the periods in which Christianity converted a large part of the world, it was a crusading faith. That was true of the Apostles, of the early church fathers, of the Jesuits in China or South America, but also of the great Protestant leaders such as Luther or Wesley. As Luther wrote, "The Gospel cannot be introduced without tumult, scandal and rebellion . . . the world of God is a sword, a war, a destruction, a scandal, a ruin, a poison." Luther was a great man, but not a moderate one.

Whether or not Khomeini would have used Luther's words, this was also the attitude of the Ayatollah. It was the way in which he made and maintained the Islamic revolution in Iran. A year after his death, millions of Iranians walked fifteen miles to his tomb, in searing heat, to show their devotion to his memory and to their faith. Some, no doubt, died on that dreadful journey. But they died in the expectation of paradise. Islam's appeal is not just a question of political power. Nations without a faith are always exposed to nations that have faith.

Echo the crushing slogan of disavowal of pagans and apostates of world arrogance, headed by the criminal U.S.A.

—AYATOLLAH KHOMEINI
to pilgrims in Mecca, 1987

The revival of Islam has many opponents. Certainly, the current leaders of many Middle Eastern countries are in that number. But Khomeini himself believed that the greatest enemy was the secular modernism that he personified in the "Great Satan," the United States. That is the essentially antireligious influence that had inspired the regime of the Shah, and threatened—as in Britain it undoubtedly does threaten—to subvert the faith of the Islamic people. Pope John Paul II views the materialism of the West in much the same way.

As an idea the atheistic materialism that had its most perverse expression in Communism has always been present in the world. It was the leading idolatry of ancient Rome as much as it is of modern New York. But its main centers of power are somewhat remote from Islam. They are to be found in the newly competing centers of economic progress, in Western Europe, North America, and Japan. There are, of course, outposts in the Middle East, but they can be regarded as secondary.

There are five counterpowers that are nearest to areas of Islamic ferment, and are likely to suffer for it. They are Russia, Turkey, India, the secular and pro-Western regimes of the Middle East, and the Zionist state of Israel.

Russia has been weakened by economic collapse and the loss of the czar's empire. Nevertheless, Russia's military retains its historic interest in controlling the regions of Central Asia to its south. By treaty, Russia will continue to control nuclear weapons stationed in Kazakhstan. And Russian nationalists have expressed strong solidarity with the millions of Russians still living in all the Islamic former republics of the Soviet Union. It is likely, therefore, that Russia will continue to play a major role in Central Asia and will seek to block Iran's aspirations to create a fundamentalist Islamic empire in the region.

The second power that will contest the rise of fundamentalism in the Islamic states in Central Asia is Turkey. The Turks were a great power in region for centuries. Although Turkey is a westernized and secular nation with its own fundamentalist movement, Turks may prove to be the most formidable adversaries to the fundamentalism supported by Iran. The Turks bring historic linguistic and ethnic advantages to this struggle, which they may carry into Iran itself. The Turks are closely related to the Azeris and the Turkmen, groups that constitute sizable minorities within Iran. Northwest Iran is home to 14 million Azeris, while Northeastern Iran is populated by some 2 million Turkmen. Secessionist movements in both regions are being encouraged by Turkey. With tribalism on the rise, it is possible that Iranian Azeris will indeed secede to Azerbaijan, while the Turkmen secede to Turkmenistan. A crack-up of Iran would be a major blow to the fundamentalist revolutionary movement.

Iran also appears ready to exploit and aggravate ethnic tensions in an effort to destabilize Turkey. The Ansar Corps of the Qods Force are said to be funding the PKK (Kurdish Workers Party), the terrorist group active in fomenting violence in Kurdish regions of southeastern Turkey. However, unless the world depression is sufficiently severe as to provoke a triumph of Islamic fundamentalism in Turkey itself, the Turks will prove to be a formidable counterpower to any fundamentalist advance into Central Asia that appears to be a cover for Iranian ambitions.

The next groups of opposed powers are the secular dictatorships of the Middle East, like Algeria, in loose alliance with pro-Western regimes like that of Egypt. These are really more closely aligned than they may at first appear. The current Egyptian government, after all, is the direct descendant of the regime of President Nasser. When he was alive, authoritarian nationalist socialism seemed to offer a real alternative to Islamic fundamentalism. The Algerian regime, born in a struggle for independence, has followed much the same trail to disillusionment that Egypt followed under Nasser. Socialism, in both cases, was merely a strategy for development. Its failure in Egypt led Nasser's successor, Anwar Sadat, to turn to the West as a matter of material advantage. The West offered more aid and better prospects for economic development.

Regimes of Nasserite character were still in power in 1992 in Syria and Iraq, as well as in Algeria. Iraq's war with Iran, and the Algerian crackdown on fundamentalists show how real the hostility between the two systems is. But as Saddam Hussein quickly realized after his invasion of Kuwait, the real drawing power of ideas is on the side of Islam. He sounded much like Khomeini in calling on all Moslems to defend Mecca from the spear of the infidels, whom he was keen to identify with the United States. In the wake of the war, Saddam was barely able to save his regime from a fundamentalist uprising. The likelihood is that as the 1990s wear on, Islam will eventually absorb the secular regimes, including the pro-Western secular regime in Egypt. Islam has a prophet and they do not.

India, like the Soviet Union, is a multi-ethnic empire forged in the time of colonialism. The animosities between its Islamic populations and the Hindu majority were already a cause of the fissuring of the British India. It is likely that as the forces of devolution gather strength, India will again be split apart. Cracks are showing in at least three provinces as we write— Jammu, Kashmir and the Punjab. The Indian authorities blame Pakistan for Islamic ferment. But an upsurge of Hindu militance, typified by the destruction of a 16th century mosque in Ayodhya by a Hindu mob, aggravates animosities on both sides. It is likely that the two countries will go to war in the 1990s, as separatist movements in India become more violent, a war that has a potential to prove devastating. We assume that both India and Pakistan have access to nuclear weapons. As the example of the Soviet Union proved, nuclear arsenals do not prevent separatists violence and disintegration. But they could be fired in anger where both sides are motivated by tribal hatreds.

The Danger to Israel

Obviously, Israel is in the greatest danger, a danger made much greater by the benighted character of the government that came to power in 1990. There was a period, from the death of Nasser to the fall of the Shah, when a determined Israeli government might have made a general peace with a largely moderate group of neighbors. That opportunity was missed. If Islamic fanaticism continues to increase, fueled by failures of economic development to provide a secure life for millions of Moslems in surrounding countries, and sparked by major triumphs in reclaiming the Islamic independence of the former Soviet states, then the threat to Israel will become even more acute. It is no longer even likely that Israel has the advantage of a monopoly of nuclear weapons in the region. One must assume that Iran has nuclear weapons and the capability to deliver them. Given the leaky state of Russian arsenals, and the poverty of Russian scientists, it is possible that any of the Arab states and even Islamic terrorist groups may secure nuclear weapons. Israel may discover that is has little deterrent advantage.

Islam is, therefore, likely to become steadily more powerful in political terms during the 1990s. This is not only a consequence of the collapse of Communism, it is also another symptom of the collapse of large power centers, and the reversion to more ancient forms of disorder. As the power equation in the world moves back to reflect the kind of balance that existed five centuries ago, our headlines will come to more nearly match those of five centuries ago as well. By the end of the century, if the second and deeper stage of the depression we have forecast does not arrive, the gradual depletion of the world's oil resources will again have raised the price of oil. Much of that oil, including vast quantities in the former Soviet Asian states, will be controlled by Islamic governments. And Islam will become a growing force in Europe itself. No doubt, Islam will be held back, as throughout history, by internecine conflict—the Iran-Iraq War was the largest conflict in the world of the 1980s. But the trend of power and the threat to the interests of neighboring nations is inescapable.

CHAPTER EIGHT

LINEAR EXPECTATIONS IN A NONLINEAR WORLD

HOW THE TELESCOPE LED US TO COMPUTE;

HOW THE COMPUTER CAN HELP US TO SEE

Nature and Nature's laws lay hid in night:
God said, let Newton be! and all was light.

—ALEXANDER POPE's epitaph for
Sir Isaac Newton

I do not know what I may appear to the world, but to myself I seem to have been
only a boy playing on the sea-shore, and diverting myself in now and then finding
a smoother pebble or a prettier shell than ordinary, whilst the great ocean of truth
lay all undiscovered before me.

—SIR ISAAC NEWTON

THE MECHANICAL INTUITION

TOLSTOY TALKS of false conclusions woven thread by thread into the fabric of our lives. It is a telling metaphor from the earliest stages of industrialism. Great novelists have not yet adopted the metaphors of the postindustrial age. They don't speak of "false conclusions programmed into our lives like a computer virus." People don't yet think that way. Far more than we can easily imagine, our perceptions of reality, our "conclusions," true and false,

245

are informed directly and indirectly by technology. Much of this volume is a discussion of the impact of technology, especially weapons technology, on political and economic life. Ironically, an impact of past technology on present perceptions has been to blind us to the dangers of abrupt change that the new technology implies. Our contemporary worldview, while a great improvement over most past systems of thought, nonetheless has blind spots. One is our mechanical intuition—the unconscious expectation that the political economy should function like a machine. We fool ourselves in potentially crucial ways because we expect reality to fall into simpler patterns than it actually does. There is no better illustration of this misapprehension than the following headline from page one of the October 15, 1989, issue of the *Washington Post*:

"The Market" Defies Logic, Explanation

This false conclusion, like many others, can be traced to a mathematically naive assumption that complex systems like the market ought to behave in a mechanical way, like a teeter-totter, with outcomes strictly proportioned to the known influences. When the *Post*'s Steven Pearlstein wrote that the market defies "common sense," he was paying unconscious homage to a seventeenth-century mathematical model of reality pioneered by Sir Isaac Newton. Sir Isaac's brainstorms have informed a large part of the educated "common sense" of the Industrial Age. He described a universe that operates according to mechanical principles, with change occurring on a gradual, proportionate basis.

Now a higher stage of technology has laid the groundwork for a Postindustrial Revolution, as well as a postindustrial science. The advent of powerful computers has given students of many different disciplines new means of analyzing complex systems. The human economy in all its forms is such a complex system. The deeper science has probed into nature, the more it has become clear that complex systems at every scale, from the organs of our bodies to the supergalaxies in space, incorporate different forms of order than those that our minds have been trained to perceive. This is epitomized by the new mathematics of chaos. Strictly speaking, chaos is only a subset of the larger realm of nonlinear dynamics. But the very fact that "chaos" has become the nickname of this whole realm of discovery betrays the extent to which its findings confound older, "common sense" perceptions. "Chaos" sounds like what happens when the Three Stooges direct traffic. In everyday speech, "chaos" means "utter confusion" and "disorder." The mathematics of chaos reveals hidden order by examining apparent disorder at a higher level of abstraction.

Much time and trouble stands between us and the day when these emerging mathematical insights will inform a new intuition of "common sense," as second-nature as the old patterns of perception. Meanwhile, it is important to understand the deficiencies of "common sense" at all times and places, and realize how much our perceptions of reality can be distorted by prevailing systems of thought.

As Thomas Kuhn has explained, the primary element in any investigation is the assumption that some order or pattern exists to be discovered. Kuhn's famous work, *The Structure of Scientific Revolutions*, details how turning points in the history of science involve shifts from one paradigm, or pattern of understanding, to another. These paradigms are just as crucial in everyday life as they are in rigorous scientific investigation. In ways that are never obvious, what "makes sense" to you is a function of the paradigm that is an unconscious part of your understanding.

We explore these points and their broad implications below, beginning with an example from New Guinea, where peoples with a pre-Newtonian mindset came into contact with the industrial world. Their reactions offer a vivid object lesson on the limitations of what "makes sense."

Stephen King Meets the Civil Air Patrol

The mountains of New Guinea are home to some of the strangest airstrips in the world. They are the work of natives who wear nose ornaments, and who stand with one foot in the primitive past. They look out into the world of modern technology, scanning the skies for cargo planes, whose arrival they have expected for up to half a century. By night, they build bonfires to illuminate runways carved from the jungle. Each strip resembles a World War II air base, complete with tumble-down hangars, a radio shack, a beacon tower, and even homemade planes, all modeled out of sticks, leaves, and bamboo. Anthropologist Marvin Harris explains:

> They are expecting the arrival of an important flight: cargo planes filled with canned food, clothing, portable radios, wrist watches, and motorcycles. The planes will be piloted by ancestors who have come back to life. Why the delay? A man goes inside the radio shack and gives instructions into the tin-can microphone. The message goes out over an antenna constructed of string and vines: "Do you read me? Roger and out."

In other words, the natives expect their dead ancestors to fly home and spread around the bounty from a supernatural shopping spree. This is the type of story line you would expect if Stephen King had collaborated with Margaret

Mead. But no one of their imagination was required to concoct the cargo cults. Like primitive peoples everywhere, the cargo cultists held a firm belief "that those who possessed wealth were under the obligation to give it away," wrote Marvin Harris. The foundation of this primitive egalitarianism is the fact that in primitive conditions everyone has more or else equal physical power. It therefore becomes almost impossible for anyone to obtain more of life's good things than he and his immediate family can effectively protect. Whenever anyone in a primitive society obtains something desirable, he is obliged either to hide it or to give it away. When primitive peoples covet some products they desire, their "common sense" tells them they ought to get these products as a gift. The cargo cults arose spontaneously to express this common conception. This is evident from the many versions of the cargo prophecy.

Supernatural Bills of Lading

Anthropologists tell us that the peoples of New Guinea and Melanesia have invented many stories about the mysteries of "cargo"—the products introduced by whites or the Japanese from abroad. Just about the only element these fantasies share, other than their utter misunderstanding of the way industrial society works, is the expectation that someone, man or god, will convey to the natives the products they covet free of charge. Otherwise, you can shop among the cargo prophecies for your choice of comic details. In the New Hebrides, the local people somehow concluded that a World War II soldier, a certain sergeant of the medical corps, John Frum, was King of America. He would someday dispatch Liberator bombers "with a cargo of milk and ice cream," wrote Marvin Harris. On the Bismarck Archipelago, an enterprising native in 1968 led his followers in a tax rebellion. By this method, the "cult members saved $75,000 to 'buy' Lyndon Johnson." They intended "to make him king of New Hanover" if he would reveal the secrets of cargo. At about the same time, a prophet named Yaliwan Mathias convinced his followers that the cargo cornucopia was hidden beneath a large U.S. Air Force survey marker atop Mount Turu. In May 1971, he led a group to the site where they eagerly dug up the concrete slab, a back-breaking job. When they could find no cargo, they assumed it was because "the authorities had taken it away." Among the West Irians, who apparently accepted the argument that industrial products come from factories, prophets forecast that "whole factories and steel mills" would be delivered by cargo ship.

What "Makes Sense"

Although the cargo cultists have lately taken up guns to reinforce their claims on "cargo," their long-held fantasies say a lot about the way the human mind works. Notice particularly the way that technological progress was incorporated over the years—without much altering the primitive pattern of understanding. At first, the natives in coastal areas expected their windfalls to be delivered in giant canoes. Later, they looked for sailing ships. And later still, they waited for phantom steamships bearing bolts of calico and tinned sardines. More recently, they have looked for airplanes of a modern type, which would disgorge the latest model of automobile.

Turbo-Charging the Stone Age

The cargo cultists have generally coveted the most modern products, and even imagined that they would be delivered in the most modern means of conveyance. Yet they resisted modernizing their conception of the way the world works. In effect, they wanted a new radio they could wire into a vine.

To the minds of the natives, the products introduced as cargo from abroad were understood in very traditional terms. Like primitive societies generally, the New Guinea cultures were short on scientific explanations and long on magic. It would take us deeper into New Guinea than we want to go to detail all the reasons why the cargo fantasy—so preposterous to us—made sense to the local people. A simple way of saying it is that natives operated with a magical rather than a mechanical intuition. The wondrous products were seen not as the output of industrial processes, but as the fruit of a secret that, once revealed, would spare them from toil.

It was only with great difficulty that the cargo cultists could be convinced otherwise. The Australian government, which administered New Guinea as a colony until 1975, found to its surprise that even a show-and-tell tour of Australian factories, mills, and warehouses did not necessarily dispel the fantasy. In one famous case of a cargo prophet named Yali, efforts to confide a modern understanding of production and trade backfired spectacularly. Factories belching smoke were one thing, but they did not answer the natives' longstanding question—why "the white men are hiding the cargo secret."

Learning Facts from the Fantasy

Attempts by natives of New Guinea and Melanesia to come to grips with changed circumstances were for generations a complete muddle—although they behaved in ways they thought made perfect sense. They diverted much energy carving useless airstrips in the jungle, digging up concrete slabs, and saving funds to buy Lyndon Johnson. So long as the natives stuck with the patterns of understanding informed by their old cultures, it was almost guaranteed that modern technology would be beyond their comprehension.

In effect, the paradigm or worldview that accompanies a culture is like a software program. It enables people to process information by suggesting an underlying pattern of reality in which information fits together. The inability of the natives to make modern details fit comprehensibly into a Stone Age mindset leads us to some important points—with application far beyond the rain forests of New Guinea or the New Hebrides.

1. What matters most in "making sense" of life is the underlying pattern of reality that people believe exists. Details standing by themselves are usually unintelligible, not just to persons of a Stone Age background, but to anyone.

2. What seems to "make sense" may actually be a delusion arising from a "blind spot" or defect in the local paradigm of understanding.

3. Any mindset will take adequate account of the facts that are relevant in the economic and political setting in which it emerged. Hunters will be alert to details indicating the presence of game. Farmers will distinguish the quality of seed. Industrial mechanics will understand wrenches. But all paradigms are incomplete. If one comprehensive paradigm could suffice in all circumstances, human understanding would probably be informed by instinct.

4. Facts that are economically irrelevant and do not fit comfortably into an existing worldview or paradigm will generally be misinterpreted or ignored. The ability to remain oblivious to nonessential facts may have helped focus human attention on what was necessary to survive under primeval conditions. This could have been quite important to a species struggling to live by its wits in many different ecological niches.

5. The more primitive the economic conditions under which a culture emerges, the less likely it is to realistically comprehend a broad range of facts.

6. An existing paradigm is seldom dispelled by evidence alone. As Keith Thomas has written, "Such systems of belief possess a resilience which makes them virtually immune to external argument." A people whose culture grossly misinterprets certain facts will not necessarily reason their way to a more encompassing worldview until forced to do so by the brunt of economic necessity or military defeat. Reason does not alter values.

7. The tendency to preserve counterproductive and unrealistic worldviews

is enhanced when the fantasies they incorporate encourage the redistribution of wealth.

8. During times of trauma, when worldviews are most subject to adjustment, there is a tendency for people to incline toward irrational intrepretations of events. This leads to two subsidiary observations:

9. In the primitive conditions under which human societies emerged, functions now fulfilled by governments and capital markets were handled through religions and taboos. Under such conditions, apparently irrational reactions to stress may have had a survival value by encouraging adherence to new sects or prophecies that helped people overcome common difficulties and took discontinuities into account.

10. Characteristics of mind that may have helped humans survive—such as the capacity to remain oblivious to previously irrelevant facts and the tendency toward irrationality under stress—may now be liabilities. In a modern setting, economies and political institutions depend upon rational interpretation of rapidly changing facts to function effectively. The comic cargo cult of a primitive society may become a Nazi party when a modern society is traumatized.

11. Although it may not be obvious, the example of the cargo cults is another illustration of the pervasive nonlinearity of life.

A Nonlinear World

A mighty flame followeth a tiny spark.

—DANTE

If this last point is not immediately apparent, we hope it will be by the end of this chapter. "Nonlinearity" is a characteristic of natural systems at every level. They are frequently marked by abrupt "phase transitions," with outcomes apparently disproportionate to their causes, like Dante's "mighty flame" that followed "a tiny spark." Contrary to common expectation, cause and effect often do not move in a simple straight line, but interact in cycles, "with the effect feeding back on the cause and perhaps amplifying it," in the words of Gary Taubes.

Perhaps the most famous example of nonlinearity is the "straw that broke the camel's back." Under most circumstances, it would be a trying task to kill a camel with a straw. The weight of one straw, by itself, would scarcely slow a camel down. Indeed, every straw that can be added to a bale will represent only the tiniest possible addition of weight. But clearly there is some weight that the animal's overburdened spine cannot support. Locating that point may be difficult. But that does not make it any the less real. Load one straw too many and the camel's back breaks. That is a nonlinear event.

There are far more nonlinear events than most people realize. Even the electronics of the human brain are organized according to a nonlinear dynamic, so you are employing nonlinearity as you think about this sentence. Brain waves—the signals given off by the firing of neurons—appear to be random and erratic. In fact they are highly organized in a nonlinear fashion. And the more nonlinear, the better. Recent research demonstrates that when neurons in your brain fire in a regular, periodic way, you are in trouble. Either you are incredibly dull or, worse, you are about to have an epileptic seizure. The sparks of genius travel a nonlinear path.

> Our studies have led us as well to the discovery in the brain of chaos—complex behavior that seems random but actually has some hidden order. The chaos is evident in the tendency of vast collections of neurons to shift abruptly and simultaneously from one complex activity pattern to another in response to the smallest of inputs.
>
> —WALTER P. FREEMAN,
> Professor of Neurobiology, University
> of California, Berkeley

This may be true not by chance but by necessity. Computational learning theorists tell us that all nontrivial computation depends upon nonlinear dynamics. To achieve innovation and higher-order computation, even an artificial brain would have to be organized to accommodate nonlinear functions. In effect, "artificial brain waves" would have to be irregular.

What is true of the physical brain is reflected in the operations of the mind. Patterns and paradigms of understanding help you sort through the hubbub of data that reach your attention. These paradigms incorporate innumerable nonlinearities in their everyday operation. A great part of what is puzzling about the way people process information can be explained by these often overlooked nonlinearities. They account for many of the wide differences in time awareness, organizational capacity, literacy, numeracy, and moral values that can be observed between peoples. These differences are not innate. Human nature is the same everywhere. The frequently irrational human beings found howling at the moon by anthropologists and their calculating, rational cousins described in economics textbooks actually behave according to similar principles, but in a way that can be seen only by taking nonlinearity into account.

Multiple paradigms of understanding are necessitated by the complexity of an environment that has always been subject to abrupt change. When these "phase transitions" occur, such as the arrival of white men in the South Pacific, previously functional paradigms can rapidly become dysfunctional. Hence, the cargo prophecies. The Stone Age cultures of New Guinea accustomed natives to look to "great men" for bounty. In that sense, there was a kind of gruff logic in their looking to buy Lyndon Johnson. But taken as a set of ideas about how to realize the desire for a better life, the cargo prophecies could hardly have been more absurd.

Like much of the recurring absurdity of life, the cargo prophecies are examples of developments that occur during phase transitions. We are now undergoing such a transition. In the past, these shifts have been periods of bewilderment, as old patterns of understanding suddenly became inadequate, leading people to make clusters of stupid decisions.

The Gods Speak in Times of Trouble

The stress that builds during such periods seems to add extra cement to the irrational sentiments that bind groups together. When times are good, the gods say nothing. But during hard times, which often arrive abruptly, the range of the sacred is expanded, and many ears can hear the whispers of the gods. Consequently, times of stress are times when delusions, taboos, and apparently irrational behavior abound. Later in this book we argue that much of this apparent irrationality serves a purpose in helping groups and individuals to survive. At least, it used to.

Nonlinear dynamics are the foundation of mental shortcuts that save us from the trouble of keeping our information constantly up to date. They bring us to the critical state where higher-level computations are possible, and keep us from betting the whole wad on the sometimes false assumption that tomorrow's environment will be in all crucial ways similar to today's.

Nonlinearity is a pervasive feature of human existence that has nevertheless remained largely invisible because it falls in a paradigmatic blind spot in the modern worldview. Just as the cargo cultists could observe modern products without understanding, so even the most educated persons in the West have generally failed to appreciate the nonlinear character of life and its profound implications for economics, politics, and human history. In a famous exaggeration, Lord Keynes said that even "madmen in authority" were the slaves of "some defunct economist." It is more true to say that we have all been slaves to a defunct physicist, Sir Isaac Newton. We continue to reckon with a telescope, and have not yet learned to see with a computer.

Linear Expectations

There is much evidence that human expectations tend to be linear. Most of the time, most people expect current conditions to continue for the indefinite future. It is almost an unnatural act for a man to leave home with an umbrella on a sunny day. Call it optimism, faith in the future, or just reluctance to see the party end, there is a presumption that the environment is stable. This is why cities are built on floodplains and fault lines. A similar presumption makes the gambler double his bet or the farmer plant additional crops on reclaimed land the year after a good harvest. Wherever prosperity exists, it is natural for people to expect prosperity to continue. For this reason, much of the history of human society is a record of astonishment. Time and again, people have marginalized their affairs, rendering themselves increasingly crisis-prone. They have gone into debt, extending claims on resources to an extreme that could be supported only if current conditions were sustained uninterrupted into the future. Time and again these hopes have been disappointed.

Whenever prosperity has seemed permanent, some apparently minute change—a shift in wind patterns in the upper atmosphere that altered the fall of rains and the flow of rivers, a mutation in the genetic composition of a virus or bacterium to produce a new form of pestilence for which human beings or their food stocks had no defense, or a technological twist like the addition of a stirrup to the riding gear of horses—could produce astonishingly large nonlinear shifts in the organization of human society.

The failure to recognize or anticipate these nonlinear transformations has been a common characteristic of almost all societies. In most times and places, the understanding of cause and effect has been too meager to allow much grasp of the dynamic processes by which societies change. Our own period would be an exception, if not for a paradigmatic blind spot—our expectation that a complex system like the economy functions on a linear basis, like a machine.

Science Follows Technology

Contrary to the general assumption that technology is an offshoot of science, the primacy is really the other way around. Great advances in science tend to occur after technological innovation has given the human mind access to a broader range of information. The Dutch invention of the refracting telescope in 1608 was such a primary innovation. It was quickly improved upon by Galileo, who ushered in a flood of new observations about the nature of reality. He scanned the solar system, discovered the moons of Jupiter, and dramatically improved understanding of the character of trajectories, virtual velocities, specific gravity, and more. It was in this environment of rapid scientific discovery that the apple hit Newton's head. It inspired him to work through thoughts that led to the theory of gravitation. Along the way, the need to solve a problem of mechanics, particularly the need to find the velocity of motion when the distance covered over a given time is known, led Newton to invent differential calculus.

What Newton saw peering into his new telescope was far less important that the computations it inspired him to make. More than one might imagine, Newton's revelations have influenced our perceptions of reality, especially economic reality. When he and others developed a grasp of the motions of the heavenly bodies, they described a universe that appeared to be stable.* Using the principles of Newtonian physics, it was possible centuries ago to predict with fair accuracy where the planets would be in the solar system today. The apparent stability of these arrangements had a great impact on understanding. The greater part of this impact was paradigmatic. The way that human beings saw the world was fundamentally altered by the discoveries of science in ways that reached far beyond the immediate impact of science.

Newtonian physics gave rise to the metaphor of a clockwork universe. It seemed to suggest that all of reality was governed in an orderly fashion by simple laws. It was as if God had wound up a clock and let it go. Its unwinding was destined to proceed in an orderly, intelligible fashion as the meshing gears moved the hands steadily, and predictably forward, one tick at a time. This was not a metaphorical construct that prepared people to think in terms of sharp, discontinuous, and "chaotic" movements from one moment to the next. Whatever was being measured, whether time or quantity, no one expected to see the dials reading 12 at one moment and then 4:30 a second later. Everything was to proceed steadily and continuously toward its predictable destination.

Even religious concepts were altered by Newton's discoveries. The greatest minds of the eighteenth century thought in terms of a laissez-faire God, a giant clockmaker in the sky, who set the world going and then left the cogs and pieces to grind out a rather orderly destiny.

Later, when geologists sharpened perception of upheaval in history, this was integrated into the linear conceptions of reality through the adoption of the Darwinian concept of evolution. This held that the dramatic variations in life recorded in fossil evidence were simply the work of chance, unfolding over millions and even billions of years. A time scale of this magnitude made a joke of the natural history accepted in Newton's lifetime. In 1650, James

---

*Newton himself was aware of nonlinearity. As we describe later, Newton was not a Newtonian.

Usher, the archbishop of Armagh, working backward through scripture, had fixed the date of the Creation of the universe as one fine morning in October 4004 B.C. As the discoveries of science proceeded, the role of God seemed to be pushed further and further from an immediate relevance in human affairs. The laissez-faire God of the clockwork universe was no longer merely taking a "hands off" attitude. By the twentieth century, "God was dead."

Organized religion, instead of attempting to further a spiritual understanding of human life, shifted its focus toward the attempt to achieve a heaven on earth. As the scale of governments and commercial enterprises rose, religious figures were more tempted to talk in terms of social justice than of the ultimate justice of God. They turned more frequently to the state to replace God as a mechanism for righting the wrongs of this world. Partly this reflected the fact that governments and markets were increasingly performing functions that previously had been fulfilled by religions. Belief in scientific technique encouraged people to suppose that government could intervene effectively, using "scientific" principles of economic management to assure material prosperity, counter unemployment, and redistribute wealth. The state, in many respects, had come to take God's place, but it was an intellectual preeminence based not upon theology, but upon physics and mathematics, especially those branches of physics and mathematics that predominated as societies industrialized.

The Industrial Paradigm

An essential characteristic of the mechanical relations Newton elucidated was that they involve linear components. If change is smooth and continuous, it can be modeled mathematically and solutions found through calculus. By and large, this is true of most of the physical properties that humans had to manipulate in order to launch the Industrial Revolution. Physicist Paul Davies put it this way:

> Linearity is not a property of waves alone; it is also possessed by electric and magnetic fields, weak gravitational fields, stresses and strains in many materials, heat flow, diffusion of gases and liquids and much more. The greater part of modern science and technology stems directly from the fortunate fact that so much of what is of interest and importance in modern society involves linear systems. Roughly speaking, a linear system is one in which the whole is simply the sum of its parts. Thus, however complex a linear system may be it can always be understood as merely the conjunction or superposition or peaceful coexistence of many simple elements that are present together but do not 'get in each other's way'. Such systems can therefore be decomposed or analysed or reduced to their

independent component parts. It is not surprising that the major burden of scientific research so far has been towards the development of techniques for studying and controlling linear systems.

Because so much of modern problem-solving in science and technology involves calculations where relations are linear, the presumption of linearity has become second nature. In a sense, the mind has been programmed to expect such a relationship, much as computers are programmed to process information according to certain principles. It is natural for people to carry the mathematical assumptions and techniques appropriate to linear systems to other areas. Where they do not work well, as is the case in most dynamic systems, this is treated more or less like static temporarily interfering with a broadcast on a favorite channel. James Gleick describes it this way:

> Confronted with a nonlinear system, scientists would have to substitute linear approximations or find some other uncertain backdoor approach. Textbooks showed students only the rare nonlinear systems that would give way to such techniques. . . . Nonlinear systems with real chaos were rarely learned. When people stumbled across such things—and people did—all their training argued for dismissing them as aberrations. Only a few were able to remember that the solvable, orderly, linear systems were the aberrations. Only a few, that is, understood how nonlinear nature is in its soul.

The existence of nonlinear relationships remains genuinely invisible to most people.

This has been reflected in the development of social studies. So great was the influence of Newtonian physics on social research that Auguste Comte, the founder of sociology, proposed that the new discipline be known as "the physics of society." The emulation of Newtonian conceptions in the study of economics was even more eager. Karl Marx, particularly, laid claims to a "scientific" foundation for his thoughts, which, as Don Lavoie put it, were to be "in a strictly Newtonian sense, a study of the 'laws of motion of the capitalist system' analogous to the physical laws of motion of planetary systems."

The early stages in the quantification of economic relationships employed techniques borrowed from the sciences, especially physics. Seeing that Newton's calculus could solve problems in physics, economists sought to apply the same mathematical techniques to economic problems. But economics is not mechanical physics. To make the mathematics work required that the economy be conceived in unrealistic ways. Some of the nonlinear features of the economy that otherwise made it unsuitable to differential equations had to be assumed away. The result was the model of the economy existing in an imaginary state of equilibrium, a concept lifted from physics. "Equilibrium" is a static state in which opposing forces exactly balance one another. Employing such a model was more than an attempt to formalize the *ceteris paribus* technique, one of the most valuable aids in reasoning. It was the creation of a closed system of independent parts, all conceived as fitting together in a linear, even a mechanical way. Necessary assumptions of this model were that everyone had perfect knowledge, that all expectations were identical, and that all resources were already allocated to their most valued use. It implied that economies are or ought to be continuous, orderly, and stable.

Equilibrium Football

The trouble with this view is that it bears about as much resemblance to the real economy as a waxworks does to life. If the same mental constructs were applied to analyze other forms of activity, their shortcomings would be obvious to everyone. Imagine, for example, an equilibrium model of a football game. In equilibrium football, all the players would converge perfectly on the ball because they would know exactly where it would go. The players would have no trouble doing this because they would never make a mistake. The ball would never bounce in a strange way. There would be no missed passes. No penalties. Nor injuries either. Time would never run out because no time would ever elapse. And the game would never be called on account of bad weather, or because rowdy fans flocked onto the field. Such a model would hold little interest for most football coaches, players, or fans of the game. It would give no hint at all about who would win and how. It implies that no play is better than another because the adjustments necessary to counter any scoring attempt—whether a fake, a pass, or a power run up the middle—are automatically known and executed perfectly. By definition, no one can win in equilibrium. The game is a zero-zero tie. There are no stars. No losers. No one faints from all the excitement.

This does not mean, of course, that nothing useful could be learned from an equilibrium model of football. If nothing else, such a model shows the principle of compensation at work in its most virile form—where every advantage is immediately and magically counteracted. But whatever the value of these insights, they come at the expense of masking the process by which the game proceeds. This is the problem with most conventional economic models.

Masking Change and Discontinuity

By definition, a stop-frame analysis will not capture motion. It will tell us little about how the economic process unfolds from moment to moment. And as others have pointed out, it will tell even less about long-run changes. Indeed, it masks the importance of time. The longer the time over which action is frozen, the greater the departure from reality. It is therefore hardly surprising that economic theory is weakest when it comes to explaining long-run change and discontinuity.

Nor is it surprising that mechanical assumptions about perfect foresight and computational abilities mask important questions about how people really perceive and act upon their possible choices. By stipulating that knowledge is "given," economists have largely closed off the lines of inquiry that could explain how economic change affects the way people think. The demand for information not only shifts as the economy changes, but the willingness of people to process it accurately also changes. Persons in different circumstances respond to information differently, not just because they have different incentives to put the information to use, but because they have different incentives to seek it out in the first place, and even different incentives to think rationally or objectively about what they know. We explore some of the consequences of these factors in explaining questions as diverse as Third World poverty, the pathological behaviors of the underclass, conspiracy theories, the immolation of Jews in the Black Death, the Spanish Inquisition, and the insanity of German politics after the Great Depression.

In effect, economists following in Newton's footsteps defined out of existence some of the more vital questions about how information is transmitted and how prices are set. In the process, they fundamentally misrepresented the character of the economy as a complex system. The economy is not closed but open. It is interdependent with many influences in a complex environment and subject to discontinuous, nonlinear change.

In the mid-twentieth century, the ideological power of the Newtonian "paradigm," or worldview, in social studies reached its height. Early computers increased the ease of computation, and thus made econometric modeling practical. Flush with their new tools, economists boldly announced that they could control the economy in the same mechanical way that engineers control boilers. They imagined themselves fine-tuning variables like fiscal policy to increase output, lower unemployment, and regulate inflation. It sounded like a great idea to minds conditioned to expect linear relationships. And it yielded occasional approximations of success—when the relationships between various components were stable. But when they were not, even trivial changes in inputs could produce chaotically different outcomes. Hence the dismal record of economic forecasting, government economic management, and centrally planned economies.

Lags in Revising Basic Paradigms

In strict logic, enough is already known about nonlinear dynamics to thoroughly discredit many of the widely shared conceits of economists. But ideas can be discredited without being discarded, especially if they form an essential component of a worldview, or paradigm, of understanding. The notion that the sun rotated around the earth had been discredited by the Ionian astronomers Aristarchus and Hipparchus in 400 B.C. Yet two thousand years later, in 1632, Galileo was imprisoned by the Inquisition for arguing that the earth revolves around the sun.

This is hardly the only example of a considerable lag between the introduction of evidence and its broad acceptance. Fully three centuries lapsed between Newton's birth and the high tide of the Newtonian paradigm in social thought. Ironically, Newton himself was not a Newtonian in worldview. He was well aware of nonlinearity. He considered it evidence of God's hand in the universe. His vision of history was that of a seventeenth-century alchemist who believed in the distinctly nonlinear concept of the Apocalypse. He devoted a great portion of his time and genius to elucidating apocalyptic literature, including the prophecies of Daniel and the Book of Revelation.

The lag between the advent of new technology and the realization of its full impact on human understanding is likely to continue. Just as Newtonian physics set in motion waves of cause and effect that peaked long after the death of Newton himself, so it will take generations, though probably not centuries, before the full impact of computer technology is felt in changing the way educated people in the leading economies think about the organization of reality. This revolution in thinking is bound to be accelerated by the coming economic and political shock of world depression.

CHAPTER NINE

THE REMAKING OF THE COSMOPOLITAN MIND

The dice of God are always loaded.

—RALPH WALDO EMERSON

SOMEDAY POWERFUL computers, and the nonlinear science they make possible, may inspire a new worldview as distant from current perceptions as we are from Newton's alchemy or the Stone Age fantasies of New Guinea. In time, it will be possible to employ Artificial Intelligence and dynamical systems simulations to build more realistic nonlinear models of the economy and much else. No doubt, these new models will improve upon our understanding in ways we cannot now predict. They will also color our perceptions of much else. Many aspects of the way we view the world are roundabout consequences of technology.

Even though we cannot anticipate the full impact of the emerging paradigm, we can pierce at least some of the mental blinders that until now have masked the way the world works. High-speed computers are, in essence, the telescopes that enable us to look beyond the Newtonian universe. We now know that complex systems do not necessarily operate with mechanical, regular, and continuous relationships. Cause and effect can interact in far more complicated ways. And this has consequences. It should alert us to look with new respect at the interconnectedness of events. Apparently trivial causes operating at a great remove from where their effects are finally felt can produce sweeping changes. This means that the surest prediction about the future is that it will be full of surprises.

The computer also tells us to look again at the boundaries between chance and necessity. Developments now treated as random, and which even seem random to simple statistical tests, may actually be deterministic when analyzed in higher dimensions. As computational power expands the number of dimensions in which calculations can be made, the realm of the random is likely to shrivel.

> Revived memories of antiquity, the Turkish advance, the new horizons opening beyond, all encouraged Europe to see itself as civilization confronting barbarism. But the Renaissance was an affair of aristocracy and intelligentsia, confronting also their own illiterate masses.
>
> —V. G. Kiernan

Simply recognizing these long-overlooked natural patterns suggests insights that will be gradually incorporated into the cosmopolitan worldview of the 1990s. Just as the early intellectual repercussions of the Gunpowder Revolution in the Renaissance were not immediately felt or comprehended by everyone, so the feedback from the Information Revolution will not immediately revolutionize mass culture. But the new information does have implications that may interest you as an investor and a thinking citizen. Many of these insights would not likely have occurred to analysts even a few years ago. Because computers have made it possible to understand some nonlinear relationships, they have brought all nonlinear relationships more clearly into focus. Some of the important economic and political implications of the new perspective were touched upon in the last chapter. Others we explore below and later. Among them:

1. The fact that cause and effect operate in cycles, as well as in a straight line, implies that more effort should be invested in analyzing the economic long wave and the other cycles of history. This is likely to happen as the work of notepad historians is transformed by the computer.

2. Evidence that has long been "hidden in plain view" can now be understood as part of a necessary response to discontinuity in the human environment. The existence of sex, for example, may be a statement from nature that economic disturbances are an inherent feature of the human niche. The human life span also may be an indirect measure of the length of the economic long wave.

3. The pervasive importance of nonlinear change suggests that economic

models that assume continuity are inadequate, not just because they mask long-term change, but also because they mask many types of phase transition, including discontinuities in the way that people calculate and respond to incentives.

4. The narrowing of the realm of the random, along with closer attention to interconnectedness, will destroy intellectual respectability of moral and cultural relativism.

5. Pronouncements by academics that have long misled investors can now be understood as paradigmatic mistakes. This suggests some follow-on points of special interest:

- The "efficient market hypothesis" is false; investors' interpretations of events are not immediately reflected in price.
- There is nonlinear dependence in market returns, patterns that persist for decades, and may recur over the centuries.
- Factors that are presently unidentified may have an impact in informing patterns in markets that have heretofore been attributed to chance alone.
- Capital markets are asymmetric; in progressive countries they tend to rise slowly and fall abruptly.
- The greatest drops are likely in the richest markets, and the most rapid rises in poor ones.

6. The new dynamical systems analysis of the political economy does not mean the end of liberalism; rather, it should give rise to a new, nonlinear liberalism in which free markets and inequality of wealth are understood as essential to the health of the system as a whole.

7. As appreciation of the hidden dependencies between events grows, it will become increasingly evident that political authorities are incapable of benign economic planning.

8. Attempts to suppress the fluctuations of the business cycle may increase dangers of a system failure. What appear to be annoying fluctuations and volatility may actually be essential to the economy's vitality as a dynamic system.

9. The bogus "historical materialism" of Marxist theory will be further exposed as appreciation grows for the dependencies between cultural and legal concomitants and economic development. Marxist systems trip over these hidden dependencies in practice by incorporating unsustainable contradictions between features of open and closed societies.

10. As the political economy comes increasingly to be seen as a dynamic system, open to the environment, more attention will be paid to those crucial variables at the margins that can have the greatest impact in precipitating nonlinear change—the factors that we have described as "megapolitical."

11. Improved understanding of the way the world works may have far-reaching consequences equivalent to the violation of taboos in primitive societies. For example, as it becomes clear that apparently unconnected events are not as random as they seem, innovation may be inhibited. A more realistic appreciation of the cyclical nature of history, which implies unequal potential between different stages of the cycles, may undermine belief in progress and complicate the transmission of positive values between generations. It could even contribute to a growth of fatalism, pessimism, and market closure. Every time a Bart Simpson ceases to believe in progress, the economy becomes more vulnerable to another spitball in the neck.

12. As we have suggested, religion is likely to make an intellectual as well as social comeback, as for the first time in centuries science appears to buttress rather than undermine the belief that human history could be unfolding according to a predestined plan.

13. There will be a sharper clash between those who uphold the values of Western civilization, including the universality of human nature, and irridentist groups who divide along ethnic and racial lines.

We can only hope to explore some of the important implications of the revolutionary new paradigm in this book. Even a cursory overview, however, should be enough to show that the world economy is far more vulnerable to a system failure than most people would imagine. The day before an earthquake, the great city gleams in the sun, with scarcely a hint that beneath the surface, pressures are building along the fault lines.

THE CYCLES OF HISTORY

> *A time like ours will not be moved,*
> *for it lives with no memory and no aspirations,*
> *caring no more about its past than about its future.*
>
> —ANTONIN ARTAUD

Evidence that nonlinear dynamics permeate nature, with cause and effect operating in complex ways, gives credence to the view that there are patterns or cycles of history, including long-term economic cycles. In *Blood in the Streets*, we wrote about a cycle of hegemony, in which world economic conditions fluctuate between prosperity and depression as great powers rise and fall. When one nation enjoys cheap military predominance, along with disproportionate shares of manufacturing output and financial power, the world tends to enjoy free trade and monetary stability, and thus prosperity. When the predominant power fades, borders and barriers proliferate, access to markets is curtailed, and debts are repudiated. Often, major wars begin at a time when the predominant power has weakened, but when several nations are wealthy enough to fight. Some authorities have suggested that there is a war cycle of about fifty years corresponding closely with peaks in the long wave. Although there is much evidence supporting the existence of such cycles, it has been roundly ignored, in part because it does not fit comfortably with contemporary visions of the way the world works. Where the cycles of history are concerned, we have averted our eyes from an important body of knowledge that was well studied centuries ago.

At the takeoff stage of the Industrial Revolution in the late eighteenth century, many of the best minds were fascinated by the rise and fall of nations. Edward Gibbon's *The Decline and Fall of the Roman Empire* appeared in its first volume in 1776, the same year that Adam Smith published *The Wealth of Nations*. Their contemporary, Adam Ferguson, authored *A History of the Roman Republic*, and an even earlier *Essay on the History of Civil Society* (1767), which detailed the cycles through which societies progress and decay. Another neglected masterpiece of this literature is William Playfair's *Decline and Fall of Powerful and Wealthy Nations*, which we have quoted at length. These books deal systematically with the question of national decline. They have something important to tell us. In spite of their sometimes quaint language, they speak to the current circumstances of the United States of America, as they did to those of Great Britain earlier in this century. It is impossible to read them without being struck with how much history does repeat itself, or, as Harry Truman said, "The only news is the history we don't know."

Those who deny the cycles of history have grouped theories about power transitions and the economic long wave in the same league with astrology and Mother Shipton's fortune-telling—without coming to grips with basic evidence that economic performance could be dependent on conditions that evolve through stages over time.

The Long Wave

Short-term fluctuations of the business cycle seem to be superimposed upon larger movements, which include power cycles and cycles of war. Sometimes these larger movements are known as "long cycles," the "long wave," or "the K-wave" after the work of N. D. Kondratieff, a maverick Russian agricultural expert. Kondratieff published a theory of economic long cycles in a series of articles in the early 1920s. Unhappily, his research was cut short. After his initial findings were published, Kondratieff's views were subjected to severe criticism in the Kremlin. He was dismissed to Siberia, where he died, a victim of Stalin's purges. The official epitaph was that notions of a long wave were "reactionary and wrong." Nonetheless, his fundamental observation survives. He described the long cycle as follows:

> The upswing of the first long wave embraced the period from 1782 to 1814—that is, 25 years. Its decline begins in 1814 and ends in 1849, a period of 35 years. The cycle, therefore was completed in 60 years. The rise of the second wave begins in 1849 and ends in 1873, lasting 24 years. . . . The decline of the second wave begins in 1873 ending in 1896—a period of 23 years. The length of the second wave is 47 years. The upward movement of the third wave begins in 1896 and ends in 1920, its duration being 24 years. The decline of the second wave, according to all data, begins in 1920.

Notice that Kondratieff himself did not claim that long waves arrive and depart regularly like clockwork. He merely says that he expected long waves to be "of average length of about 50 years."

The idea that such patterns of depression and regeneration recur is not as preposterous as most experts have claimed. In the first place, it fits with the facts of the past. Major depressions have been rare events, recurring about twice a century. Furthermore, the long wave thesis is supported by evidence that shows how economic activity has varied substantially from one period to another. This evidence includes overlapping or connected cycles in prices, growth rates, product innovation, agriculture, industrial production, and real wages.

There is also evidence that the long wave and business cycles in general are not a merely modern phenomenon that arose with industrialism. Records of the mintage and fluctuating value of Italian coinage from the Middle Ages "forcefully bring out the existence of both secular changes and long waves."

Evidence of long waves is overlooked for the same reason that natives of New Guinea overlooked hints about the true nature of industrialism—because it does not fit comfortably into the received worldview.

Depressions Fit the Rhythm of Nature

Disturbances analogous to economic depressions are characteristic of many complex systems in nature. Paleo-ecologists, for example, have established that spectacular forest fires in Yellowstone Park, in which vast numbers of acres are consumed, such as that in the summer of 1988, "occur every 200 or 300 years." In effect, there is a "long wave" of forest growth, followed by a major conflagration and a slow period of regeneration. William H. Romme and Don G. Despain point out that forest systems evolve through various stages of succession. Growth is most luxuriant and varied immediately after a major fire. For quite logical reasons, the forest is not very flammable during the recovery period when a few widely spaced saplings and low-lying vegetation keep the forest floor moist. Neither are major fires likely during the many decades when "the treetops rise too far above the forest floor to be easily ignited from below." But during the "climax stage," when the understory of old-growth forests is littered with dead trees and rotting underbrush, a spectacular fire is almost inevitable. It is only a matter of time until lightning strikes in a dry season and the whole flammable mixture explodes.*

Raising the Exponents in the Equation of Contraction

The long cycle of economic life appears to be shorter than the long cycle of forest growth in Yellowstone Park, and, we hope, less combustible. Yet both cycles may function in inherently similar ways. Just as it is impossible to prevent or suppress spectacular forest fires by putting out every small fire over time, so too, economic policies that aim to prevent depression by forestalling bankruptcies and enlarging debts may only increase the severity of the ultimate disturbance. The mounds of debt paper issued by politicians in the leading countries, especially the United States, may merely be littering the understory of the economy with combustible material. When the spark is lit, it will produce a "mighty flame."

Of course, many people no longer believe that the long cycle of boom and bust still operates. They imagine that the climax of the cycle—the period of credit collapse and deflation—is now impossible because politicians have determined to prevent it. This is not the place to go into an extensive analysis of why this view is mistaken. We shall save that for another chapter. Suffice

*This pattern of growth and conflagration is not unique to Yellowstone. Some Florida pine forests, for example, actually require fires in order to survive. The Florida pines have evolved so that their cones will not open to release their seeds unless they are heated to a high temperature by fire.

it to say that the populations of the leading industrial countries evidence a touching faith in the powers of politicians. This may not be quite as obviously silly as the proclamation of "the end of history," but it arises from the same vision that sees the present as independent and disconnected from the past. It isn't.

A CYCLE OF CENTURIES?

It is even possible that there are supercycles of five hundred or a thousand years. As we suggested earlier, the history of Western civilization seems to divide into such segments.

The five centuries prior to the birth of Christ were a period of growth and intensification of the ancient economy.

The next five centuries were a period of gradual decline, culminating in the collapse of the Roman Empire in the late fifth century. As William Playfair put it, "When Rome was at its highest pitch of greatness . . . will be seen to be at the birth of Christ, that is, during the reign of Augustus, and by the same means it will be found declining gradually till the year 490." Rome was snuffed out, as Thomas Malthus said, by "clouds of barbarians" that "seemed to collect from all points of the northern hemisphere. Gathering fresh darkness, and terror, as they rolled on, the congregated bodies at length obscured the sun of Italy, and sank the whole world in universal night."

The five centuries after Rome's fall in Western Europe saw a steep descent into barbarism, when commerce and public order collapsed in what we now know as the Dark Ages.

Then sometime around the end of the tenth century, "Western Europe ceased being the wrack left behind by the ebb of the Roman Empire and began being something new and vital." As historian Alfred Crosby put it, "populations, towns, and trade began to revive." Five centuries of relatively slow revival, now known as the Middle Ages, brought a rebirth of money, arithmetic, history, biography, time awareness, more social mobility, and early signs of self-expression, including the revival of verbal skills, and romantic love.

Then five centuries later, at the end of the fifteenth century, the Gunpowder Revolution ushered in the age of modern expansion.

Whether these periods of history just happened to fall into convenient five-century divisions, constituting a down cycle of a thousand years, followed by an up cycle of so far similar length, is beyond our ability to say. It is clear, however, that history involves more complex patterns than is generally acknowledged.

As Antigone tells us, "there is a law that is everywhere in force." Whether we know it or not, we must obey that law. Our fates, like those of our fathers, are bound together in an intricate system of interactions, with linkages stretching deep into the past. Until human beings evolve into another species, we will continue to live with cycles of boom and bust. The better we come to understand them, the more wisely we can prepare for the future. Unfortunately, these patterns are very little appreciated, as, indeed, is history itself.

How Historians Help Us to Ignore History

Our present Western outlook on history is an extraordinarily contradictory one. While our historical horizon has been expanding vastly in both the space dimension and the time dimension, our historical vision—what we actually do see, in contrast to what we now could see if we chose—has been contracting rapidly to the narrow field of what a horse sees between its blinkers or what a U-boat commander sees through his periscope.

—ARNOLD J. TOYNBEE

Some of the failure to perceive historic regularities is due to a natural limitation of perspective. Human experience is narrow compared to the scale of the events involved. The very largest patterns or cycles seem to involve time scales of centuries or millennia—far longer than a human lifetime. Such patterns are therefore beyond the reach of simple observation. To understand them, one must study the past. This is a job that modern information techniques simplify, but that modern culture and circumstances have discouraged. If we are to see into the past, we must stand on the backs of historians.

Unhappily, today's historians won't stand still for such an exercise. Part of the reason that they find so little evidence of regularities is that they seldom look for them. In spite of the fact that professional historians have developed and refined knowledge of the past as never before, they have largely abandoned the old-fashioned notion that history has lessons. As a result, history as a discipline has less to tell us about the way the world works than it did two centuries ago. This is true for a variety of reasons.

1. Perversely, the glut of historians in the world is a contributing cause to the decline in the practical value of the work they do. There are so many historians that the optimal strategy for accommodating them all has been to divide the work of history into almost infinitesimal specializations. With some honorable exceptions, this is what they have done. Historians have sought academic status by turning the microscope to its highest power in examining

some episode in minute detail. One will study "Prussian Plans for Constitutional Reform in 1808"; another, "Pontchartrain and the Grain Trade During the Famine of 1693." Still another is the world's authority on "The
Denigration of Lieutenant-Colonel Charles a Court Repington." These are no
doubt worthy studies. But they are focused at a level of detail that is not
calculated to reveal long-term historic patterns. To recognize patterns requires
taking an overview, and resorting to simplifying generalizations. But such
generalizations are professionally dangerous for academic historians. Almost
any really useful generalization will take insufficient account of some fact or
detail, and will thus be subject to criticisms that could not be leveled at
narrowly focused research. That is why you will find thousands of studies
that nitpick a narrow topic for every attempt to develop an overview of broad
historic patterns. With few exceptions, historians as a group have become
narrow specialists, with a vested interest in complexity. As has often been
said of specialists, "they know more and more about less and less."

2. Almost all historians are employed in universities, foundations, or public
institutions under terms that free them from having to sell their work directly
in the market. Once professors achieve tenure, they may divert themselves
more or less as they please—golfing, or documenting the evolution of loud
check trousers. For the most part, their circumstances do not oblige them to
take account of the public's interest in a practical history, with lessons that
can be applied like a thirty-day diet plan. If historians had to sing for their
supper, there would be fewer of them, and their focus would change. They
might or might not produce better history, but more of what they did produce
would involve an attempt to recognize history's patterns.

3. The search for historic patterns can be politically and ideologically embarrassing. Both sides in the warmed-over nineteenth-century debate on socialism are agreed in supporting a general scheme of progress in human affairs.
For non-Marxists, this reflects a more or less inherited belief in an ever-
brighter future. For Marxists, there is a perception of having grasped history's
"laws of motion," which are imagined to point toward the eventual triumph
of the working class. Neither view fits comfortably with the search for patterns
in human affairs. The very existence of such patterns implies that history
fluctuates cyclically, that societies fall as well as rise. The common adherence
to the doctrine of progress is a socially positive feature, but it nonetheless
discourages recognition of the full range of patterns of human interaction.

4. It is rare to find a historian with money or a interest in markets. It is
rarer still to find a historian who actively trades in markets. As a consequence,

few historians are familiar enough with the lore of markets to recognize the patterns and factors that recur from one episode to another.*

5. Historians, like almost everyone else, have tended to share a limited vision of the range of patterns that exist to be discovered. They continue to reckon with a telescope, and have not yet begun to see with a computer. In particular, there is a broad presumption among many historians that future developments are more or less random and therefore unpredictable.

The Computer Replaces the Notepad

These factors have combined to make history less useful than it should be. But this is bound to change as the notepad gives way to the computer. The complex, high-dimensional models made possible by improved computational capacity will soon come to the attention of historians. This is not as unlikely as it may seem, in that one of the pioneers of nonlinear dynamics was a wealthy English mathematician, L. F. Richardson, who sought to develop better techniques for analyzing such questions as the patterns of war. Even though he worked without the benefit of modern computers, Richardson's insights proved to have significant mathematical importance. It is only a matter of time until students of social phenomena catch up with mathematicians in recognizing the application of the now much-improved nonlinear dynamic tools of analysis. To even dream of using such nonlinear models, they will have to focus on longer-term developments that could generate time series lengthy enough to be analyzed by the new methods. A six-dimensional model won't have much to say about "The Denigration of Lieutenant-Colonel Charles a Court Repington." But it may give insights into broader patterns of historic change.

As we discuss in more detail below, these high-dimensional analyses already reveal that chance plays a smaller role in apparently random events than is now widely believed. Not only has the computer revealed new patterns that permeate complex systems in nature, it has all but antiquated the specialized research paradigm of the age of the notepad. The day is rapidly approaching when it will no longer make sense to devote an academic career to specializing in a narrow topic. At one time, finding all there is to know about "The Denigration of Lieutenant-Colonel Charles a Court Repington"

---

*A notable exception to this sweeping generalization is Charles A. Kindleberger, whose *Manias, Panics, and Crashes: A History of Financial Crises*, New York: Basic Books, 1978, offers a wealth of keen observation.

was no doubt a scholar's ticket to tenure. But it will soon be the work of a computer programmer. Why send a bright person to a library to sift through papers for five years when a computer can do the sifting in a few minutes? Much of the material is already on file. Practically every newspaper, magazine, official document, or academic paper published in the last half of the twentieth century has been committed to a computerized retrieval system in one form or another. So have many publications, original papers, and materials from earlier times. Before long, the force of technology, if not the power of ideas, will drive historians from the confines of their specialties to take a broader view. This, indeed, has already begun. The authors of many of the works we cite as references pull together details and ideas from what were recently many different disciplines. Others will be obliged to follow them in exploring history's patterns because that is work a computer cannot yet do. The result is bound to be a more lively effort to organize the record of the past in ways that develop keener insights about the future.

Luckily, we do not have to wait for historians to raise their sights in order to begin to understand history's message. We need only look more closely at what is already known about the fluctuations that permeate life.

"Dangers, Surprises, Devastations"

Among the powerful implications of the new nonlinear dynamics is the light it sheds on facets of reality that have been "hidden in plain view." These argue with the whole weight of nature that prosperity can never be permanent. The thought that it can be is contrary to the very character of complex systems. Indeed, it is contradicted by the most profound evidence of life.

For example, the fact that all advanced species employ sexual reproduction, rather than asexual cloning, testifies to the fact that more or less abrupt changes in environment are inherent to the conditions of life on earth. If this were not the case, sexually reproduced organisms would have lost out to asexual in the competition to survive. As Robin Fox put it, "It remains a constant theoretical problem how sexual reproduction can have arisen, since any favourable mutation in an asexually reproducing organism can be immediately and rapidly replicated, while its sexual competitor must dilute the next-generation effect through breeding. Even inbreeding will not help for sexual competitors, since it is bound to be slower than in the asexual, and also will produce lethal homozygotes." In essence, asexual cloning would allow species to mass produce the individuals who were best suited to survive under existing conditions. By contrast, sexual reproduction is a means of enforcing diversity in the gene pool, and thereby assuring the survival of traits that may have no present value but will perhaps be crucial to survival in the future. Sexual reproduction, in essence, prevents species from betting their futures on the continuation of current conditions. This makes sense only if current conditions are subject to abrupt change. The fact that humans, like all higher animals, reproduce sexually rather than clone their young is a hint from nature that discontinuity is an inherent feature of the human niche.*

Death and Discontinuity

Another such hint, disquieting though it may be, is provided by death. The human life span of "three score and ten, or if by strength, four score," is implicit evidence of a survival value in turnover of the generations no less frequently than every fifty to sixty years. Otherwise, so limited a life span would serve no survival function. The life spans of species are not all fixed at the same point, but vary from just a few moments to more than a thousand years. A butterfly that you see outside your window may survive only a few hours as an adult, just long enough to reproduce and then die. Some of the fat, lazy carp lolling in the ponds of the Imperial Gardens in Tokyo were alive when President Millard Fillmore sent Commodore Perry to Japan to negotiate a commercial opening in 1852. Sequoia trees still growing in California had already taken root when William the Conqueror set sail for England. Some bristle cone pines were alive six thousand years ago, when Bishop Usher said the world began.

The reasons that humans do not share the life spans of butterflies, on one extreme, or bristle cone pines on the other, are determined by practical considerations of survival. We live at the top of the food chain, a position that is too complex and precarious for behavior to be controlled by simple genetic programming or instinct. Our survival requires intelligent behavior. To learn more complex, intelligent responses to a changing environment takes time. It requires more complex brains, which require a long gestation period, followed by years in which children are educated or programmed, to cope with the particular circumstances of time and place that form their local environment. The fact that humans live longer than butterflies is evidence of greater complexity and vulnerability to change in our niche than theirs. Human society would be impossible if we had a life span of hours or days.

The more interesting question, however, is why we do not live 969 years, like Methuselah. After all, in biological terms, there is a substantial investment

---

*Confirmation of the value of sex, if it were needed, has kindly been provided by computational theorists. They have begun to employ "genetic algorithms" that short-circuit the time required to solve complex computations, by mixing randomly selected samples, equivalent to the mixing of the genomes in sexual reproduction.

in the life of each human. Why does the species prosper by cutting that life short? The explanation must point to some survival advantage to compensate for the loss of acquired immunities, skills, and survival traits among individuals who reach maturity. Here, too, the answer must be found in the propensity of the environment to undergo nonlinear change. This increases the likelihood of some crisis that can be resolved only through heroic or risky behavior—such as taking a dangerous hunting trip or confronting an enemy in combat. In this respect, a very long life expectancy could be a detriment to any group for whom it was a common characteristic because it would encourage timidity. An individual with nine hundred years to live has nine hundred years to lose. An individual with nine hundred months may not be a daredevil, Evel Knievel leaping over Hell's Canyon on his motorcycle, but he is more likely to be. By and large, life is cheapened as life expectancy falls. If individuals lived for the better part of a thousand years, a single life would be so dear that risky or heroic behaviors, such as fighting for the group—or even childbirth—would diminish.

This might doom the group, or it might not, but it is certainly true that longer life slows the turnover of generations, thus diminishing the adjustment of the gene pool to new conditions. It is written that Methuselah was 187 years old when he fathered his first child. At that rate, there would have been just three generations in the five hundred years since Columbus sailed west looking for China. Three generations instead of twenty-five. The drop in the turnover and diversity of the gene pool would be staggering. Going back twenty-five generations, you have 33,554,432 ancestors—enough to people a country rather than fill a room. Such genetic diversity optimizes survival— but only in an environment subject to discontinuous change.*

---

*The assumption that one had 33,554,432 grandparents twenty-five generations ago is more a mathematical than a genetic certainty. Assuming that there were five generations to a century, it is apparent that, at least for persons of British origin, many of the ancestors must have been the same individuals who were our grandparents many times over through different lines of descent. It is estimated that the entire population of the British Isles in 1500 was four million or fewer. If every person then living had given birth to offspring, all of whom lived, he would on average have been a grandparent of each person of British descent 8.38 times. Of course, the actual number must be higher. Many persons living in 1500 would have died without offspring, and some of those offspring would not have had descendants who survived for more than a few generations. In effect, almost everyone descended from the small British populations of five centuries ago must be related.

The Long Wave and Human Life Span

Long wave crises in the economy recurring every fifty to sixty years are often associated with human life span. It is commonly argued that individuals who experienced the previous crisis must die out before their descendants can repeat their mistakes. There is logic in this. But it is possible that the causality is reversed. Humans may be limited to an adult life span of fifty to sixty years because crises recur with that rough frequency. Such a limit on life span may optimize the flexibility of response by insuring that the same generation is seldom in command during two successive discontinuities. In this respect, economic historian S. B. Saul reports:

> The most amusing version of this entrepreneurial-decline argument came from the Master of a Cambridge college who attributed much of Britain's deficiencies to the invention of false teeth! He argued that this enabled older industrialists to eat better and live longer and also be less embarrassed at attending Board Meetings, thus continuing for longer than before their conservative influence on industrial behavior.

The argument has the taint of silliness about it, but it is certainly true that you need not worry about old fogies contributing to institutional rigidity if all the fogies die young.

A more encompassing perspective on institutional rigidity was spelled out by Mancur Olson. He argued in *The Rise and Decline of Nations* that resistance to change caused by the predominance of special interest groups in stable societies is a major contributing factor to economic malfunction. Presumably, the level of institutional rigidity would be even greater if those who held power could continue at their posts for centuries. You need think only of what society would be like if William the Conqueror were still living to appreciate how the social advantages of population turnover could be part of its genetic advantage.

It is difficult to even imagine how the Industrial Revolution in England, for example, could have proceeded under his stewardship. Indeed, it is difficult to imagine how much of the history of the past millennium could have unfolded if all its major struggles had been fought out by William and his contemporaries, engaged in terms of the understandings and values they would have brought with them from the eleventh century. The fact that death requires that all human understanding be relearned anew is an advantage as well as a disadvantage. To the extent that longer life spans would strengthen personal allegiances and limit intellectual flexibility and learning, cementing old values into place, they would tend to petrify social arrangements. If nothing else, they would necessitate wrenching and violent upheavals to facilitate change.

Although we do not often think about it, death is a primary mechanism by which the species adapts itself to discontinuous change. If the human niche on earth were stable, a more static gene pool would do no harm, and the species would prosper by retaining accumulated strategies and knowledge attained by individuals who reached adulthood. In that case, we would expect the human life span to be far longer than it is. The fact that the life span is seventy to eighty years argues that the human evolutionary environment made it impossible for humans to be as unchanging and inflexible as a stand of sequoias. In a sense, the human life span may well be one of the better indicators of prehistoric economic statistics, suggesting crises of one kind or another recurring with that approximate frequency. There is no direct evidence for this hypothesis, of course. No one was gathering reports of animal kills and the collection of nuts and fruits one hundred thousand years ago. But indirect evidence abounds of periodic fluctuations in what Darwin called "the economy of nature."

It is possible that nineteenth-century economist W. Stanley Jevons was thinking along the right lines after all in attributing cycles to "cosmical variations of which we have evidence in the frequency of sunspots, auroras, and magnetic perturbations." Unfortunately, his original formulation was overly mechanical and soon discredited. While Jevons was clearly mistaken in assigning a simple and direct link between solar fluctuations and the economy, "cosmical variations" may be the ultimate engine of the fluctuations that long ago set the human life span, and may still influence the cycles of economic prosperity. Unfortunately, too little is known about the earthly effects of "cosmical variations" to establish a clear chain of causation linking what happens on the sun to events on earth. There is also established evidence of climatic fluctuations associated with the gravitational pull of the nearer planets on the earth's orbit. "Calculations mapping these planetary alignments far into the past have shown that they affect our relation to the sun in three major cycles of 96,000, 41,000 and 21,000 years."

Changes in wind patterns and rainfall arising from turbulence in the sun and the cycles of planetary alignment are the wellspring of climatic variation. Even a small shift in the prevailing currents or winds can produce startling variations in weather. Witness the drought that struck North America's grain basket in the summer of 1988. As reported in the *New York Times*, the drought was "caused by massive, naturally occurring forces in the tropical Pacific Ocean and had little to do with global warming caused by the greenhouse effect." The same phenomenon caused "unusually heavy monsoon rains that in 1988 brought record floods, death and misery to Bangladesh."

Just as cloning, or multiple asexual reproduction of the currently successful members of the population, is an option negated by nature, so is the indefinite continuation of individual life. Both sex and death, two undeniably large features of human existence, operate together to insure diversity, preventing the species from betting its future on the continuation of current conditions. Both tell us that the world we live in has long been subject to dramatic change—not only at infrequent intervals that mark the comings and goings of ice ages, but on a smaller scale at the approximate frequency of a human lifetime. Discontinuity is inherent in the rhythm of nature.

REALITY AND ECONOMIC THEORY

Some readers may dispute the relevance of these speculations for current circumstances. Admittedly, they are merely hints from the prehistoric darkness. But they are hints worth noting because they suggest that the order or pattern of reality is rather different from that commonly assumed in the study of economies.

Hidden Necessity in "Random" Events

This is nowhere more startling and potentially far-reaching than in the uncovering of "pseudorandom" phenomena. As reported in the *Journal of Monetary Economics*, these are examples in nature of "completely deterministic processes that generate behavior which looks random." Their discovery implies a major reversal of intellectual fashion. To an extent that is seldom appreciated, many opinions about economic and political life are conditioned by a view that practically everything is random and unpredictable, and therefore independent of everything else. This implies a wide range for permissible behavior because it narrows the set of consequences that need to be considered. In its extreme form, it also implies that economic progress is independent of the cultures and values that people hold, and that no objective or rational judgments can be made about them. The cultural relativists cannot see the causal connections between primitive cultures and economic backwardness, corruption, nepotism, and technical incompetence. They cannot tell whether it is better to be a witch doctor or a mechanical engineer.

This silliness has its roots in the very developments that freed Western civilization from witch doctors and their equivalents. An impact of science through most of the modern period has been to identify and broaden the range of apparent randomness in life. The primitive mind believes that all things are connected—in magical ways. Because cause and effect are so little understood in primitive societies, false connections are attributed between events. If a crow flies over your house and croaks three times, you or someone in your family will die. If your neighbor happens to walk by at the moment your cow gives birth to a deformed calf, it was he who crippled your calf. His guilt can be tested by burning his flesh with a hot iron. If the wound festers, he is guilty. Such are the fantasies common to a premodern mind. Webs of portent, superstition, and bewitchment are woven between unconnected events, in ways that bind down the economy, ensnaring rich and poor alike.

Modern science was the scissors that cut through these false connections. As the understanding of cause and effect developed, it freed individuals to behave in ways that previously would have been foreclosed. You can now take a stroll in the country with little danger that you will be blamed for the sickness of every cow you pass, or taxed for similar coincidences. Most people now realize that you are not responsible for the farmer's bad luck. But this realization spread only after science began to explain the true causes of previously mysterious happenings. In this sense, each advance in the attribution of causality was like a court order dismissing unjustly indicted suspects.

As more direct cause-and-effect relationships were exposed, everything that could not be traced in a direct way to a given cause was considered independent and only randomly connected. From what we now know, however, the assumption of independence and randomness was overdone. Some guilty suspects were set free. Larger systems were assumed to be merely the sum of their parts, with every part independent, like the parts of a clock. Even within the realms that science could predict, the larger determinants came to be seen as random. In a peculiar way, chance became the ordering principle of science, from chance mutations in evolution to the "random walk" said to characterize the behavior of capital markets. While this enthusiasm for randomness represented a great improvement over magical thinking, it led to false conclusions. In the zeal to describe everything as a matter of chance, many hidden and subtle connections were overlooked. In the process, cause and effect have been partially decoupled.

Now the computer is enabling us to better see the dependencies and hitherto hidden connections between events. What appears random to the eye and tests as random according to simple statistical measures may actually be the outcome of deterministic systems. Even complex systems that are not completely deterministic may be less random than they seem, incorporating nonlinear dependence. This means, in some cases, that there is a kind of "memory" at work in nonlinear dynamic systems. Apparently random outcomes are dependent on previous outcomes. Until there is a fundamental change in the system, results will tend to persist in reflecting past events.

The Rebirth of Consequences

If human events are less independent than they have seemed, then many combinations of action and belief that now appear plausible will be seen at a higher level of abstraction to be contradictory and self-defeating. Consider this analogy. You can fiddle around all you please rearranging the furniture in your living room because there are few or no dependencies between the location of your whitewashed wicker lamp and your loveseat. Each piece is independent and can be stationed anywhere you please. But you cannot be so free and easy in rearranging the organs of your body. Their locations do involve intricate dependencies. The greater the number of dependencies between actions or events, the more perilous it becomes "to shuffle the furniture."

As the computer clarifies connections between events, it will cut the scientific ground from under the flabby moral and cultural relativism that has dominated the progressive countries in recent decades. The perception that practically everything is random, including cultural and moral values, has contributed to a false conclusion that no set of values is better or more useful than another. This will change as we come to see that features of culture are causally connected to the stage of economic development. Such apparently independent questions as whether a society believes in a narrow or universal human nature; its treatment of time and chronology; the degree of commitment to education, accurate biography, and history; the role of mythology, superstition, and magic; even the degree of interpersonal honesty are all connected to economic development and social mobility. Or so we believe.

In his fascinating and suggestive study, *Hierarchy, History & Human Nature*, Donald E. Brown has shown that artistic styles are not random, but have tended to vary broadly with the character of the societies that produced them. Before the invention of photography, open societies from the Greeks onward almost invariably gave rise to realistic art. Closed, hierarchical societies, by contrast, have tended to produce art of a highly stylized, nonrepresentational kind. Such societies tend to represent individuals symbolically, identifying persons through the symbols of their rank rather than depicting their individual characteristics. By contrast, individual portraiture of a realistic kind— as well as its literary analog, biography—has been produced almost exclusively by open societies. You can practically measure the degree of economic mobility in past societies by the degree of realism in art. Roman art became steadily more stylized and less realistic as the Roman economy sank into destitution. During the Dark Ages realism disappeared altogether. You could no longer recognize the individual who was the subject of an art work by looking at the work itself. Realism made a comeback in the medieval period, but only at the time of the Gunpowder Revolution was there a true Renaissance of realism, including a rediscovery of perspective, and realistic sculpture of a standard to match that in ancient Greece or Rome.

Upon consideration, these characteristics of closed and open societies make sense. They complement the principles that societies must invent and reinvent to define themselves and provide guidance to their members. Closed societies, such as precolonial India, or Christian Europe of a thousand years ago, afforded individuals little practical opportunity to advance according to their merit. This closure was even more strict in principle than it was in fact. The few who were perched precariously atop a social pyramid in which the many were miserable at the bottom had strong incentives to promulgate ideologies to justify these arrangements as ordained by heaven. The surest way to do this has been to state that the perquisites of wealth and power are a birthright—a matter of status rather than accomplishment. That is exactly what the leaders of stagnant societies have proclaimed throughout history. They have denied the universality of human nature, proclaiming that all people did not share the same nature, or deserve the same rights. Generally, they have attempted to make their title to life's good things hereditary by prohibiting intermarriage between individuals of different social status. By so doing, those who dominated closed societies made a good genealogy among the more important of all assets. It is no surprise, therefore, that the highest caste of the Indian elite traced their ancestry to mythic figures, while the lords, dukes, and earls of Christian Europe claimed as forebears the early saints and church fathers.

These examples suggest why closed societies have tended to falsify their histories. A claim of descent from mythic figures is most unlikely to withstand scrutiny in an environment where accurate records are kept and understanding of the past is animated by a disinterested concern to know what really happened. To the contrary, the importance of bogus genealogies in legitimizing the exercise of power and privilege is obviously in conflict with the requirements of sound historiography. This is why closed societies, like Rome in its dotage, have elevated myth above history. Rather than seeking out a realistic understanding of what actually happened, with specific chronologies and sequences of events, closed societies have tended to understand their pasts in terms of myth. The makers of myth, of course, can alter their tales to incorporate elements that in historical terms are simply lies. Thus it is not a coincidence that societies that seek to foreclose economic mobility shun realistic depiction of individuals, and even turn away from realistic accounts of their own histories. The cultural corollaries of open and closed societies are not so random as they may seem.

As this becomes clearer, it will discredit some contemporary ideologies, in much the same fashion as the development of the telescope doomed the medieval vision of the earth as the center of the universe. It may not be possible, for example, to have a modern society that retains the values of hunting and gathering cultures, as some in Africa and the aboriginal tribes in North America, Australia, and elsewhere have attempted. And the spectacular failure of Marxist-Leninist systems can be understood in a new light.

They incorporated profound functional contradictions. On the one hand, Marxists believed in progress, science, and the universality of human nature. They also placed a dogmatic emphasis on realism in art. These are all features of open societies. More ambiguously, they pretended to an objective "scientific" interest in history, which was frequently short-circuited by blatant attempts to disguise what really happened, edit events, and airbrush away inconvenient faces from old photographs. The attempt to maintain a closed economy could not be reconciled in functional terms with the cultural expressions of science, progress, and individualism. In their stable forms, closed systems have been associated with the suppression of science, inexact chronologies, and the denial that all humans share the same nature. Closed systems also are associated with symbolism rather than realism in art. The "cult of personality" characteristic of Marxist dictatorships is a powerful, though inadvertent, expression of individualism. The dictator whose face is plastered everywhere and glorified in heroic statues is a specific individual. He is depicted in a flattering but still realistic fashion, and it is he as a person, not the symbol of his station or an anonymous everyman, that we know. As the dependencies between culture and economies are drawn more clearly into focus in the future, it will become more obvious that Communism was always rent with severe functional contradictions.

A Clash of Cultures

There will be other consequences of better understanding of dependencies. Educated people will come to be less tolerant of perverse cultures, like the culture of the slums. They will be seen, not as benign instances of diversity, but as the social equivalent of computer viruses, mental programs that waste the lives of those infected with them and endanger the lives of others. Recognition that open societies believe that all humans share the same nature will undercut and clash with the growing political assertions of separatism, and with claims for special treatment based upon ethnicity or race. Racial or ethnic quotas, which have been justified under the rhetoric of equal economic opportunity, will come to be seen as inimical to economic opportunity. They are instances of reward based upon status rather than achievement. They go hand-in-hand with economic closure and stagnation. In the past, those societies that have treated persons differently, based upon who they are, rather than what they do, have faltered economically, and opportunity has been foreclosed for almost everyone.

Better recognition of the dependencies between culture and economic performance means an end to the temporizing of values that characterized the postwar world. In the next few years, there will be a powerful reassertion of the universal values of Western civilization. School curricula, at least those in schools patronized by successful people, will be redesigned to emphasize the values of successful living. The notion that the values of Western civilization are no more relevant to a modern economy than those of hunting and gathering tribes will be dismissed as the nonsense it always was.

But this understanding will not, in itself, diminish the growing power of small groups. The bold reassertion of irredentist, racial, and tribal identities is based upon a megapolitical fact: the growing military effectiveness of small groups. Historically, whenever the real power of any group increases, ideologies arise to justify that new power. As the example of the cargo cults shows, ideologies may be remote from the facts and still be believed. Ironically, new knowledge, made possible by microtechnology that underscores the negative consequences of tribalism is also undermining the power of governments to prevent ancient animosities from flaring into the open again. Thus political divisions and debate are likely to become more highly charged, as government becomes less capable of composing differences and maintaining order.

Interventionism Discredited

Much of the plausibility of government intervention in the economy is based upon the assumption that the politicians are shuffling furniture, rather than organs. In the past, the dependencies that existed were hidden or unnoticed. Now higher levels of analysis will expose consequences that previously could be ignored. This will foreclose more actions than it will open. Typically, it is far easier to interfere disastrously with complex systems than to improve upon them with naive experimentation. Any idiot could find one hundred lethal ways to rearrange body parts without coming close to bettering the natural arrangement. So it is with much government economic planning and interventions to change behavior. In many cases, planners would literally have to see in higher dimensions in order to navigate between dependent events. As this becomes clear, what little respectability remains for the dying ideology of socialism will disappear.

Nonlinear Liberalism

Ironically, the scientific eclipse of the more extreme claims of methodological individualism will reinforce the liberal, free market view. This is ironic because it has normally been those opposed to operation of markets who have placed the greatest emphasis upon viewing society as a whole, rather than merely toting it up as a sum of independent parts. Now we see that they were at least partially correct, but not in the way they thought. The fact that the economy is a complex system and complex systems are more than the sum of their parts does not make many forms of government intervention any more likely to succeed. The economy still must be understood in terms of individual human action. It is linear locally, but nonlinear globally. The holistic analysis implies that the costs of many interventions may be higher than previously thought because they spread a wider net of perverse consequences. These consequences, in turn, set off more consequences. Which set off still more consequences. Which compound over time.

Indeed, the very presumption that policy should aim to smother the fluctuations of a complex system like the economy appears to be a profound mistake, analogous to the attempt to suppress irregularities in the heartbeat. Contrary to what you might suppose, the danger of sudden heart attack is greatest when the heart beats most regularly. Similarly, the danger of system failure may be increased in many cases by policies that aim to stabilize present conditions. Objectives such as extinguishing fires in the national parks or enlarging debts to prevent economic slumps are inherently self-defeating. They temporarily forestall an unwanted outcome, but only at the cost of exposing the system to a more spectacular crisis in the end.

The new understanding will also narrow the range of tolerable personal and commercial behavior. This is analogous to the revelation that ambient smoke has unwholesome and potentially deadly consequences for those who breathe it. Before this was understood, smokers could puff away without recrimination in almost any company, a fact that is unmistakably captured in old movies. They leave little doubt as to why Humphrey Bogart succumbed to lung cancer. He is shown with a cigarette on his lips in practically every scene. Not so today. Heroes and heroines who smoke are few and far between in contemporary cinema. New knowledge of the consequences of smoking has made lighting up in public, at least in the United States, a less acceptable behavior. By the same token, new revelations of hidden consequences will have a restraining impact on other forms of behavior, including environmental disruption, creation of indisposable waste, and fouling the air and water with poisons.*

Economic Nihilism?

If there is a depression as we expect, one of its consquences is likely to be a thoroughgoing disillusionment with government, and government promises of intervention to forestall fluctuations of the business cycle. Nonetheless, so long as governments retain substantial resources at their disposal, there will always be a demand for rationalizations of far-reaching government action. It will no doubt take some time for a new coherent rationalization for economic closure to be concocted. It will probably not emerge until after the coming slump bottoms out. The power of decentralizing technologies insures that whatever this new ideology is, it will claim far less comprehensive powers for central authority than those proposed under socialism. Most likely, it will take the new knowledge of dependencies between events into account, and turn it in some fashion around ecological concerns, which point in some cases to the need to prevent private entrepreneurs from exploiting the public commons with pollution and other costs.

This new ideology of modified closure that will compete with nonlinear liberalism in the politics of the future will probably emerge first in America. In the Great Depression, an Englishman, Lord Keynes, was the philosopher of economic closure. The same internal dynamic that turned Britain away from open markets in its twilight is likely to be at work in America, though much modified by disillusionment and the decentralizing impact of the Information Revolution. In the meantime, retrenchment will be the political force of the 1990s, competing not with a coherent ideology of government, but with a common opinion that may be characterized, as Nobel economist James Buchanan has written, by "what is essentially an attitude of nihilism toward economic organization."

---

*No waste is truly indisposable. But it is certainly true that the difficulty and cost of disposing of many forms of waste are much higher than previously thought. A pricing structure that fully accounted for these costs would foreclose the use of some products and resources because they would no longer pay.

Religion Replaces Ideology?

We are speculating about the extent to which presently obscure connections will be made more visible by future knowledge. How accurate our speculations prove to be is a matter to be seen. Much depends on the soundness of our hunch that rapidly increasing computational capacity will reveal a considerable degree of nonlinear deterministic dependence in apparently random phenomena. The earliest probes in that direction are equivalent to the first shaky flights of the Wright Brothers' plane. There is good reason to believe that further improvements in computational capacity will take us from the treetops to the stars. They may reveal entirely new principles of nature implied by the capacity of complex systems to organize themselves across many different scales. To a much greater extent than educated opinion has heretofore supposed, we are likely to discover that the ordering of complex systems is not random, but destined to happen according to nature's laws. As physicist Paul Davies has put it, nature's capacity to organize in complex ways may be predestined, part of a "cosmic blueprint." The Revolution of the 1990s may include an intellectual as well as a social revival of religion.

Pseudorandomness in the Economy

Already, nonlinear scientists are looking for evidence of pseudorandom phenomena in physics, chemistry, ecology, climatology, biology, and, of course, economics. Because this line of inquiry is so new, it will be many years before the full range of pseudorandom systems is explored and identified. There is reason to believe, however, that current tests may underestimate the extent of pseudorandomness in the economy and markets. We simply don't know how many relationships that textbooks now tell us are random are actually biased by some hidden order.

Another thing we don't know is how many pseudorandom events can be predicted. The fact that a system is completely deterministic does not mean that it is predictable. And as the angel proved to Jimmy Stewart in *It's a Wonderful Life*, there may be an interesting range of contingent predictability. In any event, the realm of phenomena that appear random to human eyes will always be large. Even entirely deterministic systems may be impossible to forecast. A random number generator, for example, is a deterministic system. But it is a system that cannot be predicted within the dimensions accessible to a human mind. It is very unlikely that it will ever be otherwise. There will be little more scientific warrant for fatalism in the 1990s than the Puritans had in Newton's time.

Even in less constrained circumstances, prediction may be very difficult without, in effect, "reading the mind of God." The now-famous Butterfly Effect describes how the flapping of a butterfly's wings in China can change the weather in New York. It is in most cases an instructive exaggeration—an apt way of imagining how very small factors can alter outcomes significantly in a nonlinear world. To foresee them all would involve omniscience. And that means omniscience across all dimensions. In the past philosophers talked about omniscience without the computational capacity to build high-dimensional models. Now that it has begun to be available, it creates milestones of a sort, light-years measuring empty space, against which the full impossibility of the observations and calculations required can be gauged. Certainly, high-dimensional models can tell us more than we now know. The extent to which the wide variety of pseudorandom phenomena can be forecast will be a matter for discovery in the next century.

> The substitution of a downward for an upward tendency often takes place suddenly and violently, whereas there is, as a rule, no such sharp turning point when an upward is substituted for a downward tendency.
>
> —LORD KEYNES

The fundamental nonlinearity in nature should alert us to expect a different pattern of economic ups and downs from what economists have traditionally suggested. For one thing, nonlinearity makes a hash of the much-touted "efficient market hypothesis." This is the view, championed more by academics than investors, that all new information is instantly and completely reflected in market prices. This could be true in a linear world. It is far less plausible where apparently small influences can produce disproportionate or discontinuous changes.

You can see this by imagining the market impact of an announcement that Abdul intends to load one more straw on the ever-aching camel's back. What will the result be? If the straw merely slowed the beast proportionately, the expected outcome would be trivial, but economically positive. The productivity of hauling would rise. And so would the profits of the caravan, by one straw's worth. But if another straw were the weight that would break the camel's back, it would put the expedition out of business. Or worse. It could even subject the owners to attack by animal rights terrorists. What should an investor expect? There is no simple answer. In a world of many camels and many straws there are bound to be surprises. Nonlinear change will confound "common sense" hopes about the future.

The fact that "investors' interpretation of events is not reflected immediately in price" is a reflection of nonlinear dependence or the persistence of sentiment in the face of the facts. This provides a foundation for a "memory effect" and strange seasonal tendencies that are observable over the decades.

THE JANUARY EFFECT

For example, there is substantial evidence documenting an unusual upward bias in returns on certain types of securities in January. This bias appears to prevail in most industrial countries, and even be stronger outside the United States. It has often been attributed to seasonal selling of shares of small companies for tax losses in December. But other factors we cannot now identify may also be involved.

AUTUMN CRASHES

Even more mysterious is the strange tendency for major crashes to occur in the autumn, especially in October. Why this should be has never been explained convincingly. Yet it is hardly a new phenomenon. As long ago as December 1857, a Mr. Langton read a paper to the Manchester Statistical Society attempting to detail why financial crises were common in the autumn. His theory could not have covered the major crashes on September 18, 1873, and October 29, 1929, let alone the subsequent crashes on October 6, 1932, October 18, 1937, October 19, 1987, and October 13, 1989. Each of these dramatic drops, among the largest ever recorded, occurred in the fall. Of the fifteen largest one-day declines in the Dow-Jones average since 1928, ten fell between September 24 and November 11. The old view would be to argue that this is merely coincidence, which, of course, is possible. More likely, some factor we do not now understand increases the vulnerability to sell-offs in the fall.

Nonlinearity and the "Buy and Hold" Strategy

For humans to have long survived in a nonlinear environment has required complex adjustments that profoundly shape life. We argue elsewhere in this book that many of the peculiarities of cultures, including taboos and religious doctrines, are, in some measure, functional responses to the limitations of human forecasting abilities. Even the basic laziness of humankind may be a trait that increases the prospect of survival in a nonlinear world.

One way to handle the prospect of discontinuity is to ignore it altogether, which is how many people behave. They act as if the major trend in place would persist forever, and are suitably stunned when it doesn't. In economic theorizing, this leads to the recurring fantasy of a "New Era" in which economic slumps are to be a thing of the past. In politics, it leads the public to swallow any promise of government action to suppress discontinuity. And in investment, the aversion to discontinuity has its heretofore most profitable expression—the "buy and hold" strategy.

When the long-term trend is up, as it has been for most of the modern period, and you are investing in a stable society, it makes sense to buy and hold. This has been an easy way to make money. If you are not rich today, you would be had your ancestors for the past two centuries bought and held stocks, especially in the United States and Britain, the two predominant powers of the period. The long-term trend has been up. When you buy and hold, you hitch your fortune to the long-term trend. You make money so long as the trend stays in force. Most of the time it has carried on. But not always. There have been significant discontinuities, including World War I, the Great Depression, World War II, and the oil shocks, which rattled markets and drove prices down.

The asymmetrical behavior of markets during these breaks from trend is another confirming evidence that the alleged "randomness" of markets is an illusion. As Keynes understood, the downturns in markets are often more violent than the periods of gain. This is to be expected when the economy is suddenly destabilized in a period of progress.

The opposite type of asymmetry—sharp rises followed by gentle declines to new lows—is rare, because the market sentiment it would reflect—a persistent bias toward lower values—is incompatible with the continued existence of capital markets. We saw something like that in the United States following the "Sucker's Rally" that peaked in April 1930. Prices sank lower and lower until the Dow scraped bottom at 41.22 on July 8, 1932. Even those few years during which stocks fell by almost 90 percent from their highs so shook the faith in progress that many openly doubted that the system could survive. If stock prices were to turn down and stay down for a generation while the economy regressed, the persistent faith in progress would be replaced by a persistent gloom. Under those conditions, growth would probably have to reemerge in a nonlinear fashion, "suddenly and violently," as it did in the Industrial Revolution.

Asymmetrical Buying and Selling Opportunities

Evidence that the market does not instantly and fully reflect all information helps explain the persistence of inefficient forms of saving in backward societies. It also suggests that developing countries that suffer from a lack of fully functioning capital markets would benefit from foreign investment. In a sense, the failure of people in depressed conditions to see opportunities is the flip side of the coin to the failure of participants in progressive markets to anticipate downside discontinuities. Both reflect important aspects of reality. Only individuals who already incorporate an assumption of progress in their expectations are likely to place their money at risk under conditions of uncertainity. Backward societies are generally unstable. Their economies are narrowly based, and subject to more frequent political shocks, revolutions, and abrupt departures from the trend of economic growth. Therefore, markets probably need to be seen shooting straight up to attract broad participation from domestic investors.

Still another implication of the nonlinearity embedded in life is that the persistent positive bias that characterizes markets in progressive countries is likely to result in a dearth of short-sellers in bull markets. In other words, most investors in rich countries will overlook opportunities to make money from negative developments, just as there is a dearth of buyers in backward societies. Here is where an alert observer may find an opportunity to make money.

It will often be possible, especially during bull market conditions, to obtain higher than ordinary returns, simply by following the professional short-sellers. If nonlinear dependence exists on the level that we have suggested, there will be an asymmetry that can be exploited. In futures markets, which are more genuinely two-way markets than share markets, if negative sentiment on heating oil, for example, reaches an extreme, heating oil is probably a buy. By the same token, if everyone thinks that oil can only go up, it is probably poised to drop instead. This is the essence of the "contrarian" strategy of investing—waiting until market sentiment reaches an extreme and doing the opposite. But the contrarian principle may not apply to short-selling, especially in relatively illiquid sectors of the stock market.

If you see everyone racing to buy an individual share that "can only go up," it is most likely too late to buy. However, if short-sellers start ganging up on an individual stock, it does not necessarily mean it is too late to sell. If the price has not yet fallen substantially, the fact that short-sellers are circling around, licking their chops, is a hint that should not be ignored. If you go to a national park and look out over the horizon, you cannot tell where in that region a healthy animal may be. But you can tell where an unhealthy animal is, by watching for the buzzards circling overhead. Short-sellers give a similar hint in stock markets.

As a group, the short-sellers are likely to be smarter than the buyers. Any share, especially in the OTC market, that has a heavy short interest and has not yet taken a tumble is likely to fall disproportionately to the market as a whole whenever the bad news sinks in.

Ironically, the best place to look for a market to go straight down is in the richest country. It is there that the bias towards optimism is likely to be most acute. The best place to find a stock that will shoot straight up is in an underdeveloped market in a poor country, because savings there will tend to be hidden under the mattress, and potential investors will persistently overlook opportunities.

Dangers of Market Closure

We have been lucky in the United States, Canada, Britain, and the other leading capitalist countries that economic growth has been robust for the last two centuries. Because all economic shocks have proven transitory, they have not undermined persistent faith in progress, at least among investors. Every major drop in the economy has been followed by a return to the trend of growth. But a spectacular crisis or a long downturn could produce a major shift of sentiment. In an extreme case, it could even lead to a closure of markets themselves. If economic decline disappointed the expectation of progress over the lives of a whole generation of investors, it would be hard to keep capital markets functioning. Savings would tend to regress toward less efficient forms, such as gold jewelry, or the preference for large families, the most common form of saving in traditional societies.

It could be quite important to know that you may not be able to depend upon a gradual recognition in the market to signal that a depression is coming to trigger a change in your plans. You may need to anticipate discontinuities in order to avoid being overwhelmed by them.

CHAPTER TEN

DRUGS, DELUSIONS, AND THE IMPERIAL CULTURE OF THE SLUMS

From the wild Irish slums of the 19th century Eastern seaboard to the riot-torn suburbs of Los Angeles, there is one unmistakable lesson in American history: a community that allows a large number of young men (and women) to grow up in broken families, dominated by women, never acquiring any stable relationship to male authority, never acquiring any set of rational expectations about the future . . . that community asks for and gets chaos.

—DANIEL PATRICK MOYNIHAN, 1965

THE FALLING capacity of governments to maintain order is a global problem, dictated by the power equation. Yet its manifestations differ from country to country. Just as a flood will first inundate low-lying areas, while persons living on hills and mountains remain dry and secure, so the rising tide of violence in the world has first swamped the regions of lowest development. Backward countries, which never achieved modern market economies or institutions that could operate effectively at a large scale, have suffered first. The Communist countries followed them into political breakdown and economic slump, for reasons we have already analyzed. The Western industrial countries appear to have been spared this unhappiness. But look again.

Rioting that swept Los Angeles, San Francisco, Toronto, and other cities in the spring of 1992 was merely a first surge of a rising tide of violence and disorder that will drown many urban neighborhoods in the West. The *Economist* wrote of the Toxeth region of south Liverpool:

291

The houses are crumbling, weeds flourish, shops are boarded up and the street-signs are painted in the Rastafarians' green, red and yellow stripes. Except for the drizzle, it could be a third-world country that has run out of cash.

The backwash of the same technological developments that destroyed the empires and reversed the trend toward larger and larger enterprises has reversed centuries of cultural progress in calming criminal violence. New lifeways and perverse values that encourage aggressive behavior spread in the hollowed ruins of industrial cities. Areas like Liverpool's Ward 8 are prey to disorder like that which has washed over the Third World. They are regions where the rule of law has only minimal reach. Power on the streets is shared with criminal gangs that compete in the only thriving enterprises in the region: larceny, extortion, drug dealing. These neighborhoods are the dead ends of civilization, where racial and ethnic differences have been magnified into widening cultural divisions. "Whites are not welcome. Television crews, the only whites much interested in going there, have to apply to local leaders for an escort, and even then may lose the contents of their car to a rival gang." A wicked feedback of perverse incentives reinforces the criminal values and delusional thinking that trap the underclass in poverty. This trap is shut all the tighter because its outlines are hidden by the miasma of race.

The False Assumption of Economic "Normality"

To clear away some of this fog involves a detour out of the ghetto to discuss the broader issues of how values and culture affect the way people behave. This is among the more important subjects of the 1990s. The way people perceive the world, and their willingness to respond to opportunities in the marketplace, are not quite what economists usually suppose.

In the last chapter we explored some of the impact of enhanced computational power in sharpening the perception of the way the world works among the educated. But this is hardly the complete story. Only the educated are likely to be impressed with the new, high-tech understandings of complex systems and how they operate. The technology that is shedding a new light on the organization of reality is also speeding the division of culture into fractured segments. The result is what Richard Bernstein has called "a new tribalism, a heightened awareness of ethnic and racial separateness." The cultural gaps between the educated, cosmopolitan elite and those left behind at the bottom grow wider by the moment. Whole sections of human society seem condemned to move further away from understanding how the world is organized and how they can succeed in it.

The conventional view of economic rationality begs the question of how people think or process information by assuming that it is done perfectly, instantly, and without exertion. This unrealistic assumption accounts for some of the wide discrepancies between the economist's view of how humans behave and the accounts from anthropologists, psychologists, and sociologists. Of course, not even economists would pretend that the assumption of perfect knowledge and instantaneous calculation is true. But it is a falsehood justified on grounds that there is no real discontinuity, or sharp break, between the "normal action" that may be expected "from the members of an industrial group" and economically "abnormal" behavior—a category that covers everything from simple laziness, to mistakes in calculation, to the apparently perverse and self-destructive behaviors of the underclass.

The quotations are from Alfred Marshall. He spelled out the theoretical backing for the conventional view of economic rationality in 1890. In the preface to the first edition of his *Principles of Economics,* Marshall emphasized the importance of what he called the "Principle of Continuity." He claimed

that there is a continuous gradation from the actions of "city men," which are based on deliberate and far-reaching calculations, and are executed with vigor and ability, to those of ordinary people who have neither the power nor the will to conduct their affairs in a business-like way.

Marshall's assumption of continuity implies at least two notions that are generally accepted: (1) Cultural differences do not create large gaps (or to put it in terms of the computer, programming failures) in the way people think and act; and (2) a surge of economic prosperity or a sudden decline will have no real impact upon the way the participants in an economy calculate.

CULTURAL GAPS AND SHOE SIZES

We believe otherwise. Even though human nature is the same everywhere, there are significant discontinuities or breaks in the ways that individuals process information.

There is a very great distance between the way that "city men" or professional investors in the City of London, Wall Street, Frankfurt, or Tokyo process and act upon information, and the way that the "unbusiness-like classes" behave. In today's terms, the "unbusiness-like classes" include a lot of people. To get an idea of how many, just look around. Visit the supermarket checkout counter and read the headlines on some of the best-selling tabloids:

"Japanese terminal lets anyone visit the past—and future!"

"Dead hubby's tattoo appears on widow."

"Life After Death Nightmare! Young nurse lives two lives—one now and the other in 1842."

"Astonishing new medical study proves . . . Your Shoe Size Tells How Long You'll Live: Calculate your life span with easy-to-read chart inside!"

These stories all reflect the mentality of people who can fathom the "easy-to-read chart inside." Millions think that Elvis Presley is alive. And pro wrestling is real. If you think they are grinding gears, think of the millions of others who cannot read at all. And the additional millions who can't figure out their shoe size, let alone anticipate the impact of the national debt on future bond yields. Recent estimates suggest that fully one-third of the adult population of the United States cannot perform simple arithmetic calculations. Anything more complicated than flicking to the channel with the music videos, and they are over their heads.

The gradations between these modes of calculating and pursuing ends are not continuous or imperceptibly small. They involve real gaps. For example, there is an obvious and wide gap between those who are literate and numerate and those who are not. This gap is magnified by additional training and professional experience. As Sidney Pollard documented in his study of the Industrial Revolution, this gap has probably been widening since the eighteenth century. It has continued to widen with the increase in educational differentiation inherent in the growing complexity of mental work. A striking evidence of this is provided in the magnification of computational abilities among those who are skilled in using computers. They enable their users to perform certain calculations up to a billion times faster than the person who is scratching along with a pencil and paper, let alone the poor sod who is still reckoning on his fingers.

Language and Computation

There are further educational gaps determined by the ability to understand different languages. An opportunity that is first made known in Japanese will be more or less totally inaccessible to those who do not speak Japanese until it is translated into other tongues. There is no meaningful sense in which languages "shade into one another" the way truly continuous phenomena do. The regional differences in inflection and expression between French spoken a hundred yards from the German border and that spoken in Paris are minuscule compared to the differences between French and German.

It is absurd to assume, as has been the tendency, among a great many Western anthropologists and sociologists, that all traces of Africa were erased from the

Negro's mind because he learned English. The very nature of the English the Negro spoke and still speaks drops the lie on that idea.

—LeRoi Jones

There are profound effects on the capacity to think and visualize that arise from vocabulary and grammar. It is well established, for example, that primitive peoples who survive by direct interaction with nature have much more extensive vocabularies for describing the physical world than do modern peoples. Eskimos are said to have more than one hundred words for "snow." The distinctions conveyed by these words cannot easily be noticed by the modern tourist to the Arctic Circle.

By the same token, primitive peoples usually have "no words for abstract concepts." Their "languages, which are intimately adjusted to their way of life, tend to prevent the free movement of their minds into new regions of experience."

Another feature of primitive languages and cultures is that they have a poorly developed concept of time, with no clear distinction between past, present, and future. This was strongly emphasized by Benjamin Whorf in an extensive study of the Hopi Indian language. He found that "the Hopi language contains no words, grammatical forms, constructions, or expressions that refer to time or any of its aspects." The Hopi have little or no sense of the future, a feature that they share with many primitive groups, and, indeed, with all animals. Like animals, they live in the "eternal present."

The intuition of time is not universal to human beings. It must be learned. Before the age of about thirty months, all children appear "to live only in the present." Only gradually do children reduce the "relative proportion of present-oriented statements." The leading historian of time, G. J. Whitrow, concludes that "it is only in Indo-European languages that distinctions between past, present, and future have been fully developed." This is not an ethnocentric view, but a descriptive fact. Like a software program, human understanding is tailored to fit the particular circumstances in which it emerged. Everyone's ancestors lived in cultures with little or no sense of futurity. "Old English," as it was spoken "before the Norman Conquest, contained no distinct words for the future tense." A confused or missing future tense is both cause and effect of living mainly in the present, with a low regard for long-term consequences.

Developing a clear sense of time and the future requires an "abstract conceptual framework" that is a specific function of language and culture. This is why children who do not grow up in a modern Western culture often have great difficulty judging the passage of time. Intelligent children in Uganda, for example, variously reported a two-hour bus trip to have lasted for as little as ten minutes and as much as six hours. Whitrow elaborates:

> Also, Australian aborigine children of similar mental capacity to white children find it extremely difficult to tell time by the clock—something that most Western children usually have learned to do successfully by the age of 6 or 7. The aborigine children can read the hands of the clock as a memory exercise, but they find it difficult to relate the time they read on the clock to the actual time of day.

A similar language and conceptual handicap seems to be at work among the children of the slums, who are notoriously poor at higher-order thinking. Seldom do those from the lowest rung of the underclass develop math and science skills. A big part of the reason is that they grow up speaking ghetto dialects that do not convey the same abstract conceptual framework as standard English. Ghetto dialects do not employ tense as an essential feature of grammar. Trying to comprehend mathematical problems in black English is like trying to do a spread sheet on a Nintendo program.

Academic studies of black English show that even the rare words in underclass black speech that seem to suggest a tense because they end in *ed*, like *throwed, frozed,* or *strucked,* are merely coincidences that do not refer "to tense or to time categories at all." Eleanor Wilson Orr, reflecting on her experience as a teacher in Washington, D.C., concluded that black inner-city students, in contrast to those who came from the black middle class, were unable to understand basic processes underlying math because of their language. The problem was not poor vocabulary, but a "lack of concepts" that led to an 80 to 90 percent failure rate. Orr's book, *Twice As Less: Black English and Performance of Black Students in Mathematics and Science,* outlines the broad conceptual gaps that hamper students whose home speech employs pidgin and Creole grammar rather than standard English. As J. L. Dillard put it, "There is much reason to believe that structural and historical differences between Black English and the English spoken by most other Americans have practical consequences which take them out of purely academic concerns."

Learned Helplessness

These examples show that there are considerable gaps or discontinuities in the capacity to process and act "rationally" on information. These gaps would be real, even if they were merely educational. They are more than that. They are also informed by incentives that make it "economically rational" for some individuals and groups to adopt counterproductive habits of mind and behavior. The incentive to calculate in an exacting way, to recognize opportunities and act on them "with vigor and ability," varies widely with circumstances.

We need not drift onto the shoals of biochemical determinism to note that variations in response to incentives may have chemical analogs. Research in the chemistry of the brain shows that apathetic, helpless behavior is a learned state. Experimenters put rats in boxes with lids, and applied mild electric shocks of the kind a human might get after shuffling across a carpet and touching a door knob. The shocks were unpleasant but not harmful. The rats responded in the natural way by attempting to leap out of the boxes. But the closed lids frustrated their escape. After repeated failure, they ceased to try. Even when the lids were removed, and the shocks reapplied, the rats remained apathetic. They no longer sought escape from unhappiness, even though the obstacle that previously held them back had been removed.

Researchers found that the brains of the rats with learned helplessness were depleted of noradrenaline. Interestingly, cocaine releases noradrenaline in the brain, which may account for its great appeal in underclass communities. It gives a temporary boost to otherwise apathetic persons, increasing their aggressiveness and sense of purpose. This high is merely temporary, however. It is the biological equivalent of a credit card spending spree. Cocaine depletes the noradrenaline in the brain, leaving those who use it in quantity even more apathetic and wiped out.

Taboos

Drug addiction is a special and extreme case of a discontinuity in the willingess of individuals to respond to opportunities. Yet even where simple profit maximizing is not stalled by addiction or learned helplessness, it may be inhibited by social pressures or taboos that apply to certain individuals or groups, and not at all to others. One would not expect a fundamentalist Christian to seize opportunities to sell liquor on Sundays, or devout Jews to peddle pork sausage. Likewise, there was a wide gap between the capacity of someone like Ray Kroc, the McDonald's tycoon, to automate the sale of hamburger, and that of a devout Hindu who believes that cows are sacred.

These are obvious and perhaps trivial examples, but there is a larger issue involved. The premise of economic rationality, which holds that individuals act to increase their surplus of reward over cost, is probably the deepest truth of human life. But it does not necessarily imply that people act rationally in the scientific sense. People are naturally lazy and present-centered. They may neglect the facts, employ techniques that are scientifically preposterous, and override immediate cost/benefit considerations to conform to apparently counterproductive values.

These anomalies reflect the high value of immediate satisfaction and the fact that effort is costly. To gather and process information requires work. It is just as if an individual who wished to update his perceptions were obliged to scale a twelve-foot wall in order to look around. After repeating this exercise a few times, even the more energetic among us would tend to "make do" with old information. This is what happens. Humans employ many shortcuts to economize on information and avoid the necessity of computing anew what is most profitable in each circumstance. These shortcuts parade under a variety of names. Some are simply "habits." More complex or overriding responses involve "values." As Mancur Olson has shrewdly noted, "values reflect what used to pay." They incorporate cost/benefit calculations from the past.

Time Lags and Economic Calculations

The difficulties and costs of instantaneous calculations across a broad range of phenomena introduce many time lags into human life. Values typically reflect calculations of behavior that paid during the lifetime of one's parents or earlier. Even the recognition of some fundamental economic relationships may lag long behind the facts. We suggested in the last chapter how new understanding of nonlinear dynamics has led to a recognition of the persistence of sentiment in markets. Some historians have suggested that perceptions of overall economic prospects tend to lag about fifty years, or approximately one adult lifetime, behind the facts. An interesting statistical support for this idea was provided by population historians E. A. Wrigley and R. S. Schofield. They analyzed the gross reproduction rate in England from 1550 through 1800. During much of that period, most of the English population lived by subsistence farming. There was also a growing urban population who worked for wages that provided for a living that just skirted the edge of subsistence. The productivity of farming was appallingly low. Famines and epidemics were common until the eighteenth century. Having too many children to feed at a time when real wages were insufficient meant hunger for everyone or even starvation. As a result, they speculate that primitive forms of contraception were used, including postponement of the marriage age. The reproduction rate fluctuated considerably.

In analyzing the relationship between the live birth rate and real wages in the premodern period they expected to find that the birth rate went up with income. They found a correlation, but not what they expected. Wrigley and Schofield argued that the birth rate did indeed follow the pattern of changes in real wages. Every time wages rose, people chose to have more children. When wages fell, the reproduction rate also fell. But the response was long delayed. As they put it, "in each case also the fertility change took place about half a century later than that in real wages." The only times when real wages and fertility moved in common were when the long-term wage trend continued in the same direction for more than a half century.

For a modern investor accustomed to dealing in a liquid market where prices fluctuate from moment to moment, it may be hard to appreciate the fact that reproduction decisions were among the most important economic variables in the lives of persons living at or near subsistence. Yet they were. It may be significant that the lags in perceiving or acting upon fundamental changes in these relationships approximated the adult lifetime, and, perhaps not coincidentally, the average length of the long cycle.

We believe that it is common even today for values that reflect complex cost/benefit analyses to lag about half a century behind the economic realities by which they were informed. It is apparent, for example, that many political attitudes in the United States, Britain, and other industrial countries are still colored by the impact of the Great Depression and World War II. Similar lags may be in evidence in the long-delayed popular repudiation of the oppressive Communist regimes in the Soviet Union and Eastern Europe.

Stagnation and Perverse Values

Since the state of equilibrium between survival and starvation which they normally experience is often finely balanced, it is not surprising that they usually consider it dangerous to deviate from their traditional customs and habits.

—G. J. WHITROW

In stagnant societies, where social mobility is effectively foreclosed or inhibited for generations, powerful inhibitions may block adjustments in behavior that are needed to take advantage of opportunities for advancement. It may require a major change or discontinuity before impoverished persons update their information or "values" to reflect changed circumstances.

The nearer people sink to subsistence, the less likely it is that their behavior will be organized through markets in ways that optimize efficiency. This has been true in a remarkable number of settings, in backward and primitive societies from the closed village systems of the Far East to peasant societies in India, Africa, and elsewhere. Efficient forms of property relations encourage opportunities for innovation. This is precisely why they are resisted. The truly poor often cannot afford innovation. It increases the variability of results. A peasant who experiments with a new seed or a new planting method not only increases the chance of a bumper harvest, he also increases the chance that his crop will fail altogether and he and his family will either starve or become a burden on near relatives who also sneak by above the bare margins of subsistence.

More surprising to people accustomed to living far above subsistence: The alternative of startling success is also threatening in hidebound societies—not necessarily to the person who succeeds, but to his relatives. This is true for basic economic reasons. It threatens the relatives with substantial losses—the disappearance of their investments in the individuals themselves. Modern economists speak of "human capital" investments as a factor in productivity. In subsistence societies, such as many of the traditional societies of Africa, "human capital" is a fact. The largest investments available are often investments in marriage and children, investments that are generally so large that they must be syndicated among the relatives.

This requires some explanation. The examples that follow are primarily from Africa, to tie them more closely to the rest of the discussion. But the points are universal points that apply to traditional societies on every continent. Such societies in Africa, as elsewhere, were based upon the family. Kinship meant everything, not because the people who lived in these cultures necessarily cared more for their kin as a matter of personal inclination, but because they depended on them for functions that are handled by insurance companies, banks, capital markets, and governments in wealthier societies. For example, individuals were obligated to support their relatives, with the obligation varying roughly with the degree of genetic relatedness. Children provided the nearest approximation of an old-age pension for parents. Children therefore were economic assets. If aged parents were entitled to live in the homes of their married sons, as was usually the case, some compensation had to be arranged for the parents of the bride. The result was the bride price. Bernard Murstein, a leading expert on marriage and family customs, put it this way:

> The bride price is the giving of compensation—in the form of livestock, implements, or cash—to the father of the bride as part of the marriage procedure. In some African societies the practice of payments or "gifts" continues for years and years.

The power of the family in African subsistence societies is reflected by the prevalence of arranged marriages. It also largely explains the practice of polygamy, or the habit of richer men in traditional African societies taking more than one wife. Poor men with few close kin sometimes could not afford to marry because they could not raise the bride price. Likewise, a barren Nuer woman with a few cattle in the southern Sudan could become the legal husband of another woman. This was not a lesbian relationship, but an investment. The richer woman paid the bride price for the wife, and delegated sexual rights to a male relative or friend. But the female husband retained economic rights to the children. If "daughters are born she is entitled to the bride-price when they marry," Murstein writes.

In traditional societies, especially those in Africa, children were seldom abandoned by their fathers because they were valuable assets—one of the few viable forms of investment. Neither was it common for traditional African husbands to abandon their wives. To do so meant forfeiting the bride price, a large investment that took years to accumulate. Abandonment could alienate the husband from his own family and in some cases invite violent retribution.

Where there are few other forms of investment or capital markets, marriage is an investment decision that normally dominates other economic considerations. Upward mobility, however, tends to disrupt these arrangements. An individual who took up new ways of doing things in closed societies threatened to unravel his kin's claims. If he became rich, he might be tempted to leave the region and desert his obligations. Indeed, the very workings of closed societies sometimes push those rare individuals who are upwardly mobile away from their kin. This appears to have often been the case in India. Because of the need to fabricate genealogies to enter high-status occupations, it was not easy for the nouveau riche to carry their kin along on a trip up the social ladder. One cannot pretend to be a member of an aristocratic caste and at the same time be harboring relatives from a poor village.

For these reasons, relatives tended to look askance at any type of innovation. It might be costly or destabilizing, whether it succeeded or failed. That being the case, it was quite rational for impoverished peoples to develop social mores and modes of thinking that inhibit innovation. By rigidly fixing behavior, they protected their existing investments in family and kinship arrangements in a generally stagnant economy.

This is yet another reason why traditional cultures are dysfunctional in a modern market environment. They rigidly stereotype behavior with strict moral injunctions, enforced by stiff penalties. These work in closed systems, but they stifle free thought and innovation.

"Rationality" Varies with Incentives

Far more than we imagine, "rational" behavior and even rational thought vary according to economic incentives. Where rewards for accurate calculation are high, as they are among investors, economic and scientific rationality are likely to coincide. A trader with a multi-million-dollar bond portfolio would be forfeiting a small fortune to overlook causal relationships that could make a point or two difference in yields. He cannot afford to waste a lifetime updating his conception of economic fundamentals. The very poor, by contrast, can well afford to overlook any cause-and-effect relationship in the bond markets. They can attribute the movement of bond prices to a conspiracy of pixies and not lose a penny for it.

Only where rewards for economic exertion are high or rising do you find little conduct that is economically "abnormal," to use Marshall's words. Abnormal behavior may be rational in the deeper sense that it conforms to values that economize on the need to calculate, or provides a pretext for redistribution of wealth. But it is scientifically irrational in that it reflects a blindness to immediate incentives and a disregard for cause and effect. Economically abnormal behavior includes an unwillingness "to undergo a certain exertion for a certain pecuniary reward." Where rewards are low or falling, individuals and the groups with which they closely interact may lack a lively reason to exert themselves. Even worse, they may have strong incentives to adopt values that further limit their willingness to respond to opportunities in the market. When incentivies to respond to pecuniary rewards diminish, incentives to think rationally and behave in productive ways decline with them. Major depressions tend to stimulate an upsurge in delusional thinking and even generate long-lasting inhibitions that foreclose individual options "to seek the best markets in which to buy and sell."

In short, values as well as mechanical computational capacities can produce significant gaps in the ability of individuals to behave in an "economically normal" way. A person who knows how to read and write may still be very poor at employing "deliberate and far-reaching calculations," and unable to execute plans. This is one reason that problems of development in backward countries or among the urban underclass are so intractable. The scarcity of competent industrial labor and enterprise that is endemic in backward societies is not a coincidental or random feature of those places, but a function of perverse incentives. Similar incentive traps are a major factor inhibiting the success of the chronically unemployed minorities in big cities in America, Britain, and elsewhere. The failure of foresight and even common sense that seems to prevail among the urban underclass and the populations of Third World countries is evidence of discontinuities. It shows that economic rationality and scientific rationality do not always coincide.

ECONOMIC GROWTH AND "THE MAN OF THE FUTURE"

It is often forgotten today that the emergence of a modern population capable of "stable, reliable, and disciplined" economic effort was, to quote Alexander Gerschenkron, "a difficult and protracted process." This was true even in Britain, a nation that had long been rich and socially mobile by comparative standards. He specifically observes that industrial revolutions seem frequently to depend upon discontinuities. They appear to require an "eruptive" or revolutionary stage that involves rapid growth on a large scale in order to throw off the counterproductive values and behavior characteristic of backwardness.

In this respect, it is interesting that each nation that has emerged at the top of the world economy has developed a reputation for an extraordinarily able, energetic, and exacting work force, a reputation for "economic rationality" that has not long outlasted its period of rapid growth. For example, English industrial workers of the middle of the nineteenth century enjoyed an esteem reserved for Japanese workers today. As the nineteenth-century German writer Schulze-Gaevernitz put it, the English worker was "the man of the future . . . born and educated for the machine . . . [who] does not find his equal in the past." This reputation faded after the Great Depression of the late nineteenth century—a period of very high unemployment in Britain accompanied by a marked fall in the growth of labor productivity and income growth. The Trafalgar Square riots of 1886, in particular, gave a big boost to the "new unions" that organized unskilled and semi-skilled workers. They demonstrated a raw power that frightened the wealthy. Faced with dangers of social unrest, opinion soon forgot the arguments for the liberal employment market and skimpy public payments to the poor that characterized England during its period of dramatic growth.

In the early twentieth century, American workers began to develop the reputation for superior quality work that had previously been associated with the English. Observers in London cast an envious eye toward the United States, where workers were credited with "superior technical education," and greater flexibility than their British counterparts. "Even the drier climate was cited as one reason why the migrant European toiled more energetically and productively over there," according to Vivian Vane. Meanwhile, Americans widely believed that the British decline was directly connected to the introduction of the dole, which created perverse incentives to shirk work. Peter Fearon wrote:

> Britain seemed to display a lack of vigour when compared to the US, a condition which was worsened, as many North Americans believed, by national welfare

policies. US newspapers reported the despair of unemployed British families existing on dole payments and contrasted their lot with American citizens who had no such public benefits to erode their initiative.

The intervention of the Great Depression of the 1930s brought mass unemployment in the United States, and a considerable change in the values of the work force. American workers turned to welfare and unions that began to deprecate "hustle" in the same fashion that the British unions had before them.

Today, of course, the great growth region of the world is the rim of Asia. Workers in Taiwan, Hong Kong, and especially Japan are now "the men of the future." Comparative accounts emphasize their superior education (which is to say, they have worked harder to learn more), and the fact that they toil "more energetically and productively over there." As it happens, welfare spending in Asia is minimal or nonexistent. If past patterns hold, the next severe depression will bring a perverse change in the values of the Asian work force in the same fashion that the previous two depressions struck first Britain and then the United States. The dole will be introduced on a larger scale. Workers will turn to unions and featherbedding. They will work less exactingly and invest less effort in education. Periods of protracted income stagnation reduce the return from hard work. When something pays less, you get less of it.

The Fracturing of Culture

As increasing computational capacity brings more information within the reach of people who live by use of their minds in the Information Age, it is likely to speed the rate at which old intellectual capital is outmoded. This will tend to speed the breakdown and fragmentation of culture. As culture fragments, and governments lose the capacity to enforce laws and maintain order, especially in urban slums, violence will increase and so will the number of persons without the skills needed to prosper in a modern market economy.

The problem of the underclass would be difficult enough if it simply represented the fracturing of culture. Far more than in the past, persons who live in close physical proximity may no longer share the common experiences that in crucial ways inform culture. Microtechnology has facilitated a market choice of widely different channels of instruction, entertainment, and information, with the result that people who live within miles or even blocks of one another may have radically different values, habits, and ways of relating to the world. In effect, the Information Age has led to a vertical division of culture, which now overlaps the old geographic divisions. In the past, one could identify a person's culture simply by knowing the county or city where he grew up. But no longer. Culture is rapidly fissuring, like a monumental piece of glass being shattered into shards.

At the top, there is a culture of achievement, shared to a remarkable extent by the educated and well-to-do across the globe. Instant communications, reinforced by easy travel between continents, have melded the tastes, habits, and values of the wealthy in a new cosmopolitan version of Western culture. This is the culture of men and women who are future-oriented. They read. Listen to Mozart. And seek the same adornments with the proceeds of similar investments. Wealthy Japanese may still pay top dollar for samurai swords. But they also pay top dollar for van Goghs and Shakespeare folios.

The division of culture has almost as many fine gradations as cable television has channels. To some extent, these divisions of taste and values track education. They also track the faint shadows of religious affiliation and hobbies, as well as unassimilated ethnic cultures. There is even an alienated class of wealthy eccentrics, of whom Andy Warhol was a kind of hero. The *New York Times* records that Warhol died with ninety-six gold watches. A man who has ninety-six gold watches is either a jeweler, a collector, or sick.

There is a much larger group in America whose members have ceased believing what their parents taught them, yet show a bewildered credulity to almost any proposition their parents would have laughed at. Shirley MacLaine produces best-sellers on what could be called the idiot occult, a mixture of reincarnation, extraterrestrials, and sex. Her charm makes them forgivable, but cannot save them from being ridiculous.

The small ads, even of respectable magazines, show a weird variety of sects and beliefs competing for attention. In an issue of *Harper's* the small ads make much more bizarre reading than the text; they are a jumble of astrology, offers of phallic posters, and proposals of marriage by Asian women.

The culture of achievement has many divisions, and it would certainly be a mistake to suppose that those who provide for their own livelihoods share a common worldview in the way that culture once informed opinion. Yet in spite of the many gradations of taste, and the retreat into cults and quackery, many of the fractured subcultures in the advanced economies still share one crucial civilizing feature. They largely adhere to nonviolent norms of conduct. This is a cultural trait that "first took root among the urban upper and middle classes," according to historian of violence Ted Robert Gurr. It spread during recent centuries as megapolitical power allowed the consolidation of political jurisdictions and the scale of economies rose. Gurr put it this way:

The thesis that sensitization to violence spread from the social center to the periphery and from upper to lower classes is intrinsically plausible as an explanation of some basic features of violent crime, past and present. . . . The further down the class and status ladder, then and now, the more common is interpersonal violence, because the lower classes did not assimilate and still have not wholly assimilated the aggression-inhibiting values of the middle and upper classes.

Unhappily, the trend toward the acceptance of "aggression-inhibiting values" appears to have been halted and reversed about the time of the onset of the last depression in 1930. Since that time there has been a common trend toward the resurgence of crime and violence in Western societies. This parallels the reversal in the power equation that has made it increasingly costly to project military force from the center to the periphery. In the six decades since 1930, interpersonal violence has reverted to levels common in the early nineteenth century. And in some urban centers of the United States, all the progress of eight centuries in suppressing violence has been reversed. Violence is now worse than in medieval Europe, when people were "enmeshed in a culture that accepted, even glorified, many forms of brutality and aggressive behavior," writes Gurr.

The growing rejection of upper- and middle-class values by the poor is a potent explanation, not only for the self-reinforcing trend toward violence, but for poverty itself. Far more than is commonly acknowledged, poverty is not the cause but the consequence of perverse values and antisocial behavior.

199 Chances in 200 of Escaping Poverty

An American's chance of staying poor is less than ½% if he or she does the following three things: (a) completes high school; (b) gets and stays married; (c) stays employed, even if initially only at the minimum wage. Americans who fail these three requirements have an up-to-80 times greater chance of staying for a long time below the official poverty line, and breeding sad generations there.

—ECONOMIST, April 25, 1987

Anyone who cultivates basic skills and the discipline of work can capitalize on the social mobility of the marketplace. As the *Economist* reported, the odds *in favor* of escaping poverty in the postwar United States were 200:1 for anyone who took these three simple steps:

1. Finished high school.
2. Refrained from having children out of wedlock.
3. Took a job, even if at the minimum wage, and did not quit except to take another job.

These are not mysterious steps that could be taken only by initiates in the higher circles of society. They are common-sense behaviors anyone could follow if he wished. The underclass do not. They choose impoverishing behavior—"out-of-wedlock births, school inattendance, dismissing a $5-an-hour job as 'chump change.'"

They are abetted in the wasting of their lives by the perverse incentives of entitlement programs that impose effective tax rates of 100 percent or more on those who shun welfare to take a job. In many cases, the total value of food stamps, rent subsidies, welfare payments, income supplements, and free medical care and other services exceeds the after-tax income that can be earned in unskilled work. And welfare entitlements, by definition, can be realized with little or no daily effort. You don't have to rise in the morning and rush through a crowd of commuters to secure your livelihood. The welfare recipients who take jobs are not only required to meet a schedule not of their own making, they are heavily taxed on their earnings, while they lose benefits that would otherwise come to them for free. Under such circumstances, employment is often a long-term investment for the very poor rather than an immediately profitable act. It pays off only over the longer term, by qualifying individuals for better jobs as they gain experience and work skills.

Lax law enforcement also makes illiteracy, idleness, and illegitimacy more attractive. Children who can make one hundred dollars per hour as thieves or drug dealers are less likely to be impressed with the rigors of learning to read or keeping a minimum-wage job that may pay off in a better life only in the future. Estimates that professional criminals commit 150 to 175 crimes a year underscore the higher hourly return available through a career in crime. Even if the average crime takes two hours to complete, which is probably an overestimate, that means that the professional criminal works less than an hour a day. To earn an honest living takes eight to ten times as much effort. Count time out for court appearances and occasional trips to jail and crime is still a lifetime of idleness. Pete Hamill quotes a New York City cop: "Crime isn't a job, . . . but it is an occupation. So these guys make it their life for a while and then get slammed into the prison system. They're more or less happy there. It's the way they grew up, the state paying everything. Lock-in welfare. In the joint, they don't have to care for women, raise children, open bank accounts, plead for mortgages, bust their asses to make ends meet."

THE CULTURE OF CRIME

It may be said . . . that the existence of a powerful system of criminal values and relationships in low income areas is the product of a cumulative process extending back into the history of the community and the city. It is related both to the general character of the urban world and to the fact that the population in these communities has long occupied a disadvantageous position. It has developed in somewhat the same way as have all social traditions, that is, as a means of satisfying certain needs within the limits of a particular social and economic framework.

—C. SHAW and H. MACKAY,
Juvenile Delinquency and Urban Areas,
1942

Those at the bottom of the cultural divide do not orient their behavior toward the future, and have "low self-control." Preoccupied with immediate pleasure, and inattentive to the long term, they do not educate themselves, or firmly attach themselves to the labor force. In puritan terms, they are irresponsible and self-indulgent. These are people for whom whole clusters of deviant and criminal behavior come easily. Michael Gottfredson and Travis Hirschi, authors of *A General Theory of Crime,* put it this way:

> . . . the same people who use drugs also steal cars, commit burglaries, assault and rob others and drive recklessly. . . .
> The versatility of offenders goes beyond conventional crime categories to include alcohol abuse, spouse and child abuse, accidents, truancy from school and work, and sexual promiscuity. Research repeatedly shows that these behaviors are consistently found together in the same people.

These people are more isolated geographically than their contemporaries, depending on television and radio for contact with the larger world. Their culture is that of the slums. To a far greater extent than is openly acknowledged, the culture of the slums is a culture of crime.

THE RACE QUESTION

The logic of the criminal culture is much the same in all-white regions of South East London, like Gorer Lane, as it is in impoverished black communities. In such environments where people "have thrived on criminal activities for generations," the local culture takes a benign attitude toward law-breaking and other irresponsible, self-indulgent behavior. There is a "cultural heritage" of crime, well explored by Janet Foster in *Villains: Crime and Community in the Inner City.* Her study is based upon white populations who could not have been victims of racial discrimination by the largely white British society. Yet they evidence similar social pathologies to ghetto blacks: broken families, child abuse, juvenile delinquency, high dropout rates, substandard use of language, weak labor force attachment, drug addiction, antagonistic attitudes toward the police, and isolation from the mainstream of society.

There is only one essential difference between the culture of the white criminal slums and that of the black underclass. That is the confusion of race. No one who visits Gorer Lane is likely to come away with the view that white people are mostly criminals and uneducable. Nor do successful whites in Mayfair feel obliged to rationalize and exonerate the failings of their "brothers" in the white slums. But the culture of the black underclass is wrongly thought to have some racial component. For some nonblacks, the behavior of blacks in the slums has seemed to tarnish the reputation of all blacks. And some blacks themselves have appeared to believe that their self-pride is at risk unless they defend the virtues of a "black culture," which to a large extent turns out to be a culture of the slums.

Both extremes of this emotional and highly inarticulate debate are wrong. Culture has no genetic or racial component. Human nature is the same everywhere. As we have emphasized throughout, cultures are like software programs. They facilitate success or survival in certain environments but are dysfunctional in others. In today's world, the culture of success is the cosmopolitan Western culture. It is no less a culture for black achievement than it is for white or Oriental. The many millions of blacks who succeed in the larger society do so by adopting the values and habits conducive to success. They are in no sense abandoning "black culture" because there is no such thing. Culture is not racial but circumstantial.

Man is the child of customs, not the child of his ancestors.

—IBN KHALDUN

The misidentification of slum culture as specifically black, and its adornment with the Rastafarian's green, red, and yellow colors of Africa, have been profoundly counterproductive and misleading. It has harmed blacks who believed it. The rites, myths, and rituals of tribal Africa have little role to play in informing successful behavior in the computer age.

Indeed, the artifacts of premodern African cultures only compound the economically "abnormal" behavior of the underclass. We have already suggested how the underclass is hindered by the grammar of "black English," and its present-centered conception of time. Another harmful carryover from African cultures is the reliance on rite and ritual over technique as means of obtaining what one wants. This is exemplified by behaviors such as eating dirt, which are surprisingly widespread among blacks in rural areas. A 1971 study showed that one in four adult women in Holmes County, Mississippi, ate dirt on a regular basis. There is also a residue of African superstition, including the cults of Santeria, which have significant Hispanic followings. Small stores in many underclass neighborhoods sell voodoo paraphernalia, including ingredients used in casting spells and curses.

But any specifically African features of underclass life are largely coloration of a culture that shares its main elements with the culture of white criminal slums. They include "idleness of young males, illegitimacy, alcoholism, drug abuse, criminality, illiteracy." Underclass culture, black and white, shares perverse features of warrior societies, which include diminished forward vision and a lack of verbal skills. Much of this warrior mentality of the slums has probably been reinvented to suit the violent circumstances of slum life.

DRUGS AND VIOLENCE

It may be worth noting that drug use in the slums, black and white, has much in common with the use of drugs in primitive societies to encourage violent behavior. The most violent societies in nature, like the Yanomamo Indians of South America, take drugs in quantity, and behave with extraordinary savagery. Approximately one-quarter of male Yanomamos die fighting—a ratio that is not far above the death rate for black males in some inner-city neighborhoods. Heavy drug use is implicated in both cases. Intoxication with crack cocaine, for example, seems to stimulate violent behavior.

> In Wayne B. Bennett's world of cocaine dealing and armed robbery, he is known as "Jamaican Wayne" and he lives by a code of conduct that is an unseen but crucial part of the carnage and lawlessness that have marked the District's drug violence. . . .
> Bennett is serving a six-to-18 year sentence for the Gallatin Street shooting and two armed robberies, and he says the code of conduct is the same in Washington's crowded prison system as it is on the street: Never back down, even from what appears to be a trivial confrontation. Be willing to kill or die to defend your honor. Protect your reputation and manhood at all costs, lest you lose the respect of your friends.
>
> —LEON DASH,
> "A Crack Dealer's Creed"

Because the underclass live in an environment that is effectively without law, drug dealers and others who work outside the law resolve contract disputes and turf battles with violence. They cannot go to court to obtain performance on contracts, collect debts, or sue for remedy when another dealer delivers low-quality drugs. They cannot call the police when another thug steals their drugs or money. Only when would-be aggressors know that you will not back down are you likely to minimize what could otherwise be constant physical challenges to defend your property or yourself. This places a premium on an apparently irrational willingness not to flinch when threatened.

When you may face a life-and-death challenge at any moment, valor is more important than persuasive ability or discretion. In such circumstances, it may not seem to pay to regard long-term consequences and make constructive plans for the future. This is especially true if there is a high prospect that any constructive plans you make will be thwarted by the violent intervention of others.

In this respect, the crack culture of America's inner cities is much like that of warrior culture of the Dark Ages. Both are largely illiterate and innumerate, and both have an extreme sense of valor. You cannot turn your back. Roland, a count in Charlemagne's guard who was immortalized in medieval epics, refused to blow his horn to call for reinforcements until his comrades were wiped out. Like the street hipsters who must stand fast for their valor, Roland could not back down. The inner-city crack dealers would understand the *Song of Roland* better than middle-class students.

> . . . They saw indeed, they heard; but what avail'd
> Of sight or sense of hearing, all things rolling
> Like the unreal imagery of dreams,
> In wild confusion mix'd?
>
> —AESCHYLUS,
> *Prometheus Chained*

The violent environment of underclass life may also contribute in unexpected ways to the decline of verbal skills. During the Dark Ages, when European society was thoroughly violence-ridden, even the few who were literate were remarkably bad at expressing themselves. As Colin Morris wrote, "What cannot be verbalized can scarcely be thought, and before 1050 the capacity of most writers to express themselves was poor." It was so poor, in fact, that if you read the description of Charlemagne written in the eighth century, you would have no idea what he really looked like. The physical features attributed to him were not his at all, but those of other persons living centuries earlier, descriptions copied by his court chronicler from Roman texts. Charlemagne was the most famous king of the Dark Ages, yet his contemporaries could not say what he looked like. This was not as strange as it may seem. It is rare for people who survive by violence to cultivate verbal skills.

No Racial Values

A uniform conception of human nature that denies, at least within a given society, the existence or relevance of racial or specieslike distinctions and, on the contrary, asserts that people (disregarding sex and age) are basically alike except for differences induced by their differing environments, is perhaps the most fundamental of all the concomitants of the open society.

—DONALD E. BROWN,
Hierarchy, History, & Human Nature

Do not be captured by a sense of universality given you by the Eurocentric viewpoint.

—MOLEFI KETE ASANTE,
Temple University

The values of African societies were functional in the settings in which they emerged. But they were in no sense particularly "black values" because other peoples in hunting/gathering or pastoral settings developed very similar cultural clues to help them organize their lives. Today, these values are like the file cards used in the first computers. They don't fit the 1990s. The same would be true if one could locate a tribe of white people in a similar stage of economic development to traditional African societies, say the Picts or the Scots, as they were a thousand or more years ago. They would be as hopeless at coping with postindustrial life as are the Masai or the Zulu today. Not for genetic, but for cultural reasons.

In historic times, "tribes" of white people have gone through many cultural stages. It would obviously be silly to speak of any one of these as the permanent culture of whites. Is it a characteristic of whites to wear animal skins and burn cities because the tribes that overran the Roman Empire did that? We think not. And it is just as mistaken to think of "black culture" as defined by the habits and values of blacks as they are found in any African society, much less in the criminal slums of inner cities.

The growing habit of identifying cultures as racially specific—now the rage among black educational theorists, like Professor Asante—fundamentally misconstrues the basis of culture. Any people of whatever race will tend to develop similar cultures when thrown into the same circumstances. When knowledge of North American Indian cultures was first introduced to Europe in the seventeenth century, learned Europeans immediately recognized the similarity of the habits and institutions of the Indians to those of "the ancient inhabitants of Europe," the Germans who sacked the Roman Empire. The prominent eighteenth-century historian William Robertson later made fun of the fallacy that peoples who share similar cultures must be genetically related. He concluded with a point that should be taken to heart by the black leaders who are noisily pushing for "Afrocentric" culture today. Robertson said, "The human mind, whenever it is placed in the same situation, will, in ages the most distant, and in countries the most remote, assume the same form, and be distinguished by the same manners." To consciously inculcate young children in a modern setting with tidbits of culture and values from tribal societies is to confuse them at best, and most likely condemn them to fail. It is to teach them not to tell time, and then be surprised when they miss the bus.

Racism and Ghetto Life

There is another minority whose situation may be more instructive. I refer to Asian-Americans. Neither the newly arrived Southeast Asians nor the earlier-arriving Japanese-Americans, Chinese-Americans, and Korean-Americans are loved by white people. But these groups have spent little time and energy proving that white people don't love them.

While our myth is that racism accounts for our shortcomings, their belief is that their own efforts can make the difference, no matter what white people think.

—WILLIAM RASPBERRY

It is wicked to hate anyone because of race. And there is plenty of wickedness in life. We do not doubt that blacks living in multi-ethnic societies like the United States and Great Britain have been held back by small-minded discrimination, and even by legal bars to their progress. But if you wish to understand the world, and forecast how it might change, it would be a mistake to assume that racism explains the present dilemma of the underclass. There is ample evidence from around the world that ethnic groups who were victims of intense discrimination were nonetheless economically successful. Jews, for example, have been hounded from country to country. Yet they have been highly successful in the face of discrimination. Orientals were long forbidden by law from owning property in California. And Japanese-Americans were confined in detention camps as recently as 1945. When World War II ended, they literally had to start their lives over from scratch. Yet they are now the highest-income ethnic group in the United States.

It's a black thing, you wouldn't understand.

—T-SHIRT SLOGAN,
Washington, D.C.

Claims of "racism" do not explain the failures of the underclass. But they bode ill for the future of major cities in the United States, and, to a lesser extent, Europe. They fit into an ancient pattern of delusional thinking among the poor that has often culminated in violence. That such claims are now so prominent is itself a hint both of megapolitical vulnerability and economic closure to come.

MAU-MAUING THE ESTABLISHMENT

Because centralized urban living is increasingly susceptible to disruption, the potential for intimidation is also increasing. As it rises, those who might be able to influence their followers to either resort to violence or desist from it have real bargaining power. And they have learned to use it. Intimidation and threats of violence rose over the quarter-century before 1990, and some black leaders played no small role in this.

To understand why, consider that black organizers were the principal, and perhaps only, beneficiaries of the urban rioting that swept American cities in the late 1960s. When black mobs rampaged through Detroit, Washington, Los Angeles, and other cities, government and business responded by pouring large sums into community relations and "development" efforts. These mostly involved hiring and contracting with black leaders and community organizations. Within the limits set by economic distress and the growing bankruptcy of government, the pattern was repeated in the wake of the devastating riots in Los Angeles. If society felt threatened, they received the ransom payments.

The idea that there is a distinctly black culture may not stand to much scrutiny. And its counterproductive effects on blacks as a group are evident in statistics recording the rapid breakdown of black family life, and the spread of crime, drug addiction, and violence in black communities. But these disasters have been made to pay, especially for black leaders. Delusion, denial, and the retreat into black racism grew in the 1980s, not in proportion to the good they did for blacks in general, but in proportion to the resources they enabled some black leaders to leverage out of an increasingly vulnerable society. Thus black educational theorists and social workers who bemoaned "cultural genocide" could speak as ever more indignant victims. They demanded ever greater recompense, such as more funding for their programs to emphasize "Afrocentric" education and "black culture."

AL SHARPTON, MYTHMAKER

Not to be left out, provocateurs like the Reverend Al Sharpton have taken the depreciation crisis of the center cities to some of its gaudiest extremes. Sharpton has operated what could be politely described as shakedown operations. For example, news reports indicate that Sharpton threatened to picket the highly successful Michael Jackson concert tour in 1984 "unless the black community shared in the concert take," as reported by James Kunin in *People*. As a result, Sharpton was "paid handsomely for 'his community relations work,' " wrote Kunin. He was later charged with grand theft of $250,000 from the National Youth Movement, which prosecutors allege was used to funnel cash extorted from concert promoters.

Sharpton is most famous as the choreographer of a long-running comic opera over the fabricated abduction and rape of Tawana Brawley, a New York teenager. Brawley claimed that she had been kidnapped near Wappingers Falls, New York, and repeatedly raped by six white men, one of whom wore a badge. Police investigators could not find evidence to corroborate the charges. A grand jury was later told that Brawley had run away from home and was attending a four-day party in a crack-infested neighborhood during the time of her alleged abduction. Evidence suggested that she had faked evidence of an assault, covered herself with excrement, and even crawled into a plastic garbage bag to await discovery. Further, it appeared that Sharpton knew her story was "a pack of lies," according to the *New York Post*. Nonetheless, Sharpton and associates Alton Maddox, Jr., and C. Vernon Mason repeatedly claimed that Tawana Brawley was a victim of a "racist" legal system that would not prosecute her assailants. The trio unleashed a barrage of allegations of complicity in various "white racist" crimes and cover-ups, involving everyone from the Attorney General of New York to the Irish Republican Army. Maddox compounded this lurid fantasy by alleging that New York Attorney General Robert Abrams masturbated over photographs of Tawana Brawley.

Such claims, however remote from the facts, contribute to the volatile atmosphere of urban life. They serve to heighten the risk of violence, and thus reinforce the purposes of those who make them. Alton Maddox is quoted as insisting "I don't care 'bout no facts" in the *People* article. His distaste for a straightforward or objective account of what actually happens has much in common with the professional mythmakers of caste-bound societies, like the Vahivancas of India. The Vahivancas "create myths" for a living. They draw up fabricated genealogies that upwardly mobile Hindus use to trace their lineage to higher castes. In closed societies like India, where success depends upon status rather than personal accomplishment, a well-fabricated claim is useful whether or not it is true. A Vahivanca cares little for the facts, but adjusts his myths to fit "the social life of his patrons."

In a sense, Al Sharpton and associates are professional mythmakers like the Vahivancas. They fabricate status, but of a kind that has never before been sought. The status they fabricate is not that of a higher caste, but the status of victim. By the peculiar logic of the welfare state—which seeks to prevent anyone from losing—to be a victim is to be a winner. The more victimized one is, the higher the recompense he can claim. This is reflected by the avalanche of lawsuits that bury American courts. It is also evident in the statements of many black spokesmen, who lay claim to hereditary status as victims, simply by being black. The case of Tawana Brawley demonstrates how the rewards of being a victim work against maintaining a clear understanding of what really happens. Brawley and her advisors profited by concocting and promoting a fantasy of victimization. For their purposes, the facts mattered little. All that mattered was that the story was broadcast far and wide by the media, making it an instant myth.

Partly because of the role of the media, the more lurid and inflammatory claims attract publicity and are therefore more useful in organizing shakedowns. Provocateurs like Maddox and Sharpton use "black culture" to vindicate black criminals, like the Central Park gang rapists, and to justify threats of violence, which the broader society is invited to avoid through payoffs. The same "logic of irrationality" has led a former Milwaukee city official, Mike McGee, to claim that black crack babies are somehow the victims of whites. He has organized a private militia to back his demands for higher compensation for his community of victims. As reported in the *Economist*: "His uncompromising message: unless some $100 million is invested in Milwaukee's black areas by 1995, the militia will take matters into its own hands with a reign of terror against the white way of life." When the Los Angeles riots stoked media interest in problems of the inner cities, McGee was featured on national television enlarging his ideas to the whole United States.

The turn away from analytic rationality and the blinking of facts by black leaders are sell signals for the central city. Historically, the claim for rewards based on status rather than achievement has been associated with economic decline. And that, in turn, encourages dishonesty, counterproductive behavior, and delusional thinking.

Destitution and Delusional Thinking

A general characteristic of the destitute is that they are prone to delusional thinking. They are far more likely than the rich to believe in black magic, the evil eye, predestination, astrology, and confining cultural taboos. These taboos, such as the Indian injunction against eating cows, predominate among peoples who subsist at the margin of survival, with few assets and little access to credit or capital markets. Simplifying greatly, subsistence taboos and delusions are a substitute for capital and reliance upon the insurance value of money.

The lower the prospect of upward mobility, the more rational it is for the poor to adopt an anti-scientific, delusional worldview. In place of technology, they employ magic. In place of independent investigation, they opt for orthodoxy. Instead of history, they prefer myths. In place of biography, they venerate heroes. And they generally substitute kin-based behavioral allegiances for the impersonal honesty required by the market. If you depend upon your relatives for survival, you cannot afford to be an objective judge of their standards of honesty in dealing with strangers.

Backwardness and Dishonesty

Low standards of honesty that prevail in the underdeveloped countries and in many poorer communities in the West are important obstacles to growth. They were overcome only with difficulty in the industrialization of England and other countries. Although it is largely forgotten now, dishonesty in English government and commerce was rampant until well into the Industrial Revolution. As John Carswell wrote: "The conception of loyalty to a firm, as distinct from obligation to an individual, which is so engrained in our business system, was quite alien. . . . What we should call embezzlement and fraudulent conversion flourished in consequence—but these crimes were unknown to the English law until the end of the eighteenth century. . . . The victim of a bogus prospectus or a fraudulent agent had only himself to blame for lack of 'common prudence.' False pretences was not an offense until 1757."

Counterproductive behaviors and delusional thinking generally follow a functional logic, even when they involve sloppy morality or are out of touch with the facts. They are informed by incentives that become more compelling the more impoverished one becomes. These incentives have a sharper bite in premodern, closed social systems, and in Third World societies where traditional values linger. But the record of modern depressions suggests that any significant increase in poverty will lead to a dramatic surge in delusional thinking. Whereas an isolated individual who adapts to personal failure in delusional ways may be seen as illogical or even mentally ill, when large numbers succumb to the same incentives, the result is a cultural and political phenomenon. In either case, adopting delusional thinking serves the same function for the poor.

> *Yet, ah! why should they know their fate.*
> *Since sorrow never comes too late,*
> *And happiness too swiftly flies?*
> *Thought would destroy their paradise.*
> *No more;—where ignorance is bliss*
> *'Tis folly to be wise.*
>
> —THOMAS GRAY

Poor people generally have only a minimal ability to control events, so attribution of cause and effect in ways remote from the facts may be "the best adjustment the individual can make to an apparently hopeless situation," writes George M. Foster. Frequently, delusions provide solace. They take the burden of failure off the individual and place it elsewhere. In its passive form, delusional thinking puts the blame on fate. Whatever happens is God's will. The more active form of delusional thinking places the blame on other humans, who become scapegoats. This has happened time and again, often enough to provide the basis of predictions that can help you understand what may happen over the decade of the 1990s.

Scapegoating, Conspiracies, and Redistribution

Jealousy of the worldly success of *conversos* (or New Christians), combined with the suspicion that they were crypto-Jews, therefore, helps to explain why they became the chief victims of fifteenth-century mob violence. This violence was also undoubtedly linked with royal debasements of the coinage, severe price inflation, increases in taxation, and monetary reductions.

—ANGUS MACKAY

A rational basis for scapegoating from the point of view of the impoverished is that it often provides an excuse for redistributing wealth. This practical feature makes scapegoating a more attractive form of delusion, especially in economies where some individuals are far enough above subsistence to have some wealth to redistribute. It is to be expected that sudden ill fortune will be widely attributed to the magical conniving of scapegoats. These scapegoats may be practically anyone who seems luckier: wealthier peasant neighbors, foreign devils, international bankers, or Jews. The ugly rioting against foreigners in Germany and the widespread hallucination in Japan that foreign "Jewish investment houses" caused Japanese stocks to crash testify to the universality of scapegoating.

Whether the scapegoats are imagined to perpetrate their deeds through black magic or through other means roughly depends upon the scientific credulity of those with whom the delusion is shared. This, in turn, probably involves a wealth effect. The impoverished in more developed societies are more likely to adopt delusions that involve at least some semblance of economic motivation. But whatever the exact means by which it is imagined that the scapegoats cause the misfortune of those who fail, many elements of the delusion are quite similar. At times of significant income drops they almost invariably involve conspiracies, whether at the village or the global level.

What appears at first approach to be a surprising coincidence in the content of these delusions across time and cultures is, on second thought, exactly what should be expected. The similarities are dictated by the function of the delusion—to exonerate the loser from responsibility for his misfortune. The poor man's pig cannot simply die. It must have been killed by the village "sorcerer," who usually just happens to be the person in the village who is most successful at fattening his own pigs. It is not incidental that the farmer with pigs is also likely to be most able to bear the burden of redistribution.

For the sorcerer or conspirator to achieve this amazing feat requires that he possess occult knowledge not generally available. It also requires that the inner circle to which the sorcerer belongs have some wicked purpose. This could be devil worship, cannibalism, repugnant sexual practices, a commitment to enslave the world—or whatever seems likely to disqualify the conspiracy from common sympathy. The wicked purpose is essential. Otherwise, the loser is still subject to the reproach that he failed to obtain the powerful knowledge himself. To be entirely exonerated, it must appear that he could not be privy to the occult knowledge without forgoing his moral standing—or even risking his soul. And, of course, the delusion that racial exclusion prohibits blacks from getting life's good things serves the same function. The logic of this delusion is much the same, whether it is the poor villager in Africa blaming his dead pig on a neighbor, the Roman pagans attacking early Christians as a cannibal conspiracy, or Midwestern farmers in the depression of the 1890s blaming their debt woes on "Jewish bankers and British gold."

Debtors in debtor countries usually blame their woes on their creditors, a pattern that almost guarantees that the list of scapegoats from the coming crisis will be extended from Jews, whites, the Trilateral Commission, the Queen of England, and the international banks to include the Japanese. Many Americans, especially those employed in smokestack industries, will blame the coming slump on some diabolical Oriental conspiracy. There will be talk of a "secret plan" to reduce the United States to pauperism so that Japanese carmakers can put urban laborers out of work and Korean grocers can cash their welfare checks.

The similarity of these delusions from one case to the next is so great that it is difficult to discern where one ends and another begins. Norman Cohn described a

> specific fantasy which can be traced back to Antiquity. The essence of the fantasy was that there existed, somewhere in the midst of the great society, another society, small and clandestine, which not only threatened the existence of the great society but was also addicted to practices which were felt to be wholly abominable.

In premodern societies, where the scapegoats themselves may have shared a belief in the efficacy of magic, fear of the evil eye seems to have encouraged income redistribution. As Lawrence Stone put it, "Fear of being bewitched must have acted as a powerful incentive to the financially secure in the prime of life to be kind and generous to the old, the sick, and the poor." In societies where the scapegoats are unlikely to fear being bewitched, there is the danger of more active political measures motivated by delusional thinking.

Some of these actions, like the tortures of witches by the Inquisition, had the not-incidental effect of allowing those who identified the conspiracy to seize the property of their victims. Inquisitors in Germany in the early thirteenth century claimed that leading citizens were in league with the Devil. Allegedly, they were flying to and from orgies where they were said to have kissed the Devil's bottom and carried on in other unmentionable ways. Those who were charged with participating in these devilish conspiracies were tortured mercilessly. If they confessed, as most did, their property was taken.

Usually, though not always, delusional thinking masks an element of theft. The victims of the delusion are usually those with something to steal.

In light of this analysis, it is no surprise that politics tends to take frightening turns in the wake of economic depressions. The rise of the Nazis to power in Germany in 1933 followed the steepest drop of real income in any industrial country during the last depression. This led on to the concentration camps and the gas chambers. Such horrors have tended to coincide with economic destitution, whether of the pagan middle class in late Rome, when Christians were fed to the lions, or the drought-wracked Castilian farmers of the fifteenth century, who went on violent rampages when their crops failed, slaughtering Jews and *conversos*.

THE EFFECTS OF TELEVISION

Television could facilitate the spread of delusions and conspiracy theories in the 1990s. We argued in the last chapter that the impact of improved computational technology in creating a new paradigm for understanding complex systems will be to sharpen the understanding of educated opinion. But little of this will necessarily spill over into the slums and into the marginal neighborhoods that could become slums. There, technology will have other consequences for the way humans think. For mass culture, or cultures, television will play an important role that cannot be ignored.

The global impact of TV is not wholly bad, of course. Its positive dimensions were well illustrated by the role of the mass communication media in the collapse of Communism in Eastern Europe. The totalitarian systems fell, in part, because radio and television allowed people to see that they were not alone in wishing change. From East Germany to Rumania, dictators stumbled over people who could no longer be kept in the dark when the television was on.

Yet there are also negative influences of broadcasting that relate directly to a coming upsurge of scapegoating, conspiracies, and delusional politics. Television drowns out the abstract. It enables people to see, but discourages them from taking an interest in what cannot be seen. Abstractions are far more difficult to portray on television than they are on the printed page. This has important implications. "The liberation from the visual," as Oswald Spengler wrote, has been called one of the great achievements of the Western mind. Abstractions are the basis of all higher-order thinking. As we explained earlier in this chapter, primitive societies are distinguished by larger vocabularies for description of certain aspects of the physical world, and the almost complete absence of words for abstractions. If "liberation from the visual" was indeed a great achievement of Western culture, then many minds are once again being bound to visual impressions.

The mere fact that the eye is engaged in television implies that it should be satisfied by watching some kind of action. Abstractions, by their nature, are not visible. TV is particularly ill suited to the coverage of economics, which is almost an entirely abstract field of understanding. TV is even poor in focusing on public affairs, the photogenic half-brother of economics. Coverage is limited almost exclusively to the transmission of small excerpts of live or recently completed events, with voice-over commentary. TV is a medium where drama and confrontations attract a larger audience than calm discussion. Al Sharpton, who describes himself as "media wise," has commanded more air time in America's largest television market from the "hungry media" than any sober analyst of the causes of poverty. He has done it by firing off

"charges so outlandish and reckless they sometimes verged on the halluci-
natory," as reported in *People*.

There is little abstract analysis on TV. The nearest that television comes to
abstraction is in what are called in the industry "talking heads," interview
shows or short segments of news analysis by commentators. "Talking heads"
programs have weak audience appeal. The most successful in the United
States, such as the "MacNeil/Lehrer Newshour" or "Wall Street Week," are
public television programs with a narrow upper-income audience.

By reasserting the primacy of the visual over the abstract in mass culture,
TV may help remake the modern mind in another way. Even as computers
allow the educated to grasp the patterns in life at a new, higher level of
abstraction, TV drowns out abstraction for the uneducated. Never before in
history have the cultures of people living in the same terrain split in this way.
It is a split that is likely to grow as mass broadcasting gives way to multi-
channel cable, satellite, and VCR systems, allowing viewers greater choice
over the programming they watch. In the early decades of television, when
there were only a few program choices, anyone who watched TV eight hours
a day was obliged to expose himself to at least some coverage of public affairs.
Everyone watched "I Love Lucy." This is no longer so. If you so choose, you
could watch nothing but music video. Canada could disappear and you would
never hear about it until it became a song.

Television may also have contributed to a disturbing shriveling of the time
horizon of the public. Past and future are shallow in broadcasting. The visual
imperative is as powerful in the coverage of the past, or discussion of the
future, as it is the present. There is no such thing as a thirty-second take of
the future, much less a one-second take of the future, which is the average
length of visual images on American news programs. Consequently, TV offers
little forward vision, beyond scheduling information about programs to be
aired later in the day.

The minimal historic information that appears on TV is restricted to one-
or two-second excerpts of old news clips, and a few still shots of past events.
But these are seldom aired because their visual quality is poor, and those
more than a few decades old are not in color. It is probable that the strongest
sense of the past on television is conveyed by old movies and costume dramas,
which seem to appeal more to audience segments already interested in history
rather than to the great majority. Otherwise, old programs would have higher
ratings than they do.

The sense of the past for one who draws his information mainly from
television can be even more shallow than in primitive societies. Even the
most backward peoples, who have no clear measurement of time, manage
at least a vague sense of the succession of events extending back for about

half a century. Test results of young Americans who grew up watching eight or more hours of television a day show that their grasp of historic events is remarkably weak. Great numbers cannot identify Winston Churchill, or say when World War II was fought. Even someone who has seen *Casablanca* ten times may have only a sketchy grasp of the chronology of the twentieth century.

The effects of television viewing in drying up the historic sense and diminishing the abstract have probably been most fully felt in the United States, where more people have watched more TV longer than anywhere else. The collapse of the public's time horizon and attention span could reduce long-term savings and economic growth. The widely noted deterioration in the ability of young Americans to do conceptual thinking and mathematics is quite possibly a roundabout consequence of television viewing. So, indeed, may be their lack of grounding in basic principles of behavior.

To a surprising extent, many American children in recent years have been reared in front of a television set. They more or less go about their own business without close instruction from a parent. In this respect, American childhood in 1991 is in some respects nearer to childhood of primitive tribes than it is to the middle- and upper-class childhood of Americans sixty years ago. An eighteenth-century description of American Indian family life described it this way:

> Every one does what he pleases. A father and mother with their children, live like persons whom chance has brought together, and whom no common bond unites. Their manner of educating their children is suitable to this principle. They never chastise or punish them, even during their infancy. As they advance in years, they allow them to be entirely masters of their own actions, and responsible to no body.

This description could be fairly applied to American children in the age of television.

TELEVISION AND VIOLENCE

Television viewing may be a factor in the startling increase in violence that has tended to follow ten to fifteen years after television is introduced in a society. Dr. Brandon Centerwall, professor of epidemiology at the University of Washington, has linked the doubling of murder rates among white populations in three countries to TV viewing. He limited his study to whites because they were the first to own televisions. He believes that the twenty-five hours a week children spend before the set reduces the time they have available for developing social skills. It is more likely that repetitious viewing of violent acts reduces inhibitions against resorting to violence. People tend to imitate behaviors they see. The fact that youth are becoming desensitized to violence could well be connected to the constant exposure to violence on television. In any event, children who cannot comprehend "Do unto others as you would have others do unto you" are not likely to make much headway in understanding mathematically more elaborate abstractions.

This is a problem because many important developments can be understood only in abstract form. The interrelationship between the budget deficit and future living standards is not even potentially the subject of the kind of human drama that "Death by Drug Addiction" is. The military action to force General Manuel Noriega from power in Panama could easily be depicted in a TV miniseries. The link between the dead junkie or a gang battle on the streets of Chicago and narco-militarism involves a few steps to be sure. But these are all steps that can be traced visually, following in the footsteps of individuals. The link goes from the junkie, to his pusher, who is a person, to the wholesale drug cartel, to the drug smugglers, to the corrupt Latin officials in link with the drug cartel. All the links in the chain are comprised of actions motivated by incentives that are comprehensible to anyone.

On the other hand, the links between the budget deficit and the lower living standards have no direct correlation with motives at all. They cannot be traced by following in the footsteps of anyone. The budget deficit was caused by the fiscal actions of Congress, whose members all deny, and rightly so, that their intention was to reduce American competitiveness, slow economic growth, and lower living standards. We would argue that this is exactly the effect of their actions. But this cannot be demonstrated by drama. It can be demonstrated only by argument.

Coming: Widespread Belief in Conspiracies

If, as we suggest, TV has helped to drown out abstract thinking, this has troubling consequences. It means that when crises do occur, and thereafter require explanation, their causes are unlikely to be grasped. If our argument is correct, conspiracy theories in an age of television will be more widely popular than in the immediate past when abstract thinking played a larger role in "public reason" than it does today. The tendency to dramatize and personalize outcomes could also contribute to the popularity of conspiracy theories. Such theories flourish when and where people are overtaken by events they do not like and cannot readily understand. Lacking an emotionally satisfying explanation, they invent one.

As examples we list below suggest, the most luxuriant growth of the conspiracy underbrush was in black communities as the nineties opened. This is
because economic conditions there deteriorated more sharply in the 1980s
than elsewhere. But everywhere people feel a sense of loss or defeat, they
blame the Conspiracy, with a capital C. It is an all-purpose cabal of the wealthy
and powerful who are imagined to be secretly responsible for everything from
global warming to New York Yankee manager Billy Martin's fatal traffic
accident. If a farmer loses his farm, the conspirators took it away. Is there an
AIDS plague? "A Chicago city official says that 'the AIDS epidemic is a result
of doctors, especially Jewish ones, who inject the AIDS virus in blacks.' " Do
groceries cost more in poor neighborhoods? The manipulators wanted it that
way. Do crack-addicted mothers give birth to sickly babies who tend to die?
There must be a white plot to kill black babies. Was the black mayor of
Washington, D.C., a junkie, videotaped smoking crack cocaine by the FBI?
There must be a "plan" among white people to wrest control of the city away
from blacks. The editor of a weekly in Washington called for blacks to respond
to the alleged "white conspiracy" against Marion Barry with "a good old-
fashioned, blood-soaking race war."

> *Pullin' out a silly club so you stand*
> *With a fake-ass badge and a gun in your hand*
> *Take off the gun so you can see what's up*
> *And we'll go at it, punk, and I'm a f—— you up . . .*

> —N.W.A. (NIGGERS WITH ATTITUDE), 1989

The seeds are being sown for racial confrontations and disorder at an unprecedented level. The riots in Los Angeles, Toronto, and other North American cities in the spring of 1992 are only the first installments of a violent
urban depreciation crisis. Much of this violence will originate with angry
blacks, who are among the main economic losers from the decline of high-
paying manufacturing jobs in urban America. There is already ample evidence
of black scapegoating of Jews, Orientals, and whites. The falling demand for
poorly educated assembly-line workers from the mid-seventies on has deepened the ranks of the black underclass. In a severe recession or depression,
large numbers of unemployed blacks could affiliate with the political message
of the underclass "black culture." In 1988, according to *Money* magazine,
"manufacturing occupations such as machine operators and laborers were
the largest single job group for black men." Chairman William Gibson of the
NAACP commented, "A lot of the black middle class is fewer than two
paychecks away from being in the underclass."

The Bad Rap on Africa

Black rap musicians are the heralds of a new imperial culture. Advocacy of racial hatred and violence against whites did not originate with Sister Souljah in the spring of 1992. It has been a major subtext of black rap music for years, as analyzed in the first edition of this book. Rap singers and others who extol the underclass in terms of symbols and traditions thought to be indigenous to Africa are rationalizing a criminal life-style. What they proclaim as "black culture" is not a traditional culture, but a perverse modern culture in an African robe. It mixes up self-indulgent consumerism, influences of television, and the values of the violent underworld.

The resulting mixture is not appropriate for success in the cosmopolitan economy of the Information Age, nor does it preserve the coherence and moral structure of traditional African societies. They were cultures of strong families, not cultures of irresponsibility in which 60 percent of children were born illegitimate, as they were among blacks in the United States in 1990. Traditional African cultures were not cultures of crime, in which 25 percent or more of the young men were imprisoned as in the modern United States. The murder rate of black men in Africa was not one in thirty murdered by their fellows.

THE POLITICIZATION OF CRIME

Recently in the Amsterdam News, a black-oriented weekly, the Rev. Lawrence E. Lucas, pastor of Resurrection Roman Catholic Church in Harlem, advised black parents to tell their children not to trust the police or the white-dominated media. He also wrote that a major mission of the criminal justice system is "putting young black males in jails by any means necessary so that lower class whites can exercise authority, supremacy and make a nice living."

—*NEW YORK TIMES*, September 9, 1990

The culture of the slums rationalizes and politicizes crime. This has become so overt that black juries blink at overt evidence of crimes by blacks out of racial solidarity. This was evident in the 1990 trial of Marion Barry, where a jury of two whites and ten blacks could not agree to a guilty verdict on numerous felony charges. News reports of other jury deliberations suggested that all-black juries acquitted black defendants of crimes as serious as murder, simply because one or more jurors were politically adamant against sending more blacks to prison. Race-based denial will be a growing phenomenon in the 1990s.

The Perverse Success of a Failing Culture

Birth rates have tended to fall as income rose since the early nineteenth century. But never in history have cultural groups been able to sustain more offspring than they could support from their own resources. Never until now. For the first time in tens of thousands of generations, a group is growing in numbers and influence precisely because it adheres to counterproductive values. This reverses the normal logic of evolution. Normally, it is the individuals who are most successful in their niche who leave behind the most offspring. The next generation is therefore more or less automatically inculcated with whatever values make for success in that environment. Not so with the underclass as the twentieth century draws to a close. It has become the most rapidly growing segment of the population, not because those who are part of it follow an economically successful life strategy, but because they don't.

The welfare state has made failure pay in evolutionary terms. Underclass women give birth to 60 percent more children than middle-class women—black or white. But even this statistic underestimates the impact on the population. Underclass women not only have more children, they also give birth at a younger age, leading to a geometric rise in the underclass population over time. This was highlighted when the *Guinness Book of World Records* named Delores Davis as the world's youngest great-grandmother at the age of forty-four. Davis is a Kentucky resident who dropped out of school to give birth, as did her daughter and then her granddaughter. By the year 2010, four times as many individuals joining the work force will have been born the children of unwed mothers. One-third will have been born to teenagers. Continuation of this trend would mean that each successive cohort entering the work force in the next century will contain a larger proportion of disadvantaged or underclass individuals.

This increases tremendously the demands upon education to correct widening cultural gaps. One might as well ask an old lady to bend a steel bar with her bare hands. Evidence shows that the deficit in educational skills, otherwise known as the "human capital deficit," is widening rather than closing. In its 1983 report, *A Nation at Risk,* the National Commission on Excellence in Education summarized the situation this way: "For the first time in the history of the country, the educational skills of one generation will not surpass, will not equal, will not even approach those of their parents." A more recent survey of the National Assessment of Educational Progress came to an even more grim conclusion. It found that among young adults aged twenty-one through twenty-five, only about 60 percent of whites, 40 percent of Hispanics, and 25 percent of blacks could "locate information in a news article or an almanac." "Only 44% of whites, 20% of Hispanics, and 8% of blacks could correctly determine change due from the purchase of a restaurant meal." And just 25 percent of young whites, 7 percent of young Hispanics, and 3 percent of young blacks could comprehend a bus schedule. Whole sections of human society are condemned to fall further behind in understanding how the world is organized, and in supporting themselves in the Information Age.

The culture of the slums has become an imperial culture. It grows in influence not because of its strengths as a life strategy, but because of its failures. Perverse values have been reinforced by political developments since the 1960s—which in turn were a response to the increasing vulnerability of the nation-state to violence organized by small groups.

To be a loser, a victim, is now an asset that can be utilized to demand payoffs from the larger society. And in some ways, the more irrational the claims by the victim, the more effective they are. Irrationality makes the implied shakedown more threatening. The breakdown of law enforcement has further compounded the incentive traps of the welfare state by increasing the returns from antisocial behavior. Crime pays, especially for black criminals, whose misbehavior is rationalized as never before.

As a consequence, the underclass has gone from a tiny subculture in inner cities during the 1960s to become a dominant culture in many urban areas today. The rapid growth of the underclass has meant a dramatic increase in violence, drug addiction, and social disintegration among blacks. In 1965, only 17 percent of all black babies were born illegitimate. In 1990, the number was 61 percent. And, the *Economist* reported, about "three-quarters of black babies born in the big inner cities of America were births to unwed mothers; of these, half were to teenagers." The large number of births to teenage girls and unwed mothers compounds the problems of poverty, but increases the raw power of the underclass. The current differential in births between the middle class of all races and the underclass will reshape the megapolitical geography of North America.

Especially worrisome are untold thousands of "crack babies" born each year to drug-addicted mothers. The first crack babies to reach school age in 1989 showed early signs of sociopathic behavior. Sociopathic behavior patterns normally appear to be established by the age of eight.

The concentration of growing populations of disgruntled and impoverished people in cities dependent upon vulnerable infrastructure is fraught with dangers. Not the least of these is a strong likelihood that the social solidarity that underlies the welfare state will be broken apart in the years to come. The steadily escalating costs of supporting dependent populations will try the patience of the more successful in an economic downturn. And a growing demographic divide will destroy the credibility of the promise that current generations of Americans who are paying heavy payroll taxes will realize a return on that investment. Consider that the crack baby generation is meant to pay the unfunded intergenerational transfers known as "Social Security" and "Medicare." It is highly unlikely, to say the least, that an increasingly nonwhite and impoverished work force will tolerate employment taxes of up to 50 percent of payroll to keep the largely white Baby Boom retirees in leisure.

But that is a problem for the next century.

Civil Disorder

There are other, more immediate dangers of social explosion to be considered. You do not need to ponder long to realize what these dangers are. They are spelled out in the lyrics of best-selling rap songs:

> *When I'm called off,*
> *I got a sawed off*
> *Squeeze the trigger and*
> *bodies are hauled off . . .*

> —ICE CUBE, N.W.A.

The two predominant powers of the past two centuries, Great Britain and the United States, are both exposed to dangers of violence and disorder that could spill out of inner cities during the 1990s, animated by a new imperial culture: the culture of the slums. The United States, of course, stands in far greater danger. There is more crack cocaine in use in American slums than in British ones. The American underclass is far larger, and its culture is more chauvinistic.

It is spreading for demographic reasons. And its influence is also widening for economic reasons. It pays. The self-indulgent, violent, present-centered behavior glorified in much rap music is also glorified by heavy metal—rap's white counterpart. In one best-selling song, the lyrics claim that happiness could be achieved by killing a lover who nagged.

Heavy metal music is not only violent and sociopathic, it is also racist. It is white racist and anti-black. There is an obvious danger that unskilled whites may make blacks the scapegoats for their distress, just as underclass blacks are already making whites and Korean greengrocers the scapegoats for their troubles. With two increasingly aggressive and irrational groups seeking to tag one another with the blame for their failure, a social explosion is possible.

Delusional Politics

The powerful impulse to fix blame on scapegoats is likely to find expression in politics with a highly delusional element. In urban areas where blacks constitute majorities, there may be overt anti-white regimes. They could well confiscate the property of whites through indirect means, such as allowing services and infrastructure in white neighborhoods to break down, and by defaulting on bonds, mostly owned by whites.

But because whites outnumber blacks, the larger danger in the 1990s will be of delusional political programs supported by the white majority. The rise of the Nazi party in Germany after 1929, with its occult emphasis upon race, followed the steepest drop of living standards in any industrial country. German unemployment rose to 30.1 percent. Germany then, like the United States today, entered the depression with a financial and banking system that was "highly unstable." Germany then, like America in 1990, was dependent upon foreign borrowing to finance artificially high living standards. The withdrawal of foreign funds compelled German leaders to follow a contractionary budget policy, slashing government spending and raising taxes. The result was "a paranoia about bankers' conspiracies" and a revulsion by the public against what was seen as mostly "hot air" coming from "corrupt" democratic institutions. As living standards plunged, delusional thinking gripped an entire nation.

If there is a major economic contraction in the 1990s, it is likely to lead to sharp curtailment of government spending and tax increases in major metropolitan areas. Deep reductions in military manpower levels will also affect blacks more than whites, because of the high concentration of blacks in the armed forces. The same will be true of almost all federal government manpower reductions. Government at the state and local levels also employs disproportionate numbers of blacks. City governments are particularly likely to face budget crises, as we explore in more detail in a coming chapter. Welfare payments will be cut in real terms. Housing subsidies will be reduced. Even police protection is likely to be cut back because there simply will not be the money to continue funding programs at current levels. In cities where local governments are the main employers of the black middle class, as administrators and teachers, cutbacks will further inflame animosities.

THE DEPRECIATION CRISIS OF CENTRAL CITIES

Amid the bleak menace of the boarded-up tenements and burnt-out apartment blocks of the no-man's-land on the rim of Harlem, the use of "crack," a highly addictive cocaine derivative unknown before 1984, has turned this urban landscape into a battle-ravaged area more akin to Beirut, or to Berlin in 1945, than to one of the world's largest cities in an industrially advanced country.

—CINDY FAZEY, *Financial Times,*
February 19, 1989

Many major American cities are extremely vulnerable, centralized organizations that depend upon overtaxed infrastructure, much of it more than a century old. An island city like New York is particularly at risk. New York is the most centralized, densely populated metropolis in America. Practically everything it requires to survive must be imported by train, truck, and ship, or brought in cables and pipes like electricity and water. Hundreds of thousands of vehicles pass in and out of Manhattan every day. Trains of food and shiploads of newsprint arrive while garbage scows depart. By 1991, a landfill in Staten Island may become the world's largest man-made object, exceeding the cubic volume of the Great Wall of China.

New York is highly vulnerable to sabotage, terrorism, and simple infrastructure breakdown. It depends for its viability on the assumption that the overwhelming majority of its inhabitants will adhere to civilized lifeways. Tunnels, bridges, pumping stations, power lines, are all practically unguarded. Many could not be guarded. They are artifacts of a "brittle power," left over from the age of large-scale organizations and social order that could be shattered with a blow. The wonder is that some henchman of Saddam Hussein or a terrorist group or a criminal gang has not already held the city to ransom by sabotaging crucial facilities. Simply turning off the electricity brings the city to a halt. The Sendero Luminoso, the nihilist guerrilla band who terrorize Peru, have many times turned off the lights in Lima, shut off the water, and closed down the sewage systems. It would be militarily easier to disrupt New York, and the damage done would be greater.

As the 1990s unfold, New York could become as violent as Rio de Janeiro, with a new class warfare waged in the streets by muggers, kidnappers, and criminal terrorists. It is not uncommon for criminal bands in Brazil to "assault entire apartment buildings, systematically looting them, floor by floor." Something similar could happen in New York.

By the year 2000, New York could be a Gotham City without Batman. Currently thriving buildings could stand empty. The communications, banking, and financial industries now headquartered in New York are likely to be downsized, file for bankruptcy, or flee the city. Midtown Manhattan could end up like downtown Detroit, a rapidly depreciating shell, prey to beggars and criminals. Other cities particularly at risk because of their high concentrations of underclass population are Miami, Dallas, Philadelphia, Chicago, Houston, Baltimore, and Washington, D.C. But practically every city with a large underclass is at risk. Presumably, if Councilman McGee is a man of his word, and tries to wage his promised "reign of terror," Milwaukee will be an unhappy place by 1995.

CRIMINAL GANGS AND GUERRILLA WAR

Lacking an infrastructure capable of securing property and policing the safety of individuals, Third World countries have fallen prey to economic destitution, rampant crime, corrupt police, and guerrilla war. In these circumstances, the distinction between ordinary criminal gangs plundering the public and guerrilla movements imposing "taxes" has blurred. This is especially true as modern technology has made it easier for rebellions to sustain themselves with little or no outside help. This was vividly demonstrated in Mozambique, where the Renamo movement showed how cheap, hand-held computers could be used to orchestrate a bootstrap rebellion. It appeared to be only a matter of time before the techniques applied in Mozambique spread elsewhere.

The connection between crime and political upheaval has been even more spectacularly demonstrated in countries like Lebanon, Colombia, and Peru, major centers of drug traffic. There, the breakdown of order was hastened by drug lords with bankrolls larger than those of governments. There is also a close connection between drug dealing and terrorism. Edward Mortimer wrote in the *Financial Times*: "Most terrorist groups finance themselves wholly or partly by criminal activity—bank-robbery, extortion and drugs."

Third World–style violence has already been imported into the city streets and once quiet countryside of America. So much crack cocaine is being diverted through rural areas that they are experiencing an unprecedented level of violence. The murder capital of the United States is not Washington, D.C., or even Detroit, but Albany, Georgia. And that is surprising to anyone in Washington, because the drug lords and junkies have made America's capital a "City Under Siege." A local television station runs a nightly report under that name detailing the gun battles that ring out over the city as the politicians sleep.

When Mikhail Gorbachev said, "We can hear threats of approaching chaos

and talk of a threatened coup, and even of civil war," he prophetically acknowledged a collapse of what had been the globe's leading totalitarian state.
The danger of disruption of civil society in America has not been as frankly
acknowledged by America's leaders. Nor has there been much public understanding of how the threat to public order is heightened by the drug trade.
It gives criminal gangs a vested interest in destroying a legal system already
exposed to growing megapolitical danger.

The drug lords are the wealthiest people on the planet. The *Economist*
estimates profits from the cocaine trade alone in the United States at ninety-
five billion dollars annually. This is considerably more than the total economy
of Saudi Arabia, with all its oil wealth. It is greater than the military budget
of West Germany, France, Great Britain, China, or even Japan. Ninety-five
billion dollars is only marginally less than the nominal military spending of
the Soviet Union. It is far greater than the combined expenditures on law
enforcement by all levels of government in the United States. The drug cartels
are not rinky-dink, back-alley criminals. They are financial superpowers,
endowed with all the worst possible traits for attacking the foundations of
social order. They are unscrupulous. Violent. Adept at clandestine organization. And richer than governments.

They not only threaten domestic peace, they are now a force to reckon
with in international affairs. They finance guerrilla wars, or suppress them,
as their interests dictate, and they can outbid even the U.S. government for
the allegiance of often corruptible foreign leaders. Illegal drug profits have
literally bankrolled the enemies of civil society—given them gigantic sums
with which to finance the development of criminal gangs, purchase weapons,
bribe police and judicial officials, and if that fails, employ murderers and
terrorists to shoot down anyone who stands in their way, from the local
school crossing guard to the Justices of the Supreme Court.

Nothing could be better calculated to destroy the foundations of economic
progress than to hand billions of annual cocaine profits to murderous drug
lords on terms that give them a vested interest in destroying the rule of law.
America has literally funded an internal enemy and invited attack on the
system at its most vulnerable points.

A stable system of property rights, an honest police force, and a dependable
judiciary are historical accidents, rare in the experience of the world. They
are hard to create, and easy to destroy, especially under current technological
conditions, which make it easy for small groups to wield effective military
power. You need only look at countries like Colombia and Lebanon, where
organized authority has always been weak, to see the havoc that results where
enfeebled authorities are unable to enforce the reach of law against its heavily

armed antagonists. Not coincidentally, drug dealers have played a major role in financing and arming paramilitary organizations in both countries to provide security for the drug trade.

Telepresence and Drug Legalization

Before the 1990s come to end, it is likely that America will learn from the evidence of the Soviet Union cracking up that the logic of disorder can overtake even superpowers. To prevent police and prosecutors from being corrupted, the prohibition against drugs may well be abandoned, just as the prohibition against alcohol was abandoned soon after the last depression bottomed out.

A factor contributing to this decision will be the continued rapid advancement of computational power. It has been growing at an exponential rate since about 1970. By the middle 1990s, "artificial reality" machines will be available that will create stunning computer images of artificial worlds. Such technology is already available in crude form. NASA has a program for computational fluid dynamics in which operators get the sensation of stepping out and opening a window with their hands to enter. They exit the program by closing the window. This is part of a growing development in which computer-driven systems will be tied in with physical and mental processes.

Improvements in fiber optics and high-resolution television technology will make "telepresence" a reality sometime in the 1990s. Telepresence will provide individuals with a realistic sensation of being practically anywhere, or doing practically anything. As the *Wall Street Journal* has reported, these artificial reality machines will "use remarkably crisp pictures and sound to 'deliver' a viewer to a pristine tropical beach, to a big football game or to a quiet mountaintop retreat. Japanese researchers envision golfers practicing their swings in front of three-dimensional simulations of courses." Telepresence will also enable people to travel with Sergeant Pepper in a yellow submarine, go with Mr. Spock on a Star Trek, or enter the world of the Hobbits. Practically any construct reality that could be imagined, could be made to seem real.

People who don't like reality as it is will be able to make up their own realities and enter them on a real-time basis. Artificial reality will make at least some uses of hallucinogenic drugs obsolete. It will breech the taboo against altering reality, but do it in a technological rather than a pharmaceutical way, thus antiquating part of the reason that drug use is banned. Telepresence, of course, will not directly affect the chemistry of the brain, but if controlling their own artificial realities gives people satisfaction, it may substitute for drugs.

Of course, the technological equivalent to the drug culture will have some of the same drawbacks as drugs. Individuals who can retreat into an artificial reality will care less about understanding or changing the real reality, which still exists when someone pulls the plug and the music stops. Nonetheless, technological dependence has a great advantage over drug dependence. The flow of funds it generates brings people into the mainstream economy and culture. The "pushers" of artificial reality will not have incentives to destroy social peace and the whole legal system.

Legalization would also minimize the strength of nihilistic drug cartels and guerrilla movements supported by drugs in already weakened Third World countries, not to mention cities in the West. It is the wad of easy cash that has encouraged kids in urban areas to abandon school and turn to the streets. It is the drug money that pays for the murderous antics of the Sendero Luminoso. Without the many billions a year of illegal drug profits that line the pockets of drug lords and criminal gangs, they would be less able to corrupt, subvert, and terrorize society.

Already a Shooting War

As the 1980s ended, there was a shooting war going on in Washington, D.C. In the worst months, the murder rate approached two a day. At that pace, almost one person in a thousand living in Washington could be murdered in a single year. Given a normal expectation of life, that would mean a Washington resident has about a one in fifteen chance of dying by murder rather than by any other cause. It may occur, as in the case of one prominent lawyer, when a killer guns him down as his car pauses for a red light within the shadow of the U.S. Capitol. It is more likely to be, like the case of three drug dealers, in a fight over turf on the streets.

The murder rates are much lower among the white population and among women. About 10 percent of Washingtonians fall into the highest risk category of young black males. If only half of those killed are in this category—and estimates are higher than that—then one young black man in two hundred could be murdered in Washington, D.C, in a year.

That means that a black boy of fifteen living in the capital city of the United States has one chance in ten of being murdered before he reaches the age of thirty-five. The casualty rate is much higher than that of Northern Ireland or the West Bank, with their much higher populations.

The white population is indeed afraid, and the black population is both afraid and angry. One well-known black columnist asked in 1989 for the U.S. Army to take over the policing of Washington to restore order. Martial law for Washington is a striking proposal.

Washington is not the only city in America to suffer from this epidemic of violence. The same is true of New York, Miami, and Los Angeles, where the Hispanics are suffering in equal degree to the blacks, as some seventy thousand gang members battle one another and police for control of the city's streets. In Detroit, which is also a leading contender for the title "murder capital of the United States," violent motorists shoot each other on the freeway—a feature of disorder that has also spread to Southern California. A popular bumper sticker in Los Angeles reads, "Don't shoot, I'll pull over."

Compared with the United States, Britain is still relatively free of murder, and still much less penetrated by crack. European murder rates tend to bunch together at about a quarter of those of the United States. Nevertheless, some of the conditions that have caused the rise in violence in the United States are present in Britain. Criminals can obtain guns, in spite of stiff gun laws. The drug businesses, with their enormous wealth, are international, and keen to expand their European markets. Britain, and France as well, have depressed inner cities with minority racial groups. There is a culture of the slums that grows with drug use. The statistics for serious crime show a long-term rise. Twenty-five years ago most of New York was as safe as London is now, and London is becoming less safe.

The public in America is now more concerned with violence and crime than with the threat of foreign powers. That was already becoming evident before the Soviet Union collapsed. Increasingly, the problems of disorder in the world are local problems. Street by street, neighborhood by neighborhood, violence and criminality are impinging on people's lives in most unwelcome ways. If the capital city of the United States can be almost destroyed by drugs, violence, and urban poverty—even before the depression reaches its deepest stages—no other city can regard itself as safe.

The rising tide of disorder in the world will be felt first in the West, not in political collapse as in the Soviet Union, but in the collapse of neighborhoods, and a rising tide of violence and crime. This will lead to greater candor about the destructive culture of the slums. But clearer thinking about the role per-verse culture plays in pauperizing cities will probably come too late to prevent society at large from paying a dear price for the breakdown of black families. Urban areas with concentrated underclass populations will suffer an inten-sified depreciation crisis. Banks, S & Ls, insurance companies, and private families will suffer a massive write-off of capital and infrastructure invested in these now overly centralized and vulnerable locations. Even buildings in other center cities, untouched by the rioting in Los Angeles or the rioting to come, will lose value as if they had been charred by the flames. In conditions of growing disorder and rapidly changing information technology, cities will no longer be centers of productivity. They will be centers of high costs, crime, and decay, ever more vulnerable to civil unrest.

The heavy welfare and make-work spending that temporized the effects of cultural failure, while making it worse, will no longer be supportable. City governments will be profoundly insolvent. Because subtle threats will no longer suffice to engineer redistribution, threats of violence will escalate. There will be more Mike McGees, and more battalions of black militia promising to make war on "the white way of life."

Yet the consequences of urban bankruptcy will not be all bad. The condescending intellectual fashion for holding blacks to lower standards of behavior will fade in the 1990s, as bankrupt ideas tend to do. The 13 percent of affluent black families will come to have their accomplishments appreciated as more evidence of their own individual effort, rather than the tarnished trophies of entitlement. One of the more wicked consequences of the temporizing of black racism is the way that it devalued the solid accomplishments of middle-class and affluent blacks. Never in history have successful individuals sought to be viewed as victims. A clearer recognition that black poverty is a problem of culture, not race, will free middle-class blacks from condescension, and liberate them from the guilts and burdens of underclass failure. A successful black is no more responsible for the antisocial behavior in the criminal slums than is any white or Oriental who succeeds in the modern marketplace.

In summary, we expect the revolution of the 1990s to heighten the confrontation between mainstream culture and the imperial culture of the slums. This clash will be manifested in a rise of "irrational" and criminal behavior, and an increasing military problem of maintaining social order in inner cities. There will not only be a danger of increasing anti-white violence by underclass blacks, there will also be a danger that economically disadvantaged whites will blame all blacks for their problems. Periods of abrupt change are often times when societies are stressed, torn by violence, overtaken by mass movements that appeal to emotion rather than reason. This could become startlingly evident when the music stops.

CHAPTER ELEVEN

DEFLATION AHEAD

FINANCIAL FALLOUT IN THE ATOMIC AGE

Where the army is, prices are high; when prices rise the wealth of the people is exhausted.

—SUN TZU,
The Art of War, chapter II, 12,
circa 400 B.C.

MOST PEOPLE believe that another debt deflation is no more likely than an invasion from Mars. And they behave accordingly. The average resident of English-speaking countries is deeply in debt, with the largest part of his assets invested in real estate. This is a gamble on inflation. For most real estate and other tangible assets to hold their 1990 value, let alone appreciate, inflation must rise sharply—as it seemed to be doing during the Kuwait-Iraq crisis. Even a modest deflation would send inflated real estate, collectibles, and many other assets tumbling, wiping out many individuals, families, and businesses. Yet in spite of the huge investment stake we all have in understanding the dynamics of deflation, most individuals refuse to think about it, relying upon political promises that there will never be another depression.

Deflation More Likely Than People Think

You have heard the reasoning before. . . . Politicians have high-speed printing presses. They can make them run as fast as they please. In a choice, they would always want to inflate. Therefore, there can never be deflation.

It is a sweet, simple argument. If it were true, it would make your job as an investor incredibly easy. All you would have to do to make a fortune is place a whole-hog bet on inflation. Just hock every asset you have, run your credit to the limit, buy some gold, and lie back to wait for the silly politicians to float your easy chair down to paradise on a river of red ink.

We don't think it is that simple. Those who say that government has the power to prevent deflation are right. But they are answering the wrong question. Obviously, the government can print all the money it wants. It can slap any number of zeros on a piece of paper and raise the nominal money supply to a higher power. This has always been true. But it is a mistake to stop your inquiry there, because you have merely answered a misleading question. One could just as well say that "the government has the power to prevent you from dying of cancer." It can. By taking you out and shooting you first. But the cure in that case, like the printing-press cure for deflation, is worse than the disease.

The key to understanding the danger of deflation is to recognize that the process of deflation is less transparent than the process of inflation. Inflation corresponds to an understandable motive on the part of politicians. It is easy to see how they could benefit from printing money. The early stages of inflation are often periods of boom. Easy money makes people feel richer than they are. The inflationary euphoria is good for reelection prospects. Politicians tend to prosper when their constituents prosper. So if inflating puts more money in everybody's pockets, it is clear why politicians are tempted to do it.

Inflation is particularly attractive to politicians in an economy with many organized special interests, what Mancur Olson calls "distributional coalitions." These groups obtain special favors for themselves—such as subsidies, price supports, and monopolistic wages that are usually specified in nominal dollars. This means that inflation can devalue the loot that these groups extract from society. A dairy price support, for example, will be less costly to taxpayers and consumers if the dollar loses 10 percent of its value. A monopolistic wage that is 20 percent too high for prevailing conditions will cause less unemployment if inflation reduces it in real terms by 10 percent. For these reasons, modest inflation may in some respects increase real output. It is one of the few ways that weakened governments can loosen the stranglehold of special interests over the economy. They demand more than the economy can afford, perhaps even than the economy produces. If the total of their demands comes to an impossible 110 percent of output, a weak government can say yes to everyone, and use inflation as a convenient gimmick for devaluing its impossible promises.

No Motive to Deflate

Of course, we don't pretend that major episodes of inflation in rich countries are solely explained by political expediency. Outside shocks like the OPEC embargo or world war that politicians would seldom court for short-term electoral effect also play a role. But the chronic inflations in the postwar world certainly do seem to fit the institutional interests of politicians. Inflations correspond with a political motive that makes sense.

Deflation, on the other hand, doesn't. Deflation makes many people poor. It reduces real output by tightening the stranglehold of special interests over the economy. Political rigidities and fixed prices that slow economic growth and waste resources when money is losing its value will waste even more when cash suddenly becomes worth more. A monopolistic wage rate that is 20 percent too high for prevailing conditions would generate still more unemployment if deflation raised the value of money. The loss of output due to monopolies and special interests like labor unions and professional lobbies under deflation is much worse than it is with modest inflation. Making their constituents poor is not a rational act for politicians under most circumstances. Therefore it is difficult for many to understand how deflation could come about. Politicians apparently have no motive to set about to slash the money supply. So why do deflations happen?

We answer that question in this chapter. Just as some stimulants in small doses make those who use them feel giddy, while larger doses are deadly, so there is a point where too much inflation is worse than none at all. As an ironic example, consider that British secret agents were said to have spread Argentine money through that country to undermine the economy during the Falklands War. If printing more money always made things better, governments at war would not counterfeit one another's currency as an act of economic sabotage.

SOME DANGER SIGNS OF IMPENDING DEFLATION

We have studied past deflations in an attempt to understand the dynamic process involved. *Blood in the Streets* spelled out some of our conclusions as of 1986. We believe that deflation is much more likely at some times than others. Just as tornadoes or hurricanes occur only under certain atmospheric conditions, so spontaneous deflation and depression are not everyday dangers. They are only likely as delayed reactions to a significant discontinuity, such as a change in political barriers, technological revolution, or a geopolitical shock. Deflation is a delayed compensation for inflation.

The world economy was buffeted in the early 1970s. The collapse of the international monetary system of fixed exchange rates based on gold disrupted price signals. And a dramatic geopolitical event—the oil shock of 1973—transferred trillions in wealth. At the same time, the economy began to experience a profound megapolitical transformaation based upon the microchip. These developments present many parallels wih the conditions that led to deflation in the 1930s, as we argued in *Blood in the Streets* and elsewhere in this volume.

There are also a number of more technical warning signs of impending deflation.

Danger Sign Number One . . .

A rising percentage of debt compared to nominal GNP. In the United States in 1992, the ratio was approaching 195 percent, as compared to about 140 percent in 1929.

Danger Sign Number Two . . .

A record of extraordinarily high returns in many forms of investment a decade or more ago. An unweighted average for all fifteen investments listed in the frequently quoted Salomon Brothers study showed an average compound rate of return of 16.6 percent over the decade June 1970 to June 1980. The average compound growth rate of corporate profits since 1872 has been only 4 percent. And there have been many periods when the rate was much lower. Hypernormal returns like those of the 1970s, following decades of stable growth, are a danger sign that a period of subnormal growth is likely to ensue. Extraordinarily high profits during World War I were followed by lower than ordinary profits during the twenties and a massive fall-off of profits in the 1930s. For the first five years of the 1980s, the unweighted average compound rate of growth for all fifteen investments tracked by Salomon was just .8 percent.

Danger Sign Number Three . . .

Debt compounding faster than income. As the end approaches, it is typical for everyone to borrow with abandon. The trillions in debt added in the United States and other economies in the 1980s, however, have no parallel in their magnitude in any previous credit bubble. In the mid-eighties, net debt issuance in the United States reached an astonishing ten times the personal savings rate. For the decade as a whole, total debt grew by 11 percent, while nominal GNP grew by just 8 percent. A growing ratio of debt to income is inevitable if the real rate of interest exceeds the rate of growth of the economy. This was the case in the United States throughout the 1980s. There is clearly a limit to the percentage of income that can be devoted to debt service. It can jump from 20 percent to 40 percent. A further jump to 80 percent is highly unlikely. But still another doubling to 160 percent is mathematically impossible.

Danger Sign Number Four . . .

A falling ratio of M-2 to the monetary base. The money supply is not entirely in the hands of the authorities. They can expand the monetary base. But the market determines how much of that monetary base is turned into money. As we write in November 1992, the money multiplier points once again to deflation. M-2, the most frequently watched measure of the money supply, has barely reached the lower range of the Federal Reserve's growth targets for 1992—in spite of a massive increase in the monetary base and low interest rates. The monetary base has increased almost five times faster than M-2.

As the accompanying chart shows, the money multiplier has slowed significantly from its peak in the late 1980s. The last time this happened, in the late 1920s, it took more than a decade before the deflationary impulse bottomed out.

Danger Sign Number Five . . .

A falling ratio of money supply to debt. A feature of deflationary periods is that debt grows in proportion to the money supply. By 1990, a measure of the U.S. money supply (M-2) divided by total debt was at a level lower than that of the 1930s, and about at par with the level seen during the deflationary 1890s.

Danger Sign Number Six . . .

A money supply (M-3) more than twelve times greater than the Treasury's stock of monetary gold. In their interesting book, *Power Cycles*, William and Douglas Kirkland point out that high levels of money relative to gold reserves have been danger signals of deflation. The depression of 1873 began with a ratio of 12:1. In 1929, it was 15:1. In 1990, it was 32:1. Of course, since gold no longer plays an active role in the monetary system, it might appear that this ratio is of no interest today. But be cautious. One cannot be too

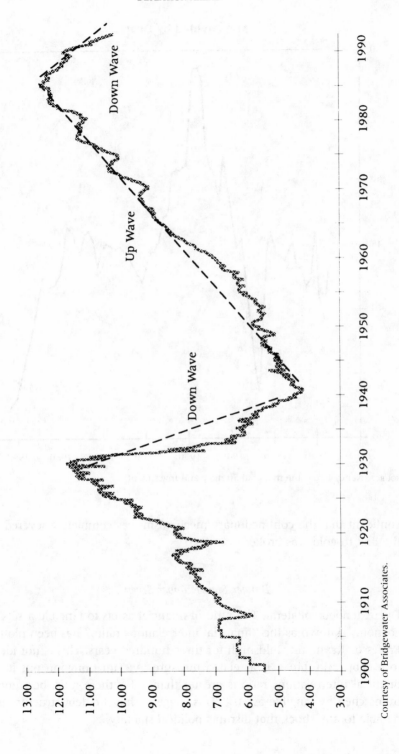

The Money Multiplier: M2 / Monetary Base

Down Wave

Up Wave

Down Wave

Courtesy of Bridgewater Associates.

M-2 Divided by Debt

SOURCE: Nancy Lazar, International Strategy and Investment

confident that the contractionary mechanism was completely severed when the link to gold was broken.

Danger Sign Number Seven . . .

Overextended collateral. The ratio of financial assets to tangible assets in an economy, known as the "financial interrelations ratio," has been plotted by Professor Raymond Goldsmith for three hundred years. This is not identical to a debt ratio, but it is a related measure. As Tim Congdon put it, if the financial interrelations ratio is greater than 1:1, "there must be some debt unmatched by tangible assets." This suggests that the debt structure is vulnerable to any shock that disrupts political stability.

Danger Sign Number Eight . . .

Foreign debt defaults. In the panic of 1837, American debt to lenders in London went into default, along with Latin American obligations. In the Great Depression that began in 1873, Latin American and Egyptian debt went into default. In the Great Depression beginning in 1929, Central European and, yes, Latin American debt went into default or was repudiated. By the late 1980s, Eastern European, African, and Latin American debt was in default. History repeats itself.

Danger Sign Number Nine . . .

Financial scandals. The top of a financial assets boom before a deflation begins is usually marked by financial scandals. Such was the case in the nineteenth century with the Crédit Mobilier Scandal, just one of many incidents that led Mark Twain to describe the 1870s as the "Gilded Age." By that he meant that most of the apparent gold of the time was brass that someone was trying to sell as gold. The twenties were a similar fast-buck period, capped by the Hatry Scandal and the famous frauds of Ivar Kreuger, the Match King. In the late 1980s, newspaper headlines trumpeted scandals on Wall Street involving Ivan Boesky, Michael Milken, and a large supporting cast. These scandals were compounded by a larger scandal on Main Street, where S & L operators played fast and loose with other people's money.

None of these signs in themselves necessarily proves that deflation lies ahead. But they should warn you to look more closely at the dynamics of deflation. We would also argue that massive federal deficits and the near insolvency of the banking system in the United States are warning signs of pending deflation. But to cite these would be to beg the question. Those who expect runaway inflation would also point to the same examples as primary evidence of easy money to come.

Is Deflation Possible?

If stopping deflation were as simple as turning on the presses, then a question immediately arises: "Why was there ever deflation?" Printing presses are an invention of the fifteenth century. Every country in the 1930s had access to high-speed presses that could have cranked out paper money in any denomination. It would have been just as cheap and easy to print ten-thousand-dollar bills as it was to print one-dollar bills. Yet deflationary depression swept the world. Why?

To understand the danger of deflation you need to pose the right question. It is not *whether* governments have the power to print money. It is: *"When do the benefits of printing money exceed the costs?"* If political authorities could benefit only from inflation, and not be harmed, they would obviously print more money in higher denominations than they do.

Those who estimate the chance of deflation at zero are missing several facets of a complex situation:

1. As we have emphasized, they have misunderstood the nonlinear character of the economy as a complex system. Nonlinear systems typically operate through stages or cycles, with rapid phase transitions from one period to the next. This is characteristic of the economy in practice, if not in theory.

2. They are too readily dismissing the relevance of past experience. The chronic inflation since World War II is a historical anomaly. There have been ups and downs since the beginning of time. The Book of Genesis tells us that seven lean years followed seven bountiful years. It would truly be remarkable if the cycle of boom and bust has been eliminated.

3. They ignore the costs of runaway inflation, which exceed those of deflation. In advanced economies, the damage done by destroying the bond market is greater than the stimulative effect of eliminating all debt. Only countries without advanced capital markets like those in Latin America and Africa have dared to have runaway inflations. The fact that average inflation in 1992 was in single digits in the advanced countries that borrow in their own currencies is itself evidence of potent deflationary feedback mechanisms.

Civic Myths from the 1930s

The sky is shaking. We'd better get ready to hold up the sky.

—SENATOR RICHARD SHELBY

You are told the dangers of deflation were finally and magically overcome by political tricks learned in the 1930s.

What were these tricks? That government would prevent depressions by spending money, even by spending money that it didn't have. Where would that money come from? It would be borrowed. If borrowing proved impossible, it would be printed. In short, the magic new invention to prevent depression was for government to spend money and if necessary to print money. Such a treatment can be envisioned as a patentable discovery only by someone who knows little of the behavior of governments in the past. Practically all governments have enjoyed spending money—the more the better. And they have been equally keen to print money or use other devices for debasing the currency—where they found a profit in doing so.

If lavish spending accompanied by inflation could have prevented economic decline, Rome would still rule the world. Higher spending and more inflation were tried over and over, until inflation reached levels that can be considered remarkable for an economy with metallic money. Reay Tannahill wrote, "Money was so seriously devalued that a measure of wheat which, in Egypt, had cost six *drachmai* in the first century A.D., cost two million shortly after A.D. 344."

Indeed, a willingness to spend, with or without resources to meet the bills, has been such prevalent behavior among political authorities through all times that the more interesting historic question is not, "How is it that it took governments until the twentieth century to discover the magic of deficit spending and inflation?" Rather, it is, "What are the factors that have prevailed in prosperous countries that account for the rare rectitude of political leaders who did not spend money out of an empty pocket and inflate the currency?" Any serious attempt to answer that bring you face to face with the fact that the inflationary remedy for deflationary depression is nothing new. Nor is it self-evidently a remedy.

The New Deal Did Not Cure the Depression

The depression of the 1930s was the most severe in American history, in terms of unemployment and the fall of output. Popular culture credits the New Deal with rescuing the economy from collapse. This is wrong. The National Bureau of Economic Research dates the recovery to March 1933. The stock market rebounded from the nadir of depression in July 1932. The recovery after the New Deal was instituted from 1933 forward was actually less robust than the recoveries from previous depressions. It was not until the actual outbreak of World War II in Europe, a decade after the depression began, that U.S. industrial output exceeded its 1929 highs. From 1929 to 1939, adult unemployment averaged 18 percent.

DEPRESSION IN THE THIRD WORLD

It is far too simple to think that government demand management and loose fiscal policy can easily counter worldwide forces making for contraction or revolutionizing the structure of industry. If printing money to finance deficits at unlimited levels really prevented economic downturn, no country in Africa or Latin America would have experienced falling living standards over the past three decades. In fact, many have. Among those turning in the worst performances are Guiana, Gambia, the Maldives, and Nicaragua, which, along with the late Soviet Union, were champion deficit spenders.

One could argue that inept administration or other factors prevented the deficit tonic from giving a lift to these unhappy countries. Yet the fact that government demand management has failed so conspicuously in so many places since World War II does not encourage optimism about the political guarantee to stop depression. Quite the contrary. A prescription that has widely failed, while appearing to work in a comparative handful of rich countries, can hardly be the basis of complacency about the future.

Chronic Unemployment in Europe

What is more, evidence from industrial countries has begun to accumulate that should alert a thinking observer to the weakness of the Keynesian prescription, even if nothing were known of the abysmal experience of the developing countries. In the advanced nations where labor unions continue to dominate a large share of total employment and exercise political power, the growth of new jobs has slowed and the unemployment rate has crept upwards. This is true in practically every country of Western Europe. It is merely a way of saying that political authorities do not know how to manage the economy to achieve a more complete industrial boom. Not one new job has been created in Western Europe for more than a decade. If governments, even in countries like Germany, Sweden, and France, cannot create jobs at tolerable costs during times of relative prosperity, what is the basis of confidence that they can do so in the face of true depression conditions?

The idea that government can easily interrupt or suppress economic cycles is more a civic myth than a fact. The claim made by John Kenneth Galbraith and others that the Great Depression emerged because the U.S. government in 1929 was content to allow the market to operate without intervention is simply untrue. Indeed, it is remote from the facts. President Herbert Hoover intervened vigorously but without success. Even a massive stimulus program and an "easy money" policy that led to negative T-bill rates in 1933 did not prevent deflation.

Central Banks Cannot Create Capital

It is all too simple to think that central banks have magic powers. They don't. They can create liquidity by creating debt. But this is not the same thing as creating capital. Any time a central bank monetizes an asset by buying it, in essence, with printing-press money, it also creates a liability. Only the market can create capital by valuing assets above liabilities. Turning on the presses at a higher speed destroys more wealth than it creates.

This is evident in a number of ways. For example, backward countries with high levels of inflation have few financial assets in proportion to tangible assets. Even their tangible assets like land and buildings tend to be valued at low levels. By contrast, land and buildings tend to be worth a great deal more in a country with a high proportion of financial assets. Switzerland, the nation with the best anti-inflation record, has tangible assets worth far more than those in backward countries. A building in downtown Geneva or Zurich will be worth many times more than a comparable structure in a city like Lagos or Buenos Aires. A condo at Crans-Montana will sell for the price of a whole mountain near San Carlos de Bariloche.* A higher ratio of financial assets to tangible assets usually means that the valuations of both are higher.

A high financial interrelations ratio reflects the capital that a society can create when inflation is controlled. The gain in wealth is tremendous. But this added wealth is at risk if inflation is allowed to run wild. That is why inflation at runaway levels is rare in advanced countries. They seldom allow inflation to exceed the levels that are compatible with continued economic growth. Hyperinflation, however, is much more common in backward countries that do not borrow their own currencies. A hyperinflation that would wipe out the bond market is much less costly in a country that has no bond market. Backward countries with few financial assets compared to tangible assets permit hyperinflation because they have less to lose.

In more advanced countries, the market is itself a potent deflationary mechanism. Politicians are stopped from inflating wildly because people who have financial assets like bonds that would be harmed by hyperinflation can sell them. For example, if it appeared to everyone that the U.S. government intended to rapidly inflate away the national debt, then most holders of U.S. Treasury bonds would dump them, driving up interest rates. The effect would therefore be just the opposite of what the politicians would wish. The stronger

---

*San Carlos de Bariloche is a transplanted Alpine village near Mt. Tronador, Argentina, founded by Swiss immigrants.

the appearance that the authorities are following an inflationary policy, the higher interest rates will go, and thus the more rapidly capital will disappear.

   This, of course, does not mean that there cannot be hyperinflation in rich countries. But it does mean that the economic and political gains of such a policy are likely to be more than canceled by its high costs. Indeed it is possible that the attempt to counter deflation by political expedients has the effect of increasing the strength of the impulse making for contraction—just as attempting to prevent forest fires only postpones and enlarges the ultimate conflagration. The notion that easy money is a magic tonic that can counter the forces of contraction is likely to seem more alluring as an argument than it proves to be as a fact. In 1929, neither the Federal Reserve nor the Bank of England could overcome the worldwide forces making for contraction just by manipulating numbers on their balance sheets. Economic historian Joseph W. Davis put it this way:

> ... A careful reading of a mass of contemporary literature and an analysis of economic and financial developments in 1930 yield little or no support for the views (a) that Federal Reserve policy in that year was open to serious criticism, or (b) that flooding of the money supply by the Federal Reserve System would have effectively checked the contraction or moderated the current and ensuing collapse. With enterprise "collapsed," the forces making for contraction were too strong to be overcome by the stimulus of artificially reducing short-term money rates below the very low levels actually reached.

Our bet is that the central banks today could not do much better.

Statistical Illusions Feed Bigger Illusions

There is evidence that some of the effects for which policy-makers are given credit in smoothing the fluctuations of the business cycle since World War II are merely statistical illusions. So argues economist Christina Romer of the University of California. She has pointed out defects in the conventional measures of commodity prices that are used to infer the volatility of economic growth. For example, the measure of industrial production used prior to 1919 included only forty commodities, rather than the two hundred that have been included since then in Federal Reserve Board statistics. When the postwar economy is measured according to the methods used prior to 1919, a funny thing happens. It appears that business cycle fluctuations in America have been of the same magnitude since World War II as they were prior to World War I. Only in the period between the wars was there substantially more fluctuation. This is exactly what should be expected. Furniture will tumble more during an earthquake than on a calm day. It was precisely in the inter-war period that the economy was working off the collapse of the international monetary system, and the shattering of trade and property relatons that ac-companied World War I. It should not come as a surprise that the full impact of the bloody war that began in August 1914 could not be absorbed in an afternoon, or even in a season.

DEFLATION IS A LONG-TERM PROCESS

There is no reason to assume that the crisis was started by a deliberate deflationary action on the part of the monetary authorities, or that deflation itself is anything but a secondary phenomenon, a process induced by the maladjustments of in-dustry left over from the boom.

—F. A. HAYEK, 1933

Deflation is not a willful act of perversity by authorities, but the culmination of an historic process that takes years to unfold. Deflation is not something that politicians choose, any more than people choose to have cancer, midriff bulge, or the infirmities of old age. Sometimes, however, the system as a whole is led to outcomes that no one would prefer, and that are tolerable only in comparison to alternatives that are even worse. The outbreak of war is such an outcome. So is deflation.

By studying past booms and collapses, we have identified at least a few of the regularities that seem to be at work from one episode to another. The process works something like this:

The Inflationary Stage

1. Some shock, often a war, sets the process in motion by disturbing the system. It alters property rights, encourages monetary instability, and raises real asset prices.

2. This leads to extraordinarily high rates of return in real assets, especially for debtors, who gain disproportionately. The high rates of return seem to justify massive new investment.

3. A credit binge ensues, as people borrow at accelerated rates to capture the extraordinary profits. Real estate, in particular, rises in value.

4. Institutions and contracts are adjusted to reflect the inflation. Debt maturities shorten. Nominal and real interest rates rise.

5. Nonetheless, a credit binge continues, as investors now accustomed to high rates of return calculate that they can continue to earn supernormal profits.

6. Financial as well as real assets are purchased on a basis of increasing leverage, and a bull market in stocks follows, though not yet a drooling frenzy.

Then Comes the Deflationary Stage . . .

7. Profitability declines toward more normal levels as investment matures and new output is brought onto the market.

8. Commodity prices decline.

9. The farm economy goes into recession.

10. Interest rates fall, and as they do, hot money moves into financial assets, further stimulating the stock market.

11. As opportunities in the real economy subside, investment is concentrated on financial assets, leading to a stock market blow-off.

12. The boom is self-limiting because debt contracted at high interest rates compounds faster than income, eventually requiring that owners of leveraged assets liquefy their holdings, thus driving asset prices down.

13. Real estate sags.

14. Some trigger such as credit squeeze, a major bankruptcy, fraud, or simply the slowing of the real economy reveals the overvaluation of assets.

15. The stock market crashes, credit contraction intensifies, the money supply implodes, and depression ensues, with returns on previous investment falling to subnormal rates.

16. Real interest rates skyrocket, even as nominal interest rates fall, further reducing economic activity.

17. Unemployment skyrockets because real wage rates rise.

18. Wages and prices are cut as the system winds down.

19. Bingo. You have been in deflation for some time.

More to the Story

Although the foregoing sequence is obviously stylized, it captures something of the dynamic process that has already begun to unfold in the slow-motion deflation of the 1990s. We don't pretend that there is anything ironclad about this account. It is meant to hint at a complex historical process by which the system compensates for a shock. It is interesting that booms have reached their greatest extremes during power transitions. The reason is that shocks or property rights disturbances have been most intense then. The lesser cycles that did not involve world wars have tended to be shorter, and less dramatic. But wherever local systems have been disturbed, the inflation/deflation cycle has had locally severe effects. Such was the case with the Revolutionary War in the United States. It was followed by deflationary depression in the United States by 1785.

Timing?

There are several markers, like beacons in a fog, that can give us further hints about the time scale over which this process unfolds. Those that we have identified suggest that the world was well into the early stages of deflation as 1993 began. Consider:

1. There was evidence of a power transition, with financial and manufacturing predominance transferring to Japan.

2. The end of the credit cycle in the last five depressions has in each case been signaled by a peak in commodity prices 9 to 10 years prior to the crash in asset markets in the leading country. As detailed in Chapter Four, Tokyo's 1990 crash fits that pattern exactly. It is a strong hint that the world had already entered the first stage of depression.

Another reason to suppose that the downturn of the early 1990s was a depression in its early stages and not a normal recession that will run its course, is the period of time that has elapsed since the initial shock that raised returns on investment. In the past, the range of time has been from fifteen to twenty-two years. Examples:

- The Dutch joined the Thirty Years War with Spain in 1621. The tulipomania completely collapsed in 1637. Elapsed time: sixteen years.
- The world war of the early eighteenth century, the War of Spanish Succession, began in 1701. Both the Mississippi Scheme in France and

the South Sea Bubble in England collapsed in the fall of 1720. Elapsed
time: nineteen years.

- The Napoleonic world war of the early nineteenth century began in
  1803. The London market crashed in December 1825. Elapsed time:
  twenty-two years.
- A long worldwide depression began in 1873, accompanied by a 40
  percent drop in the British price level. This deflation emerged in the
  wake of a number of conflicts, including the Crimean War of twenty
  years earlier (1853–56) and the American Civil War of twelve years
  earlier (1861–65). The Austro-Prussian War (1866) and the Franco-
  Prussian War (1870–71) also may have played a role, especially in the
  property collapse in Germany and Austria after payment of the French
  indemnity. Elapsed time from onset of Crimean War: twenty years.
- World War I began in 1914, and the stock market collapsed in October
  1929. Elapsed time: fifteen years.

The shock that set in motion the current cycle was spread over several
years, with the Vietnam-induced repudiation of the international monetary
system occurring in 1971, and the OPEC property rights shock in 1973.
Elapsed time to 1990: a minimum of nineteen years.

By 1992 we had already gone four years longer than the complete cycle
from shock to crash in the last depression.

War and the Monetary Cycle

A closer look at the actual experience of the 1930s and the conditions under
which recovery emerged casts further doubt on the assumption that modern
societies are deflation-proof. We have argued that government spending *per
se* did not cure the depression. Then what did? The answer is obvious, but
not simple. World War II. The outbreak of a devastating war in Europe and
the Pacific did restore demand to languishing sectors. Far from confirming
the hypothesis that government spending can easily prevent depression, the
World War II experience raises many doubts. Its effect did not merely rest
with the fact that war was expensive. Rather, a great part of World War II's
impact was that it curtailed supply, destroyed competitive capital, killed tal-
ented personnel, and reorganized world monetary, trade, and property rights.

World War II was the most destructive war in history. By the time the
fighting was over, America was the only prewar economic power to emerge
with its plant and equipment intact, let alone augmented. Industrial capacity
in the European nations and Japan had been largely flattened by the fighting.
In Japan, for example, about 35 percent of national wealth was destroyed in

1944 alone. Europe was equally destitute. Many factories and even whole cities had been bombed to rubble. The productivity of the surviving resources was dramatically reduced because parts and materials upon which they depended were no longer available. In some cases, the factories were isolated from their markets because bridges were down, railways had been torn up, or occupying troops blocked the way.

The effect of the war, therefore, was to greatly augment the relative demand for U.S. goods in the world—a development that stands in stark contrast to effects of simply spending money. It was the depletion of the capacity of competitors that explains the vast increase in the U.S. total share of world manufacturing output. What is less obvious, but more important for the long-term prospects for deflation, is the way that the war altered the long-standing relationship between military power and sound money.

The Persistence of Inflation Since World War II

The remarkable feature of the postwar world has been the magnitude and persistence of inflation. All previous inflations in American history were wiped away with amazing regularity in deflations. No previous climb in the price level lasted as long as twenty-five years. And none was shorter than twenty.

Prices peaked in 1814 after a twenty-three-year rise from 1791.

They peaked again in 1864 after rising from 1844.

And our century's first inflation peaked in 1920 after a twenty-four-year rise from 1896.

As of 1992, sixty years had passed since the wholesale commodity price lows of 1932. Prices were still rising.

Many people will tell you that this means that deflation is a thing of the past, as extinct as Herbert Hoover's high collar or his wife's corset. Is our current inflation really different? And if so, why?

To us, the expectation of perpetual inflation is only slightly less credible than perpetual motion. But ours is an old-fashioned view, influenced by the old-fashioned hunch that "what goes up must come down." In a world of leveraged buyouts and multi-trillion-dollar debts, this view has taken on the character of contrary thinking. Those expecting ever more inflation are certainly going with the trend. But so were the people who bought gold at eight hundred dollars an ounce. The chart of the inflation rate over the past five centuries looks a lot like gold's chart before it crashed—only more extreme.

Here are the facts. The trend in inflation has been up since the bottom of the last depression, a long time by the scale of a human life. Taking an even longer view, prices have been rising for five hundred years, over the whole

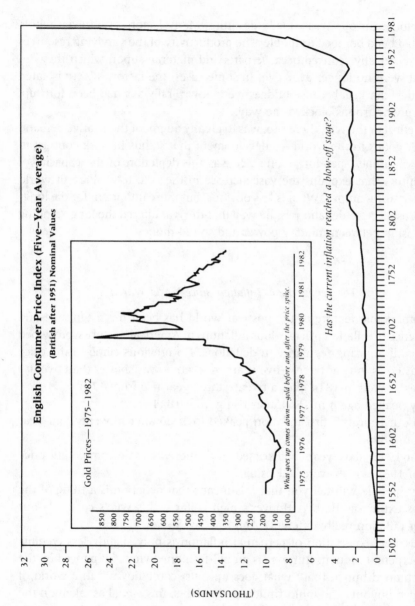

English Consumer Price Index (Five–Year Average)

(British after 1951) Nominal Values

Gold Prices—1975–1982

What goes up comes down—gold before and after the price spike.

Has the current inflation reached a blow-off stage?

SOURCE: South English consumer prices, 1500–1950, from E. H. Phelps-Brown and Sheila V. Hopkins, "Seven Centuries of the Prices of Consumables," cited in Joshua S. Goldstein, *Long Cycles: Prosperity and War in the Modern Age.* British consumer prices, 1951–83, from *Economic Statistics, 1900–1983*, compiled and edited by Thelma Leisner.

period of Western predominance in the world. But they have never risen in quite the way they have in the past fifty years.

Past Inflations

Early statistics are undependable. But what we do know suggests that English consumer prices rose by almost 400 percent during the century from 1500 to 1600. During the seventeenth century, prices continued to rise overall, but at a slower pace of just 46 percent for the century. From 1700 to 1800, inflation again accelerated, with consumer prices rising by 133 percent. During the nineteenth century, English consumer prices actually fell by 37 percent. The uptrend resumed in the twentieth century, but on an unprecedented scale. British consumer prices rose by more than 3000 percent from 1900 to 1983. Almost all the gain occurred after 1935.

Prices in the United States and other industrial countries show a similar explosion. U.S. wholesale prices have risen about 1000 percent during this century. These were up just 15 percent to 1932.

The Teeter-Totter Breaks

The current inflation has been more severe than those of the previous four centuries combined. This is not because the increase in inflation in any given year has been higher than ever before. It is because inflation has become uncharacteristically persistent. There have been no deflationary years to offset the compounding of prices during the inflationary years. The old teeter-totter on which inflation and deflation took turns riding up and down seems to have broken. The half-century prior to 1990 was unique as the only such period over the past five centuries when the number of deflationary years did not approximately match the number of inflationary years.

Even in the sixteenth century, the most inflationary prior to the twentieth, prices fell during forty-three years. Among those forty-three deflationary years was 1558, when the best records show that prices fell by more than 40 percent. Here is the record of South English Consumer Prices, which captures the inflation and deflation in the London area:

	Inflationary years	Deflationary years
The sixteenth century	57	43
The seventeenth century	46	54

| The eighteenth century | 53 | 47 |
| The nineteenth century | 47 | 53 |

During the four hundred years prior to 1900, prices on average fell during 49.25 years of each century.

This pattern was not sharply changed in the first half of the twentieth century. English consumer prices fell during seventeen years prior to 1950. There were fewer years of deflation than usual, but not significantly so. The startling change occurs after 1950. Using the *Economist*'s index for all consumer prices in Britain, they have not fallen during any year since 1950. In the United States, they fell once, by an almost invisible margin in 1959. The record is only slightly different among the few "strong currency" countries. Japanese consumer prices fell during the period 1986–87, as they did in Germany. The German mark, the strongest Group of Seven currency since 1950, has nonetheless lost an average of 2.7 percent of its purchasing power per year—for a compound loss of about two-thirds of its 1950 value.

Taking a longer view, it is clear that inflation has been uncharacteristically severe and persistent since 1950. Will this continue? The usual response of those who expect perpetual inflation is to point out that more paper money is circulating today than ever before. This is true. It is the easy part of a two-part answer. The hard part is to explain why governments have gotten away with creating more money than they did in the past. Answer that and you come closer to understanding how the current round of inflation may come to an end.

WAR AND INFLATION

Any systematic explanation of the inflation cycle must include some account of the role of war. Inflation is the monetary footprint of war. As you can see from the accompanying chart, the tops of previous inflationary surges in America were closely associated with war. The deflationary years occurred by and large when the nation was at peace.

It is not surprising that the nineteenth century was the most deflationary in modern history. It was also the most peaceful. War was underway only 40 percent of the time—as compared to 80 percent of the time in the eighteenth century and 95 percent of the time in the sixteenth and seventeenth centuries. Most of the years when wholesale prices fell during the nineteenth century were years when wars were not underway. Likewise, periods of falling consumer prices during previous centuries in England were periods when England was at peace, or engaged in only minor fighting.

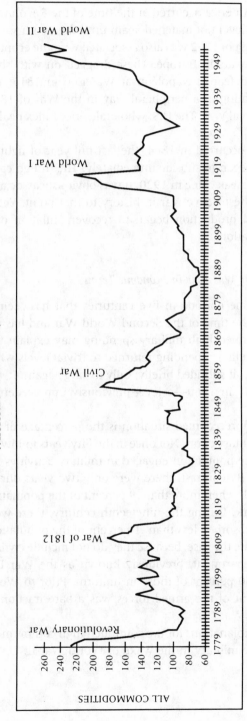

Wholesale Price Index, 1779–1951

ALL COMMODITIES

The first great inflation in America occurred at the time of the Revolution. It was severe. Prices rose to a level not matched again until this century. The upturn of prices from the trough in 1792 was also associated with the eruption of the French Revolutionary wars in Europe. These dragged on with short intermissions until the final defeat of Napoléon at Waterloo in 1815. The U.S. entered the fighting in a peripheral way in the War of 1812. The U.S. wholesale price index peaked with the fighting in 1814.

The next major price peak occurred in 1864, the last full year of fighting during the Civil War. Prices began to subside immediately. The trough came in 1896. The next inflationary peak came in 1920. It was obviously associated with World War I, the most destructive conflict in history to that point. Yet as troops were demobilized and production began to recover, inflation duly slowed, then turned into deflation.

Almost all the current inflation has occurred since 1953.

SOURCE: U. S. Historical Statistics, Bureau of the Census, Washington, DC, 1975

The first great inflation in America occurred at the time of the Revolution. It was severe. Prices rose to a level not matched again until this century. The upturn of prices from the trough in 1792 was also associated with the eruption of the French Revolutionary wars in Europe. These dragged on with short intermissions until the final defeat of Napoléon at Waterloo in 1815. The United States entered the fighting in a peripheral way in the War of 1812, known elsewhere as the Colonial War. The U.S. wholesale price index peaked with the fighting in 1814.

The next major price peak occurred in 1864, the last full year of fighting during the Civil War. Prices began to subside immediately. The trough came in 1896. The next inflationary peak came in 1920. It was obviously associated with World War I, the most destructive war in history to that point. Yet as troops were demobilized and production began to recover, inflation duly slowed, then turned into deflation.

The Cold War Was War in Economic Terms

The current inflation is the one episode in five centuries that has seemed different. It was launched at the time of the Second World War and has not come down yet. Why? Continued high military spending may explain this puzzle. After previous wars, military spending returned to trivial levels when the fighting stopped. This time, it subsided briefly, only to surge again. It was still almost 10 percent of GNP in 1960—a level previously unprecedented except in war.

Another measure of this unprecedented situation is the percentage of the U.S. population engaged in military effort. Not once in the fifty years following 1940 did the percentage of the population engaged in military activities fall below .9 percent of the total. By contrast, there were only two years during the previous century and a half when more than .9 percent of the population was dedicated to military work. During the nineteenth century, there were fifty years when the military absorbed less than .1 percent of the population. These figures actually understate the case, because they do not include civilian employees of the Defense Department, previously known as the War Department, who equal about 50 percent of those in uniform. Prior to World War II, the civilian component of the armed forces was a bare fraction of what it has been since World War II.

There are several possible explanations for the continued high commitment of people and resources to the military in the wake of World War II.

Empire

1. In the early years after World War II, the United States became the predominant power in a new world order, taking over the role previously performed by Great Britain. More on that below.

The Bomb and Inflation

2. Technological change required "front-loading" of military effort. As we have emphasized, the technological shift of advantage from the offense to the defense dramatically raised the costs of conventional weapons. Thus it was relatively more costly for the United States to maintain a military power advantage equivalent to that enjoyed by Great Britain early in this century.

But the advent of nuclear weaponry appears to have had a more decisive impact. The bomb made monetary and fiscal rectitude a smaller factor in the preservation of state power than it had been in the past. Part of the impact of nuclear weapons has been to shorten the expected duration of the next great war.

In the past, a strong credit rating and low bond yields were among the more important factors in securing victory in protracted conflicts. Strategic missiles and hydrogen bombs implied that there would be no protracted wars among the great powers. They therefore seemed to necessitate a strategy of deterrence—spending a lot of money immediately—in order to deter attack. Even if high military spending were known to be ruinous in the long run, it seemed preferable to running a greater risk of near-term annihilation.

U.S. Wealth Cushions Costs

3. As we suggested above, World War II was one of history's rare profitable wars for its chief victor, the United States. The fighting was almost entirely on foreign soil. It resulted in massive liquidation of the plant and capital of most of America's competitors. As a result, U.S. financial resources after the war were overwhelming enough to sustain an otherwise crushing burden of military spending without serious trouble for decades.

Communism Increased Tolerance of U.S. Inflation

4. When monetary and fiscal trouble began to surface around the time of Vietnam, the United States had help in exporting inflation to its allies because of the menacing character of Soviet ideology. The hostile attitude of Communist leaders toward capital assured that foreign investors would not peel

away from the United States and side with Russia as U.S. bond yields rose.

American allies, especially Germany and Japan, were willing to coordinate central bank policies and use other devices to finance U.S. budget deficits and import American inflation as preferable alternatives to actually assuming the costs of defending themselves. Japanese insurance companies, for example, could be persuaded to buy American bonds. They were then compensated through roundabout mechanisms for their capital losses. The allies knew that an American credit crisis would necessitate budgetary contraction and, most likely, a reduction in American defense subsidies. Prior to the death of the Soviet Union, the menacing character of Communism was a powerful inducement to cooperate in extending the inflationary Cold War status quo.

Taken together, these factors and others allowed the United States to continue military spending for several decades at levels that would have been more rapidly ruinous in the past. Eventually, however, the burdens of military spending did become ruinous. Among the results has been the most extreme and persistent inflation in modern history.

The connection between war and inflation goes beyond the obvious fact that wars are inflationary. War and war-induced inflations are linked together in a continuous historical process. War causes inflation. Inflation causes economic decline or even bankruptcy that necessitates peace. Peace frees resources for productive use. More production raises output and lowers prices. As wealth increases, war becomes more affordable. It breaks out again. More war creates inflation, and the cycle repeats.

An interesting book, *Long Cycles: Prosperity and War in the Modern Age* by Joshua Goldstein, highlights the importance of some of these connections. Goldstein argues that war is the crucial link that transmits disturbances through the price mechanism and the production process. He marshals impressive statistical evidence and analysis in support of this conclusion. His argument suggests yet another dimension to the feedback mechanisms that make ever-rising inflation difficult to sustain.

We believe that rising debt levels create economic feedback that forces a deflationary reaction. Put simply, debt cannot indefinitely compound faster than income.

Military Power Required Sound Money

The influence of war and military spending on prices and production is also self-limiting. A level of military spending high enough to materially alter the price level will also undermine the economic capacity of a country to continue spending. In the past, even the richest nations were too poor to sustain the costs of mobilization for full-scale war on more than a temporary basis. Before the French Revolution, battles between states were mainly engagements of maneuver, often fought by mercenaries, and sometimes involving only small detachments of men. Wars may have been more frequent, but they were far less intense, what Gibbon described as "temperate and indecisive contests." They had to be. No government could afford to continually siphon off significant percentages of national wealth for military purposes without courting bankruptcy—and thus military weakness.

As Dr. Samuel Johnson wrote in 1749:

> Yet Reason frowns on War's unequal Game,
> Where wasted Nations raise a single Name,
> And mortgag'd States their Grandsires Wreathes regret,
> From Age to Age in everlasting Debt.

Neither could governments afford wild inflation. If they attempted to wipe away their "everlasting debt" with the printing press, they would have lost further access to the credit markets, greatly diminishing their strategic position. When nations lost the financial capacity to fight, they often lost wars.

In his best-selling book, *The Rise and Fall of the Great Powers,* Paul Kennedy emphasized the importance of financial stability, "sound money, secure credit, and regular repayment of debt" in producing military success. In one case after another, the leading powers were powers because they were rich. "Success in war depended upon the length of one's purse." First Spain, then the Netherlands, and later England came to dominate much of the world because of their extraordinary financial capacities to wage war.

These nations failed when they reached the limits of their capacities to finance the costs of war. Spain was bankrupted in 1596, when interest on the national debt took a large fraction of the national revenues, variously reported as from 40 percent to 66 percent. The result was that Spain was forced to withdraw from wars it could no longer afford. The bankruptcy of Spain produced a period of peace known as "The Breathing Spell."

Dutch finance was the strongest in Europe even before the Dutch became militarily predominant. Dutch capital continued to play a major role in financing British wars. When Britain allowed its creditworthiness to decline during the time of the American Revolution, the Dutch withdrew their financial support, with unfavorable consequences from the British point of view.

Later, as we emphasized in *Blood in the Streets,* the end of British military hegemony occurred when the costs of maintaining the British Empire exhausted the fiscal resources available. Britain's economy was taxed at a disproportionately high level to meet the costs of maintaining world order. Because Britain was for many years spending a higher portion of its national output for military purposes than the United States, British competitiveness was hampered. In time, British wealth was simply insufficient to support an ever more costly military mission. This ultimately left Britain dependent upon foreign borrowings to finance military measures. Appeasement during the deflationary 1930s was a fiscal and monetary policy, not a strategic vision.

The last depression was a period of widespread disarmament. In April 1930, President Herbert Hoover signed a strategic arms treaty that was to have "lifted the burden of militarism from the backs of mankind." Then, as in 1992, pacifism and isolationism were on the rise. Politicians who listened to the mood of their constituents made much of the virtues of international law, and treaties were forwarded as a civilized alternative to military vigilance.

Common Bankruptcy Requires Disarmament

A similar pattern is repeating itself in the 1990s, but on a larger scale. The Cold War kept U.S. military spending at historically high levels for decades, burdening the economy and reducing American industrial competitiveness. Soviet military spending was an even heavier burden to that backward economy. As Li Chuan wrote in the Tang Dynasty, "Now when the army marches abroad, the treasury will be emptied at home." This has happened. The Soviet Union died a bankrupt. The United States suffers with massive budget deficits and a growing burden of external debt. Its manufacturing sector has lost ground for years to the Japanese, who spend a bare one percent of GNP on military spending. The Germans also have enjoyed a better reputation in world markets, and a higher level of exports per head, while devoting half the U.S. percentage to military spending.

The fiscal and monetary pressures caused by the declining economic competitiveness of the United States and the death of the Soviet Union will force a continuation of the trend to lower military spending as a percentage of output. Just as Spain, the Netherlands, and England were obliged by sheer economic necessity to cut military spending because they ran out of cash, so will the United States, especially after the death of its Cold War enemy, the Soviet Union.

We have already seen the early stages of disarmament, predicted in *Blood in the Streets*. With the election of President Clinton, military spending in the United States will fall sharply. By the mid-1990s, U.S. military spending will have been cut by one-third to two-thirds in real terms. Parts of this savings will come from major reductions of the U.S. military personnel abroad, especially in Europe, where the NATO allies will no longer be menaced by

Communism. As military spending is cut in real as well as relative terms, U.S. industrial competitiveness will increase, and so will output.

The sudden dampening of conflict and trends to lower military spending are deflationary. Prices fall when fighting stops and personnel are demobilized. It is no coincidence that the nineteenth century, the only deflationary century in modern history, was also the most peaceful, with wars underway in only half as many years as the previous three centuries.

In economic terms, the period since 1940 has been equivalent to fifty years of war. It was a half-century of unprecedented military outlays for weapons of unprecedented destructive might. If our argument is correct, what went up will soon come down. The release of real resources, including highly able personnel, from military employment will set the stage for a long-delayed drop in the price level, not just in the United States, but around the world. Inflation has risen far outside its long-term trend, with a persistence that is characteristic of price charts during a blow-off phase. This is not the time to buy into inflation by increasing your debt burden, or betting heavily on companies that do. At least some of the unique factors that permitted high military spending to sustain high inflation are coming to an end. The coming deflation will be the economic fallout of the atomic age.

CHAPTER TWELVE

CLUES FROM THE PAST

A PROLOGUE TO DEPRESSION

Paradoxical as it may seem, the riches of nations can be measured by the violence of the crises which they experience.

—CLEMENT JUGLAR,
Des Crises Commerciales, 1889

LET US tell you a story of a nation in depression. It is a true story. It illustrates many of the common features and consequences of severe economic slumps. If a slump hits in the 1990s, it could have similar consequences. In most times and places, depressions have generated wild swings of inflation and deflation, successively impoverishing creditors and debtors alike, bankrupting governments and bringing on a collapse of crucial public services. In many cases, the social upheavals lead to revolution or a major change in the form of government.

The story we are about to tell illustrates these tendencies well. It is the story of a newly independent country. Mainly agricultural, most of its residents earn their livelihoods from subsistence or barter farming. Most of the few manufactured necessities they can afford are imported from abroad, resulting in a large trade deficit and a mounting burden of foreign debt. Its government, like many new governments, is weak and ineffectual.

Most members of the national assembly seldom bother to turn up for appointed sessions. On occasions when they do appear their physical safety is sometimes threatened by angry mobs or mutinous troops. The government finances are "chaotic." The national assembly cannot pay the troops their promised wages.

As the depression deepens, the national assembly itself is obliged to take to the road, like a band of vagabonds, to stay a step ahead of the mob. The government, "facing utter bankruptcy," makes laughing stocks of the few citizens incautious enough to lend it money. The government's debt securities are so depreciated that they sell for less than fifteen cents on the dollar. The implied interest rate on the national debt skyrockets to 40 percent. But this is just an implied rate, not an actual yield. Interest payments on both domestic and foreign debt are in default. In many places, the hapless creditors are in the absurd situation of having their property confiscated "for non-payment of taxes" allegedly levied "to pay them interest on their securities."

As so often happens, authorities lacking a better expedient resort to printing paper money. In one of the few commercial centers, the value of local paper money tumbles by 92 percent in thirty months. What was the equivalent of a dollar becomes just eight cents. Some local government debts are discharged at "the depreciated ratio of a thousand to one." As the local paper money is discharged or discredited, an automatic deflation sets in. People prefer to do business in stronger foreign currencies that circulate in inadequate amounts. As a consequence, real wholesale prices tumble by more than 60 percent in just a few years.

As real wealth shrinks, the country suffers the classic symptoms of economic and political instability. Attempts at tax collection are redoubled even as public services go on a downward spiral. The interior of the country is so impoverished that the imposition of a head tax of just three dollars a year precipitates open rebellions. Armed bands roam the interior, forcibly preventing courts from sitting. As the depression bites into spending power, merchants find their stocks of unsold goods far exceed what they could plausibly hope to sell at a profit. They clamor for protectionist laws to cut off the import of foreign goods. The national government, however, is too weak to enforce such counterproductive measures. In an effort to keep prices high, local areas erect their own barriers to stall or penalize the shipment of goods from anywhere—even domestic goods from neighboring jurisdictions. The result is rampant smuggling in a growing black market.

As commercial distress multiplies, the entire financial system teeters on the brink of collapse. Banks fail. Checks written by the largest bank in the country regularly bounce. The local currency is worthless in foreign commerce. The indebted nation, dependent on foreign bankers to keep even a minimal trade afloat, finds its foreign credit gone. As chaos mounts, impoverished debtors look for scapegoats. Here and there, angry mobs attack the homes and persons of the rich. Politicians seeking office campaign on promises to repudiate the national debt and inflate away private debt with more paper money.

Newspapers report that desperate debtors in the backwoods are organizing an armed rebellion supported by foreign agents. The rebels group together under the command of a mysterious "Committee of Seventeen." The papers report that the rebels' aim is nothing less than to establish a radical form of communism. It is widely reported and widely believed that they intend to seize all property in the country and redistribute it equally. An alarmed local governor begs the national assembly for help in restoring order. Little is forthcoming. Wealthy citizens are so frightened that they take up a collection in foreign money to privately pay the loyal troops.

Such is the portrait of a nation overpowered by depression and political collapse. A commentator captured the mood of the time with the observation that people "ceased to care whether the Republic lived or died." With debtors in revolt and the government floundering, a leading general determines that the time has come to take charge. "Something must be done, or the fabric must fall, for it certainly is tottering." He wants stronger actions to maintain law and order and fend off the danger of communism. Other wealthy citizens join him in organizing a new government that can take effective measures to enforce austerity. The public greets him with open arms.

This is a story that has been repeated in one form or another throughout the world in this century. You have read many versions of it in the newspaper. This particular version would hardly seem farfetched, unless, of course, we told you that the nation in question was the United States. Yet everything we have just recounted did happen. It happened during the depression of the 1780s. This was the depression that wiped away the greatest inflation of American history—the greatest, that is, prior to the current period. Not surprisingly, therefore, it saw the greatest collapse of asset values in American history. What goes up must come down. The index of all commodity prices fell from 226 to just 85 in a decade, a breathtaking collapse.

Historian Samuel Eliot Morison wrote of a situation that "was very bad and rumor made it seem worse." He observed:

> With trade at a standstill, farm produce a drug in the market, no employment for common labor, and little specie in circulation, court judgments for debts or overdue taxes could in most cases be enforced only by stripping a farmer of his real estate, his cattle, and his furniture. In Worcester County alone, 92 persons were imprisoned for debt in 1785.

As the situation worsened in 1786, armed bands of impoverished debtors forcibly prohibited courts from sitting, including the Court of Quarter Sessions of Worcester County. Violence was most intense in New England and the Northeast, where population pressures combined with depleted soil to press subsistence farmers to desperation. Rioting mobs intent on preventing the enforcement of judgments against debtors struck in many areas, including New York, Connecticut, Vermont, New Hampshire, Rhode Island, and Massachusetts.

In Massachusetts, Connecticut, and Rhode Island, the discontent was organized along military lines. Thousands of men, commanded by continental army veterans and current officers of the Massachusetts state militia, were organized into rebel regiments. The rebel soldiers were drilled and paid three shillings a day. In other words, a serious effort was begun to change the law through physical force.

The most important military engagement of these revolts was Shays's Rebellion, a battle for a federal arsenal at Springfield, Massachusetts, on January 25, 1787. A band of twelve hundred rebels under the command of Captain Daniel Shays was dispersed with the aid of bitter cold. Temperatures as low as thirty degrees below zero had thinned the rebel ranks, confusing communications between three separate contingents and making it difficult for the attackers to fire their muskets. The troops at the arsenal held the day, in part because they had cannon, while the rebels did not. If the weather had been warmer, the rebel force on the field would have been augmented by at least eight hundred men. The battle for the arsenal probably would have begun earlier. It might have turned out differently. As it was, minor skirmishes continued through the summer of 1787.

> Their creed is, that the property of the United States has been protected from the confiscations of Britain by the joint exertions of all, and therefore ought to be the common property of all; and he that attempts opposition to this creed is an enemy to equality and justice and ought to be swept from the face of the earth.
>
> —GENERAL HENRY KNOX,
> Commander, U.S. forces,
> on New England rebels in 1786

It may have been farfetched to think that communist revolution was underway. But that is what General George Washington did think. He was responding to a report written by one of his trusted friends, General Henry Knox, on October 23, 1786. General Knox, who, as Secretary at War under the Articles of Confederation, was commander of United States forces, implored Washington to take a hand in radically restructuring the government.

"What is to give us security against the violence of lawless men? Our government must be braced, changed or altered to secure our lives and property,"
according to General Knox. Knox's letter to Washington was reprinted or
appeared in some version in practically every newspaper in the United States.
Knox claimed that the rebels' "real aim was nothing less than a common
division of all property." According to historian Forrest McDonald, Knox told
Washington that the rebels "intended to march on Boston, loot the Bank of
Massachusetts, recruit additional rebels in New Hampshire and Rhode Island,
and then march southward with the intention of redistributing all property."

The story of the United States of America in the depression of the 1780s
is remarkable precisely because it reflects the common characteristics of
depressions in all times and places. No country is immune from instability.
Wherever you look throughout history, human beings have responded in
remarkably similar ways in the face of sharply falling incomes. This is not to
say, of course, that all depressions are the same. Far from it. No episode is
exactly like another. Nevertheless, many of the features that distinguish
depressions from one another are broadly predictable. Among the more important variables:

1. Market drops are most severe in the most advanced countries.
2. Depressions are most intense at times when there is no predominant
   nation controlling an overwhelming share of financial resources and
   military power.
3. Poor countries suffer more acute instability than rich ones.
4. Creditor countries are more stable than debtors.
5. The intensity of an economic slump is roughly proportioned to the
   degree of debt outstanding when the downturn begins.
6. The more asset prices have been inflated during the boom, the further
   they tend to fall when it ends.
7. Unemployment tends to be greater as the scale of enterprise rises.
8. War in the wake of depression raises prices and tends to mobilize
   output.
9. The deeper the depression, the more likely it is to stimulate a change
   in the methods and magnitude of income redistribution.
10. The deeper the depression, the more it will stimulate migration.
11. Nations with open frontiers are more stable than those with closed
    frontiers and population pressures.
12. The deeper the drop in income, the more pronounced the rise of
    delusional thinking and conspiracy theories, and the more violent
    the retribution against scapegoats.

13. The longer the depression, the more traumatic its effect in altering orientations towards work and the future.
14. The longer and deeper the depression, the greater the chance that it will lead to a closure of the economy.
15. The more stable the country, the greater the likelihood that debt liquidation will take a deflationary course. Inflationary depressions generally result in the government being overthrown.

We will discuss these characteristics and others at greater length, with special attention to the chief puzzle of any depression—what becomes of the value of money.

Distinguishing "Recessions" from "Depressions"

Before World War II, it was common to refer to any business cycle downturn as a "depression." This confused the short-term cycles, normally inventory cycles that recur about every four to five years—what we now call "recessions"—with the deeper depressions, which are infrequent events, recurring every fifty to sixty years. Depressions seem to be driven more by weaknesses in balance sheets than by errors in ordering and stocking of goods.

The difference between a recession and a depression can be described in terms of that old-fashioned toy, the yo-yo. When it is operating successfully, the yo-yo goes up and down on its string, and each fall is followed by a rebound. If the operator makes a mistake, however, the wooden sphere falls to the end of the string, and can only be restarted when it has been completely rewound.

A recession is a downturn that automatically rights itself, normally after little more than a year. A depression requires longer to play itself out. In a deep slump, the economy may unravel for years. The contraction of 1929 took three and half years to hit bottom in the United States. The U.S. economy shrank by 30 percent. The fall was so severe that the United States did not surpass its 1929 output until 1939. The depression of 1837 deepened for four years before the recovery began. After the economy started down in the depression of 1873, it continued to fall for five years, five months.

Recessions are sometimes local in character, affecting one nation only. They are often relatively mild, resulting in only shallow drops in gross national product and the other statistical measures of economic output. For example, the U.S. 1981–82 recession, considered the most severe of the postwar period, caused just a 2 percent drop in GNP. The economy recovered to surpass its 1981 output by 1983. Recessions often last less than a year, and seldom drag on for more than eighteen months.

Depressions, on the other hand, are usually global in scope. They tend to be most severe in the most advanced countries, but are felt even in remote and backward areas. In Indochina in the 1930s, for example, the peasant farming economy was upset when the world depression led to a one-dollar fall in the price of rice. This led to widespread rioting and the abandonment of 560,000 acres in cultivation. The guerrilla wars that flared into the open after World War II were set in motion by the bitter reaction of peasants to the impoverishment that followed the collapse of the world price of rice.

To summarize, recessions are brief, shallow episodes of contraction. They recur, on average, every four to five years in mature industrial economies, like the United States and Great Britain. Depressions, by contrast, are rare events, occurring every fifty to sixty years. They can cause steep drops in output. They tend to last two to three times longer than recessions, and require a longer recovery period.

Inflation or Deflation?

Some slumps are accompanied by dramatic depreciations of currency. These are inflationary depressions. Other depressions have been deflationary. They raise the value of cash. Whether a depression will be deflationary or inflationary is sometimes difficult to predict. The question is whether the collapse of purchasing power is accompanied by a selective or wholesale wipeout of creditors. In either event, purchasing power tumbles. Therefore the real demand for commodities always falls. Real wealth declines, undermining the collateral upon which the structure of debt rests.

In richer, more stable countries, the deflation is accepted. Bad debts are liquidated and solid credit instruments rise in value. In failing, less stable societies, the government attempts to paper over insolvency with printing press money. Nominal interest rates rise, shortening the time horizon by reducing the future value of money to nothing. In an inflationary runoff, real income generally falls even further than in deflation. Most, if not all, debts are wiped away by the inflation and the government is typically overthrown.

Instability and Depression

The countries that have maintained constitutional stability in spite of the destabilizing impact of wars and depressions are few in number. Not coincidentally, they are all rich countries that have had deflationary rather than inflationary depressions. Foremost among them are Great Britain and the United States, the two predominant English-speaking powers of the past two centuries. Other than tiny Switzerland, and arguably Sweden, all the nations that have maintained their constitutional stability over the whole industrial period have been English-speaking allies of the United States and Britain. They include Canada, Australia, New Zealand, and some lesser colonies and appendages.

By contrast, Germany, France, Holland, Spain, Italy, Portugal, and the other cosmopolitan nations of Europe have all suffered through different forms of government since the eighteenth century. Each either was conquered in war or succumbed to internal collapse. The governments of the rising powers of the Pacific, Japan and China, are new since World War II. Among the lesser economies, the record of stability is even more sorry. In Asia, Africa, and Latin America, governments come and go like Elizabeth Taylor's husbands.

Political instability and depression feed on one another. Instability causes economies to weaken. Depression, in turn, undermines political stability. The more income drops, the more likely it is that political institutions will abruptly change for the worse, thus harming prospects for recovery. There is a potential of a downward spiral in any global depression unless some leading nations are stable enough to anchor the system. Since inflationary depressions are politically destabilizing, the leading powers must be strong enough to endure a deflationary economic shock.

The five centuries of economic progress since 1490 have differed from most of past history in that the conditions for growth have remained intact through many shocks. Business cycle slumps, wars, droughts, and plagues have not prevented an increase in prosperity in the West from generation to generation.

While it would be a mistake to forget that depressions automatically lay the groundwork for recovery, it is also important to recognize that the cycle of rebirth may be dependent upon conditions that are subject to change. As a stark example, consider that no observer of economic conditions at the twilight of Rome could have lived long enough to witness the next "long-wave upturn." It was not a matter of waiting twenty to twenty-five years. Economies went into decline and wound down for centuries. We are not saying that such a catastrophe is likely today. But it would be wrong to conclude that some inherent engine of rebirth automatically restores sagging economies as a matter of clockwork. The economies of much of Asia, Africa, and the Americas had experienced little or no growth for centuries before they were opened to European contact and their institutions forcibly changed. A reversion to old forms of misgovernment and institutional weakness could hobble growth into the indefinite future.

If all governments were as unstable, and therefore corrupt and arbitrary as those in underdeveloped countries, it would be far more difficult to restart the world economy once it sank into depression. Economic slumps might have to proceed further before they hit bottom.

Depression and Destitution

Just as a protracted head cold can become pneumonia, a protracted depression, accompanied by political instability, could extend into something worse than depression—destitution. At some times and places, the forward progress of economies has been broken and replaced by long-term decline. This was true throughout Europe in the centuries after Rome fell. It is true of some African countries today. Dozens of economies, from Ethiopia to Mozambique, are not just temporarily depressed. They are collapsing. Falling apart at the seams. When slumps extend from years to decades, and the infrastructure decays, the roads fall apart, bridges wash away, and copper wire from the telephone lines is hammered into bracelets, this is not a temporary departure from the path of economic growth. It is something more permanent. The end of the line. As Theodore Burton said in 1902,

> Depression runs its course and disappears. Poverty remains. The study of periods of depression reveals the fact that there are alternate seasons of activity and dulness in trade and industry, but that these alternate seasons do not, in a series of years, prevent an increase of prosperity. Poverty describes a permanent loss or abatement of prosperity. Progressive and highly developed countries suffer from depression; unprogressive and decayed countries suffer from poverty.

We believe that the conditions under which countries become "unprogressive and decayed" are in large measure determined by megapolitical circumstances. Unfortunately, megapolitics has turned in directions that make it cheaper and easier for disgruntled individuals or small groups to wreak vengeance and havoc on the wider community. If the argument of this book is correct, the consequences of this depression on major industrial countries, especially the United States, will be more trying than any similar episode since the eighteenth century.

Clues from the Past

> In the summer of 1929, then, there was a fairly general expectation (1) that an economic contraction was in prospect . . . , and (2) that a more or less severe fall in the stock market from the heights to which it had risen was inevitable. Neither prospect was viewed with alarm generally, and the timing seemed unpredictable. . . . The Federal Reserve . . . and the Hoover Administration, with a reputed superman at its head, were trusted to prevent either contraction or fall from going to extremes and to reverse the contraction in good time, if indeed the economy

and the stock market did not recover without substantial government interposition.

—JOSEPH W. DAVIS,
The World Between the Wars

At the end of 1929, the *New York Times* looked back on the year to identify its biggest story. It was Admiral Byrd's trip to the South Pole. There is a hint in this that is worth noting. Like the dog that did not bark, the failure to recognize the evidence of impending depression tells you again that expectations are linear. The smartest reporters in the world could not see the importance of the stock market crash in 1929. Their grandsons and granddaughters are unlikely to do better in the 1990s.

The economy had already turned down in August 1929. It was many months later, after the crash, after the Suckers' Rally, afer a slow year with no recovery, after the banks started to collapse, that people began to realize what had hit them. By then, it was too late to prepare adequately.

In the summer of 1990, there was general agreement that the economy was slowing. Yet just as in 1929, few viewed the situation "with alarm." Most people assumed that the Federal Reserve and the administration were prepared to stop a contraction "from going to extremes."

Complacency

If recession should threaten serious consequences for business (as is not indicated at present) there is little doubt that the Federal Reserve System would take steps to ease the money market and so check the movement.

—HARVARD ECONOMIC SOCIETY,
October 19, 1929

The immense, and false, assumption was that the authorities could counteract a depression if one began. This proved untrue in 1930. It is no more likely to be true in the 1990s. Even recognizing that a slump is underway is often beyond the vision of the authorities. Consider that the 1973–75 recession began in November 1973, but, reported the *Wall Street Journal,* "as late as August, 1974, Arthur F. Burns, the Federal Reserve chairman, was assuring Congress that the economy was still expanding."

Widespread complacency is not the only parallel between the situation in 1990 and that on the eve of the last Great Depression. The list is long:

1. Both decades began after a darker decade, in which the predominant power had been challenged militarily, World War I for Britain and Vietnam for the United States.

2. In both cases, the predominant nation had abandoned gold, and as a result, much of the world experienced the symptoms of the inflation/deflation cycle we explored in the last chapter.

3. In the late teens and twenties, and again in the 1970s and 1980s, wide currency fluctuations confused the terms of trade, thus reducing the efficiency of international markets.

4. There was widespread disorder on the periphery in both periods, undermining the security of investment in backward countries. In the 1980s, the flight of capital became, as it was in the 1920s, a major factor straining world flows.

5. In both decades, bond yields fell, and financial distortions were papered over by an outflow of money from the rising financial power, which maintained low domestic interest rates and thus tempted its investors to seek higher returns abroad. "American capital seemed to come from a bottomless well." "Borrowers and lenders had entered an unreal world in which the possibility of disaster had been dismissed. Many countries came to rely upon this flow of American money and their economies would face serious problems of adjustment if its flow was stemmed." For the eighties, change "American" capital to "Japanese."

6. In both decades, the center of gravity in the world financial system shifted: from London to New York in the 1920s, from New York to Tokyo in the eighties.

7. Both the twenties and eighties were decades of lower inflation, in which major tax cuts extended credit booms by raising the after-tax return to lenders. In the 1920s, U.S. personal income tax rates were cut from 77 percent to 25 percent. In the 1980s, they were cut from 70 percent to 28 percent.

8. In both the twenties and eighties consumption spending fueled by debt was the main engine of growth. As an economic historian wrote of the twenties, "The public had gone into debt on a large scale to finance purchases of homes, [and] consumer durables. . . ."

9. In both decades, job growth was in services, not manufacturing. Manufacturing jobs declined, along with the number of manufacturing firms.

10. There were sharp falls in union membership in both the twenties and eighties. In the twenties, union membership fell by more than 30 percent.

11. Both decades saw a growth of speculation, and strong bull markets on Wall Street. The eighties were only the second decade in the century in which stocks had risen five years in a row.

12. The effect of the bull market and secular changes in the economy was to concentrate wealth in the hands of savers, thus increasing the disparity of income between the rich and poor. Real income gains during the 1920s were minimal for wage earners. The lower 93 percent of the nonfarm population lost income from 1923 to 1929. Likewise, workers with only a high school education lost income during the 1980s.

13. Both decades saw wealth and business glamorized, and politics took a conservative turn, with Republican presidents in the White House.

14. Both decades experienced strong construction booms, with a tremendous growth of home mortgage debt in both decades.

15. Both decades gave rise to the conviction that prosperity was now permanent. In the 1920s, economists spoke of a "New Era" in which the business cycle would be a thing of the past. In the 1980s, economists like Ed Yardini proclaimed that there might never be another recession.

16. In both decades, banks sought new outlets because blue-chip companies no longer needed the banks to borrow.

17. Both decades saw widespread bank failures, particularly connected with sour real estate loans. From 1921 through 1929, 5,421 banks failed in the United States, a liquidation process that has no parallel except in the 1980s, with the savings and loan debacle, Penn Square, and the Texas bank insolvencies.

18. There was a bull market in trade associations in the 1920s and again in the 1980s.

19. Farming went into depression early in both decades, but recovered, and farm income rose during most of each decade.

20. In both the 1920s and 1980s, there were significant drives, culminating in legislation, to curtail immigration into the United States.

21. In the twenties, law enforcement was diverted by a concerted nation-

wide effort to prohibit the use of alcohol. In the eighties, the latter-day version of Prohibition was the "War on Drugs."

22. In both decades there were considerable moves toward disarmament, with far greater progress being made in the twenties, but the movement of the late eighties was more startling.

23. In both decades, efforts to negotiate tariff reductions and bring about European unity were proposed. In the late twenties, the aim was a "United States of Europe." In the eighties, more progress seems to have been made in achieving an integrated, twelve-member European Community.

Some similarities between the conditions in the two decades are striking. Still others could be cited. It may even turn out that both depressions will have begun far from the places where most sophisticated investors fixed their attentions. If true, this will be confirmed only in hindsight, after official statistics in the United States, Europe, and Japan acknowledge that a recession has begun. The depression of 1929 did not begin on Wall Street. It did not even begin in 1929. It began in 1927 when economies at the periphery, like Australia and the Dutch East Indies, began to wind down. By 1928, the slump had taken hold in Latin America and Eastern Europe. Brazil, Argentina, Finland, Poland, and even Germany were all in depression before Wall Street's bull market ended. There may well be a parallel in the 1990s. As we write, Finland, Brazil, and Poland were once again in depression, a condition they shared with much of South America, Africa, and all of Eastern Europe and the former Soviet Union.

The 1980s Were Not the 1920s

The many parallels between the twenties and the eighties do hint that a depression may be coming. But they do not mean that the 1990s will be a carbon copy of the 1930s. To the contrary. They may be very different. In the United States in particular, many conditions in the 1980s diverged from those in the twenties. Some of these differences are implicit in the fact that the United States is now the declining rather than the rising power. The role that the United States played in the twenties has been supplanted by Japan, while the United States is in a situation much like that of Britain, but worse. Consider:

1. In the twenties, the United States was the world's leading creditor. In the eighties, it was the world's largest debtor.

2. The federal government had a budget surplus each year from 1920 through 1930. From 1980 through 1990, the United States ran massive deficits. The national debt was reduced by more than 33 percent during the twenties. It increased by 342 percent during the eighties. In the twenties, the debt was mostly of long maturity. In the eighties, the average maturity of the marketable debt was just six years, and most of it was in short-term instruments that had to be rolled over frequently.

3. In the twenties, the United States was on the gold standard. The United States had the lion's share of the world's gold reserves. In the eighties, the dollar was a pure fiat currency, and American monetary reserves had dwindled to just 9 percent of the world total, down from 50 percent in 1952. Gold reserves were also a far smaller fraction of the total volume of outstanding dollar liabilities.

4. In the twenties, the U.S. government had almost no unfunded liabilities outside of meager veterans' benefits and pensions. Today, unfunded liabilities, off-budget borrowing, loan and deposit guarantees, government pensions, and unfunded Social Security obligations amount to approximately fourteen trillion dollars. As of 1992, according to an estimate compiled from government data, federal liabilities exceeded assets by 16 trillion dollars.

5. In the twenties, the United States ran a significant trade surplus. In the eighties, it ran the largest deficit of any trading nation in the history of the world.

6. The twenties were a decade of high savings and high gross domestic investment in the American economy. The eighties were a decade of record low savings and low investment.

7. Productivity growth in the United States skyrocketed by more than 50 percent in the 1920s. It was stagnant in the eighties, just as British productivity growth had been in the 1920s.

8. Helped along by high productivity growth, prices remained stable during the 1920s. During the eighties, inflation was half as virulent as in the seventies, but consumer prices for the decade still rose by 53 percent. Interestingly, if productivity growth in the United States had matched that in the twenties, prices in the eighties could have remained stable. Part of the reason they did not was the heavy weighting of services—which have experienced little or no productivity growth in the CPI. Real goods prices fell by 4 percent to 5 percent annually during the 1980s relative to services.

9. In the 1920s, the United States had the lowest interest rates in the world. The average annual yield on long-term U.S. government securities in 1929

was 3.6 percent. During the eighties, U.S. rates were far higher than those in Germany, Switzerland, Holland, and Japan. In the summer of 1990, U.S. long bonds yielded 8.9 percent. Other interest rates were equivalently lower in the twenties. The ten-year average of mortgage rates in Manhattan for the decade was just 5.89 percent, while the average rate on farm loans nationally was 6.2 percent. High-grade corporate bonds issued in 1929 yielded just 5 percent, while New York state municipal bonds yielded 4.5 percent. By contrast, in 1990, mortgage rates were at 10 percent or higher, high-grade corporate bonds were yielding 9 to 10 percent, and New York tax-exempt municipals averaged 7.3 percent.

10. In 1929, American corporations were loaded with cash. In 1990, they were hocked to the gills. Interest payments were taking a record share of cash flow, almost a quarter of every dollar. This broke the record set at the depths of the 1974 recession. Normally interest burdens do not peak until a recession reaches bottom.

11. In 1929, Argentine and most other foreign debt was selling at par. The 1920s were, in A. D. Noyes's words, a "defaultless era in foreign lending." In August 1990, Argentine debt was worth 14 cents on the dollar. Brazil's foreign debt was worth 24.75 cents, Mexican debt was at 43 cents, and the debt of Chile, the sterling foreign debtor of the eighties, was worth only 67 cents.

12. In 1929, the unemployment rate in the United States was 3.2 percent. In 1990, the unemployment rate was 5.4 percent, about midway between the U.S. and British levels in the twenties.

13. Only 51 percent of the American population lived in communities of more than twenty-five hundred persons in 1920. Almost 22 percent of the work force was on the farm. By 1980, the United States was overwhelmingly urban, and only 2.6 percent of the work force was employed in agriculture. There were therefore far fewer persons who were likely to be self-sufficient in food.

14. Total military spending in 1929 was just .6 percent of GNP. Military employment was trivial, and there were few military contractors dependent on government. Total federal purchases of goods and services came to just $18 billion in 1982 dollars. In the 1980s, by contrast, the military budget was ten times higher as a percentage of GNP, and military contracting was a mainstay of many communities. Total defense purchases were $254.7 billion.

15. Government spent just 3.2 percent of GNP in 1929. Less than 10 percent of the civilian work force was employed by governments at all levels. The only nonemployees receiving checks from the federal government were military pensioners and a few retirees. Total federal payments were just $700 million. There was no Social Security. There was no dole for the unemployed. There was no aid to families with dependent children nor were there food stamps. The few destitute who were supported—widows, orphans, the blind—were wards of state and local governments. They had to be judged "deserving" as well as poor to qualify for aid. Most were housed in low-cost institutions like poor houses and orphanages under supervision. Total public welfare expenditures in the United States in 1927, a recession year, were just $151 million in a population of 121.9 million. Adjusted for inflation, per capita welfare expenditures in 1927 were about $7.50 in 1982 dollars. In the 1980s, by contrast, government employed 21.2 percent of the work force, and many millions were dependent on government transfer programs. In 1989, these totaled $539.5 billion in 1982 dollars, or $2,159 per capita. Total transfer payments at all levels of government had increased by 29,000 percent.

16. Outside of the farm community, there were few Americans in the twenties who expected the government to provide for them or make good their losses. Indeed, the common opinion was that entitlements sapped initiative. In this respect, there was little or no racial division. Most blacks were Republicans, who voted overwhelmingly for Harding, Coolidge, and Hoover. In the eighties, by contrast, the entitlement mentality was a fixture of American life. There was a widespread belief that government should absorb or forestall losses, and compensate for real or perceived inequities. This carried over to the legal system, where an avalanche of lawsuits demanded compensation for unhappy outcomes that would not have been compensable in any other society in the history of the world.

17. In the twenties, total federal, state, and local tax collections equaled only 13 percent of personal income. By 1989, tax collections had swollen to 36.8 percent of personal income.

18. In the 1920s, families were larger, and they served many of the functions that government assumed in the later decades of the century. There were few single-parent households. It was not unusual for several generations to live together, providing mutual support. In the 1980s, the family with both the husband and wife living under the same roof with children was now a minority life-style. The population was broken into many more households.

Grandparents commonly lived in another house, and even far away from their adult children.

19. In spite of Prohibition, the United States was largely a law-abiding nation in the twenties. By the 1980s, there was an unprecedented wave of crime and bad manners in America.

20. The United States was far wealthier in the 1980s than in the 1920s. In inflation-adjusted terms, real personal consumption was more than five times higher.

This catalog could be extended. The points of distinction and difference between the economic situation of the United States in 1990 and in 1929 were many. Unhappily, the U.S. position was worse than it had been in 1929, in spite of the great growth of the economy. Governments at all levels were far less solvent. In 1929, there was no gap between the government's promises and the means to meet them. Spending was modest. Taxes were low. The powder was dry. The political authorities had room to maneuver because they had promised little. Notwithstanding lower living standards than those sixty years later, the public in 1929 may have had a greater capacity to withstand an economic shock than the public of the 1990s. People were less dependent, better mannered, more family-oriented, and more used to taking care of themselves.

More Deadweight on the Safety Line

The federal government entered the nineties spending six hundred million dollars a day out of an empty pocket. Its credit was in hock. Outstanding promises and contingent obligations were vast, and trillions of them could conceivably be triggered almost simultaneously by depression conditions. The prevailing view in Washington was that no economically significant bankruptcy could be tolerated. By implication this was a way of saying that it costs nothing to forestall bankruptcies by extending a credit guarantee or enlarging a debt.

The trouble with this philosophy of finance, unfortunately, is that it is an invitation to total ruin. Everyone cannot be bailed out by everyone else, just as climbers who are tied together by a safety line cannot all fall off the mountain at once and be held aloft by one another. For the rescue to work, someone must still be clinging to a solid handhold above the ravine. The greater the deadweight tugging on the safety line, the greater the chance that everyone will tumble down together.

In 1992, transfer payments plus government wages and salaries accounted for an astonishing 61.2 percent of all salaries and wages earned in the private sector. Record high portions of the public were totally dependent upon the government. If the political safety line were to fail, they would tumble in a free-fall from a greater height than ever before. The government would have few means to cushion a hard landing below because politicians had already mortgaged revenues for years to come.

CHAPTER THIRTEEN

WHEN THE MUSIC STOPS

WHY THE WELFARE STATE COULD COLLAPSE

IN THE 1990s

Always pay; for first or last, you must pay your entire debt. Persons and events may stand for a time between you and justice, but it is only a postponement. You must pay at last your own debt. If you are wise, you will dread a prosperity which only loads you with more.

—RALPH WALDO EMERSON

THE JUNKIFICATION OF T-BONDS

In MAY of 1990, *Grant's Interest Rate Observer* held a conference on the credit-worthiness of the U.S. government. It is notable that such a conference was even held. Since the ratification of the Constitution, the federal government's credit has generally been beyond reproach. There were a few troubled moments during the Civil War. There was also a strange notch up in rates during the dark days of the Great Depression. But throughout most of American history, the U.S. government has been able to borrow for long terms at low rates.

However, with the S & L fiasco looming large on the horizon, compounded by the weaking condition of commercial banks, some thoughtful investors began to wonder whether there is a limit to the good credit of the government.

The answer is plainly "yes." There is a limit to everything. The more immediate question is where the limit falls.

Higher Taxes Solve Everything?

Former Reagan Budget Director David Stockman was a featured speaker at the conference. He strongly argued that the U.S. political system is in balance with economic reality. In his view, spending and taxable resources have stayed in equilibrium over the long term. The Treasury's deposit insurance liabilities were nothing new. He foresaw a "peace dividend" that would free 2 percent to 3 percent of GNP to pay for domestic spending. Furthermore, he argued, the federal government could raise taxes by an additional 5 percent of GNP. This would bring the U.S. tax burden up to the level that prevails in Europe. Therefore there was little likelihood that the Treasury would have to pay a premium for credit risk.

If Stockman's view is correct, bonds would be good buys not just in the short run, but over the next thirty years. Bond yields should fall as taxes rise, lifting the capital value of zero-coupon Treasury bonds. A drop in bond yields to 6 percent, which is historically high, would have approximately doubled the value of the Treasury 2016 zeros from 1990 prices. In effect, if Stockman were right, buying the zeros could be an easy way for U.S. investors to pay for coming federal tax increases. Capital gains on the zeros would compensate for much of the loss due to higher taxes.

The Bear Case

Sounds great. Private credit demand shriveled in 1991 and 1992, allowing government borrowing to absorb 70 percent of all credit activity. Consequently, Treasury bonds were able to rally, though the rally was far short of what might have been expected given the weakness of the economy. But over the longer term, we doubt that the market will handle the government's credit demands with quite the calm that Stockman suggests. A closer analysis shows that his arithmetic works only on a static basis. If deflationary debt liquidation gets underway, it may be difficult to fund the government's cash requirements. You can't simply raise taxes by 5 percent of GDP in a downturn without crunching the GDP as well.

Contrary to what David Stockman suggests, the economy and the political system may not be in equilibrium. There is evidence of significant departure from past practice, with liabilities growing far faster than the economy since the late 1960s. For example, the U.S. government's lending not included in the federal budget grew at a compound rate of 16.4 percent during the 1970s and 19.2 percent from 1980 to 1989. The federal deficit itself is compounding at a 17.5 percent annual rate as we write, which is more than triple the nominal growth of the economy. This is clearly unsustainable.

Furthermore, the experience of other countries makes it doubtful that Stockman's basic thesis is correct. Looking around the globe, there appears to be no inherent equilibrium between the financial liabilities created through the political process and the ability of economies to meet those demands. Otherwise, elected governments from Italy to Canada would not find their credit under siege in the markets.

Leverage at a Historic Extreme

At the end of 1992, the American private sector was leveraged to a historic high. With a diminishing number of dollars available to cover debt, and the Treasury's liabilities set in nominal terms, a deflation could greatly increase the Treasury's real borrowing requirements. Of course, some of the burdens of spending could be eased by changes in the law. For example, deposit insurance could be reduced. Social spending could be cut sharply. The military budget could be slashed as David Stockman suggests. These are logical possibilities but not yet political ones. History shows that such steps will not be taken unless they are forced upon reluctant leaders by a crisis. As Carlo M. Cipolla wrote in *The Economic Decline of Empires:*

> It is remarkable to see how relatively numerous in declining empires are the people capable of making the right diagnosis and preaching some sensible cure. It is no less remarkable, however, that wise utterances remain generally sterile, because, as Gonzales de Cellorigo forcefully put it while watching impotently the decline of Spain, "those who can will not and those who will cannot."

Unrest Rattles Bonds

One can hope that society will adjust rationally to a difficult situation. But a severe downturn could trigger social unrest, which, in turn, could be aggravated by spending cuts and tax hikes. Yet even if no unrest develops in the United States, the troubles that beset other countries could nevertheless unnerve U.S. bond markets. For example, civil war in the former Soviet Union, the fundamentalist takeover in Saudi Arabia, or threats to stability in Europe or Japan could have a negative effect on the U.S. Treasury market. This was the case in the 1930s. U.S. Treasury rates notched up after the mutiny at the British naval garrison at Invergordon in September 1931. Sailors went on strike over pay cuts in the depths of the depression. This threat to the stability of the British Empire reverberated around the world. In the Far East, Japan invaded Manchuria. Britain abandoned the gold standard. And interest rates rose around the world.

The European monetary crisis of September 1992 bore many similarities to the monetary crisis of September 1931. While it precipitated major increases in interest rates in most of the European countries, as well as in Australia and Canada, the back-up in rates in the United States has been modest. Nonetheless, the situation is more fraught with difficulty than many suspect.

The causes of Europe's misperceived currency crises are not isolated to Europe. And they are really not issues of currency. They lie with the rapidly eroding credit-worthiness of governments and the unsustainability of the welfare state. Governments across the globe are trapped by popular entitlement programs that cannot pay their way. Structural deficits, enlarged by recession and massive bailout costs, are slipping out of control, with potentially dire consequences for unprepared investors.

The spectacle of 500 percent short-term interest rates in Sweden, compounded by Norwegian rates at 600 percent, Portuguese rates at 1000 percent, and Irish rates at an unbelievable 28,000 percent, shows the stresses that deflationary conditions can place on insolvent governments. It also highlights the danger of being in debt in an unstable environment. The credit cycle unwinding is more powerful than the capacity of governments to bring it under control. A chain reaction of crises is likely to spread as confidence erodes and markets force governments to contract the welfare state. Witness the 20-billion-krona spending cut in Sweden in September 1992. The world's leading welfare state only rolled back entitlements, while essentially privatizing unemployment compensation. It also gutted foreign aid. Similar market pressures forced Italy's Socialist government to put forward a plan for 90 trillion lire of deficit cuts. What appear to be local "currency crises" are really just installments of a global debt crisis that will force further retrenchment on credit-dependent governments.

Structural deficits are unsustainable in a low nominal growth environment once markets realize that rapid recovery is unlikely. The promise of governments to bail out insolvent banking systems and finance unemployment benefits ultimately must be paid either from budget surpluses or by depreciation of the currency. With budgets chronically in deficit in most countries, the expectation of currency depreciation can lead rapidly to a crisis. Funds flow out of the currencies of the countries whose credit is in doubt, resulting in the highly contractionary phenomenon of interest rates rising as economies weaken. The effect is to take away much of the freedom that governments seem to have to finance their deficits through inflation. Governments facing the need to finance massive structural deficits due to the slowdown in economic activity may find that markets can set the price of funding high enough to offset any stimulative gains from inflation. If so, there will be no alternative to direct debt liquidation, and the second, deeper stage of depression.

Watch international bond prices carefully, particularly Italian bonds. There is a widespread sense that Italy's deadlocked political system cannot make the tough cuts that will be necessary to close the structural deficit. Events there may provide a preview of how other G7 countries, including the United States, will respond to the inability of the national government to continue funding the welfare state in a time of depression.

These will not remain theoretical issues for long. They are likely to be put to the test early in the Clinton administration, and on terms much like those imagined by David Stockman in his optimistic assessment in 1990. Military spending will be cut. Taxes will be raised. If the new president follows the counsel he is likely to receive, his economic program will be an unintentional laboratory test of David Stockman's view that the credit of the U.S. government will always answer whatever calls are put on it. It will also test a number of other longstanding civic hypotheses.

The Coming Test of Conventional Wisdom

Perhaps the biggest of these is the idea that active government measures can turn back the tide of depression. Most economists and professionals in the investment community have never doubted this. They have little patience for our thesis that the downturn of the 1990s is a credit cycle unwinding and not an ordinary postwar recession. Some would acknowledge that the debt burdens of the 1980s helped slow recovery. This gives them an explanation for their failure to foresee the dragged-out character of the slump. But they do not really accept the idea that excessive debt has limited the growth potential of the economy.

Most economists and almost all of the investment community continue to expect the U.S. economy to recover without widespread debt liquidation. They may pay lip service to the idea that the debt burden has slowed recovery. But the full implications of that idea have not been faced. They do not doubt for a minute that a sustainable recovery can be engineered without disturbing or lightening the debt load.

In fact, the worst thing that they could imagine is actually liquidating any considerable amount of debt—an unpleasantness which in logic might be a necessary step to clear the decks for recovery. Clearly, if you really thought that someone was slowed to a halt because of a heavy weight strapped to his back, you would favor shedding enough of the burden to make movement possible again.

That is not the case with the conventional economists who talk about the debt burden. They do not concede that any level of debt stands in the way of rapid income growth. Yet if there ever was a time when debt posed a structural impediment to growth, it was in the early 1990s.

Debt Burden Heavier Than Ever

Total debt at the end of 1992 was considerably heavier than at the outset of previous depressions. Sustainable recoveries from the other credit cycle unwindings began only after a considerable portion of the existing debt was paid off or liquidated. Hence the dragged-out nature of recovery from depression which normally takes about four years—as opposed to the rapid recovery from an ordinary inventory cycle recession—which averages about eleven months.

If debt liquidation is insufficient, growth potential will remain sluggish even after recovery sets in. This is a lesson of the 1930s, when politicians made the most concerted efforts at avoiding liquidation prior to today. The result was a decade when growth averaged just 2 percent.

By implication, the sustainable growth potential of the economy should be even lower now, because of the refusal of policy makers to allow markets to clear the excess debt. Even where individuals and firms have gone into liquidation, most of the obligations of banking systems have been refunded at full face value, keeping the debt structure more or less intact. By our estimate, $3 to $4 trillion in excess debt is still to be liquidated.

The authorities, along with almost all conventional economists, continue to look in the other direction. They believe that recovery can be engineered by adding debt. That is the thrust of the standard macroeconomic tools—more government spending out of an empty pocket and easy money to stimulate private credit demand. To be sure, the huge fiscal deficits at the federal level in the United States have somewhat dampened enthusiasm for fiscal stimulus. With government borrowing now absorbing 70 percent of total credit activity, even some conventional economists have begun to wonder whether still higher deficits would not do more harm than good. But to this point there has been little retreat from the view that easy money and more spending can get the economy moving again. There is a particularly firm conviction among business economists that feeding reserves into the banking system at an artificially low price will assure a pick-up in nominal growth, with a variable lag of about eighteen months.

We doubt this for several reasons. First of all, there is a structural impediment that limits the price reduction of credit. Nominal interest rates in the banking system cannot fall below zero. Banks cannot pay people to take money away. Furthermore, people who borrow money must be able to retire their debt. This limits the willingness of creditors to lend and of borrowers to use the available reserves to create loans. At interest rates above zero, investment generated by new debt must produce a rise in income higher than the interest rate, and sufficient to amortize the principal. Otherwise, any additional debt is contractionary. In the downturn of the 1990s, the debt is not paying its way. The American economy has grown, if it has grown, by running down the national balance sheet. The increase in the gross public debt alone for 1991 and 1992 was more than double the total reported nominal growth for the two years.

Debt levels, at about $2.00 for every dollar of economic activity, are too large to be sustained out of cash flow. As soon as balance sheets are depleted, a deeper crisis of asset liquidation is likely. The situation is equivalent to that of a once rich family, earning $100,000 a year and spending $140,000, $400,000 in debt. Unable to service its debt and still live beyond its means, the family decides to hock its remaining assets, and spend still more. Now its debt is $440,000, and its income has barely grown at all. This policy does not prevent a fall in the family's living standard; it merely postpones the inevitable. At the end of the day, the family faces an even worse crisis. When its remaining credit is finally exhausted, it will be forced to curtail spending far more drastically than would have been necessary years earlier. Its living standard will plunge.

This is just the prospect that is likely to face America sometime in the term of President Clinton. His administration will test whether government can successfully contain depression by aggressively refunding bad debt and deploying public credit when private demand is slack. The crux of the issue is whether running down the balance sheet buys recuperative time or merely postpones the inevitable. We suspect that it is a policy of postponement, not prevention. It is the equivalent of encouraging a man who is afloat over his head to tread water rather than turn back to shore. Unless he is able to regain solid footing, he will eventually become exhausted and drown. So it is with an economy floundering in red ink. The multi-trillion-dollar losses suffered due to malinvestments in the 1980s are real. They can only be disguised until the good credit of governments is exhausted.

Can Depression Be Contained?

Running huge debts to postpone a further decline in living standards has been considered a policy success by the few observers, like David Levy of the Jerome Levy Institute, who acknowledge that the current environment is a depression. Indeed, Levy worries that the government deficit may be too small to offset the implosion of the private economy. But this may be a multi-trillion-dollar mistake. As deep as the government's pockets appear in comparison to those of individuals or corporations, even the good credit of the Treasury is a limited resource.

In the early 1990s, transfusions from the public purse kept the pulse of economic activity from faltering even more than it did in the United States as in all the advanced economies. But this cannot continue indefinitely. If a second and deeper stage of depression is to be avoided, growth must be rekindled at a pace that significantly narrows the deficit and allows the government's balance sheet to be restored. Those who speak optimistically about a "contained depression" beg the question. They assume that technological growth will counteract the drag of debt and justify massive new investment, investment that will not only pay its way, but implicitly pay the way for all the trillions in malinvestments accumulated at the expense of excess debt. It would be delightful if this were to happen. But history suggests that once nominal growth slows in a heavily indebted economy it is difficult to engineer a sustained recovery until the excess debt is eliminated.

The fundamental problem blocking real recovery is not consumer psychology, but consumer liquidity. Too many people are tapped out to allow for vigorous growth. Just as after 1929, there has been a surge of permanent job losses, not temporary layoffs. Only 15 percent of those who lost jobs in the downturn of the 1990s have been re-hired. Exports provided three-quarters of the measly 1 percent annual growth reported in the United States during the Bush administration. With foreign economies weakening, even that source of strength is thrown into doubt. Furthermore, the savings rate through 1992 was staggering along at an anemic 4.3 percent. In a debt-burdened economy with low savings, any recovery presupposes a degree of borrowing in the private sector that will tend to raise interest rates. This would imply sharply higher long rates in the double-digit range—which would probably short-circuit recovery by themselves.

A return to deflationary conditions could mean a considerable risk of a credit "reset"—or higher yields on Treasury obligations. The market has not focused on the full measure of the Treasury's exposure in the event of greater banking trouble or a wider drop in real estate values. Nor is it likely to until a crisis makes the evidence of insolvency unavoidable.

Gambling Away the Welfare State?

To a degree that is not yet understood, the Congress may have gambled away the welfare state. Future revenues required to pay for government spending at levels taken for granted since World War II were mortgaged through deposit insurance and credit guarantees into a whole-hog bet on property prices. So long as real property continued to rise, the costs of these guarantees appeared to be negligible. But watch out below when property prices fall. As the S & L debacle demonstrated, the costs of imprudent promises could become ruinous very quickly. In effect, the cornerstone of the welfare state was laid in shifting sands of real estate. If real estate were to fall by 50 percent across the United States, the welfare state could well fall with it. That is the message lurking in the numbers.

It isn't necessary to imagine a doomsday scenario in which all loans go bad at once to foresee a point where the ability of the Treasury to meet its liabilities at tolerable interest rates would be overwhelmed.

"Déjà Vu *All Over Again*"

Slight doubts on the part of the creditors would bring the whole flow of funds to a halt. . . . Bruning was guiding the economy within a very narrow range of options. His high civil servants—Trendelenburg and Schaffer—looked more and more desperately for ways of saving money, even as they realised that the budgetary deflation was helping to undermine political stability as civil servants mutinied and the unemployed took to street warfare.

—HAROLD JAMES,
on Weimar fiscal policy in 1930

The situation of the United States in the 1990s could prove as tricky as that which Germany faced after 1929. Like Germany in the 1920s, the United States borrowed heavily from abroad during the 1980s to increase living standards rather than to invest. A Reichsbank Statistical Department report complained in the spring of 1929 that "Germany instead of allowing the free development of forces in a state based on work is increasingly a state of pensioners and welfare beneficiaries." What was thought true of the pre-depression German economy also appeared to be true of America's entitlement economy in 1990. Deficit spending in both eras reflected deep divisions in society. Tax-consuming constituencies felt victimized and entitled to greater benefits, while taxpaying constituencies doubted the value of much public spending. The expedient of borrowing from abroad to compose the differences was equivalent to climbing to a higher diving board. In Weimar Germany the withdrawal of foreign credit forced the government to take the plunge.

The Germans were forced by threat of withdrawal of foreign credit to run "highly restrictive government budgets . . . at the turn of 1929–30." As economic historian Harold James put it, "The necessity of spending cuts combined with pressure for tax reductions and a need actually to *increase* revenue (in order to reduce the scale of the funding problem) imposed great strains." Curiously, the eve of the depression saw Weimar political parties battling over replacing "damaging" capital gains taxes with consumption taxes, especially taxes on beer. Like the Congress in 1990, the German politicians were unable to agree on systematic reform of the budget. "The parties continued to reject any spending cut or tax increase that might affect their electorate particularly severely."

The falling away of revenues during 1930, however, forced the government to take far more unpopular measures than those previously rejected as infeasible. Income taxes were raised sharply. Unemployment compensation was slashed by 27 percent. All nonpermanent government employees were dismissed. Further hiring was frozen. Civil service pay was cut, first by 6 percent, then by another 8 percent. "Reductions in other areas of state spending were in fact much more drastic than the pay cuts." Loans and subsidies were cut by more than 25 percent. Spending on housing plunged by 60 percent. Wherever possible, the central government delegated spending responsibility to the German states without providing the means to pay for it. The government of Bavaria complained that it was "left with odious taxes and falling revenues."

Weimar Germany's dependence on foreign credit to finance its budget forced the authorities to adopt a restrictive, deflationary budget as the depression deepened. This was true in spite of the fact that hyperinflation in the early twenties had already more or less wiped out the German savings, mortgage, and bond markets. Weimar Germany therefore had fewer financial assets to protect. We believe that a major reason why underdeveloped economies are more prone to inflationary than deflationary crises is that the great majority of assets in such economies are tangible assets, like land, mineral deposits, buildings, livestock, equipment, and inventories that cannot be completely wiped out by inflation. A plot of land and a buffalo will still be worth something, no matter how ruthlessly governments devalue the currency.

By contrast, developed economies have more financial assets than tangible assets. They therefore have more to lose if inflation wipes away the value of money. Bank deposits, bonds, mortgages, and insurance claims become worthless if money becomes worthless. Germany had already suffered with a hyperinflationary wipeout in 1923. As a result, the structure of assets in the German economy when the depression began was more like that of an underdeveloped country like India than that of other modern economies. German financial assets in 1929 totaled just 39 percent of tangible assets, as compared to 30 percent in India, 129 percent in the United States, 142 percent in Japan, 165 percent in Switzerland, and 245 percent in Britain. Because so many German financial assets had already been wiped out, the play of political pressures might have made it easier for Germany to solve its deficits with inflation than is usually the case for industrial countries. Yet the Weimar government was still forced to run a restrictive fiscal policy that aggravated deflation. It had almost no choice because it depended on hot foreign cash to finance the deficits. Only later, after the foreign credit had totally evaporated, and parliamentary government had been scrapped, did the Germans turn to inflation under Hitler.

THE FEDERAL DEBT TRAP

Our sins and our debts are often more than we think.

—ENGLISH PROVERB

The U.S. government could find that it has stumbled into a debt trap in the 1990s similar to that Germany faced after 1929. There is no previous American experience of deficits of the magnitude of those in the 1980s. Not only has new federal debt been added at a record rate, but total debt was skyrocketing as a percentage of the economy. After decades of stability at a little more than 130 percent of GNP, debt skyrocketed to about 200 percent of GNP by 1992. The United States had one foot in a dangerous debt trap in which real interest on the national debt compounds faster than the real growth of the economy. In the eighties, debt expanded at an 11 percent annual clip, while the nominal GNP grew by 8 percent. The U.S. position was further weakened because of growing dependence on foreign capital. A large foreign debt increases the vulnerability to a debt trap as Germany found because the government cannot force foreign holders to purchase additional securities, nor prohibit the sale of securities already held.

During the 1980s, the United States became dependent upon a large inflow of foreign money, particularly Japanese money, to finance U.S. deficits. Japanese investors bought about 30 percent of thirty-year U.S. Treasury bonds. But just because they bought long-term obligations does not mean that the Japanese or anyone else had a long-term commitment to financing the U.S. deficit. In fact, as Marc Faber points out, the average holding period for foreign bonds among the Japanese in 1990 was just three months. In 1929, the average maturity of the U.S. public debt was more than twenty years. By 1992, maturities had shortened to about five years. A federal liquidity squeeze in a downturn would mean sharply higher costs for financing the current deficit, as well as higher costs for rolling over existing debt.

As the 1981–82 recession began, the budget deficit was running at an annual rate of about $50 billion and when the recession ended the deficit rate topped $200 billion.

—ALFRED L. MALABRE, JR.,
Wall Street Journal

Merely the threat of widespread foreign selling of U.S. Treasury obligations could drive already high interest rates higher, and force the government to take what would previously have been considered drastic measures to cut spending and raise taxes in a downturn. This is all the more likely because the potential U.S. deficit in a depression of the 1990s would be far worse than Germany's in 1930 and 1931. The German government was spending only 10 percent of GNP in 1930. Compared to the United States in 1990, Weimar Germany was a model of fiscal sobriety.

Deficit Quadruples in Depression

The budget deficit has quadrupled in the past two recessions. In 1990, the deficit was running at about $200 billion, without fully accounting for the S & L bailout. By this analogy, the deficit would leap to $800 billion, an amount so staggering that it would swamp credit markets, necessitating unprecedented cuts in government spending.

Closer consideration shows that this is not as ridiculous as it may seem. In the depression of the 1930s, receipts fell by 50 percent at their low. Even after massive tax increases in 1932, receipts in 1933 were down by 41 percent from 1929. A similar drop from 1990 levels would put federal receipts at less than $600 billion, when total spending was $1.230 trillion in 1990. Adjust for the higher spending triggered automatically by a slump and you have a deficit of $800 billion or more.

The Off-Budget Liquidity Squeeze

Bankers Will Fight Deposit Insurance Guarantee—
Would Cause, Not Avert Panics, They Argue;
Bad Banking Would Be Encouraged
And Honesty Discredited, Say Foes.

—*NEW YORK TIMES* HEADLINE,
March 26, 1933

Without reforms to cut the Treasury's obligations to absorb losses, the deficit could head even higher than $800 billion. The on-budget deficit would be compounded by an avalanche of defaults involving off-budget obligations. Just because the government insures against some form of trouble does not mean it can't happen. In fact, many financial accidents are more likely precisely *because* the government absorbs all losses. Consider the S & L example. According to *Money* magazine, total costs could exceed $530 billion. More conservative, present-value estimates of losses by the end of the eighties were between $200 and $300 billion.

Failures on such a massive scale would have been impossible if the government had not assured depositors that their money was safe no matter how banks invested it. This is hardly a new realization, as the headline from the *New York Times* quoted above indicates. That story went on to report on the disastrous experience of deposit insurance guarantee laws at the state level. Here are crucial excerpts from the article as it appeared on the front page of the *New York Times* finance section on March 26, 1933.

> Although the banking community is prepared to accept a rigid revision of the banking laws, there is one proposal that bankers here still vigorously oppose— any plan for guaranteeing bank deposits. Attempts to guarantee deposits, the bankers say, have always ended disastrously. . . .
>
> A study of the operations of guarantee laws was made last year by Thomas B. Paton, general counsel of the American Bankers Association, and the bankers rest their case on his brief. Mr. Paton found that from 1908 to 1917, guarantee laws were enacted in eight states: Oklahoma, 1908; Kansas, 1909; Texas, 1909; Nebraska, 1909; Mississippi, 1914; South Dakota, 1915; North Dakota, 1917, and Washington, 1917. "Disastrous results," he said, "led to repeal in 1923 of the Oklahoma law, in 1927 of the Texas law, in 1929 of the Kansas, North Dakota and Washington laws, and in 1930 of the Nebraska law. . . ."
>
> The chief arguments of the bankers against a bank deposit guarantee law is that it encourages bad banking, discredits honesty, ability and conservatism, and would cause and not avert panics. They say the public must eventually pay. . . .

Congress ignored the evidence in creating federal deposit insurance because doing so was in the interest of powerful rural congressmen. Note that all the states that enacted deposit insurance in the early part of the century were large states with extensive farm economies. There was little or no pressure for deposit insurance from financial centers like Boston, New York, Chicago, or San Francisco. But small-town politicians and small-town bankers did have a reason to guarantee deposits. They wanted to forestall the development of a national banking network of the kind that serves other modern economies. To preserve small, inefficient banks required isolating them from market processes. This meant not only limiting competition by banks across state lines. It also required finding a way to attract low-cost funds into what were often small, unstable institutions. Federal deposit guarantees fit that latter requirement. In effect, the local banks were drawing on the good credit of the Treasury to cancel much of the high risk of small-town banking. The beneficiaries were not so much the small depositors as members of Congress, along with the owners and managers of locally controlled banks that otherwise would have disappeared. The local bankers stayed in business isolated from competition longer than would have been the case otherwise. They became major campaign contributors.

The myth, of course, is that Congress was motivated to protect small depositors to prevent them from being wiped out in another depression. While this no doubt played a role in engendering popular acceptance of the deposit insurance scheme, the idea that the depression resulted in massive losses to depositors is much exaggerated. In fact, total losses by depositors in banks that failed from 1929 through 1933 were just $1.413 billion. Adjusting for inflation, the losses to taxpayers caused by deposit insurance in the 1980s were at least *twenty times higher than all the losses from bank failures during the Great Depression*.

This does not even account for opportunity costs of malinvestments in empty office buildings that will have to be torn down, abandoned strip malls, and housing projects that failed. When the government counts the GNP, it does not subtract the sums that were lost by loan officers at now insolvent financial institutions.

The Surprise of Decembers to Come

For some time it has been obvious that many banks, including some large banks, were facing a severe crunch. A law that went into effect on December 19, 1992, requires that banks with less than 2 percent capital be shut down. The anticipation of a surge of bank closures after December 19 was described throughout 1992 as a "December Surprise."

According to Veribanc, the FDIC had a backlog of 204 banks awaiting closure and 1,044 institutions on its problem bank list. Forty to eighty of these institutions were critically insolvent. As we write, however, it appears that the surprise will be that the government lacks the money to close these banks. The FDIC is insolvent. Capital and liquidity restraints of the same sort that are hampering banks may prohibit the government from recognizing the insolvency of banks it is legally required to close.

While the FDIC retains the capacity to borrow from the Treasury, its capacity to borrow at the scale required to liquidate the weak banks would imply a $50 billion to $100 billion new call on money markets. The alternative of aggressively liquidating the FDIC's $44 billion portfolio of bad assets would also accelerate deflationary pressures. It would hasten the bankruptcy of other weak institutions whose collateral would be undercut by the real estate liquidation. The uptick in short-term interest rates in the United States during the autumn of 1992 has been read as a bull sign indicating a recovery. Another reading is that lower rates are an invitation to a gigantic supply of government debt that the markets do not wish to accommodate at prices below 3 percent.

Bank analyst John Rickmeier thinks that some of the biggest banks in the United States could face funding problems on a massive scale if psychology shifted for one reason or another. Every time the banks report, there is a potential for bad news to change psychology. There is also an awareness of growing losses to uninsured depositors as Congress has attempted to trim back the costs of politically embarrassing bank bailouts. Depositor losses at failed banks jumped from $33 million in all of 1991 to $208 million in the first nine months of 1992.*

The lowest-rated American banks, including the "too-big-to-fail" banks, have $600 billion in assets, of which only $500 billion appeared to be performing in 1992. The capital of these banks is far less than $100 billion. They are insolvent. They are vulnerable to meltdown because a large portion of their liabilities is in uninsured forms. Deposits in amounts above $100,000, Eurodollars, and other uninsured instruments account for $250 billion.

The uninsured liabilities of banks considered "too big to fail" were roughly equivalent to 90 percent of the total of the Federal Reserve's current holdings of government securities. Any disruption that changes psychology and causes the withdrawal of funds from the weak banks could create a greater crisis than any so far in the downturn. Beware of these systemic risks. And closely watch your uninsured deposits.

A process which has already been damaging the world's banking system clearly has further to go. Banks are losing confidence in their customers, and the customers are losing confidence in their banks. The banks are losing confidence in their customers because too many of their loans have proved bad, first to the Third World, but now to domestic customers, including home owners. There is no longer a feeling that the bank can rely on the people it knows; and the way banking is now organized, banks do not know their customers in the way they used to.

Customers are also losing confidence in their banks. That is partly because too many banks have gone to the edge of financial stability. When a bank's credit rating is downgraded, it damages the confidence of its customers as well as of its creditors. And few banks have proved reliable supporters of businesses during the recession. Oddly enough, it is in the recovery phase,

*Data furnished by Veribanc, Inc., Post Office Box 461, Wakefield, Massachusetts 01880.

when business security is rapidly improving, that banks are most likely to ask for loans to be reduced.

The combined effect is that money will tend to flow only toward the strongest banks, and that banks will make loans only to the strongest borrowers. We shall get a two tier system, in which the triple A banks will lend at low rates to triple A customers, and second-rate banks and second-rate borrowers will be left out in the cold.

Confidence—trust—is the basis of the whole financial system. There is not as much trust about as there was. And as the losses of uninsured depositors compound, there could be still less. The dimensions of a crisis in confidence could be huge. Note that it would probably take an FDIC cash outlay of about $50 billion just to close Citibank. Cash outlays for banks with assets in excess in $1 billion have been running at about 30 percent of assets. Citibanks' total assets are $169 billion.

Citibank is not likely to be closed, whatever its difficulties, but many other banks could be targets for closure, and they will require cash outlays of 25 percent to 30 percent of total assets. President-elect Clinton has indicated that he would like to see the problem tackled early on. If this happens, expect it to add to the massive charges against the Treasury.

Deposit insurance is hardly the only high-risk credit guarantee that the federal government has issued. Total guarantees and liabilities are in the trillions. The risks in these unfunded promises are not only hidden from plain view, they are concentrated to a startling extent. A great many have the common feature of being triggered by a general fall in the price of real estate. Merely regional declines in real estate have already necessitated an S & L bailout that will be by far the most expensive financial debacle in history. This happened while real estate in most regions remained healthy. A generalized fall of real estate would escalate the costs of S & L guarantees by more hundreds of billions, bringing many of the already "bailed out" banks back for more. It would also undermine the recovery value of the Resolution Trust Corporation's huge real estate portfolio.

Any such drop would also spill over to commercial banks. As we write, there were already hints the Treasury's balances were being used to prop up insolvent banks, including some of the biggest in the United States. The difficulties of making such a federal levitation act succeed would be far greater than the bailout of the Texas banks in the late eighties. Note that banks in the Dallas Federal Reserve district represent less than 5 percent of bank deposits, while California represents more than 20 percent. The New York and New England districts, where real estate had already begun to fall by 1990, account for more than 30 percent of deposits. Taken together, the areas where real estate weakness was intensifying in 1992 are more than twelve times as

significant in the banking system as Texas was in the mid-eighties. As of
September 1990, commercial banks had almost three-quarters of a trillion
dollars in real estate exposure, approximately 25 percent of all banking assets.
Delinquency rates were at 11 percent in Arizona, 9.8 percent in Massachusetts,
8.6 percent in Rhode Island, almost 8 percent in Connecticut, and almost 7
percent in New York.

Additional Liabilities

Banks and S & Ls are not the only real estate investors, of course. Even many
of the ostensibly uninsured lenders and owners, like insurance companies
and pension funds, cannot lose in a big way without transferring their liabilities to the Treasury through the Pension Benefit Guarantee Board. The
PBGB has been running in the red almost from its inception. It insures $800
billion in pension benefits that are indirectly tied to real asset values—as well
as to the health of the corporate economy.

There is more. The Treasury is also exposed to another $800 billion in
guarantees of mortgages through agencies such as the FHA, Freddie Mac,
Fannie Mae, Ginnie Mae, the VA, the Farm Credit System, Farmer Mac, and
the Federal Home Loan Banks. Even Sallie Mae, the student loan agency, is
a major holder of home equity loans—with $35.5 billion in loans outstanding
as of 1989. Sallie Mae was an exception in one respect. It had sufficient capital
to cover 2.9 percent of its obligations. Most of the other government-sponsored credit agencies had capital bases so thin that they would have been
insolvent had they been thrifts. Practically without exception, these government-sponsored credit agencies are lending at below-market standards, with
as little as $1 of capital supporting $160 in loans. For an excellent in-depth
study of the frightening risks of government-sponsored enterprises, see *A State
of Risk* by Tom Stanton.

Many agencies fail to document their loans adequately, or even maintain
their books. The FHA, for example, was not fully audited for ten years because
of the lack of a usable accounting system. The FHA was said to hold $17
billion in mortgage losses in 1990. Ginnie Mae was hit by the default of seven
companies that were servicing more than $10 billion of mortgages. Its losses
were mounting. This was even before a downturn began.

A hint of things to come was provided by a GAO audit of the Farmers
Home Administration. It found a 40 percent default rate. A downturn could
spread such massive defaults throughout the government's loan and loan
guarantee programs. It is hard to see how such losses could be easily absorbed
in the budget. The full logical implications of the situation are psychologically

unthinkable. A 50 percent drop in residential real estate prices could bring the U.S. government to the brink of insolvency.

The very idea seems preposterous.

Yet if you work through the numbers, it is hard to imagine how even the federal Treasury could fund the guarantees that it has given. Anyone who thinks about the true financial condition of the U.S. government must be frightened. A special committee of the Social and Economic Congress of Japan, including Yoshio Okawara, former Ambassador to Washington, has warned Japanese investors that Congress may default on the national debt.

The Largest Put Option of All Time

In effect, the U.S. Treasury is like an insurance company without reserves. Congress has gambled the good credit of the country by writing trillions of dollars of coverage against the fall of real estate prices in the United States. If real estate continues to weaken broadly or very far, the consequences could be more serious than most investors have imagined. The avalanche of losses could create a mismatch between current obligations and assets unprecedented since U.S. Treasury paper sold for less than fifteen cents on the dollar in the eighteenth century.

To put it another way, the government is like a highly leveraged futures trader who has bet everything on the proposition that a certain price will rise. If the market goes the other way, as we think it will, the power of leverage could be brought into play to create losses of an unmanageable kind.

WHAT GOES UP COMES DOWN

Everybody was making money on land, prices were climbing to incredible heights, and those who came to scoff remained to speculate.

—FREDERICK LEWIS ALLEN
on real estate in the 1920s

In many parts of the United States and the world, property prices have skyrocketed since the 1970s. Many think that such gains are permanent. We doubt it. Reliable statistics on property prices are skimpy, and few date back before World War II. But the numbers that do exist suggest that real estate tends to give up most of its inflationary gains during each depression period. This not only has unhappy consequences for the balance sheet of the gov-

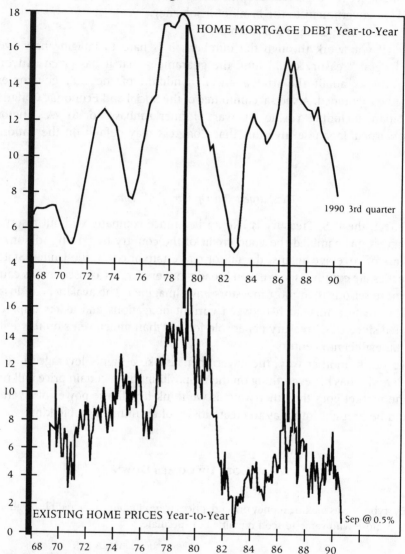

Deleverage Leads to Deflation

An acceleration in mortgage debt growth leads to an acceleration in home prices.
A slowdown in mortgage debt growth leads to falling home prices.

SOURCE: C. J. Lawrence

ernment, it also implies a dramatic loss of net worth for most middle-class families—a factor that will feed back into politics.

In every case we can find, the boom periods before previous depressions have produced inflationary gains in property prices. These gains were never uniform across regions, and local effects amplified or even canceled small fluctuations. Yet generally speaking, real property has tended to appreciate or depreciate in line with monetary forces of the economy. When inflation was extreme, property prices rose higher, and subsequently fell further when deflation took hold. In short, the higher prices rose, the harder they fell.

Our forecast of a real estate crash in *Blood in the Streets* spelled out many of the reasons that prices have already begun to sag. Rather than repeat a lengthy argument here, we urge you to take a look at chapter 8 of that book. Alternatively, look at the real estate section of the newspaper and talk with your neighbors. Either should provide evidence that real property prices can fall. The question for the moment is whether these price falls will be significant enough to trigger the put option on which politicians have gambled the future of the welfare state. The answer may well be yes, if real estate falls as far in the coming depression as it did in the last two.

Total Inflationary Gain Wiped Out

A casual look at the Commerce Department data on home prices in the twentieth century would belie this conclusion, in part because U.S. statistics are formatted to start with 1929 as a base year. For example, at the Department of Commerce the price index for private homes in twenty-two major U.S. cities shows a fall from 100 in 1929 to 75.7 in 1933. This is a drop of 24.3 percent. It is hardly trivial. But it is more frightening when put in context. The depression-era drop in U.S. housing prices (understated in the government statistics) wiped out the *total gain* during the inflationary boom dating back to World War I. In 1914, the index stood at 78.1—higher than in 1933.

Similarly, the index of the average value of farm real estate per acre in the United States (1967 = 100) rose from 28 in 1914 to a high of 48 in the early twenties. It then tumbled to a low of 19 in 1933. The total gain in farm land from the inflationary boom was wiped out in the depression. At the bottom, land was worth 33 percent *less* than it had been before the boom began.

The twenties were a period of a tremendous building boom. A higher percentage of the total economy was devoted to housing construction than at any time in American history. From 1921 to 1930, approximately $61 billion (in 1929 dollars) was invested in the construction of new private homes. Another $4 to $5 billion was spent on additions and alterations to existing homes. In spite of the huge investment in new and improved housing, total nonfarm residential wealth in the United States tumbled from $108.4 billion in 1929 to just $81.3 billion at its low in 1935. This was 12 percent below the comparable figure for 1920.

Similar Pattern in Britain

British data show a similar pattern in prices of private homes and farm land for the previous "Great Depression" that began in 1873. It, too, wiped out the whole inflationary gain during the preceding boom. Private houses in Britain rose in value by 13 percent from the period 1851–52 to their peak in the years 1876–77. They then declined by 19 percent over the next thirty-five years. In 1912, they were 9 percent lower than they had been in the period 1851–52.

The value of British farm land also tumbled. Tax records show that rental values rose by 24 percent from 1846 to 1875. This entire gain was then wiped out, as values dropped by 37 percent over the next twenty years. By 1900, income yields from British farm land were 17 percent lower than they had been in 1846.

Evidence from the past two depressions shows that deflation reduced the value of the average home each time by wiping out the inflationary gain of the previous boom. Values of farm land fell even further, setting at levels about 15 percent below where they stood when the boom began. It would be too simple to pretend that such averages capture all the elements that will determine how far real estate prices could fall in the 1990s. Yet it is chilling to note that a similar retracement today would drop the price of the average American home by two-thirds or more and reduce the value of farm land to an average of about two hundred dollars an acre.

If you are among the millions who have a high percentage of your wealth in real estate, take note. The danger of being wiped out, or having a large portion of your assets eroded, may be greater than you may think. In 1989, the average price of existing homes in America was approximately one hundred thousand dollars. A drop back to the prices of 1973 would mean a loss of almost sixty-five thousand dollars in capital, enough to wipe out the average homeowner, whose mortgage debt in 1989 came to 49.2 percent of equity. Even if another downturn had a less pronounced impact on real estate prices than previous depressions, it could still wipe out the entire equity of many property owners—especially of persons who have purchased recently.

Those who have held houses for a long time, including most older home-owners, have little or no mortgage debt. For the overall mortgage debt in owner-occupied real estate to reach 49.2 percent, more recent borrowers had to be leveraged to the hilt. There is no doubt that debt has skyrocketed as housing gains have slowed. Total mortgage debt was just 40 percent in 1985, up from 25 percent in 1952.

For older owners, housing has been a substitute for financial savings. Before these paper windfalls generated during the seventies and eighties can be converted to cash, however, new buyers must be found. Most of these buyers will not have sufficient cash reserves to pay 50 percent down. Therefore, mortgage lenders will have to absorb a growing share of the housing market risk for prices to remain stable at 1990 levels. They are unlikely to do this. Losses on real estate loans have been the main cause of increasing losses in the banking system. Creditors normally react to rising losses by curtailing lending, imposing higher qualifications on borrowers, and raising loan rates higher than they would be otherwise.

As this trend becomes apparent, aging homeowners, who are depending on their homes to provide retirement security, will try to sell. This will push prices down further. Paul Hewitt estimates that "the predicted trade-up market among the Baby Boom generation (born 1946–1964) may not fully materialize if a growing number of middle-class boomers elect to remain in housing they consider merely adequate, rather than risk their equity in large luxury homes."

A combination of demographic trends, the deflationary fallout from the end of the Cold War, and the breakdown of infrastructure in urban areas could make housing perform poorly. This would hit the middle class hard, endangering the savings of millions. It could be just one of several factors contributing to the evaporation of retirement.

Wealth Disparities to Increase

. . . the dying ashes spreading on the air the fat savour of wealth.

—AESCHYLUS

The last depression reduced the inequality of wealth. The tumble in the stock market and the losses from repudiated foreign bonds were borne almost entirely by the wealthy. Furthermore, the wealthy owned a larger percentage of the nation's real estate wealth in 1929 than they did in 1990. However, the coming depression may increase inequality rather than reduce it because the lion's share of the losses may come in real estate, which has been bid to more fantastic heights by the Cold War inflation. The middle class have the largest proportion of their assets in real estate.

Deflation raises the value of financial assets relative to tangible assets. The rich are therefore likely to gain proportionately for the not very mysterious reason that the rich as a group have a greater proportion of their wealth in financial assets. On average, the top 10 percent of income earners have only about 15 percent of their assets in housing as opposed to over 50 percent for the middle class. Fifty-five percent of American families have negative financial assets. Their debts exceed the value of all the stocks, bonds, bank deposits, and other financial assets they have. This is disproportionately true of black families.

> We can actually pinpoint 1990 as the year of the world's greatest depression ever. . . . The germ of this calamity has already been planted by the misguided fiscal policy of the Reagan Administration. During the 1920s, the pro-business, pro-affluent tax cuts caused a sharply higher concentration of wealth, which eventually led to the collapse of the economy. During the 1980s, the pro-wealthy tax cuts are producing the same effects. The inequity of wealth is now climbing at an unprecedented pace. Within a few years, this inequity will surpass even its peak reached in 1929. This is because currently there are two factors operating to raise the disparity. Low or zero taxes paid by the affluent is only one cause. The historically high rate of interest, itself the product of wealth concentration, is another.
>
> —Professor Ravi Batra,
> *The Great Depression of 1990*

Batra's theory that "pro-affluent tax cuts" have set the stage for depression has obvious charm for many politicians and interest groups—even though it is demonstrably false. The top 1 percent of income earners pay twenty-four times their proportionate share of total federal income tax, an amount that increased by more than 10 percent since the 1981 tax cuts. If the rich are getting richer, it is in spite of the fact that their share of the total tax burden has gone up.

Nonetheless, the delusion that the rich pay "low or zero" tax resonates with a deep wish to increase the redistribution of income. You will hear more about it in the months and years to come. Before long, half the people you meet will have it in the back of their heads that, if a depression begins, it was because of inequality of wealth.

This is unfortunate, because if the bottom does fall out of the economy, as we believe it may, the political strife will be aggravated if people believe that the rich are the source of their miseries. Take note, and, if you have money, try not to show it. The advice, "If you've got it, flaunt it," was composed during a boom. It does not suit depressed circumstances.

Depressions are always periods of abrupt political change. What seem like harmless, crank obsessions, like Batra's plan for a wealth tax, could be voted into law, especially at the state level, if the unemployment rate again tops 20 percent. During the nineteenth century, most states had personal property taxes that included all assets, presumably even stocks and bonds. These taxes were drawn in an age when most assets were tangible assets, like real estate, livestock, farm implements, and buildings that could not be hidden. Personal property taxes are not well suited for an age of intangible assets that can be moved or hidden. But this won't necessarily prevent some hard-pressed state and local governments from reaching for confiscatory personal property taxes in a slump—especially in jurisdictions where the owners will be a racial or ethnic minority distinct from the majority of voters.

A wealth tax at the national level is also a possibility, in spite of the fact that it would be an obvious violation of the U.S. Constitution. The constitutional amendment that provided for an income tax did not repeal the earlier ban on a capital tax. But such niceties may not withstand the rush of circumstances. Remember, Franklin Roosevelt confiscated gold, which was a clear infringement of the prohibition against taking property without compensation. Indeed, it was an idea so radical at the time that a member of Roosevelt's own cabinet described it as "the end of Western civilization as we know it." And of course, more moderate policies, such as a steep hike in the income tax, are possibilities, in spite of increasingly footloose wealth. Herbert Hoover more than doubled the top federal tax rate in the last depression. Such policies, which would have been entirely unthinkable a few years earlier, may be attempted again in the 1990s.

Such taxes would mainly be vindictive, not economically useful. Wealth is an antidote to depression, not its cause. A wealth tax would make the rich poorer or send them abroad. It would do nothing to stop a depression or strengthen the overall economy. To the contrary, confiscatory taxes would reduce savings, discourage work, and increase indebtedness. To pay a tax on wealth, much of which is illiquid, would require either reduced savings or more borrowing. It would discourage investment in start-up companies that do not pay dividends, and retard the economy in other ways. In the past, the severity of depressions has been correlated to the amount of debt outstanding when they started. The more debt, the deeper the downturn. Professor Batra's "cure" for depression would make matters worse. But this is not to say that it won't happen.

A New Taboo on Debt?

A more positive sign for America's future and those who invest in it would be the emergence of a new taboo on debt. When people have suffered from overindulging in some practice, rules often change in the wake of a trauma to place it off limits. The bitter experience of debt default and debt bondage by taxpayers could lead to at least a partial repudiation of the high-tax policies that encourage debt. That would be far more constructive for the future.

Diverting Attention from the Real Problem

The delusion that the rich as a group are to blame for depression deflects attention from the real problem—the fact that American society has indulged in economic profligacy. Both government and society have lived beyond their means. Vast sums were wasted. Debt skyrocketed. And so did counterproductive behavior. These are intimately connected causes of economic decline. The balance sheet of the United States has been run into the ground, not by the rich, but by politicians catering to constituencies who want something for nothing.

As we analyze in detail elsewhere, part of the problem has been the growth of income redistribution—which reflects the deteriorating capacity of governments to maintain order. The political etiquette of this process has served to disguise the degree to which many of the poor contribute to their own plight. For reasons we have canvassed at length, a major cause of poverty and rising social disorder are the life-style choices of the poor themselves. Chronic failure to take advantage of abundant educational opportunities, for example, assures that incomes among the lower class will not rise in a period when returns from manual work fall.

Yet we hear very little overt criticism of the unwillingness among the poor to apply themselves. Quite the opposite. The common response is to exonerate the poor for their part in economic decline, while the more productive and successful are blamed. This makes about as much sense as a farmer beating his most productive milk cows because the rest of his herd has gone dry. The rising tide of resentment against achievement is a negative indicator for the future.

Inequality Not a Hamper to Growth

Inequality of wealth, *per se*, is not necessarily a negative for economic growth. Where the poor have a low propensity to save, inequality of income is essential for economic growth. As economic historian Carlo Cipolla points out, "a high concentration of wealth is an indispensable condition to the formation of savings" under some circumstances. A growing disparity of assets is sometimes a sign of rapid progress. It spurs people with little income to adjust their behavior and values in imitation of those who succeed. Inequality exploded during the takeoff phases of industrialization. This did not stifle growth. The compound growth rate of some economies in the nineteenth century, when inequality was high, exceeded that during the twentieth century, when inequality of wealth has generally been lower.

Rising inequality may also be a sign of a society in decline. The burdens of high taxes fall hardest on the poor—even if the rich pay the lion's share. As Playfair observed long ago, "Long before a country is as highly taxed as the majority of its inhabitants will bear, those who are the least able to pay are crushed, and reduced to absolute poverty."

Everyone is better off, rich and poor alike, when total wealth rises. Those who have little are worse off when a tumbling stock market wipes out billions of dollars of assets—even if they end up with a higher proportion of a shriveling pie.

High Inflation Led to Lower Tax Rates

The decline in marginal tax rates has helped increase the value of some financial assets, such as bonds, by raising their real returns. But the full story is quite different from what Batra and others suggest. The closer you examine it, the nearer you come to an understanding of the mechanism that really triggers deflation—the explosive compounding of debt.

In both the 1920s and the 1980s, so-called "pro-affluent" marginal tax rate reductions were enacted in the wake of high inflation and interest rates spiking to peaks unprecedented in the previous three or four decades. These unexpected bouts of inflation, associated in the teens with the breakdown of British power in World War I, and in the seventies with the decline of the United States, rewarded debtors and cost creditors dearly. This created an imbalance in returns between savings and borrowing that had to be redressed. Higher real interest rates were one solution. These, indeed, characterized both the 1920s and the 1980s. But the rise of real rates was tempered in each case by changes in the tax code. Congress cut marginal rates, effectively increasing the return to creditors. This lowered real interest rates for debtors, and thus kept the credit bubbles from popping.

These measures were compelled by the desire of politicians to secure easy credit for debtors. They were not payoffs to the rich for political contributions, although they were no doubt gratefully received. This may be judged from the fact that Congress even repealed the withholding tax on foreign interest earned in the United States during the 1980s. Foreign creditors are hardly a popular or powerful lobby on Capitol Hill. They have no votes. And they make few political contributions.

We expect that taxes on the rich will rise in the coming depression, especially income taxes, because deflation increases the return to creditors. It will no longer be quite as necessary for politicians to encourage creditors, so they will be tempted to encourage borrowers and redistribute income by imposing higher marginal rates against which interest payments will be deductible.

The irony, of course, is that the more successful the attempt to scapegoat the rich becomes, the more it will drive the system toward extremes of deflation or hyperinflation. The tendency to hoard cash and withdraw it from active investment rises as societies become less stable. When investment flows are correspondingly reduced, deflationary pressures increase. These, in turn, compound instability, increasing the incentive to hoard. Historically, as Cipolla notes, hoarding has been endemic "in areas and periods suffering from political and military turmoil."

Deflation, Not Speculation, Raises Financial Asset Values

In any event, Ravi Batra's idea that the rich get richer prior to a depression because they can afford to speculate explains nothing. The rich can always afford to speculate, but they don't always get richer. Look at the Hunt Brothers. They certainly had the wherewithal to speculate during the 1980s. They lost billions.

Clearly, it is not the fact that individuals are affluent that accounts for any gains they make in the predepression period. It is their choice of assets. Those who gain from the early stages of deflation are the owners of financial assets. About 20 percent of these are persons with middle-class incomes or lower. Federal Reserve statistics on the distribution of assets tell the story:

Percentage of various assets owned by the top 10% of income-earners:						
30%	28%	32%	92%	72%	85%	80%
Houses	Savings accounts	CDs	Muni bonds	Other bonds	Stocks	Mutual funds
Source: *Federal Reserve Bulletin*, March 1986						

As the chart indicates, middle-class people have the greatest part of their wealth in assets that do not appreciate during a deflationary financial asset boom. In fact, most middle-class assets are real assets: houses (first and second), land, automobiles, furniture, etc. Many families have negative financial assets. They owe debts greater than the value of all the stocks, bonds, and other financial assets they have. This is a recipe for disaster during a deflationary period.

It also explains a part of the widening divergence in wealth between the middle class and the upper stratum of investors. While it is true that investment in financial assets (or investment of any kind) is easier for the rich, because they can afford greater diversification, practically anyone could buy at least a few shares of stock or bond mutual funds. The average individual could have bought quite a few. Mean middle-class net worth in 1983 was approximately seventy-five thousand dollars. If that amount had been invested in blue-chip stocks in 1983, it would have grown to almost two hundred thousand dollars by July 1990.

Few middle-class investors did invest in stocks. Fully 80 percent of all mutual funds and 85 percent of all publicly traded stocks in 1983 were owned by the rich. Since the stock market has skyrocketed since then, while the house and the savings account haven't, it should be obvious why the rich are getting relatively richer. It is no more mysterious than the fact that the people who bet on the winning horses cash the tickets.

It is true that the share of total wealth owned by the rich tends to rise on the eve of a depression. But this is not the cause of a depression. It is a symptom of the powerful deflationary forces at work. The actual cause and effect are practically the opposite of those suggested by Professor Batra. It is not growth in the assets of the rich that causes the depression. It is the approach of the depression that causes a deflationary financial assets boom. Stocks and bonds go up in value. The rich gain proportionately more because they hold more of their wealth in stocks and bonds.

The domestic disparity of wealth would be even greater than it is if not for the fact that U.S. deficits have been financed with the help of massive capital inflows from abroad. Since every dollar of debt must be someone's asset, increased net indebtedness by Americans inevitably raises the share of financial assets owned abroad. Many of the creditors who have benefited from the early stages of deflation are not Americans, but Japanese, British, German, and Latin American investors. Their wealth has risen sharply relative to that of average Americans, who have continued to sink deeper into debt. According to an estimate published in the *American Banker*, the average family is living beyond its means by about ten thousand dollars.

During the 1980s Gross Domestic Expenditures (GDE) have increased sharply relative to Gross Domestic Product (GDP). In 1986, domestic spending exceeded output by an astonishing 5.4 percent. Americans as a group consumed more than they produced. For the eighties as a whole, Americans consumed 97 percent of what they produced, as compared to an average of 90 percent in Europe and just 85 percent in Japan. In the future, Americans will be obliged to produce more than they consume. American living standards, including the pay in manufacturing industries, will have to fall sharply in real terms. The wealth of foreigners relative to Americans will inevitably increase.

As ordinary middle-class living standards fall, the Americans with the best hope of emerging unscathed will be Americans who are investors. Those who are able to invest abroad will tend to gain more (or lose less) than those who depend almost entirely upon wage or salary income in U.S. dollars to support their life-style. This implies even wider wealth disparities after the day of reckoning. But as Donald Trump kindly demonstrated, many of the high and mighty who invested primarily in real estate will also be brought low.

Propensity to Consume Likely to Fall

The need to build financial assets will be a major factor lowering the itch to consume in the United States and Great Britain during the 1990s. This move to build financial assets implies belt tightening and lower living standards during the transition, but ultimately higher living standards as productive values gain broader acceptance and increased investment finds expression in higher productivity. In the long run, a society is likely to be better off placing a larger portion of its savings into financial investment rather than housing.

Of course, this may seem academic to those who have purchased houses or condos near the top. They stand to lose much or all of their real estate investments. Some have no investment. Many properties in the late eighties were changing hands with down payments of 10 percent or even lower. Some houses even sold for negative down payments. They carried mortgages greater than 100 percent of the sale price. Numerous such examples were listed in the October 1, 1988, issue of the *Washington Post*. For example, a mortgage of $136,350 was placed on a house in Poolesville, Maryland, that sold for $135,000. Since real estate brokerage fees and closing costs typically consume 6 to 7 percent of the sale price, any owner who purchases for 10 percent down, let alone a negative down payment, really has no equity at all. It is not a question, therefore, of waiting for a major appreciation of the property to recover investment. The buyer has no investment to protect. If prices fall, he would most likely walk away.

History shows that the fall in prices has just begun. Housing prices had fallen behind the rate of inflation in 80 percent of America by 1987. In oil-producing areas, Alaska, Colorado, Louisiana, Wyoming, Oklahoma, and Texas, prices had tumbled. Banks in Texas in the late eighties were giving away expensive houses for free to sound credit risks for borrowing large sums of money. In

England, too, prices fell in 1989 by the greatest amount since World War II.

We have enjoyed the greatest real property boom in history since the late 1960s. If history is a guide, we are due for the greatest collapse in history. When real estate prices fall, they usually stay down for a long time.

The shrewd investor should take note, and build cash to buy property when the music stops. You should also note the possible consequences of this scenario for the government's finances and politics. The fact that there will be far fewer capital gains in real estate to tax will be the least of these.

Exchange Controls

The U.S. government's credibility will fall sharply as the recession bites into revenues, and the deficit rises. Caught in a cash crunch, dependent upon foreign credit, the authorities will have little room to maneuver when the music stops. A slowdown, much less a retreat of foreign capital, would bring pressures for exchange controls and currency investment restrictions. These would intensify as the U.S. dollar is replaced by the yen and the German mark as the world's reserve currency.

Capital restrictions are common throughout the world. They were instituted by three countries of the European community during the currency crisis in the fall of 1992. They are almost universal among debtor countries. Even creditor nations, such as Japan and Taiwan, have only recently abandoned currency and investment restrictions. Korea still employs them. They were imposed in Britain in the first week of World War II, lasting in various forms for forty years until Margaret Thatcher came to power in 1979. When sterling again became a convertible currency for non-UK residents in the 1950s it remained a blocked currency for British subjects. Investment outside the United Kingdom was restricted. In effect, London was a haven for foreign capital, but a prison for domestic capital. This sorry state of affairs lasted for decades, depriving many British investors of higher profits than they might have earned abroad. As you consider the future, remember, it is unusual for a debtor country to allow its citizens free latitude to move capital outside its borders.

Eating the Seed Corn

The limited financial reserves of households are likely to be depleted early in the coming slump, leaving less cash to finance red ink by governments at all levels. In the depression of the 1930s, national savings were negative between 1931 and 1934. With many more households more deeply in debt, we would expect personal savings to turn negative more quickly. Since the household sector is a creditor of government and business, it is likely that national savings will again be negative, but on a much larger scale than in the 1930s. The country will be eating its seed corn. It is unlikely that the corporate sector will contribute many profits to ease the burden of financing the deficit. The corporate sector had negative savings rates from 1930 through 1940, even though it entered the depression highly liquid compared to today. This time, corporate debt stood at 40 percent of GNP before the downturn began. In such a situation, many assets would have to be liquidated to raise cash needed to feed the demands of government.

You might even see government mandate that a significant fraction of capital in regulated pension plans be devoted to financing the deficit. You could be obliged to buy Treasury bonds for your IRA or 401(k) plan. Employee benefit funds could be required to hold a large fraction of their assets in Treasury bonds. The danger of such moves will overhang the stock market, depressing prices more than might otherwise seem appropriate.

Dramatic Deficits for States and Localities

In the late summer of 1990, states and localities were already facing their largest aggregate deficit in history—$31.4 billion. They will face much larger deficits before the 1990s end. The fall of property tax receipts will be partic- ularly severe as property values drop and families fall behind on their tax payments. Property taxes account for approximately 20 percent of all state and local revenues, but are three-quarters of income for some localities.

This means bankruptcy for these communities if property values fall to the same degree they did in the last depression. The creaky nature of the property tax assessment system will cushion the fall in tax receipts for the first year or two, but at the cost of making the eventual contraction more severe. Here's why. Governments desperate for revenue will not lower tax bills in proportion to the fall of property values. As a result, homeowners and commercial real estate investors will flock to challenge tax bills based upon now-inflated assessments. The assessment appeals system will be swamped.

In 1930 and 1931, the collapse of the local appeals systems under the weight of these challenges had the effect of spurring tax delinquencies. Tax- payers who thought their bills were outrageously high stopped paying. Many could not pay. Delinquency rates for property tax collection skyrocketed— reaching as high as 66 percent in Shreveport, Louisiana.

The allure of not paying grew as the depression deepened, because the tax sale system also collapsed. Tax-title buyers were "wiped out" by the collapse of real estate. Taxpayers realized they no longer faced an immediate prospect of having their properties auctioned for failure to pay. Property tax compliance tumbled.

Extreme economic pressures led to a widespread tax revolt throughout the United States in the early thirties. These revolts were often organized and financed by large property holders, trying to force a reduction in assessments. The owners of downtown office buildings in Chicago organized one of the more widespread and successful of these efforts. With the Chicago collection and appeals process in a particular muddle, 53.4 percent of taxes went unpaid in the period 1931–32.

> A lot of people bought when prices were going up; now they're going down. More of these people view walking away as an option. It happened in Texas and Arizona, and now it's happening in the Northeast. It's not a massive problem, but it could become one.
>
> —KENNETH ROSEN, Chairman,
> Center for Real Estate
> and Urban Economics

In spite of the fact that tax payments are escrowed with mortgage contracts today, it is likely that a widespread revolt will diminish receipts by state and local governments. If property prices drop to the same degree they fell in the last depression, the squeeze on owners would be even tighter today. Inflation has been greater during the Cold War, and property tax rates are now much higher than in 1929. A two-thousand-dollar property tax bill that would be burdensome on a property worth one hundred thousand dollars would be intolerable if applied to a property now worth just thirty-three thousand dollars. The relative tax burden would be more than *eight* times heavier. Many people would simply walk away from their homes, abandoning their mortgages as well as their property tax bills.

Tax Reform Makes Muni Bond Default More Likely

State and local taxes as a portion of income more than doubled from 1929 to 1932. It is unlikely that such an increase would be tolerated in the 1990s. A widespread tax revolt such as that which hit New Jersey in 1990 will largely bar attempts to hike taxes or raise rates to stabilize revenues. In states and locales with an initiative and referendum process, it is likely that spending and taxes will be slashed. The organized opposition to economizing in government will be limited mainly to the tax-consuming groups. There will be very little participation in tax-raising initiatives from the financial community.

Unlike the situation after 1929, when banks were major holders of state and municipal securities, and thus lent large sums in "tax anticipation notes" to keep municipalities going, banks in the 1990s will be less interested in protecting their investments in local government. They have much smaller investments to protect. Tax reform in 1986 discouraged banks from holding municipal securities. In their eagerness to prevent banks and others from escaping federal taxes, politicians have knocked away an important prop shoring up local government finances in times of distress. The limits on new tax-free issues by local government had a similar effect in driving investment banks out of the municipal bond business. Large bond holders and dealers were among the most influential groups in the rescue of local governments from popular tax revolts from 1930 through 1934.

It is likely that many municipalities and state agencies will default on their debts in the 1990s, and reschedule them like Third World countries. These defaults are likely to be far more widespread than in the 1930s and less easy to remedy. In the thirties, with the exception of "tax anticipation notes" that were floated to cover short-term cash shortfalls during the depths of the depression, 95 percent of all state and municipal issues were general obligation issues. They were backed by the "full faith and credit" of the issuing governments. Not so today. A whole kennel of cats and dogs issues, including revenue bonds and paper of independent authorities, carry greatly diluted commitments of states and localities. Hospital bonds. Housing bonds. Sewer bonds. School bonds. These obligations have grown like Topsy because they don't always have to be approved by voters. And the agencies themselves could go out of business much more easily than the states themselves. As Jonathan Laing rightly put it, many state and municipal issues are "as subject to vicissitudes of the general business cycle as the private companies securing the bonds." Most of the bonds that did go into default in the 1930s were ultimately redeemed and back interest was paid within a decade because the borrowing agencies wished to return to the market.

This time, many borrowing agencies may disappear altogether. And some localities could easily go legally bankrupt to shed their obligations. The "full faith and credit" of many municipalities won't be worth much.

There is a likelihood of a surge of downgrades in asset prices of municipal bonds that will be triggered by defaults and redemptions of muni bond mutual funds that will drive down prices in illiquid markets. We anticipate a multi-stage process of collapse for instruments of state, municipality, and agency debt—much like that undergone by Third World debt during the 1980s. At first, weak issues will sell above 90. They will then notch down to about 70, where some will tend to stabilize for a time. The next resting place will be about 50. And the last stop before the frame shop buys the obligations to sell

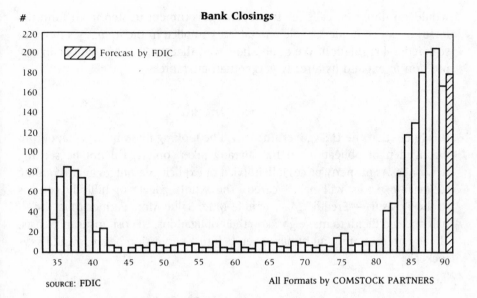

Bank Closings

SOURCE: FDIC   All Formats by COMSTOCK PARTNERS

on Sundays to strollers in the park is 15. Be aware of these price points if you intend to hold low-grade municipal bonds as a speculation.

Financial Institutions to Fail

Banks, S & Ls, and insurance companies are likely to fail in record numbers in the 1990s, as mortgages go into default, properties are abandoned, and the flow of new funds into development projects dries up. Insurance companies were mostly in sound shape in the depression of the thirties. Defaults on obligations to policy holders were prevented by strong companies stepping in to fulfill the policies of the few companies that did go broke. Today, insurance companies are generally more solvent than S & Ls and banks, precisely because they are not directly insured by the government. But the insurance field has become less conservative over the past six decades. There have been increasing failures in the industry, which are costing the larger companies so much money that they have abandoned their longtime opposition to federal regulation. They see the danger ahead, and hope to avoid common responsibility for losses that could mount in the 1990s.

Many insurers have large liabilities to meet high-interest annuities, which they have funded with risky investments, including junk bonds. Others will find their solvency strained if real property prices tumble as forecast. There would no doubt be calls for the federal government to step in to fund the losses to policy holders, which are already implicit in the industry's move to seek federal regulation. We doubt, however, that the Treasury will be in any position to expand its already gargantuan guarantees.

Guarantees Triggered

It is likely that the U.S. government will be looking for ways to escape from the burden of obligations it has already taken on. It will not be seeking new ones. As property prices fall, implicit or explicit guarantees against falling real estate prices will be triggered. The whole gaggle of hillbilly cousins to the Treasury—Freddie Mac, Fannie Mae, Sallie Mae, Farmer Mac, etc.—will find it difficult to make good on their obligations. Deposit insurance costs, already an escalating nightmare even before a depression began, would sky-rocket.

Inflating Around the Problem?

Perhaps the very difficulty of meeting all these obligations encourages people to believe that they will never have to be met. Printing press money sounds like a trick that could keep the price of real estate high, and erode the value of insurance obligations, credit guarantees, and debt outstanding.

This is probably one of the reasons that highly leveraged corporations continued to gain on the stock market through the first stages of the slump. Buyers may have reasoned that if there was a downturn, the weakness of the government's credit posture meant that we would get lots of inflation, which would wipe out corporate debt, now approaching 40 percent of GNP, and raise the value of shares.

Most people would assume that the government will step up to bail out large debtors, an assumption that is closely linked to the assumption that debts will be wiped away by inflation. It is certainly possible that the Treasury would seek to cover its liabilities with Argentine money. They could seek to offset deflation of collateral by printing cash to buy back T-bonds from the market. But such gestures would show up immediately in the weekly Federal Reserve reports. To holders of trillions in bonds, the threat of inflation devaluing their assets would be real. The market would adjust by demanding higher rates. Bond prices would fall. The economy might slip into even a deeper stall. Wealth would be driven into forms like coin hoards and gold that are not subject to repudiation by politicians. The net result could be to make things worse. For the Treasury to persist in inflating its liabilities in the face of troubles it will face in the downturn would amount to a conscious choice of inflation at Latin American levels. This is possible. But we have already indicated why the weight of probabilities favors a deflationary solution to the debt crisis.

Hyperinflation Unlikely

The United States has too many financial assets that would be wiped away by hyperinflation for that to be a ready alternative to deflation. Advanced countries have not experienced hyperinflation except in conditions when they were already deranged by defeat in war. The U.S. government would lose more than it could gain by attempting to cure the coming credit crisis with inflation. That makes inflation less likely, but not impossible.

Much depends on how delusional and unstable politics becomes. The election of 1992 showed that the depression did have a decisive impact on politics. Bill Clinton won the White House in an unusual result. He is the first man ever elected president who carried a majority of the popular vote in only one state—Arkansas. Analysis of the returns shows that the Republican defeat was almost entirely due to the weak economy. At the time of the 1992 election, income had fallen for almost 70 percent of families, with household liquidity at depression levels in many areas, including California, New York, and most of the other heavily populated states that contribute most of the electoral votes needed to win the White House.

Bush ran best in the Rocky Mountain states, where household liquidity is highest. One of the reasons for the relatively strong economies in that region is the flood of people leaving California. The influx of relatively affluent new residents into thinly populated areas is keeping property prices from falling while providing better employment opportunities than are available in the more industrialized states.

Ross Perot won 19 percent of the vote, in spite of running one of the weirdest campaigns in history. Had he not dropped out of the race and then later made apparently bizarre charges about George Bush tampering with his daughter's wedding, he might have won, becoming the first independent elected since George Washington.

We suspect that there may be a hidden logic that matches political personalities to the needs of the time, which gave Perot a particularly strong boost. Although it has not been widely noticed, we saw Perot as a figure much like Herbert Hoover. Hoover was a self-made man who became the highest paid executive in the world before World War I. Hoover was not only rich but, like Perot, had a reputation as a superman who knew how to get things done. Like Perot, Hoover was a pragmatist by disposition, and a man whose political allegiances were open to question. Hoover was offered the

Democratic presidential nomination in 1920, after having served as an advisor to Woodrow Wilson. It wasn't obvious whether he was a Democrat or a Republican, and he could have been either. Perot took that all the way by running as an independent.

Perot, like Hoover, would serve without pay. Perot's metaphors about the political system as an engine, which he would duck "under the hood to tinker with," are strangely reminiscent of Hoover, who was also an engineer, and talked of making the engine of the economy go. Likewise, Hoover was a protectionist, as Perot seems to be. Hoover, like Perot, was also a believer in active government management to target emerging industries, which he pursued in pushing federal support for the radio and airplane industries. Perot is like Hoover in another respect. He is clearly an innovator in political campaigning. It is now forgotten that Herbert Hoover was the first incumbent president to break with the quaint conceit that presidents should not take their case for re-election to the people. He barnstormed throughout the United States to answer what he described as Roosevelt's "lies." Like Perot, Hoover invented his own method of campaigning.

While Perot did not win in 1992, he might be elected in 1996 if the economy weakens as we expect. Perhaps there is an element of necessity as well as chance in the coincidence of political roles played by Harding and Reagan, and Coolidge and Bush. Harding and Reagan were both what might be called "good times" conservatives. They were both elderly men who were great speakers. They articulated the need for American society to return to more normal conditions after a decade of high inflation and disruption. Neither was much of a hands-on administrator. Each administration was touched to some extent by scandal. Each was succeeded by his inarticulate vice-president. Coolidge seldom had anything to say. And Bush, in spite of his Yale education, seemed to have a hard time expressing himself.

Perhaps these characteristics reflect the needs of an electorate at different stages in the unwinding of the credit cycle. The demand for eloquence accompanies the waning of the inflationary decade and the yearning to return the country to a more comfortable style of life. During the relatively benign stages of disinflation, a credit boom begins, and conservatism takes a different form. People don't want to be disturbed, and they choose a president who is not likely to impinge very much on their private concerns.

Finally, as the cycle winds to an end, the public at least subconsciously understands the jeopardy of the situation, and turns to a businessman with a reputation for having made a super-success of everything to keep the economy going.

That is somewhat strained, but the pattern makes a certain amount of sense. If a convincing recovery from the depression has not begun by the end of

Clinton's term in 1996, conventional politics could be thoroughly discredited and the electorate in the United States could clamor for a man on a white horse. The fact that the Democratic Party won control over the White House as well as both houses of Congress puts it in great jeopardy. Unless President Clinton and the Congress respond with remarkable deftness to the challenge of debt liquidation, they can look forward to presiding over the death of the welfare state. They may well be trapped and politically destroyed by the coming paradigm shift. If the political system survives in anything like its present form, the Democratic Party could be thoroughly discredited, not winning the White House again for at least a generation.

This is why the defeat of George Bush could turn out to be blessing in disguise for the Republican Party. It could also be a blessing for the country. If a Democrat is in the White House when the music stops, that could shave four years off the recovery process by allowing the welfare state to have a mercifully rapid death. If Bush had squeaked back to victory, the collapse of the economy on his watch would have given the false impression that "free markets" and "limited government" had failed, because these are his rhetorical stances. The world would have had to endure four painful, indecisive years, followed by a Democratic victory, in which still more extreme state intervention would have been tried only to fail. The Democrats may also lose control of Congress, perhaps even to a new party. The experience in Germany after 1929 was that log-rolling and political paralysis in a highly organized economy led to the widespread discredit of parliamentary institutions.

The Democrats could also be disadvantaged by the appearance of being the party of income redistribution. It is widely, but incorrectly, assumed that the public mood in a time of depression turns immediately toward income redistribution as a solution. In fact, two separate reactions occur. Those without assets or those in organized groups suffering substantial losses blame others for their woes and seek political relief through redistribution. But those with assets or prospects are thereby asked to pay much higher taxes. They tend to fiercely resist, so long as their own financial survival is at stake. In an all-out test between taxpayers and tax consumers, the taxpayers are likely to win— provided they are not a small minority. This is why retrenchment has been the political response to most of the depressions in American history. Retrenchment carried the day in the depression of the 1780s. It also carried the day in the depressions of the nineteenth century. While mega-political conditions were more favorable from the point of view of creditors in the early stages of American history, stability and prosperity still depend upon creditors not being wiped out.

The first real triumph of redistribution as a political theme in a depression was William Jennings Bryan's capture of the 1896 Democratic presidential nomination from President Grover Cleveland. This happened at the very end of a long-wave economic downturn in which prices had essentially been falling for more than twenty years. Cleveland had built his reputation as an advocate of austerity as mayor of Buffalo and later as governor of New York. Cleveland vetoed measures to redistribute income to the poor, including a bill that would have forced down fares on New York City's elevated railways. He also vetoed higher pensions for Civil War veterans and pushed the repeal of the inflationary Sherman Silver Purchase Act, which committed the Treasury to buy 4,500,000 ounces of silver each month. Cleveland's strong stands against inflation and income redistribution made him very popular until the end of his last term, when debtors came to be better organized politically in the South and West through the Populist movement.

Revolt of the Middle Classes

Printed and spoken abuse of government is seen and heard on all sides.

—CARL SANDBURG, 1932

In 1929, retrenchment was once again the predominant popular reaction, although it did not find immediate expression in the policies of government. The initial popular reaction to the depression after 1929 was to blame it on excessive government spending. Most citizens who worked in the private sector were obliged to deflate their living standards and household budgets in line with the contraction of the economy. Governments did not retrench as much as had previously been the case. Partly this was because Herbert Hoover was an advocate rather than an opponent of government action to dampen the business cycle. Hoover encouraged local governments to spend. He tried to keep wage rates up, including those for government employees. Nonetheless, there was a strong popular push to cut public expenses. Government spending was a small portion of the economy in 1929 by 1990 standards. Yet most citizens believed that they were getting little for their tax dollars. There were angry cries to slash spending. Harold Bettenheim, editor of *American City* magazine, an opponent of budget-cutting, observed:

It has become fashionable to decry government and taxes. Demands for indiscriminate budget-slashing are the order of the day. So-called economy leagues are springing up all over the country. Embattled taxpayers are organizing strikes. Fluent orators are taking to the air to attack government and the costs of government.

The American Municipal Association, an organization of city governments, lamented that "there are a great many people with whom the need for economy in government has become such an obsession or mania that they have become violent and destructive opponents of all government." Historian James T. Paterson remarked, "As tax revenue dwindled and unemployment increased economy in government became a magic word."

In short, the initial reaction to the depression was a political demand to cut government spending. Candidates elected to governorships in 1930 and 1932 were generally strong advocates of economy in government. Paterson reports, "Retrenchment dominated the governors' messages of 1931 and thereafter." Even Franklin Roosevelt ran and was elected in 1932 on a platform of slashing government spending by 25 percent and balancing the budget. Roosevelt denounced Hoover for "the greatest spending administration in peace times in all our history." He asked voters "very simply to assign to me the task of reducing the annual operating expenses of your national government."

It was only after the economy stabilized and the household sector ceased having to lower its own consumption that demands for retrenchment began to slacken. The national mood of retrenchment that helped elect Roosevelt is even more likely to dominate in a slump in the 1990s. Taxes as a percentage of income were more than three times higher in 1990 than they were in 1929. The government was far less solvent. Its huge overhang of debt forecloses any significant spending initiatives. The disappointment of easy promises to prevent depression and preserve citizens from losses will likely lead to a reaction. Historically, people who have been harmed by indulging in a practice like falling into debt have invented taboos and stern principles to discourage repetition of such behavior. The political candidate or party that captures the White House in 1996 will probably win on the basis of a promise of improved financial management, which implies a program of retrenchment. It could establish a new era in American politics that could last for half a century or more.

The Market Defeats Monetization

There is no doubt that a conscious decision could be made to ruin creditors and keep the spending going at all costs. But after tentative experiments failed, it would have to be a conscious decision. The market has already adjusted to the practice of inflating to cover the deficit. That battle was fought in the 1970s. A large part of the inflation of the 1970s was caused by monetizing the deficit. As the cumulative deficit rose, the money supply ballooned to absorb it. The market reacted by making a great many structural adjustments, the most basic of which were shorter maturities and higher interest rates. The maturities on the national debt stopped shriveling only when the Treasury started increasing the percentage of the deficit that was borrowed rather than printed in the mid-seventies.

The Treasury turned from inflating to borrowing to cover the massive deficits—because that was the cheapest way to get the money. The result was a major change in the rate of money growth compared to deficit growth. The cumulative deficit since 1960 has risen to a huge proportion of the broader money supply—almost two-thirds. This is more than three times its percentage in 1975. In effect, the huge floating debt is a hostage against significant inflation. For Washington to monetize the debt would require, by implication, a doubling of the core money supply, M-2, in a very short period. Such a massive increase in the money supply would drive interest rates to ruinous levels.

The result would be just the opposite of what is wanted. Runaway rates would collapse the economy, especially the real estate sector, which depends upon the ready availability of credit. While nominal values of real estate would rise, the gains would be offset by devastating losses in financial assets. The multi-trillion-dollar bond markets would be battered. So would capital spending by state and local governments, which is largely financed in the bond markets.

The losses implied by a concerted inflation would cripple an advanced economy. This is why no country that borrows its own currency has ever followed such a course, especially when it depends upon a major inflow of foreign dollars to finance current needs, as the United States does now. There is nothing stopping anyone from selling Treasury debt and sending proceeds overseas at the speed of light. As Kent Davis has rightly said, "The quickest way Uncle Sam can run out of money is to print more of it. In today's environment, the markets can withhold a trillion dollars quicker than the government can print it."

Lower Spending, Higher Taxes

If a fall of real estate precipitates an avalanche of cash demands on the Treasury, the inflationary solution will probably be blocked by the market— just as it was blocked in Germany in 1930. The only way the government will have to pay its bills will be to pay them. That will mean taking the scissors to both sides of the spending equation: obligations will be pared drastically, and the citizenry squeezed for more revenues. What may happen will be far different from what most people expect.

Taxes Raised

Tax rates will be raised, especially taxes on corporations and the rich. Top rates will probably not return to the 70 percent range from which they fell. It is unlikely that the public will believe the "tax more, save less" school of economics that became so prominent in public thinking after 1933. Carl Schneider of the International Association of Public Works Officials declared in September 1933, "We haven't taxed enough in the past, taking the country as a whole. We have saved too much." Few serious people will be convinced in the 1990s that America has taxed too little and saved too much. Furthermore, the increased mobility of wealth in the Information Age is a megapolitical fact that cannot be completely overriden. It will be far harder to impose a severance tax on ideas than it is to tax mines or factories.

Exactly how the public will respond is hard to predict. It is possible, though perhaps not likely, that public opinion will move sharply in favor of a tax system designed to increase savings, rather than debt.

A value-added levy may be instituted, along with a more hefty tax on gasoline, which would dampen consumer spending, and reduce the trade deficit, probably turning it into surplus.

Farewell to the Welfare State

Even more astonishing, given current expectations, the need to narrow a gaping deficit will result in government spending being slashed. Although few will be convinced by the arguments we spelled out earlier about the need to curtail income redistribution and thus reduce pauperism, circumstances will force the hand of authorities. Programs will be cut sharply or even abolished.

- Federal banking deposit guarantees will be trimmed or abandoned. In order to escape ruinous costs for funding losses from collapsing banks and S & Ls, the government will be obliged to curtail guarantees, just as state governments in the United States were forced to do by circumstances. Instead of borrowing from the market to pay off insured depositors, the government will probably offer a combination of cash, perhaps as little as ten thousand dollars, and low-yield IOUs. In order to facilitate recovery, the government will need a very steep yield curve. Deposit insurance at a time of profound uncertainty works against this goal of restoring the solvency of government. It extends assurances of safety to the funding operations of deposit-taking institutions. So an investor who wants to be sure that his money is "absolutely safe" is not obliged to buy Treasury debt as he was in the last depression. This makes bank rates lower than they would be and T-bill rates higher. The government will need to make T-bill rates as nearly invisible as it can in order to restore its solvency and thus lay the foundation for recovery. That means lifting the guarantees that have been spread to many other forms of investment.

• Many implied Treasury guarantees may go uncovered. The U.S. Treasury is not obligated to pay the bad debts of most of the government-sponsored enterprises, so it probably would not. You might see the bankruptcy of government-sponsored enterprises, with creditors paid off with hybrid instruments, like the "certificates of value" that were foisted upon the creditors of the Penn Central Railroad in the 1970s. The same practice will probably be extended to holders of defaulted mortgages. Their bad paper will be replaced by some other form of questionable paper, or zero-coupon obligation, set for redemption in the distant future.

• Military spending will be cut by as much as two-thirds. Military force levels will be greatly reduced, as the United States will largely abandon the effort to police international trouble spots.

• Unprecedented numbers of government employees will be fired. Civil service pay will be cut one or more times. The economies of Washington, D.C., and most state capitals will suffer more than usual as spending is slashed and government work forces are reduced. In the depression of the 1930s, it was an advantage to be a federal employee or a well-connected government contractor. Federal employees were always paid. Their incomes rose in real terms because of deflation. Efforts to keep wage rates high led to uniformly high rates of pay for the employees of government contractors, who were some of the more grateful political contributors of the 1930s. The advantages of federal employment may disappear in the 1990s, as they largely disappeared in England after the depression of the 1930s. Governments under severe financial distress in the coming slump will be unable to maintain the relative purchasing power of their senior employees. It is unlikely that the federal government employees in the United States will go unpaid, as some state and local employees will. But they will almost certainly lose real spending power. This drop in pay will be yet another factor that will contribute to widespread privatization of government services in the late 1990s. Able government employees will come to favor privatization over the objection of their unions. They have a clear interest in shrinking the public sector to eliminate services that could be performed by the market. The smaller the public sector, the easier it would be to bring its pay up to the market level. Several years of slump and pay cuts will make the public sector community less antagonistic to the one reform that would result in their being paid more.

- Public schools will be largely privatized by the year 2000. The fall of real estate prices will remove the financial advantage that contributed to support of public schools by many upper-middle-class families. They have tended to seek out areas of strong public schools and purchase properties in the areas served by such schools. Typically housing prices rise to reflect the high caliber of public schools in the areas where they do perform well. Because home mortgage interest was deductible, the after-tax cost of sending children to public schools became minimal in some locales during the time of rising property values. One could move into a community, buy a house, send children through high school, and sell out at a profit. Such an approach is much less attractive when property prices are falling. Falling property prices make private schools and public school choice more attractive. Many locales will give up public schools altogether in the 1990s and offer voucher programs to parents as a lower-cost alternative to maintaining the grotesque overheads of the public schools. In the last depression, there were serious proposals to close the public schools in Chicago and elsewhere. But these were rejected in the end because no coherent alternative was offered. In the 1990s, the public schools will prove far less popular than they did in the 1930s. With educational results steadily deteriorating, public schools are unlikely to survive the trauma of depression in their current, costly form. Class sizes in public schools that do survive will be increased. Many teachers and school administrators will get the axe.

- Government spending on housing will tumble, in part because of the tumble in real estate values. It will be too obviously ridiculous to build housing at public expense when a vast inventory of repossessed properties is coming into the hands of the federal government. Housing expenditures took one of the biggest cuts in Weimar Germany, and will probably repeat that distinction in the United States during the 1990s.

- Outlays for health care and pensions will also be trimmed. Retirement was essentially an invention of the Great Depression. It was meant not only to shore up the private income of the elderly, but to free jobs that were in short supply. A combination of collapsing work force skills among the young and the insolvency of the government will lead to a radical reworking of retirement programs. Benefits will become more modest, and they will probably be means tested. Indexing will be abolished under deflationary conditions. Remaining barriers to work force participation by the elderly will be dropped.

- Programs for helping the poor will be reorganized with the object of reducing costs—and altering the antisocial behavior of the underclass. The result will be a modern-day equivalent to the English Poor Law Amendment of 1834. It was undertaken to reduce pauperism and discourage able-bodied people from seeking relief as an alternative to work. This reform was later sharply criticized when English opinion shifted in favor of income redistribution late in the nineteenth century. But the reforms of 1834 succeeded in cutting the percentage of the population on relief from 8.8 percent in 1834 to 4.3 percent in 1860. In the 1990s, the poor house will make a comeback, at first in the guise of a shelter for the homeless. The virtues of orphanages and retirement homes also will be rediscovered, as mounting Medicaid and AFDC costs overwhelm strapped budgets.
- Spending on decontamination of nuclear weapons plants and the clean-up of other toxic waste sites will be stretched out and delayed.
- The sale of assets and privatization will be an important method by which governments attempt to return to solvency. However, in many areas, public infrastructure will continue to run down, because the capital sums required to replace falling bridges, potholed roads, and crumbling dams will not be available. Insolvent governments will lack the funds to invest and private firms will find it unwise. From 1929 through 1933, and then again after 1936, there were major expansions of public infrastructure of all kinds. A similar program during a depression of the 1990s will depend upon interest rates being lowered to levels where insolvent governments can afford to spend themselves or attract private investors. To a larger extent than ever before, repair and upgrading of public infrastructure including wastewater treatment facilities, airports, jails, bridges, highways, and dams will be privatized.
- Agricultural subsidies will be curtailed. Attempts to shore up farm income in a more protectionist environment will center on regulation, and mandated use of methanol in automobiles.
- Other government subsidies to life in remote rural areas, like cheap postage, subsidized electricity, cheap farm credit, etc., will be curtailed. As a result, more small towns in the northern plains that lack a sufficient tax base to finance repair of infrastructure or a sufficient market to attract private investors will disappear.
- One or more rural states, following Nevada's example in legalizing gambling early in the last depression, will lift the laws against drug use in an attempt to raise tax revenues and obtain an economic advantage.

- Big cities and aging surburbs with crumbling infrastructures will also be hard hit as the level of violence rises and the tax revenues to pay for services and infrastructure maintenance fall away. Public services like libraries, recreation, and arts programs will be starved for funds. The quality of services now taken for granted, like water treatment and waste disposal, may become highly uneven. It is even possible that local governments wrestling with tax revolts will more or less intentionally allow water and sewer mishaps to dramatize their demands for funds. Garbage collection will be cut, and even police protection may shrink along with the economy. City officials facing widespread tax strikes after 1930 frequently spoke in apocalyptic terms of the consequences of further falls in tax revenue. An article in the *National Municipal Review* declared, "Water would cease to flow from faucets. Sewer pumps would stop. . . . Millions of school children would roam the streets. Criminals and lunatics would break from their cells." What was fantasy in the 1930s may not be in the 1990s.
- There will be a major migration within the United States and Canada as upscale citizens flee to select semi-rural enclaves with high income and education profiles that have sufficient infrastructure to support greater population densities.

OPTIMISM ABOUT THE TRANSITION CRISIS

These developments would decisively alter the political landscape of the United States. We are optimists in believing that America will take a deflationary course, and thus retain its institutions. But make no mistake. At the depths of the coming depression, the very survival of the U.S. government will be widely questioned. Disillusionment and delusion will abound. Violence will be widespread. Tribal and nihilistic antagonisms will lead to greater terrorism, especially in the cities of America. In the country, Indian tribes will exploit their ambiguous legal status to demand sovereignty. More or less lawless regions will spread from the inner cities to the suburbs. Even some remote areas will revert to nineteenth-century conditions, in which homesteaders take over public lands, and operate economies outside the law. Canada, America's weaker neighbor to the north, will probably split apart. Some Canadian provinces may seek to ally themselves with the United States. Some American states may seek broader autonomy from Washington.

Needless to say, the outcome of the intensifying struggles between those who support themselves and those who live by entitlement will be unhappy for both sides. Even if advocates of the cosmopolitan Western culture of achievement are victorious politically, as we expect, there will be many moments of uncertainty. Events could take turns that are impossible to foresee. If we are wrong in being optimistic about the ultimate triumph of existing American institutions, hyperinflation and even revolution will be possibilities.

Megapolitical Foundations of American Stability

At what point, then, is the approach of danger to be expected? I answer, If it ever reach us it must spring up amongst us; it cannot come from abroad. If destruction be our lot we must ourselves be its author and finisher. As a nation of freemen we must live through all time, or die by suicide.

—ABRAHAM LINCOLN

We are optimistic because America remains largely a middle-class nation, built upon what was a strong megapolitical foundation. The first English settlers found an open continent, remarkably free of predators, pathogens, and powerful neighbors. The soil was rich and plentiful. The weather was temperate. If ever there was a land destined to yield prosperity for its inhabitants, it was the territory that became the United States. America's fortune was endowed by the land. Many millions of acres of surplus, tillable land were still being claimed by homesteaders right through the early decades of the twentieth century. This land not only provided a solid economic footing, it provided an unusual measure of political stability during the early period when farming was the predominant occupation. The fact that much of America was climatically ill-suited for plantation farming assured a broader ownership of land than was common in settlement colonies either in the Deep South of the United States or in Latin America.

Climatic Accidents Boost the Republic

The boundary between slaveholding and free states within the United States was set along a climatic boundary, where grain farming was more profitable than labor-intensive plantation farming. Crops like cotton, sugar, rice, and tobacco were grown on larger plantations with slave labor. If all of America had been blessed with temperate rather than subtropical weather, the Civil War might have been unnecessary.

Even though large plantation farmers were not and could not have been a political majority in the antebellum South of the United States, Americans fought a bloody Civil War, in large part because of the destabilizing impact of plantation farming that predominated in the southern tier of states. Interestingly, the split of sympathies between the northern and southern causes was generally determined along lines that matched crop patterns. The mountainous regions of the Deep South, where plantation farming was impractical climatically, and yeoman farming predominated, were generally pro-Union. The western, mountainous counties of Virginia seceded to form the new state of West Virginia for just this reason. This was not so much a border state phenomenon as a reflection of these basic megapolitical conditions. When Sherman marched through Appalachia, he was greeted as a liberator. Even in Deep South Alabama, there were strong secessionist movements in the pro-Union mountainous north of the state.

Within the border states themselves, divisions of opinion reflected the basic megapolitical reality. In Maryland, for instance, Confederate sympathizers predominated in the flat southern and eastern plains of the state, while the population was largely pro-Union to the north on the Piedmont plateau, where yeoman farming predominated. Barbara Frietchie, the Maryland resident immortalized in a bad poem for enjoining southern troops to "shoot, if you must, this old gray head, but spare your country's flag," was a resident of the Piedmont highlands.

While the Civil War demonstrated that the climatic and geographic dimensions of megapolitics in North America fell short of perfection, they did provide a stable foundation for popular government. During the founding centuries of the American experience, the emergence of a strong bulwark of yeoman freeholders was practically guaranteed by the interaction of climatic conditions and the impact of European and cosmopolitan diseases. The advantageous immune systems of the settlers, programmed through centuries of survival of endemic measles, chicken pox, mumps, and other "childhood diseases," practically assured triumph over indigenous Indian populations on the frontier, whose gene pools were maladjusted to survive the microbiological environment of a fixed agricultural society. As the largely white settler populations pushed west, they pushed the Indian population before them. They might have done so even without resort to an unquestionably superior weapons technology, simply by virtue of their unseen and inadvertent microbiological superiority.

Although it may not have been precisely true that anyone could "make a million," anyone could secure a homestead. During all the years that America remained an agricultural economy, this helped insure that the country retained its yeoman, middle-class base. The basic tension between the inequality of income and property and the equality of votes in a democratic system assures political instability if too large a percentage of total wealth is concentrated in a few hands. Under those conditions, the temptation by the many poor to use the vote to redistribute the property of the rich is too obvious to

ignore. But even the dramatic increase in return to education and the deflationary assets boom that has increased the wealth of savers in comparison to
those who consume their whole income have not altered the basic middle-
class composition of the American nation. Most of the redistribution that
takes place in the American political system is from one middle-class constituency to another.

Too Much Redistribution Undermines Stability

Thus the United States appears to have an ample cushion to maintain the
dominance of property owners in the national electorate. The U.S. distribution
of wealth is very different from that in unstable agricultural societies where
land ownership is more completely locked up, and political violence is correlated with inequality. In the Information Age, the key to earning income
is education, which can never be locked up or monopolized the way that
land or natural resources can be. At a time when economies of scale and
capital requirements are generally falling, the prospects for upward mobility
are in many respects more open than they have ever been. This is true quite
apart from any inequality in the current ownership of financial assets.

The biggest cause of the current increase in inequality in America, and in
some other advanced countries as well, is the pokey speed at which poorly
educated segments of society have adjusted to the dramatic fall-off in jobs
that require a strong back rather than a brain. In the 1950s, in both America
and Western Europe, 70 percent of people were employed in jobs where they
used their hands. Just 30 percent were "use-of-brain" workers. Now the ratio
has almost reversed. As Mickey Kaus points out, "In 1973 college graduates
made only 15 percent more than mere high school graduates; by 1982 the
differential was 49 percent." Narrowing the income gap requires narrowing
the gap in education and skills between the poor and the rich.

Unhappily, however, this has been very slow to happen. Part of the reason
is that there is too much income redistribution. Too many programs and
unachievable political promises have not only slowed the speed of adjustment
to the new realities, they have subsidized the growth of a counterproductive
slum culture, which we analyzed in detail. Welfare entitlements encourage
too many uneducated, unmarried women to have children. They then lack
the family cohesion and cultural values to educate themselves and stay out
of trouble.

Another part of the gap in income is due to overindulgence in current
consumption, another facet of life in the 1980s that could not be redressed
by more income redistribution. Part of the reason that Americans save so little
is the assurance that they will be protected from many of the high-cost con-

tingencies, like retirement security and medical care in old age, that induce savings in the first place. Too much income redistribution and too much income equality can actually undermine stability.

The poor and even much of America's middle class, unlike the thrifty pioneers who laid the foundation of American prosperity, spend every penny that comes into their hands. This is not a life-style that will stand the test of time. Nor is it one that can be justified by the exigencies of the moment. Some will say, of course, that middle-class people are "unable to save."

But this cannot be true.

It cannot be true of today's poor as it would have been for the poor in pre-industrial societies. In most cases, even today's poor enjoy a standard of real consumption many times higher than that of the rich of a few centuries ago. They simply fail to utilize their resources—including their time—wisely. And the poorer they are, the worse they tend to do. The poorest people in Western societies tend to bear and rear children irresponsibly, as well as indulge in crime, drug abuse, and alcoholism more than productive citizens. These behaviors seldom lead to the development of skills or economic success. What is worse, they are destabilizing in an environment where adverse megapolitical trends make it difficult to stop law-breaking.

The most urgent need in the 1990s is to increase the payoff from accomplishment and law-abiding behavior. The countries that will best adapt to the Revolution of the 1990s are those with the highest incomes and most productive citizens—like Switzerland and Japan. Rather than penalizing the successful, and making it more difficult to become and remain affluent, a rational policy for America would aim for the opposite result. It would reduce taxes. And reduce the unsustainable burdens of transfer payments, income redistribution, and guarantees against failure that are the essence of the welfare state. When you subsidize poverty and failure, you get more of both.

A Third Great Rollback of Income Redistribution?

It appears to the pauper that the Government has undertaken to repeal, in his favor, the ordinary laws of nature; to enact that the children shall not suffer for the misconduct of their parents, the wife for that of the husband, or the husband for that of the wife; that no one shall lose the means of comfortable subsistence, whatever be his indolence, prodigality, or vice; in short that the penalty which, after all, must be paid by some one for idleness and improvidence, is to fall, not on the guilty person or on his family, but on the proprietors of the lands and houses encumbered by his settlement. Can we wonder if the uneducated are seduced into approving a system which aims its allurements at all the weakest parts of our nature—which offers marriage to the young, security to the anxious, ease to the lazy, and impunity to the profligate?

—THE ROYAL COMMISSION
ON THE POOR LAW, 1834

Part of the cycle of progress in Western civilization since the end of the fifteenth century has been a series of radical reinterpretations in the nature and form of income redistribution. Two of the changes most closely associated with spurts of progress were rollbacks of redistribution aimed directly at reshaping the culture of the unskilled.

The first of these began to take shape in Switzerland and Germany in the early decades of the sixteenth century. The rise of capitalism was associated with the Protestant Reformation—religious reforms that reduced elements of income redistribution by curtailing feasts and deemphasizing the importance of alms-giving as a route to redemption. An important element of this transformation took hold in a second stage in the seventeenth century—the rise of Puritanism in England. Simplifying crudely, the "Genevas of Lancashire" emerged as the economy was transformed with the rise of cloth-making and growing international trade in commodities. The Puritans were "the merchants and middle sort of men," described by R. H. Tawney in *Religion and the Rise of Capitalism,* as "humble to God and haughty to man." They distinguished themselves from the "spendthrift aristocracy" and the "basest and lowest sort" of poor, neither of whom worked very hard.

The Puritans rejected the paternalism and deference of traditional agricultural society. As social historian David Underdown points out, they sought instead to "emphasize the moral and cultural distinctions which marked them off from their poorer, less disciplined neighbors and to use their power to reform society according to their own principles of order and godliness." This meant placing the burden of failure squarely on the poor, whose poverty was taken as evidence that they were not among the elect of God. The Puritans were in no mood to support anyone in idleness. A contemporary observer noted that the greater their religious zeal, "the greater their inclination to trade and industry." As Tyndale's translation put it, "And the Lord was with Joseph, and he was a luckie felowe." Anyone who was not lucky, or working at being lucky, the Lord was not with. The Puritans were willing not only to slash income redistribution to the poor, the medicants, and the vagrant, they were willing to go much further than would be needed in late-twentieth-century America. The Puritans were ready to consign the able-bodied indigent to eternal damnation, "amid the blare of trumpets."

We have already analyzed many other features of this cultural revolution. It was an example of a major retrenchment in income redistribution, which, notwithstanding its zealous nature, played a constructive role in altering the culture and behavior of the poor. It was the tough love of the sixteenth and seventeenth centuries.

A second great reform in the spread of middle-class values was the rollback of welfare payments as the Industrial Revolution transformed England in the early nineteenth century. The Poor Law Amendment of 1834 sharply curtailed "outdoor relief"—or welfare payments to the able-bodied. This reform also made it more difficult to qualify for relief. It once again shifted the blame for failure from society to the individual pauper who, in "the large majority of cases," was judged to have failed because of "gin drinking, carelessness and recklessness."

The new Poor Law was less theological and more overtly economic in its rationalization. It provided a safety net in the form of alms houses where the truly destitute could find shelter and food. While it was administered un-evenly—relief payments to the able-bodied poor continued in some areas—the reform achieved its aims. There was a dramatic drop in the percentage of the British population receiving relief. In just twenty-five years, dependence on welfare fell by 50 percent. Similar policies were adopted in the United States and elsewhere, making it difficult for the idle to qualify for relief at public expense.

The surprise of the 1990s is that there could be another rollback of income redistribution. The sheer fiscal impossibility of continuing to subsidize the growth of discontented and unskilled populations of poor may force the issue far more than most people would think possible. Such reforms will certainly cause a cultural confrontation. But if such a confrontation is released by the coming depression, the social cost of dramatic reforms will fall for that very reason. They may be necessary to stability and even the survival of American institutions over the long run.

The Future of Redistribution

One of the factors that helped destabilize the Weimar Republic prior to the Nazi takeover was a sweeping redistribution of wealth. The hyperinflation, punitive taxes, and other redistributive programs instituted by the Weimar politicians effectively wiped out the savings of Germany's domestic creditors. Because the rich save a great deal more than the middle class or poor, wealth taken from the rich and the upper middle class was principally consumed rather than saved. This left a huge savings deficit for the country as a whole. As we have seen, to make up that deficit governments at all levels in Germany were obliged to finance their budgets on foreign borrowing. Dependence upon foreign creditors necessitated the adoption of highly contractionary budget policies analyzed earlier in this chapter.

To put the matter in another way, a large pool of domestic savings tends to increase stability of a modern economy. Since the rich save a higher proportion of income than the poor or middle classes, income and wealth can be too equally distributed to preserve economic and political stability under current megapolitical conditions. This is not to say that a democratic system could withstand having 90 percent of the income earned by 10 percent of the population.

But that is not the situation in America. We believe that Americans, facing high costs of failed programs, will react in favor of retrenchment and privatization. There will certainly be some reaction to insure that "the rich pay their share." But the twilight of the welfare state may be drawing near. During the depression, the public may demand action to reform incentives that govern the expenditure of public money. It may be wishful thinking, but we believe that American institutions will survive the next slump.

Every representative or democratic popular government that has been stable, has been stable because of an economic foundation that assured that the predominant mass of voters were yeoman freeholders or members of the middle class. The classic Greek city-states, Rome during its republican period, the medieval trading republics, like Venice, and the modern industrial democracies all kept their popular governments only so long as megapolitical conditions and the military balance of power prohibited too many of the poor from becoming voters or the voters from becoming too poor. Productive Americans will see the threat that emerges with a growing underclass, and take action to narrow the gap in skills that underlies the growing gap in income.

In spite of troublesome signs that America's middle class will be adversely affected in the coming depression, we believe that America will continue to be a middle-class nation. With the threat of Communism effectively dead as a lure for dissident opinion in the West, intellectual arguments in favor of redistribution will be increasingly museum pieces. As military spending shrinks, the consensus that supported the big government of the Cold War period will break apart. The wealthy, in particular, who tended to be strong supporters of the Cold War to fend off Communism, will no longer have strong reasons to support a costly government. The same will be true in varying degrees for financially independent members of the middle class. As a result, there will be less tolerance of high taxes, not more. There will be a snap back in public opinion in the direction of the old Yankee virtue, and its motto, "Make do, wear it out, when it's gone, do without." The political balance will be reasserted in support of savings and sound values that stand the test of time.

Just as the welfare state was forged in the depression of the 1930s, so it may be dismantled in the depression of the 1990s. The year 1989 brought proof that socialist systems that attempted to prohibit anyone from making a profit could not stand the test of time. By 1999, we may well have discovered that the corollary is true. The welfare state that attempted to prevent anyone from taking a loss may prove to be an anachronism that could not long outlast the end of the Cold War.

CHAPTER FOURTEEN

THE ESCAPE FROM HIGH COSTS

THE PRIVATE ECONOMY IN THE SLUMP OF THE

1990s

Take Care to Sell Your Horse before He Dies
The Art of Life Is Passing Losses on.

—ROBERT FROST

THE ARGUMENT of this book is an invitation to think the unthinkable. It challenges the central faith of postwar consumerism—that the welfare state can prevent depression. We suspect it cannot. If this heresy is correct, the whole superstructure of economic assumptions upon which many people have based their lives will give way, like a house built on rotten planking. To calculate where the pieces will fall is a trick of trigonometry. We do not pretend to have gotten all the angles right. To the contrary. What follows is merely a rough outline of how a second stage of depression in the 1990s could affect various sectors of the economy. You will want to form ideas of how your job or business could be affected, where the bust will hit hardest, and what industries and regions will fare best.

These are only some of the crucial questions for the 1990s. Will industries that performed well in the depression of the 1930s repeat that performance? And if not, which industries will fare the best? Will politicians thwart recovery by resorting to wild inflation or instituting cartels and counterproductive measures to keep prices high? And closer to home, how will growing violence and infrastructure breakdown affect your decision about where to live?

Our focus in what follows is on the United States. If you live in another country, you should be able to extrapolate from the American example on the basis of information in other chapters and what you already know.

Bear in mind as you read that our forward vision is nearsighted at best. There is no way that we can accurately anticipate many details of time and place in advance of the actual events. Causes have consequences that can sometimes be foreseen in broad outline. But where human action is concerned, the complexity of the interactions is such that events may turn out differently from the way we imagine. We can only give you hints that can serve to stimulate your thinking about probable outcomes. History is still in the hands of individuals, who by their actions perform God's miracles.

HOW THE DEPRESSION MIGHT UNFOLD

Not even the ingenuities of debt
Could save it from its losses being met.
—ROBERT FROST

"You can depend on the fact that the slump will first be considered merely a brief recession. It will be blamed on Saddam Hussein and higher oil prices or some other gust of unfavorable wind. Even strong hints of trouble to come, like the collapse of the Japanese stock market or major bankruptcies, will not dramatically sway expectations." So we wrote in the first edition of this book. And so it was. This is a logical consequence of nonlinear dependence, or the persistence of sentiment in the face of the facts. Evidence of weakness will make people cautious and even bearish in the short term. But they will expect a rapid recovery. And there may indeed be one or more periods of positive news before the credit cycle comes to an end.

On January 1, 1930, the *New York Times* published its Annual Financial Report. These were three of the headings: " 'Normal Prosperity' Is Forecast for 1930. Some Clouds on Horizon. Many Heartening Factors." The report contained a number of individual forecasts, almost all of which showed the same qualified optimism.

"Cleveland is optimistic. Chicago sees slow period. New England hopeful. Texas farmers have cash. Philadelphia is cheerful. Georgia sees prosperity. Secretary Lamont predicts progress." Wall Street shared in this mood: "General price rise ends 1929 stock trading with Wall Street moderately bullish for 1930." Note the recurrence of the qualifications—"moderately bullish" sounds such a reasonable thing to be.

The analysis that dominated the forecast for 1930 was well argued. With a change of dates and replacing one or two names, such as "Hoover" with "Bush," it would have made an entirely plausible article for January 1992. Another name change of "Clinton" for "Hoover" with a later dateline may also work.

We doubt if one could have had better-informed advice than the *New York Times* offered readers in 1930. It sounds remarkably like the consensus of well-informed opinion as we write.

We can forecast with firm conviction that the government will not acknowledge that a depression has begun until it has been underway for eighteen months to two years.

The Scapegoat Search as Confirmation

A major confirmation of the onset of depression will be a concerted effort on the part of political authorities to locate scapegoats for the slump. Every slump and market crash in history has been blamed upon something other than a decline in economic prospects. The pattern is infallible. The blame is fixed partly on some technical factor: short-selling, margin abuse, etc.; and partly on some fraud or peculation of wicked manipulators. In 1720, it was Sir George Caswall and the Directors of the South Sea Company who were judged to have ruined the London Stock Market. The Panic of 1837 was blamed on Nicholas Biddle. The crash of 1873 was the work of Jay Cooke. In 1893 the blame fell on James M. Waterbury and "international bankers." In 1929, the "international bankers" came in for another tarring, along with President Herbert Hoover, short-selling, and "unregulated securities markets." In the 1990s, Bill Clinton will be blamed, along with program trading and derivative instruments like options and futures, the Japanese and foreigners in general, and members of other tribes—the blacks, the whites, the Hispanics.

"Sustaining the Morale of the People"

The same medieval mentality that outlawed short-selling when it was known as "forestalling" will be back at work attacking the structure of free auction markets when the slump becomes unmistakable. We had hints of this with the work of the Brady Commission after the 1987 crash. Its investigation differed from the parliamentary search for scapegoats in 1720 only in that Brady had a new high-tech villain: the computer. All the computer does is make calculations quickly—just what people would do themselves if they had greater computational capabilities. Brady's recommendations for restricting markets will no doubt be back in force as the slump of the 1990s deepens.

The search for scapegoats is in many respects silly. But it unintentionally makes a point that you should take to heart. When the news is bad and apt to get worse you cannot draw your bearings about the economy or the market from channels of mass communication. Can you imagine a major newspaper (much less the leaders of a country) saying that stocks fell because objective conditions no longer supported their further rise? Has it ever been recognized politically that a market has topped out? Or that an economy needed to go through a painful slump to facilitate a transition and shake out dead wood? In every case of which we know, politicians have continued to pretend that all was well long after events provided impressive evidence to the contrary. This is a game that President Hoover, in retirement, described as "sustaining the morale of the people."

In spite of these often well-intended gestures, the economy will shift into a contraction that government will be powerless to abate. Asset prices, especially real estate and stocks, will tumble. Credit will contract. Governments hungry for reelection will panic as the asset deflation gathers force. Their first response will be an attempt to counter the contraction with easy money. The Federal Reserve and other central banks, especially the Bank of Japan, could buy up the bad debts of insolvent institutions, like big banks and industrial corporations. The Bundesbank could monetize the reunification bonds and move to shore up weak German companies, like Krupp. In the United States, the Fed could buy Los Angeles's overdue notes, or pump money into New York City's till to forestall budget cuts. In short, the socialization of losses could be taken to greater extremes. The bad debts of all large borrowers could be added to the government's balance sheet. Central banks could essentially become national pawn shops—economy-wide holding companies of insolvent institutions. They could end up owning many banks, perhaps some insurance companies, and a great deal of real estate.

The Threat of Inflation

We do not know how long this first stage will last, because we do not know how concerted and reckless the government's attempt to rescue bad debts will be. The assumption that it will go to extremes permeates the financial life of the United States as well as other advanced democracies. But this assumption is based upon promises intended to forestall a credit collapse. Once such a collapse has clearly begun, authorities will probably move to minimize the damage in a bad situation by abandoning the attempt to pay every bad debt from Little Diamede Island to Key West. But they will not back down until the market has shown them that they must. Few will be persuaded by the arguments spelled out in this book and elsewhere suggesting that deflation would be less costly than runaway inflation. These arguments will have to be proven by the markets.

Paradoxically, that is more apt to happen when markets are focusing on the dangers of inflation. Therefore, you can expect that fears and alarms about pending inflation will be on everyone's lips, even as asset deflation takes hold. The newspapers are likely to run page one headlines about inflationary actions. Analysts who closely follow central bank policy will warn of debasement of the currency and dangers of Latin American–style inflation. You may even see signs that the reflation is working. Some news reports will say that the economy is getting stronger. The stock market could rise in one or more suckers' rallies. Indeed, you may read the kind of news that fooled investors on April 1, 1930.

News That Will Be Reprinted in the 1990s

If you had read the financial news on April Fool's Day, 1930, you would have seen the following comments in the *Wall Street Journal:*

"It has been a remarkable market since the first of the year, or as one broker expressed it, 'a bull market extraordinary.' Stocks of some companies that will show a falling off of earnings in the first quarter of the current year have advanced a great deal, some 25, 50 and 75 points."

"It is said that scrap copper is getting very scarce."

". . . the market is again on the first pages of the daily newspapers."

". . . current news on industrial progress has for a week or two been visibly less favorable than it was or appeared to be most of the time throughout the winter."

"Extraordinarily easy money and stability in the commodity markets are important factors working to that end [making for prosperity]. The tariff is still an obstacle in the channel."

"Movement of stock prices since the first of the year has been of decidedly cheerful augury."

"Radio Inventory Difficulty Over."

"The improvement in the position of the savings banks of New York has continued during March."

". . . fundamental credit conditions have undergone a marked change for ease not only in this country but all over the world."

From the *New York Times:*

"An accumulation of buying orders that had piled up over the weekend sent prices sharply higher at the opening of stock markets yesterday."

"Bullish activities were resumed last month and prices and averages advanced to their highest levels of the year and broke through the levels made at the end of last October. *The New York Times*'s averages gained 12.75 points for the month. This is the largest gain in any one month since last July."

" '. . . It has been agreed to that the Committee on Rules shall report a rule sending the tariff bill to conference.' "

"March Money Rates Show Sharp Declines."

" 'An outstanding development is the sharp drop in interest rates, marking the end of a period of credit strain and bringing rates to the lowest point in several years. In its bearing on general business conditions the advent of really cheap money has been widely heralded, and rightly so, as the most important and promising feature in the general situation. That cheap money is a tonic for the recuperation of business has been proven by long experience.' "— quoting the April bulletin of the National City Bank.

"Money rates declined rapidly to the lowest levels since early in 1925, the April 1 review of the Federal Reserve Bank of New York states, and accompanying this ease in money, the bond market in March made a vigorous recovery. . . . 'The recovery of the bond market,' the review says, 'was of special importance because various programs of public works and other new undertakings have been dependent on the possibility of the sale of bonds in considerable quantities.' "

"A large proportion of all the industrial groups had a materially higher margin of net profit for the full year 1929 than for 1928. The outstanding example is the steel group, which expanded net earnings 66 per cent further."

COUNTING ON EASY MONEY

Such is the news you would have read in the two papers that offered the finest financial coverage in America in 1930. Here and there were hints of trouble. A destructive trade bill was nearing passage. But there was also plenty to feed the imagination of a bull. Notice that contrary to what is now supposed, the economy did not fall into the abyss on the day the stock market crashed. By All Fools' Day, 1930, the tone was optimistic. Attention to rising stock prices had all but overshadowed lingering concern about the events of "last October."

Also notice the recurring references to monetary policy. Contrary to the current wisdom that stupidly tight money turned the '29 stock market crash into depression, accounts of 1930 speak of "extreme ease of money."

The point is not that financial coverage in 1930 was woefully bad, nor that investors in 1930 were chronic optimists. As the accounts quoted above indicate, analysis of business and investment prospects in 1930 depended on relationships and indicators similar to those we use today. Protectionist trade legislation was seen as a far less important indicator of future economic trends than "easy money."

That what seemed to be easy money at the time was denounced later as "too tight" may only show that the dynamic of contraction works behind the scenes. More muscular attempts to counter that dynamic process by inflating faster would paradoxically strengthen the deflationary impulse. This is especially likely in the 1990s, as the experience of inflation is closer to investors than it was in the 1930s. As the 1920s ended, there were plenty of bad debts to go around, but balance sheets were clean compared to the stable rags on which corporations and governments post their numbers today.

Against this background, nervous bond holders will be on guard against government attempts to monetize everyone's bad paper. The appearance of rapid debasement of the currency would send bonds tumbling. Gold would skyrocket.

A Foolhardy Policy

Determined reflation, because of its disastrous consequences, would be a foolhardy policy. We expect and hope that the authorities will submit to the dictates of the market, and take steps to restore the economy and the government to solvency. This would mean deflation—letting the bad debt be liquidated.

This chapter is written optimistically, on the assumption that the American constitutional system will prove stable enough to hold together, in spite of the adverse megapolitical trends. It is a guess that we will have a crash landing, rather than a disintegration in flight. Deflation will prevail over inflation. Creditors will prevail over debtors. Financial assets will be selectively repudiated through default, not obliterated by inflation.

This optimistic reading does not depend upon creditors being more numerous than debtors, but on markets being more powerful than governments. The power of markets, however, is a long-run power, a power that asserts itself over decades. It took seventy years to destroy socialism. The view that the power of markets will soon prevail over the welfare state's policy of socializing losses is a guess based on the cycles of history, current megapolitical conditions, and the magnitude of debts outstanding as the 1990s began. But bear in mind that this is a guess. It may be wrong. There may be another cycle of reflation left in the system before the phase transition occurs.

If events prove that we are not yet at the point where further inflation would be self-defeating, we are very near. A concerted attempt by political authorities to override market disciplines and write down debt through inflation would lead, in the extreme, to the disappearance of credit altogether— an outcome that would doom a modern political economy.

The logic of this is clear. Of course, one cannot be too sure of applying logic to politics. The fact that a policy could be destructive does not preclude it from happening. And it is also true that destruction can take different forms. Gorbachev could have fired on the demonstrators in East Berlin, but he could not have saved Communism in East Germany. Political authorities in the United States and other Western countries may take a stand to defend the welfare state against the demonstrators in the bond markets just as Erich Honecker wanted Gorbachev to take a stand against the Lutheran church workers and the reformers in the streets. Lord Rees-Mogg leans more to the view that governments will press blindly ahead with inflation, in spite of the destruction that would involve. James Davidson believes that the costs of ruthless inflation will be higher and more obvious early in the process, thus short-circuiting the reflation. But those are both weightings of probabilities divorced from knowledge of the actual details of the immediate market setting in which the decisions will be made.

Political authorities will surely attempt to lighten debt loads by depreciating the value of money. But the market will understand this even better than the politicians. A hunter with a visible snare catches few rabbits. Creditors will seek to stay one step ahead of the authorities, to avoid being tagged with the losses through inflation or currency depreciation.

The lesson of September 1992 is a re-affirmation of a central theme of this book: markets are more powerful than governments. The European Exchange Rate Mechanism cracked apart because the Bank of England was no match for George Soros. Even with tens of billions of Deutsch marks to spend defending an artificially high value of the pound, the British government was obliged by the market to beat a humiliating retreat. Given a similar circumstance, it would happen again.

The major economic drama of the middle-1990s will be the struggle between the market and government over the liquidation of debt. Political authorities will prefer to wipe away debt surreptitiously through inflation. But to inflate away bad debts also means inflating away good credits. Market participants will seek to preserve the value of their assets denominated in money. To the extent that they succeed, they will make it harder to repay excessive debt in cheap money, and thus make the system more vulnerable to overt default and deflation. As monetary policy is loosened, in increasingly desperate efforts to reliquify the economy, the market may force a deflationary response. Inflationary depression would wipe out the financial economy, and probably lead to the overthrow of the government. Because all of society's bad debts would be the bad debts of government, the temptation to repudiate the debts by repudiating the government would grow. In effect, the capital value of the Constitution would tumble. This would expose society to the full measure of destabilization implied by the present power equation in the world. The megapolitics of devolution could take hold, threatening to make the United States a Northern Hemisphere, balkanized version of Argentina.

Deflationary depression would write down the value of tangible assets that are the collateral for many loans in the banking system, but it would increase the value of sound financial assets, including the value of government debt. Deflationary depression would expose social conflicts papered over by welfare state spending.

You can expect additional currency crises and worse. Governments facing the need to finance massive structural deficits due to the slowdown in economic activity may find that markets can set the price of funding high enough to offset any stimulative gains from inflation. If so, there will be no alternative to direct debt liquidation, and the second, deeper stage of depression. Watch bond prices carefully. There is a limit to everything, including the good credit of governments. When theirs is exhausted, even the governments of the richest industrial countries will face the dilemma Sweden answered with 500 percent interest rates and deep cuts in government spending. When it appears that authorities are most determined to inflate depression away that very perception could put the economy on the verge of again slipping into the deflationary vortex.

Deflation and hyperinflation are not remote polar opposites, but the male and female of the same species. You should prepare yourself for either outcome, which means remaining alert to the dangers of both.

Either form of depression would greatly curtail the availability of credit, send the real demand for commodities tumbling, and depress living standards in real terms. The danger of deflation, of course, requires the greater thought and preparation, because it represents a reversal of the trend.

Warning Signs of Deflation

There are some early signals to watch for confirmation of the deflationary depression scenario:

- Continued shrinkage of M-2 as a multiple of the monetary base.
- Continued, double-digit increases in the portion of the money supply that is held as cash.
- A flight from high-risk bank instruments such as jumbo CDs and a widening of the spread or gap between Treasury bills and Eurodollars. In trading parlance this is known as the Ted spread.
- A dramatic drop in the market price of freely trading instruments that mimic the valuation of bank collateral.
- Falling commodity prices. But note that a rising nominal price of gold implies that either the crunch is still ahead or it is already passed. At the end of past credit cycles, the *real* price of gold has bottomed at or near the end of the credit cycle, then risen sharply.
- Continued declines in real estate, in spite of "easy money."
- A fall in loan demand in the face of falling interest rates.

This last point is particularly important. The Fed immediately dropped the discount rate in 1929 from 6 percent to 5 percent. Within two weeks, the rate had been pushed down to 4.5 percent. By March 13 of 1930, it stood at 3.5 percent. In the weeks after the crash, "the system expanded credit enormously." Nonetheless, after the crisis subsided, falling interest rates were not accompanied by a growth of money aggregates. A repeat of this would be an early confirmation of a coming deflationary collapse.

Credit Revulsion

The timidity of the banking system appears to have been general and widespread. Indeed, the 1939 survey found that over half of the reasons given for credit refusals by banks were "bank policy"; only a third were because of "the condition of the borrowing concern."

—MICHAEL A. BERNSTEIN,
The Great Depression

A common feature of economic slumps is credit revulsion. Even good borrowers find their welcome mat withdrawn. When the music stops, the attitude of lenders hardens. Banks will slash credit and call loans even to good customers. They will be driven to do this, in part, because of growing demands to hold cash. When the public raises its demands for currency, the banks have no choice but to shrink. Each time commercial banks obtain currency refills for their customers, they must reduce their reserve accounts with the central bank. If the customers suddenly prefer low-leverage money—cash—the banks are obliged by the logic of leverage to reduce their lending. A dollar in the banking system can be leveraged 10:1. A dollar in a mattress is not leveraged at all.

Note that the money supply is much more than merely cash in people's pockets. M-3, the broad measure of money, currently includes in addition to currency: traveler's checks, checking accounts, other "checkable" deposits like NOWs and Super NOWs, savings deposits, small time deposits, overnight repurchase agreements, overnight Eurodollars, money market funds, money market deposit accounts, large time deposits, institutional money funds, term repurchase agreements, and term Eurodollars. Of all the components of the money supply, currency involves the least leverage of all.

Following the stock market crash in 1929, currency grew by 16 percent annually until early 1933. This was a contributing factor to the shrinkage of the overall money supply. Deflation happened in spite of the fact that the Fed, by the account of its chief economist, "embarked on a policy of easy money which it pursued through the depression." The Fed kept the monetary base expanding at a 4 percent annual rate from 1929 through 1933, yet the overall money supply collapsed, partly because of strong public demand for no-leverage money. As we complete the editorial process on this book in the fall of 1992, M-3, the broad measure of the U.S. money supply, has grown by a meager 1.7 percent rate for the past year. We don't pretend that such a short-term movement has great significance for the future. Indeed, we rather expect that authorities will soon try to speed the growth of money in an attempt to fend off asset deflation and rescue insolvent debtors. But it is interesting that the slowdown in broader money measures has been accompanied by a 12.4 percent increase in the supply of currency in the economy. It could be an early sign of the movement away from high-leverage money.

When deflation lowers interest rates, the loss of real income by holding cash may not be significant compared to the risk of losing your capital due to default of banks or other institutions. The average yield on three-month Treasury securities in 1933 was an almost invisible 0.515 percent. For a brief time, it was even negative. So those who chose to hold cash were not throwing away high-interest income. Watch the growth of currency as a crucial sign that the economy is headed for a deflationary contraction.

SLOW DEATH OF COLLATERAL

With the value of real estate collateral falling, the true market value of construction and other real estate loans will fall. Bankers and other lenders, like their predecessors after 1929, will not wish to magically turn one dollar of cash into a loan worth just eighty cents, much less sixty cents. When the value of collateral falls, and the public's demand to hold cash rises, even easy money at the Fed may not stop deflation.

Cash could be hard to come by, and idle credit lines may be withdrawn. If your business has seasonal needs, anticipatory borrowing may make sense. If you cannot secure irrevocable letters of credit, you may wish to borrow now. You can place the cash you realize from anticipatory borrowing in interest-bearing accounts, and absorb the loss as a price of doing business. It could be cheaper than dealing with a loan shark, as many small businesses were forced to do in the last depression.

Durables in the Dumps

The falling rates of profit have a purging effect: less efficient businesses, which might have been able to survive in the expansion phase, have to close. Only the more progressive firms survive the depression, and in this way this phase of the cycle generates technical, and other, progress.

—HAROLD JAMES

The consumer, whose spending accounts for two-thirds of the economy, will retrench as the slowdown becomes obvious. The first spending to be dropped or postponed will be the purchase of durable goods. In the 1930s, real spending on furniture dropped by about 50 percent. Spending on new and used autos plunged by almost 70 percent. Sales of radios, televisions (yes, there were televisions in 1929), and musical instruments fell by more than 80 percent.*

*In the week the stock market crashed in October 1929, New York television actors made news themselves with a protest of the heavy makeup they were obliged to wear in order to have their expressions visible on primitive 1929 televisions.

These drops came from levels of absolute spending that are low compared to those today. It seems certain that consumers will sharply curtail durable spending in any slump in the 1990s. This means fewer new automobiles, boats, pieces of furniture, and household appliances. The auto industry was weak even before Saddam Hussein invaded Kuwait. It will get weaker. The boat industry, more of a luxury market, was in recession for the last three or four years of the eighties. If your livelihood revolves around selling new cars, boats, furniture, or appliances, look for ways to diversify or try to sell your business.

The American auto industry is particularly vulnerable because it was forced to compete on quality in the 1980s by foreign competition. This has put it on slippery footing. In the depression of the 1930s, auto companies discovered that their products from the 1920s had been too good. The country was well stocked with new cars, and when purchasing power tumbled in 1930, so did auto sales. A similar pattern could repeat itself in the 1990s, with the added wrinkle that manufacturers have extended warranties up to seven years or seventy thousand miles. It won't be much fun to be an auto dealer doing warranty work, but selling only an occasional vehicle.

In general, dealer as well as consumer finances were remarkably weak in 1990, considering the strength of auto sales during the long upturn. Indeed, part of the problem was the extended bull market in auto sales. It was sustained in part by the expedient of easing credit standards for auto loans and extending payment periods as far as seven years. Many innovative new loans were made between 1986 and 1988, some requiring no money down. Indeed, some even provided "cash back." These loans to weak borrowers had the interesting characteristic that they lasted longer than the cars did. As a consequence, many would-be car buyers were "upside down" as the 1990s began. They owed more money on their old vehicles than the vehicles were worth.

As a group, auto dealers were only somewhat better off than their customers. Many had very thin margins and were heavily in debt. They were vulnerable to defaults by buyers and lessees. We expect many dealers to fail when new car sales and leases stall in a slump. This will increase the opening for nondealer repair of autos.

Eventually, of course, old loans will be paid off, down payments will be accumulated, and a replacement cycle will kick in. Consumer durables, like worn-out autos, will one day be replaced. This, however, will be a matter of years, not months. There is a huge excess capacity for auto production around the world, which has been expanded by aggressive Japanese construction of off-shore plants. A 70 percent drop in auto sales, like that in the last depression, would threaten to close high-cost auto plants, which are mainly owned by the big three American companies. Japanese companies have perfected what is known as "lean production," an intermediate step in the transition away from mass production. American companies, especially GM, have appeared to suffer from diseconomies of scale. They are too big to respond quickly to market changes. It takes them one to two years longer to develop and build new cars than their Japanese competition. Many European producers will also suffer in a slump, as they are hampered by old-fashioned mass production methods, even when they produce few cars. The number of auto companies is likely to fall in a slump.

Importers and Exporters to Suffer

An early consequence of past depression has been the closure of economies to foreign competition. Tariff barriers, like the infamous Smoot-Hawley bill of 1930, closed U.S. markets to foreign competition. Similar political moves to close markets are likely in the 1990s, with high-value products like automobiles featuring prominently in protectionist measures. Protectionist sentiment was rising in the 1980s, even before a slump began. It is likely to lead once again to pernicious legislation in the 1990s, which will place importers and exporters in difficulty.

Capital Goods

Capital goods markets will be hit hard for several reasons. In the first place, it usually makes little sense to invest in increasing capacity in a market where excess capacity is already a problem. Furthermore, the most active capital goods markets are for the production of tangible, often durable products. You have much less developed capital goods markets to produce the products that may be innovations in the next depression. Many of the areas to which we should look for innovations are information-based rather than natural resource–based products. A good example is biotechnology. You need to invest in biotech research. But the need for capital goods to fabricate biotech products is minimal. The natural process is the productive process.

Even minor recessions tend to sharply lower outlays for capital goods. If you deal in this field, you may want to find a way out, unless you have a product that East Germans must buy, and one that rapidly pays for itself to boot.

Defense

Capital goods for the defense industry are particularly vulnerable, notwithstanding the chaos in Russia and other manifestations of trouble in the world. The fact that General Dynamics appears to be getting out of the defense business as we write is a strong hint of much deeper cuts to come.* There will be a reorientation of America's military forces, with more emphasis upon confronting terrorists and projecting power into the Third World. This will mean new weapons better suited to small-scale warfare, especially in desert conditions. Smaller tanks and improved air- and sealift capacity may result. But overall military spending is still likely to plunge, as we argued earlier.

Construction

Another thing you can be assured of is that construction will be one of the weaker industries in a depression. Homebuilding will be especially weak. Private construction in general will trickle to a halt, except perhaps in the select areas that benefit by the flight from the cities. Even government contractors will face hard times. In this respect, the slump of the 1990s could be deeper for the construction industry than that of the 1930s. According to Standard & Poor's, the percentage of building in the economy fell in half in the 1930s.

As we have already emphasized, governments at all levels were far more solvent in 1929 than they are today. Long-term interest rates were low. The strength of government balance sheets enabled public works spending to increase early in the depression, and help offset some of its deadening effects on private construction spending. The index of new construction was at a value of 96 in 1929 on a base in which the period 1947–49 equals 100. That means that in 1929, total construction in the United States was practically at the same level that it reached two decades later in 1949. In 1929, private construction was at 98 percent of the 1949 level, while public construction was at 92 percent.

When the depression began, private construction plunged, but public construction increased. Herbert Hoover organized the equivalent of an eighty-billion-dollar stimulus package in today's terms during the first two years of the depression. By 1931, public construction was up to 115. Private construction, meanwhile, continued falling, dropping by more than 80 percent by

---

*"Swords Into Shares General Dynamics Contemplates Selling Its Remaining Units Arms Maker May Seek Gains for Stockholders in Sales of Its 'Core Businesses.' " *Wall Street Journal,* November 3, 1992.

1933. Even by 1940, recovery was still incomplete. The index of private construction was at 60—almost 40 percent below its 1929 level. In terms of the floor area of buildings erected, construction of private factories plunged by more than 90 percent. Private residences fell by more than 80 percent. Hospital construction fell by three-quarters. The value of utility construction plunged by 86 percent.

During the first four years of the Roosevelt administration, public construction turned down again, sinking to a level below that of the predepression period. The public construction boom under Roosevelt didn't happen until 1936, when spending on public construction soared to almost 40 percent above its 1929 level. This was seven years after the depression began. It was a tough time to be in the construction business.

It was also a tough time to be a supplier of raw materials to contractors. One of the hardest-hit sectors of the building supply area was lumber. Little lumber is used now in public construction. Public projects use more steel, more cement, more brick and stone. A slump in the 1990s would be bad for all those sectors.

Consumer Goods

People continue to eat, even in a depression. But the composition of spending on food changes. In the early stages of a slump, people whose incomes are squeezed will buy lower-quality items. More chicken, less steak and salmon. They will get their vegetables from the ketchup, or settle for something out of the can, not fresh or frozen. Spending on food will drop quickly, but it will be a shallow decline compared to other consumer areas.

In the 1930s, the prices of finished foods fell much less than the prices of meats and other farm products. Bread, for example, fell 20 percent from an average of 8.8 cents a loaf in 1929 to a low of 7 cents in 1932. The price of flour, by contrast, fell 37 percent—about equal to the average fall in wholesale food prices in general. Products from the farm, meanwhile, like butter, milk, eggs, meats, fruits, and vegetables, tumbled almost 60 percent. Officially, the government calculated that the price of eating at home fell by 37 percent. Nonetheless, the percentage of personal consumption spending going for food held steady at around 27 percent.

Less Spending on Fashion

Most North Americans today own many more clothes than ever before. In a real depression, spending on fashion could tumble. Money spent on clothing, accessories, and jewelry plunged by more than 50 percent in the 1930s. Not only did absolute spending fall, but the percentage of income devoted to clothing purchases fell by 18 percent. In 1990, personal spending for clothes was many times higher in absolute terms than in 1929. It is hard to know whether this means there is more slack in the system to cushion any fall, or whether there is a much greater distance to the bottom. In any event, it would take many years before most people would physically wear out the clothes they now have in their closets.

Spending on personal care items fell by 40 percent in the 1930s—another field that is more glutted at today's higher standard of living than it was in 1929. The same goes for gadgets and gift items. Gift shops will be a bad business in the 1990s.

Pawn Shops a Growth Industry?

Of course, not all industries suffer in a depression. Some do well. Those firms experiencing rapid secular growth when the slump begins will suffer less and recover more rapidly. A few companies selling high-tech products will be on the list. There are also certain types of activity that tend to prosper when times are hard. Repair firms do well for obvious reasons. Consumers will have less money to spend on replacing automobiles, appliances, and other durable goods, so the old stuff gets patched up when it breaks down. Pawn shops prosper in hard times. They lend at high interest rates on fully secured collateral. Usually, they advance only a small fraction of the value of items that are pawned, so they could make money even if none of the items was ever redeemed. Cash America, a public company that operates pawn shops, will no doubt do a booming business in the coming decade.

THE AMWAY DECADE

Another type of business that prospers in hard times is the informal business run from the home. Among the fields suited to home entrepreneurs are computer programming, database management and analysis, desktop publishing, accounting, consulting services, marketing, tax preparation, mail order, maid service, baby sitting, tutoring, elder care, catering, home security, dog walking, and more. Some of these cottage industries have already turned to franchising. ServiceMaster, a home cleaning franchise, had forty-two hundred franchises in 1990, according to *Home Office Computing* magazine. Barter organizations and part-time sales jobs can also be operated from the home, which points to success for direct selling organizations in a slump. The

1990s will be a decade of Tupperware parties, Avon ladies, and Amway dealers.

SERVICES

Many believe that services are depression-proof. This is wrong. Spending on services is relatively stable in an ordinary recession, because most recessions are inventory adjustments. A depression is a different story. Services are slower to fall, in some cases, but when they do, they take longer to recover. This was the experience in the United States in the 1930s. Per capita personal consumption spending on services was $1,803 (1982 dollars) in 1929. Even then, services took more of the consumer's income than staples, which averaged $1,735 per capita. As the depression deepened, spending of all kinds fell, with durable goods taking the biggest hit—over 50 percent. By 1936, spending on nondurable goods had recovered to surpass its 1929 level in real terms. Even durable goods spending had recovered to 1929 levels by 1941. But real personal spending on services did not match 1929 levels until 1946— a full decade after spending on nondurable goods had recovered.

A similar pattern was played out in Latin America's inflationary depressions during the 1980s. People who could no longer afford haircuts stopped going to the barber. Eventually, they bought a scissors or clippers and cut one another's hair. Or just let their hair grow. They may have looked silly. But that matters less when everyone else looks silly, too.

In a depression, the service sector is like a shoal of fish trapped on a beach with the tide receding. As real income falls, many service companies starve for customers. Many consumers no longer find it cost-efficient to purchase services they can perform more cheaply for themselves. So they don't. Once they get out of the habit, it may take another generation coming of age with a higher income to restore demand.

The reason that services rise as income rises is that the opportunity costs of doing certain things for yourself, like fixing a meal or ironing your shirts, rise. This pushes more household and personal chores into the market. If you are making hundreds of thousands a year, spending one hundred dollars a head to eat "Veal Boogie Woogie" is a bargain. It economizes your time. You find it cheaper to pay someone else to get you dinner rather than take a few hours to make it yourself and then clean up. But when Sherman McCoy loses his job, he can heat up some chili or eat a hot dog. He does not have to keep the limo driver hovering outside, or worry about hailing a cab. It is amazing how many services you can do without when your income falls.

Restaurants Hit Hard

Restaurants, particularly, will feel the services slump. Especially joints selling Veal Boogie Woogie. Expense account dining, already placed on a diet by tax reform, will take another cinch or two in its belt in a downturn. For the first several years of a slump, expensive restaurants will suffer. So will high-end restaurant chains and suppliers. Consumers will be value-driven. Among publicly traded restaurant chains, those specializing in Italian and Mexican food with low costs will tend to gain market share. Poor people's food will sell in an ethnic dress.

Medical Services

Financially strapped families will also reduce their spending on medical and dental services. This will be compounded by the effects of budget stringency on government spending for medicine. Physicians, dentists, optometrists, and other health practitioners fared poorly in the depression of the 1930s. In the 1930s, spending on medical care of all kinds fell by about one-third, although the percentage of personal income going to health rose slightly. Because so much more of the health dollar today is being spent by government, there is a possibility of more abrupt cutbacks, especially in controversial or expensive treatments that do not extend life expectancy in proportion to their cost. Financially strapped locales will curtail or even eliminate spending on whole categories of medical procedure, as Oregon has already attempted.

Firms operating nursing homes and drug detoxification centers will experience a sharp reduction in paying customers. Drug addicts will be fired or arrested in a depression. Insurance coverage will change to reflect the hardening attitude of society toward drug addiction, alcoholism, and "illnesses" that reflect life-style choices. When potential employees are eager and plentiful, there will be less reason for employers to foot the bill for personal difficulties. Even legal pressures in that direction will tend to be resolved in keeping with the revised attitudes of the 1990s.

Legal Services

The great bull market in lawsuits and legal work in the postwar world will come to an end in the coming slump. The United States, which has the greatest redundancy of lawyers of any society in history, will see greater unemployment among lawyers than elsewhere. Most commercial transactions that support the legal profession—other than bankruptcy—will fall off rapidly as the slump deepens. There will be fewer incorporations, fewer public offerings, fewer private placements, fewer joint ventures, and, of course, fewer real estate transactions. There will even be fewer divorces, as economic necessity will tend to hold couples together.

As the slump deepens, state legislatures in the United States will begin to reform the practice of law to gain a competitive advantage in attracting business. They will be pressed from a variety of quarters to deflate the grotesque costs and unpredictability of the tort system, and limit preposterous punitive damages. The insurance industry, suffering from an increase in claims, lower premium income, and falling return on its investments, will lead the reform effort. The medical establishment will join the effort to cut lawyers down to size. As resources shrink, the inflation of medical costs due to the peculiarities of the American legal system will become less tolerable. Its effects in lowering profits will grow more important. And its adverse impact on the delivery of medical services will be further highlighted. The early success of laws limiting malpractice awards will lead to expanded restrictions on suits over failed medical care, especially for care provided through programs for the poor. Local governments, school boards, and other authorities will also seek relief from ruinous litigation, such as the nine-million-dollar award pinned on New York's subway authority by lawyers for a drunk who lost an arm after falling on the tracks in an alcoholic stupor. Increasingly insolvent governments will be unable to pay such absurd awards, so they will join a reform effort to see them abolished.

Within three to four years of the onset of the slump there will be significant reforms in the practice of law in the United States. The direction of some of these reforms will be much the same as the reform of English law in the crisis-ridden seventeenth century. At that time a popular movement in reaction to high legal costs forced the legal establishment to pare costs. As legal historian Donald Veall put it:

> Some of the seventeenth century arguments have a modern ring. Most of the popular prejudices about the law and the lawyers, in all countries and at all times, found a place in the pamphlet literature of the 1640s and 1650s. The arguments for and against the abolition of the death penalty for theft at once bring to mind the controversy in our own times about the abolition of the death penalty altogether. Then, as now, there was the case for and against the jury system. Was there an effective answer to the law's delays? What were the proper punishments for criminals? Was severity or clemency in punishment the better policy? Why were the costs of litigation so great? Did the answer to all those questions require modification of the legal system?

The seventeenth-century reformers were particularly concerned that the high cost of defending lawsuits was an invitation to blackmail. In seventeenth-century England, as in modern America, innocent litigants were required to pay ruinous legal fees to defend frivolous or inventive lawsuits. These fees were not automatically reimbursed if the suits proved groundless. A member of the seventeenth-century parliamentary committee set up to investigate complaints about excessive legal costs and delays, G. Norburie, wrote:

> What a miserable thing it is that the plaintiff should bring the defendant from the farthest part of England to answer an idle bill, which done, he will perhaps, quarrel at some part of the answer, get it referred to a Master of the Chancery and consequently overruled for insufficient; and so having vexed and put him to great expense, leave him at the end to wipe his nose on his sleeve for any recompense he shall get, be the cause ever so ridiculous.

In most of the civilized world, the seventeenth-century abuse of requiring the victims of absurd lawsuits to vindicate themselves through bankruptcy has been abolished. In modern England, anyone who brings a lawsuit that fails automatically is charged with meeting the legal bills of the party he has sued. Not so in America. In U.S. courts, groundless actions often carry no cost to the plaintiffs. Lawsuits can be undertaken by prospecting lawyers on a contingency fee basis, with no downside risk of paying the costs of those required to answer the suit. As a result, U.S. courts are far more crowded than any other legal system in the world. Many parties who are sued find it financially rational to settle with their tormentors, however groundless the case, simply to avoid shelling out still more money to see it through an increasingly costly and unpredictable legal process. Our bet is that the American rule will be discarded in the coming depression. This and other legal reforms will cost many thousands of lawyers their jobs.

Businesses and institutions that cater to the legal profession will also shrivel as legions of lawyers are disbanded.

Office Buildings in a Slump

The profitability of downtown office buildings, in particular, will tumble. Law firms are major users of office space in center cities. In the depression of the 1930s, the economics of operating office buildings were grim. Many operators had overmortgaged during the building boom of the 1920s. As prices dropped, they found they could no longer profitably dispose of their assets. But it was difficult to hang on and make a profit. One survey estimated that operating expenses of a typical office building actually rose by 2 percent from 1927 to

1932, in spite of deflation. On the other hand, net revenues fell by 70 percent. It was not a good time to be a commercial landlord. We suspect that this pattern will be repeated in the 1990s, especially in major cities that have disproportionate concentrations of lawyers. Technology is making it ever less important to be physically centralized to do business. Many transactions that would have taken place in offices in the 1980s, will be concluded by tele-commuting in the future. Improved voice recognition systems will displace the need for many thousands of stenographers, allowing even the law firms that stay in business to get by with smaller offices.

Oil

Access to oil was a major factor in the outcome of two world wars in this century. As the Iraq-Kuwait crisis emphasized, oil is still the lifeblood of the economy, although its importance in economic growth is shrinking as the economy moves into the Information Age. Oil can also provide an illustration of the difficulty of extrapolating directly from past depressions to guess how the next one will unfold. You cannot simply conclude that because an industry was profitable in the depression of the 1930s it would be profitable in another depression today.

Oil was perhaps the strongest of all industries in the last depression. It enjoyed a wide gap over other industries throughout the period, in terms of output, demand, and profitability. Oil was one of only three industries (the others being food and tobacco) to report net profits in 1932, the deepest year of depression.

Oil Not Depression-Proof

Nonetheless, it would be a mistake to assume that the oil industry is inherently depression-proof. Some of the factors that made for oil's strength in the thirties are no longer present. The industry was lucky to be in a dynamic growth phase when the world slump began. Gasoline retailing was the strongest of all retail sectors. In spite of a decline in auto sales, the annual per car con-sumption of gasoline rose from 525 gallons to 648 gallons during the thirties. The number of retail gasoline stations increased rapidly through the depths of depression. Dynamic growth in the chemical feedstock industry, which uses oil as a raw material, led to the introduction of 53 new basic products in the 1930s. More new petrochemical products were developed in the thirties than in the forties and fifties combined. Even the farm sector contributed to increased oil demand in the 1930s. Further mechanization of agriculture led to an increase of 750,000 in the number of tractors in use during the thirties.

Why Similar Strength Is Unlikely

None of these factors is likely to be repeated. For the most part, this is obvious. The maturing of the sectors with which petroleum is most closely associated practically rules out countertrend growth. Use of oil in railroading and aviation, for example, is not going to increase if the economy slumps. Neither is it likely that tractor use will rise in another depression, nor that innovations in auto design will increase the use of gasoline per car. In fact, auto use is likely to decline. The number of vehicles on the American highway was far higher in 1990 than in the 1930s, with 1.1 registered vehicle per licensed driver. This growth is partly attributable to increased population dispersal and the dramatic rise in the number of individuals employed. From 1960 to 1990, the U.S. population increased by roughly 30 percent, and the number of households increased by 50 percent, while the number of registered vehicles jumped 200 percent.

Unemployment would chop the need for multiple vehicles because it would reduce the number of members per household working, as well as reduce the number of households. Unemployed children would move home with their parents, and elderly parents might move in with their children.

During the 1990s, the roads and highways in America may actually deteriorate. Much of the interstate highway system is at the end of its designed life. Bankrupt governments have been slow to make needed repairs, replace crumbling bridges, and expand the system to meet new demand. A downturn might threaten as well increased public works construction. The experience of the late eighties was that infrastructure spending was cut in order to fund current consumption. It fell from an average of 2.5 percent of GNP in most of the postwar period, to about 1 percent in the end of the 1980s. When budget pressures intensify in a deeper slump, spending on roads, bridges, and airports may be cut further. The net result could be lower gasoline demand.

Given the political environment, with sensitivity over imported oil supplies and their contribution to the trade deficit, no significant substitution of oil for other energy sources is likely. Indeed, oil import fees and higher gasoline taxes are likely to raise the relative cost of oil compared to other fuels. When the U.S. dollar falls from its perch as the world's reserve currency, a development that is quite likely in the 1990s, you could see dramatic and draconian reductions in U.S. oil imports, not unlike those experienced by Third World countries in the 1970s and '80s. Unable to pay for their oil, they had to make do with less. The drastic reductions of oil use proposed by conservationists in the 1970s and 1980s could be imposed by *force majeure* in the 1990s. This would imply a growth in demand for domestic oil, as well as alternative energy supplies and technologies. Natural gas, in particular, is likely to enjoy enhanced demand. This implies a relatively bright future for natural gas suppliers, and industries that service natural gas and build natural gas boilers, turbines, and the like.

There will undoubtedly be concerted efforts to impair the efficiency of market pricing of gasoline and other petroleum products in a slump. The government will be more bankrupt than it was in the 1930s, which will increase the tendency for relief measures to be regulatory in nature, including measures requiring the private provision of income supplements to the poor. Since transportation is an "essential," gasoline marketers are vulnerable, not only to income transfers to the poor, but also to transfers to other groups. For example, further mandated use of uneconomical ethanol blends is likely as foreign exchange pressures build on the dollar. The United States may well follow in Brazil's footsteps in fostering a domestic alcohol program in the hothouse atmosphere of trade protectionism. This will lower the profits of much of the energy sector in a depression.

The petroleum industry will no longer be a preferred credit risk as it was in the 1930s. The widespread banking failures in Texas, the Continental Illinois crisis, problems with the Hunt brothers, the Texaco bankruptcy, etc., have put the credit rating of the oil business down several notches from the high level it enjoyed in the past. Oil companies were able to borrow as they pleased, during even the darkest days of 1932. Today, they may not be so well regarded in a general downturn, which could make it difficult to sell industry-specific assets as the credit crisis develops.

Insurance Problems and Rising Driving Costs

Changes in the legal system will curtail driving during the next depression. In the thirties, auto insurance was essentially voluntary. Persons who could not afford insurance (but could afford gas) drove anyway. While hundreds of thousands of cars were stored and the number of autos in use fell by 10 percent during the first three years of the depression, the ratio of cars in use per capita rose during the decade of the thirties from one in 5.2 persons to one in 4.5. Over the whole decade, the operating costs of driving a car fell sharply. This allowed for increased driving and increased gasoline use, in spite of the pressure on incomes.

Today, circumstances are different. A rapid decline in the overall operating costs of driving a car to offset a decline in income is unlikely. Insurance costs have risen significantly because repair costs have risen in relative terms and legal liabilities exist that were unimagined half a century ago. A major rise in unemployment combined with the workings of the mandatory "uninsured motorists laws" would put many drivers off the roads—if the laws could be enforced. The impact would be especially strong in low-income urban areas. A significant fall in the number of cars in use in some areas is possible. Obviously, this would have a negative impact on the profitability of marginal gasoline stations, fast-food operations, and almost any business in low-income neighborhoods. It will also increase the financial risk of driving in urban areas where you may be involved in an accident with a driver who has neither insurance nor the financial capacity to be responsible for the losses he creates.

Weak Industries Get Weaker

The industries that fared worst in the 1930s were the ones that had been the least profitable in the 1920s. This is contrary to what you might think. Industries that have restructured and downsized in the years before a depression begins could be expected to prove lean and mean. Instead, they seem only to be emaciated and weakened. This is not necessarily because they are managed less competently. Rather, they are in long-term secular decline, which makes it far more difficult for management to turn a profit. Industries in secular decline throughout the 1980s, such as oil, steel, and mining, are likely to be even harder hit in a depression.

The fate of an industry in secular decline is illustrated by the fate of the American textile industry in the Great Depression. Textiles had been losing ground to lower-cost foreign competition during the 1920s, with profit margins squeezed by excess capacity. Textiles also suffered in the depression because output of nondurable products tends to stay high, while profits plunge. Textiles as a group showed a deficit even before the crash, losing money in 1926. Even before the depression became general, demand for textiles was much curtailed and consumer income was insufficient to keep the industry profitable. Half of all textile firms lost money in 1929, three-quarters in 1930. The industry as a whole was in the red from 1931 to 1933, and again in 1935 and 1938. By the end of the depression, many firms were out of business, particularly the high-cost New England firms that operated with the oldest technology and unionized labor. We expect high-cost producers in most industries to suffer in the coming slump.

Necessities May Not Be Profitable

Of course, not all textile or apparel firms were unprofitable in the 1930s. If you look at the exceptions in the textile and apparel field, you can see something that could be important in sorting out investment opportunities in the 1990s. Surprisingly, luxury goods do better in a depression than basic necessities. This requires some explaining. You might expect that luxury sales would fall away and only necessities would be purchased during a slump. But this is only half true. The majority whose spending power has fallen will spend the little money they have on necessities. But that does not mean that the people who purvey those necessities are going to make much of a profit.

It makes no difference whether the industry makes a product that is "essential." Bread is an essential. But baking has often been less profitable than selling diamonds, which are not necessities. Many products of the textile industry are essential. Most of the time, people have to wear clothes, especially in the northern climates. That did not keep the textile industry in profits in the last depression.

Luxury Goods

By 1932 the purchasing power of those still employed had risen greatly because of rapid deflation. Because these income recipients tended to be businessmen and professionals, the demand for luxury items, high-priced durables such as large cars, and nonessential services such as entertainment and tourism rose.

—MICHAEL A. BERNSTEIN,
The Great Depression

When the dust settles after a depression has bottomed, the people who are in solid financial condition have more money to spend, not less. As the 1930s progressed, the marketing of most goods was skewed to emphasize luxury, enhanced comfort, or high fashion, because of the skewing of the income distribution. The market split with the large majority of families and unattached individuals spending their few dollars on low-cost commodities, and the minority setting a trend that continued after recovery toward high-income spending behavior. The net effect of the fall in income and weakness of the economy was to increase the competition for the high-income market. Companies began to stress luxury, greater service, higher-quality foods, silks (and rayons) rather than cottons, higher-octane gas, etc.

There was a tremendous upgrading of the luxury of the automobile in the 1930s. Manufacturers introduced heaters, radios, electric starters, automatic transmission, power steering, and other features to make the automobile easier and more luxurious to drive. The car of the thirties was very different from the Model T Ford, which was a commodity that did not change much from year to year.

Luxury Sales Slip at the Onset of Slumps

It is important to bear in mind, however, that sales of luxury goods tend to falter in the early stages of a slump. They recover only after the depression bottoms out and the stock market has resumed its upturn.

Stories in the January 1, 1930, issue of the *New York Times* reported the complete confidence of most of America about economic prospects for 1930, in spite of the stock market crash. Most people did not care about the stock market because they held few or no stocks. Those who did have stocks and knew their prices cared. As a first effect, luxury sales dried up. This is partly because richer people are more sophisticated about the economy, and it was mainly they who were hurt when the stock market crashed.

In the first round, the people who buy big BMWs will stop short. Three to four years later, when the dust settles, and they realize that their business is not going to collapse, they will resume spending in a big way. Unless the society has become so violent that no one can risk marketing with an emphasis on luxury, you will see a growing tilt in that direction as the 1990s wear on. Products will be regeared to appeal to the upscale buyer. Luxury travel and consumption will increase while downscale won't.

Luxury, Quality, and Style

As we mentioned earlier, the American auto industry, in the period before the Great Depression, was intent upon improving the quality of its product and making it last longer. A headline on a business report in the *New York Times*, January 1, 1930, reads, "Auto Industry Confident For The New Year— Better Cars At Lower Prices." A year or two later, the automakers were not so confident. They found to their dismay that people with cars that lasted for long periods were reluctant to buy new ones when the economy crumbled. Auto executives found that they could not compete on price alone. They decided to place less emphasis on making their cars last longer, and put a heavier emphasis on style. In a sense, this was another reflection of the gearing of the market to high-income spending behavior. The rich bought new clothes to be fashionable. They also bought new cars to be fashionable.

When America emerged from World War II as the richest nation on earth, everyone adopted high-income spending behavior. American cars continued to be sold more on fashion than those in Europe or Japan.

Specialty Lines and Fashion Changes

In the recovery from the next slump, many industries will tend to move toward specialty lines and fashion changes with luxury orientation to maximize their profits and reduce price competition.

Much product innovation will also come in expensive wrapping. Before the decade is out, if you are still affluent, you will be able to live in a computer-driven house that turns on the lights by your favorite chair at reading time, and draws your bath to exactly the temperature that you desire.

Designer Foods

During the 1930s, there was a big increase in the per capita consumption of what were known as luxury foods. Consumption of citrus foods jumped as did ice cream and beef. This will have analogs in the 1990s. We are at the threshold of tremendous changes in the food industry due to the advent of biotechnology and new ways of processing and preparing foods. You will see designer foods, and far higher quality vegetables and fruits. Before the nineties are out, brand-name tomatoes will appear that can be cut with a fork and don't taste like cardboard.

Brand Loyalty Evaporates

When demand falls as it does in a depression, competition for the remaining customers is abnormally intense. This was especially true in the thirties in fields enjoying dynamic growth, such as tobacco products, gasoline sales, and better processed foods. When the depression began, for example, gasoline was sold from tankers at railheads. Crankcase oil was scooped from large drums. There was practically no service. Within a few years, this was totally changed. New stations were designed. Service attendants ran to greet each customer. They washed windshields, checked oil levels, and put air in their customers' tires. They also offered repair facilities, credit services, "service with a smile," etc. As gasoline retailers sought to outdo one another, they invested large sums in marketing and capital improvements. Oil company advertising costs alone in the mid-thirties amounted to 20 percent of the value of gasoline purchases.

In light of this experience, another depression should be viewed as an opportunity to compete. Depressions are periods when brand loyalties in practically any product line are up for grabs. This means that advertising is important for positioning and repositioning products. Companies that trade on identifiable brands will be vulnerable to new competition, especially if they sell cheap products that are technologically easy to produce. Coca-Cola's lock on the cola market, for example, was challenged in the depression by Pepsi, which originally was a low-cost competitor. This is a matter to bear in mind when reviewing your portfolio. Companies with big names but weak balance sheets, like Marriott, may not survive. Brands that do not go hand-in-hand with superior products will not be worth premium prices.

Media Profits Suffer

Although advertising and positioning are perhaps more important in depressions than in normal economic periods, this does not make newspapers and magazines profitable. To the contrary. Newspapers, especially, will lose revenue because most of the advertising dollars they receive are not from product innovators, but from small companies and individuals competing to sell products that cannot be easily repositioned. Furniture stores, car dealers, grocery chains, and department stores are the major sources of ad revenue for newspapers. Even receipts from classified ads dry up as real estate transactions wind down.

Revenues for television and radio stations will also dwindle, especially in competitive markets. Radio stations and local TV, like newspapers, will suffer from the fall-off in advertising dollars in local markets, as car dealers, furniture stores, etc., go out of business. The growth of satellite, fiber optic, and cable television alternatives will undermine the economic standing of the major TV networks. And the growth potential of technologically anachronistic cable television will itself be limited by fiber optic telephone networks and satellite broadcast.

Bear Markets Hurt Emerging Firms

One of many reasons for the long lag in recovery from depressions is that there is a basic change in the composition of the national output. The demand for labor may be lower in the emerging firms than in the dying industries, which tend to be of larger scale. Another is that the new industries generally are more dependent on the capital markets than the old, mature industries.

A big, rusting steel company can have a lot of cash in the bank, and many assets to work its way through as it heads over the hill to oblivion. Even in a depression, its land and buildings will be worth something. Its old machines will sell for scrap value. It has tangible assets that represent collateral for credit.

But small, emerging firms tend not to have that advantage. A new company may do fairly well in the upsurge of a bull market because it can go to its investment bank when it needs more cash to obtain another private placement or an initial public offering. It can raise cash to keep itself going, as it works through the development process. However, when financial markets crash and a credit crunch develops, the very companies in dynamic growth sectors that need additional funding to make a go of it are locked out of capital markets. That is a perverse feedback loop that slows the recovery during major economic transitions.

It is also a warning sign of longer-term stagnation because companies in information-based activities where the product cycle is short, and where there are few tangible assets to serve as collateral for lending, depend more upon effective government to justify investment than do firms of a similar scale operating with tangible assets. An efficient judicial system, and honest and effective recording of patents, are more essential for recovery of investment in a software company than a brewery. If you lend money to a brewer, you don't have to worry very much about whether his recipe for light beer is protected by the patent office. If all fails, you can still recover the vats and the rest of the plumbing. Not so with the software company. Its tangible assets are likely to consist of little more than some computers, file cabinets, and desks.

Changes in the Work Force

Even though *The Feminine Mystique* was published in the 1960s, the major move out of the household by women really began in the last depression. It was then, for the first time in peacetime, that women became deeply involved as participants in the cash economy. It is for this reason that the sector of the apparel industry that focused upon women's clothes did better than the one that focused upon men's clothes.

As women got out of the house, this increased the market for household appliances that eased cleaning jobs, and made it easier to wash clothes, get dinner on the table, and so forth. The number of refrigerators, washing machines, vacuum cleaners, irons, toasters, coffee makers, and radios went way up during the depression. Appliances we now take for granted as fixtures of the home were introduced into the household economy during the last depression.

The movement of women into the workplace contributed to the fortunes of another successful industry during the last depression—the tobacco industry. One reason was the terrific one-time surge of women buying cigarettes. Women started to smoke cigarettes in the workplace during the depression.

In another depression there will be little scope for an increase in the number of workers per household unless we move to polygamous marriage, repeal the child labor laws, or return to extended family living, with more than two generations under the same roof. Only the last of these possibilities seems plausible. Nonetheless, there will be obvious dangers of falling household income. A greater proportion of the total population was involved in the work force in the late eighties than ever. Many families living near or at the margin had both husband and wife working. They depended on that dual income to meet their mortgages, their car payments, and their credit card bills. Both must keep their jobs to support their life-style. When a family depends upon two wage earners as opposed to one, the chances are higher that the income stream will be interrupted. One or the other may suffer some stage of unemployment in a severe downturn.

Often it may be the higher-paid worker, usually the husband. This certainly was the case in the rust bucket when middle managers of industrial plants as well as highly paid union workers were laid off in the recessions of the early eighties. In many cases, the wife kept her job and the husband stayed home. This will recur more widely in the 1990s. As a result, you can expect increased demand for the utensils and other components of the production of food and services within the home aimed especially at househusbands. There will also be a specialized market aimed at unsupervised children, who will more or less have the run of the home in many households where both parents keep their jobs. There are lively possibilities for combining computerization with home utensils and products that will change the way the household economy operates.

In any event, there will be at least a temporary reversal of the long-term trend toward the movement of most household services and products into the market. The service sector could suffer more than most people now imagine.

Cartels to Come

If the transition occurs as slowly as we think it may, it is not going to be over in a couple of years. It is likely to drag on for at least four years, and could last longer. This "crisis of transition" may not be as easy to overcome politically as it was in the 1930s because we entered the last depression with advantages not now enjoyed. Because the U.S. government in particular is insolvent at its current level of promises, you almost can count on seeing more regulation that will do the wrong thing. It will protect dying industries, suppress innovation, and slow the transition to the new economy. The glacial pace of court action to resolve bankruptcy filings and provide clear titles to repossessed properties will also inevitably retard the adjustment process.

The representatives of the new economy—the new firms that will come into existence, the new employees who will someday be hired—do not have any present political coherence or organization. They do not wield a bloc vote. By contrast, large numbers are employed in the old industries. The old industries are threatened with falling demand, falling profits, and worse. Their employees face transitional unemployment and perhaps structural unemployment.

Politicians Will Make Things Worse

Politically, the representatives of the unemployed, underemployed, and unemployable are going to push to "make jobs," in spite of the insolvency of the government. The government will seek to create work through regulation. These policies will be implemented in conjunction with the industries with falling demand, perhaps by mandating a very short work week, or requiring that successful firms "adopt" dysfunctional individuals for "training."

The prospect of another round of counterproductive regulation is one of the strongest arguments for the *laissez-faire* prejudice in politics. It is not necessarily true that government can never do anything that would be beneficial. Wise and knowing leaders, in theory, could encourage rather than retard necessary developments. They could facilitate the liquidation of inefficient firms, and encourage workers to adopt productive values and adapt to changes in technology.

But the political reality is otherwise. There is a strong temptation to use whatever power government has in these transitional moments to retard the progress of the country rather than to encourage it. In many more cases than not, politicians actually encourage constituents to adopt counterproductive values and resist changing their behavior to comply with signals in the market. We would be better off with the old rule that said government should not step in to try to improve things. Nine times out of ten, the politicians will not improve things. They will make them worse.

This was certainly the case in the 1930s. Controls on output and prices set up by the National Recovery Administration "protected lethargic and inefficient firms." Almost none of the NRA Boards had representatives of independent business. Nor did they have representatives of the dynamic sectors of faltering industries like steel. They did not represent the few steel companies that were profitable or innovative. The companies that successfully adjusted to the new realities and made money had no input in the direction of the New Deal cartels. The political high ground was controlled by the losers. The same tendency will be in evidence in the 1990s. You will see efforts to curtail output and to restrict innovation.

In the last depression, mature industries suffered lower profits, slower recovery, and greater regulation than did emerging industries. Those who felt that the demand for their products was inflexible, or "inelastic" in the language of economists, "were obsessed with the specter of overproduction." Thus industries like steel, textiles, and oil vigorously sought government regulation. Where demand was inelastic, price discounting did little to stimulate demand or improve capacity utilization.

If demand for your product is relatively price-inelastic, you are not going to be able to utilize your excess capacity much better if you cut prices. You will not be able to better amortize your equipment. You are just going to sell at a lower price. Under those conditions, the political process will be employed to stop and squelch adjustment. As a result, a lengthy adjustment process may unfold even more slowly because of political impediments.

In the thirties, the object of regulation was almost invariably to curtail output and stifle innovation. Price controls were largely designed to keep producer prices high. Today, there may be a higher likelihood of regulation of output and product mix to guarantee profits to the politically best-connected firms, with differential prices to reward powerful industrial customers or favored consumers.

"Stimulation" Will Not Stimulate

Efforts to "stimulate" growth in the 1990s are likely to prove more counterproductive than in the 1930s. They borrow from the future in a futile effort to sustain the past. Consider the reasons why:

1. The same kind of public works spending that was very productive in the last depression would be a waste today. Lots of new highways, for example, would not pay off as they did in the past. Improvement of highways had a dramatic effect beginning in the 1930s in increasing the number of autos in use and amplifying other activity that depended on autos, like building of suburbs and shopping centers. There will be much more modest effects today. The number of autos in use is not likely to go up no matter how many roads are built. Congestion can be much more efficiently handled by peak-load pricing than by pouring more concrete.

2. Even during the last depression, when industrialism was still advancing toward its mature phase, political efforts to "stimulate" the economy usually involved subsidizing the faltering sectors of industry and impeding the emerging sectors. This tendency to retard is bound to be more pronounced because of the much more frightening impact of information technology in reducing economies to scale, reducing the demand for unskilled labor, breaking down

the barriers between occupations, and shifting the distribution of income toward the better educated.

3. Investments in the "industrial base" in an attempt to preserve high-wage jobs for voters with low skills are destined to show meager returns. They are force-feeding more capital into a declining sector. For example, Clinton's plan to create "manufacturing extension centers" modeled on the agricultural extension centers of the last century are no more likely to halt the decline of manufacturing than agriculture extension services were to reverse the decline of farming. The reason that manufacturing is in decline is not that private business is unaware of how to manufacture, but because information technology is supplanting industrial technology as the main area of value-added activity. At best, political manipulations can slow the general decline in the standard of living, while creating larger pockets of dependency.

4. Most "stimulation" involves either overt or thinly disguised income redistribution, which tends to delay the necessary adjustment in skills among poorly educated segments of the population who are prepared to work on the assembly line but not to contribute to the development of intellectual property.

5. Redistribution also diminishes incentives to save, while reducing the capital of those who do most of the saving. A clear case is provided in the U.S. election, where candidate Clinton promised to assure everyone of health care, and lend every student the money to go to college, regardless of income. This is to be paid for by higher taxes on the rich. If people no longer feel the need to save either to protect themselves against medical emergency or to educate their children, their savings rate is likely to decline. The ability of the rich to save obviously will be undercut by higher taxes.

6. The tendency to regulate higher costs onto operating businesses to facilitate income redistribution is a common feature of political systems under stress, and is remarkably evident today both in Europe and North America. But these higher burdens make the local economy less competitive, and thus impede recovery.

7. A common feature of all stimulative initiatives, especially those that involve little but income redistribution, without a substantial investment component, is that they expand government debt. This runs down the national balance sheet, increasing the debt service burden without increasing earning capacity. In logic, this means a deeper depression in the end.

The Attempt to Revive the Past

There are many experts, of course, who will say that the key to making America prosper again is to revive manufacturing. Their prescription to do this is to focus incentives in ways that encourage longterm, fixed investment. It sounds plausible when viewed from a conventional perspective. But it is backward-looking and probably won't work.

The reason fixed investment is lagging is that its productivity has fallen. Most or all of the industries that figured in the post–World War II boom now face satured markets with worldwide overcapacity. Force-feeding additional capital into fixed investment in the manufacturing side will only aggravate the longterm problem by increasing the overcapacity. It also takes resources away from the small business sector which creates new jobs.

Saturated or slowly growing replacement markets with overcapacity require companies to compete by increasing productivity. This is a good thing in itself. But higher productivity with flat markets means fewer jobs. Short of buying the products directly and giving them away, which is obviously ruinous, there is little that can be done to rescue oldline manufacturing in aggregate.

The hope for the future lies in incubating new products and services, in other words, in entrepreneurship. To do that, *flexibility* and *adaptability* must be the hallmarks of the economy and government policy. Legions of small businesses should be encouraged to form. Many ideas need to be tested in the market place in order to come up with the 20 to 30 major innovations that will create vigorous economic growth.

Unfortunately, that is not likely to be the path that policy takes.

Privatization of Government Services

One positive development that is likely is the privatization of government services. With or without the support of government employees, a major area of growth in the 1990s will be the privatization of functions now performed badly by governments.

The breakdown of order in urban areas will place a premium on security services. Anti-theft devices and more sophisticated security systems will be in demand. Community groups will supplement declining police patrols with private security details. More corporations will hire outside services to protect their premises against invasion by criminals. Karate studios and martial arts training programs will be profitable. And wealthy individuals will increasingly hire bodyguards, as is common in Latin America.

The collapse of urban infrastructure will oblige individuals to supplement the quality of public services in other ways. Water purification systems, for example, will be necessities in bankrupt cities. Another important feature of the privatization of infrastructure like sewage treatment plants is that it offers hope for the banking system. Sewage plants can and should be privatized as utilities, which pay taxes. Their operations are perfectly suited for bank financing, because they have significant collateral and they will certainly have ongoing revenue streams. Banks need a new, dependable outlet for financing to replace inventory financing, which was their main business. Now it is rapidly disappearing. Computerization has reduced the importance of inventories, and the falling product cycle has made it risky for banks to finance areas of high tech growth. What seems to be the last word in a computer program, for example, could be rendered obsolete overnight. That won't happen with sewage.

There will be a tremendous growth in private educational services, including for-profit and nonprofit schools, as companies such as Project Edison and Educational Alternatives have already begun to show since the first edition of this book was published. The tribalization of society, and the seizure of school curricula in urban areas by militants pushing "Afrocentric" education, substantially undermines the reason that school systems were operated by governments in the first place. That was not to secure a better education. Overwhelming evidence shows that private schools are more effective instruments of learning. Schools were kept largely under government management to facilitate indoctrination with middle-class culture and the ideas of citizenship. The rising power of small groups and the rebirth of tribal thinking make the principal purpose of public schools, acculturating students, obsolete. Where "Afrocentric" and other eccentric curricula have come to dominate, public schools are now actually counterproductive to their original purpose. And they are certainly not doing the job of education, which has now come to be too important to leave in the hands of bureaucrats.

Therefore, it is more likely than most people now imagine that public schools in the United States will more or less disappear in the coming decade. Educational entrepreneurs will enjoy a rare opportunity to compete in providing effective elementary and secondary education to children whose parents will be able to spend vouchers on their services.

Telepresence in the University

The advent of telepresence could have an impact by the end of the 1990s in improving the quality and lowering the costs of university education. The availability of real-time, high-quality imagery and sound would enable universities to syndicate the best lecturers nationwide and even internationally. The top authorities who are the most entertaining and effective speakers could literally be "on stage" practically anywhere the high-quality telepresence systems could be plugged in. This would enable universities to cut costs. They could dispense with many costly tenured posts, and substitute lower-rank proctors and teaching assistants. Many of the full professors do little teaching anyway. Their research activities may come to be supported only by larger, better-endowed institutions, and by private foundations and corporate funds.

On the Road Again

The construction and maintenance of highways will be increasingly turned over to private companies that will recover their investments by collecting tolls on bridges and major arteries. These privately financed roads will be able to adopt new technologies that governments in the United States have proven slow to use. For example, advances in photonics and electronics make it possible to identify an automobile traveling on a highway, over a bridge, or through a tunnel, and bill its owner monthly for usage. Weight sensors could be employed to detect overweight vehicles. They could either be charged a stiff toll proportionate to the costs they impose by destroying the roadbed, or they could be barred and their loads redistributed to smaller, more economical vehicles. Private firms could utilize such technologies to make investments in highways a paying proposition, thus keeping the infrastructure up-to-date.

Federal and state highway maintenance has fallen miserably behind what would be required simply to preserve the road system of the 1950s. Official estimates suggest that 60 percent of the urban highway system is in fair or poor condition. Forty-two percent of America's 575,607 bridges are classified as obsolete or structurally deficient. A conservative estimate of repair costs is five hundred billion dollars. Since governments are utterly without free funds, they will undoubtedly raise the gasoline tax steeply, and turn increasingly to private entrepreneurs to finance needed infrastructure.

The move to high-tech roadways may be encouraged by auto companies seeking to appeal to high-income drivers with more sophisticated technologies that outmode older cars. One feature that Honda and other manufacturers are now trying to perfect is built-in electronic mapping. This would literally tell the driver where he is going. In interactive versions, it would also allow drivers to know that traffic jams were ahead and take alternative routes. In effect, this would be a higher-tech version of the CB that would interact with highway monitoring services. Some of these systems would work off highly precise satellite navigation that can pinpoint vehicle locations within a few feet.

Such technologies could be an essential step in the evolution of more modern traffic control. The Japanese and Asian "Dragons" are leading the way in the development of high-tech highway systems that manage traffic.

In Europe, Project Prometheus looks to bring an intelligent highway system on-line in the 1990s. Norway has already introduced Premid, a fully automated toll system that uses electronic scanners and special identity plates to debit tolls electronically without requiring vehicles to stop. Such systems will make privately financed toll roads and bridges more practical than ever before.

Of course, not every pothole will be a target for privatization and repair. In many urban areas in the United States, social disintegration and violence will preclude the investment of considerable sums in high-tech toll systems. An unguarded highway or bridge would have more gate-crashers than a rock concert in an open field. Around-the-clock patrols would be needed to apprehend toll-evaders, and to protect scanning systems from vandals and criminals who did not wish their whereabouts to be noted. Therefore, the advantages of a privately funded infrastructure will be limited to those areas that serve mainly commercial traffic, or orderly, middle-class drivers. Elsewhere, more decay should be expected. When you escape from the high-cost metropolis, you may have to drive slowly to avoid having your undercarriage battered by potholes.

Heading for the Hills

The more you think about it, the more likely it is that the coming depression will alter your ideas of where you want to live. If we are correct, the 1990s could well be a footloose decade. The coming slump will dramatically alter the regions of opportunity in America and the world. Many people will literally head for the hills to escape the high costs of urban disintegration.

THE FIFTH MIGRATION

Aversion to New York is passing like an airborne virus among the city's people, even among those with money—money to buy their way out of the public schools, the crumbling neighborhoods, the subway, all the things that are supposed to make life here unlivable.

The young man from Utah murdered in the subway while defending his mother against thugs was the last straw. Before him was the assistant district attorney, a kind and generous man shot as he went to pick up doughnuts at a bodega. The murdered baby, his walker's merry fabric blotted with blood. The man at the telephone booth who suddenly wasn't on the line anymore, killed while he talked to a friend. . . . They live in a city where people are disposable, and not even the garbage is safe.

—ANNA QUINDLEN,
New York Times

An enduring image of the last depression in America is that of the uprooted poor, with all their possessions tied to the back of a dusty Model T Ford. In literature and old movies, these unhappy pilgrims are always making their way to California, where they intend to find jobs, cheap oranges, and sunny weather.

While the reality of depression migration differed from the myths, it is true that depressions are periods of extraordinary population shifts. That important fact could hold clues to what happens in the future. There have been four major depressions in U.S. history. Each coincided with a major migration. Now demographers have spotted the beginnings of what looks like "the fifth migration." It is another intriguing hint that America's fifth depression is coming. So far as we know, no one has ever said that a migration was a characteristic feature of depression. Yet in the American experience, at least, the dates of the four major migrations of the past correspond strikingly with the down phases of economic activity.

The periods of deflation as reflected by changes in U.S. wholesale prices coincide with the four major periods of migration as calculated by demographers. The overlap may be coincidental, but we doubt it.

The Flight from Suburbia

Dr. Jack Lessinger, author of *Regions of Opportunity*, has identified a new shift in population that will have a major impact on business and investment in the 1990s and the early part of the next century: "The abandonment of suburbia begins the fifth major migration since the American revolution." If this perception is accurate, as we suspect it is, it may also be an unrecognized leading indicator of depression. Each of the four previous migrations of American life was already underway prior to the depression with which it was associated.

Migration Patterns in America Hard to Discern

With the exception of gypsies, no culture is so attuned to moving as are Americans. America began as a nation of migrants. Wanderlust remains a national habit. Indeed, the whole of American history celebrates the westward push from the old world on the eastern shores of the Atlantic through a new continent to the Pacific. The settlement and westward expansion of America are so well celebrated that the casual recollection of American history does not distinguish the ebbs and flows of the great migrations. Nor is it likely that many people would have an accurate perception of current population movements without resorting to a study of the data.

Why People Move in Times of Depression

The great migrations of American life have not been one uninterrupted wagon train. People moved. Then they stayed put. They built homes, cleared land, and erected fences. They or their children moved again only when events gave them powerful motives to do so. Those motives had to be powerful in the centuries before our own, because the rigors of travel and the challenge of living on the frontier were great. The desire to escape persecution and live in freedom was a powerful motive. Another was a desire to escape poverty and ruin, conditions that are felt more acutely in times of depression.

It is no surprise, therefore, that the great surges of foreign immigration into America, as well as the waves of internal migration, have coincided with depressions abroad and at home. Robert Louis Stevenson left a marvelous record of such a migration in his volume *The Amateur Emigrant*. It recounts his journey in 1879 on a sailing ship to New York, and a further trip across America to San Francisco, where he joined his future wife. Most of Stevenson's fellow passengers were refugees from depression. He wrote:

> Labouring mankind had in the last years, and throughout Great Britain, sustained a prolonged and crushing series of defeats. I had heard vaguely of these reverses; of whole streets of houses standing deserted by the Tyne, the cellar-doors broken and removed for firewood; of homeless men loitering at the street-corners of Glasgow with their chests beside them; of closed factories, useless strikes, and starving girls. . . . A turn of the market may be a calamity as disastrous as the French retreat from Moscow. . . . Thus it was only now, when I found myself involved in the rout, that I began to appreciate how sharp had been the battle. We were a company of the rejected; the drunken, the incompetent, the weak, the prodigal, all who had been unable to prevail against the circumstances in the one land, were now fleeing pitifully to another; and though one or two might still succeed, all had already failed. We were a shipful of failures, the broken men of England.

When opportunity is cut off in one direction, people will move in another. Where there is freedom to move, the process is practically as automatic as that which inclines plants toward sunshine. It is all part of the mechanism through which individuals actively seek their happiness and societies maintain their balance.

Neither Migrations Nor Depressions End in a Year

The fact that depressions are associated with major migrations, while recessions during bull phases are not, is a distinction that should not be ignored.

Depressions are more than inventory adjustments. They are reorganizations of the economy. Old patterns, old structures, old ways of doing things, even old patterns of settlement, are subject to far-reaching change. Such transitions, by their nature, are long-term. You cannot build a new city in a day. Nor tear one down. This is why the recovery in a depression cannot be as immediate as the recovery from recession.

Migrations to the Frontier

Empty continents swarm, as at the bo's'un's whistle, with industrious hands, and whole new empires are domesticated to the service of man.

—ROBERT LOUIS STEVENSON

The first three American migrations involved dramatic rearrangement of the nation's capital and structures as activity shifted from one location to the next. Not only were cities built, but whole states and regions were peopled with pioneers, most of whom had not done well in the established areas.

The first American migration coincided with the depression of the 1780s, a downturn no longer remembered today. But this "lost depression" made a major mark on American history. As we recounted in an earlier chapter, it was a contributing factor to the overthrow of the Articles of Confederation and adoption of the U.S. Constitution. The migration to the frontier associated with this depression began a trend that has continued until today—of declining relative population in what were the predominant states among the first thirteen colonies. Massachusetts, New York, Pennsylvania, and Virginia lost population to new regions to the north and south, such as Vermont, New Hampshire, and Georgia.

The second migration took up the decades of depression from the 1820s through the 1840s. It was a period of expansion westward and southward through the Ohio and Mississippi valleys.

The third migration (1873 through 1900) marked the settlement of the western United States and emergence of industrial and trading cities in the Midwest and West, like Chicago, Minneapolis, San Francisco, Portland, and Seattle.

The Migration of the Affluent

The fourth migration of American life, the move to suburbia, was the first to involve a movement within the boundaries of a settled nation rather than a migration to the frontier. It was also the first in which the new regions of opportunity—the emerging suburbs—attracted primarily the more wealthy members of society, rather than the "failures," to use Stevenson's term.

The fourth migration was only incidentally a migration of Okies and movie stars to California. It was more significantly the move to suburbia. It took place throughout America, and is dated by the demographers as having begun in 1929. The first stirrings of this migration, however, were evident earlier. An intelligent observer could have spotted the growth of suburbs by the middle twenties. By 1929, the Connecticut suburbs of New York were already so jammed with commuters who had grown rich in the bull market that choice properties were selling for as much as a million dollars. As Jim Grant points out, this was actually the top of the market for that type of suburban property. The million-dollar houses in Greenwich of 1929 "changed hands for as little as $75,000 in the 1930s." Suburbia began with a migration of the rich.

Throughout the entire migration period, ending with the recession of 1958, new suburbanites tended to have higher incomes than those left behind within the city boundaries.

THE ESCAPE FROM COSTS

A good portion of the opportunity that beckoned in the suburbs was the opportunity to evade costs. In the beginning, new suburbs enjoyed significantly lower taxes. They did not have well-established and often corrupt urban governments. The suburbs were safer, cleaner, and free of congestion. It was possible to buy a property with a yard and a garden. As Jack Lessinger put it, "Americans migrated to the suburbs by the million to preside as little kings and queens over their one-sixth acre domains. There, plumbers and steel-workers indulged themselves in a regal lifestyle that exceeded their parents' wildest expectations."

The Decline of Suburbia

In recent decades, suburbs have begun to decline. In many cases, they have become rundown, congested, polluted, and almost as crime-ridden as center cities. The quality of schools has slipped. Taxes have gone up.

We have already explained how technological change weakened the capacity of labor unions to redistribute income from investors to factory workers. The full implications of this development have yet to be felt. Wider income gaps are just the first consequence. As income comes to be more directly proportioned to education and skills, communities where the skill level of the work force is deficient will be candidates for long-term decline. Not only will unskilled workers tend to lose income relative to investors, their children will be likely to fall even further behind because of the evaporation of high-paying jobs for unskilled work, and adverse cultural changes that reduce the influence of middle- and upper-class values.

According to the Hudson Institute, "between now and the year 2000, for the first time in history, a majority of all new jobs will require postsecondary education." A high concentration of poorly educated, unskilled individuals entering the job markets in major metropolitan areas argues that these are unlikely to be centers of dynamic growth. Quite the contrary. The big cities and many of their suburban neighbors will be centers of high costs.

> Apathetic residents in ethnic and blue collar neighborhoods tolerate corrupt judges, police and politicians. As is true with many decaying cities, litter and potholes are everywhere. People sleep on sidewalks. The stench of urine and human feces often permeates downtown streets, subway tunnels, and even City Hall.
>
> —*WALL STREET JOURNAL*
> on Philadelphia, "City in Crisis"

It is likely that large Northeastern cities, especially New York, Washington, and Philadelphia, will suffer fiscally and physically in the coming slump. We have already indicated some of Manhattan's vulnerabilities as an overly centralized island metropolis. Like Calcutta, where the last sewer pipe was laid in 1896, New York is living on infrastructure investments made long ago. There will be little money to rebuild unless large sums are diverted from social spending and income redistribution—an outcome that will be achieved only under extreme fiscal duress.

Philadelphia was already teetering on the brink of bankruptcy in 1990. Its entrenched municipal bureaucracy "consumes an enormous percentage of general funds." The *Philadelphia Story* of the 1990s will not star Katharine Hepburn and Cary Grant. It will be a story without stars, only extras: the unlucky who cannot afford to leave, drug addicts, the homeless, and the legions of city employees who do little badly.

Not to be outdone, Washington, D.C., suffered under one of the more corrupt and incompetent governments outside the Third World. In 1990, Washington spent twice as much per citizen as the average for state and local governments. It spent two thousand dollars per capita more than even New York City, and had a payroll three times as large as the average big city. One in every ten residents of Washington was employed by city government. In spite of massive overstaffing, productivity was abysmal. For example, a study scrutinized the city's costly low-interest rehab loan program. Auditors found that a city bureaucrat could process an average of only one loan application every three months. It cost eleven thousand dollars in administrative expenses for each twenty-thousand-dollar loan. Not coincidentally Washington was facing a massive deficit, which political leaders hoped to close by yet another tax increase.

Compounding other burdens will be growing crime and violence, which often increase in depression. This upsurge in violence is likely to compound a long-term trend toward more violent behavior among blacks. For example, the black murder rate in Philadelphia rose by more than 850 percent from the nineteenth century to the 1950s. Black murder rates in New York and Washington shot up by almost 50 percent during the 1930s. A repetition of this pattern in the depression of the 1990s would make these already violent urban areas even more dangerous to live in.

Another unhappy contributing factor to the decline of the metropolis will be the mounting requirement for care of tens of thousands of impoverished AIDS patients. Not only is AIDS an overwhelmingly metropolitan epidemic, but urban areas are magnets for those from smaller communities who happen to be infected.

THE LIGHTS MAY GO OFF

What happens when the lights go off in a city of 10 million people? Not just for one night, like New York City's Great Blackout in the 1970s, but for at least six hours a day for months on end? That's the experience . . . in Buenos Aires, Argentina. . . .

Since mid-December, SEGBA (Servicios Electricos de Gran Buenos Aires) has been implementing rolling blackouts, neighborhood by neighborhood, in Argentina's great commercial and industrial center and capital city. The result: an estimated $42 million a day in lost industrial production and commercial activity; angry and embittered citizens. . . .

Household appliances are off. Refrigerators defrost, and food can spoil. Electric clocks are useless (do you want to reset them twice a day?). Washing and vacuuming must be rescheduled to fit the blackout schedule.

No more shopping for a week's groceries. Buy only for the day. Sales of dairy products and fish plummet in the stores and restaurants.

—DAVID RUSK

A major downturn would reduce demand for all forms of energy. But if it is accompanied by political instability and terrorism, the fall-off in demand may not be enough to head off blackouts and brownouts in the 1990s. The whole centralized power grid is an artifact from the time when violence was falling, and economies of scale in the production process were high and rising. The power grid is now vulnerable to sabotage and breakdown. The vulnerability to breakdown has been compounded by a continuing shift in the composition of the demand for energy. From the first oil shock in 1973 through 1989, demand for electricity rose by more than 50 percent, while demand for all other forms of energy declined. Utilities, however, especially in the Northeast, have been unsuccessful in bringing major new plants on line to extend their capacity. Partly this is because of mistaken estimates of future demand. The long lead time—about fourteen years to build a major generating station—makes mistaken estimates of future electricity demand from the early seventies problems for the 1990s. The margin of extra capacity in the American electrical grid steadily declined throughout the 1980s.

This could be important in establishing the areas of greatest economic potential in the 1990s. If we are mistaken about deflation, and the debts of the government are liquidated by hyperinflation, electric utilities would be prime losers, in spite of their high debt ratios. More important than the fact that their debts would be wiped away is the fact that their prices are regulated. Politicized utility commissions would be unlikely to allow rates to rise far enough and rapidly enough to preserve the capital base of the companies. As in Argentina, the lights could go off.

Even a deflationary outcome may not bail out the utilities. Widespread delinquencies and defaults by customers in misgoverned cities, and even takeovers by militant urban governments, are dangers. The margins of excess generating capacity in some areas of the United States are below 15 percent. Before the 1980s, reserve capacity below 25 percent was considered inadequate. Demand for energy in the form of electricity could be skewed further by the introduction of functional electric cars in the 1990s. General Motors has plans to market the unfortunately named "Impact," an electric automobile that can outrace a Mazda Miata. Unlike the clunky electric vehicles that poke around Europe delivering milk, the new electric cars could become popular for passenger travel. This is especially likely in the event that a foreign exchange crisis and new taxes raise the price of gasoline.

Any breakdown of current generating facilities due to sabotage, old age, or diminished availability of fuel could result in your having to think about electricity, something you probably don't do very much now. You could face brownouts, blackouts, or even rotating Argentine-style shutdowns. These are most likely in the Northeast. American states with the greatest electric generating problems include: Connecticut, Maine, Massachusetts, New Hampshire, Rhode Island, Vermont, New York, New Jersey, Delaware, Pennsylvania, Maryland, and Michigan. Even rural areas in these states may not be far enough removed from the problems of big cities because they are tied to them by the power grid.

Garbage with No Place to Go

The states with power grid problems are the same ones where garbage is piling up. North Atlantic and Mid-Central states are particularly at risk. Landfill locations are filling up, as they always do. But political pressures have delayed approval of new sites. New York's famous garbage scow with nowhere to go will sail the seas again in the 1990s. Or it will simply dump its load in the ocean.

A WAY OUT

At a time of increasingly footloose industry and an information-based economy, those who can escape the high costs of urban and suburban decline will tend to do so. Technological change will encourage this transition. The advent of telepresence, for example, will reduce the necessity for travel to attend business meetings and to interact in informal ways. If and when the mysteries of superconductivity are mastered at normal temperatures, high-speed rail lines will make it possible for individuals to commute to cities from hundreds of miles away. Even the remote possibility that such a development could be brought on-line could make the carcasses of dying or defunct railroads valuable. They possess an asset that could not be duplicated today, a right-of-way that would speed the route of escape from the crime-ridden, high-cost metropolis.

This flight from high costs has already begun. We expect it to continue. Opportunities will expand in regions of lower costs, which happen to be the "exurbs," select rural or semi-rural areas beyond the normal commuting range of big cities. These exurbs have been growing at twice the rate of the country as a whole in recent years.

Only 4 percent of the U.S. population lived in these high-growth exurbs at the time of the 1980 census. Since the exurban counties cover a land area larger than that which houses half the U.S. population, the potential for additional growth is high. The exurbs could double or quadruple in population and still retain the attractive characteristics of semi-rural life. The migration to selected small towns has only begun.

The exurban areas that will be the new center of growth typically have underused assets and old buildings that can be restored. Many also have sufficient infrastructure to support higher population, because they once did. Most of the dynamic new exurban areas were in decline for much of this century. In many of these areas land is relatively cheap. Populations are literate. Crime is low.

Aspen Is the Future

Should a depression occur today, the factors encouraging a migration to small towns and open spaces would feed on themselves. In a period of generally weaker social cohesion and crime, the flight of the higher-income groups away from the inner cities and suburbs would accelerate. The exurbs would be the only place for them to go. In this respect, Aspen is probably a community of the future—a wealthy small town with many of the cultural amenities of a city: world-class music, good restaurants, even a smattering of theatre. Property prices in Aspen will no doubt come down in the coming slump. But Aspen will be an even more desirable location in the 1990s than areas that are not exurban havens. We expect more Aspens to emerge.

Already, only 17 percent of households with incomes of fifty thousand dollars or more are within central cities, but 89.2 percent are within standard metropolitan areas. Many of these suburban areas are in long-term decline. Even a marginal movement of upper-income individuals from the suburbs into the underpopulated exurbs could produce dramatic growth in those areas.

TAKE THE HINT

The intelligent investor looks for every hint he can find about the future. Here you have one. If Professor Lessinger and other demographers are correct in believing that a fifth migration is now underway, this will mark a transformation of the American economy of a magnitude always associated with depression in the past. The horizons of opportunity will move away from high-cost metropolitan regions into those small towns that can offer amenities that high-income residents seek. Normally these include rural beauty, major recreational facilities, one or more local educational or cultural institutions, and a critical mass of high-income, well-educated neighbors. The Bitterroot Valley in Montana could become a major growth area in the Fifth Migration. The dusty ghost towns of western Iowa or the regions abutting Dakota Indian reservations probably won't be.

As the wealthy "vote with their feet," it will be a painful, unhappy transition for millions of poorly educated city dwellers left behind in the decaying metropolis. "The rejected; the drunken, the incompetent, the weak, the prodigal," to borrow Stevenson's words, will have to pick themselves up, screw up a bit of mild optimism, and join the migration back to small towns. To succeed, they will also have to adopt a modern version of small-town values. Some will.

For those lucky enough to have skills and money, a depression will be a less trying challenge. But it will require thought and preparation. Now would not be too soon to start scanning a map and laying out a plan for joining and profiting from the Fifth Migration. We include in appendix 4 a listing of counties that in our judgment offer particularly attractive destinations for the Fifth Migration. The prudent investor will begin to plan his strategy for adaptation now.

CHAPTER FIFTEEN

RATIONAL LIVING IN AN AGE OF CRISIS

The remedy is for people to stop watching the ticker, listening to the radio, drinking bootleg gin, and dancing to jazz; forget the "new economics" and prosperity founded upon spending and gambling, and return to the old economics and prosperity based upon savings and working.

—T. W. LAMONT, 1930

MANY PEOPLE feel that we are on the edge of an unknown period. The Cold War has come to an end. They know the world is going to be very different, but they don't yet know quite what to do about it. This final chapter is an attempt to carry forward some of the major themes we have explored, and offer you some qualified advice. One needs to look forward to a new world in the twenty-first century.

A FAREWELL TO SOCIALISM

Most historians, looking back at this century, will start off by saying that it was the century of socialism. Although socialism was invented in the nineteenth century—Marx is a nineteenth-century figure—no major power had converted to a socialist system by the time this century opened. You could say that welfare socialism began first under Bismarck, and it was the first important development of socialism as a government activity. Nonetheless, at the end of the nineteenth century, it was still possible that socialism might prove to be nothing more than an intellectual fad that would pass away without changing the real world to a substantial degree.

At the end of the twentieth century, we know how much socialism changed the real world. Every major country, almost every country at all, has gone through a socialist transformation in line with its own particular character and traditions. There was a socialist revolution in the Soviet Union in 1917. The New Deal was socialism applied to American conditions. There was a vast extension of the activities of the state, primarily in terms of activity designed to shield people from failure and insure against losses. The expenditures of the central governments skyrocketed, as did direct intervention in the economy by governments. In Britain, the first Labour government with an overall majority was elected in 1945, coinciding precisely with the beginning of the postwar period. That created a semi-socialist society in which something like half the economic activity in Britain was transferred from private to state activity.

If one looks at the expenditures of governments, they were, at the start of the twentieth century, around 10 percent. Over the past ninety years, they have risen throughout the world, and vary between 30 and 35 percent at the low end, to about 50 to 55 percent at the high end, in nonsocialist countries. Historians will say that this was the century in which society changed from a predominantly individualist to a predominantly state-organized economy. Yet, when one looks at it, one can see that this great wave is now in clear decline.

There is no country in the world in which the megapolitical conditions that destroyed socialism have not been accompanied by a critique of socialism that is extremely powerful. There is no country in the world that is not looking at the activities of the state and asking itself whether these things may not be done better if they were returned to private action. And particularly striking is the reaction against socialism of the century's once militant Marxist giants, China and the former Soviet Union. During the 1980s there were major reform movements in both countries essentially directed at reducing the grip of socialism in their society. In China, as recently as the middle 1970s, it was illegal to sell your second-hand bicycle to your next-door neighbor, because that was an interference with the right of the state to direct commerce. Now we have in China a new economic policy that is introducing, on a quite remarkable scale, personal opportunity and the opportunity to develop at least small businesses on a personal basis. The Chinese looked at the two great examples near to them—the Soviet Union and Japan—and they saw what an astonishing success the Japanese economy had been in the period since the Second World War and they saw what an astonishing failure the Soviet economy had been. In spite of the setback to reform after Tiananmen Square, there can be little doubt that the days of socialism in China are numbered.

The failure of socialism brought on economic collapse and the death of the

Soviet Union. The leadership of Russia has now made a commitment to junk the command system and move to a free market. If Mr. Yeltsin survives, which one has to regard as very doubtful, he can do it only by restoring private property and the other essential elements of capitalism.

The socialism that attempted to forbid the making of profit is clearly dead. The question still to be tested during the 1990s is whether the socialism that seeks to forbid losses can stand the test of time. We doubt it. Mainstream economists, of course, believe otherwise. They think that welfare state programs instituted to insure against loss "stabilized the economy without weakening its free and efficient features," to quote Herbert Stein. But the financial crises of the 1990s may bring proof that government cannot protect everyone against insolvency without becoming insolvent itself.

The perverse effects of insuring against loss have greatly enlarged the ultimate loss that society and individuals must bear. To cite a spectacular and unarguable example, deposit insurance has cost taxpayers in the United States at least twenty times more in real terms than the total losses to uninsured bank depositors in the Great Depression. Yet the moral hazard of insuring against loss has cost society more than money. It has wasted lives. Welfare programs made victimization an asset, and thus provided a powerful added impetus to the tribalization of multi-ethnic societies. Welfare programs discouraged the poor from conforming to middle-class values—at the very time such values became more crucial.

Two of the profound differences between middle-class culture and the culture of the poor are the value they place on education, and the degree to which they are sensitized to violence. Entitlement spending broke the long-term trend that had deepened the acceptance of upper- and middle-class values among the poor. As a result, education declined and violence increased. Perversely, this happened just as technological change was wiping away most of the high-paying jobs open to people without education. At the same time, adverse megapolitical trends were making the economy more vulnerable to violence.

The cultural consequences of the welfare state did indeed "weaken the free and efficient features" of the market by subsidizing counterproductive behavior. Entitlement spending encouraged the breakdown of family life among the poor. This has had terrible consequences. Drug abuse has become epidemic. Centuries of progress in dampening violence and crime have been squandered in a few generations. The breakdown of order now threatens the viability of some of America's largest cities. This implies not only gigantic losses as urban real estate and infrastructure depreciate, it also means more human misery than we have been accustomed to seeing in advanced economies.

This is clearly evident in what were the two richest cities in America when the last depression began—New York and Detroit. New York was the financial capital of the world. Detroit was the manufacturing capital. In 1929, *Life* magazine ran a major story entitled "Detroit—It Changed the World's Pattern of Life and Is Now the Fourth City in the Land." At that time, the Detroit River was the busiest waterway in the world, as raw materials and finished manufactured products came and went. Today, both New York and Detroit are rapidly falling apart. New York is crumbling by the moment. And Detroit is even more of an urban desert. As Marc Faber has said, "It would not be too much of an exaggeration to compare the inner city of Detroit with Berlin at the end of the Second World War. Once-proud commercial buildings and beautiful mansions have been deserted or burned down. Racial tensions have caused the white population to abandon the inner city and move to the suburbs. The drive from downtown Detroit to the elegant suburb of Grosse Pointe is like a trip from Soweto to swanky Sandton in Johannesburg. It is hard to believe that what was the richest city in the world in the 1920s could decay as much as it has."

The reaction to the perverse consequences of welfare socialism has been a political movement to the right. This has been most evident in America, the richest country of the Cold War period, and the most ethnically diverse. A movement to the right arose in the 1970s and has been dominant in the politics of the advanced world of the 1980s. One can see that socialism is now in substantial retreat. This does not mean that it is going to go away completely. The social and political pressures on politicians who promise too much and then try to fulfill it have not disappeared. It has proven remarkably difficult for governments all around the world to control these political pressures, let alone to reduce their state expenditures. And not all governments really wish to do so.

If one looks at the difficulties the United States has had in the control of the budget, it is evident that many of the pressures that led to the development of twentieth-century socialism are still there with considerable force. This, indeed, is one of the reasons to worry that the political reaction to the coming depression will veer in a right-wing populist direction. Demagogues may offer a formidable appeal to frustrated and dispossessed voters. The hope of thinking people must be that the retrenchment leads to a more enlightened, nonlinear liberalism with enhanced appreciation for the market as a complex system, not to a fascist closure of the economy.

One way or the other, the reaction to increased budget pressures could be a sweeping away of the welfare state guarantees that have had such unhappy consequences for so many. But even if the reaction is less muscular than we imagine, we can nevertheless see that socialism as an idea that convinces men's minds is now in decline. It is now seen as it truly is—an extremely inefficient and unsatisfactory way of conducting human affairs.

One of the reasons is that socialism is hampered by an extraordinarily inefficient information system. This has been made more clear by the dramatic development of computer technology, which we reviewed earlier. Whereas people have genuine information about their own affairs, the state has only the most limited and rudimentary information about what is really happening in the economy for which it is responsible. Therefore, market solutions are closer to efficient information technology than states' illusions can ever be. Socialism is undermined by the strongest and most important element in the development of modern technology itself.

The Death of Secular Consumerism

There has been another movement that doesn't exactly have a name, but we might call it secular consumerism. It is the religion of the television channels, if one might put it that way. And this, along with socialism, has been an extremely powerful force in the twentieth century. Outside the United States, it has been identified with the United States because in the Cold War period when secular consumerism was absolutely at its height, which was roughly speaking during the period of relief and thankfulness when people got back to an ordinary life after World War II, the American economy was dominant in the world. These were the last great years of the feature film, when the American communications system was totally dominant. The United States was looked to as the leading, and almost the only great, example of this consumer worship at a time when other nations felt themselves extremely poor in the aftermath of the war.

Consumerism, of course, is still a force to be reckoned with in the 1990s. But again it seems to us that it is in decline, and it will decline more dramatically as the world slump takes hold.

Consumerism belonged to a period when throughout the world secular values were ascendant. It can be linked even to the postwar development of the Middle East. Secular systems such as those of President Nasser in Egypt seemed to be the dominant attraction, rather than the religious institutions that had ruled the Middle East down to 1945.

This secular consumerism depended on its novelty for its attraction. It represented to people that a particular kind of purchasing would give them the good life. Its dynamic was that it could induce people to work hard in order to satisfy themselves with particular consumer objects.

Glass Beads and Tail Fins

When you think of it, the objects of conspicuous consumption are rather like the trade goods of the seventeenth century. For many decades, merchants going out in their ships from Europe carried with them large quantities of glass beads and baubles, the long-ago version of the Wal-Mart jewelry counter. They traded these glass beads to tribes that had never seen glass beads before. And their attraction was tremendous. The Dutch picked up Manhattan for twenty-two dollars' worth of beads. Today, of course, the relative value of beads has plunged. Yet if one sees people going round the duty-free shop in an airport and buying perfume on which the markup is nine times the actual cost, watches they don't want, bits of jewelry where the markup is absolutely colossal, which they could happily do without; if one sees people gloating over consumer advertising, literally killing one another to obtain new running shoes, one sees the effect that glass beads may have had when they were first introduced.

> Every day, an estimated 50,000 energetic, indefatigable shoppers descend—sometimes by the busload—on Lenox Square, one of Atlanta's hottest shopping spots. And many of them . . . don't really need what they are shopping for. Often they don't even know what they're after. Some buy things they never wear or rarely use; many buy and then return what they bought, then buy again and return that.
>
> —BETSY MORRIS,
> "As a Favored Pastime, Shopping Ranks High with Most Americans,"
> Wall Street Journal

Most consumers could have a very different life-style, and not feel any the worse off for the lack of many things that they now purchase. This is not even taking it from a particularly aesthetic point of view. The satisfactions of many consumer goods are very limited satisfactions. Indeed, for many people it is the act of shopping as a pastime rather than the items they buy that appears to be the main pleasure. Various surveys have shown that as many as one of six persons in America prefers shopping even to romantic love.

This secular consumerism became the motive force of much of the society of the twentieth century. And it dominated because it was the force that financed television, the standard communications systems of most of the world. The television networks are built around it. The television networks are the way in which people obtained most of their information of the world around them. Just now one sees the way in which these very powerful communications systems do seek to impose their own standards and values on the world in which we live. It seems to us that the arrogance of television, certainly the arrogance of television as we see it in the United States and the United Kingdom, is one of its most remarkable characteristics. Television people who are neither particularly wise, nor—except in a certain way— even particularly well informed, assume that the views they have to propagate are the universal views that ought to be held by the people who live in the society to which they broadcast.

Secular consumerism is now also in clear decline. We would judge it, as far as the United States is concerned, by a change of attitude that Lord Rees-Mogg has perceived in the forty years that he has been coming from England to visit the United States. When he first came, the headquarters of consumerism, New York City, really did seem to dominate American lives. New York City was and is the seat of the major television networks, which control communications in a useful alliance with the film and television studios in Los Angeles. In 1951, when Lord Rees-Mogg first visited, most Americans did look to New York City as the cultural capital of the country. Many of them even then resented it. Many did not agree with it. But they saw that New York was where the action was. Countless highly gifted young Americans made the pilgrimage to New York City and then made a pilgrimage away from New York City some years later, somewhat disillusioned.

We doubt that such dominance exists anymore. Practically everyone has heard the view expressed that the best thing to do with New York City would be to cut it off from the rest of the United States and tow it out into the Atlantic Ocean. This view is more commonly held and more firmly believed than it ever used to be. People feel that it is another world. You get this in literature. Tom Wolfe's novel about Manhattan, *The Bonfire of the Vanities*, is an extremely significant cultural event because it says that this way of life, with all its implications, was a blind alley damaging to human existence. It would be difficult to think now of a novel written about New York City in the last ten years that had the tone of confidence and excitement that almost all the novels written about New York City up until 1960 tended to show. This is a symptom of the rejection of the consumer culture. It was extremely powerful and is now increasingly seen to be a deformation rather than a fulfillment of the human spirit.

The Revival of Religion

The twilight of consumerism has coincided with another worldwide phenomenon, a fascinating revival of the force of religion in human affairs.

Perhaps the most striking example is that of Iran. It is an example that needs to be understood. On the one hand, the Ayatollah Khomeini was clearly, in some senses, a blood-thirsty maniac. An extremely dangerous and undesirable man, ruthless in his treatment of other people, who would induce torture to destroy human lives, and wage an unnecessary war that killed hundreds of thousands of his fellow citizens. A bad man by any of the standards of history. Yet, at the same time, the Ayatollah was not just another materialist dictator, of whom the twentieth century has seen so many. The revolution he led in Iran was the first significant social rejection of modern consumerism in the postwar world. Iran had a modern leader in the form of the Shah. The Shah was a figure totally convinced that a certain kind of secular modernization would answer the problems of Iran. He was convinced that, if only he could get the Iranian people to abandon their religion, to abandon their way of life, and to take up a modern plan of doing things in a technically efficient way, he would be endowing great benefits to his people. He was a modernizer. He also used torture, but that can be a modern thing. He had almost fulfilled his idea of building Iran into a twentieth-century power when the Iranians decided that the twentieth century was not a century into which they wished to be brought. They wished to preserve their traditions, and even to revert to older forms of social organization. They wished to preserve their religion. They said that religion was more important to them than the consumer standard of living that they were able to enjoy. They rejected the trade goods in a very decisive way.

We can feel a sympathy with the religious assertion that involved, however much we may feel horror at the form that it has actually taken.

This revival of religion is something that is happening throughout the world, in varying degrees. Japan may be an exception, perhaps because social order has as yet shown no signs of breaking down there, and the Japanese have only recently begun to enjoy their phase of great material abundance as the world's predominant manufacturing power. The Japanese have always been an eclectic people about religions, picking up doctrines here, there, and everywhere. Trying a little bit of Christianity, which they have had for a long time—the Jesuits arrived there in 1549, a considerable time ago. And about 1 percent of Japanese are Jesuit-trained Christians. They tried Buddhism on a rather larger scale. But the average Japanese citizen regards it as a mildly interesting thing that you do on festivals. Buddhism in modern Japan is rather like Christianity in modern France. It is something for the grandmothers and two or three days a year.

Even if the Japanese are not an example of it, this renewed interest in religion is extremely widespread. It is transforming the attitudes of South America. And not at all in a way that one would expect. There has been a great deal of attention to "liberation theology," which is Marxism decked in a priest's frock. Yet it has not been liberation theology that has actually been striking home at the imagination of the people of Latin America. On the contrary, rather unexpectedly, American Protestant evangelism, which, until a few years ago, had very little impact on Latin America with its Catholic tradition, has become an extremely potent force in most Latin American countries. In Chile, Jimmy Swaggart, the television evangelist, is a real and powerful religious influence. Something like 10 percent of the population have now moved in the direction of an evangelical Protestantism of the kind familiar in the United States.

Why is that? We are told that it is because the left-wing bias in the political action of the Roman Catholic authorities has alienated people. They want to have a religion that is both simple and direct and does not make the state a god. The directness and the simplicity of the message of a Jimmy Swaggart draws crowds. These crowds approve of his repudiation of left-wing materialism.

A similar phenomenon is underway in what used to be the Soviet Union, the bastion of official atheism for three-quarters of a century. The Orthodox Church is making a comeback, rapidly regaining its following, and even its official stature. Before long, the sycophants who ran the church during the Communist period will have been replaced by new leaders who better represent the more confident spirit of religion in a society where materialist atheism has been discredited.

What Next in America?

This brings us to the question of what will happen to the United States if a depression occurs. We feel fairly convinced that depression would not lead to a return to socialism as a popular solution. The weaker the balance sheet of the country when the slump begins, the more the reaction is likely to carry politics to the right. The left wing of the Democratic party has become a museum of old rhetoric and worn-out ideas. Liberal Democratic candidates are yesterday's men. They continue to push solutions that were tried, with very little success in most cases, over the last century. There is a lack of connection between their arguments and the needs of the time that is quite striking. We don't really believe that economic crisis will make these mummified arguments live again. America will not go back to New Deal methods and New Deal days. Whether the New Deal was right or wrong for its time is a matter that will still be debated, but at any rate, it is all over. The New Deal is part of the great historic past. It does not look like the answer for the future.

We believe that the answer people will find in the coming slump will be much nearer to the advice set forth by J. P. Morgan's crusty friend T. W. Lamont and quoted at the beginning of this chapter. There is going to be a further rejection of secular consumerism, and a return to values that will stand the test of time. Why do we say this? Much of the answer has already been canvassed. But it could be as simple as this. When someone has hold of glass beads that really don't serve a practical function, their appeal wears thin in a time of trouble. Consumerism cannot be the center of life for long. It is always shallow because it relates to the creation in people's minds of wants that suit the manufacturer rather than the consumer of the goods. This is not a condemnation of the manufacturer. But it is fundamentally a false view of society that the difference between happiness and unhappiness is how much chrome you have on the tail fin of your car.

We think it is extremely likely that the religious movement we see at work in many societies across the globe will be strengthened if we go through a very difficult economic period. Religion will be strengthened because the current thrust of science no longer undermines the religious perception of reality. Indeed, for the first time in centuries, it actually buttresses it. Religion will also be strengthened because the breakdown of social order will further discredit the attempts of the state to substitute for the social functions that religions performed in traditional societies. The rising epidemic of crime, in particular, underscores the need for more potent controls on behavior than overtaxed police and court systems can enforce. It is not a coincidence, therefore, that validly religious influence has been coming steadily to the fore in American politics.

For evidence, you need only ask yourself a question that many people have forgotten to ask, which is, how did Jimmy Carter become president of the United States? He is one of the most unusual presidents that America has ever had. He came from almost nowhere. He was not a known man before the primaries. He emerged against a group of serious competitors in the Democratic party. He defeated President Ford, who had actually performed surprisingly well in the post-Watergate trauma. Yet Carter's victory has been very little discussed because he did not go on to be a successful president. It seems to us that the answer to this question is that Carter's appeal was the appeal of the man who avowedly said that he is absolutely guided by moral standards, and based his life on religious belief. An electorate was ready for that kind of statement.

What role did religion play in the popularity of President Reagan? It did play a role, although Reagan was not a conspicuously religious man. He did, however, put forward in an extremely attractive way basic American values, which were drawn from a religious tradition. He himself had been brought up in a Protestant religious home and his character had been formed by that tradition. Most Americans who related to the same tradition recognized in President Reagan that he was like them. He may not always have been able to do what they would have liked to have done, but they thought that his heart was where their heart was.

The 1988 primaries tested the candidacy of Pat Robertson. Although he failed to win a significant percentage of the vote, he did register a degree of support that is surprising. It is highly unlikely that a television evangelist would have done as well a few decades earlier. The issues Robertson addressed are the issues that a great number of Americans would like to have political leadership address again. They feel that the United States is facing some sort of fundamental moral, religious, metaphysical challenge, which they wish to see faced and resolved. And again, one gets the feeling that the candidates who are not talking about those issues, or are not comfortable with those issues, are likely to be upstaged by them. Robertson's strength came not from his answers, necessarily, but from the fact that he was addressing himself to the questions that many Americans want to have asked. The Robertson candidacy, which attracted great financial support and an outpouring of volunteers, is a fascinating evidence of the reaction away from secular consumerism.

Dan Rather referred to the people who wanted to vote for Pat Robertson as "armies of the night." We think it interesting that this eminent television figure, who so personifies a particular view about the pluralist, modern society, should be shocked by the ordinary Americans who feel the religious issues are key issues to the future of their society. And should feel instinctively indignant that the proper business of politics and of television should be interrupted by discussion of fundamental issues such as the future of the family or the moral conduct of the nation.

Our own feeling is that Pat Robertson is not going to be the president of the United States. But he will prove to have been a preparer of the ground for someone who will carry a message of moral revival to the White House. He raised issues, and started accumulating a constituency that is not yet ready, and for which he is not the most appropriate leader. But we shall find that this great movement of opinion, which you can see starting with the Carter campaign, is going to come to a fulfillment in American politics, further down the road. It is a fulfillment that will be all the more natural if the United States, in the meantime, has been through a period of trauma and difficulty.

That is our sense of the likely present movement based in the United States and in the world, of what we regard as the most important of all the underlying forces: the basic spiritual forces that move mankind. It is particularly fascinating that these forces should be operating simultaneously in societies as different as those in modern Chile, the former Soviet Union, America, and the Middle East. What all these societies share in common is that they have been touched to a greater or lesser extent by the emptiness of secular consumerism, and the logic of megapolitical breakdown. The result is a natural feedback mechanism that leads to a revival of moral concerns.

Religion is the reflection in human conduct of the profound nonlinearity of nature. A society in which behavior is guided solely by simple, one-dimensional cost-and-reward calculations is bound to be a wicked place. Consider that a survey by the tabloid newspaper *The National Enquirer* found that one-quarter of the people interviewed on the streets of five American cities— New York, Chicago, Dallas, San Francisco, and Washington, D.C.—indicated that they would have someone "murdered if they were sure they could get away with it." The methodology of this survey could be questioned, but its frightening logic cannot be. It shows the moral risk that society runs when questions of murder are only questions of material circumstance, and nothing more. The going rate for murder for hire in Colombia is ten dollars in cash. It is a stark evidence of how low the market price for murder can be driven in a disordered, immoral environment. If the equation that determines whether murder is done were not complicated with a few exponents, circumstances could arise where almost anyone's murder would be profitable to someone. Religion adds the crucial exponents to the cost-and-reward calculus that leads human beings to act in a civilized way.

The breakdown of the justice system in the United States has made crime so profitable and pervasive as to make a strong comeback of religion almost inevitable. Ironically, religious fundamentalists blamed the Supreme Court for rulings that reduced the role of religion in civic life. Without intending to, however, the Supreme Court actually gave religion a powerful impetus. Rulings that increased the difficulty of successfully prosecuting and jailing criminals have probably contributed more to the rebirth of religion than all the tent revivalists put together.

SURVIVING THE REVOLUTION OF THE 1990s

The moral revival involves a painful process of compensation that will make the Revolution of the 1990s unpleasant for many. Surviving it will require more than financial preparation, which we address below. It will also require sound values and sound citizenship. And special measures to protect your health and the health of your family. We emphasize that these are problems of values as well as technique because the culture of consumerism has made it difficult for even a wealthy people like Americans to save and invest. Many people have no money. Literally. They are broke. Even with good jobs, and high incomes, many Americans have scarcely a nickel to spare.

They have chosen to have no money, because they preferred immediate satisfactions over the future. Even saving ten dollars a day would make the average person a millionaire on retirement if he or she began putting money aside early. But people have lately been more inclined to borrow ten dollars per day rather than save it. As the *Wall Street Journal* put it, Americans have taken on "staggering amounts of debt." This, of course, is the story of the average, and even the above-average, American consumer. If it is your story, stay tuned, the advice that follows should be of special interest to you.

15 Steps to Survival and Independence

> For wisdom is a defence, and money is a defence: but the excellency of money is that wisdom giveth life to them that have it.
>
> —ECCLESIASTES 7:12

If we are correct in thinking that a major depression is around the corner, the ideas that follow may be among the more important you have read. If you follow this advice and we prove wrong about the depression, the worst that will happen is that you will forgo some profits you might have had from staking a 100 percent long position in the stock market. Even so, you would still offset much of that opportunity cost by increased savings, which will build up your capital faster than might have been the case otherwise. If the world economy is showered with prosperity, you can write us a letter and complain that we steered you wrong.

Step 1. Get committed. Whatever your age or circumstance, remember that it is never too late to be in better charge of your own life. Your choices remain the biggest single factor that control your destiny. Seek to strengthen your moral commitments and religious faith. Reread the Ten Commandments and the Book of Ecclesiastes. A Bible is not a bad teacher of history and guide to survival in hard times. In the future as in the past, self-discipline will not only be a key to successful living, it will also be a key trait of successful investment. Recognize that it may be difficult for you and your family to adjust to changes as sweeping as those outlined in this book. It is best to make your commitment early. Lay a foundation for yourself by starting in a small way, if that is necessary. The worst thing for your inner resolve is to make a "New Year's resolution" that you later betray. A lack of credibility and disbelief in yourself are dangerous foundations for living, especially in a time of change. Make small promises to yourself. And keep them. Be on time for all appointments for two weeks. Drink no alcohol or eliminate a favorite food for two weeks. Do not jaywalk or break any traffic law for two weeks. Commit yourself, and mean it. That is the first step to surviving when the music stops.

Step 2. Involve your spouse. You will make things much harder on yourself otherwise. It is difficult to become an aggressive saver in a society still geared to consumption. You will need support. If you aren't married, get married, or find a partner with whom you can plan for the future. Be sure that your husband, wife, or partner is involved in your financial and investment decisions. Discuss your plans together. Be sure that you can both fill out your tax returns, a necessary step in case something should happen to one or the other of you.

Step 3. Act as if the depression has already begun. By the time you read this book, it may have. If not, consider yourself lucky. You have more time to put your finances in order. Immediately begin reducing your living standard to the level necessary to enable you to save 25 percent of your income. The higher your present cash flow, the greater your savings target should be. Unless you already have an adequate cash reserve, you should slash consumption spending, postpone durable goods purchases, and save every penny you can, consistent with maintaining your health. If necessary, move in with a Korean immigrant to see how it is done.

Step 4. Gather knowledge. Knowledge is not only power, it is money. Stay informed. The need to gather knowledge and realize the meaning of sound principles has probably never been greater than at this moment. Look at the past for guidance and do all you can to think ahead. Almost every famous investor is an avid reader. Life is complicated. So much more is happening than you can perceive with your unaided eye that you will be lost unless you scour the world for every thought that can be of use. And the further away you stand from divine genius, the more you need to reach, as Emerson said, "by seeking the wisdom of others." Read Benjamin Franklin's *Autobiography*. It remains a warehouse of common sense and advice for rational living.

Step 5. Master compound interest. In today's world of pocket calculators that should be easy. But most people do not understand compounding. They are stunned at how much of their monthly mortgage bill is interest. And they would be equally stunned to know that the typical person could become a millionaire by retirement simply by setting aside the cost of a margarita or a few beers each day—provided he started early. But many people never hold savings long enough to allow compounding to do its work. As Benjamin Franklin said, "Money is of a prolific generating nature. Money can beget money, and its offspring can beget more." Because of compounding, every dollar you save can be many dollars in the future.

Step 6. Stop shopping. Most Americans are spendaholics, who devote more time to shopping than they do to reading. Put away the charge cards. And stay out of stores. Don't buy anything unless you need it. The only exceptions you should entertain to this rule are purchases of storable items from small or weak suppliers that may not survive a slump. If you are particularly fond of a product or two that may no longer be produced or imported in a slump, by all means, lay a store aside. It may also pay you to lease an automobile now rather than wait until later to purchase, provided you can find a leasing company or a dealer that will not require you to guarantee the residual value. The experience of auto leasing companies offering luxury vehicles has been colored by the inflation of the 1970s and 1980s. Leases often do not adequately cover depreciation in a deflationary environment. If you will have to obtain a new car in the next two years, it may make more sense to lease now, and let the leasing company absorb the risk of deflation while you enjoy other uses of your capital. In other respects, make a conscious effort to curtail shopping. When you do shop, shop only for specific items you determine you need before you leave home. Buy nothing on impulse. And stay away from prestige items and designer labels. If you are bored, pick up a book. Every dollar you save could be worth much more in the future if asset deflation creates bargains everywhere.

Step 7. Turn off the television. Challenge your mind. Studies of TV viewers show that they burn fewer calories than people doing nothing—because their brains are switched off. Take up a hobby or diversion that makes you think. When you are tired of reading, play chess, bridge, or Scrabble. Or take up puzzle solving. The more you force yourself to think, the smarter you will be. Researchers have shown that thinking actually changes the brain's physical composition, making it chemically more active and increasing the size of key neurons. In short, you can increase your intelligence at *any* age. If the economy goes the way we think it will, your extra brain power will come in handy.

Step 8. Connect more closely to family and neighbors. You will find that as public services break down and income falls in a slump, people can help one another get along. The values of community and friendship become more apparent. Barter arrangements between friends and family allow everyone to get along better for less. One of your neighbors may need to supplement a declining pension income, but perhaps can babysit or bake a great pie. Get to know your neighbors and visit with your extended family. Find out what each of you has to contribute and how you can help one another in a constructive way.

Step 9. Do not be a victim. To think of yourself as a victim is to focus on negative thoughts and to assure yourself of failure. Indeed, it makes failure a perverse asset, like a beggar's stump. Accept responsibility for whatever situation you find yourself in, but do not blame yourself. Think positively. Ignore the negative thoughts of others. Remember that no one can make you feel bad about yourself without your permission. This is especially important if you are black, or of another minority. The 1990s will be a period of increasing tribalization, which will mislead many people into emotional and cultural dead ends. Cast your lot firmly with Western values. They are the universal values for success, as much yours by right as anyone's. If some stupid people dislike you without getting to know your capabilities as an individual, it is their loss. Remember, minorities have been economically successful in the face of discrimination throughout history by behaving in ways that lead to success. Concentrate on success and you will be successful.

Step 10. Watch the calendar, not the clock. Don't try to obtain your financial objectives instantly. Lord Beaconsfield wrote of "the alchemy of patience." It is a lovely phrase and a thought that is apt for the times. An investor today needs patience. Without it, he is unlikely to position himself for the longer term. Don't make that mistake. Let time do its work. Discipline yourself to meet long-term targets, such as monthly goals for higher savings. The difference between the successful and the ordinary person is that the successful person plans ahead. This is a truth that has stood the test of time since the fable of the grasshopper and the ant, told by Aesop. Challenges invigorate life and bring out the best in individuals as well as the worst. Plan and live for the future.

Step 11. Treasure your health. Without it, your money won't matter much. Be sure to eat nourishing foods, including plenty of green and yellow vegetables daily. Exercise to control stress. Think positively. But don't be so positive that you fail to see your doctor for regular checkups. And do not try to economize by doing without adequate health insurance. If you and your family are in generally good health, insurance with a high deductible might be in order, but cover your risks against major illness or accident.

Step 12. Don't boast. Your privacy will be of value in the future if the economy turns down. Live modestly and don't flaunt your wealth, especially when it exceeds that of others in your community. If you happen to live in an urban area that will be rapidly bankrupted in a depression, consider moving. Don't make yourself a target for disgruntled people.

Step 13. Help others. As your wealth grows, so does your responsibility. Meet that responsibility. Pay every legitimate claim on your time and your attention. Whether you live in the United States or China, do what you can to build a better future for your country and your community. To discipline yourself to save anywhere in the modern world involves standing slightly aloof from the culture of consumerism. But don't stand aloof from people. If you succeed in your commitment to save, and invest wisely, you will be a valuable person for your family and your community. When things fall apart, you will be able to help pick up the pieces.

Step 14. Defend the open society. The 1990s will be a period of delusional thinking, scapegoating, conspiracy theories, and increasing tribalization of thought. If the economic contraction is as deep as it may be, and the welfare state is trimmed back or collapses, recriminations will be widespread. There will be a danger that the repudiation of the culture of the slums will turn into an anti-black, racialist political reaction in the United States, and to equivalent tribalism elsewhere. It will be important for thinking people to reaffirm the universality of human nature, and seek to keep economies and markets open.

Step 15. Tell your children. Even the children of well-fixed families do not have a sound grounding in finance, or even a basic understanding of the economy. If you have children, teach them the value of money, and the importance of saving. Pass on sound values and the money you pass on will not be wasted.

A Necessary Foundation

Those are our fifteen points to help you prepare for the Revolution of the 1990s. If you have found nothing else in this book valuable, we hope these ideas will be. They do not constitute investment advice in themselves, but they are a necessary foundation for financial survival and independence. Even if you start with little today, you can build a significant amount of capital during a slump, when many assets fall in value and are therefore better bargains for those with money to buy.

A sound foundation for living is equally important if you have much wealth today. The risks of the 1990s will be great if you have much to protect. You will need to prepare for the possibility that political or market developments may lower your living standard. Most investors, especially American investors, are unprepared to face these risks.

A Grand Supercycle bear market would "correct" all the progress dating from the late 1700s. The downside target zone would be the price area (ideally near the low) of the previous fourth wave of lesser degree, wave (IV), which fell from 386 to 41 on the Dow. Worldwide banking failures, government bankruptcy, and eventual destruction of the paper money system might be plausible explanations for a bear phase of this magnitude.

—ROBERT PRECHTER

Americans have been complacent about dangers that investors in other wealthy nations have been forced to take seriously by painful experience. Consider what has happened in this century.

- Capital holdings were almost wiped out twice in Germany, and once in Japan.
- In France, where the franc had been a strong currency in the nineteenth century, it lost 99 percent of its value against the U.S. dollar, which itself lost 90 percent of its purchasing power during this century.
- In Britain, the richest country on earth when the century began, investors were trapped by inflation and exchange controls. As Sidney Homer wrote in *A History of Interest Rates*, British financial assets collapsed so dramatically, "there were doubts about the viability of the entire British economy, and, more important, about its political structure."

The British example is particularly telling because Britain was once in relatively the same position as America is today. The United States also shares many cultural and legal traditions with Britain. In spite of the strong tradition of freedom of capital that prevailed there prior to the sterling balances crisis, once the problems of adjustment became acute, tight exchange and capital controls were instituted.

American investors therefore will face the following risks in the 1990s:

1. Currency. This is the risk to dollar-denominated assets, in which almost all American income is earned. In an acute form, this risk becomes a risk of . . .

2. Unprecedented inflation. This could occur because of a liquidity squeeze on the U.S. Treasury during the next downturn. In the face of ballooning deficits, the requirement to fund credit guarantees, and declining tax revenue, authorities may resort to inflation, even at the risk of damaging the credit-worthiness and ultimate viability of the U.S. government.

3. Deflation. Debt liquidation in countries with more financial than tangible assets has been deflationary in the past. A deflation from current debt levels could be the most severe in history. This risk cannot be ruled out, especially in light of the impending decline in military spending around the world.

The extreme character of these monetary risks can be judged from history. Five great credit cycles have come to an end over the past three centuries, the last in 1929. On average, the price of gold in real terms rose within four years of the end of the cycle to exceed its high of a decade earlier by 8.5

percent in real terms. This implies that the inflation- (or deflation)-adjusted price of gold would exceed $925 in 1980 dollars. That comes to about $1600 in December 1990 dollars. There are only a few ways that such a tremendous leap in the price of gold could occur: (a) gold could be remonetized at a high price; (b) inflation would have to skyrocket; or (c) deflation would raise the value of each 1990 dollar to about $2.45 cents. A tremendous monetary disturbance lies in store if history repeats itself.

All three of these monetary risks could be realized in succession. In any combination, they would likely trigger further risks, such as:

4. Capital loss due to bankruptcy or default. Bank deposits and insurance values could be wiped away. Stocks could plummet. Bonds could be clipped by inflation or default.

5. Exchange and/or capital controls. They are an almost universal feature of nations with adjustment problems of the sort America is likely to face in the next downturn. Such controls might make it difficult or impossible for American investors to participate in investment opportunities arising from major transitions in the world economy.

6. Adverse political changes. Confiscatory taxes, soak-the-rich policies, and other unhappy developments cannot be ruled out. Bank accounts could be frozen, as has been the case in Latin America and elsewhere. Political authorities may decide to unilaterally alter the terms of repayment for some Treasury securities, lowering coupon yields directly or through taxation, or converting short-term obligations into long-term or even perpetual obligations. Privately owned gold held by Americans within U.S. borders could be confiscated again as it was in 1933.

7. Terrorism and violence are also grave dangers, especially in urban areas.

8. Breakdown of public infrastructure may make it unwise for you to take for granted such essentials as clean water, safe roads and bridges, police protection, and other services presently performed by governments.

We believe that such risks are higher than most prudent persons would tolerate without insurance. The odds of a private house burning down are so remote that if you had built one on the day Muhammad was born, it would have burned down just once since then. Yet few owners of small houses, let alone large ones, are so imprudent as to test the odds by going without fire insurance. As the world economy faces a period of upheaval, investment insurance against unhappy events becomes more important.

You can provide yourself with partial insurance against these contingencies.

The ideas that follow are guidelines that were formulated, in part, as extrapolations from the depression of the 1930s. In broad terms, the United States in the 1990s will be in a situation like that of Britain in the 1930s, while Japan will follow a course equivalent to that followed by the United States. The British are one cycle ahead of America; the Japanese, one cycle behind. But these are only rough guides for investment and life choices because adverse megapolitical change has moved the whole world closer to devolution and decline. The United States in 1990 was in some ways in worse financial straits than Britain sixty years earlier. We have tried to take the deterioration in the U.S. balance sheet into account in formulating the recommendations listed.

We have avoided the temptation to provide specific buy and sell recommendations on stocks, although we publish lists of companies that are exposed in various ways in the appendices. For those who would like more detailed and timely advice, we refer you to our monthly newsletter, *Strategic Investment*. It provides specific buy and sell guidance on a regular basis.

The advice that follows is based upon the assumption that America and the world will take a deflationary course in the 1990s. If this proves to be wrong, much of the advice could still be correct. You would need to adjust by purchasing the shares of heavily indebted firms to add to a core portfolio including gold. You would also wish to add a higher proportion of collectibles and real estate to an inflationary portfolio.

Guideline 1

Build cash. Liquefy your position by selling low-yielding assets, including idle land, commercial real estate, and partnership interests over which you have no control, or which you suspect will falter in a downturn. Trim your debt load. This will be much easier if you stop going into debt. If you are now in debt, it may take time for your increased savings to mount up. If you are deeply in debt, devote at least half your increased monthly savings to building a cash reserve, while accelerating the repayment of debt with the other. One trick: speed up your mortgage payments. For example, if your mortgage bill is one thousand dollars per month, see if the bank will allow you to make two payments of five hundred dollars every two weeks. If you pay just half a month in advance, a larger amount of each payment will go to retire principal. You will reduce your debt and build equity much faster—another of the secrets of compound interest. But note this caution. It probably does not make sense to pay off your mortgage entirely unless you are rolling in liquidity.

Your cash reserve should equal one year's expenses. If it is less than that, immediately curtail consumption or sell assets to raise cash. Add 10 percent to your cash reserve for each decade of life you have attained over fifty. Add another 10 percent if there are more than five members of your immediate family.

Determine the minimum cash level for yourself according to the multiple that your income is of $25,000.

Annual expenses	Age	Family	Cash needed
$25,000	<50	<5	$25,000
$25,000	50	<5	$27,500
$25,000	50	>5	$30,250
$25,000	>60	<5	$30,000
$25,000	>70	<5	$32,500
$25,000	>80	<5	$35,000

If your cash holdings are less than the minimum suggested for your circumstances, restrain yourself from taking undue risks—unless the risks you take are basically hedges of other risks. Concentrate on building cash and cash equivalents, such as short-term Treasury obligations, gold, and insured deposits in amounts less than one hundred thousand dollars. While observing the deposit insurance limit, you should not depend upon it. Select a bank as if there were no deposit insurance system.

Guideline 2

Put your business on sound footing. You know what that entails. If you cannot satisfy yourself that your business is in shape to weather a depression, try to sell it. If you can't sell at a price that is minimally acceptable, make arrangements now for an irrevocable line of credit from a dependable bank. Be cautious as you plan your capital spending. Avoid taking on new risks even if that means forgoing opportunities that might have been profitable. The task of the moment is to preserve capital.

Guideline 3

Accelerate your income. This means realizing discretionary income in the earliest possible year for tax purposes. The rates on the wealthy are headed higher as the government's insolvency crisis intensifies. Collect monies owed to you at the earliest possible date.

Guideline 4

Consider selling your home if you are holding it primarily as an investment, particularly if your equity is less than 50 percent of its appraised value, and/or your home represents more than 50 percent of your total assets. Renting is cheaper in most areas. Most private homes in 1990 still fetched huge premiums over their rental values. These premiums could fall sharply. In 1933, people bought houses for twenty-five dollars in bankruptcy auctions that had sold for four thousand dollars in 1929. While you're at it, dump any other real estate investment that does not pay its way or would be vulnerable in a depression. This is especially important if you live in a major city that is likely to be the site of violence and urban collapse. Be especially alert to your dependence upon faltering infrastructure. Don't be at the mercy of a shaky bridge that might not be repaired or replaced by bankrupt governments. For maximum safety, seek out a location in one of the exurban counties listed in appendix 4. We particularly recommend that you divest yourself of real estate in the New York metropolitan area (New York City, nearby Connecticut, and northern New Jersey) unless your total assets are so large that you would be indifferent to a sharp drop in the value of such holdings.

Guideline 5

Diversify your assets outside your home country if you have more than $250,000, particularly if you live in the United States. The dollar could fall dramatically in the coming slump, and exchange controls might prohibit you from taking advantage of opportunities in the rest of the world. The next dollar collapse could mean the end of the dollar as a reserve currency. In September 1987, the chairman of the Bank of Tokyo, Yusuke Kashiwagi, told the European Parliament that the dollar was in danger of collapsing and that emergency steps might be necessary to upgrade the yen and the deutsche mark to replace the dollar. A repetition of such dollar weakness would probably lead to its quick dethroning. This might be undertaken in conjunction with *denomi*, or redenomination of the yen. You will want to have funds in some currency other than U.S. dollars. You may also wish to purchase a safe haven abroad. If you are wealthy enough to afford it, consider purchasing a property in Switzerland, such as a chalet or condo. This could be a valuable insurance against unrest and megapolitical breakdown, as Switzerland is likely to remain safer longer than other societies. But you may need to act quickly to obtain a foothold in Switzerland because the welcome mat to wealthy foreigners could be pulled back a bit as the world becomes more disorderly.

For more information, contact Julia Guth, *International Living*, 824 East Baltimore Street, Baltimore, Maryland 21202.

Guideline 6

Bear in mind the asymmetry of markets. A major slump will make the "buy and hold" strategy unprofitable for some time. It will therefore dry up liquidity of many assets, and lead to undervaluation of some stocks that could persist for several years.

- As we have analyzed earlier, this implies that short-selling could be more profitable than usual—although this advantage will tend to dissipate as negative sentiment increases and more people enter the market on the short side.
- As in the depresion of the 1930s, brokers will organize "short squeezes" to ramp up the price of otherwise weak company shares. In the 1930s, there were fierce short squeezes such as that on Stutz Motor Company that cost naive short players 1000 percent or higher losses. Stutz was selling $1⅝ in November 1930. By December, it had shot up to $19⅛. By February, it was at $24. By March it had plunged back to $3½. By April it was back up to $23⅝. This rollercoaster short squeeze wiped out many investors who had correctly realized that the Stutz was in trouble. The underlying stock was eventually worthless. Stutz went out of business, but along the way it took out a lot of bears. The moral is that you must be nimble to avoid trouble when you sell short. It pays to maintain an adequate information network in the investment community to keep you abreast of short squeezes as they are being put together.
- Nonlinear dependence in a bear market also implies explosive upside rallies, such as typically occur in the markets of underdeveloped countries.
- The volume in the stock market will drop more sharply than the volume in futures markets.
- The futures markets will be more vulnerable to political interference than a lack of volume, though open interest in most contracts will sag. Gear your investment plans to these consequences of nonlinearity in markets. And pay careful attention to the solvency of your broker. Otherwise, you may be unable to realize the gains of trading, or even access your capital. A reputable firm with a large capital buffer is best, even if it charges higher commissions.

Guideline 7

Keep an eye on Japan in formulating your valuation of stock markets. Japan in 1990 was where the United States was in 1929. The ultimate test of how low markets in Europe and North America go will be the success of reflation efforts in Tokyo. As we write, the Japanese authorities remain confident that they can avoid the "mistakes" of the U.S. authorities after 1930, when the money supply imploded. Whether it is as easy to stop deflation as the Japanese and others now expect is a matter we shall see in the first half of the 1990s. At October 1990 prices, the S&P 500 was fairly valued in monetary terms. It was at neither a premium nor a discount. By way of reference, the Dow traded at a 75 percent discount to fair value in 1932. It was at a 50 percent discount in 1974, and again in 1982, when the bull market of the 1980s began. In the 1987 crash, the market traded down to only a 10 percent discount. If the Japanese authorities really can stabilize their financial system and do a better job of reversing deflation than the U.S. authorities did at the end of 1930, then most world markets will not trade to a deep discount in the 1990s because they will be lifted by further outflows of Japanese liquidity.

But the result may take years to unfold. The Japanese banking sector is exposed to a real estate debacle that could be fifty times more costly than the S & L collapse. In 1990, Japanese real estate was valued at more than twenty trillion dollars. Even a modest drop of 25 percent in land values could leave highly leveraged Japanese banks facing trillions in write-offs. The U.S. banks started to fail only after the depression had taken hold for about eighteen months. The stock market sensed recovery in 1932 only after the Dow traded down by almost 90 percent. The test in Japan will come after a Japanese recession has been underway for a year or more—which could extend well into the 1990s. We believe, however, that it is most unlikely that the Japanese market can rebound from the coming recession without significant damage to the financial sector from sliding real estate and stock prices.

- Expect a "Drunken M" pattern that is common to most historic panics. The pattern goes boom, panic, rally, decline. Tokyo had the boom. In 1990, it had the panic, with the market down more than the Wall Street market of 1929. There was a Japanese version of the "Suckers' Rally." We expect the market to fall off to new lows in an erosive decline. This happened in other panics, not only in 1929.
- Watch to be sure that any apparent Japanese recovery is real before you invest more than 25 percent of your capital in long positions in the stock market.
- Raise your long exposure cautiously if the Japanese market breaks

decisively above its two-hundred-day moving average after falling to 14,000 or lower.

- If the Japanese economy and market do not recover, even a drop of the Dow to 1,000 would not necessarily make it a bargain. A 1930s-style discount would put the Dow down to about 500 and the S&P at about 60. Even a deeper discount would be possible if the U.S. government mismanages its budget and the liquidation of bad debt in the banking system.

- Resume normal investment if both the Japanese and U.S. markets break to a new high. The London Stock Market recovered quickly to a new high in the 1930s, whereas the U.S. market did not surpass its 1929 high until 1954. There is a possibility that the U.S. market will evidence analogous performance to that of Japan in the 1990s, which could put the Dow at 5000 toward the end of the decade. But the insolvency of the U.S. financial sector and the government, along with megapolitical deterioration, make it unlikely that the United States will respond as well to the coming slump as Britain did in the 1930s. Place more emphasis on trading to the short side until the stock market falls enough to yield 7 percent or more. In the depression of the 1930s, the U.S. stock market was yielding 11.2 percent at the bottom.

Guideline 8

If you have sufficient funds, seek professional guidance in short-selling, purchase of growth stocks, and scavenging for assets. Our monthly investment newsletter, *Strategic Investment*, has regular contributions from across the globe. See appendix 8 for more details.

Guideline 9

Place 5 percent to 10 percent of your total assets in gold bullion and selected gold and silver coins. (For guidance on buying or selling coins at low markup, speak with William Bradford at the Bradford Exchange, at 206-385-5097.) No one knows with certainty whether the coming depression will be inflationary or deflationary. We have argued that the dangers of deflation are underestimated. Yet even with deflation, a 5 percent insurance position in precious metals is prudent and necessary because gold has historically rallied above its inflationary highs in real terms within four years of the end of the credit cycle. There is also more than a slight possibility that political and economic breakdown would force governments to revert to gold-backed money to reliquefy a bankrupt world.

Be thoughtful when purchasing gold not to store it unwisely. Remember that bank safe deposit boxes may be inaccessible if the institution is closed due to insolvency. Also recall what happened to the gold that was stored and traded with Drexel Burnham Lambert when that firm went into bankruptcy. If you are wealthy enough to purchase bullion in significant quantities, you might be well advised to store it outside the reach of local politicians, in whatever nation you live.

Guideline 10

Maintain adequate insurance and look carefully at the solvency of your insurance company. As we indicated above, your health, in particular, should never be uninsured. Never make false economies at the expense of your health. Be sure to maintain adequate cover on your life to keep your estate intact for your heirs. This means more than signing a contract and writing a check, it means looking to the safety of your insurance company. Many companies appeared to have high junk bond and real estate exposure. Be cautious. More insurance companies could find themselves in financial turmoil as the 1990s unfold. In the 1930s, all life insurance policies were paid because strong companies pooled together to meet the obligations of the few weak companies that went under. You may not be able to depend on a similar failsafe in the 1990s. There are many more weak companies, and the industry as a whole has been less conservative in its investment policies. It will be more exposed to losses when the music stops.

Guideline 11

Prepare for substantial volatility in bond markets. Interest rates on high-quality obligations in the 1970s and 1980s reached levels not seen since the second decade of the eighteenth century. From 1930 through 1935, the prices of long-term British gilts fluctuated by an average of 12.5 points per year. The minimum price move was 7 points, with the largest swing between the high and low prices being 20 points. This followed an experience of low yields and stable prices in the second half of the nineteenth century, which can now be seen as a historic anomaly made possible by extraordinary megapolitical advantages. An editor of the *Economist* declared a century ago, "For British Consols to yield more than 3% in time of peace and prosperous trade is certainly abnormal." As we write in 1992, gilts were yielding 8.7 percent and U.S. T-bonds were yielding 7.4 percent. British rates were practically three times their earlier level, while U.S. rates were also much higher. This continues a clear historic tendency for rates to rise as a nation fades from predominance as a financial power. Among the implications for bond buyers:

- U.S. rates will be higher in the 1990s than Britain's in the 1930s, and Japanese rates will be lower still.
- Real U.S. long government bond rates may not approach the 15 percent high they reached in the 1930s. But there will be a double-digit swing in real yields in the years immediately following the collapse.
- Nominal U.S. long rates can be expected to fluctuate between 4 percent and the upper teens. Real yields will probably not exceed a high of about 12 percent—based upon real yields at the end of 1990. Bonds will be better buys near the top of this expected nominal interest rate range.
- Investors who buy bonds for yield should hedge their capital with puts.
- Zero-coupon Treasuries will be excellent trading vehicles for tax-advantaged investors at the upper range of the yield spread, because they trade essentially like long-dated options. Your broker will give you a chart that shows the gain (or loss) that can be had for zeros of different maturities at various interest rates.
- There will be a widening spread between high-quality and lower-quality debt instruments.
- Corporate bond defaults will skyrocket. Standard & Poor's, the credit rating agency, downgraded a record number of 206 corporate issues in the second quarter of 1990, compared to just 50 upgrades. This is before the downturn has officially begun. With corporate debt service taking a record percentage of cash flow, the coming downturn will lead to record bankruptcies. Trim back questionable corporate bond holdings.
- State and local bond defaults also look likely to swell to large numbers in the downturn. In 1990, five states had already experienced a decline in year-over-year receipts: Maine, Massachusetts, Michigan, New Hampshire, and New York. As spending in even most slumping states has continued to skyrocket, timely payment on debt instruments may require layoffs and significant local discomfort. Trim away holdings of bonds issued by municipalities rated below AA.

Guideline 12

Place tax-sheltered retirement funds in German and Japanese government bonds, as well as German mark– and Swiss franc–denominated zero-coupon bonds. Of course, you should invest less in zeros if you are five years or less from retirement. If you are a North American or a resident of an English-speaking country, buy single-premium annuities denominated in Swiss francs, German marks, or Japanese yen. The more money you have, the more sense it makes to meet some of your insurance and retirement needs by purchasing life insurance abroad. Remember, all of your wealth could be treated as a honey pot by greedy politicians. Put your money some place where they cannot get at it.

Money on deposit inside the United States could be converted involuntarily into American Treasury instruments with a low coupon and a long maturity. Great Britain, during its period of financial crisis, substituted perpetual notes for higher-yielding, more attractive British Treasury obligations. The danger of a similar maneuver in the United States will grow as the budget deficit balloons in the 1990s. If you are fired from a job and obtain a 401(k) distribution, roll it over into a self-directed IRA to avoid penalty taxes.

Guideline 13

The private provision of services now provided by government should be both a theme to explore in investment and an imperative in your personal life.

- The bankruptcy of municipal governments, for example, will threaten the quality of city water. Firms that supply small-scale water purifying systems should profit. You should have such a backup system for your family. Even before the downturn began, two-thirds of Americans worried about contamination of public drinking supplies.
- For-profit education services, like Education Alternatives of Minnesota, should be part of a growth industry in the 1990s as the public schools collapse.
- The upsurge of violence will increase the appeal of private security services. If you are very rich, it might be prudent to hire a personal bodyguard. As an alternative, you should consider acquiring weapons as a last resort to defend your family if you live in an area where public order is breaking down and cannot afford to leave. You may not be able to depend upon the police for protection.
- If you live in a neighborhood of single-family homes and other alternatives for protecting your family are distasteful or impractical, try to form a neighborhood association that can organize patrols and make your neighborhood less attractive to criminals. Congressional testimony suggested that active security patrols can reduce victimization by 20 to 60 percent. These efforts can pay for themselves. Economists Mitchell Joelson and Charles M. Carey have concluded that the average value

of an urban single-family house in the United States goes up by about
$330 for each 1 percent reduction in crime rates.

* The breakdown of public transportation infrastructure may drive new
  growth industries. One alternative will be the privately funded highway, with high-tech toll debiting procedures. New technology will also
  allow people to sidestep many of the consequences of traffic jams on
  public thoroughfares. Aeronautics engineer Paul Moller's flying car, the
  M200X, for example, could allow four people to cruise at 322 miles
  an hour without traveling on the roads at all. It could take off and land
  vertically.

To a larger extent than is now imagined, the megapolitics of devolution
will lead to the replacement of public services with private alternatives.

Guideline 14

Start now to form a consortium of like-minded partners with whom you
would like to work. Gear your ambitions to your current level of capital,
experience, and your age. If you have little money, or are just starting out,
form a loan circle with a group of friends or relatives whom you trust. This
is a technique that has been used with great success by many ethnic groups,
such as Koreans. The group comes together, pools its capital, and lends it
first to the member of the group considered by the others most likely to make
a success of an idea for a small business. He or she then repays the money,
and it is lent to another. Through this method it is possible to incubate many
small businesses. But you must only invite dependable partners into your
loan circle.

If you are wealthier and more established, your group could focus on
scavenging assets and restructuring businesses as the slump unfolds. The U.S.
government is destined to become the world's largest pawn shop, converting
and liquidating assets inherited from bankrupt financial institutions, failed
government-sponsored enterprises, and citizens defaulting on government-
insured mortgages. You will be able to pick up assets at pennies on the dollar
from:

Resolution Trust Corporation
Fannie Mae
Freddie Mac
Department of Housing and Urban Development
FDIC
Department of Veterans Affairs

Small Business Administration
Internal Revenue Service
U.S. Marshal's Office

State and local governments will also come into large inventories of property, some of it abandoned for nonpayment of taxes. And many banks, insurance companies, and other holders of nonperforming assets will be forced to liquidate their positions at deep discounts. The opportunities to purchase assets at fire-sale prices were already significant in 1990. They will improve as the depression arrives. To take advantage of opportunities to buy assets for a nickel on the dollar, it may be important for you to develop your own sources of financing through the partnership route because conventional avenues to cash and credit to take on large-scale projects will disappear in the economic downturn. As far as possible, government will attempt to deny access to distressed sales to small purchasers as a gesture at keeping prices high.

- If you are not a lawyer, it may be wise to include a lawyer in your circle to lower costs and facilitate completion of contracts and other negotiations.
- Don't overlook opportunities to scavenge assets in declining and out-of-favor industries. They have a crucial advantage in that physical assets represent an unusually high percentage of total assets in their operations. This could be helpful in establishing collateral when the economy reliquefies. One of the advantages of operating a declining industry in a declining region (North America) is that you have extraordinary opportunities to capture orphaned assets for negligible cash investments during periods of stress. A surging industry with rapidly rising demand seldom affords great restructuring bargains. When poorly run companies in a growth industry fail, as they sometimes do, there are usually active cash bidders for their assets. But industries with a recent history of unprofitability tend to attract less interest. For want of cash bidders, assets pass to persons who have the know-how to turn them around.
- If you become successful and take on more than one project, be careful to isolate the projects from one another financially so that if one fails it will not drag down the others.

There are few better ways to make really big money than restructuring distressed assets. See appendix 5 for important addresses of agencies that will have inventories of distressed property to sell.

Guideline 15

Don't expect a recovery in less than three to four years unless the Japanese are able to roll back the tide, which seems unlikely. If this is a depression and not merely a recession, the recovery will not begin until all the bad news has been faced. This will be a matter of years, not months. Not the least of the reasons is that court procedures for filing and settling bankruptcy, repossessing defaulted properties, and clearing title can be expected to drag out for years. The incredible inefficiency of the American legal system, far more ponderous in 1990 than in the 1930s, assures that the debt liquidation will require many years. The recovery will not begin until the yield curve is very steep, with short interest rates trading at minimal values, while long rates are a significant multiple of the short rates. Note that a three-percentage-point spread could be the foundation of recovery if the short rates were trading at 1 percent and long rates at 4 percent. This would not be the case if short rates were at 7 percent and long rates at 10 percent. It is the difference between long rates being 400 percent higher and 30 percent higher. Lending long must become very profitable before confidence will be restored and a sound foundation for recovery is laid.

False Dawns

It is important that you recognize the high likelihood of a long liquidation process and not be misled by economic false dawns and reports of recovery before the bad debts have all been faced. As we suggested in the last chapter, the economic news from April Fool's Day, 1930, may also hold lessons for today. The financial press then was talking about "A Bull Market Extraordinary," big corporate profits, the dangers of inflation, and "easy money." In fact, the world was facing the worst depression in history. There could hardly be a better reminder that you need a contrary source of judgment. Analysis of business and investment prospects in 1930 depended on relationships and indicators similar to those that fascinate investors today. Then as now, the evaluations of investors reflected nonlinear dependence on results from the immediate past. No one expected a worldwide debt liquidation, so press reports were misleadingly optimistic. You will have to look very carefully at the news for evidence that the credit problems have been resolved before you can expect a recovery. This will not happen until all the bad debt has been washed out. And that means all the bad debt. The insolvent banks will have to be liquidated or reorganized before this can occur. And insolvent governments will have to shed tasks and obligations, and reliquefy economies with sound money.

How to Buy U.S. Treasury Securities

In the meantime, large sums of cash may no longer be safe in some of the world's largest banks. To protect your liquid funds we recommend that you buy Treasury bills to park cash. U.S. Treasury bills will remain the lowest-risk debt instruments issued in America. If our fears about the banking system are realized, cash balances held in savings accounts or certificates of deposit may be unavailable for your use, even if they are "insured."

Treasury bills have another advantage. The income from them is exempt from state and local tax. In some areas, this can be a considerable advantage.

Treasury bills are issued in maturities of three, six, and twelve months. They are sold in multiples of five thousand dollars, with the exception that the minimum purchase must be at least ten thousand dollars.

You can purchase Treasury securities from commerical banks or brokers. For their pains, the selling institutions normally charge you a fee or commission of twenty-five dollars and up. In addition, you typically lose one-eighth to one-quarter of a percentage point of interest due to a markup in price. If you sell before maturity, you will pay another commission, and lose another one-eighth to one-quarter point on the sale.

The commissions and fees charged by commercial banks and brokers for Treasury securities are probably as low as they could be and still cover their costs. If you place significant sums in Treasury bills for safekeeping, be sure that those securities are registered in your name, and held separately from the assets of the bank or broker. Otherwise, if the worst happened, you might find yourself as merely another creditor of a bankrupt institution, in the same spot as a depositor—but possibly without insurance.

To avoid this possibility, and save yourself the fees and commissions, you can buy new Treasury securities directly from the Federal Reserve. It is easy.

All you have to do is submit a letter to a regional or branch office of the Federal Reserve Bank. Say that you wish to place a noncompetitive tender for whatever sum of Treasury bills you wish to buy. This means that you have agreed to accept the average yield or interest rate determined in the competitive auction. By agreeing to accept the average yield, you make life much simpler for yourself as a buyer. Include along with your letter a check payable to the Federal Reserve in the face amount of the T-bill you wish to buy. Also enclose a W-9 tax form, which is available at any Fed branch.

If you wish, you can also obtain a noncompetitive tender form from the Fed and fill it out. This form has a space to specify the securities you wish to buy. If you intend to buy notes or bonds, you must indicate the name in which they are to be registered.

Your bid must either be delivered to the Federal Reserve Bank by 1:00 P.M. Eastern time on the day of the auction, or, if mailed, be postmarked by midnight the preceding day.

Federal Reserve Banks	
Boston	600 Atlantic Avenue Boston, MA 02106
New York	33 Liberty Street New York, NY 10045
Philadelphia	10 Independence Mall Philadelphia, PA 19105
Richmond	701 Byrd Street Richmond, VA 23219
Atlanta	104 Marietta St. N.W. Atlanta, GA 30303
Cleveland	1455 E. Sixth Street Cleveland, OH 44101
Minneapolis	250 Marquette Avenue Minneapolis, MN 55480
Chicago	230 S. LaSalle Street Chicago, IL 60690
St. Louis	411 Locust Street St. Louis, MO 63166
Kansas City	925 Grand Avenue Kansas City, MO 64198
Dallas	400 S. Akard Street Dallas, TX 75222
San Francisco	101 Market Street San Francisco, CA 94105

When the rates are decided, you will receive a check refunding the discount from face value of the T-bills you bought, along with your receipt. T-bills do not pay interest periodically. They are redeemed at face value.

Residents of Canada, Britain, and other Western industrial countries should explore the methods of buying local Treasury instruments. International investors should look to purchase Treasury securities of other nations as well.

Hedging Against Debt Liquidation

Even a conservative investor may wish to profit from the necessary liquidation of much of the banking sector by selling short the shares of money center banks. In appendix 2 we list some of the more vulnerable banks that appeared to be insolvent in 1990 or were likely to become insolvent. A conservative portfolio could also include hedges on credit risk in U.S. dollar–denominated securities. These hedges could protect you against losses due to financial instability or heightened credit risk in U.S. markets. A specific hedge that we explain in appendix 1 involves the sale of Eurodollar contracts matched against the purchase of U.S. Treasury bills in the futures market.

Between the Best and the Worst

In investment there is always a better and worse course, but they may be very difficult to find. In 1989 it might have seemed reasonable for an American investor to put funds into the Japanese stock market. An investment of $100,000 in September 1989 would have been worth just $60,000 in September 1990. It would have seemed more speculative to invest $100,000 in Mexico. Yet an investment at that time of $100,000 would have grown to be worth more than $160,000.

In looking at the present world prospect for investment, we should, therefore, start by assuming that many of the things that we expect will not happen. That in itself is something of a comfort at present, as most of those expectations are very gloomy. The view spelled out in this book may seem very dark. But as we have emphasized, it is actually optimistic. We expect responsible people to win the contest for culture and control of governments in advanced countries, an assumption that might well be challenged as unrealistic. We expect markets to recover and society to mend its wounds, in spite of the movement of megapolitics toward devolution. As we look ahead at the 1990s, we expect neither the best nor the worst to happen, but the worst is the less likely of the two.

There is good reason for this. All market systems are self-balancing in principle, although they can oscillate to a high degree. When prices rise too far or too fast, sellers are brought into the market, and when prices fall we see new buyers. These countervailing forces are often harder to identify than the main forces guiding the market, but they are always there. Whether markets are going up or down, they are always marching into enemy territory; their lines of communication are becoming longer, and the resistance is becoming stronger.

Where markets are allowed to function, economic suffering, however savage, is only temporary. It is laying a foundation for a stronger prosperity ahead. In investment, it is when things look their best that false values are being created. It is when things look their worst that the foundation for growth is being rebuilt. If you are feeling gloomy about prospects now, you may have reason to be cheerful when the 1990s have come to an end.

Bright Lights from the Gloom

> All places that the eye of heaven visits
> Are to a wise man ports and happy havens.
> Teach thy necessity to reason thus;
> There is no virtue like necessity.
> —KING RICHARD II, I, iii

Every depression radiates unforeseen consequences across the generations. It puts those who lose fortunes in good company and motivates human ingenuity in unexpected ways. The story of an Englishman whose life illustrates this point has been much in our minds. He is a successful businessman who has fallen on hard times, as so many have. In the early sixties he inherited a farm from his father. He was not much good as a farmer, his hedges were a disgrace to the neighborhood, but he always had an eye for a bargain. He sold the farm, built up a business in textiles and leather goods, put money into other local businesses, and joined the local council.

Before he inherited the farm, as early as the fifties, he had an interest in properties, and as his business expanded, he bought more properties. By the late sixties he had reached a high point in his civic career. He was appointed the bailiff of the local market town in which he lived. His operations were on a substantial scale. He was part of the English enterprise culture before Mrs. Thatcher.

Unfortunately, it was the crisis of the mid-seventies that turned his fortunes for the worse, as it did those of many other businessmen and property people. He was overstretched. Some of his deals went sour. Unemployment was rising and money was tight. Life became a lot less pleasant for him. He had to sell most of the property he had bought, often for low prices, although he was able to keep his home. He retired from the council. There were lawsuits, even appearances in court and threats from bailiffs. For twenty years he had become steadily richer; for the next twenty years he became steadily poorer.

Who is this old man? His name is John Shakespeare; his son's name is William. The facts are recorded in Dennis Kay's *Shakespeare*. The years are correct, but the century was, of course, the sixteenth. John Shakespeare lived on until 1601, "a merry-checked old man," and saw his son's theatrical and business success.

John Shakespeare was indeed a victim of the major Elizabethan depression that began in the 1570s and continued, with some intermissions, to the end of the century. There were thousands of businessmen like him, and there have been many more thousands of businessmen destroyed in each of the depressions that have occurred at the rate of two every hundred years. What has been happening in the nineties, and the terrible damage to lives and careers, has happened again and again in the past.

The depression of the 1630s spread across Europe and incidentally destroyed the business of a collateral ancestor of Lord Rees-Mogg, William Mogg of Wincanton. He went bankrupt for £1300, an enormous sum at the time, in the trade of "banking in grain." More important, that depression also destroyed the finances of King Charles I, whose need to raise new money led to the Civil War, his defeat, and his execution.

On November 12, 1672, John Evelyn noted in his diary that "widows and orphans" had been ruined by King Charles II's stop on the Exchequer, and he added a later comment: "The credit of this bank being thus broken did exceedingly discontent the people and never did His Majesty's affairs prosper to any degree after it."

In 1721, Jonathan Swift, then dean of St. Patrick's in Dublin, wrote of the aftermath of the South Sea Bubble: "Two hundred chariots just bespoke / Are sunk in these devouring waves, / The horse drowned, the harness broke, / And here the owners find their graves." An eighteenth-century depression was as damaging to the carriage business as a twentieth-century one is to car manufacturers, which General Motors has reason to know.

The South Sea Bubble and the depression of trade that follow it ruined countless families, of both businessmen and investors. A Midland businessman who failed in trade, partly because of the depression and partly because of an unsuccessful investment in making artificual parchment, was Michael Johnson, the leading bookseller of Lichfield. Like John Shakespeare, he was a hardworking and successful businessman and a local councillor in a Midlands market town.

The 1570s depression struck when William Shakespeare was eleven years old; by a coincidence, the South Sea Bubble collapsed when Michael Johnson's son Samuel was also eleven years old. Who knows whether the one would have gone to London as a common player and the other as a bookseller's hack if their fathers' businesses had continued to prosper?

In 1780, Edmund Burke was complaining of the high rate of interest and the correspondingly low value of land. He advocated an economical reform of government. In 1782, John Walter, who was to become the first proprietor of the *Times*, in effect became bankrupt as a result of huge losses at Lloyd's caused by the American war and by the depression of the time. He called his creditors together and was able to repay them out of his subsequent earnings.

That depression, which persisted through the 1780s, caused James Davidson's ancestor Josiah Prather to lose his tobacco plantation in Southern Maryland. It also destroyed the finances of Louis XVI and led directly to the French Revolution and to his execution.

If one reads the mid-nineteenth-century novelists Dickens, Thackeray, and Trollope, they all record the debtors' prisons, the ruined banks, the distressed childhoods of the post-Napoleonic depression. Sir Walter Scott himself died in heavy debt because of his commitment to the failure of the house of Constable in the crash of 1825–26. Later in the century, the great agricultural depression of the 1870s lasted for a generation. In this century we have experienced the depression of the thirties and—more like the late nineteenth century—the longer economic malaise that has linked the inflation of the seventies to the deflation and debt of the nineties.

Since the mid-sixteenth century there have been nine of these depressions. All follow periods of excessive debt, all involve a credit crisis, all lead to a collapse of property values, all ruin independent businessmen, all have serious political consequences, and all cause high unemployment and social distress. They do have some positive results, however, in releasing energies from the businesses they destroy. With no depression, we might have had a large leather business in Stratford and a bigger bookshop in Lichfield, but no *Hamlet* and no Johnson's *Dictionary*. Perhaps even now debts are distressing the parents of an eleven-year-old child who will write the poetry of the next century.

THE SPIRALS OF HISTORY

To prepare for the 1990s means both looking back and thinking ahead. It means holding up the distorted mirror of the past to the light of present circumstances, to see among the shapes a few we can recognize as important for the future. While history never repeats itself exactly, its patterns can be useful in forming a kind of 20/100 forward vision. We observe that certain kinds of events occur repeatedly—lightning in summer rainstorms, and debt default in slumps. We try to impose a regular pattern on those occurrences, because the human mind is a pattern-creating consciousness. We fit events to one or another of the cycles that have been suggested—and quite often the cycles let us down. They predict a thunderstorm and no thunderstorm comes. They are not as reliable as Newton's heavenly cycles of the planets around the sun.

Then as soon as delay or failure has made us lose confidence in the cyclical theory, the lightning does strike and we start to believe again, or half believe.

Our own view is that cycles and patterns from the past are good ways to explore what may happen, but not the basis for forming a view of certainty. In human affairs there is no certainty about the future.

Yet the theory that history moves in spirals can help to give you an insight into what is happening. In a spiral you come closer to the same point in the previous cycle than you are to the remote point of the same cycle. If we are not making ourselves clear, think of a coiled spring on which you could paint a red line down one side. The red point on one coil will be very close to the next, but the diameter of the spring may be quite wide.

As we enter the 1990s, there is a feeling of a spiral of human history that is bringing us to a "red point" that has been marked in a strange and complex pattern. The year 1989 and its revolutionary events came precisely fifty years after the outbreak of World War II, when the survival of democracy and free markets was in doubt. But 1989 ended as 1889 had, with democracy and capitalism everywhere seeming to be on the ascendant, and mankind, despite its fears, set on a road of progress and improvement. In 1889 this was true. It was indeed another twenty-five years before the outbreak of World War I shattered the complacency and broke the growth of prosperity. Yet there was one historic event in 1889 that hardly anyone noted at the time, which was to change the world and cause the death of tens of millions. In April 1889 Adolf Hitler was born, and he was to be brought up in the nihilist atmosphere of the sub-Bohemian life of the old Austria, where he learned his resentment and anti-Semitism.

A hundred years earlier, in 1789, most Americans were celebrating the end of the feudal monarchy in France, and looking forward to France under a democratic constitution, just as they looked back to the Glorious Revolution in the years 1688–89 as a great success in establishing a new constitution of liberty. Within four years, in 1793 there was the Terror. We do not believe that the fall of the Bastille in Eastern Europe will lead to such terrible events. But it could. One must not be seduced by the moment of hope. We have been here before, repeatedly, in human history.

This strange spiral of history is a spiral of centuries and millennia. Twenty centuries ago in this decade, Rome was at its height and Christ was born. It was the peak of prosperity in antiquity, the time when interest rates reached their lowest levels until the fifteenth century. If history had been a stock, it would have been the time to sell. Rome slid downhill. At the end of the fifth century, Rome fell and Europe tumbled into the abyss of the Dark Ages. Then, again, at the end of the tenth century, there was an inflection point in the economic history of Western Europe. The recovery from the Dark Ages began, and continued for five centuries of the Middle Ages. Then once again exactly five centuries ago in this decade, history took another dramatic turn. Columbus sailed for America and Charles XIII invaded Italy with a new type of cannon. The Gunpowder Revolution exploded in Europe, launching five centuries of the most astonishing material progress in all the generations of human existence.

Now we are back at another red point on the spiral, the final decade of the twentieth century. It seems too much to believe or imagine that progress is destined to be reversed in this decade. This pattern suggests it, as another pattern suggests that lightning will strike on a summer afternoon when the thunderheads darken the sky. We can look overhead and see the clouds. We cannot see the spiral winding to the red point. We can notice the terrorists with the hand-held missiles, "the colors dripping on the map," the buildup of debt, the eclipse of another empire, the technical signs of a long economic upturn winding down. These developments all point to a deeper slump ahead. Let us hope it is no worse than a slump.

THE RECOVERY

The worst of the economic storm has passed. . . . A rapid recovery seems assured.
—HERBERT HOOVER, May 2, 1930

As we write, many would assume that the question of whether the depression of the 1990s can be contained has been rendered moot by an increasingly vigorous recovery. Growth in the U.S. during the third quarter has been reported at a revised 3.9 percent—the highest in four years. Professional investors and economists are all talking recovery. Again. Money supply growth has accelerated once more. Initial unemployment claims are down. Lumber prices have risen again in expectation of a jump in home building. Animal spirits in the boardroom appear to have picked up along with consumer confidence following the election of President Clinton. Retail sales have improved, along with prospects for a good Christmas selling season.

This may be a sign of a genuine recovery that will last for two or three years. It could also be something less—another false start in a sawtooth recovery. It has happened before. It is what we expect. Misleading signs of recovery are characteristic of depressions. Witness President Herbert Hoover's comments from 1930.

Nations that began slumping before the United States evince the same pattern. Britain has experienced several apparent surges toward recovery, only to see them fade. Norway's slump began with the plunge in oil prices in 1986. Every spring has brought new optimism in Oslo that a rebound is at hand. Yet year after year all the upturns have turned down again. A plot of Norwegian economic growth looks like the design for a particularly wicked saw.

This is what we expect for the United States. A sustained recovery is unlikely so long as the economy is burdened with almost two dollars of debt for every dollar of economic activity. When an economy is overloaded with debt, revving it up to a sustained take-off speed is like getting an overloaded airplane off a short runway. Not easy even in an odd-numbered year. With the elections looming, the Bush administration pushed the throttle as far as it could go before the November 1992 elections. The nose may be pointing up now. But any liftoff will lift interest rates and put the flight plan into a stall. You will be lucky if the next news after the reported takeoff is not the crash.

George Bush's Revenge

The depression of the 1990s has been slower to unfold than the depression of the 1930s. Events that took only a year to 18 months to happen in the 1930s, have taken 26 to 30 months this time. As a result, the presidency of Bill Clinton will have begun on a note of false hope. Many people have come to believe that a real recovery is underway, and others will believe that Clinton's program of economic stimulus can manufacture a recovery. If our analysis is right, however, there is little that any president can do except take the blame when the music stops. Even if America's depression in the 1990s is destined to be relatively mild, as Britain's was in the 1930s, it could still make Clinton one of the least popular figures of the century. If, as we believe, the bottom of the depression has been postponed beyond Bush's presidency, it is likely to appear that Clinton was responsible for renewing a downturn which in all probability never really ended.

The biggest reason that a sustainable recovery did not develop in the United States during the Bush administration is a lack of income. Consumer pockets had not been so empty in an election year since 1932. But unlike the situation when Hoover lost to Roosevelt, the second stage of depression, including the debt liquidation phase, had not yet begun. That means that Clinton could be the Hoover this time, because only a small fraction of the population believes that the downturn of the early nineties has been a depression. By the time Hoover left office, everyone alive knew the economy was in depression.

3.9 Percent Inches of Frosting on a Plate of Crumbs

The idea that there was vigorous growth in the third quarter of 1992 is mostly an illusion, produced by Hurricane Andrew and politically inspired massaging of the income accounts by the Department of Commerce. Look closely at the numbers. A revised total of about $55 billion in economic growth was reported by the government in the third quarter of 1992:

1. Insurance analysts have pointed out that up to $20 billion was due to be spent in non-recurring purchases to repair damage due to Hurricane Andrew and Typhoon Iniki. Much of that spending fell in the third quarter, though we don't know how much. Suppose half did. Multiply by four to annualize as government statisticians do, and you get $40 billion, which equates to growth of more than 0.7 percentage points on a $5.6 trillion economy. It is likely that a fifth or more of the reported growth was the statistical trail of a bad wind.

2. A total of $14 billion of spending in the third quarter was attributed to booming sales of computers, which would be good news to IBM if it were true. It wasn't. The amount actually spent on computers was just $2.4 billion. The other $11.6 billion was a statistical adjustment added to reflect the government's view of how much computational power consumers got for their money. About 20 percent of the reported increase in GDP was a measure of spending that was never spent.

3. Another layer of the reported growth was contributed by the fictitious incomes of phantom employees. As pointed out by Philip Braverman of DKB Securities, the federal government employment reports show that 400,000 jobs have been added in the economy since March, while the total of the 50 state employment reports shows a loss of 377,000 jobs. That is a difference of 777,000. It arises because the Labor Department is adding 50,000 phantom jobs each month to account for the hiring they imagine is taking place by companies too small to count. At an average of $26,500 per job, that comes to $20.6 billion in nonexistent income of phantom employees padding the annual GDP growth.

4. $40.6 billion of imaginary "non-wage component of personal income" is also included in the total of GDP. As Albert Sindlinger has demonstrated, the base numbers have been manipulated since the recovery allegedly began in 1991. The income category accounted for by dividends, interest, and the proprietor's share of small business profits was deliberately revised downward for the years immediately preceding the alleged start of recovery in 1991. The net effect of understating the previous income and overstating it during the period when the recovery is alleged to have taken place, was to raise GDP by $40.6 over what is actually was in the third quarter of 1992. It was enough to shift GDP from negative to positive in five of the seven quarters since the recovery allegedly began. According to Sindlinger, the only two quarters of positive growth were the first quarter of 1991 and the first quarter of 1992.*

*Albert Sindlinger, *Sindlinger's Consumer Outlook,* Vol. Nos. 8, 9, August—September, 1992, page 8.

What looked from a distance to be a handsome 4-inch layer cake was, on closer examination, 3.9 inches of frosting on a plate of crumbs. We have no doubt that the economy has bounced as we write. But how much is another question. Genuine growth, if any, was certainly much slower than that reported, much of it the result of non-recurring repair costs due to Hurricane Andrew. But at least the wind was real. It appears to us that $60 billion or more of reported GDP was not. Another $20 billion of the reported growth was due to the accumulation of unsold inventories. The savings rate fell from an anemic 5.3 percent, to an even lower 4.3 percent.

We see no convincing evidence of a sustainable recovery—in spite of the biggest budget deficits in history, dramatic monetary ease, and one of the steepest yield curves ever. This is also the tale told by the Index of Coincident Indicators. Because it is not widely followed, it has not been subject to optimistic distortions. The Coincident Indicators are lower as we write than they were when the recession supposedly ended in the spring of 1991. The weakness of the economy was confirmed in another way. At the ballot box. The reason that President Bush lost is that 69.6 percent of households had experienced a fall in income, the highest negative level recorded in Sindlinger's household liquidity surveys in 38 years.*

We continue to believe that the entire world economy is destined to get weaker. Because our forecasts are based on a comprehensive theory of the way the world works, the confirmation of so many individuals elements of our view suggests to us that the broadest themes of this book are true, and will be more emphatically borne out as the decade unfolds. We still expect to see a second and deeper stage of depression, an economic meltdown that would be compounded by national bankruptcy as the depression of the 1930s wasn't.

OVER-DETERMINED MELTDOWN

Most experts believe that such a meltdown is quite unlikely. We rather expect it. Such a crisis, in fact, seems to us to be over-determined. And not merely for the reasons spelled out in this book. There are other reasons for forecasting deeper depression ahead based on entirely different methodologies.

Having read this far, you are well aware of our view that changes in the technological boundary forces that determine the exercise of power are the ultimate causes of depressions. They generate property rights shocks that

*Albert Sindlinger, *Sindlinger's Consumer Outlook*, Vol. 1, Nos. 10, 11, October–November, 1992, Page 3.

radiate through the system for decades, resulting in massive malinvestment and the built-up of debt which ultimately must be liquidated.

Prices Tell All?

But ours is not the only theory of depression. Robert Prechter and his associate Dave Allman have developed a very different analysis, based upon technical price movements known as "The Elliott Wave." Prechter believes that stock price patterns over the past several centuries reflect a five-wave structure that has predictive value. He foresees stock prices correcting back to levels of the 1930s.

Prechter also has done some interesting work in comparative sociology, which amplifies his study of price movements and brings them to life. Using Elliott Wave principles, Prechter forecasts that there will be a severe depression in the 1990s that could bring the very survival of Western civilization into doubt. We find his work interesting because he comes to a more dire conclusion than we do, with a quite different argument.

Ignoring Prices Altogether

We have recently become aware of still another argument for depression. Dr. Cesare Marchetti is a physicist working in Austria who takes exactly the opposite tack from Prechter. In fact, Marchetti's approach has almost nothing in common with the work of any market-sensitive economist. Instead of arguing that price movements explain everything, Marchetti ignores prices and money altogether. He measures only physical quantities in his work— BTUs of energy consumed, or passenger miles driven, cars per capita, etc. Marchetti treats the development and penetration of innovations and products in the economy as if they were populations of living species. He argues that the growth and spread of automobiles into the markets of the Western world, for example, can be described by the same logistic equation that describes the penetration of rabbits into Australia, or any other form of ecological competition.

Using this analysis almost ten years ago, Marchetti concluded that markets for most of the products that constituted the postwar economic boom had been saturated. This implied growing profit pressures and significant job losses in established industries. Notwithstanding his unorthodox methodology, Marchetti accurately forecast the slowdown of growth worldwide and some of its specific consequences for the least flexible competitors. In an article published in 1983 he wrote:

[I]n order to slash costs one has to show the utmost flexibility at the level of engineering, labor, and management. In an old established company, let's call it GM, engineers tend to be oldish and ranked, labor rigid and greedy, management exhausted by the gratification of obtaining so much with so little swimming, when riding the tide of the boom. The young company, let's call if Toyota, still has young and experienced engineers, no labor problems as it still expands, and a management terrorized by the saturation of the local market it sees coming. You name the winner. In spite of all institutional barriers the losers will erect, my Darwinian forecast attributes to Japan half the cars produced in the world in the year 1995.

Not bad. The ongoing shakeup at GM was well anticipated and explained by Marchetti in 1983. His argument implies that there is little prospect that the world economy will escape without a deeper depression because the two features most necessary to faciliate innovation, *flexibility* and *adaptibility*, are being attacked by the political response to economic distress. As incomes come under pressure due to the slowing of growth (or saturation of markets in Marchetti's terms), a cry goes out to politicians to *slow* the pace of change by imposing rigid regulations that thwart innovation and punish entrepreneurs with stifling taxation.

Measurements taken across different dimensions point to a similar unorthodox conclusion. The depression has not reached bottom.

- We doubt that the depression has bottomed because too little of the excess debt has been liquidated and many of the benchmark events that typically occur in credit cycle unwindings have not yet happened.
- Robert Prechter thinks that a much deeper depression lies ahead because stock prices have not yet plunged to the highly depressed levels anticipated in his reading of Elliott patterns.
- Cesare Marchetti's argument implies further downward pressure for still another reason. Incomes are destined to fall until a surge of innovation develops new products of sufficient market importance to replace those on which postwar prosperity was built. Statistically, there is no evidence that this has not happened yet.

These arguments, taken from different realms, and developed years ago, all have a proven predictive value. Or at any rate, they have all been used to make forecasts that came true. They point to at least somewhat similar outcomes now. There is also the hazy Ravi Batra argument that a social cycle now marked by the predominance of "The Era of Laborers" implies a deep depression. Perhaps there are other arguments as well, any one of which is only a partial explanation for a profound pattern of events that is far more highly determined than most people believe.

Events are likely to show that politicians cannot prevent depression, as conventional economists of all persuasions, Keynesians, monetarists and supply-siders, have long advertised that they could do. Deflation is far less superficial than they have tended to believe. Ever since the 1930s, economists have beguiled themselves with the idea that all the unpleasantness of the Great Depression was due to policy mistakes, adherence to "outmoded ideas," such as the gold standard, or failure to print money and spend it fast enough. We suspect that they underestimate the comprehensiveness of contractionary forces. Just as water pumped up to an unnatural height will find its way back downhill, so when debt exceeds the carrying capacity of the economy to sustain nominal growth, you get debt liquidation. One way or another.

Economists have tended to gather at the site of the feedback loop that was most potent in any given setting, and proclaim that if it were dammed up, there would be no further problem. In fact, they would merely displace the deflationary torrent into another channel.

The economists, then and now, who blamed gold as the unique obstacle to recovery in the 1930s have indulged in wishful thinking. And it is wishful thinking that takes no account of recent mathematical insights into the structure and function of complex systems. Taking a longer view, the economy should be expected to evolve through stages like any complex system in nature. In Chapter Nine we draw an analogy between the stages of growth and transformation in the economy and those of a forest system which has its necessary liquidation phase, the conflagration in which the old growth is burned to the ground. To focus on the particular spark that sets such a blaze, or the prevailing wind that carried it from tree to tree, is to fundamentally mistake how the whole system operates. If one spark had been quenched, the forest would have been burned by another.

Returning to the example of the 1930s, it is far from clear that abandoning gold before the necessary liquidation took place would have had any effect except to transfer the problem to a different level. Witness what is happening today. The gold standard is long gone, but similar forces of contraction appear to be at work. Now it is the Bundesbank that has become the culprit that the gold standard appeared to be sixty years ago. The hope for early world recovery rests with the expectation that the Bundesbank will shift strategy soon, if not immediately. This is analogous to the exhortations and hopes that various countries should abandon the gold standard in the early 1930s.

Events now seem poised to prove that depression is not a superficial phenomenon that occurs just because a few willful leaders make mistakes. It is the culmination of a long, historic process that began decades in the past. This does not mean that nothing can be done to ameliorate it or that you cannot take steps to protect yourself and your family. But if we are correct, it would be a mistake to depend upon political promises or programs to shield you from the slump. They won't. You are more likely to be the source of help yourself than any politician is.

The message of this book is that a major change is underway in the world and that you will be better positioned if you face it by taking charge of your own financial destiny. Remember as you read that we mean our warnings to be helpful and constructive. If they stimulate your thinking in positive directions, we will consider ourselves successful.

TECHNIQUES FOR HEDGING AGAINST ECONOMIC CRISIS

THE TED SPREAD

SOMETIME IN the 1990s the United States and much of the rest of the world will face a major financial crisis, which will include the bankruptcy of many leading banking institutions. If this financial crisis materializes, it is likely to share the common features of past financial crises. Chief among these is panic. When investors are frightened, they favor safety above all else. This is why near-term government securities, known as Treasury bills, or "T-bills," tend to skyrocket in value during financial crises. Usually, the credit of the U.S. government is better than the credit of other dollar debtors.

The worried investors and fund managers who rush to buy Treasury bills often sell uninsured short-term debt instruments. Among such instruments are Eurodollars.

Both T-bills and Eurodollars are investment instruments that you can trade through banks. But trading them is made far more convenient and much cheaper by the fact that futures contracts for both are traded through the International Money Market Division of the Chicago Mercantile Exchange. These futures contracts can be bought and sold through many brokerage firms. They are regulated by the Commodity Futures Trading Commission.

The Chicago Mercantile Exchange is one of the largest futures trading exchanges in the world. It is a highly liquid market. A depression would reduce the liquidity of futures markets, but not decisively. The greater danger is that political intervention would interfere with the markets. It is typical for authorities to blame markets for foreshadowing and reflecting economic discontinuities. They may attempt to close or hamper domestic futures markets in a slump, which merely increases the necessity of keeping money outside the borders of the country in which you live.

In a typical week, about 30,000 contracts for ninety-day T-bills change hands. About 350,000 contracts for Eurodollars trade in that same period. When you consider that each contract is for a unit of one million dollars, the total value of contracts traded is staggering.

The contract months are the same for both T-bills and Eurodollars: March, June, September, and December. Minimum margin for trading each contract by itself is $1,000. The spread margin for buying and selling combinations is just $750.

Both Treasury bills and Eurodollars are discount instruments. That means that they sell at a discount from face value. Their prices are quoted to reflect the interest rate yields that each offers. The prices are calculated by subtracting the prevailing interest rate from 100.

If T-bill rates are 5 percent, T-bills will be quoted at 95. If Eurodollars are yielding 6 percent, they will be quoted at 94.

Of course, interest rates are seldom rounded off perfectly at 5 percent or 6 percent. Usually, you will see T-bills and Eurodollars quoted at rates spelled out to hundreds of a point. These small divisions are known as "basis points." Each basis point, .01, is worth twenty-five dollars.

How It Works

T-bills and Eurodollars form the basis of the Ted spread. The "T" in "Ted" comes from "*T*-bills." The "ed" comes from "*Euro*dollars." To execute a Ted spread, you buy T-bills and sell Eurodollars in equal amounts. The "spread" is equal to the price of the Eurodollars minus the price of the T-bills.

When a financial crisis begins, the Ted spread widens. The value of Treasury bills increases relative to the value of Eurodollars.

If you suspect that a financial crisis is coming, and you also suspect that T-bills will fare better than Eurodollars, you know how to profit in the event the crisis occurs. You buy the Ted spread.

Why Trade the Spread?

During most financial crises, short-term interest rates fall. Therefore, you may wonder why it is advantageous to buy a Ted spread rather than simply buying T-bills outright. There are two reasons.

First, the risk is lowered when you trade a Ted spread. If you buy T-bills, and a crisis does not eventuate, you could end up losing money quickly if interest rates happen to rise.

When you trade the Ted spread, you are usually protected against loss because of climbing short rates because Eurodollars tend to lose value faster than T-bills when rates are rising. Normally, the Ted spread will narrow when rates are falling—unless, of course, rates are falling because of financial crisis.

Another reason to trade the Ted spread outright is to get a greater kick from your margin investment. At $750 per spread on exchange minimum margin, you can trade four Ted spreads for each T-bill contract you could hold outright, while still making lower provision for margin calls in the event that the market moves against you.

$20,000 in Ted Spreads

If you are in a position to risk twenty thousand dollars, deliver twenty thousand dollars in T-bills to your broker. This will provide you with a way to earn interest on some of your margin money. Most brokers allow you to count just 90 percent of the face value of T-bills for margin purposes. Unfortunately, most brokers allow T-bills to be used for initial margin, but not for maintenance margin.

This means that if the market moves against you, you must provide cash to make up the loss sufficiently to maintain your position.

Your T-bill will provide enough initial margin to enable you to buy about twenty-four Ted spreads, which is more than we recommend. If the market moves against you by just one point, you would lose six hundred dollars, and you would face a margin call.

A more conservative approach would be to purchase ten Ted spreads, buying the nearby T-bill futures contract and selling an offsetting number of Eurodollar contracts. Presuming your broker allows you to trade on exchange minimum margin of $750 per spread, this would account for $7500 initial margin, leaving you $11,500 to meet maintenance calls without cashing in your T-bills. The Ted spread would have to narrow by 42 basis points before this happened. Such a move is hardly out of the question, but may not happen if interest rates rise or the crisis we anticipate is forth-coming.

The Extra Whammy

A way to reach for an even greater kick from a crisis is to employ a wrinkle on the Ted spread known as the "whammy." You buy a "whammy" when you purchase a nearby T-bill and sell a Eurodollar contract for delivery in a later month. Usually, the nearby T-bills gain the most from a financial crisis, while further-out Eurodollars tend to be more depressed. The margin for a whammy is the same as the margin on a Ted spread—$750 per contract.

You can't stop the advent of financial crises, but if one should come, knowing how to trade the versions of the Ted spread can give you a method to make what is basically bad news a little easier to bear.

Another Hedge Against Economic Collapse

If your circumstances permit you to take higher risk, you could seek higher profits by investing in positions likely to profit significantly if a severe recession begins. Assets could be allocated to short-selling of commodities, the purchase of long-term put options on the Japanese stock market, and trading in sovereign debt of Third World and old Communist countries.

Historically, commodity prices have fallen during times when real economic activity diminishes. Commodity prices tend to fall disproportionately when the money supply falls. This is because commodity prices are set daily in auction markets. Many other prices in the economy are not so flexible. Some prices are fixed by law, others by contract, tradition, or government regulation. When demand slows because of a deflation, inflexible prices are not free to fall. Therefore, prices that *are* free to fall, like commodity prices, take the brunt of the decline. Prices for both soft and hard commodities tumbled by between two-thirds and three-quarters during the Great Depression.

How to Profit from a Commodity Fall

No jingles to write. No envelopes to address. As with the Ted spread, deliver twenty thousand dollars in T-bills with the longest possible maturity to your broker. They will serve as your margin deposit in what could be one of the better ways of hedging against a downturn. By posting T-bills you will earn interest income on your margin money. The longer the maturity of the bills, the more interest you will earn if the economy goes soft. That is what you are betting will happen.

You now have eighteen thousand dollars to play with. For margin purposes most brokers count T-bills at 90 percent of face value ($20,000 × .9 = $18,000). Step one is complete. You now move to step two. Tell your broker to sell short three contracts of the CRB index.

THE CRB INDEX

The CRB index is an unweighted geometric composite of the prices of a basket of twenty commodities. They are: Live Cattle, Cacao, Coffee, Corn, Cotton, Crude Oil, Comex Gold, Number 2 Heating Oil, Hogs, Lumber, Oats, Orange Juice, Platinum, Pork Bellies, Comex Silver, Soybeans, Soybean Meal, Soybean Oil, World Sugar, and Chicago Wheat. In short, these are the raw materials of economic life.

When the economy is strong or inflation is rising, these commodities tend to go up in price. When the economy weakens or deflation sets in, they fall. Of course, not every commodity follows the same path. Special circumstances may raise prices for one or more items under even the most depressed of conditions. That is why there is less risk in trading a basket of many commodities as a hedge against a slump than in picking one or two crucial ones to sell. It is harder to predict how any one commodity will move than to know that if the economy slows down, demand for most commodities will fall.

The CRB index was the first basket of commodities to be traded on a futures exchange. It is quoted as a percentage of its value of 1967 (when it was 100). Its all-time high was reached on November 20, 1980, a reading of 337.6. Commodity prices then started down and continued falling as recession set in during 1981. By October

4, 1982, the CRB index had dropped by a third to 225.8. As we write, the index stands at 204, below its 1982 level.

Each full point of the index is worth $500 per contract. If the CRB is selling at $203, the value of each contract has fallen by $500. If you have two contracts, the value of each full-point move is $1,000. Three contracts means $1500. (Check to verify the present contract size of the CRB. It may have been changed since this was written.)

Entering the Trade

The more contracts you trade, the greater your gain if you are right and the higher your loss if the market moves against you. Initial margin should be around $1200 per contract. Therefore, if you sell three CRB contracts, $3600 of your $18,000 of margin credit will be spoken for. You will have a margin buffer of almost 20 points.

A cautious speculator might choose not to sell short unless the index stood above 230. The CRB has rallied above 230 many times since 1982, only to fall back again. If our theory is correct, one of these fine days, the CRB will break down and not retrace back to 230—although the expected fall of the dollar could negate some of the drop in commodity prices. Most world commodities are traded in dollar-denominated contracts.

You can place your sell order as high as you please. The higher you place it, the lower your risk of being caught in a technical retracement. You should also remember that if you try to sell short at too high a price, your order may never be filled. You may miss the trade altogether.

Margin Calls and Positional Trading

The chance of adverse swings in volatile commodity markets is more than trivial. That is why most professional traders are crucially concerned with timing. As the song said, "Tick. Tick. Tick. Timing is the thing, it's true." Unhappily, many novices entering futures markets cannot carry a tune. They sell or buy too soon, and are wiped out by short-run fluctuations.

The best way to solve this problem is to be born with the luck of the gods. An alternative is to pony up more margin money. The more ample your margin, the less chance that you will be caught by a random event that temporarily pushes prices against you. With enough margin, you can essentially reduce your risks on a "positional" trade to just one—the chance that you are fundamentally wrong about what is happening in the economy.

This is risk enough. Positional trading can offer large gains, especially if you get into the market with prices at or near the terminal of a major move. But the very fact that you are not going to be stopped out of the market if it moves against you a little ensures that it will move against you a lot before you can cut your losses. If you are mistaken, you will pay dearly.

Given this reality, traders with little experience in futures markets should risk large sums only on rare occasions when a sustained move in one direction or another seems likely. To make such a commitment, you must be confident of the fundamentals. In this case, we are. Shorting the CRB index is a bet that the economy will slow. If the argument of this book is correct, you should be able to profit all the way down to 100 or lower.

DON'T RISK CASH YOU CAN'T AFFORD TO LOSE

Of course, we could be wrong. You should not risk your money unless you are in a position to do so. In particular, you should not be trading unless you have an ample cash reserve by the terms we spelled out on page 505.

PRUDENT HEDGING

If you own a business that holds cash now but stands to lose large sums in the event of a slump, selling short the CRB now may be an excellent way of hedging your position. If there is no slump, you will lose money in the CRB but gain in your business. If there is a slump, your business may falter, but you will pick up highly leveraged returns from the decline in real activity as reflected in the drop of commodity prices. In either case, you would be better off than you will be if you do not hedge and the economy falters.

Betting $20,000 to Gain $100,000

You will essentially be risking $20,000 against a possible gain of $100,000. That is the approximate profit that would accrue if the CRB index falls as much over the next few years as it fell from the peak to the bottom in the last recession. That would put the index down to about 160, a drop of 33 percent. If you sold short at 225, you would gain 65 points. At $500 a point, times three contracts, your total gain would be $97,500. Interest income on your T-bills would round off your spare-time earnings to $100,000 or more.

What Will Happen?

What will actually happen? Nobody knows. The recession could be light. The CRB index could fall by less than it did in the period 1980–82. Or there could be a depression that would cut commodity prices as drastically as they were cut in the troughs of the last three down waves. As unlikely as that seems, prices could go down much further than people now expect. If so, it will certainly be the start of a period when it will be very hard to make money, much less at home, in your spare time. Selling short the CRB could be a lot better way of bringing in some extra cash to help you through hard times than sending a letter to Ed McMahon or throwing a Tupperware party.

TROUBLED BANKS

THE FOLLOWING BANKS with assets of about $100 million or over had financial ratios that could call their long-term health into question. The financial ratios were compiled by IDC Financial, for the first quarter of 1992. Bear in mind that financial ratings change. Many banks that seemed sound when these readings were taken were located in regions where the real estate depression had not yet begun to take hold. If property values in your area have recently taken a turn for the worse, you should seek up-to-date information from IDC Financial before assuming that banks and bank holding companies not listed here are safe.

Remember as well that factors other than those analyzed may affect the future solvency of the banks. Many banks have large bond portfolios. A significant jump in long-term interest rates would leave them exposed to capital losses.

The ratings were calculated using data prepared by IDC Financial Publishing. This information is believed to be reliable, but no warranties are given. In the case of bank holding companies that own more than one bank, the financial ratios of the holding company were used to calculate the warning flag, unless IDC did not calculate financial ratios on the holding company. Bear in mind that the bank that you deal with may not operate under the name of its bank holding company. Many banks with similar names are separately capitalized. Therefore you should be aware of the name of the ultimate owner of the bank with which you deal.

IDC can offer you an up-to-date report on the soundness of any financial institution for $25. For more recent data or to obtain information on specific banks in your area, contact IDC. They can be reached at (800) 544-5457, or in Wisconsin, at (414) 367-6497. Write to IDC Financial Publishing, P.O. Box 140, 300 Cottonwood Avenue, Hartland, Wisconsin 53029

ALABAMA:
National Commerce Corp., Birmingham

ARIZONA:
Valley National Corporation, Phoenix

CALIFORNIA:
American Republic Bancorp, Torrance
Bank of Newport
Brentwood Bank California, Los Angeles
BSD Bancorp, San Diego
Capital Bank, Downey
Capital Bank of California, Los Angeles
Commerce Bancorp, Newport Beach
Financial Center Bancorp, San Francisco
First California Bank, La Mesa
First National Corporation, San Diego
Lippo Bank, Los Angeles
MBC Corporation, Modesto
Mechanics National Bank, Paramount
Montecito Bancorp, Santa Barbara
Olympic National Bancorp, Los Angeles
Pacific Inland Bank, Anaheim
Pioneer Bancorp, Fullerton
RCB (River City Bank) Corporation, Sacramento
Security Pacific Corporation
United National Bank, Monterey Park
West Coast Bancorp, Orange
Westside Bank, Los Angeles
World Trade Bank, NA, Beverly Hills

COLORADO:
Jefferson Bank & Trust Company, Lakewood
Mountain West Banking Corp. (Vectra), Denver

CONNECTICUT:
Amity Bancorp, New Haven
BNH (Bank of New Haven) Bancshares, Inc.
Founders Bank, New Haven
LaFayette American Bancorp, Hamden
New Canaan Bank & Trust Company
North American Bancorp, Waterbury
Northeast Bancorp (Union Trust Company), New Haven

Olde Windsor Bancorp (New England Bank & Trust Company), Windsor
Westport Bancorp

DISTRICT OF COLUMBIA:
Maryland Bancshares, Inc.
New York Bankshares, Inc.
Riggs National Bank
Washington Bankshares, Inc.

FLORIDA:
American Bancorp of South, Merritt Island
Boca Bank, Boca Raton
Capital Bancorp, Miami
Continental Bancorp, Miami
County Financial Corp., North Miami
First National Bank of Bonita Springs
Florida Bay Banks, Inc., Panama City
Florida International Bank, Perrine
Guardian Bank, Boca Raton
Marsh Investments, N.V. (Consolidated Bank), Hialeah
Republic Bancshares Corp, Clearwater
Suburban Bankshares, Inc., Lake Worth

GEORGIA:
Bank South Corporation, Atlanta
Citizens Bank, Gainesville
Metro Bancorp, Douglasville
Northside Bank & Trust Company

IDAHO:
Valley Bancorporation, Idaho Falls

ILLINOIS:
Boulevard Bancorp, Inc., Chicago
DG (Downers Grove) Bancorp.
First Northbrook Bancorp
Livingston and Company SW, Chicago
Oxford Financial Corporation, Addison
Water Tower Bancorp, Chicago

IOWA:
River Cities Investment Company, Davenport

KANSAS:
Johnson County Bankshares, Shawnee Mission
One Security (Security Bank of Kansas City)

KENTUCKY:
First & Farmers Bancshares, Somerset

LOUISIANA:
Bank of Gonzales
Baton Rouge Bank & Trust Company
First Continental Bancshares, Gretna
First Guarantee Bank, Hammond
First National Bancshares, Alexandria
First National Bancshares, Houma
Hibernia Corporation, New Orleans
New Iberia Bancorp, New Iberia
Pioneer Bancshares Corp., Shreveport
Royal Windsor Holding Corp. (Jefferson Guarantee Bank), Metarie
Whitney Holding Corporation, New Orleans

MAINE:
Ocean National Bank of Kennebunkport
Peoples Heritage Financial Group, Portland

MARYLAND:
Baltimore Bancorp
Bank Maryland Corporation, Towson
Maryland Bankcorp, Inc., Lexington Park
MNC Financial, Baltimore

MASSACHUSETTS:
Baybanks, Boston
Century Bancorp, Somerville
Commerce Bank & Trust Company
Independent Bank Corporation, Rockland
Malden Trust Company
Martha's Vineyard Bancorp.
Multibank Financial Corp., Quincy

New England Bancorp, Waltham
Saugus Bank & Trust Company
Shawmut National Corporation, Boston
USA Bancorp, Boston
UST Corporation, Boston
WCC Management Corporation, Boston
Westbank Corporation, West Springfield
Woburn National Corporation

MICHIGAN:
Thumb National Bank & Trust Company, Pigeon

MINNESOTA:
Liberty Bancshares, St. Paul

MISSISSIPPI:
First Bank, McComb
Omnibank of Mantee

MISSOURI:
Cardinal Bancorp, Inc., Saint Louis
Colonial Bancshares, Saint Louis
International Bancshares, Gladstone
Jackson Exchange Bank & Trust Company
MBI Bancshares, Inc., Kansas City
Mega Bancshares, Inc., Saint Louis
Metro Bancshares, Inc., Kansas City

NEW HAMPSHIRE:
Bank of New Hampshire, Manchester
Connecticut River Bancorp, Charlestown
Finest Financial Corporation, Pelham
Granite State Bankshares, Inc., Keene
Somersworth Bank

NEW JERSEY:
BMJ (Bank of Mid-New Jersey) Financial Corp., Bordentown
Broad National Bancorp., Newark
Citizens First Bancorp., Glen Rock
Constellation Bancorp., Elizabeth
Garden State Bancshares, Jackson
High Point Financial Corp., Branchville
Independence Bancorp, Inc., Allendale
Inter-Community Bank, Springfield
MidAtlantic Corp., Edison

National Westminster Bancorp, Jersey City
Peoples Bancorp, Belleville
Ramapo Financial Corporation, Wayne
Urban National Bank, Franklin Lakes

NEW MEXICO:
CBC Incorp., Clovis

NEW YORK:
Arrow Financial Corporation, Glenn Falls
Atlantic Bank of New York
Bank Leumi Le-Israel Corp, New York
Citicorp, New York
First New York Business Bank Corp., New York
Hampton Bancshares, Southhampton
Marine Midland Banks, Buffalo
National Westminster Bancorp, New York
North Fork Bancorporation, Mattituck
UBAF Arab American Bank, New York

NORTH CAROLINA:
Barclays American Corp., Charlotte

OKLAHOMA:
American Bank & Trust Company, Tulsa
American National Bank & Trust Company, Shawnee
First Bancshares of Muskogee

PENNSYLVANIA:
Equimark Corporation, Pittsburgh
First Lehigh Bank, Walnutport
Old York Road Bancorp, Willow Grove

RHODE ISLAND:
Bay L&IB, East Greenwich
Eastland Financial Corporation, Woonsocket

SOUTH CAROLINA:
RHNB (Rock Hill) Corporation, Rock Hill

TENNESSEE:
Bank of Barlett
Community Bancshares, Inc., Germantown

TEXAS:
American Bank, NA, Woodway
Ameritex Bancshares Corp, Fort Worth
BancTexas Group, Dallas
Denson Financial Corporation, San Antonio
Brenham National Bank
Citizens National Bank in Waxahachie
Community Bankers, Inc., Granbury
Cornerstone Bancshares, Inc, Dallas
CullenFrost Bankers, Inc., San Antonio
First Bancshares of Texas, Longview
First City Bancorporation, Houston
Grayson County State Bank, Sherman
International Bank–Corpus Christi
Inwood National Bank of Dallas
Longview Financial Corporation
Med Center Bank & Trust Company, Houston
National Bancshares Corp., San Antonio
North Texas American Bancshares, Sherman
Post Oak Bank, Houston
Provident Bancorp of Texas, Dallas
State Bank & Trust Company, San Marcos
State National Bank, El Paso
Union Texas Bancorporation, Laredo
University Bancshares, Inc., Houston

VERMONT:
Independent Bankgroup, Inc., Springfield

VIRGINIA:
Independent Bank, Manassas
Suburban Bancshares, McLean
Virginia Bankshares, Richmond

SOUND BANKS

THERE ARE many sound banks in America. Here is a sampling of more or less conservative institutions that are likely to survive, come what may. Most are small institutions, with total assets of less than $50 million. A few are larger. Those with assets in excess of $1 billion are marked with an asterisk. The larger of these sound banks might make good repositories for corporate cash in amounts in excess of the insured limit.

Remember our positive opinion about these institutions is based upon a snapshot of where they stood in the first quarter of 1992. It is always possible that there could be a change of management or a change of circumstance that would adversely affect the banks on this list. Many are farm banks in rural areas that could suffer serious declines in a slump. Because these institutions are generally small, they could be transformed rapidly, either by adverse developments in the local community or by a change in banking philosophy.

Bear in mind also that many banks operate under names that are similar or sound alike. Some banks with the same name in the same state may be capitalized separately. A "Farmers & Merchants" bank with an excellent balance sheet may operate in one town while another "Farmers & Merchants" with one foot in the grave operates independently a few miles away.

We recommend that you check the latest numbers yourself with IDC Financial.

We should add that the omission of a bank from this list does not indicate that it is an unsound institution. We have merely selected a sampling of banks with strong financial ratios and large proportions of equity capital as a percentage of assets.

ALABAMA:
Brantley Bank & Trust Co.
First Bank of Fayette
First Bank of DeKalb
   County

Monroe County Bank
Peoples Bank of Greensboro

ALASKA:
First National Bank of Anchorage

Arkansas:
Arkansas State Bank, Siloam Springs
Bank of Mountain View
Farmers & Merchants Bank, Des Arc
Farmers & Merchants Bank, Prairie
Grove
Farners Bank, Greenwood
First National Bank of Izard County
First Paragould Bankshares
First Security Bancorp, Searcy

California:
*Farmers & Merchants Bank of Long
Beach
First Security Thrift Company, Orange
United Security Bank, NA, Fresno
Western Ind. National Bank, South El
Monte

Colorado:
Citicorp Savings & Independence Bank,
Denver
El Paso Bancshares, Monument
Farmers State Bank, Fort Morgan
First National Bank of Flagler

Connecticut:
Citizens National Bank, Putnam

Delaware:
*American Express Centurion Bank,
Newark
Associates National Bank, Wilmington
First National Bank of Wyoming
*Greenwood Trust Company, Newcastle
*MBNA Corporation, Newark
Primamerica, Newark
*Wilmington Trust Corporation, Wil-
mington

District of Columbia:
National Capital Bank

Florida:
First Bank of Immokalee
Peoples Bank of Graceville

Georgia:
Bank of Danielsville
Bank of Gray
Bank of Upson
Farmers & Merchants Bank, Dublin
Monogram Credit Card Bank, Roswell

Illinois:
Algonquin State Bank
Alpha Financial Corporation
Alpine Bancorporation, Inc., Rockford
Athens State Bank
Chicago City Bancorporation, Chicago
F.N.B.C. of La Grange
First Bank & Trust Company of Illinois,
Palatine
First Lansing Bancorp
Forreston State Bank
Germantown Trust & Savings Bank,
Breese
National Bank of Canton
Peterson Skiles & Co, Virginia
Poplar Grove State Bank
Reynolds State Bank
Sparbank, Inc., McHenry
Teutopolis State Bank

Indiana:
Fowler State Bank
Franklin County National Bank, Brook-
ville

Iowa:
American Savings Bank, Tripoli
Dial National Bank, Des Moines Iowa
The First National Company, Storm
Lake
Home State Bank
Kingsley State Bank
Libertyville Savings Bank
Solon State Bank
West Bancorporation, West Des Moines

Kansas:
Fort Riley National Bank

Midland Bank of Lenexa
Western State Bank, Garden City

KENTUCKY:
Area Bancshares Corporation, Owensboro
Bank of Ashland
Harrison Deposit Bank & Trust Company, Cynthiana
Kentucky Farms Bank, Catlettsburg
Peoples Bank of Bullitt County, Shepherdsville

LOUISIANA:
Bank of Montgomery
City Bank & Trust Company, New Orleans
Evangeline Bancshares, Ville Platte
First National Bank in Deridder
Jonesboro State Bank
Tri-State Bank & Trust Co, Kaplan

MAINE:
Camden National Corporation, Camden

MARYLAND:
Calvin B. Taylor Banking Corp., Berlin
Damascus Community Bank
*Mercantile Bankshares Corp, Baltimore
Middletown Valley Bank

MASSACHUSETTS:
Fidelity Management Trust Company, Boston

MICHIGAN:
Bank of Stephenson
Chelsea State Bank
Farwell State Savings Bank

MINNESOTA:
Dakota Company,Inc., Minneapolis
First National Bank of McIntosh
IDS Bank & Trust Company, Minneapolis
Marquette Bank, Mound

Marshall County State Bank, Newfolden
Northern State Bank of Thief River Falls

MISSISSIPPI:
Bank of Benoit
Bank of Okolona
Batesville Security Bank
First National Bank of Holmes County, Lexington
First National Bank of Pontotoc

MISSOURI:
Bank of Creighton
Bank of Fordland
Citizens Bank Oregon
Merchants & Planters Bank, Homersville
Midland Bancor, Inc., Kansas City

NEBRASKA:
Bank of St. Edward
First National Bank of Wisner
First National Bank of Shelby
The Lauritzen Corporation, Omaha
Mid-City Bank, Omaha
State Bank Palmer

NEW HAMPSHIRE:
First Deposit National Bank, Tilton

NEW JERSEY:
Bessemer Group, Inc., Woodbridge
Dreyfus Consumer Bank, Paramus

NEW YORK:
Bank of Holland
Canadian Imperial Bank of Commerce, New York

NORTH CAROLINA:
Avery State Bank, Newland
Bank of Granite Corporation, Granite Falls
First National Bank of Shelby

NORTH DAKOTA:
Scandia American Bank, Stanley

OHIO:
Farmers Savings Bank, Spencer
Monogram Bank USA, Symmes Township
*Provident Bancorp, Cincinnati
Saint Henry Bank
Security Banc Corporation, Springfield
Spirit of America National Bank, Milford
World Financial Network National Bank, Whitehall

OKLAHOMA:
Alva State Bank & Trust Company
First National Bank in Okeene
First National Bank of Konawa
First National Bank of Pryor
First State Bank, Harrah
Limestone National Bank, Sandy Springs
Locust Grove Bancshares, Inc.
Oklahoma State Bank, Ada
Republic Bank, Norman
Welch State Bank

OREGON:
Pacific Continental Bank, Eugene
Pioneer Trust Bank, NA, Salem

PENNSYLVANIA:
East Prospect State Bank
Financial Trust Corporation, Carlisle
New Tripoli National Bank
Peoples Bank of Unity, Pittsburgh

SOUTH CAROLINA:
Enterprise Bank of South Carolina, Ehrhardt

SOUTH DAKOTA:
Bank of Hoven
Belle Fourche Bancshares
Dial Bank, Sioux Falls
Hurley State Bank, Sioux Falls

TENNESSEE:
Bank of Cleveland
Citizens Bank & Trust Company of GRN, Rutledge
Citizens Bank, Carthage
Farmers Bank, Cornersville
First Pulaski National
Planters Bank, Maury City
Union Bank, Jamestown

TEXAS:
Citizens First Bank, Rusk
Citizens Bankers, Inc., Baytown
First National Bank in Munday
First National Bank in Pampa
First National Bank of Floydada
First National Bank of Henrietta
Muenster State Bank
Peoples National Bank, Pasadena
Peoples State Bank, Rocksprings
State Bank of La Vernia
Western National Bank, Odessa
Wilson State Bank

UTAH:
American Investment Bank, NA, Salt Lake City
American Investment Financial, Sandy
Barnes Banking Company, Kaysville
Brighton Bank, Salt Lake City
Fidelity US Depository Trust Company, Salt Lake City
Liberty Financial Corporation, Salt Lake City
Merrill Lynch National Financial, Salt Lake City
USAA Credit Card Bank, Salt Lake City
USAA Financial Services Association, Salt Lake City

VIRGINIA:
Bank of Southside Virginia Corp., Carson
Citizens & Farmers Bank, West Point

First & Citizens Bank, Monterey
First Naitonal Bank of Clifton Forge
Grundy National Bank

WASHINGTON:
Bank of Sumner
Cashmere Valley Bank
First Independent Investment Gr., Vancouver
Northwest Bancshares, Vancouver
Northwest Community Bank, Tacoma

WEST VIRGINIA:
First National Bank of Keystone

McDowell County National Bank, Welch

WISCONSIN:
Bank Alma
Citizens Bank, Delaven
First American Bank & Trust Company, Fort Atkinson
Whitewater Bancorp., Whitewater

WYOMING:
United Bancorporation of Wyoming, Jackson

APPENDIX FOUR

AREAS OF OPPORTUNITY

We BELIEVE that the exurbs, especially those with strong recreational attractions, will be growth areas in the 1990s. Demographers with higher claims to authority than we have spent years filtering through computer screens of various characteristics that point to economic growth in the future. Dr. Jack Lessinger, who proposed that "a fifth migration" (see chapter 14) could transform some rural areas of America in the 1990s, has singled out characteristics in his listing of areas of opportunity that favor lower-cost areas, with fewer cultural amenities and less-educated populations.

We have generally followed Dr. Lessinger's lead in identifying opportunity counties of the 1990s. But we also believe that some areas not singled out by Dr. Lessinger may be growth regions in the future. These are high-income rural counties with educated populations. Most add to significant recreational facilities the benefits of established educational or cultural institutions.

It may be that the events of the decade to come will reconcile these views. Perhaps both are in a way correct. Dr. Lessinger is primarily identifying regions that he believes will gain significantly in population. Our concern is to identify regions where life-style opportunities are most attractive and where more of the amenities of urban living can be found in areas of smaller population density. We believe that affluent tele-commuters would rather spend their time in Aspen, with its fine restaurants and music festival, than in a small town in Arkansas where the low income of most residents more or less rules out many of the amenities of living that attract the rich to big cities. People who cannot afford Aspen will move to Arkansas, or some similar spot. But in our view one should look at high-income rural areas as well as low-cost regions as areas of opportunity. Both share the common characteristic that they are much less ridden with crime and are more than a comfortable drive removed from big cities.

Counties that deserve special attention are those that meet Dr. Lessinger's population growth criteria and are also distinguished by high median household income, high household wealth, and a heavy concentration of adults with five or more years of college. They are:

COLORADO COUNTIES:
Hinsdale
Gunnison
San Miguel
Routt

MONTANA COUNTY:
Yellowstone National Park

WASHINGTON COUNTY:
San Juan

The following counties are also possible regions of opportunity. Those in italics are not highly rated by Dr. Lessinger, but do have characteristics that appeal to us. We believe that high-income exurbs are less likely to fall victim to the surge in crime rates that often accompanies rapid growth. Nonetheless, it is also true that some of the lower-cost exurbs, such as those in Arkansas, begin with lower crime rates. The crime index for each state as of 1988 is also included. The average figure for the United States as a whole was $5,550.

ARKANSAS COUNTIES: Crime Index
Carroll (State
Cleburne Average)
Franklin $4,200
Fulton
Grant
Hempstead
Izard
Johnson
Little River
Lonoke
Marion
Montgomery
Newton
Perry
Polk
Randolph
Sevier
Sharp
Stone
Van Buren

CALIFORNIA COUNTIES: $6,636
Alpine
Sierra

COLORADO COUNTIES: $6,178
Archuleta
Custer

Eagle
Elbert
La Plata
Ouray
Park
Pitkin
Summit
Teller

FLORIDA COUNTIES: $8,938
Gilchrist
Holmes
Jefferson
Lafayette
Liberty
Suwannee
Washington

GEORGIA COUNTIES: $6,327
Banks
Ben Hill
Brantley
Butts
Crawford
Dawson
Harris
Heard
Jasper
Lee
Long

GEORGIA COUNTIES: $6,327
(cont.)
Madison
Monroe
Murray
Oconee
Pierce
Pike
Putnam
Union
Worth

IDAHO COUNTIES: $3,973
Benewah
Boise
Fremont
Teton

ILLINOIS COUNTIES: $5,621
Johnson
Menard

INDIANA COUNTIES: $4,150
Crawford
Monroe
Ohio
Owen

IOWA COUNTIES: $4,077
Johnson
Story

KANSAS COUNTIES: $4,880
Coffey
Douglas
Jefferson
Pottawatonie

KENTUCKY COUNTIES: $3,135
Anderson
Carter
Grant

Grayson
Johnson
Knox
Lawrence
Letcher
Livingston
Magoffin
McCreary
Menifee
Russell
Shelby
Whitley

LOUISIANA COUNTIES: $5,761
Grant
Sabine

MARYLAND COUNTIES: $5,705
Garrett
Kent
Talbot

MASSACHUSETTS COUN- $4,991
TIES:
Berkshire
Nantucket

MICHIGAN COUNTIES: $6,084
Antrim
Kalkaska
Missaukee
Osceola

MISSISSIPPI COUNTIES: $3,593
Claiborne
Madison
Marshall
Tishomingo

MISSOURI COUNTIES: $4,845
Barry
Benton

Boone
Carter
Cedar
Christian
Clinton
Dent
Douglas
Hickory
Madison
Miller
Morgan
Ozark
Polk
Ray
Ripley
Stone
Warren
Wayne
Webster

MONTANA COUNTIES: $4,267
Broadwater
Jefferson
Rosebud

NEBRASKA COUNTY: $4,140
Box Butte

NEVADA COUNTIES: $6,606
Eureka
Lincoln
Storey

NEW HAMPSHIRE $3,334
COUNTIES:
Carroll
Grafton
Rockingham
Stratford

NEW MEXICO COUNTIES: $6,606

Catron
Los Alamos
Socorro
Torrance

NEW YORK COUNTIES: $6,327
Greene
Saratoga
Tompkins

NORTH CAROLINA $4,862
COUNTY:
Currituck

NORTH DAKOTA $2,728
COUNTIES:
Mercer
Morton

OREGON COUNTIES: $7,059
Benton
Morrow

SOUTH CAROLINA $5,412
COUNTIES:
Beaufort
Jasper

SOUTH DAKOTA $2,581
COUNTY:
Custer

TENNESSEE COUNTIES: $4,469
Cannon
Claiborne
De Kalb
Hickman
Lauderdale
Macon
Meigs
Moore
Union

TEXAS COUNTIES:	$8,018
Anderson	
Archer	
Austin	
Bandera	
Bastrop	
Bosque	
Brazos	
Burleson	
Callahan	
Cass	
Ellis	
Erath	
Franklin	
Freestone	
Hartley	
Hemphill	
Henderson	
Hood	
Hopkins	
Houston	
Irion	
Lee	
Live Oak	
Madison	
Panola	
Polk	
Real	
Roberts	
Rockwell	
Sabine	
San Jacinto	
Schleicher	
Somervell	
Trinity	
Van Zandt	
Williamson	
Wilson	
Wise	
Wood	
Young	

UTAH COUNTIES:	$5,579
Duchesne	
Emery	
Juab	
Kane	
Millard	
Rich	
Sanpete	
Sevier	
Summit	
Wasatch	
Wayne	

VERMONT COUNTY:	$4,241
Grand Isle	

VIRGINIA COUNTIES:	$4,177
Albemarle	
Bedford	
Caroline	
Cumberland	
Essex	
Fluvanna	
Greene	
King William	
Lancaster	
Lee	
Louisa	
Middlesex	
Shenandoah	

WASHINGTON COUNTIES:	$7,113
Ferry	
Pend Oreille	
Stevens	

WEST VIRGINIA COUNTY:	$2,239
Hampshire	

WISCONSIN COUNTIES:	$3,967
Burnett	
Florence	

Marquette   WYOMING COUNTIES: $3,967
Waushara   Converse
                                   Lincoln
                                   Platte
                                   Teton
                                   Uinta

For further information on Dr. Jack Lessinger's current forecasts, contact him at his real estate consultancy: 17004 26th Avenue, N.E., Seattle, Washington 98155.

We also believe that the following micropolitan communities merit attention as areas where the quality of life is high and likely to improve in the 1990s:

Ames, IA   Kingston, NY
Bend, OR   Laconia, NH
Bozeman, MT   Laguna Niguel, CA
Carson City, NV   Logan, UT
Coeur d'Alene, ID   Manhattan, KS
Corvallis, OR   Marshalltown, IA
Fairbanks, AK   Missoula, MT
Flagstaff, AZ   Muscatine, IA
Fredericksburg, VA   Newport, RI
Grand Junction, CO   Pocatello, ID
Helena, MT   Pullman, WA
Hilton Head, SC   Rock Springs, WY
Idaho Falls, ID   San Luis Obispo, CA
Ithaca, NY   Stillwater, OK
Keene, NH   Traverse City, MI
Key West, FL   Vero Beach, FL

APPENDIX FIVE

PURCHASING DISTRESSED PROPERTIES

THERE ARE always distress sales and property auctions in even the best of times. Under bullish circumstances, however, there are fewer bargains to be had, and those that are available are so much work to uncover that the time they take probably offsets the profit potential they provide. But the situation can be far different in a slump.

As asset values fall in a highly politicized economy, protracted efforts are made to avoid allowing the normal market channels to reflect the fall in prices. Prices for homes, office buildings, hotels, and other properties tend to decline slowly while the credit crunch pushes greater numbers of marginal borrowers into default. This means that there are often great deals to be had in distress sales, liquidations, and auctions. Especially from the government.

Unlike private liquidators, who generally have a strong incentive to realize the greatest possible value from the properties they dispose of, government liquidators have little or no personal incentive. As a consequence, they are often slow to dispose of properties, and those they do sell are seldom well advertised.

WHAT PRICE?

The growing insolvency of S & Ls and banks has created growing opportunities to purchase assets from the Resolution Trust Corporation and other government agencies. It is quite unlikely that real estate prices will bottom before the government has disposed of its vast property inventories. But rather than trying to call the bottom, let the price you will pay be governed by cash flow considerations. Make sure that any property you purchase is priced low enough to provide positive cash flow at a yield that is higher than can be obtained in relatively risk-free Treasury debt instruments. Don't count on appreciation. There may not be any.

Beware of Liens

Remember when you purchase properties at auction or directly from distressed sellers to beware of hidden legal claims. These are more likely to be a problem when purchasing from an agency like the IRS rather than the RTC. But satisfy yourself in any sale that your title is clear of claims that could prevent your realizing value from the property.

Go to the Bank

In looking for distressed property in the United States, begin at the level of the bank. For a fee of $25, IDC Financial can provide you with the names of banks in your area with high mortgage delinquencies and faltering real estate portfolios. Once you identify banks and S & Ls with property to dispose of, contact the "Real Estate Owned" sections of these banks, indicating that you might be willing to purchase a distressed property. For various reasons, the banks are sometimes willing to sell repossessed properties at concessional prices. They may even provide financing.

FREDDIE MAC, FANNIE MAE

Many private home mortgages are sold to Freddie Mac (Federal Home Loan Mortgage Association) and Fannie Mae (Federal National Mortgage Association), quasi-government corporations created to provide financing to the home market. Consequently, both these agencies often come into possession of properties when the home buyer defaults. Fannie Mae seldom sells directly to the public in good times. But its properties are sometimes auctioned. And as the real estate depression deepens, more aggressive discounting is likely.

Fannie Mae offers a free brochure, *How to Buy a Foreclosed Home*. It is available upon request at (202) 752-6527. Fannie Mae will send you a listing of its properties for sale in your area. Call (800) 553-4636.

Freddie Mac is not a forthcoming seller, and does little to help retail buyers purchase at a discount. That may change in time.

THE FDIC

According to well-informed sources in Washington, the FDIC still holds some properties taken over from banks that failed in the 1930s. As this suggests, historically the FDIC has not been a good place to pick up bargains because the FDIC has had a policy of holding assets until their nominal prices recovered to match the FDIC's original liability. When you consider that, at 5 percent interest, the present worth of one dollar forty-five years from now is just about ten cents, you can see how unprofitable the FDIC's policy of holding assets has been. It totally ignores the basic economic fact that a dollar many years from now is worth less than a dollar in hand. If the FDIC accounted for the present value of money, as it may have to do as money becomes scarcer in the 1990s, it would most probably loosen its grip on repossessed properties and auction them in lots accessible to small buyers. For information on current FDIC dispositions, contact FDIC, Liquidation Division, 550 17th Street, N.W., Washington, D.C. 20429. Phone (202) 393-8400.

RESOLUTION TRUST CORPORATION

The RTC was the largest landlord in the United States as 1990 ended. In its early operations it hoarded properties. It might better have been known as the Irresolution Trust Corporation. But eventually, it will be obliged to dispose of real estate holdings, which include many parcels of raw land, as well as office buildings, hotels, multi-family dwellings, and private homes.

As of this writing, we cannot confidently explain the best way for you to find out precisely what properties the RTC has to sell. We recommend that you contact the main operator at RTC headquarters for an explanation of the various forms in which you can access their list of properties. They may be offering printouts in your area. Or you may be obliged to subscribe to books or even an on-line data service.

OTHER DISTRESS SELLERS

An alphabet soup of other government agencies is also required to dispose of seized or repossessed properties. In many locales, the sheriff or marshal holds auctions. Contact the local courthouse.

The Department of Veterans Affairs has an inventory of tens of thousands of re-possessed homes. To get on the VA mailing list directly, you may have to be a registered real estate broker. But contact the Property Management Division of your local VA office for the latest details.

The Department of Housing and Urban Development also has tens of thousands of properties in default for disposal. They are mostly low-quality structures in blue-collar neighborhoods. But they could be interesting investments as rental properties for the right buyer. There are HUD field offices in many larger cities. Check the white pages of the telephone book, or contact HUD's Property Disposition Branch in Washington at (202) 708-4592.

The Small Business Administration is famous for financing small businesses that fail. Many die with real assets that can be purchased at auction. SBA auctions are generally run by the same private auction firms in each locale. Contact your local SBA office and ask for the list of their auctioneers. If they are not forthcoming, check under "Auctioneers" in the yellow pages and ask the local auctioneers whether they handle SBA auctions. Those that do not will know which of their competitors do.

The Internal Revenue Service and local tax collectors also auction property. Contact the Tax Sales Division at the County Court House, Sheriff's Department, Assessor's Office, or Treasury. The IRS maintains an Auction Hotline telephone number: (800) 424-1040. When you call that number they will give you a list of properties for sale in your state.

U.S. Marshals' offices sometimes conduct their own auctions. Sometimes they hire private auctioneers. Sometimes they turn to the General Services Administration. Usually, auctions are announced in classified advertisements for several days prior to an auction. Watch the newspapers in your area for U.S. Marshals' auctions and ask to be placed on the mailing list to be notified in the future.

As the credit cycle draws to an end, a much greater supply of distressed properties will have to be moved. Do not be too keen to buy properties for investment unless they offer attractive returns on a cash basis. If the slump of the 1990s reaches the extreme that is possible, you may be able to obtain assets for pennies on the dollar.

PHYSICAL PROTECTION

THE GROWING threat to physical safety from common criminals, looters—or "non-traditional shoppers," as they might prefer to be known—and terrorists calls for a response on many levels. If you cannot make yourself and your business a less attractive target of violence, it is possible that high technology may offer you a shield. New forms of composites make it possible to replace ordinary window glass in offices, shops, and even automobiles with clear substitutes that are shatterproof or even bulletproof and bombproof. Just as the breakdown of order in agricultural society led to more widespread adoption of metal armor, the breakdown of order during the information age makes the products of ArmorVision Plastics and Glass more useful than we wish they were.

This patented new glass has been tested by independent laboratories in the U.S., Israel, Spain, Hungary, and Venezuela. The President of Venezuela has adopted it for bulletproofing his automobile. The glass is bulletproof when fired on from the outside, yet occupants of the vehicle, the president's bodyguards, can shoot through the glass in the other direction. It is one-way bulletproof glass.

Any automobile can be outfitted with this new technology, and made bulletproof, with a weight increase of less than 200 pounds. The same material can be used in store windows for protection against rioters. ArmorVision also makes additional equipment to discourage carjackings. For more details, contact ArmorVision Plastics & Glass, Suite 500, 6310 San Vicente Boulevard, Los Angeles, California 90048; phone (213) 935-6222 fax: (213) 930-1362.

Still another effective high-tech discouragement to auto theft is the Vecta engine immobilizer, now in use in England. It cannot be bypassed by thieves. Direct Vecta inquiries to: Liftsonic Ltd, P.O. Box 737, Chelmsford, Essex, England CM1 3ST.

APPENDIX SEVEN

ACTION FOR POLITICAL REFORM

OUR HOPE is that, as you prepare yourself and your family for the Great Reckoning, you will take time out to be a useful citizen. Thomas Jefferson wrote that one is never permitted to "despair of the commonwealth." We agree. If you would like to do so, you can contribute to a constructive resolution of the economic and financial problems of the United States.

The *National Taxpayers Union* works to achieve much-needed economies in government, balance the budget, and reform government finances at all levels. NTU can help you support movements for economy at the state and local level. It is working for constitutional reform of the budget process and limitations on congressional terms. Contact the National Taxpayers Union at 711 Maryland Avenue, N.E., Washington, D.C. 20002. Phone: (800) TAX HALT.

The *American Alliance for Rights and Responsibilities* was founded by James Moorman, former assistant U.S. attorney general and executive director of the Sierra Club Legal Defense Fund. The AARR is working to help residents of crime-ridden neighborhoods reclaim their communities from thugs. Many effective crime prevention measures have been disallowed by court challenges based upon exaggerated sensitivity to the rights of criminals. For example, merely requiring identification of persons loitering in high-crime neighborhoods significantly improves the safety of the streets. But courts have prohibited such protective measures under prodding by groups such as the American Civil Liberties Union. The *American Alliance for Rights and Responsibilities* works to redress the imbalance in the American system in favor of protecting the lives and property of peaceful citizens. Your contributions will help support this important work. Contact the *American Alliance for Rights and Responsibilities*, 1725 17th Street, N.W., Suite 1112, Washington, D.C. 20006.

Citizens for Legal Reform, works to change the American rule that gives lawyers in the United States feasting rights on the society at large. CLF can be reached at 325 Pennsylvania Avenue, S.E., Washington, D.C. 20003.

STRATEGIC INVESTMENT AND OTHER SERVICES FROM JAMES DALE DAVIDSON AND LORD REES-MOGG

IF YOU enjoyed this book, you may enjoy reading *Strategic Investment*, the private financial advisory service edited by James Dale Davidson and Lord Rees-Mogg.

The track record of the specific recommendations has been superlative. Steve Newby, who picks *Strategic Investment*'s Undiscovered Values, was a three-time winner of the *USA Today*/Financial News Network Investment Challenge in 1990 and 1991. He turned $500,000 into $1,498,763 in just twelve weeks. *Strategic Investment* also offers monthly advice about ways to profit from geopolitical developments.

Time after time, *Strategic Investment* has scooped the world in forecasting headlines before they occurred. In its very first issue in 1984, *Strategic Investment* pinpointed a little-known member of the Soviet Politburo—Mikhail Gorbachev. Before Gorbachev had even assumed power, *Strategic Investment* sought an interview with him, and forecast that he and his wife would become international celebrities, pull back Soviet troops from around the globe, and seek cooperation with the West, rather than confrontation.

Strategic Investment analyzed the pending fall of the Berlin Wall in February 1989, ten months before the bulldozers actually started their work. Years before the banking crisis, the S & L bankruptcies, and the real estate bust became news, *Strategic Investment* told readers what to expect. Among other *Strategic Investment* bull's-eyes: the collapse of oil prices in 1986, the 1987 stock market plunge, the meltdown in Tokyo (the Nikkei Dow put warrants we recommended gained 324%), the rapid rout of Iraq in the 1991 Persian Gulf War, and the death of the Soviet Union.

A six-month trial subscription in the United States is available for just $60 (in Canada and elsewhere—US$75). Send your order to *Strategic Investment*, P.O. Box 2291, Washington, D.C. 20013-2291. *Strategic Investment* contributing editor Steve Newby is a principal of Newby & Company. He can be reached at 6116 Executive Blvd., Suite 701, Rockville, Maryland 20852.

Davidson and Rees-Mogg have launched a new service to report on investment opportunities in the new emerging area of growth, Southern China and nearby regions of the Pacific rim. A six-month trial subscription to *Asian Growth Report* is available for $60 from *Asian Growth Report*, P.O. Box 2291, Washington, D.C. 20013-2291.

If you are interested in information on operating a business from home, *Home, Inc.* is a monthly newsletter with many practical tips. An introductory one-year subscription is available for $29 from *Home, Inc.*, P.O. Box 2291, Washington, D.C. 20013-2291.

James Dale Davidson and Lord Rees-Mogg also offer private consultation to corporations and individuals and are principals in a money-management firm specializing in hedging and capital preservation. For more details, contact Davidson and Rees-Mogg at P.O. Box 2291, Washington, D.C. 20013-2291, or 17 Pall Mall, London, England SW1Y 5NB.

NOTES ON SOURCES

Introduction: Beyond the Postwar World

The comment on weapons systems and social change is from Robert O'Connell, *Of Arms and Men: A History of War, Weapons, and Aggression*, Oxford: Oxford University Press, 1989, p. 10. The details about economic developments from the 1930s are from the *Wall Street Journal*, April through August 1930. For example, "Continued Easy Credit Likely," and "Home Building Gains Foreseen," May 2, 1930; "President Cites Recovery Made," May 3, 1930; "Motor Output Trend Upward," May 8, 1930; "Branch Banking Gaining Favor," May 14, 1930; "Early Business Recovery Seen," May 20, 1930; "1930 Rail Slump and Other Days: How Recession Compares with 1921, 1908, 1894—Duration of Recessions," June 14, 1930; "Finds Outlook Better: Harvard Economic Society Says Factors Favoring Recovery Present," July 1, 1930; "Industry Grows More Hopeful: Stocks Reflect Increasing Optimism with Regard to Autumn Business Prospects," July 21, 1930; "Credit Shows Rapid Expansion: In Past Has Heralded Business Recovery—Reserve Policy Aid to Easy Money," August 1, 1930. The article on the failure of forecasting in the 1930s was "Forecasting the Depression: Harvard Versus Yale," by Kathryn M. Dominguez, Ray C. Fair, and Matthew D. Shapiro, *American Economic Review*, September 1988, pp. 595–612. The quote on the failure of the interest rate cut to significantly improve consumer confidence is from Richard Evans, "Company Collapses Reach Their Highest Level Since Recession Began: Businesses Fail at Rate of 76 a Day," *Financial Times*, November 7/8, 1992, p. 26. The quote on Japan's newly independent foreign policy is from Lewis M. Simons, "Japan to Resume Aid to Vietnam," *The Journal of Commerce*, November 9, 1992, p. A2. For more on the saturation of markets see Cesare Marchetti, "The Future," International Institute for Applied Systems Analysis, Laxenburg, Austria. Winston Churchill's comment on the occasional futility of "weak, well-meaning legislatures" is from Sir Winston Churchill, *The Second World War*, Vol. 1, *The Gathering Storm*, Boston: Houghton Mifflin, 1948, p. 190. General Dudayev's threat to bomb Russian nuclear facilities was reported in "Russian Troops at Border of Breakaway Region," *Miami Herald,* November 11, 1992, p. 8A. The comments on the use of "omen texts" and chronologies in Babylon and China to forecast events come from Donald E. Brown, *Hierarchy, History & Human Nature,* Tucson: University of Arizona Press, 1988, p. 130. Our source for comments about traders spreading arithmetic come from Frank J. Swetz, *Capitalism & Arithmetic,* La Salle, Illinois; Open Court, 1987. The argument that written language began as an answer to inventory problems in ancient agricultural societies is from Roy Harris, *The Origins of Language,* La Salle, Illinois: Open Court, 1986. Fen Kun is quoted by Robert M. Hartwell, "Historical Analogism, Public Policy, and Social Science in Eleventh- and Twelfth-Century China," *The American Historical Review,* Volume 76, Number 2, April 1971, pp. 691–92. Ralph Waldo Emerson is quoted from the essay "On Compensation," Ralph Waldo Emerson, *The Works of Ralph Waldo Emerson,* Volume I, New York: Bigelow, Brown and Co., 1924, pp. 64 and 75. Sir Martin Jacomb is quoted from "Megapolitics and the Market: A Message for Troubled Times," *The Daily Telegraph,* October 21, 1987, p. 16.

Chapter 1: The Megapolitics of Progress and Decline

An example of the tabloid treatment of the robbery of the Best Food Market can be found in "Holdup Victim Tricks Bandit into Selling His Guns: . . . Then Forces Thief to Flee Empty-Handed," *National Enquirer,* May 15, 1990, p. 8. Playfair's comment on power is quoted from William Playfair, *An Inquiry into the Permanent Causes of the Decline and Fall of Powerful and Wealthy Nations: Designed to Show How the Prosperity of the British Empire May Be Prolonged,* London: Greenland and Norris, 1805, p. 70. Jack Hirshleifer's comments on nonconstitutional politics and the "raw politics of power and conflict" come from "Toward a More General Theory of Regulation: Comment," *Economic Behavior in Adversity,* Chicago: University of Chicago Press, 1987, pp. 168 and 164. Our source for the estimate of the Stone Age population of France is Marvin Harris, *Cannibals and Kings,* New York: Vintage, 1978, p. 18. Details about migration and its consequences in the primeval economy come from Stephen Boyden, *Western Civilization in Biological Perspective: Patterns in Biohistory,* Oxford: Oxford University Press, 1987, p. 75. The authority for the conclusion that hunters and gatherers "neither collected nor maintained" food surpluses is Susan Allen Gregg, *Foragers and Farmers: Population Interaction and Agricultural Expansion in Prehistoric Europe,* Chicago: University of Chicago Press, 1988, p. 23. Boyden is the authority for the assertion that hunter-gatherer societies devote little time to collecting food, *op. cit.,* p. 69; he is also the source of details about dispute settlement, p. 63. Our source for the role of global warming in precipitating the shift to agriculture is Harris, *Cannibals and Kings,* pp. 29– 32. The dating of the transition to farming at 400 generations ago is from Boyden, *op. cit.,* p. 13. Boyden is also the source of details on the productivity of rice farming in China, *op. cit.,* p. 63. The logic of pillage is explored by Mancur Olson, *Anarchy, Autocracy, and Democracy,* forthcoming. Our authorities for the maxim that "the Treasury is the root of kings" are Carolyn Webber and Aaron Wildavsky, *A History of Taxation and Expenditure in the Western World,* New York: Simon and Schuster, 1986,

p. 38. For evidence of the importance of microbes in conquest of North and South America by European invaders, see William McNeill, *Plagues and Peoples*, Oxford: Basil Blackwell, 1976, p. 69. McNeill's comments about religion are from William McNeill, *The Rise of the West: A History of the Human Community*, Chicago: University of Chicago Press, 1963, p. 152. The quote on the logic of monotheism is from the same source, p. 162. Our authority for comments on written language is Roy Harris, *The Origin of Writing*, La Salle, Illinois: Open Court, 1986, pp. 144–45. The quote on the death of Pueblo Indian civilizations is from Iben Browning and Evelyn M. Garriss, *Past and Future History*, Burlington, Vermont: Fraser Publishing Company, p. 117. The quote on the scale of societies in Africa is from Basil Davidson, *Africa in History*, Revised Edition, New York: Collier Books, 1974, p. 59. Comments about the destitution of Africa in the early modern period are quoted from Thomas Robert Malthus, *Principle of Population*, 1802, *Works of Thomas Robert Malthus*, Volume 2, ed. E. A. Wrigley and David Souden, London: William Pickering, 1986, p. 89. The same source testifies to the high proportions of slaves in native African societies, p. 90. The logic of hydraulic societies is spelled out in Karl A. Wittfogel, *Oriental Despotism: A Comparative Study of Total Power*, New Haven: Yale University Press, 1957. The tendency toward a more closed and stratified system in Egypt is documented by Brown, *Hierarchy, History & Human Nature*, p. 127. Details on the relative cost of transportation in the ancient world are from Perry Anderson, *Passages from Antiquity to Feudalism*, London: Verso, 1974, p. 20. The relationship betwen wine and olive farming and the capacity of Greek yeomen to bear arms is noted by McNeill, *The Rise of the West, op cit.*, p. 201. The same work is the source for argument about the logic of the phalanx making equality between the hoplites an essential ingredient of classic Greek culture, p. 199. The source for high number of slaves in ancient Greece and exclusivity of freedom there is Anderson, *op. cit.*, p. 38. Details about the megapolitics of Roman society are also from Anderson, p. 60. He is the authority for the claim that three out of seven persons in Italy were slaves, p. 62, as well as the observation that Clodius contributed to free bread distribution by arming the Roman poor, p. 69. Charles Martel's shift toward heavy cavalry is described by O'Connell, *Of Arms and Men*, p. 87. That is also our source for information about the Edict of Pitres, p. 88. Philippe Contamine describes how the *ordo equestris* was indistinguishable in tenth-century France from the *ordo militaris*. The "scorned" mass of peasantry were the *imbelle* or *inerme vulgus* (unarmed); Philippe Contamine, *War in the Middle Ages*, translated by Michael Jones, Oxford: Basil Blackwell, 1984, p. 31. McNeill's comments about the logic of feudalism as an expression of weapons technology are from McNeill, *The Pursuit of Power*, Chicago: University of Chicago Press, 1982, p. 20. Carroll Quigley's comment on the arrival of the Dark Ages is from *Weapons Systems and Political Stability*, Washington: University Press of America, 1983, pp. 830–31. Our authority for details about Viking settlements on Greenland and subsequent attempts to settle North America is Alfred W. Crosby, *Ecological Imperialism: The Biological Expansion of Europe, 900–1900*, Cambridge: Cambridge University Press, 1986, pp. 41–50. For a profound discussion of the logic of money and its revival see Alexander Murray, *Reason and Society in the Middle Ages*, Oxford: The Clarendon Press, 1978, pp. 50–69. Murray is also the authority behind the quoted comment that economic revival around the year 1000 allowed the Jews "to become Europe's first *nouveaux riches*," p. 69. Playfair's quote about wealth is from *Decline and Fall*, p. 72. His comment about commerce and chivalry is from p. 63. Comments on topography are from Anderson, *op. cit.*, pp. 166, 180. Anderson is also the source for details about Flemish peasants being reduced to serfdom in Poland, p. 242. For an insightful, early recognition of the combined impact of gunpowder, the printing press, and the magnetic compass, see William Playfair, *op. cit.* Details about King Charles VIII's new cannon are from McNeill, *Pursuit of Power*, p. 89. Guicciardini's comments on the impact of new gunpowder weapons on society are quoted by Geoffrey Parker, *The Military Revolution: Military Innovation and the Rise of the West, 1500–1800*, Cambridge: Cambridge University Press, 1988, p. 10. The consequence of small arms in shifting the scale of battle in favor of larger political entities comes from Parker, p. 1. For details about the growth in scale of European states see Charles Tilly, "Reflections on the History of European State-Making," in Tilly, ed., *The Formation of National States in Western Europe*, Princeton: Princeton University Press, 1975, and Parker, *op. cit.*, p. 5. Playfair's comment on the impact of gunpowder in shifting the advantage in conflict toward the rich is from *Decline and Fall*, p. 4. His quote on the work of gunpowder in "doing away the illusions of knight-errantry" is from p. 73. Figures on per capita consumption of beer in seventeenth-century England are from Keith Thomas, *Religion and the Decline of Magic*, London: Penguin, 1978, p. 23. Munzter is quoted by Robert Blakely, *The History of Political Literature*, Volume II, London: Richard Bentley, 1855, pp. 295–96. Details about Munzter's defeat are from the same source.

Chapter 2: The Information Revolution

Richard Feynman's comments on "the possibility of maneuvering things atom by atom" is quoted from *Blood in the Streets*, New York: Summit Books, 1987, p. 264 and references. Authority for the view that serious scientists believe that nanotechnology will make self-replicating molecular "machines" practical within decades comes from Jeffrey C. MacGillvray, "The Economics of Rapidly Changing Technology," *Foresight*, No. 7, p. 5. MacGillvray's comment on future labor is from the same source. Eric Drexler's observations about the potential for molecular technology to "lobotomize, or otherwise modify entire populations" come from *Engines of Creation*, New York: Anchor Press/Doubleday, 1986, p. 176. Playfair's comments on the relativity of power are from *Decline and Fall*, pp. 7–8. The example of Chinese anarchy was suggested by Mancur Olson, *Anarchy, Autocracy, and Democracy*, forthcoming. Details of the brigand armies are from Paul Johnson, *Modern Times: The World from the Twenties to the Eighties*, New York: Harper & Row, 1983, p. 200. The official report is also quoted from *Modern Times*, as are the further details, p. 201. The incentives governments have to let citizens prosper so they can collect more taxes are explored in James Dale Davidson, "The Limits of Constitutional Determinism," in *Constitutional Economics*, ed. Richard B. McKenzie, Lexington, Mass.: Lexington Books, 1984, pp. 61–89. Also see Mancur Olson, *Anarchy, Autocracy, and Democracy*, forthcoming. Data on proportions of the work force doing mental work and physical labor are from Norman Macrae, "The Next Ages of Man," *Economist,* December 24, 1988, survey page 8. The quote from Ted Robert Gurr is taken from "The History of Violent Crime in America: An Overview," in Ted Robert Gurr, ed., *Violence in America,* Volume I, Newbury Park, Cal.: Sage Publications, 1989, p. 12. The quotes from Nathan Rosenberg and L. E. Birdzell are from *How the West Grew Rich,* New York: Basic Books, p. 113. The comment on "a stable government that reliably provides law and order" is from Mancur Olson, "Diseconomies of Scale and Development," *Cato Journal,* Volume 7, Number 1, 1987, p. 82. The economic logic of skilled personnel in Third World countries is also spelled out in the same article, p. 80. Details of the drop of overall consumption in Latin America come from Eugene Robinson, "Third World Comes to Argentina: Poverty Is Spreading in Proud Buenos Aires," *Washington Post,* October 21, 1990, pp. A25, A29. Raymond W. Goldsmith's work on the balance sheets of leading countries over recent centuries is from *Comparative National Balance Sheets: A Study of Twenty Countries, 1688–1978,* Chicago: University of Chicago Press, 1985, pp. 45, 232–41, and *passim.* Evidence on the ineffectiveness of public law enforcement is from Richard Neely, "Law and Order—Do It Yourself: The Police Can't Stop Crime, So That Leaves It Up to Us," *Washington Post,* October 21, 1990, p. C1.

Chapter 3: America Follows in Britain's Footsteps

The quote from Adam Ferguson about "an epidemical weakness of the head" is from *An Essay on the History of Civil Society,* Dublin: Boulter Grierson, 1767, p. 356. His observations about the moral atmosphere of a society heading for a fall are from p. 357. Pete Hamill's description of a "barbarized city" is from Pete Hamill, "City of the Damned: A Baby Fed to a Dog? So What? Welcome to New York," *Esquire,* December 1990, p. 61. Winston Churchill's "many itching fingers" comment is from Paul Johnson, *Modern Times, op. cit.,* p. 347. Details about Britain's fickle intelligentsia are also from *Modern Times,* pp. 348–49. "This is a 'RED FLAG' phrase today" is quoted from John Taylor, "Are You Politically Correct?" *New York,* January 21, 1991, p. 35, as are further details of political correctness on American campuses, including Catherine Stimpson's denunciation of "objectivity and intellectual rigor." Details about the female Argentine turned down for a professorship of Latin American literature because she had Italian and Jewish ancestors are from page 37. The quote about the West being "conspicuously richer and more powerful than the rest of the world" is from Nathan Rosenberg and L. E. Birdzell, Jr., "Science, Technology and the Western Miracle," *Scientific American,* November 1990, p. 42. The attack on the great books is quoted from Taylor, *op cit.,* p. 36. The quote beginning "an ostensible concern for humanity" is from Paul Johnson, *Modern Times, op. cit.,* p. 349. Details about the deficit consuming total individual income tax revenues from everyone living west of the Mississippi River come from Richard Lamm, "The Rise and Fall of American Civilization," unpublished monograph, 1988, p. 3. Jan de Vries's comments are from *The Economy of Europe in an Age of Crisis, 1600–1750,* Cambridge: Cambridge University Press, 1976, p. 123. The quote from the *Financial Times* is from the issue of February

2, 1989, p. 14. The comment about a "lamentable want of energy and enterprise" is from Correlli Barnett, *The Audit of War*, London: Macmillan, 1988, p. 56. For an interpretation of the 1973 oil shock as a follow-on effect to the decline of American power, see *Blood in the Streets*, chapter 3. Details on the composition of American trade with Japan are from Lamm, *op. cit.*, p. 4. The *Wall Street Journal* editorial on tort lawyers appeared September 21, 1990, p. A14. Details about the inefficiency of the American legal system are from James Dale Davidson, *The Squeeze*, New York: Summit Books, 1980, pp. 226–28. The quote indicating contempt for the courts is from "The Children of the Courts," *Insight*, July 30, 1990, p. 9. For evidence that crime pays, see Davidson, *The Squeeze*, p. 242. The breakdown of the criminal justice system in Los Angeles is detailed by David Freed, "L.A. System of Justice on Overload," *Los Angeles Times*, Sunday, December 16, 1990. The account of the minimal punishment faced by Calvin W. Edwards for his seventeenth conviction is from David Freed, "Crime—A Matter of Priorities," *Los Angeles Times*, Monday, December 17, 1990. The authority for limited time spent by police officers patrolling against crime is from Richard Neely, "Law and Order—Do It Yourself," *op. cit.*, p. C4. The information and quote about the mugging in the North Bronx are from Roger Lane, "On the Social Meaning of Homicide Trends in America," in Gurr, p. 55. The information on the number of cars stolen per auto theft conviction and the number of prison days spent per theft is from Morgan O. Reynolds, "Crime Pays, But So Does Imprisonment," National Center for Policy Analysis, Dallas, Texas, March 1990, p. 2. The Correlli Barnett quote is from *The Audit of War*, p. 99. Playfair's comment on education can be found in *Decline and Fall*, pp. 297, 84–85, 90–91. The Carnegie Trust inquiry of 1937–39 is reported by Barnett, *op. cit.*, p. 198. The *Economist*'s characterization of the McKinsey study appeared February 19, 1990, p. 68. The comparative number of scientists and engineers in leading countries is from "Snapshot of the Seven," *Wall Street Journal*, July 7, 1991. Details about the Convenanter tank come from Barnett, *op. cit.*, p. 162. Cost estimates for procurement of twenty-five major weapons systems come from J. Peter Grace, *Burning Money*, New York: Macmillan, 1984, p. 188. The assembly line defects are detailed by Lamm, *op. cit.*, p. 4. The positive comments about American economic prospects are from Joseph S. Nye, Jr., "The Misleading Metaphor of Decline," *Atlantic*, March 1990, pp. 86–94. Professor Charles Hulten's comments about decline as a statistical illusion are from Charles R. Hulten, "Is the U.S. Economy in Decline?" *The American Enterprise*, May/June 1990, p. 62. The decline of real weekly earnings is detailed in "Running to Stand Still," *Economist*, November 10, 1990, p. 19. The quote is from p. 22. The comment about the relative unimportance of earning additional wealth is from Herbert Stein, "The U.S. Economy: A Visitor's Guide," *The American Enterprise*, July/August 1990, p. 7. The information on the comparative costs of Heimlich's experimental cancer therapy are from a speech by Dr. Henry Heimlich, The Eris Society, Aspen, Colorado, August 5, 1992. The figures on the depth and duration of Britain's downturn in the 1930s are from Tim Congdon; "Look at the Figures: It's Just as Bad as the 1930s," *Daily Telegraph*, July 30, 1992. Keynes's boast about English wealth in the 1930s is from Joseph S. Davis, *The World Between the Wars, 1919–1939*, Baltimore: The Johns Hopkins University Press, 1975. p. 254. The quote from Playfair about history repeating itself is from *Decline and Fall*, p. xiv. The murder rate in Dodge City in 1871 is reported in Roger D. McGrath, "Violence and Lawlessness on the Western Frontier," in Gurr, *Violence in America, op. cit.*, p. 134.

Chapter 4: Japan Follows in America's Footsteps

The plot of "Silent Fleet" is reported by Alan Murray and Urban C. Lehner, "U.S., Japan Struggle to Redefine Relations as Resentment Grows," *Wall Street Journal*, June 13, 1990, p. A1. Professor Kamiya's comments are quoted from Fuji Kamiya, "Japan, Russia: No Love Lost," *Journal of Commerce*, November 9, 1992, translated and reprinted from *Asaki Shimbun*. For an analysis of "the 'exploitation' of the great by the small" see Mancur Olson, *The Logic of Collective Action: Public Goods and the Theory of Groups*, Cambridge: Harvard University Press, 1965, pp. 35–36, and Mancur Olson and Richard Zeckhauser, "An Economic Theory of Alliances," *Review of Economics and Statistics*, XLVIII (August 1966), pp. 266–79. The quote about the danger to French ministers from farmers is taken from "France Seen Continuing Defiant Stance in Talks," *Journal of Commerce*, November 9, 1992. The quote about "brutal price falls" and threats to public order is from William Drozdiak, "EC plans 'Big Bang' on Public Works to Revive Europe Unity," *International Herald Tribune*, November 18, 1992, p. 2. Data on national balance sheets are from Goldsmith, *Comparative National Balance Sheets*, p. 45. Details about the long-term interest rates come from Sidney Homer, *A History of Interest Rates*, Second Edition, New Brunswick: Rutgers University Press, 1977, p. 503. The quote from Sir Martin Jacomb is from "Megapolitics and the Market: A Message for Troubled Times," *op. cit.* For more on Dutch predominance in the early seventeenth century, see Jack S. Levy, *War in the Modern Great Power System 1495–1975*, Lexington, Kentucky: The University of Kentucky Press, 1983, p. 37. Details about tulipomania are from Charles Mackay, *Extraordinary Popular Delusions and the Madness of Crowds*, New York: Farrar, Straus and Giroux, 1932. The authority for the statements about seventeenth-century in terest rates is Homer, *A History of Interest Rates*, pp. 158–59. The Duke de St. Simon's plan to declare France bankrupt is reported by Mackay, *op. cit.* Mackay is also the authority for details about the South Sea Bubble stocks, *op. cit.*, p. 55. An overview of eighteenth-century depression is provided by Anthony J. Little, *Deceleration in the Eighteenth-Century British Economy*, London: Croom Helm, 1976. The figures for direct foreign investment by Japanese companies in 1991 are from Paul Blustein, "Japan's 'Bubble' Bursts Amid Tumble in Land, Stock Values," *Washington Post*, April 20, 1992, p. A12. The material on rental values and for Tokyo office space and the calculation for the projected site values are from Alexander Kinmonti and Kaiko Ohtsuki, "Tokyo Commercial Property: Supply, Demand, Rents, and Values," Morgan Stanley, August 3, 1992. The authority for examples of extraordinary excesses in Japanese property markets is Maggie Mahar, "Shaky Foundation: Speculation Kites Japan's Realty Boom," *Barron's*, November 9, 1987, p. 18. Details and the quote about the low quality of Japanese residential structures come from Andrew Tanzer, "Land of the Rising Billionaires," *Forbes*, July 27, 1987, pp. 77 and 68. The claim that Japanese farmers control a disproportionate share of the votes at election time is from Mahar, *op. cit.*, p. 20. Losses for the *Tokkin* funds are reported in "One Patient, Two Cures," *op. cit.* pp. 91–92. Information about the Japanese response to the asset collapse and the quote from Christopher Wood are taken from conversations during the summer and autumn of 1992. For more information see, Christopher Wood, *The Bubble Economy: Japan's Extraordinary Speculative Boom of the '80s and the Dramatic Bust of the '90s*, New York: Atlantic Monthly Press, 1992. For details about social reform and economic collapse in Argentina, see George Pendle, *A History of Latin America*, London: Penguin Books, pp. 204–10.

Chapter 5: The New Germany and Europe in the 1990s

Our forecast of the coming fall of the Berlin Wall was published several times in *Strategic Investment*, most prominently as the lead story in the February 13, 1989, issue. On European empires as "the lords of human kind," see V. G. Kiernan, *The Lords of Human Kind*, New York: Columbia University Press, 1986. On the restocking of other continents with European flora and fauna, see Alfred W. Crosby, *Ecological Imperialism: The Biological Expansion of Europe, 900–1900*. On the crucial role of Europeans in forcing modernization on India, China, Indonesia, and Africa, see Kiernan, *op. cit.*, p. 17 and *passim*. Details about the "demographic time bomb" are from Jean-Claude Chesnais, "The Africanization of Europe?" *The American Enterprise*, May/June 1990. For evidence of philosophers postulating a major division between Eastern and Western Europe, see Anderson, *Passages from Antiquity to Feudalism*, p. 206. Anderson explores some of the megapolitical reasons that Eastern European peasants were not as free to run away as their contemporaries in the West, pp. 251–53. Playfair's observations on the collapse of Poland are from *Decline and Fall*, p. 75. Hegel's dismissal of Eastern Europe as having not fully participated in "the sphere of Occidental Reason" is from G. W. F. Hegel, *The Philosophy of History*, London, 1878, p. 363, quoted in Anderson, *op. cit.*, pp. 15–16. For more on the Italian debt see Tim Congdon, *The Debt Threat*, Oxford: Blackwell, 1988, p. 102. On EC trade protectionism directed against Japan, see "EC's Auto Plan Would Keep Japan at Bay: 1992 Unification Effort Smacks of Protectionism," *Wall Street Journal*, October 27, 1988, p. A14. Details about the World Economic Conference of 1927, and the futile attempts to form a "United States of Europe," are from Davis, *The World Between the Wars*.

Chapter 6: Latin America Takes Over Communism and Other Ironies of the End of the Cold War

"Circumstances make men just as men make circumstances" is from Karl Marx and Friedrich Engels, *The German Ideology*, New York: International Publishers, 1947, p. 29. The quote about "social revolution" and "the material forces of production in society" is from Karl Marx, *A Contribution to the Critique of Political Economy*, New York: International Library Publishing Co., 1904, p. 12. The quote on prediction "with the precision of natural science" is from the same source. The comment from Engels about causes "to be sought . . . in changes in the mode of production" is from *Herr Eugen*

Duhring's Revolution in Science, New York: International Publishers, 1939, p. 292. Kindelberger's analysis of the contributing causes to the depression of the 1930s is taken from Charles Kindelberger, *The World in Depression,* Berkeley: University of California Press, 1973, p. 289. The quote about Germany and Japan assuming larger roles in world affairs is taken from *Strategic Investment,* June 14, 1992. For examples of Soviet environmental damage see Jack Wheeler, "Soviet Eco-Catastrophes," *Strategic Investment,* August 20, 1990. The calculation that Russia's GDP could be raised by closing down its goods-producing sector is from Kent Davis, *Kent Davis Economic-Political Review,* November 16, 1992, p. 6. The quote about the impossibility of selling Trabant automobiles is from Peter F. Drucker, "Junk Central Europe's Factories and Start Over," *The Wall Street Journal,* July 19, 1990, p. A10. So is the quote about the Witkowice and Tunstram. Points about the lack of stable government in the USSR are based on arguments spelled out by Mancur Olson in "Diseconomies of Scale and Development," pp. 77–97. On Bolivia's currency reform, see "Bolivia's Inflation Triumph Holds Perils: Austerity Plan Wins Praise but Economy Continues to Stumble," by Jonathan Kandell, *Wall Street Journal,* September 9, 1989, p. A14. For a better understanding of how backward transportation and communications systems make an inflationary policy more likely, see Olson, "Diseconomies of Scale and Development," pp. 77–97. The quote from Olson is from p. 87. On the contribution of inequality of wealth to savings in early modern Europe see Carlo M. Cipolla, *Before the Industrial Revolution: European Society and Economy, 1000–1700,* Second Edition, London: Methuen, 1981, pp. 25–42. Official estimates of illegal weapons in private hands in the USSR are cited by Vladimir Bukovsky, "In Russia, Is It 1905 Again?" *Wall Street Journal,* November 27, 1989.

Chapter 7: Muhammad Replaces Marx

Comments on the social function of religions are from A. R. Radcliffe-Brown, "Religion and Society," in *Structure and Function in Primitive Society,* London: Cohen & West, 1952, pp. 153–77. For more on incentive traps and "public goods" problems see Olson, *The Logic of Collective Action,* and Garrett Hardin, *Filters Against Folly,* New York: Penguin, 1985. "The tragedy of the commons" is described by Hardin, pp. 90–101. Details about the Maring Pig Wars are from Marvin Harris, *Cows, Pigs, Wars and Witches: The Riddles of Culture,* New York: Vintage Books, 1978, pp. 39–50. Harris describes the ecological background of pork taboos in the Middle East in the same volume, p. 37. Robertson Smith's comment that behavior is "rigorously fixed" in primitive religions is from Radcliffe-Brown, p. 156. Basil Davidson's comment on the mandatory character of African religions is from Davidson, *Africa in History,* p. 5. St. Bernard is quoted by Colin Morris, *The Discovery of the Individual, 1050–1200,* London: SPCK, 1972, p. 62. The quote about religion becoming "primarily a matter of belief" is from Radcliffe-Brown, p. 155. On religious diversity in the Roman Empire, see *The Cambridge Ancient History,* Volume XII, ed. S. A. Cook, F. E. Adcock, *et al.,* Cambridge: At the University Press, 1971, p. 419. The comment quoted about Rome "abandoned to inroad, to pillage, and at last to conquest, on her frontier" is from Adam Ferguson,

An Essay on the History of Civil Society, p. 311. On East German security officers running Third World secret police, see Jack Wheeler, "Behind the Lines," *Strategic Investment*, August 1990, p. 3. The comment about the U.S. military not being designed for fighting in the Third World is from Andy Pasztor and John J. Failka, "U.S. Military Lacks Some Tools It Needs in the Middle East Crisis," *Wall Street Journal*, August 28, 1990. Details on the British fight to calm Iraq in 1920 are from Keith Jeffrey, *The British Army and the Crisis of Empire, 1918–22*, Manchester: Manchester University Press, 1984, pp. 133–55. Details about the suppression of the Iraqi rebellion in 1941 are from Wm. Roger Louis, *The British Empire in the Middle East, 1945–51*, Oxford: Oxford University Press, 1985, p. 324. Estimate of the cost of the U.S. "over-the-horizon" naval flotilla is from Selig S. Harrison and Clyde V. Prestowitz, "From the Cold War to Global Economic Struggle," *International Herald Tribune*, July 9, 1990, p. 6. The comment on the quality of U.S. helicopters is from Andy Pasztor and John J. Failka, *op. cit.*, p. A1. Churchill's concern about the costs of suppressing unrest in Iraq are noted by Jeffrey, pp. 148–50. Details about crime rates in various countries are from "Crime Around the Globe," *Business Traveler*, June 1988, p. 19. The comment about The Prophet hoping to use "the mere terror of his name to make complete security reign throughout Arabia" is from *The Encyclopaedia Britannica*, Eleventh Edition, Volume XVII, New York: Encyclopaedia Britannica, 1911, p. 408. The arguments of John Locke on the importance of free interest rates are from *Works of John Locke*, Volume V, pp. 4–18, quoted in Sidney Homer, *A History of Interest Rates*, p. 80. For an analysis of the importance of freeholders to military success in antiquity see Robert O'Connell, *Of Arms and Men*, pp. 36–37; Perry Anderson, *Passages from Antiquity to Feudalism*, p. 33. Details of usury in Rome are from Anderson, pp. 67–82. Huldreich Zwingli's arguments in favor of lending at interest are reported by Homer, *op. cit.*, p. 80. Other details about the abolition of usury provisions are from the same source. Details about migration are from Jean-Claude Chesnais, "The Africanization of Europe?" *The American Enterprise*, May/June 1990, p. 23. Albert Sauvy is quoted by the same source.

Chapter 8: Linear Expectations in a Nonlinear World

Our account of the New Guinea cargo cults is taken from Marvin Harris, *Cows, Pigs, Wars and Witches: The Riddles of Culture*. The quotations are from pp. 114, 130, 115 twice, 116, 117 twice, and 121. The quotation about the immunity to external argument of systems is from Keith Thomans, *Religion and the Decline of Magic*, London: Penguin, 1988, p. 767. The comment about cause and effect interacting in cycles is from Gary Taubes, "The Body Chaotic," *Discover*, May 1989, p. 64. Taubes is also the authority for our assertion that regular, periodic brain activity implies either stupidity or epilepsy, p. 66. The quote about chaos in the brain is from Walter J. Freeman, "The Physiology of Perception," *Scientific American*, February 1991, p. 78. The source for our view that all nontrivial computation depends upon nonlinear dynamics is James Crutchfield. He writes: "This is as true of ferromagnets at the Curie temperature as it is of digital or analog computers considered as physical systems and of evolving biological organisms." See James P. Crutchfield, "Inferring the Dynamic, Quantifying

Physical Complexity," in N. B. Abraham, ed., *Quantitative Measures of Complex Dynamical Systems,* New York: Plenum, 1989, p. 11. Paul Davies's comments on linearity are from *The Cosmic Blueprint: New Discoveries in Nature's Creative Ability to Order the Universe,* New York: Simon and Schuster, 1988, pp. 24–25. James Gleick's observations about the nonlinearity of nature are from *Chaos: Making a New Science,* New York: Penguin Books, 1988, p. 68. The quotation about the Newtonian foundation of Marx's search for the "laws of motion of the capitalist system" is from Don Lavoie, "Economic Chaos or Spontaneous Order? Implications for Political Economy of the New View of Science," *The Cato Journal,* Volume 8, Number 3, 1989, p. 613. For further analysis of the defects of conventional economic models, see F. A. Hayek, *Individualism and Economic Order,* Chicago: Gateway Editions, 1972, pp. 14–15, 33–56, 77–91; Israel M. Kirzner, *Competition and Entrepreneurship,* Chicago: University of Chicago Press, 1973, *passim*; and Gerhard Mensch, Charles Coutinho, and Klaus Kaasch, "Changing Capital Values and Propensity to Innovate," in Christopher Freeman, ed., *Long Waves in the World Economy,* London: Francis Pinter, 1984, p. 38. For an exposition of the deficiencies of mechanical assumptions about perfect foresight and computational abilities, see Jacques Lesourne, *A Theory of the Individual for Economic Analysis,* Amsterdam: North-Holland Publishing Company, 1977, pp. 1–14. For more on the Ionian astronomers, see Carroll Quigley, *The Evolution of Civilizations,* Indianapolis: Liberty Press, 1988, p. 39.

Chapter 9: The Remaking of the Cosmopolitan Mind

V. G. Kiernan's comment about the Renaissance as "an affair of aristocracy and intelligentsia" is from Kiernan, *The Lords of Human Kind,* p. 12. For evidence of a war cycle of about fifty years, see Joshua S. Goldstein, *Long Cycles: Prosperity and War in the Modern Age,* New Haven: Yale University Press, 1988, p. 230–44. Evidence that economic performance could be dependent on conditions that evolve through stages over time is spelled out in *Blood in the Streets* and references. For a more scholarly summary of evidence relating to the long wave and power cycles, see Goldstein, *op. cit., passim,* especially pp. 21–174. Kondratieff's description of his long wave is from N. B. Kondratieff, "The Long Wave of Economic Life," *Review of Economic Statistics,* Number 17, November 1935, pp. 106–7. For further evidence of overlapping or connected cycles see Goldstein, *op. cit.,* pp. 195–233. For evidence of premodern long waves see Robert S. Lopez, Review of *Studi di Storia della Moneta,* by Carlo M. Cipolla, *Speculum,* Volume 24, Number 4 (1949), p. 559. The long cycle of forest fires in Yellowstone Park is explained in William H. Romme and Don G. Despain, "The Yellowstone Fires," *Scientific American,* Volume 261, Number 5, November 1989. The quotes are from pp. 44 and 42. The Playfair quote on the fall of Rome is from *Decline and Fall,* p. 79. The Malthus comment on "clouds of barbarians" is from Malthus, "An Essay on the Principle of Population," in *The Works of Thomas Robert Malthus,* Volume I, ed. E. A. Wrigley and David Souden, London: William Pickering, 1986, p. 20. The quote on revival at the end of the tenth century is from Alfred W. Crosby, *Ecological Imperialism: The Biological Expansion of Europe, 900–1900,* p. 44. Evidence for the rebirth of money, arithmetic, history, biography, time awareness, social mobility, etc., can be found in many authorities. See particularly Colin Morris, *The Discovery of the Individual: 1050–1200, passim,* and Alexander Murray, *Reason and Society in the Middle Ages,* p. 55f. The history studies referred to appeared in *Journal of Modern History* Volume 52, Number 1, 1979. L. F. Richardson's work, though done earlier in this century, was only published posthumously in 1960. See Lewis F. Richardson, *Statistics of Deadly Quarrels,* ed. Quincy Wright and C. C. Lienau, Pittsburgh: Boxwood Press, 1960, and Lewis F. Richardson, "The Problem of Contiguity," appendix to *Statistics of Deadly Quarrels.* Robin Fox is quoted from "The Conditions of Sexual Evolution," in Philippe Aries and Andre Bejin, eds., *Western Sexuality: Practice and Precept in Past and Present Times,* New York: Basil Blackwell, 1985, p. 1. S. B. Saul's report on the managerial impact of false teeth is quoted from S. B. Saul, *The Myth of the Great Depression 1873–1896,* Second Edition, London: Macmillan, 1985, p. 47. For more on institutional rigidity see Mancur Olson, *The Rise and Decline of Nations,* New Haven: Yale University Press, 1982, and William Playfair, *Decline and Fall.* Playfair anticipates many Public Choice arguments, particularly in Book II, Chapter IV, where he discusses "causes arising from the encroachments of public and privileged bodies; and of those who have a common interest on those who have no common interest." For Jevons on cycles see W. Stanley Jevons, *Investigations in Currency and Finance,* ed. Foxwell, London, 1884, p. 78, cited in Marc Faber, *The Great Money Illusion,* Hong Kong: Longman, 1988, p. 164. There are numerous sunspot cycles. A simple sunspot cycle of 11.125 years is doubled to create a 22.25-year sunspot cycle. There is also a sunspot tidal cycle of 44.5 years, and a 178-year sunspot cycle. See Iben Browning and Evelyn M. Garriss, *Past and Future History, op. cit.,* p. 13. Effects associated with the sunspot tidal cycle of 44.5 years suggest themselves on naive grounds as in some measure influencing the human adult life span. But this could be mistaken. For a summary of recent research supporting the connection between sunspot activity and the weather, see Marcia Bartusiak, "The Sunspot Syndrome," *Discover,* November 1989, pp. 44–52. For an authoritative review of the impact of past climates on man, see T. M. L. Wigley, M. J. Ingram, and G. Farmer, eds., *Climate and History,* Cambridge: Cambridge University Press, 1988. For evidence of climatic fluctuations associated with the gravitational pull of the nearer planets on the earth's orbit, see R. Dale Guthrie and Mary Lee Guthrie, "On the Mammoth's Dusty Trail," *Natural History,* July 1990, p. 36. The *New York Times* report quoted on natural cycles causing the 1988 drought is by William K. Stevens, "Scientists Link '88 Drought to Natural Cycle in Tropical Pacific," *New York Times,* January 3, 1989, p. C1. The quote about "pseudorandom" phenomena is taken from William A. Brock and Chera L. Sayers, "Is the Business Cycle Characterized by Deterministic Chaos?" *Journal of Monetary Economics,* Volume 22, 1988, p. 71. The page citations from Donald Brown, *Hierarchy, History & Human Nature,* indicating that artistic styles are not random, include pp. 31, 44, 59, 121, 125–26, 134, 146–47, 155, 175, 177, 183, 205, 217, 242, 283, 288, 300, and 318. Buchanan is quoted from James Buchanan, "Socialism Is Dead; Leviathan Lives," *Wall Street Journal,* July 18, 1990, p. A8. Davies's concept of a "cosmic blueprint" is spelled out in Paul Davies, *The Cosmic Blueprint,* pp. 200–203. For an argument that current tests underestimate pseudorandomness in the economy, see W. A. Brock and A. G. Malliaris, *Differential Equations, Stability and Chaos in Dynamic Economics*, Amsterdam: North Holland, 1989, p. 311. For reports of the search for evidence of pseudorandom phenomena in many disciplines, see W. A. Brock, "Distinguishing Random and Deterministic Systems," *Journal of Economic Theory*, Volume 40, 1986, pp. 168–95; Chera L. Sayers, "Chaos and the Business Cycle," in Saul Krasner, ed., *The Ubiquity of Chaos*, forthcoming, American Association for the Advancement of Science publication; Jose A. Scheinkman and Blake LeBaron, "Nonlinear Dynamics and Stock Returns," *Journal of Business* Volume 62, Number 3, 1989, pp. 311–37. For an interpretation of the persistence of investors' sentiments in the face of the facts, see Edgar E. Peters, "Fractal Structure in the Capital Markets," *Financial Analysts Journal*, July-August 1988, p. 32. The analysis of the memory effect is on p. 36. For a full discussion on the January Effect see Robert A. Haugen and Josef Lakonsihok, *The Incredible January Effect: The Stock Market's Unsolved Mystery*, Homewood, Illinois: Dow Jones, Irwin, 1988. For a report of Langton's early attempt to identify the source of autumn crashes, see Theodore E. Burton, *Financial Crises and Periods of Industrial and Commercial Depression*, Burlington, Vermont: Fraser, 1982, p. 35. The asymmetrical behavior of markets is analyzed by Salih N. Neftci, "Are Economic Time Series Asymmetric Over the Business Cycle?" *Journal of Political Economy* Volume 92, Number 2, 1984, pp. 307–28. For a sense of the importance of the transitory nature of downturns in preserving a positive investment climate, see W. A. Brock and A. G. Malliaris, *Differential Equations, Stability and Chaos in Dynamic Economics*, p. 321 and references.

Chapter 10: Drugs, Delusions, and the Imperial Culture of the Slums

The *Economist* story on the Toxeth region of south Liverpool appeared July 22, 1989, p. 50. Richard Bernstein's comment on "a new tribalism" is from Richard Bernstein, "The Arts Catch Up with a Society in Disarray," *New York Times*, September 2, 1990, p. H2. Marshall's "Principle of Continuity" is spelled out in Alfred Marshall, *Principles of Economics*, Eighth Edition, London: Macmillan, 1979, p. vi. For evidence that the gap between the educated and uneducated has been widening since the eighteenth century, see Sidney Pollard, *The Genesis of Modern Management: A Study of the Industrial Revolution in Britain*, London: Edward Arnold, 1965, pp. 185–86. Our authority for the view that primitive peoples usually have "no words for abstract concepts" is G. J. Whitrow, *Time in History*, Oxford: Oxford University Press, 1988, p. 12. The quotes are from the same work, pp. 12, 8, 6, 13 twice, and 7. The authority for the view that ghetto dialects do not employ tense as an essential feature of grammar is J. L. Dillard, *Black English: Its History and Usage in the United States*, New York: Vintage Books, 1973, pp. 49–53, 282. The examples are from p. 52. Eleanor Wilson Orr's work is reported in "Are Words Failing Black Students?" *Insight*, January 11, 1988, pp. 62–63. The Dillard quote is from *Black English*, p. 24. The possible importance of noradrenaline in drug addiction was suggested by Durk Pearson and Sandy Shaw, private communication, August 17, 1990. The definition of "noradrenaline" is from Robert K. Barnhart, ed., *The American Heritage Dictionary of Science*, Boston: Houghton

Mifflin Company, 1986, p. 439. Wrigley and Schofield's argument about reproduction rates and real wages is from E. A. Wrigley and R. S. Schofield, *The Population History of England 1541–1871,* Cambridge, Massachusetts: Harvard, p. 418. Mary Kilbourne Matossian disputes the Wrigley and Schofield thesis, suggesting that fluctuations in English fertility arose from the consequences of ergot poisoning of rye flour, which suppressed fertility. Matossian writes: "English fertility varied with English rye and wheat prices. The higher the wheat prices, the more women ate rye bread and the less the fertility. The higher the rye prices, the more women had to eat ergoty rye bread and the less the fertility." Whether her explanation is correct cannot be easily established, in that rye prices for much of the period are unknown. See Matossian, *Poisons of the Past: Molds, Epidemics, and History,* New Haven: Yale, 1989, pp. 65–66. It may well be both explanations are valid. Fluctuations in the weather contributed to fluctuations in the price and the quality of grain, which both suppressed fertility due to ergot poisoning and reduced the desire of would-be parents to have children. For evidence of individuals being obligated to support their relatives in rough proportion to the degree of genetic relatedness, see R. Paul Shaw and Yuwa Wong, *Genetic Seeds of Warfare: Evolution, Nationalism and Patriotism,* pp. 29–31. Murstein is quoted from *Love, Sex, and Marriage Through the Ages,* New York: Springer, 1974, p. 503. The same work is the source for the quote and details about female husbands and the bride-price, pp. 505 and 504. Marshall's quotes about exertion and the other quoted phrases about markets and calculation are from *Principles of Economics.* The quote about the difficulty of economic discipline is from Alexander Gerschenkron, *Economic Backwardness in Historical Perspective,* Cambridge, Mass.: Harvard University Press, 1962, p. 9. The English worker as "the man of the future" is from the same source. For evidence of labor productivity and income growth in Britain after 1873, see S. B. Saul, *The Myth of the Great Depression 1873–1896,* p. 30. The important of the Trafalgar Square riots of 1886 is underlined by Michael Rose, *The Relief of Poverty 1834–1914,* Second Edition, London: Macmillan, 1986, p. 32. Quotes and details about British perceptions of superior American workmanship early in the twentieth century are from Vivian Vane, *The American Peril,* Manchester: Manchester University Press, 1984, p. 16. Predepression American perceptions about the doleful effects of the dole are quoted from Peter Fearon, *War, Prosperity & Depression: The U.S. Economy 1917–1945,* Oxford: Philip Allan, 1987, pp. 48–49. On divisions of culture see Judith Waldrop, "Spending by Degree," *American Demographics,* February 1990, pp. 23–26. The quotes about aggression-inhibiting values spreading down from the "urban upper and middle classes" are from Ted Robert Gurr, "Historical Trends in Violent Crime: Europe and the United States," in *Violence in America,* Volume 1, pp. 44–45 and 46. The same authority dates the growth of violence from 1930, p. 22. The low tide of violence in the West also coincides with a technological innovation—the advent of movie-going as a significant contributor to popular culture. The quote about violence in medieval Europe is from p. 45. For further details about the high odds in favor of escaping poverty, see Norman Macrae, "The Next Ages of Man," *Economist,* December 24, 1988, survey page 8. For more on the choice of impoverishing behavior see Mickey Kaus, " 'Underclass' Is a Useful Term," *Washington Post,* September 18, 1990, p. A19.

The quote of the New York policeman is from Hamill, *op. cit.*, p. 65. For documentation of "low self-control," see Michael Gottfredson and Travis Hirschi, "Criminal Behavior," *Washington Post*, September 10, 1989, p. C3. Michael Gottfredson and Travis Hirschi are quoted in the same source. The quoted descriptions and details about crime in Gorer Lane are from Janet Foster, *Villains: Crime and Community in the Inner City*, London: Routledge, 1990. On eating dirt, see Kathy Eyre, "Dishin Up Dirt—and Eating It, Too: Some Rural Black Women Continue Ancient African Practice," *Washington Post*, November 9, 1988, p. A10. The list of common characteristics of underclass life is quoted from Carolyn Lockhead, "In Poverty's Hard Clutch, Little Chance for Escape," *Insight*, April 3, 1989, pp. 8–9. For evidence of a connection between drug use and violence, see Marvin Harris, *Cows, Pigs, Wars and Witches*, pp. 59–84, and Michael Isikoff, "Users of Crack Cocaine Link Violence to Drug's Influence," *Washington Post*, March 24, 1989, p. A11. The Gurr quote is from Gurr, *op. cit.*, p. 19. Leon Dash, "A Crack Dealer's Creed," appeared in the *Washington Post*, April 3, 1989, p. A1. The statement on verbalization is from Colin Morris, *The Discovery of the Individual: 1050–1200*, pp. 7–8. Assante's attack on universality is quoted from William Raspberry, "Euro, Afro and Other Eccentric 'Centric's," *Washington Post*, September 10, 1990, p. A15. The comparison with "the ancient inhabitants of Europe" is from William Robertson, *History of Charles V*, Volume I, London, 1769, p. 209. The longer quote is from p. 211. The William Raspberry quotation is from *Reader's Digest*, August 1990, pp. 96–97. Details of the Reverend Al Sharpton's activities are from press reports, particularly James S. Kunin, "The Trials of Tawana Brawley," *People*, July 4, 1988, p. 62, and "Sharpton Charged with Grand Theft," *Washington Post*, June 30, 1989, p. A5. The allegation that Sharpton knew Tawana Brawley's story was "a pack of lies" is from Ann V. Bollinger, "Tawana's Four-Day Party," *New York Post*, June 21, 1988, pp. 4, 5, and 59, and Kunin, *op cit.*, p. 64. The comment "I don't care 'bout no facts" is also from Kunin, p. 64. Details about the Indian myth-makers are from Donald Brown, *History, Hierarchy & Human Nature*, pp. 28–29. Mike McGee's threats and demands are reported in "Prowling Black Panther," *Economist*, 18–24 August, 1990, p. 19. Carswell on honesty is quoted from John Carswell, *The South Sea Bubble*, London: Cresset Press, 1960, pp. 13–14. The logic of delusional attribution of causality is from George M. Foster, *Traditional Cultures and the Impact of Technological Change*, New York: Harper and Bros., 1962, p. 66. The economic delusions of nineteenth-century Midwestern farmers are explored by David Hale, "Britain and Japan as the Financial Bogeymen of U.S. Politics," Kemper Financial Services, Chicago, September 1987, p. 10. Cohn traces a "specific fantasy" back to antiquity in Norman Cohn, *Europe's Inner Demons: An Enquiry Inspired by the Great Witch-Hunt*, New York: New American Library, 1975, p. xi. The utility of delusions in encouraging income redistribution is explored by Lawrence Stone in "The Disenchantment of the World," *New York Review of Books*, December 2, 1971, p. 20. For details of persecution of the Jews and *conversos* in the fifteenth century, see Angus MacKay, "Climate and Popular Unrest in Late Medieval Castile," in T. M. L. Wigley et al., eds., *Climate and History*, pp. 356–76. Oswald Spengler is quoted from *The Decline of the West*, New York: The Modern Library, 1962, pp. 64–68. The description of Sharpton's media tactics is from Kunin, *op. cit.*, p. 64.

The sense of the succession of events in primitive societies is discussed by Whitrow, *op. cit.*, pp. 9–10. For evidence of the collapse of values see " 'Values' Lessons Return to the Classroom: Educators Say Kids Today Are 'Rudderless,' " *Wall Street Journal*, September 26, 1988, p. 29. The eighteenth-century description of American Indian family life is from Robertson, *op. cit.*, p. 210. The quote from the Chicago city official saying that AIDS is a plot to kill blacks is from George Kalogerakis, "Coincidence, Perhaps?" *Spy*, July 1990, p. 53. The Washington editor calling for race war is cited by Richard Harwood, "The Barry Story," *Washington Post*, August 19, 1990, p. C6. Details about blacks in manufacturing occupations are from Walter L. Updegrave, "Race and Money," *Money*, December 1989, p. 168. The quotation from William Gibson is from the same source, p. 156. For evidence of black incarceration rates see Bill McAllister, "Study: 1 in 4 Young Black Men Is in Jail or Court-Supervised," *Washington Post*, February 27, 1990, p. A3. On race-based denial see Sam Roberts, "For Some Blacks, Justice Is Not Blind to Color," *New York Times*, September 9, 1990, p. E6. Data about demography and education are from Richard Jackson, *The Retirement Century*, Indianapolis: Hudson Institute, 1990, pp. 73–74 and 75–76. Data about unwed mothers are from Macrae, *Economist*, December 24, 1988, survey page 6. Early evidence of sociopathic behavior is discussed by Gottfredson and Hirschi, *op. cit.*, p. C3. German unemployment figures are from Harold James, *The German Slump: Politics and Economics 1924–1936*, Oxford: Oxford University Press, 1986, p. 6. Comments about the banking system are from the same source, p. 23. "Paranoia about bankers' conspiracies" and the discredit of democratic institutions are from p. 60, and 7, 47, 75. For details of the vulnerability of the centralized systems, see Amory B. and L. Hunter Lovins, *Brittle Power: Energy Strategy for Natural Security*, Andover, Mass.: Brick House, 1982. On criminal gangs in Latin America see Eugene Robinson, "Crime Is Choking Rio: Whole Apartment Buildings Looted," *Washington Post*, October 4, 1990, p. A35. For percentages of underclass populations see Judith Waldrop, "Shades of Black," *American Demographics*, September 1990, p. 34. For details of the use of hand-held computers in guerrilla war see William Claiborne, "Mozambican Guerrillas Launch Attack on the PR Front," *Washington Post*, July 31, 1988, p. 28. On connection between drug dealing and terrorism see Edward Mortimer, "The Rising Curve of Violent Death," *Financial Times*, April 20, 1988, p. 22. On "telepresence" see Julie Amparano Lopez and Mary Lu Carnevale, "Fiber Optics Promises a Revolution of Sorts, If the Sharks Don't Bite," *Wall Street Journal*, July 10, 1990, p. A1.

Chapter 11: Deflation Ahead

For an exposition on "distributional coalitions," see Mancur Olson, *The Rise and Decline of Nations: Economic Growth, Stagflation, and Social Rigidities*, New Haven: Yale Univerity Press, 1982, pp. 43–47. For the logic of debt growth see Tim Congdon, *The Debt Threat*, pp. 18–19. The argument about high levels of money relative to gold reserves is from William and Douglas Kirkland, *Power Cycles*, Phoenix: Professional Communications, 1986, pp. 192–98. Details of "financial interrelations ratios" are from Raymond W. Goldsmith, *Comparative National Balance Sheets: A Study of Twenty Countries, 1688–1978*,

p. 4. The Congdon quote is from *The Debt Threat*. Details of the inflation of the Roman *drachmai* are from Reay Tannahill, *Food in History*, London: Paladin, 1975, p. 59. For more on unemployment in the 1930s, see Michael A. Bernstein, *The Great Depression: Delayed Recovery and Economic Change in America, 1929–1939*, Cambridge: Cambridge University Press, 1987, *op. cit.*, p. 21. The comment from Joseph W. Davis doubting the capacity of the Fed to prevent contraction by flooding the money supply is from *The World Between the Wars*, p. 243. For more on Hayek's views of deflation, see F. A. Hayek, Chapter 21, "The Monetary Framework," *The Constitution of Liberty*, Chicago: Gateway, 1972, pp. 324–29. For details of World War II destruction in Japan see Robert Czeschin, *The Last Wave*, p. 85. Details of price movements since the 1490s are from South English Consumer Price Index, 1495–1954, E. H. Phelps-Brown and Sheila V. Hopkins, "Seven Centuries of the Prices of Consumables," cited in Joshua S. Goldstein, *Long Cycles: Prosperity and War in the Modern Age*, Appendix B. On the incidence of war, see Jack S. Levy, *War in the Modern Great Power System: 1495–1975*, Lexington: University of Kentucky Press, 1983, p. 140. The comment by Paul Kennedy on the importance of financial stability to military strength is from Kennedy, *The Rise and Fall of the Great Powers: Economic Change and Military Conflict from 1500–2000*, New York: Random House, 1987, p. 70.

Chapter 12: Clues from the Past

On the "chaotic" nature of U.S. government finances in the eighteenth century, see Homer, *A History of Interest Rates*, p. 278. The authority for the assertion that the U.S. government was "facing utter bankruptcy" is Forrest McDonald, *E Pluribus Unum*, Indianapolis: Liberty Press, 1979, p. 243. For details on default of both domestic and foreign debt see Homer, *op cit.*, p. 278. The quote about the hapless condition of creditors is from McDonald, *op. cit.*, p. 190. The example of local governments discharging debt at "the depreciated ratio of a thousand to one" is from Samuel Eliot Morison, *The Oxford History of the American People*, Oxford: Oxford University Press, 1972, p. 302. The leading general quoted to the effect that "something must be done, or the fabric must fall, for it certainly is tottering" is George Washington. See John Alden, *George Washington: A Biography*, Baton Rouge: LSU Press, 1984, p. 228. Morison is quoted about a "very bad" situation in Morison, *op. cit.*, p. 303. Details about debt imprisonment in Worcester County are from pp. 302–3. Details about Shays's Rebellion are from McDonald, *op. cit.*, p. 255. General Knox's assertion that the rebels intended to redistribute property is discussed and quoted in Noah Brooks, *Henry Knox, a Soldier of the Revolution*, New York: Putnam's, 1900, pp. 91–92. The excerpt from Knox's letter to Washington is from the same source, p. 92. On the wide circulation of Knox's letter, see McDonald, *op. cit.*, p. 251. McDonald's characterization of the Knox letter is quoted from Forrest McDonald, *Novus Ordo Seclorum*, Lawrence, Kans.: University Press of Kansas, 1985, p. 177. Details about the shrinkage of the United States in the 1930s are from National Bureau of Economic Research, and *Economic Statistics: 1900–1983*, London: The Economist Publications, 1985. Details about rice prices and unrest in Indochina are from Samuel L. Popkin, *The Rational Peasant: The*

Political Economy of Rural Society in Vietnam, Berkeley: University of California Press, 1979, p. xix. Theodore Burton's comments on the distinction between depression and destitution are quoted from Burton, *Financial Crises and Periods of Industrial and Commercial Depression*, Burlington, Vermont: Fraser Publishing Company, 1982, p. 13. The quote about the lagged perception of authorities about the 1973–75 recession is from Alfred. L. Malabre, "If a Recession Comes, Trends to Expect," *Wall Street Journal*, August 13, 1990, p. A1. The quotes about American capital seeming to come "from a bottomless well" and the unreal atmosphere of the late 1920s are from Peter Fearon, *War, Prosperity & Depression*, pp. 84 and 131. Fearon is also the authority quoted on the consumer debt binge, p. 85; the job growth in services, p. 24; the fall in labor union membership in the 1920s, p. 64; the fall in real income for most consumers, p. 152; the abandonment of banks by blue chip companies, p. 55; widespread bank failures, p. 72. Details about the early onset of depression at the periphery are from Peter Fearon, *The Origins and Nature of the Great Slump, 1929–1932*, London: Macmillan, 1979, p. 31. Details of American monetary reserves are from *Economic Report of the President, 1990*, Washington, Table C-106, p. 415. Details of federal insolvency are from Peter G. Peterson and Neil Howe, *On Borrowed Time*, abridged version, San Francisco: Institute for Contemporary Studies, 1988, p. 8. Consumer price data are from *Economic Report of the President*, Table C-58. The fall in real goods prices relative to services is reported by John Rutledge, "Strangling the Economy," *Wall Street Journal*, October 18, 1990, p. A16. Details on yields of various securities in the 1930s are from Homer, *A History of Interest Rates*, pp. 354, 392, 394, 399. Debt yields for 1990 are from tables, *Wall Street Journal*, August 28, 1990, p. C15. A. D. Noyes words about a "defaultless era in foreign lending" are quoted in Davis, *World Between the Wars*, p. 136. The 1929 unemployment rate in the United States is from Fearon, *War, Prosperity & Depression*, p. 62. The proportions of American population on the farm are from *Economic Report of the President*, Table C-32. The level of military spending in 1929 is from Carolyn Webber and Aaron Wildavsky, *A History of Taxation and Expenditure in the Western World*, New York: Simon and Schuster, 1986, p. 470. Federal purchases of goods and services are reported in *Economic Report of the President*, Table C-2, as are further details of government spending, Table C-27. The figures on per capita welfare expenditures in 1927 were calculated by deflating numbers in Table C-80.

Chapter 13: When the Music Stops

On the weakening condition of commercial banks see Jerry Knight, "FDIC Says Real Estate Slump in Area, Northeast Is Weakening U.S. Banks," *Washington Post*, September 7, 1990. The compound growth of off-budget lending is detailed in *Report of the Secretary of the Treasury on Government Sponsored Enterprises*, Washington, May 1990, Table 2. Carlo M. Cipolla is quoted from Cipolla, ed., *The Economic Decline of Empires*, London: Methuen & Co., Ltd., 1970, p. 15. The quotations from John Crow and Donald Blenkarn are from Alan Freman, "Crow Cites Debt Scare; Canadian Entities Cause Concern," *The Globe and Mail*, December 10, 1992, p. B1. The quotation on the vulnerability of finances in Weimar Germany is from Harold James, *The German*

Slump, pp. 72 and 71; the order of the sentences has been reversed. The further details about the German experience are also from James, p. 55; "highly restrictive government budgets," p. 58; the "necessity of spending cuts," p. 59; battling over capital gains taxes and taxes on beer, pp. 55, 58–59; inability to agree on reform, p. 60; the steep rise in taxes after 1930, p. 64; unemployment compensation slashed, pp. 61, 67; firings of government employees, p. 67; civil service pay cuts, etc., p. 71; and "odious taxes and falling revenues," p. 76. Details of national balance sheets are from Goldsmith, *Comparative National Balance Sheets: A Study of Twenty Countries, 1688–1978,* p. 45. Marc Faber is quoted by Kathryn M. Welling, "Losing Their Yen," *Barron's,* August 27, 1990, p. 24. Alfred L. Malabre, Jr., is quoted from the *Wall Street Journal,* August 13, 1990, p. A1. The *Money* article referred to in the off-budget liquidity squeeze is "Closing a Door After the Money Is Gone," *Money,* September 1990, p. 32. For an accounting of total losses by depositors in banks that failed from 1929 through 1933, see Fearon, *War, Prosperity & Depression,* p. 110. For hints of Treasury's balances used to prop up insolvent banks, see Christopher Whalen, "Welcome to Brazil?" *Barron's,* September 17, 1990, p. 42. Analysis on the insolvency of the FDIC is from Charles Pillsbury, East Shore Partners, 155 Morris Avenue, Springfield, New Jersey 07081. Data on losses in uninsured deposits furnished by Veribanc, Inc., P.O. Box 461, Wakefield, MA 01880. Loan delinquency rates were reported by Jerry Knight, "FDIC Says Real Estate Slump in Area, Northeast Is Weakening U.S. Banks," *Washington Post,* September 7, 1990, p. A22. For details of British housing and land prices, see Marion Bowley, *Housing and the State,* New York: Garland Press, 1985; B. Weber, "New Index of House Rents for Great Britain," *Scottish Journal of Political Economy,* 1960, p. 235; A. K. Cairncross, *Home and Foreign Investment, 1870–1913,* Clifton, N.J.: A. M. Kelly, 1975, p. 214; J. C. Stamp, *British Incomes and Property,* London: P. S. King and Son, 1916–20, pp. 218–21, 342, 446. The source for the percentage of mortgage debt to equity in 1989 and earlier periods is Board of Governors of the Federal Reserve System, *Household Net Worth,* December 1989. Estimates on the Baby Boomer trade-up market are from Paul Hewitt, "Housing Asset Conversion in the 1990s," Indianapolis: Hudson Institute, 1990. For evidence of the revocation and abrogation of economic rights, see Michael C. Jensen and William H. Meckling, "Can the Corporation Survive?" *Financial Analysts Journal,* January-February 1978, pp. 31–37. Carlo M. Cipolla's comment about "a high concentration of wealth" is from Cipolla, *Before the Industrial Revolution,* p. 39. Playfair is quoted from *Decline and Fall,* p. 249. For details of hoarding increasing deflationary pressure and increasing in regions of turmoil, see Cipolla, *Before the Industrial Revolution,* pp. 40 and 42. On the average family living beyond its means, see *Strategic Investment,* June 9, 1987, p. 11. Details on levels of national consumption are from Jackson, *The Retirement Century,* p. 78. Data on negative savings in the depression of the 1930s are from *Historical Statistics of the United States,* Washington: Bureau of Labor Statistics, Series F 535-539. Data for tax delinquency rates are David T. Beito, *Taxpayers in Revolt: Tax Resistance During the Great Depression,* Chapel Hill: University of North Carolina Press, 1989, p. 6. The same source reports tax revolts in Chicago, pp. 60–100. Rosen is quoted from the *Wall Street Journal,* September 10, 1990, p. C1. Information about bond holders being influential in the rescue of local governments from tax revolts is from Beito, *op. cit.*, p. 42f. Laing is quoted from Jonathan R. Laing, "The New Junk? Risks Are Rising in the Vast Municipal Bond Market," *Barron's*, October 29, 1990, p. 10. The widespread discredit of parliamentary institutions is reported in James, *The German Slump*, p. 74. Sandburg is quoted by Beito, *op. cit.*, p. 73, as are Bettenheim, p. 9; the American Municipal Association, p. 127; James T. Paterson, p. 161; Franklin Roosevelt, p. 163; Carl Schneider, pp. 138–39. For evidence of the reforms of 1834 cutting the percentage of the population on relief, see Michael E. Rose, *The Relief of Poverty, 1834–1914*, London: Macmillan, 1986, p. 17. The *National Municipal Review* is quoted by Beito, *op. cit.*, p. 128. In Lincoln's words, America found itself "in the peaceful possession of the fairest portion of the earth as regards extent of territory, fertility of soil, and salubrity of climate"; see Abraham Lincoln, "Address Before the Young Men's Lyceum of Springfield, Illinois, January 27, 1838," in *The Writings of Abraham Lincoln*, New York: Lamb, 1905–06. Mickey Kaus is quoted from Kaus, "The Democrats and Joe Lunchbucket," *Washington Post*, October 29, 1990, p. A15. The Royal Commission on the Poor Law is quoted from M. A. Crowther, *The Workhouse System: 1834–1929*, London: Methuen, 1981, p. 13. On Puritans see R. H. Tawney, *Religion and the Rise of Capitalism*, New York: Mentor Books, 1947, pp. 169, 164. David Underdown is quoted from *Revel, Riot and Rebellion: Popular Politics and Culture in England 1603–1660*, Oxford: Oxford University Press, 1985, pp. 40 and 172. On blaming the poor for "gin drinking, carelessness and recklessness," see Rose, *op. cit.*, p. 10. On how dependence on welfare fell after 1834, see Rose, *op. cit.*, p. 17.

Chapter 14: The Escape from High Costs

For the report on building see *Standard & Poor's 1930s Family House Prices*, p. 135. The information about General Dynamics is from "Swords into Shares General Dynamics Contemplates Selling Its Remaining Units Arms Maker May Seek Gains for Stockholders in Sales of its 'Core Businesses,' " *Wall Street Journal*, November 3, 1992. For the value of utility construction see F. W. Dodge Corporation, *Survey of Current Business*, 1938 Supplement, p. 18. For prices of foods see *Historical Statistics of the United States*, Bureau of Labor Statistics, Series E 187-202, Retail prices, p. 213, and BLS Wholesale Price Indices, Series E 40-51, 1926 = 100; Series E 135-166, p. 211; Series G 416-469, p. 319. On home businesses see Jerry Cheslow, "The Best Business Opportunities for the 1990s," *Home Office Computing*, September 1990, p. 41. Real personal spending on services data are from *Survey of Current Business*, July 1988, Table 8.2, p. 99. Donald Veall is quoted from *The Popular Movement for Law Reform, 1640–1660*, Oxford: The Clarendon Press, 1970, p. x. The same source documents perverse legal rules as an invitation to blackmail, p. 9. G. Norburie is quoted from pp. 34–35. The source for data on the operating economies of office buildings is Beito, *Taxpayers in Revolt*, p. 44. Most of the details on the oil industry were obtained from Michael A. Bernstein, *The Great Depression*, *passim*. Textile industry details are from pp. 75, 76; the quote on durables is from p. 171; the skewing toward luxury, pp. 30 and 134; high income spending behavior, pp. 60–61; evaporation of brand loyalty, p. 201. The demand for labor will be lower in the emerging firms, pp. 146–47; the upsurge of demand by women for tobacco, pp. 71–72; NRA protecting inefficient firms, p. 202; mature industries "obsessed with the specter of overproduction," p. 203. The statement on growing aversion to New York is quoted from the *New York Times*, September 9, 1990, p. E25. Background on the Fifth Migration is from Dr. Jack Lessinger, *Regions of Opportunity*, New York: Times Books, 1986, and Jack Lessinger, "Regions of Opportunity," *American Demographics*, June 1987. Robert Louis Stevenson is quoted from *The Amateur Emigrant*, London: Hogarth Press, 1984, pp. 14–15. Lessinger is quoted from "Regions of Opportunity," *op. cit.*, p. 34. Philadelphia, "City in Crisis," is from the *Wall Street Journal*, September 21, 1990, p. A8. The quote on Philadelphia's municipal bureaucracy is from Michael Specter, "Philadephia's Story Is a Fiscal Cliffhanger: Fifth Largest City on Brink of Bankruptcy," *Washington Post*, August 26, 1990, p. A3. The black murder rate in Philadelphia is reported by Ted Robert Gurr, "Historical Trends in Violent Crime: Europe and the United States," in *Violence in America*, pp. 38–40. Murder rates in New York and Washington are also reported there, pp. 39–40.

Chapter 15: Rational Living in an Age of Crisis

The quote of Herbert Stein is from Stein, "The U.S. Economy: A Visitor's Guide," *op. cit.*, p. 7. "Detroit—It Changed the World's Pattern of Life and Is Now the Fourth City in the Land" is from Marc Faber, *Strategic Investment*, September 1990. The report on indefatigable shoppers is from Betsy Morris, "As a Favored Pastime, Shopping Ranks High with Most Americans," *Wall Street Journal*, July 30, 1987, p. 1. The *National Enquirer* murder survey is from John Blosser, "1 Person in 4 Would Have Somebody Killed—If They Weren't Found Out," *National Enquirer*, September 25, 1990, p. 33. The comment on "staggering amounts of debt" is from Morris, *op. cit.* Homer's comment on the collapse of British financial assets is from *The History of Interest Rates*, p. 428. On troubled insurance companies see Jonathan R. Laing, "Flawed Policies: Big Junk and Real-Estate Holdings Put Life Insurers at Risk," *Barron's*, October 1, 1990, pp. 10–11, 33–34, 36. The data on British gilts is from Homer, *op. cit.*, p. 416; the *Economist* is quoted in the same source, p. 200. The value of neighborhood associations is spelled out by Mitchell Joelson and Charles M. Gray in "Stimulating Community Enterprise: A Response to Fiscal Strains in the Public Sector," a study prepared for the use of the Subcommittee on Monetary and Fiscal Policy of the Joint Economic Committee, Congress of the United States, December 31, 1984, p. 21. For details on Paul Moller's flying car, the M200X, see "F O B," *Automobile Magazine*, October 1990, p. 17. The information about John Shakespeare is from Dennis Kay, *Shakespeare*, London: Sidgwick & Jackson, 1992. The quote from John Evelyn is from *Diary*, entry for 12 November, 1672, second edition, London, 1820. The quotes from Jonathan Swift are from *Poetical Works*, ed. H. Williams. Roman interest rates are reported by Homer, *op. cit.*, pp. 64, 506.

Afterword: The Recovery

The data mentioned are from Albert Sindlinger, *Sindlinger's Consumer Outlook*, Volume 1, numbers 8, 9, August–September, 1992, p. 8, and *Sindlinger's Consumer Outlook*, Volume 1, numbers 10, 11, October–November, 1992, p. 3. The passage quoted from Cesare Marchetti is from "Recession 1983: Ten More Years to Go?" *Technological Forecasting and Social Change*, number 24, p. 334. The quotes from Robert Prechter are from "A Turn in the Tidal Wave," 1989.

INDEX